The Western Humanities

SIXTH EDITION

Roy T. Matthews & F. DeWitt Platt

MICHIGAN STATE UNIVERSITY

Boston   Burr Ridge, IL   Dubuque, IA   Madison, WI   New York   San Francisco   St. Louis
Bangkok   Bogotá   Caracas   Kuala Lumpur   Lisbon   London   Madrid   Mexico City
Milan   Montreal   New Delhi   Santiago   Seoul   Singapore   Sydney   Taipei   Toronto

The McGraw-Hill Companies

Mc Graw Hill Higher Education

Published by McGraw-Hill, an imprint of The McGraw-Hill Companies, Inc., 1221 Avenue of the Americas, New York, NY 10020. Copyright © 2008. All rights reserved. No part of this publication may be reproduced or distributed in any form or by any means, or stored in a database or retrieval system, without the prior written consent of The McGraw-Hill Companies, Inc., including, but not limited to, in any network or other electronic storage or transmission, or broadcast for distance learning.

This book is printed on acid-free paper.

2 3 4 5 6 7 8 9 0 DOW/DOW 0 9 8 7

ISBN-13: 978-0-07-313637-0
ISBN-10: 0-07-313637-9

Editor in Chief: *Emily Barrosse*
Publisher: *Lisa Moore*
Marketing Manager: *Pamela Cooper*
Director of Development: *Lisa Pinto*
Developmental Editor: *Kristen Mellitt*
Project Manager: *Christina Gimlin*
Manuscript Editor: *Margaret Moore*
Art Director: *Jeanne Schreiber*
Design Manager: *Kim Menning*
Text Designer: *Glenda King*
Cover Designer: *Kim Menning*
Art Editor: *Robin Mouat*
Manager, Photo Research: *Brian Pecko*
Production Supervisor: *Randy Hurst*
Composition: *9.5/12 Palatino by Prographics*
Printing: *60# Sterling Gloss by RR Donnelley, Willard*

Credits: The credits section for this book begins on page C-1 and is considered an extension of the copyright page.

Library of Congress Cataloging-in-Publication Data
Matthews, Roy T.
    The Western humanities/Roy T. Matthews & F. DeWitt Platt.—6th ed.
        p. cm.
    Includes bibliographical references and index.
    ISBN 13: 978-0-07-313619-6 (alk. paper)
    ISBN 10: 0-07-313619-0 (alk. paper)
    1. Civilization, Western—History.   I. Platt, F. DeWitt. II. Title.

CB245.M375   2007
909'.09821—dc22

                                                                2006046966

The Internet addresses listed in the text were accurate at the time of publication. The inclusion of a Web site does not indicate an endorsement by the authors or McGraw-Hill, and McGraw-Hill does not guarantee the accuracy of the information presented at these sites.

www.mhhe.com

There is nothing nobler or more admirable than when two people who see eye to eye keep house as man and wife, confounding their enemies and delighting their friends, as they themselves know better than anyone.

—HOMER, *Odyssey*

PREFACE

This new edition of *The Western Humanities* represents a personal and cultural milestone. We claim it as a personal milestone, because for more than twenty years we have been defined by this project (which we affectionately call, "the Book")—reading, researching, writing, revising, and refining the manuscript, attending concerts, plays, operas, films, lectures, exhibitions, and gallery openings, and discussing the meaning of the Western heritage with colleagues, students, friends, and family. We also claim "the Book" as a cultural milestone because when it existed only in outline form in 1985, academia was in the midst of a culture war in which the future of textbooks devoted exclusively to Western culture seemed in doubt. Throughout the course of five editions, however, *The Western Humanities* has established itself as a strong presence on the academic scene, and we hope that in some small way it has contributed to the revitalization of arts and humanities survey courses in colleges and universities. Its reach now extends around the world—the latest translation has been published in mainland China.

With this sixth edition, we continue in the same spirit with which we first approached our subject. In the first edition, we placed Western cultural achievements within their historical context. In the second and third editions, we expanded coverage of the contributions of women and other artists outside the traditional canon. In the fourth edition, we added a multicultural dimension, with the expectation that students would gain a greater appreciation of world cultures beyond the Western traditions. In the fifth edition, we expanded our coverage of Islamic civilization, as a way of helping students to better grasp contemporary political and cultural issues. For the sixth edition, we have made the most extensive revision yet, increasing the coverage of philosophy, science, music,

and religion, broadening the definition of creativity to embrace advances in technology, and enhancing our treatment of the history of film and photography. It is our hope that the sixth edition of *The Western Humanities* will continue to assist instructors in meeting today's teaching challenges, as well as help the next generation of students understand and claim their cultural heritage.

AIMS OF *THE WESTERN HUMANITIES*

In its origin *The Western Humanities* was an outgrowth of our careers as university teachers. Instructing thousands of undergraduate students throughout the years had left us dissatisfied with available textbooks. In our eyes, the existing books failed in one of two ways: They either ignored material developments and focused exclusively on cultural artifacts without context or perspective, or they stressed political, social, and economic history with too little or too disjointed a discussion of literature and the arts. Our goal in writing this book was to balance and integrate these two elements—that is, to provide an analysis and an appreciation of cultural expression and artifacts within an interpretive historical framework.

When we sat down to write the first edition of *The Western Humanities*, we feared that the world of the late twentieth century was in danger of being engulfed by present-minded thinking. Students merely mirror the wider society when they show little knowledge of, or even concern about, the great artistic and literary monuments and movements of the Western tradition, or about the political, economic, and social milestones of Western history. In *The Western Humanities*, we address the problem of present-mindedness by discussing not only the works that were produced in successive periods but also the prevailing historical and material conditions that so powerfully influenced their form and content. Our intention is to demystify the cultural record by showing that literature and the arts do not spring forth spontaneously and independently of each other, but reflect a set of specific historical circumstances. By providing this substantial context, out of which both ideas and artifacts emerge, we hope to give students a deeper understanding of the meaning of cultural works and a broader basis for appreciating the humanities.

We also emphasize the universal aspects of creativity and expression. People everywhere have the impulse to seek answers to the mysteries of human existence; to discover or invent order in the universe; to respond creatively to nature, both inner and outer; to delight the senses and the mind with beauty and truth; to communicate their thoughts and share their visions with others. Thus, another of our intentions is to demonstrate that the desire to express oneself and to create lasting monuments has been a compelling drive in human beings since before the dawn of civilized life. We believe that this emphasis will help students see that they are not isolated from the past but belong to a tradition that began thousands of years ago.

We also aim to help students prepare themselves for the uncertainties of the future. When they examine the past and learn how earlier generations confronted and overcame crises—and managed to leave enduring legacies—students will discover that the human spirit is irrepressible. In the humanities—in philosophy, religion, art, music, literature—human beings have found answers to their deepest needs and most perplexing questions. We hope that students will be encouraged by this record as they begin to shape the world of the twenty-first century.

ORGANIZATION AND CONTENT

The twenty-two chapters of this text provide a balanced treatment of history and culture. The chapters follow a consistent organization, as described below.

An interpretive context for the humanities. The first part of every chapter covers the material conditions of the era—the historical, political, economic, and social developments. We aim to capture the essence of complex periods and to fashion a coherent narrative framework for the story of Western culture.

Cultural expression. The remaining part of each chapter is devoted to cultural expression, both in the realm of ideas (philosophy, history, religion, science) and in the realm of cultural artifact (art, music, drama, literature, and film). In this part we describe and analyze the significant cultural achievements of the age, and we examine how creative individuals responded to the challenges presented to them by their society and how they chose values and forms by which to live.

Cultural legacy. Each chapter ends with a brief section describing the cultural legacy of that era. Students will find that some ideas, movements, or artistic methods with which they are familiar have a very long history. They will also discover that the meaning and ascribed value of cultural objects and texts can change from one time and place to another. Our goal is not only to help students establish a context for their culture but to show that the humanities have developed as a dynamic series of choices made by individuals in one era and transformed by individuals in other eras.

SPECIAL FEATURES

The Sixth Edition includes a variety of features to enhance student understanding of the humanities.

- **Enounter boxes.** A special feature introduced in the fifth edition was the **Encounter**, which recounts meetings between the West and other cultures. Through text and art, each Encounter focuses on critical interchanges that influenced both cultures. As we seek to nurture global awareness in today's students, these Encounters demonstrate that cultural encounters and exchanges are an enduring part of history, with both positive and negative consequences.

- **Slices of Life features.** Formerly known as Personal Perspectives, these boxes offer students the opportunity to hear voices from the past of those who witnessed or participated in the historical and cultural events described in the text. These excerpts from primary sources and original documents are designed to bring history to life for the reader.

- **Learning through Maps.** This feature encourages students to develop geographical skills—a highly desirable ability in this age of globalization. By performing map exercises and answering map-related questions, students learn to read maps and understand historical and cultural developments within a specific geographic setting.

- **Legacy sections.** Each chapter ends with a section that conveys the enduring legacy of the traditions described in the chapter. For example, in Chapter 8, the legacy section talks about the ongoing cultural influence of medieval Islam on both modern Islam and on the West.

In addition to the chapter features, each chapter offers several important features at its conclusion:

Terminology. In the text, when a new cultural term is introduced, it is boldfaced and defined immediately. At the end of each chapter, a list of **Key Cultural Terms** appears, serving as a handy review of important words for the student to know. The **Suggestions for Further Reading** is a list, in alphabetic order by author, of one or two literary works by the major writers discussed in the chapter. We provide this list—naming a readily available edition along with an assessment of its usefulness—so that students may do some additional reading on their own. The **Suggestions for Listening** feature offers a list, in alphabetic order by composer, of musical compositions covered in each chapter. The list, with brief annotations, is provided as a follow-up to the music discussion in the chapter, so that students may listen on their own.

CHANGES TO THE SIXTH EDITION

We have made several significant changes in this sixth edition of *The Western Humanities:*

Increased global emphasis. A new final chapter on the impact of globalization and terror on the arts, fourteen new Encounter features highlighting interactions between the West and other cultures, and the addition of numerous writers, artists, and philosophers from around the world (all discussed in detail below), strengthen the book's focus on the global roots of the Western humanities. The illustration program also includes new globally-oriented images, such as a map of the Silk Road in Chapter 7, and manuscript illuminations depicting the Crusades in Chapter 9.

Reorganization and expansion of final chapters. Chapter 21 now focuses on Late Modernism, from 1945 to 1970, while a brand-new Chapter 22 is devoted to Post-Modernism, from 1970 to the present. In Chapter 21, additions include Neo-Orthodoxy; Vatican II reforms; a new and extensive section on film; a new Encounter, "The Globalization of Popular Music"; and a new Slice of Life giving the words of the first astronauts as they recalled their impressions of being on the Moon. We also discuss many individuals not covered in previous editions, such as theologian Paul Tillich; and writers and artists who had not been previously included, such as painter Willem de Kooning, sculptor Eva Hesse, and architect Eero Saarinen. In Chapter 22, we stress both globalization and terrorism and their impact across global culture, as well as include enhanced treatment of science and technology; the birth of liberation theology; the papacy of Pope John Paul II; the rise of radical Islam; the maturation of woodwind chamber music; the rise of hip-hop culture in music; a film section; an Encounter about demography and migration and their impact on globalization; and a Slice of Life dealing with the sources of Islamic terrorism. New individuals covered include novelist Zadie Smith, poet Derek Walcott, playwrights Dario Fo and Franca Rame, painters Susan Rothenberg and Sam Gilliam, sculptor Maya Lin, architect Zaha Hadid, and composer Tan Dun.

Expanded coverage of selected cultural topics. Science, for example, now appears in ten chapters, including Hellenistic Greece and Post-Modernism. Similarly, philosophy is expanded to bridge gaps in our treatment of the history of thought, with the addition of Jean Bodin, David Hume, Paul Tillich, and Christian Existentialism. Medicine is now discussed in many chapters, beginning with the Mesopotamians and Egyptians and ranging from the Greeks—with the inclusion of Hippocrates—through the Romans, the Muslims and Renaissance Europe to Post-Modern times. Religion is now given more visibility, by focusing on the growth of evangelicalism in Protestantism and the Roman Catholic Church's hostile reaction to modernity, after 1850. This enhanced coverage of religion thus presents more clearly the history of the continuing dialogue between secular culture and religion—a central feature of Western life today. And music is now expanded to provide brief but intense discussions of 23 musical works. These music discussions also serve a secondary goal: They function as "mini-Listening Guides" for students who listen along with the Music CD that is part of the ancillary materials associated with our textbook. Other noteworthy additions to music include the Encounter "The Globalization of Popular Music" in Chapter 21, and an enlarged treatment of Post-Modern music, in Chapter 22.

Expanded coverage of Technology. Technology, which in earlier editions of *The Western Humanities* had been treated as the handmaid of the arts and humanities, is presented in this sixth edition as a form of creative expression whose roots go back to prehistoric times. We show that technology is subject to the same historical and cultural forces that operate on other creative achievements in each period of history. Our coverage of technology extends to most chapters, ranging from Stone Age culture to today's nanotechnology, with a focus especially on those technologies with transformative potential, such as machines, papermaking, food production, and power sources. Along with technology, we have included sections on warfare, which is central to the human experience, embracing the military, science, technology, and governments, and we also show warfare's impact on the wider culture.

New Encounters features. An Encounter feature now appears in all 22 chapters, resulting in an addition of fourteen new episodes for this sixth edition. The new Encounters include such major cultural exchanges as the invention of the alphabet by the ancient Phoenicians, which became the alphabet for virtually all Western languages; the creation of the Silk Road, linking ancient Rome and the Far East, the world's first attempt at globalization; and the development of the civil disobedience techniques of Gandhi, the father of Indian independence. We have made the Encounters more engaging by adding a set of questions at the end of each, entitled Learning from the Encounter, a pedagogical device meant to help students understand the historical and cultural significance of these meetings.

Enhanced Slices of Life features. We have revised the Slices of Life so that this feature reflects a rich variety of voices including people of diverse religious outlook, including Christian, Muslim, Jewish, and pagan. We have also added questions to each feature, entitled Interpreting this Slice of Life, which are meant to assist students in understanding each speaker.

Enhanced art program. About 115 new artworks are included. Every illustration in the book is discussed both in the text and in a detailed caption. The new illustrations include the Cylinder Seal of Queen Pu-abi, with Banqueting Scene; one of the Vaphio Cups; Horsemen, from the west frieze of the Parthenon; a Hunt Scene from the Piazza Armerina; Arches of the Great Mosque in Cordoba; manuscript illuminations of Crusaders Attacking a Muslim Fortress and Muslims Attacking Crusaders; Ghiberti's *Gates of Paradise*; Bellini's *Mehmet II*; Holbein's *Henry VIII*; Brueghel's *Netherlandish Proverbs*; Rembrandt's etching of *Christ Preaching*; Chambers' Pagoda in Kew Gardens, London; a Gillray caricature; Ingres's *Madame Rivière*; Solar's *Drago*; the Bauhaus Workshop; Moore's *Reclining Figure*; De Kooning's *Woman and Bicycle*; a still from Bergman's *The Seventh Seal*; Rothenberg's *Butterfly*; Richter's *Betty*; and Koolhaas' Seattle Public Library. We have also introduced students to less well-known artists, such as Gerard Ter Borch, Raoul Dufy, and Childe Hassam, through their paintings of historical events.

Increased coverage of women and people of diverse origins. These additions include Encounter 13, "Indigenous Peoples and New Spain"; DeIslas's portrait of Sor Juana Inès de la Cruz, the Mexican nun and early feminist; Slice of Life 17, the testimony of Elizabeth Bentley, a working class woman, before an English parliamentary commission; Inman's portrait of *Sequoyah*, the Cherokee leader, in Encounter 18; the rise of hip hop music; two women photographers (Margaret Bourke-White and Dorothea Lange); one woman film director (Leni Riefenstahl); two African American film directors (Melvin van Peebles and Spike Lee); one Iraqi-born woman architect, living in the U.K. (Zaha Hadid); one Chinese-American architect (I. M. Pei); one Chinese-American sculptor (Maya Lin); two women sculptors (Eva Hesse and Jeanne-Claude); two women painters (Bridget Riley and Susan Rothenberg); one African American painter (Samuel Gilliam); the Jamaican-British woman writer (Zadie Smith); one woman playwright-performer (Franca Rame); one West Indian-American poet (Derek Walcott); a woodwind ensemble composed of minority musicians (Imani Winds); and a Chinese-American actor (Bruce Lee).

TEACHING AND LEARNING RESOURCES

As instructors, we are keenly aware of the problems encountered in teaching the humanities, especially to large, diverse classes. This text comes with a comprehensive package of supplementary resource materials, designed to help solve those problems.

Instructor's Manual. The sixth edition of the Instructor's Manual has been revised and expanded. For each chapter the manual includes teaching strategies and suggestions; learning objectives; key cultural terms; film, reading, and Internet site suggestions; and a detailed outline revised to accompany the sixth edition of *The Western Humanities*. References to the accompanying anthology, *Readings in the Western Humanities*, are included in each chapter so that primary source material can be easily incorporated into each lesson. In addition to chapter-by-chapter materials, the Instructor's Manual offers five basic teaching strategies and seven lecture models in the preface. The Instructor's Manual is available on the Online Learning Center.

The Image Vault. A large percentage of images from the illustration program are available to adopting instructors in digital format in **The Image Vault,** McGraw-Hill's new Web-based presentation manager. Instructors can incorporate images from The Image Vault in digital presentations that can be used in class (no Internet access required), burned to CD-ROM, or embedded in course Web pages. See www.mhhe.com/theimagevault for more details.

Music selections. An audio CD that accompanies the sixth edition covers the broad spectrum of music discussed in the text and includes pieces by such composers as Hildegard of Bingen, J. S. Bach, Igor Stravinsky, and Philip Glass.

MyHumanitiesStudio. The student content for the Online Learning Center of this new edition of *The Western Humanities* has been reorganized and newly enriched. All of the Core Concepts content previously available on DVD-ROM has been converted so that students can access the information online. Students can watch videos about various art techniques and access interactive activities designed to strengthen their understanding of visual art, dance, music, sculpture, literature, theater, architecture, and film. They will also be able to use the guided Research in Action tool to enhance their understanding of time periods, genres, and artists. We hope that this online availability will strengthen student understanding of the humanities as well as spark their own creativity. All of this information is available at www.mhhe.com/mp6 when you click on the **MyHumanitiesStudio** link.

Readings in the Western Humanities. Selections in this anthology of primary source materials are arranged chronologically to follow the 22 chapters of the text, and are divided into two volumes. Volume I covers ancient Mesopotamia through the Renaissance; Volume II, the Renaissance into the 21st century. This anthology gives students access to our literary and philosophical heritage, allowing them to experience firsthand the ideas and voices of the great writers and thinkers of the Western tradition.

ACKNOWLEDGMENTS

We are grateful to many people for their help and support in this revision of *The Western Humanities.* We continue to appreciate the many insightful comments of students and former students at Michigan State University over the years. We thank Professor Michael Mackay for his suggestions on the topic of nanotechnology. We are also grateful for the many suggestions and comments provided to us by the following reviewers:

Peter Dusenbery, Bradley University
Bobby Hom, Santa Fe Community College
James Housefield, Texas State University—San Marcos
Susan Jones, Palm Beach Atlantic University
Vance S. Martin, Parkland College
Kevin R. Morgan, St. Petersburg College
Linda J. Nelson, Davenport University
Darrell G. Olges, Florida Community College—Jacksonville
Linda Smith Tabb, Parkland College
Stephen Thomas, Community College of Denver
Paul Van Heuklom, Lincoln Land Community College
Rennie VanKampen, International Academy of Design and Technology
Richard A. Voeltz, Cameron University
Bertha Wise, Oklahoma City Community College
Margaret Woodruff-Wieding, Austin Community College

This sixth edition, for reasons beyond our control, has been a challenge in preparation. We thank Alexis Walker for her early role in this project. And, we especially thank Clare Payton for her certain and steady guidance. It was Clare's vision that sustained us through the many months of this endeavor, and she proved to be a calm and wise influence for us both. Special thanks to Lisa Moore, and, especially, Lisa Pinto, Kristen Mellitt, and Christina Gimlin, and to the entire editorial and production team at McGraw-Hill.

CONTENTS

3
CLASSICAL GREEK CIVILIZATION
The Hellenic Age *63*

4
CLASSICAL GREEK CIVILIZATION
The Hellenistic Age *93*

5
ROMAN CIVILIZATION
The Pre-Christian Centuries *119*

11
THE EARLY RENAISSANCE
Return to Classical Roots
1400–1494 *321*

12
THE HIGH RENAISSANCE
AND EARLY MANNERISM,
1494–1564 *351*

INTRODUCTION
Why Study Cultural History?

To be ignorant of what occurred before you were born is to remain always a child.

—CICERO, FIRST CENTURY B.C.E.

Anyone who cannot give an account to oneself of the past three thousand years remains in darkness, without experience, living from day to day.

—GOETHE, NINETEENTH CENTURY C.E.

The underlying premise of this book is that some basic knowledge of the Western cultural heritage is necessary for those who want to become educated human beings in charge of their own destinies. If people are not educated into their place in human history—five thousand years of relatively uninterrupted, though sometimes topsy-turvy, developments—then they are rendered powerless, subject to passing fads and outlandish beliefs. They become vulnerable to the flattery of demagogues who promise heaven on earth, or they fall prey to the misconception that present-day events are unique, without precedent in history, or superior to everything that has gone before.

Perhaps the worst that can happen is to exist in a limbo of ignorance—in Goethe's words, "living from day to day." Without knowledge of the past and the perspective it brings, people may come to believe that their contemporary world will last forever, when in reality much of it is doomed to be forgotten. In contrast to the instant obsolescence of popular culture, the study of Western culture offers an alternative that has passed the unforgiving test of time. Long after today's heroes and celebrities have fallen into oblivion, the achievements of our artistic and literary ancestors—those who have forged the Western tradition—will remain. Their works echo down the ages and seem fresh in every period. The ancient Roman writer Seneca put it well when he wrote, in the first century A.D., "Life is short but art is long."

When people realize that the rich legacy of Western culture is their own, their view of themselves and the times they live in can expand beyond the present moment. They find that they need not be confined by the limits of today but can draw on the creative insights of people who lived hundreds and even thousands of years ago. They discover that their own culture has a history and a context that give it meaning and shape. Studying and experiencing their cultural legacy can help them understand their place in today's world.

THE BOUNDARIES OF THE WEST

The subject of this text is Western culture, but what exactly do we mean, first, by "culture" and, second, by the "West"? *Culture* is a term with several meanings, but we use it here to mean the artistic and intellectual expressions of a people, their creative achievements. By the *West* we mean that part of the globe that lies west of Asia and Asia Minor and north of Africa, especially Europe—the geographical framework for much of this study.

The Western tradition is not confined exclusively to Europe as defined today, however. The contributions of peoples who lived beyond the boundaries of present-day Europe are also included in Western culture, either because they were forerunners of the West, such as those who created the first civilizations in Mesopotamia and Egypt, or because they were part of the West for periods of time, such as those who lived in the North African and Near Eastern lands bordering the

Mediterranean Sea during the Roman and early Christian eras. Regardless of geography, Western culture draws deeply from ideals forged in these lands.

When areas that had been part of the Western tradition at one time were absorbed into other cultural traditions—as happened in the seventh century in Mesopotamia, Egypt, and North Africa when the people embraced the Muslim faith—then they are generally no longer included in Western cultural history. Because of the enormous influence of Islamic civilization on Western civilization, however, we do include in this volume both an account of Islamic history and a description and appreciation of Islamic culture. Different in many ways from our own, the rich tradition of Islam has an important place in today's world.

After about 1500, with voyages and explorations reaching the farthest parts of the globe, the European focus of Western culture that had held for centuries began to dissolve. Starting from this time, the almost exclusively European mold was broken and Western values and ideals began to be exported throughout the world, largely through the efforts of missionaries, soldiers, colonists, and merchants. Coinciding with this development and further complicating the pattern of change were the actions of those who imported and enslaved countless numbers of black Africans to work on plantations in North and South America. The interplay of Western culture with many previously isolated cultures, whether desired or not, forever changed all who were touched by the process.

The Westernization of the globe that has been going on ever since 1500 is perhaps the dominant theme of our time. What human greed, missionary zeal, and dreams of empire failed to accomplish before 1900 was achieved during the twentieth century by modern technology, the media, and popular culture. The world today is a global village, much of it dominated by Western values and styles of life. In our time, Westernization has become a two-way interchange. When artists and writers from other cultures adopt Western forms or ideas, they are not only Westernizing their own traditions but also injecting fresh sensibilities and habits of thought into the Western tradition. The globalization of culture means that a South American novel or a Japanese film can be as accessible to Western audiences as a European painting, and yet carry with it an intriguingly new vocabulary of cultural symbols and meanings.

HISTORICAL PERIODS AND CULTURAL STYLES

In cultural history, the past is often divided into historical periods and cultural styles. A historical period is an interval of time that has a certain unity because it is characterized by the prevalence of a unique culture, ideology, or technology, or because it is bounded by defining historical events, such as the death of a military leader like Alexander the Great or a political upheaval like the fall of Rome. A cultural style is a combination of features of artistic or literary expression, execution, or performance that defines a particular school or era. A historical period may have the identical time frame as a cultural style, or it may embrace more than one style simultaneously or two styles successively. Each chapter of this survey focuses on a historical period and includes significant aspects of culture—usually the arts, architecture, literature, religion, music, and philosophy—organized around a discussion of the relevant style or styles appropriate to that time.

The survey begins with prehistory, the era before writing was invented, setting forth the emergence of human beings from an obscure past. After the appearance of writing in about 3000 B.C.E., the Western cultural heritage is divided into three sweeping historical periods: ancient, medieval, and modern.

The ancient period dates from 3000 B.C.E. to 500 C.E. (Timeline 1). During these thirty-five hundred years the light of Western civilization begins to shine in Mesopotamia and Egypt, shines more brightly still in eighth-century-B.C.E. Greece and Rome, loses some of its luster when Greece succumbs to Rome in 146 B.C.E., and finally is snuffed out when the Roman Empire collapses in the fifth century C.E. Coinciding with these historical periods are the cultural styles of Mesopotamia; Egypt; Greece, including Archaic, Classical (or Hellenic), and Hellenistic styles; and Rome, including Republican and Imperial styles.

The medieval period, or the Middle Ages, covers events between 500 and 1500 C.E., a one-thousand-year span that is further divided into three subperiods (Timeline 2). The Early Middle Ages (500–1000) is typified by frequent barbarian invasions and political chaos so that civilization itself is threatened and barely survives. No single international style characterizes this turbulent period, though several regional styles flourish. The High Middle Ages (1000–1300) is a period of stability and the zenith of medieval culture. Two successive styles appear, the Romanesque and the Gothic, with the latter dominating culture for the rest of the medieval period. The Late Middle Ages (1300–1500) is a transitional period in which the medieval age is dying and the modern age is struggling to be born.

The modern period begins in about 1400 (there is often overlap between historical periods) and continues today (Timeline 3). With the advent of the modern period, a new way of defining historical changes starts

Timeline 1   THE ANCIENT WORLD

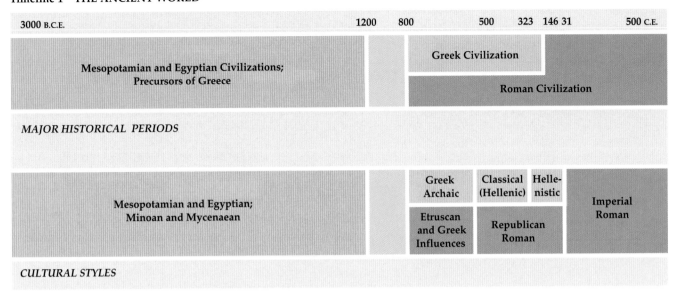

way they are expressed, especially in the Mannerist style.

The Reformation is followed by the Scientific Revolution (1600–1700), a movement that results in the abandonment of ancient science and the birth of modern science. Radical in its conclusions, the Scientific Revolution is somewhat out of touch with the style of its age, which is known as the Baroque. This magnificent style is devoted to overwhelming the senses through theatrical and sensuous effects and is associated with the attempts of the Roman Catholic Church to reassert its authority in the world.

The Scientific Revolution gives impetus to the Enlightenment (1700–1800), a movement that pledges to reform politics and society according to the principles

to make more sense—the division of history into movements, the activities of large groups of people united to achieve a common goal. The modern period consists of waves of movements that aim to change the world in some specific way.

The first modern movement is the Renaissance (1400–1600), or "rebirth," which attempts to revive the cultural values of ancient Greece and Rome. It is accompanied by two successive styles, Renaissance and Mannerism. The next significant movement is the Reformation (1500–1600), which is dedicated to restoring Christianity to the ideals of the early church set forth in the Bible. Although it does not spawn a specific style, this religious upheaval does have a profound impact on the subjects of the arts and literature and the

Timeline 2   THE MEDIEVAL WORLD

500		1000	1150	1300	1500
Early Middle Ages			High Middle Ages		Late Middle Ages

MAJOR HISTORICAL PERIODS

| | Regional Styles | | Romanesque | Gothic | |

CULTURAL STYLES

Timeline 3   THE MODERN WORLD

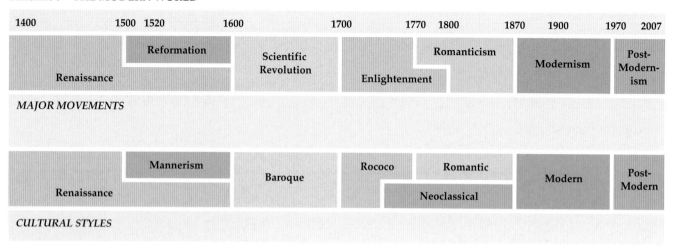

of the new science. In stylistic terms the eighteenth century is schizophrenic, dominated first by the Rococo, an extravagant and fanciful style that represents the last phase of the Baroque, and then by the Neoclassical, a style inspired by the works of ancient Greece and Rome and reflective of the principles of the Scientific Revolution. Before the eighteenth century is over, the Enlightenment calls forth its antithesis, Romanticism (1770–1870), a movement centered on feeling, fantasy, and everything that cannot be proven scientifically. The Romantic style, marked by a revived taste for the Gothic and a love of nature, is the perfect accompaniment to this movement.

Toward the end of the nineteenth century, Modernism (1870–1970) arises, bent on destroying every vestige of both the Greco-Roman tradition and the Christian faith and on fashioning new ways of understanding that are independent of the past. Since 1970, Post-Modernism has emerged, a movement that tries to make peace with the past by embracing old forms of expression while at the same time adopting a global and multivoiced perspective.

Although every cultural period is marked by innovation and creativity, our treatment of them in this book varies somewhat, with more space and greater weight given to the achievements of certain times. We make these adjustments because some periods or styles are more significant than others, especially in the defining influence that their achievements have had on our own era. For example, some styles seem to tower over the rest, such as Classicism in fifth-century-B.C.E. Greece, the High Renaissance of sixteenth-century Italy, and Modernism in the mid–twentieth century, as compared with other styles, such as that of the Early Middle Ages or the seventeenth-century Baroque.

AN INTEGRATED APPROACH TO CULTURAL HISTORY

Our approach to the Western heritage in this book is to root cultural achievements in their historical settings, showing how the material conditions—the political, social, and economic events of each period—influenced their creation. About one third of each chapter is devoted to an interpretive discussion of material history, and the remaining two thirds are devoted to the arts, architecture, philosophy, religion, literature, and music of the period. These two aspects of history do not occur separately, of course, and one of our aims is to show how they are intertwined.

As just one example of this integrated approach, consider the Gothic cathedral, that lofty, light-filled house of worship marked by pointed arches, towering spires, and radiant stained-glass windows. Gothic cathedrals were erected during the High Middle Ages, following a bleak period when urban life had virtually ceased. Although religion was still the dominant force in European life, trade was starting to flourish once again, town life was reviving, and urban dwellers were beginning to prosper. In part as testimonials to their new wealth, cities and towns commissioned architects and hired workers to erect these soaring churches, which dominated the landscape for miles around and proclaimed the economic well-being of their makers.

We adopt an integrated approach to Western culture not just in considering how the arts are related to material conditions but also in looking for the common themes, aspirations, and ideas that permeate the artistic and literary expressions of every individual era. The creative accomplishments of an age tend to reflect a shared perspective, even when that perspective

INTRODUCTION   **xxi**

is not explicitly recognized at the time. Thus, each period possesses a unique outlook that can be analyzed in the cultural record. A good example of this phenomenon is Classical Greece in the fifth century B.C.E., when the ideal of moderation, or balance in all things, played a major role in sculpture, architecture, philosophy, religion, and tragic drama. The cultural record in other periods is not always as clear as that in ancient Greece, but shared qualities can often be uncovered that distinguish the varied aspects of culture in an era to form a unifying thread.

A corollary of this idea is that creative individuals and their works are very much influenced by the times in which they live. This is not to say that incomparable geniuses—such as Shakespeare in Renaissance England—do not appear and rise above their own ages, speaking directly to the human mind and heart in every age that follows. Yet even Shakespeare reflected the political attitudes and social patterns of his time. Though a man for the ages, he still regarded monarchy as the correct form of government and women as the inferiors of men.

THE SELECTION OF CULTURAL WORKS

The Western cultural heritage is vast, and any selection of works for a survey text reflects choices made by the authors. All the works we chose to include have had a significant impact on Western culture, but for different reasons. We chose some because they blazed a new trail, such as Picasso's *Demoiselles d'Avignon* (see Figure 19.22), which marked the advent of Cubism in painting, or Fielding's *Tom Jones*, one of the earliest novels. Other works were included because they seemed to embody a style to perfection, such as the regal statue called *Poseidon* (or *Zeus*) (see Figure 3.21), executed in the Classical style of fifth-century-B.C.E. Athens, or Dante's *Divine Comedy*, which epitomized

the ideals of the High Middle Ages. On occasion, we chose works on a particular topic, such as the biblical story of David and Goliath, and demonstrated how different sculptors interpreted it, as in sculptures by Donatello (see Figure 11.11), Verrocchio (see Figure 11.12), and Michelangelo (see Figure 12.20). Still other works caught our attention because they served as links between successive styles, as is the case with Giotto's frescoes (see Figure 10.20), or because they represented the end of an age or an artistic style, as in the haunting sculpture called *The Last Pagan* (see Figure 7.12). Finally, we included some works, especially paintings, simply because of their great beauty, such as Ingres's *Madame Rivière* (see Figure 17.7).

Through all the ages of Western cultural history, through all the shifting styles and tastes embodied in painting, sculpture, architecture, poetry, and song, there glows a creative spark that can be found in human beings in every period. This diversity is a hallmark of the Western experience, and we celebrate it in this book.

A CHALLENGE TO THE READER

The purpose of all education is and should be self-knowledge. This goal was first established by the ancient Greeks in their injunction to "Know thyself," the inscription carved above the entrance to Apollo's temple at Delphi. Self-knowledge means awareness of oneself and one's place in society and the world. Reaching this goal is not easy, because becoming an educated human being is a lifelong process, requiring time, energy, and commitment. But all journeys begin with a single step, and we intend this volume as a first step toward understanding and defining oneself in terms of one's historical and cultural heritage. Our challenge to the reader is to use this book to begin the long journey to self-knowledge.

A HUMANITIES PRIMER
How to Understand the Arts

INTRODUCTION

We can all appreciate the arts. We can find pleasure or interest in paintings, music, poems, novels, films, and many other art forms, both contemporary and historical. We don't need to know very much about art to know what we like, because we bring ourselves to the work: What we like has as much to do with who we are as with the art itself.

Many of us, for example, will respond positively to a painting like Leonardo da Vinci's *The Virgin of the Rocks*. The faces of the Madonna and angel are lovely; we may have seen images like these on Christmas cards or in other commercial reproductions. We respond with what English poet William Wordsworth calls the "first careless rapture," which activates our imaginations and establishes a connection between us and the work of art. However, if this is all we see, if we never move from a subjective reaction, we can only appreciate the surface, the immediate form, and then, perhaps subconsciously, accept without question the values it implies. We appreciate, but we do not understand.

Sometimes we cannot appreciate because we do not understand. We may reject Picasso's *Les Demoiselles d'Avignon*, for it presents us with images of women that we may not be able to recognize. These women may make us uncomfortable, and the values they imply may frighten us rather than please or reassure us. Rather than rapture, we may experience disgust; but when we realize that this painting is considered a groundbreaking work, we may wonder what we're missing and be willing to look deeper. (*The Virgin of the Rocks* and *Les Demoiselles d'Avignon* are discussed in the text on page 345 and pages 605–7, respectively.)

LEONARDO DA VINCI. *The Virgin of the Rocks.*

To understand a work of art (a building, a poem, a song, a symphony), we need to keep our "rapture" (our emotional response and connection) but make it less "careless," less superficial and subjective, less restricted to that which we recognize. We need to enrich our appreciation by searching for a meaning that goes beyond ourselves. This involves understanding the intent or goal of the artist, the elements of form present in the work, the ways in which those elements contribute to the artist's goal, the context within which the artwork evolved, and the connections of the work to other works. Understanding an artwork requires intellectual involvement as well as an emotional connection. The purpose of this primer is to provide you with some of the tools you will need to understand, as well as appreciate, literature, art, and music.

APPROACHES TO THE ANALYSIS OF LITERATURE, ART, AND MUSIC

When we analyze a work of art, we ask two questions: What is the artist trying to do, and how well is it done? We want to identify the intent of the work, and we want to evaluate its execution. To answer these questions, we can examine the formal elements of the work—an approach known as formalism—and we can explore its context—known as contextualism.

Formalism

A formal analysis is concerned with the aesthetic (artistic) elements of a work separate from context. This type of analysis focuses on medium and technique. The context of the work—where, when, and by whom a work was created—may be interesting, but is considered unnecessary to formalist interpretation and understanding. A formal analysis of a painting, sculpture, or architectural structure examines its line, shape, color, texture, and composition, as well as the artist's technical ability within the medium used; it is not concerned with anything extraneous to the work itself. A formal analysis of a literary work, such as a short story or novel, would explore the relationships among theme, plot, characters, and setting, as well as how well the resources of language—word choice, tone, imagery, symbol, and so on—are used to support the other elements. A formal analysis of a film would also explore theme, plot, characters (as developed both verbally and nonverbally), and setting, as well as how the resources of cinematography—camera techniques, lighting, sound, editing, and so on—support the other elements.

A formal analysis of *The Virgin of the Rocks* would examine the artist's use of perspective, the arrangement of figures as they relate to each other and to the grotto that surrounds them, the technical use of color and line, the dramatic interplay of light and shadow (known as *chiaroscuro*). The same technical considerations would be explored in a formal analysis of *Les Demoiselles d'Avignon*. The fact that the two paintings were completed in 1483 and 1907, respectively, would be important only in terms of the technology and mediums available to the artists. In a formal analysis, time and place exist only within the work.

PABLO PICASSO. *Les Demoiselles d'Avignon.*

Contextualism

In contrast, a contextual analysis focuses on factors outside the work: why it was created, in response to what artistic, social, cultural, historical, and political forces, events, and trends; who the artist is, and what his or her intent and motives were in creating the work; how the work fits in with other works of the same genre of the same or different eras; and how the work fits in with the rest of the artist's body of work. Time and place are very important.

A contextual analysis of the da Vinci and Picasso paintings would include information about where and when each painting was completed; the conditions from which it arose; the prevailing artistic styles of the times; the life circumstances of the artists; and so on.

The paintings alone do not provide enough information for contextual inquiry. Similarly, contextual analysis of a novel by Dostoevsky would consider both his personal circumstances and the conditions in Russia and Europe when he wrote. A contextual analysis of a chorale and fugue by Bach would include information on Bach's life, his religious beliefs, and the political climate of Germany in the eighteenth century.

An Integrated Approach

In a strictly contextual analysis of an artwork, the work itself can sometimes be lost in the exploration of context. In a strictly formal analysis, important knowledge that can contribute to understanding may remain unknown. The most effective analyses, therefore, combine and integrate the two approaches, examining the formal elements of the work and exploring the context within which it was created. Such an approach is more effective and, in a sense, more honest than either the formal or the contextual approach alone. A work of art, whether a poem or a painting, a cathedral or a cantata, is a complex entity, as are the relationships it fosters between the artist and the art and between the art and its audience. The integrative approach recognizes these relationships and their complexity. This is the approach to artistic and cultural analysis most frequently used in *The Western Humanities.*

A Variety of Perspectives

Many students and critics of culture, while taking an integrative approach, are also especially interested in looking at things from a particular perspective, a set of interests or a way of thinking that informs and influences their investigations and interpretations. Common perspectives are the psychological, the feminist, the religious, the economic, and the historical.

People working from a psychological perspective look for meaning in the psychological features of the work, such as sexual and symbolic associations; they do a kind of retroactive psychological analysis of the artist. They might look for meaning in the facial expressions, gestures, and body positions of Mary and the angel in *The Virgin of the Rocks.* They might be interested in da Vinci's attitudes toward women and his relationships with them, and they might compare this painting with the *Mona Lisa* in a search for clues about who he was.

Someone working from a feminist perspective would examine the art itself and the context in which it arose from a woman's point of view. To take a feminist perspective is to ask how the work depicts women, what it says about women and their relationships in general, and how it may or may not reflect a patriarchal society. Many people have discussed the apparent hatred of women that seems to come through in Picasso's *Les Demoiselles d'Avignon.* At the same time, the work, in its size (8 feet by 7 feet 8 inches) and in the unblinking attitude of its subjects, suggests that these women have a kind of raw power. Feminist critics focus on such considerations.

Analysis from a religious perspective is often appropriate when a work of art originated in a religious context. The soaring spires and cruciform floor plans of medieval cathedrals reveal religious meaning, for example, as do Renaissance paintings depicting biblical characters. Many contemporary works of art and literature also have religious content. Religious analyses look to the use of symbolism, the representation of theological doctrines and beliefs, and intercultural connections and influences for meaning.

Someone approaching a work of art from an economic perspective focuses on its economic content—the roles and relationships associated with wealth. Often drawing upon Marx's contention that class is the defining consideration in all human relationships and endeavors, an economic analysis would examine both purpose and content: Was the work created as a display of power by the rich? How does it depict people of different classes? What is the artist saying about the distribution of wealth?

The historical perspective is perhaps the most encompassing of all perspectives, because it can include explorations of psychological, religious, and economic issues, as well as questions about class and gender in various times and places. Historical analysis requires an understanding of the significant events of the time and how they affect the individual and shape the culture. *The Western Humanities* most often takes a historical perspective in its views of art and culture.

The Vocabulary of Analysis

Certain terms and concepts are fundamental to the analysis of any artwork. We review several such general concepts and terms here, before moving on to a consideration of more specific art forms.

Any artwork requires a relationship between itself and its audience. **Audience** is the group for whom a work of art, architecture, literature, drama, film, or music is intended. The audience may be a single person, such as the Medici ruler to whom Machiavelli dedicated his political treatise *The Prince.* The audience can be a small group of people with access to the work, such as the monks who dined in the room where Leonardo da Vinci painted *The Last Supper* on the wall.

The audience can also be a special group of people with common interests or education; for example, films like *There's Something about Mary* and *Scream* are intended for a youthful audience. Sometimes the audience is limited by its own understanding of the art; we often feel excluded from what we don't understand. Consequently, some art requires an educated audience.

Composition is the arrangement of constituent elements in an individual work. In music, composition also refers to the process of creating the work.

Content is the subject matter of the work; content can be based on mythology, religion, history, current events, personal history, or almost any idea or feeling deemed appropriate by the artist.

Context is the setting in which the art arose, its own time and place. Context includes the political, economic, social, and cultural conditions of the time; it can also include the personal conditions and circumstances that shape the artist's vision.

A **convention** is an agreed-upon practice, device, technique, or form. A sonnet, for example, is a fourteen-line poem with certain specified rhyme schemes. A poem is not a sonnet unless it follows this formal convention. A convention of the theater is the "willing suspension of disbelief": We know that the events taking place before our eyes are not real, but we agree to believe in them for the duration of the play. Often, conventions in the arts are established as much by political powerbrokers as by artists. The Medicis and the Renaissance popes, for example, wanted portraits and paintings that glorified their reigns, and conventions in Renaissance art reflect these demands. Today, museum directors, wealthy individuals, and government funding agencies play a role in influencing the direction of contemporary art by supporting and showing the work of artists whose conventions they agree with or think are important.

Genre is the type or class to which a work of art, literature, drama, or music belongs, depending on its style, form, or content. In literature, for example, the novel is a genre in itself; the short story is another genre. In music, symphonies, operas, and tone poems are all different genres. Beginning in the Renaissance, genres were carefully distinguished from one another, and a definite set of conventions was expected whenever a new work in a particular genre was created.

The **medium** is the material from which an art object is made—marble or bronze, for example, in sculpture, or water colors or oils in painting. (The plural of *medium* in this sense is often *mediums;* when *medium* is used to refer to a means of mass communication, such as radio or television, the plural is *media*.)

Style is the combination of distinctive elements of creative execution and expression, in terms of both form and content. Artists, artistic schools, movements, and periods can be characterized by their style. Styles often evolve out of existing styles, as when High Renaissance style evolved into Mannerism in the sixteenth century, or in reaction to styles that are perceived as worn out or excessive, as when Impressionism arose to challenge Realism in the nineteenth century.

When we talk about **technique,** we are referring to the systematic procedure whereby a particular creative task is performed. If we were discussing a dancer's technique, we might be referring to the way he executes leaps and turns; a painter's technique might be the way she applies paint to a canvas with broad, swirling brushstrokes.

The dominant idea of a work, the message or emotion the artist intends to convey, is known as the **theme.** The theme, then, is the embodiment of the artist's intent. In a novel, for example, the theme is the abstract concept that is made concrete by character, plot, setting, and other linguistic and structural elements of the work. We often evaluate the theme of a work in terms of how well it speaks to the human condition, how accurate its truth is, how valuable its message or observation is. We usually make these judgments by exploring the extent to which the theme confirms or denies our own experience.

In addition to these general concepts and terms, each art form has its own vocabulary. These more specific terms will be introduced in the sections that follow on literary, artistic, and musical analysis, along with brief illustrative analyses in each area. These informal illustrations are meant not as definitive analyses but as examples of the kinds of productive questions you can ask as you approach a creative work. The analyses differ in their depth and level of detail.

LITERARY ANALYSIS

Literary analysis begins with a consideration of various literary genres and forms. A work of literature is written either in **prose,** the ordinary language used in speaking and writing, or in **poetry,** a more imaginative and concentrated form of expression usually marked by meter, rhythm, or rhyme. Part of poetry's effect comes from the sound of words; it can often best be appreciated when spoken or read aloud. Prose is often divided into nonfiction (essays, biography, autobiography) and fiction (short stories, novels).

In literature, *genre* refers both to form—essay, short story, novel, poem, play, film script, television script—and to specific type within a form—tragedy, comedy, epic, lyric, and so on. According to Aristotle, a **tragedy** must have a tragic hero—a person of high stature who is brought down by his own excessive pride (*hubris*); he doesn't necessarily die at the end, but whatever his greatness was based upon is lost. A **comedy** is a story with a complicated and amusing plot; it usually ends with a happy and peaceful resolution of any conflicts. An **epic** poem, novel, or film is a relatively long recounting of the life of a hero or the glorious history of a people. A **lyric** poem is a short, subjective poem usually expressing an intense personal emotion. In a general sense, an epic tells a story and a lyric expresses an idea or feeling. Lyric poetry includes ballads (dramatic verse meant to be sung or recited, often by more than one singer or speaker), elegies (short, serious meditations, usually on death or other significant themes), odes (short lyric poems dealing with a single theme), and sonnets (formal fourteen-line poems identified by the arrangement of lines as either Italian [Petrarchan] or English [Shakespearean]).

In literature, the author's intent—the message or emotion the author wishes to convey—is usually discussed as the theme of the work. In an essay, the theme is articulated as the thesis: the idea or conclusion that the essay will prove or support. In a novel, story, or play, we infer the theme from the content and the development of ideas and imagery.

In fiction, the action of the story, what Aristotle calls "the arrangement of incidents," is the **plot.** There may be a primary plot that becomes the vehicle by which the theme is expressed, with subplots related to secondary (or even tertiary) themes. Plot can be evaluated by how well it supports the theme. Plot can also be evaluated according to criteria established by Aristotle in his *Poetics*. According to these criteria, the action expressed should be whole, with a beginning that does not follow or depend on anything else, a middle that logically follows what went before, and an end, or logical culmination of all prior action. The plot should be unified, so that every action is necessary and interrelated with all other actions. Few works of fiction adhere to these criteria completely; nevertheless, the criteria do provide a way of beginning to think about how a plot works.

Characters are also important both for themselves and for their effect on the plot and support of the theme. **Characters** provide the human focus, the embodiment, of the theme; they act out and are affected by the plot. The protagonist, or primary character, of the work is changed by the dramatic action of the plot and thus is a dynamic character; static characters remain unchanged throughout the story. An antagonist is a character in direct opposition to the protagonist. Some characters are stock characters, representing a type rather than an individual human being: the romantic fool, the nosy neighbor, the wise old woman, the vain beauty, the plain girl or dumb boy with a heart of gold.

Readers need to believe that characters' actions are authentic reactions to various events. The believability of a work of fiction—the writer's ability to express the truth—is called verisimilitude. Even in works of science fiction or fantasy, where events occur that could not occur in reality, readers must believe that what characters say and do make sense under the conditions described.

The background against which the action takes place is the **setting.** It can include the geographical location, the environment (political, social, economic) in which the characters live, the historical time in which the action takes place, and the culture and customs of the time, place, and people.

The story or poem is told from the point of view of the **narrator.** The narrator is not necessarily identical with the author of the work. The narrator (or **narrative voice**) can be examined and analyzed like any other element of the work. When a narrator seems to know everything and is not limited by time or place, the work has an omniscient point of view. Such a narrator tells us what everyone is thinking, feeling, and doing. When the story is told from the perspective of a single character who can relate only what he or she knows or witnesses, the work has a first-person point of view. Such a narrator is limited in his or her understanding. Thus, we need to consider the narrator in order to judge how accurate or complete the narrative is.

Sometimes a narrator proves to be unreliable, and we have to piece together an account of the story ourselves. Other times an author uses multiple narrators to tell a story from multiple points of view. William Faulkner uses this device in his novel *The Sound and the Fury* to show that a story can be fully told only when several different characters have a chance to speak. Japanese film director Akira Kurosawa uses a similar device in *Rashomon* to show that there are many equally valid—or invalid—versions of the truth.

A literary analysis of a drama, whether a play for the stage or a film script, will consider not only the elements already mentioned—theme, plot, character, setting, language, and so on—but also the technical considerations specific to the form. In theater, these would include the work of the director, who interprets the play and directs the actors, as well as stage design, light and sound design, costumes, makeup, and so on. In film, technical considerations would include direction, editing, cinematography, musical score, special effects, and so on.

Let's turn now to a poem by Shakespeare and see how to approach it to enrich our understanding. Identifying a poem's intent and evaluating its execution is called an *explication,* from the French *explication de texte.* An explication is a detailed analysis of a poem's meaning, focusing on narrative voice, setting, rhyme, meter, words, and images. An explication begins with what is immediately evident about the poem as a whole, followed by a more careful examination of its parts.

William Shakespeare (1564–1616) was not just a great playwright; he was also a great poet. His works portray human emotions, motives, and relationships that we recognize today as well as the conditions and concerns of his time. In this sense, they are an example of aesthetic universality, the enduring connection between a work of art and its audience.

Shakespeare's sonnets are his most personal work. Scholars disagree about whether they are generic love poems or are addressed to a specific person and, if the latter, who that person might be. Formally, an English (or Shakespearean) sonnet is a 14-line poem consisting of three 4-line stanzas, or quatrains, each with its own rhyme scheme, and a concluding 2-line stanza, or couplet, that provides commentary on the preceding stanzas. The rhyme scheme in a Shakespearean sonnet is abab cdcd efef gg; that is, the first and third lines of each quatrain rhyme with each other, as do the second and fourth lines, though the rhymes are different in each quatrain. The last two lines rhyme with each other.

The meter of most Shakespearean sonnets is iambic pentameter; that is, each line has five feet, or units ("pentameter"), and each foot consists of an iamb, an unaccented syllable followed by an accented syllable (as in *alone*). An example of iambic pentameter is, "My mistress' eyes are nothing like the sun"; each foot consists of an unaccented and an accented syllable, and there are five feet. Unrhymed iambic pentameter—the verse of most of Shakespeare's plays—is known as **blank verse.**

Sonnet 130 ("My mistress' eyes are nothing like the sun") is a poem that not only illustrates sonnet form but also showcases Shakespeare's wit and his attitude toward certain conventions of his time. The poem was originally written in Elizabethan English, which looks and sounds quite different from modern English. We reproduce it in modern English, as is customary today for Shakespeare's works.

Sonnet 130

My mistress' eyes are nothing like the sun;
Coral is far more red than her lips' red;
If snow be white, why then her breasts are dun;
If hairs be wires, black wires grow on her head.

I have seen roses damask'd, red and white,
But no such roses see I in her cheeks,
And in some perfumes is there more delight
Than in the breath that from my mistress reeks.

I love to hear her speak, yet well I know
That music hath a far more pleasing sound;

I grant I never saw a goddess go,
My mistress when she walks treads on the ground.

And yet, by heaven, I think my love as rare
As any she belied with false compare.

Because the poet's intent may not be immediately evident, paraphrasing each line or stanza can point the reader to the theme or meaning intended by the poet. Let's begin, then, by paraphrasing the lines:

My mistress' eyes are nothing like the sun;
The speaker's lover's eyes are not bright.
Coral is far more red than her lips' red;
Her lips are not very red, certainly not as red as coral.
If snow be white, why then her breasts are dun;
Her breasts are mottled in color, not as white as snow.
If hairs be wires, black wires grow on her head.
Her hair is black (not blond, as was the conventional beauty standard then, when poets referred to women's hair as "golden wires").

I have seen roses damask'd, red and white,
But no such roses see I in her cheeks,
Her cheeks are not rosy.
And in some perfumes is there more delight
Than in the breath that from my mistress reeks.
Her breath doesn't smell as sweet as perfume.

I love to hear her speak, yet well I know
That music hath a far more pleasing sound;
Her voice doesn't sound as melodious as music.
I grant I never saw a goddess go,
My mistress when she walks treads on the ground.
Although the speaker has never seen a goddess walk, he knows his lover does not float above ground, as goddesses are supposed to do, but walks on the ground, a mortal woman.

And yet, by heaven, I think my love as rare
As any she belied with false compare.
His lover is as rare and valuable as any idealized woman glorified by false poetic comparisons.

Remember that to analyze a poem, we ask questions like, What is the theme of the poem, the poet's intent? How does Shakespeare support his point with specific images? From the paraphrased lines it is clear that the narrator is stating that his love is a real woman who walks upon the ground, not an unattainable ideal to be worshiped from afar. Idealized qualities are irrelevant to how he feels about her; the qualities he loves are the ones that make her human.

Closely examining each line of a poem helps to reveal the rhyme scheme (abab cdcd efef gg), the meter (iambic pentameter), and thus the form of the poem (sonnet). Explication of the formal elements of the poem would also include examining the use of language (such as word choice, imagery, comparisons, metaphors), the tone of the narrative voice, and so on.

To understand the context of the poem, we would consider the cultural climate of the time (was "courtly love" a prevalent cultural theme?); common contemporary poetic conventions (were many other poets proclaiming their eternal love for idealized women?); and the political, social, and economic conditions (what roles were open to women in Elizabethan England, and how were they changing? What influence might Queen Elizabeth have had on the poet's point of view? What comments about his society is Shakespeare making?)

Finally, we might consider how honest and accurate we find the emotional content of the poem to be, how relevant its truth. Are Shakespeare's observations germane to today, a time when the mass media present us with a nearly unattainable ideal as the epitome of female beauty?

✄ FINE ARTS ANALYSIS

As with literature, knowledge of a particular vocabulary helps us "speak the language" of art critics. The terms introduced here are in addition to those discussed earlier, such as *medium* and *technique.* They apply to all the visual arts, including drawing and painting, sculpture—the art of shaping material (such as wood, stone, or marble) into three-dimensional works of art—and architecture—the art and science of designing, planning, and building structures, usually for human habitation. In architecture, the critic would also pay attention to the blending of artistry and functionality (how well the structure fulfills its purpose).

Generally, art is more or less representational or more or less abstract. **Representational art** is true to human perception and presents a likeness of the world much as it appears to the naked eye. An important convention of representational art is **perspective,** the appearance of depth and distance on a two-dimensional surface. **Abstract art** presents a subjective view of the world, the artist's emotions or ideas; some abstract art simply presents color, line, or shape for its own sake.

The formal elements of visual art include line, shape, texture, color, composition, and so on. **Line** is the mark made by the artist, whether with pencil, pen, or paintbrush. Lines can be straight or curved, thick or thin, light or dark, spare or plentiful. **Color** is the use in the artwork of hues found in nature; **color** can enhance the sense of reality presented in a visual image, or it can distort it, depending on how it is used. The primary colors are red, blue, and yellow, and the secondary colors are orange (a combination of red and yellow), green (a combination of yellow and blue), and purple (a combination of blue and red). Blue, green, and purple hues are "cool" colors that appear to recede from the eye; red, yellow, and orange are "warm" colors that appear to move forward. Color has sym-

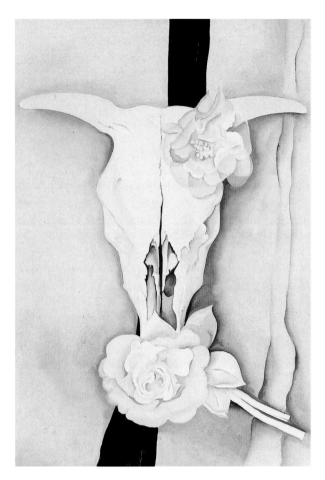

GEORGIA O'KEEFFE. *Cow's Skull with Calico Roses.*

bolic associations within specific historical and cultural settings. For example, in Western culture, white is a symbol of purity and is worn by brides. In Eastern cultures, white is a symbol of death; Chinese brides wear red to symbolize good luck.

How the artist arranges the work is referred to as the composition. Often the artist controls how the eye moves from one part to another by means of the composition. Through the composition the artist leads us to see the artwork in a particular way. The setting of an artwork is the time and place depicted in a representational work, as defined by visual cues—the people, how they are dressed, what they are doing, and so on.

With these terms in hand, let's consider *Cow's Skull with Calico Roses* by Georgia O'Keeffe (1887–1986), painted in 1931. What is the artist's intent? How well is that intent executed? Front and center we see the cow's skull, placed so the strong vertical line of the skull, accentuated by the skull's vertical midline crack, aligns with the center of the canvas. A broad band of black extending from the top of the canvas to the bottom behind the skull further reinforces the vertical axis, as do the wavy lines on the right. The skull's horns form a shorter, secondary horizontal line, creating a cross shape. At the bottom of the canvas, the black band seems to open; its expansion to the left is balanced by the rose stem in the lower right and the right-of-center rose at the top. The image overall is balanced and symmetrical, conveying a sense of stillness and repose rather than dynamic action.

The artist has not used broad or bold lines in her painting; rather, the lines of the skull and flowers are drawn delicately against the background; shading suggests contours and subtleties of lighting, and shadows blend softly. The surface is shallow and flat, conveying little sense of depth. The background material is ambiguous; is it cloth, paper, parchment, or some other material? The skull appears to float in front of this background. At the same time, the black band behind the skull seems to open into a mysterious space that recedes from the viewer.

The colors of the painting are muted, subtle, neutral—shades of black, gray, cream, and white. A slightly different color tone comes from the inside of the broken skull, where shades of tan and ochre are revealed. Within this world of muted tones, the white skull stands out rather starkly against the off-white background, and the flowers show up silvery gray against the white, beige, and black. The colors are quiet, almost somber, with a balance between the heavy black band and the other lighter-colored surfaces.

What are we to make of the image itself—a skull dressed up with cloth flowers? The animal almost appears to be eating or nuzzling one flower, and the other adorns its forehead. Many artists have used human skulls to remind us of our mortality, and in this painting suggestions of death and spirituality are reinforced, perhaps to the subconscious mind, by the cross shape that underlies the composition. In this context, the cow skull strikes an odd and discordant note. Cow skulls are often used to suggest the unforgiving nature of the desert, where animals and humans alike perish in a waterless, forbidding landscape. Here, the skull is transformed, first by its placement in an abstract setting and second by its adornment with artificial flowers. Is the image morbid, macabre? Is it humorous, playful, ironic? Or are we meant simply to see the skull in a new way, as a unique and interesting object, apart from the living animal it once was? Aged in the desert, bleached by the sun, the skull, though evocative of death, has its own stark beauty. The flowers too have their beauty; at the same time, the artist makes it clear that they are calico, not real. They are artificial, created by human hands to resemble living flowers.

Although the skull and flowers are painted realistically, the ambiguous background suggests that the artist is moving toward abstraction, toward an expression of feeling and mood rather than pure representation. The overall feeling evoked by the painting is one of contemplation, meditation. Faced with the juxtaposition of these incongruous objects, we are reminded of the intimate relationships between life and death, beauty and ugliness, art and nature.

How can we augment our appreciation and understanding of this painting with contextual knowledge? Georgia O'Keeffe grew up on a farm in Wisconsin, where she reveled in every detail of nature, bringing to it an attention and appreciation that would later be reflected in her paintings. She knew from an early age that she wanted to be an artist, and she studied art in Chicago and New York, developing a highly refined technique that quickly became recognized as uniquely her own. Among important early influences were the paintings and theories of Russian abstract artist Wassily Kandinsky, who believed that art and especially color had powerful spiritual effects. In 1929 O'Keeffe visited Taos, New Mexico, for the first time, where she became enraptured by the desert, the light, the colors of the landscape, the expanse of the sky. She was especially intrigued by bones—their form, shape, color, texture—and she shipped boxes of them back to her studio in New York to paint. Eventually she spent more and more time in the Southwest, developing a style that blended realism and abstraction. Her trademark was the selection and abstraction of an object or a view in nature, which she then transformed in accordance with her inner vision. She became known for her particular way of seeing and for her ability to enable others to see the same way.

When she painted *Cow's Skull with Calico Roses*, O'Keeffe was at a difficult time in her personal life. Perhaps depression led her to paint in subdued colors (rather than the brilliant colors of earlier and later paintings) and to focus on bones and other images of death (rather than the images of flowers for which she was already famous). Some have suggested that the seemingly suspended nature of the skull in this painting was suggestive of her own unsettled frame of mind. Whether or not personal details like these help us appreciate and understand the work, what is clear is that when we contemplate *Cow's Skull with Calico Roses,* we see not just the beauty of natural forms but also the power of nature to transform objects and the power of the artist to transform them once again.

MUSICAL ANALYSIS

Like literature and art, music has its own vocabulary, and we need to be familiar with it in order to analyze a composition. A basic distinction we can apply to music is the one between religious music, or **sacred music**—

such as Gregorian chants, Masses, requiems, and hymns—and **secular music**—such as symphonies, songs, and dances. Another distinction we can make is between vocal or choral music, which is sung and generally has lyrics (words), and instrumental music, which is written for and performed on instruments.

In music, composers choose among many different **forms,** or particular structures or arrangements of elements. Symphonies, songs, concertos, string quartets, sonatas, Masses, and operas are some of the many different forms in which composers may write their music. As in literature and the visual arts, various musical forms have been more or less popular according to the styles and fashions of the time. The madrigal, for example, was a popular vocal form of the Renaissance period; the church cantata was a common form in the Baroque period; and the symphony became the most important orchestral form beginning in the eighteenth century.

Music itself is a combination of tone, tempo, and texture. **Tone** is a musical sound of definite pitch (pitch is determined by the frequency of the air waves producing the sound). A set pattern of tones (or notes) arranged from low to high (or high to low) is known as a **scale.** The modern Western scale is the familiar do, re, mi, fa, sol, la, ti, do, with half steps in between the tones. In other cultures, more or fewer tones may be distinguished in a scale. The term tone can also refer to the quality of a sound. **Tempo** is the rate of speed of a musical passage, usually set or suggested by the composer. **Texture** describes the number and the nature of the voices or instruments employed and how the parts are combined. In music a theme is a characteristic musical idea upon which a composition is built or developed.

Melody is a succession of musical tones, usually having a distinctive musical shape, or line, and a definite rhythm (the recurrent alternation of accented and unaccented beats). **Harmony** is the simultaneous combination of two or more tones, producing a chord. More generally, harmony refers to the chordal characteristics of a work and the way in which chords interact with one another.

Music differs from literature and the visual arts in some important ways. First, unlike visual art, which does not change after the artist finishes it, music begins when the composition is complete. Like drama, music is lifeless until it is interpreted and performed. The written music represents the composer's intent, but the actual execution of the work is up to conductors and musicians.

A second difference is the fleeting, temporal nature of music. When we listen to live music, we hear it once and it's gone. We cannot study it like a painting or reread a passage as we can in a novel. Of course, recording devices and musical notation enable us to re-

visit music again and again, but by its very nature, music exists in time in a way that literature and the visual arts do not. For this reason, it is often particularly difficult to appreciate or understand a piece of music on first hearing; instead, we have to listen to it repeatedly.

Music is also more difficult to describe in words than literature or the visual arts. At best, words can only approximate, suggest, and refer to sounds. Sometimes it's helpful to use imagery from other sense modalities to describe a piece of music. What visual images does the work evoke? What colors? What textures? If you were to choreograph the work, how would the dancers move?

Finally, when we analyze a painting, we can reproduce it for our audience, and when we analyze a poem, we can reprint it. When we analyze music, we often have to hope that members of our audience know the work and can "hear" it in their heads. Alternatively, we can hope to generate enough interest in the work that they will want to make a point of hearing it themselves.

With these few basics in mind, let's consider a well-known musical work, *Rhapsody in Blue,* by George Gershwin (1898–1937). Even if you don't know this piece by name, it's very likely that you've heard it. It's been used in ads and in the sound tracks of numerous movies, including *Fantasia 2000;* it is also a standard accompaniment to images of New York City.

Imagine that you're seated in a concert hall and hearing this piece performed by a symphony orchestra (probably a "pops" orchestra, one that performs more popular classical music). When listening to a new piece of music or one you're not terribly familiar with, it's a good idea to simply try to get a sense of its general mood and character—again, focusing on the creator's intent. What emotions or ideas is the composer trying to convey? What musical elements does the composer use to execute that intent?

You'll notice, first of all, that the work is written for a small orchestra and a solo piano, the same instrumental configuration you would expect for a classical piano concerto (a concerto is a work for one or a few instruments and an orchestra, with much of its interest coming from the contrasts between the solo voice and the ensemble voice). But the opening notes of *Rhapsody in Blue* reveal something other than classical intentions: a solo clarinet begins low and sweeps up the scale in a seemingly endless "smear" of sound, finally reaching a high note, briefly holding it, and then plunging into the playful, zigzag melody that becomes one of the major themes of the work. Within moments, the orchestra enters and repeats the theme in the strings and brass, to be followed by the entry of the solo piano. Throughout the work, piano and orchestra alternate and combine to sing out beautiful melodies and create a varied and colorful texture. Variety also comes from different instrumentation of the themes and tunes, played first by a slinky muted trumpet, then by a sweet solo violin, later by a whole lush string section or a brash horn section.

You'll notice too the constant changes in tempo, now slower, now faster, almost as if the work is being improvised. Complex, syncopated, off-the-beat rhythms give the piece a jazzy feeling, and the combination of tones evokes the blues, a style of music in which certain notes are "bent," or lowered slightly in pitch, creating a particular sound and mood. The general feeling of the piece is upbeat, exciting, energetic, suggestive of a bustling city busy with people on the go. It may also make you think of Fred Astaire and Ginger Rogers movies you've seen on late-night TV—sophisticated, playful, casually elegant—and in fact, Gershwin wrote the music for some of their films.

What can we learn about this work from its title? Musical works often reveal their form in their title ("Fifth Symphony," "Violin Concerto in D," and so on). A rhapsody is a composition of irregular form with an improvisatory character. Although you may have heard themes, repetitions, and echoes in *Rhapsody in Blue,* you probably were not able to discern a regular form such as might be apparent in a classical sonata or symphony. The word *rhapsody* also suggests rapture, elation, bliss, ecstasy—perhaps the feelings conveyed by that soaring first phrase on the clarinet. *Blue,* on the other hand, suggests the melancholy of the blues. The dissonance created by the combination of the two terms—like the combinations and contrasts in the music—creates an energetic tension that arouses our curiosity and heightens our interest.

In making these observations about *Rhapsody in Blue,* we've been noticing many of the formal elements of a musical work and answering questions that can be asked about any composition: What is the form of the work? What kind of instrumentation has the composer chosen? What is the primary melodic theme of the work? What tempos are used? How do the instruments or voices work together to create the texture? What is the overall mood of the piece—joyful, sad, calm, wild, a combination?

Now, at your imaginary concert, there may be notes in the program that will provide you with some context for the work. You'll find that George Gershwin was a gifted and classically trained pianist who quit school at 15 and went to work in Tin Pan Alley, a district in New York City where popular songs were written and published. His goal in writing *Rhapsody in Blue* (1924) was to blend classical and popular music, to put the energy and style of jazz into a symphonic format.

Many listeners "see" and "hear" New York City in this piece. Gershwin created his own unique idiom, a fast-paced blend of rhythm, melody, and harmony that followed certain rules of composition but gave the impression of improvisation. He went on to write musicals, more serious compositions like the opera *Porgy and Bess,* and music for Hollywood films, all in his distinctive style. Information like this can help you begin to compare *Rhapsody in Blue* both with other works of the time and with other works by Gershwin. As in any analysis, integrating the formal and the contextual rounds out your interpretation and understanding of the work.

CONCLUSION

These three brief analyses should give you some ideas about how literature, art, and music can be approached in productive ways. By taking the time to look more closely, we gain access to the great works of our culture. This statement leads us to another issue: What makes a work "great"? Why do some works of art have relevance long beyond their time, while others are forgotten soon after their designated "fifteen minutes of fame"? These questions have been debated throughout history. One answer is that great art reflects some truth of human experience that speaks to us across the centuries. The voice of Shakespeare, the paintings of Georgia O'Keeffe, and the music of George Gershwin have a universal quality that doesn't depend on the styles of the time. Great art also enriches us and makes us feel that we share a little more of the human experience than we did before.

As both a student of the humanities and an audience member, you have the opportunity to appreciate and understand the arts. Despite the formal nature of academic inquiry, an aesthetic analysis is a personal endeavor. In looking closely at a creative work, seeking the creator's intent and evaluating its execution, you enrich your appreciation of the work with understanding; you bring the emotional reaction you first experienced to its intellectual completion. As twentieth-century composer Arnold Schoenberg once wrote, "You get from a work about as much as you are able to give to it yourself." This primer has been intended to help you learn how to bring more of yourself to works of art, to couple your subjective appreciation with intellectual understanding. With these tools in hand, you won't have to say you don't know much about art but you know what you like; you'll be able to say you know *about* what you like.

1 PREHISTORY AND NEAR EASTERN CIVILIZATIONS

A Western man or woman born early in the past century has seen more change in a lifetime than previous generations experienced over hundreds of years. Despite this rapid change in modern times, Western civilization stands firmly on a foundation that is almost five thousand years old, and people in the West often return to that foundation to discover their heritage and to reexamine their values. As further changes occur, the past becomes increasingly important as a guide to the future.

Before we begin to explore this heritage and what it means today, we need to discuss two important terms—*culture* and *civilization*. **Culture** usually refers to the sum of human endeavors: methods and practices for survival; political, economic, and social institutions; and values, beliefs, and the arts. **Civilization,** on the other hand, refers to the way people live in a complex political, economic, and social structure, usually in an urban setting, usually after making certain technological and artistic advances and sharing a refinement of thought, manners, and taste. Culture is passed from one generation to another by human behavior, speech, and artifacts; civilization is transmitted primarily by writing (Figure 1.1). The term *culture* can also be used to refer to the creative, artistic, and intellectual expressions of a civilization. We will use the term in both of these senses. In the words of Matthew Arnold, the nineteenth-century English poet and critic, culture is "the best that has been thought and said." To this we would add, "and done."

◀ **Detail** *The Great Sphinx.* Ca. 2560 B.C.E. 65′ high × 240′ long. Giza, Egypt.

1

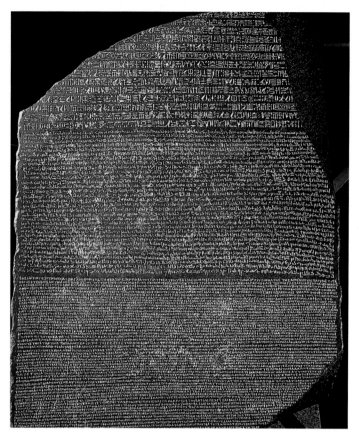

Figure 1.1 Rosetta Stone. Ca. 197–196 B.C.E. British Museum. *Although scholars knew that Egypt had a writing system, they were unable to solve the mystery of hieroglyphics until the nineteenth century. The key was provided by the Rosetta Stone, discovered by members of Napoleon's expedition when he invaded Egypt in 1799. On the stone the same event is described in hieroglyphics, in Egyptian cursive script, and in Greek. By comparing the Greek text with the other two, scholars were able to decipher both Egyptian scripts. This discovery marks the origin of modern Egyptology.*

PREHISTORY AND EARLY CULTURES

Where and when does the story of human culture begin? The latest evidence from paleoanthropology, the study of early human life, indicates that human beings originated in the distant past in lands far from western Europe. Human development thus begins during prehistory, long before our predecessors compiled—or could compile—written records of their cultures. The first ancestors of human beings probably appeared four to five million years ago. In comparison, lifeforms appeared on earth an estimated two to three billion years ago, and the planet itself is believed to have formed some four to six billion years ago.

The periods of time involved in these processes are so vast that only metaphors can make them comprehensible. If we take the seven-day week, made familiar by the biblical account of creation, and combine it with recent scientific estimates about when the earth and life began, then the following analogy may be made. The earth was created just after midnight on the first day, the first life appeared at about noon on the fourth day, and the early ancestors of human beings didn't show up until about 11 P.M. on the seventh day. To complete the analogy, the birth of civilization occurred almost an hour later, in the last tenth of a second before midnight on the last day of the week.

Paleolithic Period

Although the record of human evolution is obscure, sufficient evidence exists to show that hominids, the earliest primate ancestors of modern humans, probably originated in eastern Africa. From among them, about two million years ago, in the Pliocene epoch, the genus *Homo* evolved, a form marked by a larger brain and the ability to adapt somewhat to the environment. Hominids of the *Homo* genus made and used tools and developed rudimentary cultures. Anthropologists designate this earliest cultural period as the **Paleolithic**, or Old Stone Age. It corresponds to the geological period known as the Pleistocene epoch, or Ice Age, the time of extensive climate changes caused by the advance and retreat of massive glaciers (Timeline 1.1).

Stone Age culture spread widely over a vast area, but remains of hominid life are scarce. Evidence indicates that hominids lived in packs, followed herds of wandering animals, and ate wild seasonal fruits and vegetables. Anthropologists believe that duties and work divided along sex lines as all-male teams hunted game for meat and fur while females and children gathered plant foods, prepared meals, and tended the young. During the night, all sought shelter together in caves for safety and refuge against the elements. This way of life hinged on cooperation and food sharing among small social groups.

In the early Old Stone Age, or Lower Paleolithic, hominids invented crude stone tools, used fire, and probably developed speech—a major breakthrough that allowed them to communicate in ways denied other animals. Their first tools were simple choppers and, somewhat later, hand axes. In the Middle Paleolithic, more advanced hominids developed pointed tools and scrapers, which they chiseled with precision and care. In the Upper Paleolithic, double-faced blades became common.

By about 200,000 B.C.E., the species *Homo sapiens* had evolved from earlier hominids. More fully developed physically and mentally, they slowly spread through-

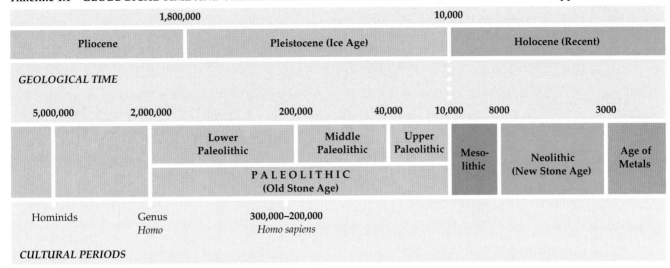

Timeline 1.1 GEOLOGICAL TIME AND PREHISTORIC CULTURAL PERIODS   All dates approximate and B.C.E.

out the Eastern Hemisphere and eventually migrated into the Western Hemisphere over the land bridge between Siberia and Alaska. Their more sophisticated tools included bows and arrows, fishhooks, and needles. They lived together cooperatively, buried their dead with rituals, and began to paint and sculpt. Especially through their cave paintings and carved figurines, our ancestors made a breakthrough to symbolic thought.

Ice Age cave paintings of reindeer, bison, rhinoceroses, lions, and horses in Altamira, Spain, and in Lascaux and the Ardèche region of France date from the Upper Paleolithic and are the earliest examples of human art (Figure 1.2). The purposes of the paintings in the Chauvet caves in the Ardèche region remain a mystery, but those at Altamira and Lascaux were probably used as part of ceremonies and rituals before hunting. By painting numerous wild animals pierced with arrows, the artists were attempting to ensure a successful hunt.

Another type of Upper Paleolithic art is seen in the carved female figurine found at Willendorf, Austria (Figure 1.3). Made of limestone, the statue is faceless and rotund. The distended stomach and full breasts suggest that the figure may have been used as a fertility symbol and an image of a mother goddess, representing the creative power of nature. As a mythological figure, the mother goddess appeared in many ancient cultures, beginning in Paleolithic times; approximately thirty thousand miniature sculptures in clay, marble, bone, copper, and gold have been uncovered at about three thousand sites in southeastern Europe alone. The supremacy of the mother goddess was expressed in the earliest myths of creation, which told of the life-giving and nurturing powers of the female.

This figurine from Willendorf, with its emphasized breasts, navel, and vulva, symbolic of creativity, may have been used in religious ceremonies to ensure the propagation of the tribe or to guarantee a bountiful supply of food. The statue also reveals the aesthetic interests of the sculptor, who took care to depict the goddess's hands resting on her breasts and her hair in tightly knit rows.

Neolithic Period

As the last glaciers retreated from Europe, during the Holocene (Recent) epoch of geological time, human beings were forced to adapt to new living conditions. Their stone tools became more advanced and included knives and hammers. Following the Mesolithic transitional period (about 10,000–8000 B.C.E.), a transformation occurred that has been called the most important event in human history: Hunters and gatherers became farmers and herders. Thus began the **Neolithic** period, or New Stone Age (about 8000 B.C.E.). In Southeast Asia, Central America, parts of South America, and the Near East, human beings ceased their nomadic existence and learned to domesticate wild animals. They learned to plow the earth and sow seeds, providing themselves with a much more reliable food supply, which in turn encouraged the development of permanent settlements and eventually the rise of urban centers. This agrarian pattern of life dominated the West until about two hundred years ago.

Precisely why and how the agrarian revolution came at this time is a hotly debated topic among anthropologists. Nonetheless, most agree that with the retreat of the last glaciers from Europe, methods of

Figure 1.2   Herd of Rhinoceroses. Ca. 32,000–30,000 B.C.E. Chauvet Cave, Ardèche region, France. *This naturalistic detail of a panel painting includes lions, bison, and a young mammoth (not visible here) moving across a vast expanse of the cave wall. The repeated black lines of the rhinoceroses' horns and backs create a sense of depth and give energy to the work.*

food gathering changed dramatically, causing either surpluses or shortages. In some areas, grain surpluses allowed populations to grow, which led to forced migrations as the number of humans outstripped the available food. In less productive lands, the people began to experiment with domesticating animals and planting grains. These innovations in marginal lands caused food production to rise, soon matching that found in more fertile areas, so that eventually a uniform agricultural economy spread to many parts of the globe. Thus, economic causes accounted for the transformation from food-gathering to food-producing cultures.

The agricultural revolution expanded across the Near East and probably into Europe and Africa. Between 6000 and 3000 B.C.E., human beings also learned to mine and use copper, signifying the end of the Neo-

lithic period and ushering in the Age of Metals. In about 3000 B.C.E., artisans combined copper and tin to produce bronze, a strong alloy, which they used in their tools, weapons, and jewelry.

The Bronze Age, which extended from about 3000 to about 1200 B.C.E., gave rise to two major civilizations in the Near East. The earlier developed in Mesopotamia, the land between the Tigris and Euphrates Rivers (in present-day Iraq), and the other, probably emerging just slightly later, originated along the Nile River in Egypt. Mesopotamian and Egyptian civilizations shared certain characteristics: Both were ruled by kings who were in turn supported by a priestly caste; the rulers' power was shared by a few educated elites; their economies were slave-based; their societies were stratified, with class privileges at the upper end; and palaces and religious edifices were built for ceremonial

Technology in Early Cultures

From earliest times, human creativity expressed itself in myriad ways. Artistically, this resulted in expressions in the arts and humanities. Technologically, this led to inventions and discoveries that often reshaped human existence. By and large, these technological innovations involved the making and using of tools, which extended human abilities in powerful and sometimes surprising ways. With certain achievements, the effects grew so powerful as to have a transformative effect on human culture. So pervasive is our tool-making capacity that scholars coined the term **homo faber**—Latin for "human fabricator"—to denote this aspect of human endeavor.

Stone Age Technology The stone tools that the hominids invented during the Lower Paleolithic period allowed human life to survive, but very little significant change occurred over vast stretches of time. Similarly, *Homo sapiens,* who sprang from the hominids, continued to live a nomadic existence, exploiting and developing the same tools, until the Mesolithic period.

The Mesolithic period, while brief, proved to be a turning point in human history. As *Homo sapiens* became farmers and herders, they gained knowledge about agriculture and they developed wooden tools and other technologies for managing the processes. Along with the domestication of animals, the animal-drawn plow was introduced to Mesopotamia, thus increasing the yield of crops. As noted above, the greater production of food was a major factor in the rise of what we call civilization. Humans were now well on the road to finding new, faster, and more efficient ways of living and thriving.

Before civilization emerged, however, the final stage of prehistory occurred, the Neolithic period, when many new technologies began. After 3500 B.C.E., the rise of these new technologies was incredibly rapid, making this one of the most fruitful eras for change that the world has ever known. In transportation the changes included two innovations: the boat (with and without sails) and the wheel—each with enormous potential for commerce, travel, and warfare. In construction and building, the discovery and use of kiln-fired bricks made houses, temples, and palaces possible. In the domestic arts, there came five new technologies: weaving, dyeing (using animal and vegetable dyes), tanning, pottery making (both plain and kiln-fired), and the making of oil lamps. In farming, there was now large-scale irrigation in the Near East, with many new plants under cultivation, such as wheat (emmer), flax, millet, barley, and spices. Of the innovations made at the end of the Neolithic period, none compares with the invention of writing,

Figure 1.3 Figurine from Willendorf. Ca. 25,000 B.C.E. Ht. 4⅜". Museum Naturhistorisches, Vienna. *Discovered in about 1908 C.E., this female statuette measures just under 5 inches high. Carved from limestone, it still shows evidence of having been painted red. Many other statues like it have been discovered, but this one remains the most famous because of the unusual balance it strikes between symbolism and realism.*

and governmental purposes. These early civilizations made deep and lasting impressions on their neighbors and successors that helped shape life in the Western world.

Copper and tin were in short supply in Egypt and Mesopotamia. To ensure a continuous supply of these metals, complex trading ties and mining operations had to be established. Copper was found in neighboring Anatolia, but tin was quite scarce, as it was mined in only a few places, in modern Serbia and Bulgaria at first, and in Cornwall, in modern England, after 2500 B.C.E. Royal leadership was essential for supplying the raw materials and protecting production. Thus, bronze technology encouraged the founding of the first organized states and the rise of urbanized life.

Figure 1.4   Banquet Scene. Ca. 2550–2400 B.C.E. Lapis lazuli, ht. 1⅞", diameter 1". British Museum. Cylinder seal (left) and modern impression of a cylinder seal (right). *This cylinder seal, found in the Royal Cemetery of Ur, depicts a banqueting scene—a joyous activity among Mesopotamia's elite. In the upper register, on the right, a female figure sits enthroned, attended by two female servants. She raises a cup (probably of beer) to a seated male figure, who returns her salute with his own cup. The man is attended by two male servants. In the lower register, two other male celebrants, attended by male servants, join in the festivities. Cuneiform inscriptions on the cylinder identify its owner as Queen Pu-abi.*

which happened first in Mesopotamia, an event that forecast the end of the "silence" of the prehistoric period.

Bronze Age Technology   Beginning civilizations appeared as the Stone Age yielded to the Bronze Age, the first period in the Age of Metals. A herald of the Age of Metals was the mastery of gold and silver metalworking. Gold and silver were first reduced from their ores after 3500 B.C.E., but their scarcity made them too precious for general use.

The shift from stone tools to bronze tools occurred at first in only a few areas in the Near East, China, and Southeast Asia. Elsewhere, and especially in Europe, Mesoamerica, and the Andes of South America, stone continued as the dominant material for tools. Even in the modern world, stone retains its usefulness, as in such products as mortars and pestles, cutting boards, building materials, and flooring.

From Mesopotamia, where the earliest successful bronze was produced by anonymous artisans, this metalworking tradition was transmitted to Egypt, Greece, and elsewhere. It produced a host of new technologies. Writing is the hallmark of this period, with Egyptians putting words on papyrus, a flat writing surface made from pressed reeds, and Mesopotamians incising words on clay tablets. In Egypt, artisans also pioneered the use of vellum, or parchment, a material prepared from animal skin, which was more flexible and durable than papyrus.

Other technologies improved the lives of the peoples. Construction methods moved along two different paths: In Egypt, stone building techniques arose, and in Mesopotamia, stepped temples, made of dried bricks, became the chief building style. Advances in transport were made, with sailboats plying their wares on Egypt's Nile and wooden ships maneuvering in the Mediterranean. Domestic life made extraordinary advances, with many changes that are still part of life today, including the baking of bread in ovens, the brewing of beer (Figure 1.4), and the distilling of perfumes in Mesopotamia. In Egypt and Mesopotamia, the making of glass and the fermenting of wine became common, and, in Egypt, the invention of hand mirrors and the sundial clock lent new perspectives to experience. Urban culture also led to the widespread use of calendars, in both Egypt and Mesopotamia.

Iron Age Technology   The Iron Age began in about 1200 B.C.E., but the making of iron has been dated to about 2000 B.C.E. Iron technology soon led to new devices, fashioned from either iron or steel, such as iron-tipped plows, weaponry, buckets, and locks and keys. Warriors quickly realized that sturdy iron defeats fragile bronze every time. Indeed, some wars between 1200 and 1000 B.C.E. are thought by scholars to have had their outcomes determined by which side wielded iron weapons, as in the victories won by the Sea Peoples against the Bronze Age Egyptians. The Bronze Age was definitely over.

LEARNING THROUGH MAPS

Map 1.1 ANCIENT MESOPOTAMIA AND EGYPT

This map shows the two earliest civilizations of the Near East: Mesopotamia and Egypt. **Notice** that much of Mesopotamia is contained within the area known as the Fertile Crescent and that Egypt is settled mainly along the Nile River. **Locate** the cities in Mesopotamia and Egypt. **Compare and contrast** the role and importance of rivers in these civilizations. **Why** was Egypt less exposed to external influences than was Mesopotamia?

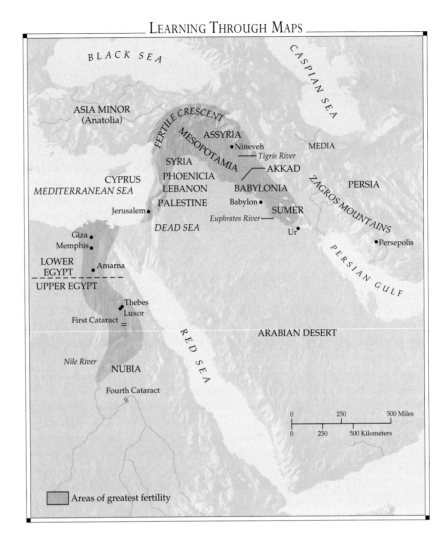

THE CIVILIZATIONS OF THE TIGRIS AND EUPHRATES RIVER VALLEY: MESOPOTAMIA

The Tigris-Euphrates river valley forms part of what is known as the Fertile Crescent, which starts at the Persian Gulf, runs slightly northwestward through the Tigris-Euphrates valley, and then turns westerly to the Mediterranean Sea and curves south along the shoreline toward Egypt (Map 1.1). This arc of land contained some of the most arable soil in the Near East, many of the heavily traveled trade routes, and most of the early centers of civilization.

Mesopotamia is a Greek word meaning "land between the two rivers." The hill country and Zagros Mountains rise to the east of the Tigris-Euphrates valley, and the vast Arabian desert stretches to the west. The twin rivers course down to the Persian Gulf, draining an area approximately 600 miles long and 250 miles wide. Near the mouth of the gulf, on the river delta, human wanderers settled in about 6000 B.C.E.,

founding villages and tilling the land. Despite heat, marshes, unpredictable and violent floods, and invaders who came from both the mountains and the desert, some of these communities prospered and grew.

The Sumerian, Akkadian, and Babylonian Kingdoms

Three successive civilizations—Sumerian, Akkadian, and Babylonian—flourished in Mesopotamia for nearly fifteen hundred years (Timeline 1.2). Indeed, as historian Samuel Kramer asserts, "History began at Sumer."

The rulers of Sumer created an exalted image of a just and stable society with a rich cultural life. Sumer's most inspirational king, Gilgamesh [GILL-guh-mesh], ruled during the first dynasty (about 2700 B.C.E.) of Ur, a state centered between the rivers. His heroic adventures and exploits were later immortalized in the poem

Timeline 1.2   MESOPOTAMIAN CIVILIZATIONS   All dates approximate and B.C.E.

3000	2350	2000	1600
Sumerian	Akkadian	Babylonian	

The Epic of Gilgamesh. A later ruler, Urukagina, is known for reforming law codes and revitalizing the economy near the end of the Sumerian period (2350 B.C.E.). But Urukagina's successors were unable to maintain Sumer's power, and the cities became easy prey for the Akkadians of northern Mesopotamia.

The Akkadian dynasties, lasting from about 2350 to about 2000 B.C.E., incorporated Sumerian culture into their own society and carried this hybrid civilization far beyond the Tigris-Euphrates valley. According to legends—which are similar to the later story of the Hebrew leader Moses—Sargon (r. about 2334–2279 B.C.E.), the first and greatest Akkadian ruler, was born of lowly origins and abandoned at birth in the reed marshes; yet Sargon survived and rose to prominence at the Sumerian court. Excavated inscriptions reveal that Sargon conquered the Sumerians and founded a far-flung empire to the east and northeast. At its height, Sargon's power was felt from Egypt to India, but his successors, lacking his intelligence and skill, could not maintain the Akkadian empire. The incursions of the Guti tribes from the Zagros Mountains brought about the final collapse of the weakened Akkadian empire and the division of southern Mesopotamia into petty kingdoms.

Babylonia was the third civilization in Mesopotamia. From northern Mesopotamia, their power base, the Babylonians governed the entire valley from about 2000 to 1600 B.C.E. Under their most successful military leader and renowned lawgiver, Hammurabi [ham-uh-RAHB-e] (r. 1792–1750 B.C.E.), the Babylonians reached their political and cultural ascendancy. However, the Hittites, centered in Asia Minor, invaded Babylon in about 1600 B.C.E. and toppled the dynasty of Hammurabi.

Agriculture dominated the economy of Mesopotamia. Harsh living conditions and unpredictable floods forced the inhabitants to learn to control the rivers through irrigation systems and cooperative tilling of the soil. Farmers eventually dug a complex canal system to irrigate their cultivated plots, which might have been some distance from the river. As production increased, prosperity allowed larger populations to thrive. Villages soon grew into small cities—with populations ranging from 10,000 to 50,000—surrounded by hamlets and tilled fields. Trade developed with nearby areas, and wheeled vehicles—perfected by the Sumerians—and sailboats carried goods up and down Mesopotamia and eventually throughout the Fertile Crescent.

By the beginning of the Bronze Age, the family had replaced the tribe or clan as the basic unit in society. Families now owned their lands outright, and, under the general direction of the religious and secular authorities, they worked their fields and maintained the irrigation ditches. Marriages were arranged by parents, with economics an essential consideration. According to the law codes, women possessed some rights, such as holding property; however, a wife was clearly under her husband's power. Divorce was easier for men than for women, and women were punished more severely than men for breaking moral and marital laws. Recent scholarship has suggested that women's status and roles became more limited as Mesopotamian society became more complex. In sum, Mesopotamian women were originally able to participate actively in economic, religious, and political life as long as their dependence on and obligation to male kin and husbands were observed, but they progressively lost their relative independence because rulers extended the concept of patriarchy (rule by the fathers) from family practice into public law.

The political structure reflected the order and functions of the social system. At the top stood the ruler, who was supported by an army, a bureaucracy, a judicial system, and a priesthood. The ruler usually obtained advice from prominent leaders, meeting in council, who constituted the next layer of the social order: rich landowners, wealthy merchants, priests, and military chiefs. The next group consisted of artisans, craftspeople, and petty businesspeople and traders. Below them were small landowners and tenant farmers. At the bottom of the social scale were serfs and slaves, who either had been captured in war or had fallen into debt.

The Cradle of Civilization

The three Mesopotamian civilizations responded to the same geography, climate, and natural resources, and their cultures reflected that shared background. The Sumerians were probably the most influential: From Sumer came writing, the lunar calendar, a mathematical computation system, medical and scientific discoveries, and architectural and technological innovations. However, each civilization, through its religion, literature, law, and art, deeply affected other Near Eastern people.

Writing Thousands of clay tablets inscribed with the wedge-shaped symbols of Sumerian script have been uncovered in Mesopotamia, indicating that the Sumerians had developed a form of writing by 3000 B.C.E. With the invention of writing, people no longer had to rely on memory, speech, and person-to-person interactions to communicate and transmit information. Instead, they could accumulate a permanent body of knowledge and pass it on from one generation to the next. With writing came the possibility of civilization.

At first, the Sumerians needed a simple way to record agricultural and business information and the deeds and sayings of their rulers. Their earliest symbols were **pictograms,** or pictures, carefully drawn to represent particular objects. To these they added **ideograms,** pictures drawn to represent ideas or concepts. A simple drawing of a bowl, for example, could be used to mean "food." As these pictures became more stylized, meaning began to be transferred from the represented object to the sign itself; that is, the sign began to stand for a word rather than an object.

Later, Sumerian scribes and writers identified the syllabic sounds of spoken words and created **phonograms,** symbols for separate speech sounds, borrowing from and building on the earlier pictograms and ideograms. These simplified and standardized symbols eventually resulted in a phonetic writing system of syllable-based sounds that, when combined, produced words (Figure 1.5). It was left to later civilizations to separate vowel sounds from syllables and thus create a true alphabet, based on individual speech sounds (see Encounter).

The Sumerians could now express complex, abstract concepts, and their system could extend to other languages. The Akkadians and the Babylonians adopted and modified the Sumerian script to keep records and preserve their literature, including *The Epic of Gilgamesh* and the Code of Hammurabi. By the end of the Bronze Age (about 1200 B.C.E.), other written languages existed, but Akkadian-Sumerian was the language of diplomacy and trade in the Near East.

The Sumerian writing system has been labeled **cuneiform,** a term derived from the Latin word *cuneus,* which means "wedge." Using wedge-shaped reeds or styluses, scribes pressed the symbols into wet clay tablets, and artists and craftspeople, wielding metal tools, incised the script into stone monuments or cylindrical pillars. Preserved for thousands of years in hardened clay and stone, cuneiform writing has provided invaluable insight into ancient Mesopotamian culture.

Religion Sumerian, Akkadian, and Babylonian religions, despite individual differences, shared many basic attitudes and concepts that became the foundation for other Near Eastern belief systems. The underlying beliefs of Mesopotamian religion were that the gods had created human beings to serve them, that the gods were in complete control, and that powerless mortals had no choice but to obey and worship these deities. The hostile climate and unpredictable rivers made life precarious, and the gods appeared capricious. The Mesopotamians held a vague notion of a shadowy netherworld where the dead rested, but they did not believe in an afterlife as such or any rewards or punishments upon death. Happiness seldom was an earthly goal; pessimism ran as a constant theme throughout their religion and literature.

Mesopotamian religion had three important characteristics. It was **polytheistic**—many gods and goddesses existed and often competed with one another; it was **anthropomorphic**—the deities possessed human

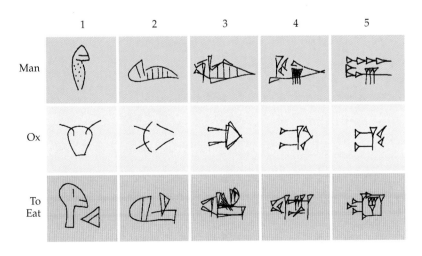

Figure 1.5 Sumerian Cuneiform Writing. Ca. 3000–1000 B.C.E. *The columns illustrate the evolution of Sumerian writing from pictograms to script. Column 1 shows the pictogram: a man, an ox, and the verb "to eat" (represented by the mouth and a bowl). In column 2, the pictographic symbols have been turned 90 degrees, as the Sumerians did in their first writing. Columns 3 and 4 show how the script changed between 2500 and 1800 B.C.E. Column 5 is an Assyrian adaptation of the Sumerian cuneiform script.*

ENCOUNTER

The Phoenicians and the Alphabet

The small kingdom of Phoenicia taught the alphabet to the ancient Greeks and, thus, to the West. The Phoenicians invented the alphabet, the basis of their writing and reading, to support the interchange of material goods and ideas with their neighbors.

Around 3000 B.C.E., the Phoenicians, a people of mixed Syrian and Palestinian ancestry, settled along a narrow strip of land on the western coast of the Mediterranean, north of Palestine and to the south and east of the Lebanon Mountains, in what is modern-day Lebanon. The Phoenicians never became a major political or military force due to their small population, limited natural resources, and geographic vulnerability, but they did establish a string of semi-independent and prosperous city-states down the Lebanese coast, governed by local rulers.

In the early years, they irrigated and cultivated the fertile hills above the coast, growing grains and fruits, but by 2500 B.C.E., they could no longer support their growing population in this small territory. Hemmed in by more powerful neighbors, who prevented them from expanding, and constantly being threatened with invasions, the Phoenicians turned to manufacturing, trade, and commerce for their survival.

They traveled the overland trade routes along the Fertile Crescent and into Mesopotamia and exported many items, including cedar and fir trees for constructing temples and palaces. By 1200 B.C.E., they had begun redirecting their commercial interests to the sea, building boats and transporting goods around the Mediterranean basin. One of their leading exports was dyed textiles, and the most famous of these was a cloth of purple dye, which the Greeks called "phoinix"—a word that came to identify the Phoenician people. By the seventh century B.C.E., the Phoenicians had also developed a glass industry, and their fine metal and ivory artworks indicate that they were importing gold, silver, an precious stones from as far away as India and Africa.

In the late twelfth century B.C.E., the Phoenicians began to found colonies on islands and along the Mediterranean coastline—not for conquests but for trade and commerce. These commercial emporiums, which reached their zenith in the eighth century, were equipped with port facilities and shipyards and were established close to one another, to serve as stopovers for travelers and as marketplaces for traders. Only later, because of the sea raiders and pirates, did the Phoenicians fortify these seaports. Meanwhile, using seafaring skills and spurred by commercial interests, they sailed down the western coast of Africa and sent ships to the British Isles, in search of tin.

In time, the colonies also became outposts for Phoenician culture and intellectual and artistic achievements. Phoenician art, architecture, and literature were often inferior to that of their contemporaries, and, in any case, most of their achievements have not survived. Nevertheless, their encounters with other societies led to the spread of the Phoenician alphabetic writing system throughout the Classical world.

As early as 1400 B.C.E., the Phoenicians had created a syllabic writing system, probably based on Egyptian **hieroglyphics**—a system of pictographs—and/or Sumerian cuneiform. Writing, understandably, helped them communicate more effectively and efficiently with their colonies and trading partners. They simplified the pictograms, ideograms, phonograms, and syl-

form and had their own personalities and unique traits; and it was **pantheistic**—hundreds of divinities were found everywhere, in nature and throughout the universe. Since Mesopotamians thought of their gods in human form with all the strengths and weaknesses of mortals, they believed their deities lived in the same way as people did, and they were pragmatic in approaching the supernatural powers. For example, they believed that their deities held council, made decisions, and ordered the forces of nature to wreak havoc or to bestow plenty on mortals.

Mesopotamians divided the deities into the sky gods and the earth gods. In these two categories were the four major deities: Anu, the heaven god; Enlil, the air god; Enki, the water god; and Ninhursag, the mother goddess. Enlil emerged as the most powerful god for the Sumerians. He gave mortals the plough and the pickax, and he brought forth for humanity all the productive forces of the universe, such as trees, grains, and "whatever was needful."

Rituals, ceremonies, and the priesthood were absolutely essential to Mesopotamian religion. Although the average Mesopotamian might participate in worship services, the priests played the central role in all religious functions. They also controlled and administered large parcels of land, which enhanced their power in economic and political matters. Priests carefully formulated and consciously followed the procedures for rites and rituals, which were written down and stored in their temples. This cultic literature

NORTH SEMITIC			GREEK		ETRUSCAN	LATIN	
EARLY PHOENICIAN	EARLY HEBREW	PHOENICIAN	EARLY	CLASSICAL	EARLY	EARLY	CLASSICAL
ᴋ	ᴋ	✗	◁	A	ᴀ	A	A
𝟡	𝟡	𝟫	𝟪	B	ᴙ		B
ꓘ	ꓹ	ꓶ	ꓶ	Γ	ꓹ		C
△	◁	◁	△	△	⋂	◊	D

Phoenician, Greek, Hebrew, Etruscan, and Roman letters.

Encounter figure 1.1   First Four Letters of the Alphabet—A Comparison. *This table presents, in comparative form, the opening four letters of the Phoenician, Greek, Hebrew, Etruscan, and Roman alphabets. The early Phoenician letters predated the rest, and other peoples adapted those letters into their writing styles.*

labic systems of earlier forms of writing into an alphabetic system. A sign for a particular object, such as one for a cow or tree, was given a Phoenician name and a new symbol, in which the letter was given the initial sound of the name of the object it represented. Thus, the sign became a sound. This collection of signs came to be known as an *alphabet*—the word itself a combination of the first two letters of the Phoenician system: aleph, or the letter *a*, and beth, or the letter *b*. The Phoenician alphabet consisted of twenty-two letters. It read from right to left, as is typical of Semitic languages, of which Phoenician is one. The letters were all consonants, and later the Greeks turned some of the consonants into vowels. The Greeks passed their modified alphabet to the Etruscans in Italy, to the Copts in Egypt, and to the Slavonic clans in eastern Europe. The Etruscans introduced the alphabet to the Romans, who made it part of their written language, Latin.

The Hebrews, Arabs, and other Semitic peoples adapted the Phoenician alphabet for themselves. It evolved into several branches of languages, including Aramaic, which was spoken for centuries across southwestern Asia and became the basis of the modern Syriac and Arabic alphabet. The alphabet is Phoenicia's lasting contribution to modern civilization.

Learning from the Encounter   **Why** did the Phoenicians never become a powerful military kingdom? **How** did the Phoenicians capitalize on their geographical location to become a trading society? **Describe** the colonies founded by the Phoenicians. **What** were the bases of the Phoenician alphabetic writing system, and **how** did the Phoenicians create a new system? **What** impact has this system had on other languages?

not only told the Mesopotamians how to worship but also informed them about their deities' origins, characteristics, and deeds. Religious myths and instructions constituted a major part of Mesopotamian literature and made writing an essential part of the culture.

Literature   Of the surviving epics, tales, and legends that offer glimpses into the Mesopotamian mind, the most famous is *The Epic of Gilgamesh*. King Gilgamesh, whose reign in about 2700 B.C.E. is well documented, became a larger-than-life hero in Sumerian folk tales (Figure 1.6). In all probability, the Gilgamesh epic began as an oral poem and was not written on clay tablets for hundreds of years. The most complete

surviving version, from 600 B.C.E., was based on a Babylonian copy written in Akkadian and dating from about 1600 B.C.E. Although this poem influenced other Near Eastern writings with its characters, plot, and themes, *The Epic of Gilgamesh* stands on its own as a poetic utterance worthy of being favorably compared with later Greek and Roman epics.

Through its royal hero, *The Epic of Gilgamesh* focuses on fundamental themes that concern warriors in an aristocratic society: the need to be brave in the face of danger, the choice of death before dishonor, the conflict between companionship and sexual pleasure, the power of the gods over weak mortals, and the finality of death. Above all, it deals with human beings' vain quest for immortality. As the tale begins, the

Figure 1.6   Gilgamesh Fighting a Lion. Ca. 2500–2000 B.C.E. Cylinder seal (left) and modern impression of a cylinder seal (right). British Museum. *The separate scenes, rolled out on this impression from the seal, which is about 1 inch high, depict the Sumerian hero in one of his many battles against beasts. The artist heightens the intensity of the physical struggle by placing Gilgamesh, with his legs bent and arms locked around the lion, at a sharp angle under the animal to muster his brute strength against his foe.*

extravagant and despotic policies of Gilgamesh have led his subjects to pray for relief. In response, a goddess creates from clay a "wild man" of tremendous physical strength and sends him to kill Gilgamesh. But Enkidu, as he is called, is instead tamed by a woman's love, loses his innocence, wrestles Gilgamesh to a draw, and becomes his boon companion.

As the epic unfolds, Gilgamesh chooses friendship with Enkidu rather than the love offered by the goddess Ishtar. Gilgamesh is punished for this choice by being made to watch helplessly as Enkidu dies from an illness sent by the gods. Forced to confront the fate awaiting all mortals, a grieving Gilgamesh begins a search for immortality.

The next section of the epic, which details Gilgamesh's search, includes the Sumerian tale of the great flood, which parallels the later Hebrew story of Noah and the ark. Although the Sumerian account of the flood was probably a later addition to the original story of Gilgamesh, the episode does fit into the narrative and reinforces one of the epic's major themes: the inescapable mortality of human beings. Gilgamesh hears the story of the flood from its sole survivor, Utnapishtim. Utnapishtim tells Gilgamesh how he built an ark and loaded it with animals and his family, how the waters rose, and how he released birds from the ark to discover if the waters were receding. The old man then explains how the gods, feeling sorry for the last remaining human, granted him immortality. Utnapishtim refuses to divulge the secret of eternal life to Gilgamesh, but the old man's wife blurts out where a plant may be found that will renew youth but not give immortality. Although Gilgamesh locates the plant, he loses it on his journey home. Gilgamesh, seeing the city of Uruk, which he had built, realizes that

the deeds humans do on earth are the measure of their immortality and that death is inevitable.

The Epic of Gilgamesh is essentially a secular morality tale. Gilgamesh's triumphs and failures mirror the lives of all mortals, and the Sumerians saw themselves in Gilgamesh's change from an overly confident and powerful hero to a doubting and fearful human being. Those who, like Gilgamesh, ignore the power of the deities have to pay a heavy price for their pride.

Mesopotamia also gave the world the first known literary figure, Enheduanna (fl. 2330 B.C.E.), an Akkadian poet who wrote in the Sumerian language. Made priestess of temples in the Sumerian cities of Ur (see Figure 1.11) and Uruk by her father, King Sargon, she used her priestly offices and literary gifts to further his political goal of uniting the Sumerians and the Akkadians. In these posts, she composed hymns to both Sumerian and Akkadian deities, and these hymns— some of which have been identified—became models for later poets. Enheduanna was especially devoted to Inanna, the Sumerian goddess of love, and she made this deity the subject of her best-known literary work, *The Exaltation of Inanna*. In this work, Enheduanna exalted, or raised, Inanna to supremacy in the Sumerian pantheon, her tribute for what she believed was Inanna's role in Sargon's triumph over a general uprising at the end of his reign.

Law   The Mesopotamians produced the fairest law codes before that of the Hebrews. The central theme of Sumerian law, whose first existing records date from about 2050 B.C.E., was justice. From the earliest times, the Sumerian kings understood justice to mean "the straight thing"—that is, dealing fairly with all their subjects and prohibiting the exploitation of the weak

SLICE OF LIFE
A Sumerian Father Lectures His Son

ANONYMOUS
Found on Clay Tablets

In this Sumerian text, dating from about 1700 B.C.E., a father rebukes his son for leading a wayward life and admonishes him to reform.

"Where did you go?"

"I did not go anywhere."

"If you did not go anywhere, why do you idle about? Go to school, stand before your 'school-father,' recite your assignment, open your schoolbag, write your tablet, let your 'big brother' write your new tablet for you. After you have finished your assignment and reported to your monitor, come to me, and do not wander about in the street. . . .

"You who wander about in the public square, would you achieve success? Then seek out the first generations. Go to school, it will be of benefit to you. My son, seek out the first generations, inquire of them.

"Perverse one over whom I stand watch—I would not be a man did I not stand watch over my son—I spoke to my kin, compared its men, but found none like you among them. . . .

"I, never in all my life did I make you carry reeds in the canebrake. The reed rushes which the young and the little carry, you, never in your life did you carry them. I never said to you 'Follow my caravans.' I never sent you to work, to plow my field. I never sent you to work to dig up my field. I never sent you to work as a laborer. 'Go, work and support me,' I never in my life said to you.

"Others like you support their parents by working. . . .

"I, night and day am I tortured because of you. Night and day you waste in pleasures. You have accumulated much wealth, have expanded far and wide, have become fat, big, broad, powerful, and puffed. But your kin waits expectantly for your misfortune, and will rejoice at it because you looked not to your humanity."

Interpreting This Slice of Life The key to interpreting this Slice of Life is to determine the tone of the father's speech to his son. *Tone* means "manner of speaking." **What** tone does the speaker manifest here? **List** three words that assist you in identifying the tone of voice. **How** does the father define *family*, and what expectations does the father have for his son? **To which** class do the father and his son belong? **Explain. What** are the father's values regarding education, worldly success, and family honor? **Which** Sumerian values in this text are shared by families in American culture?

---

by the strong. This concept of equity applied especially to economic matters, such as debts, contracts, and titles to land.

The most important set of laws from Mesopotamian civilization is that of the Babylonian king Hammurabi. Dating from about 1700 B.C.E., the Code of Hammurabi was found preserved on a seven-foot-high black stone **stele,** or pillar. At the top, Hammurabi is depicted standing in front of Shamash, the Babylonian and Sumerian god of justice. Like other ancient lawgivers (Moses, for example), Hammurabi received the legal code from a deity. Below the two figures are carved the prologue, the collection of laws, and an epilogue (Figure 1.7). The prologue lists Hammurabi's accomplishments and sings his praises while making it clear that the gods are the source of his power to establish "law and justice." The epilogue warns future rulers to carry out these laws or else be subject to defeat and ruin.

The laws concerning punishment for crimes are based on the judicial principle of *lex talionis*, or retaliation, which demands an "eye for an eye," although Hammurabi's code often substitutes payments in kind for damages done. Every major area of civil and criminal law was covered in the code, including property rights, sales, contracts, inheritance, adoption, prices and wages, sexual relations (much more severely restricted for women than for men), medical malpractice, and personal rights for women, children, and slaves. Hammurabi's code, like other Mesopotamian laws, was only one part of a complex judicial system that encompassed judges, courts, trials, legal proceedings, and contracts.

Science, Mathematics, and Medicine Mesopotamian science was strongly influenced by the region's polytheistic, anthropomorphic, and pantheistic religion. The Mesopotamians believed that a knowledge and understanding of the natural world was related to their deities' personalities and acts. Priests performed ceremonies and rituals not only to placate the gods and goddesses and to fend off their disruptive powers

Figure 1.7   Code of Hammurabi. Ca. 1700 B.C.E. Basalt, ht. approx. 3'. Louvre. *Hammurabi stands on the left, his hand raised before his mouth in the traditional Mesopotamian gesture of devotion, and Shamash, the sun god and protector of truth and justice, sits on the right. The cult of Shamash (in Sumeria, Utu) emerged from the earliest times, and this god's representation—flames shooting from the shoulders and hands holding symbols of power—was established in the Sumerian period. The relief, with its incised folds of cloth and ceremonial chair, is carved deep enough into the hard stone stele (7'4") to suggest a three-dimensional sculpture.*

but also to deal with practical matters, such as land surveys, irrigation projects, sickness, and disease. Thus, Mesopotamia's priests were also astronomers, mathematicians, and purveyors of medicine.

Knowing that the deities were powerful and capricious, the priests were convinced that they could avert some of the divine wrath by observing, studying, and calculating the heavens—the abode of most of the gods. The priests assumed that by understanding the movements of the stars, moon, and sun they could forecast natural calamities, such as floods, pestilence, and crop failure, which constantly befell their people. Around 3500 B.C.E., the priests in Sumer invented a calendar based on the movements of the moon. In this calendar, a "month" equaled twenty-eight days, but the year was divided into thireen, not twelve, months. They then used this lunar calendar to make more accurate plans for the future. Once they were able to calculate the seasonal pattern of nature, they instituted a festival celebrating the New Year, which recognized

the end of the growing season and the arrival of the next season.

Mathematics probably developed out of the need to measure and allocate land, build dams, remove dirt, pay workers, and regulate water. The Mesopotamian number system, which was likely influenced by their system of weights and coinage, used 60, not 100, as its base. Our calculation of degrees, minutes, and seconds evolved from this system. Later societies, like the Babylonian, built on this system to fashion more complex formulas, theorems, and equations, which aided shopkeepers in managing their businesses and astronomers in mapping the heavens and plotting navigation charts.

Although the oldest surviving records of Mesopotamian medicine can be dated only to about 1600 B.C.E., these texts, preserved on stone tablets, represent earlier centuries of medical practice and tradition. In these texts, the author connected disease with supernatural forces such as deities, ghosts, and spirits. Remedies involved the patient making sacrifices to the gods. At the same time, these texts counseled various treatments, such as administering potions made from herbs or plants. Their diagnostic methods and curative practices, while outdated, followed a set of logical steps. First, the patient was examined to determine the nature of the disease and advised how to cure it. Then, the patient was sent to a healer, who prescribed certain medications or applied bandages or plasters. Additional evidence for Mesopotamian medicine comes from the Code of Hammurabi, in which doctors were held accountable for their mistakes and duly fined or punished. What contributions the Mesopotamians made to medicine tended to be lost over the centuries. It was the Egyptians who came to be viewed as the most successful practitioners of medicine during ancient times and influenced later societies, especially the Greeks.

Art and Architecture   The art of Mesopotamia, like the rest of its culture, evolved from Sumerian styles to the Akkadian and Babylonian schools. Artisans worked in many forms—small seals, pottery, jewelry, vases, reliefs, and statues—and in many media—clay, stone, precious gems, gold, silver, leather, and ivory. Artifacts and crafted works from all three civilizations recorded the changing techniques of the producers as well as the shifting tastes of the consumers, whether they were rich individuals decorating their homes or officials issuing commissions for statues to adorn their temples. The temples, usually the center of the city and set on high mounds above the other structures, were often splendidly ornamented and housed exquisitely carved statues of gods and goddesses.

A fine example of Sumerian artistry is a bull's head carved on the sound box of a lyre (Figure 1.8). Working in gold leaf and semiprecious gems, the unknown artist has captured the vigor and power of the animal

Figure 1.8 Sound Box from Sumerian Lyre, from Ur. Ca. 2685 B.C.E. Wood with inlaid gold, lapis lazuli, and shell, ht. of bull's head approx. 13". University Museum, University of Pennsylvania, Philadelphia. *The lyre's sound box, on which the bull's head is carved, is a hollow chamber that increases the resonance of the sound. Music played an important role in Mesopotamian life, and patrons often commissioned the construction of elegant instruments. Thus, even at this early stage of civilization, those with wealth influenced the arts.*

Figure 1.9 Inlay from the Front of a Sound Box from Sumerian Lyre. Ca. 2685 B.C.E. *The four panels, made of ivory-colored shell inlaid onto a black background, depict mythological humans and animals. In the top panel, a man grasps two standing bulls with human heads. He may be either a god associated with the bull or a mythological figure from the* Epic of Gilgamesh. *The other panels show various animals (a hyena, a lion, a bull, and a gazelle), walking upright and behaving as humans, as they carry food and drinks or play musical instruments. In the bottom panel, the figure of the Scorpion Man is typical of the hybrid forms found in Mesopotamian art. Various theories have been offered in interpreting these scenes, including early versions of Aesopian fables, mythological stories, and humans dressed up as animals, but no consensus has been reached as to their ultimate meaning.*

in a bold and simple style. Such elegant musical instruments were played in homes and in palaces to accompany the poets and storytellers as they sang of the heroes' adventures and the deities' powers. The bull shape of the lyre reflects Sumerian religion, in which this animal was believed to possess supernatural powers. Religion may also be the inspiration for the varied creatures depicted in the four panels from the front of the sound box (Figure 1.9).

Mesopotamian artists carved thousands of figures, many on the walls of temples and palaces and others as freestanding statues. A notable early type of freestanding statue that became standard in Akkadian temples depicts a figure in a contemplative, worshiping pose, his hands folded and clasped in front of him. Many of these are likenesses of Gudea, a ruler who flourished about 2150 B.C.E. (Figure 1.10).

In contrast to the finely crafted sculpture, Mesopotamian architecture often seems uninspired, particularly the domestic architecture. Most Mesopotamian houses were square or rectangular. Even though the Mesopotamians knew about the arch, the vault, and the column, they did not employ them widely; they used primarily the basic **post-and-lintel construction** of two vertical posts capped by a horizontal lintel, or beam, for entranceways. The clay bricks used in construction limited the builders in styles and decorations, notably on the exterior. If private homes of clay bricks looked drab from the street, however, they were often attractive inside, built around an open courtyard with decorated rooms. The exteriors of temples and palaces were sometimes adorned with colored glazed bricks, mosaics, and painted cones arranged in patterns or, more rarely, with imported stone and marble.

Archeologists have not yet determined exactly how Mesopotamian cities were laid out. Urban centers were protected by walls, whose imposing and elaborately decorated gates proclaimed the city's wealth and power. The most prominent structure in each Sumerian city was the **ziggurat,** a terraced brick and mudbrick pyramid that served as the center of worship. The ziggurat resembled a hill or a stairway to the sky from which the deities could descend; or perhaps the structure was conceived as the gods' cosmic mountain. A temple of welcome for the gods stood on the top of the ziggurat, approached by sets of steps. Shrines, storehouses, and administrative offices were constructed around the base or on the several levels of the massive hill. In the low plain of the Tigris-Euphrates valley, the ziggurat literally and figuratively dominated the landscape. The Tower of Babel, described in the Jewish scriptures as reaching to the sky, may have been suggested by the Sumerian ziggurats, some of which had towers.

Figure 1.10   *Gudea.* Ca. 2150 B.C.E. Diorite, ht. 17¾". Louvre. *Little is known of Gudea, but more than thirty small statues of this Guti ruler have been found. The body and the head of this statuette were discovered separately and later joined together.*

Of the numerous ziggurats and temples that have survived, the best preserved is at Ur, in southern Mesopotamia, dedicated to the moon god, Nanna (Figure 1.11). Built in about 2100 B.C.E., this ziggurat was laid out to the four points of the compass. A central stairway led up to the highest platform, on which the major temple rested. Other cities constructed similar massive podiums in the hopes that they would please the gods and goddesses, that the rivers would be kind to them, and that life would continue. Thus, the central themes of Mesopotamian civilization manifested themselves in the ziggurats.

Figure 1.11 Ziggurat of Ur. Ca. 2100 B.C.E. Ur (Muqaiyir, Iraq). *A temple to Nanna, the moon god, stood on the top of the ziggurat, which was terraced on three levels. On the first level was an entranceway approached by two sets of steps on each side and one in the front. The base, or lowest stage, which is all that remains of this "Hill of Heaven," measures 200 by 150 feet and stands 70 feet high. In comparison, Chartres cathedral in France is 157 feet wide, with each tower over 240 feet high.*

THE CIVILIZATION OF THE NILE RIVER VALLEY: EGYPT

Another great river, the Nile, provided the setting for Egyptian civilization. Unlike the culture of the Mesopotamian valley, however, the culture of the Nile evolved continuously, responding mainly to internal changes rather than to external influences. It thus achieved a unified character that lasted for about three thousand years. Isolated by deserts on either side, Egypt developed an introspective attitude that was little influenced by neighboring cultures (such as Nubia, also called Kush, which flourished between the first and fourth cataracts, or waterfalls, of the Nile River) and that led to a sense of cultural superiority. Subjected to the annual floodings of the Nile and aware of the revolutions of the sun, Egypt saw itself as part of a cyclical pattern in a timeless world.

The periodic overflowings of the Nile made civilized life possible in Egypt. Red sandy deserts stretched east and west of the waterway. Beside the Nile's banks, however, the black alluvial soil of the narrow floodplain offered rich land for planting, although the river's gifts of water and arable land were limited. Irrigation canals and ditches plus patient, backbreaking labor were required to bring the life-giving liquid into the desert.

Because the survival and prosperity of the people depended on the Nile, the river dominated and shaped the Egyptian experience. About 95 percent of the people lived on the less than 5 percent of Egyptian land that was arable and that was located along the Nile. The resulting concentration of people led to the emergence of the agricultural village, the fundamental unit of Egyptian civilization. The reward for farm labor tended to be subsistence living, yet the perennial hope that next year's flood would bring a more bountiful harvest created an optimistic outlook that contrasted with the darker Mesopotamian view.

The Nile linked the "Two Lands," Upper and Lower Egypt, two regions whose differing geography made for two distinct ways of life. Since the Nile flows northward, Lower Egypt referred to the northern lands fed by the river's spreading delta, a region made wealthy by its fertile soil. In contrast, the harsh topography and poor farming conditions of the southern lands made Upper Egypt an area of near-subsistence living. In addition, Lower Egypt, because of its proximity to both Mediterranean and Near Eastern cultures, tended to be more cosmopolitan than the provincial, isolated lands of Upper Egypt.

The earliest Neolithic settlers in the Nile valley probably arrived in about 6000 B.C.E. These earliest Egyptians took up an agricultural life, wresting control of the surrounding lands, taming the river, and domesticating animals. In the rich alluvial soil, they cultivated barley, wheat, and vegetables for themselves and fodder for their animals. They hunted with bows and arrows and fished with nets, thereby supplementing their simple fare. They also planted flax,

Timeline 1.3   EGYPTIAN CIVILIZATION   All dates approximate and B.C.E.

6000	3100	2700	2185	2050	1800	1552	1079	525
Neolithic and Predynastic Periods	Early Dynastic Period	Old Kingdom	First Intermediate Period	Middle Kingdom	Second Intermediate Period	New Kingdom	Late Dynastic Period	Persian Conquest

from which thread was woven into linen on primitive looms. Most tools and weapons were made of stone or flint, but copper, which had to be imported, became more important after 3500 B.C.E. The early Egyptians lived in simply furnished, flat-topped houses built of sun-dried bricks. These basic patterns characterized peasant life throughout much of Egypt's history.

Continuity and Change over Three Thousand Years

Egypt stepped from the shadows of its illiterate past in about 3100 B.C.E., when Menes [MEE-neez] proclaimed himself king and united the upper and lower lands. His power reached from the Mediterranean to the first cataract of the Nile, making Egypt a state to be reckoned with in the Near East. Egypt's lengthy, complex history is conventionally divided into twenty-six dynasties, which are in turn classified into groups. The three major groups of dynasties are known as the Old Kingdom, the Middle Kingdom, and the New Kingdom. They are preceded and followed, respectively, by two dynastic groups known as the Early Dynastic Period and the Late Dynastic Period. In addition, two intermediate dynastic groupings (the First and the Second) precede and follow the Middle Kingdom (Timeline 1.3).

In the Early Dynastic Period (about 3100–2700 B.C.E.), the kings brought prosperity through their control of the economy and fostered political harmony through diplomacy and dynastic marriages. These rulers, claiming to be gods on earth, adopted the trappings of divinity and built royal tombs to ensure their immortality.

With the Old Kingdom (about 2700–2185 B.C.E.), Egypt entered a five-hundred-year period of peace and prosperity, as its political institutions matured and its language was adapted to literary uses. The most enduring accomplishment of the Old Kingdom became the pyramid—the royal tomb devised by the Fourth Dynasty kings (Figure 1.12). As the visible symbol of the kings' power, the massive pyramids served to link the rulers with the gods and the cosmos. Yet, although the kings could impress their people with divine claims, they could neither subdue the forces of nature nor make their power last forever. For reasons

not fully understood, these rulers loosened their control over the state and thus ushered in an age of political fragmentation called the First Intermediate Period.

In the First Intermediate Period (about 2185–2050 B.C.E.), civil war raged sporadically and starvation wiped out much of the populace. Eventually, a family from Thebes, in Upper Egypt, reunited the state and initiated the Middle Kingdom (about 2050–1800 B.C.E.). The new dynasty, the twelfth, fortified the southern frontier with Nubia and helped bring about a cultural renaissance, especially in literature, but unity was short-lived.

The Second Intermediate Period (about 1800–1552 B.C.E.) was an age of chaos provoked both by repeated failures of the Nile to flood and by a resurgence of local warlords. A weakened Lower Egypt succumbed to the Hyksos, Semitic-speaking invaders from Palestine. Backed by warriors in horse-drawn chariots, the Hyksos with their bronze weapons easily defeated the copper-armed Egyptians. The Hyksos era was crucial in Egypt's history because it ended the isolation that had fed a sense of cultural superiority. Egyptian nobility now joined aristocracies everywhere in employing the horse for war and sport, and Egyptian artisans fully entered the Bronze Age.

Ahmose I [AH-mos], a Theban king, drove out the Hyksos and inaugurated the New Kingdom (1552–1079 B.C.E.), the most cosmopolitan era in Egyptian history. Pursuing the Hyksos into Palestine, Ahmose conquered the foreign peoples along the way, creating the first Egyptian empire. To the northeast, Egypt's kings, now called pharaohs, pursued imperial ambitions against the cities in Palestine, Phoenicia, and Syria, a move that provoked deadly warfare with the Hittites of Anatolia. Egypt finally secured its possessions by peacefully dividing up the Near East with the Hittites and the Assyrians. To the south, the pharaohs pushed Egypt's frontiers to the Nile's fourth cataract, conquering the Nubians long in residence there. As the empire grew, Egypt's society underwent the greatest changes of its entire history, including religious innovation by a ruling family, widespread material affluence, extravagant temple building, and artistic and literary experimentation.

But imperial success declined after 1200 B.C.E., signaled by the pharaoh's growing dependence on unre-

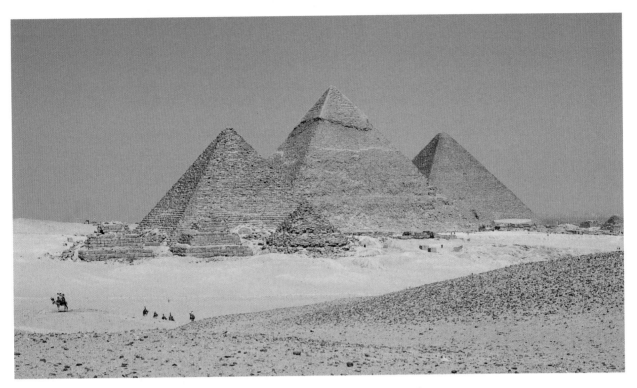

Figure 1.12   The Pyramids at Giza. Ground view from the south. Pyramid of Menkure (foreground), ca. 2525 B.C.E.; Pyramid of Khafre (center), ca. 2544 B.C.E.; Pyramid of Khufu (rear), ca. 2580 B.C.E. *The Fourth Dynasty was the Age of Pyramids, when the pyramid's characteristic shape was standardized and became a symbol of Egyptian civilization. The Great Pyramid, in the rear, was the first structure at Giza; it originally stood 480 feet high but today is only 450 feet high. All three pyramids were originally surfaced with shiny, white limestone, but this covering was stripped in later centuries by builders in nearby Cairo; the only remnant of the limestone surface is the cap on the top of the Pyramid of Khafre, in the center.*

liable foreign troops. Bands of nomads, called Sea Peoples by the Egyptians, began to disrupt trade and normal social life. Over the course of a century, the invaders forced Egypt to withdraw behind its historic borders and thus ended the empire. The success of the Sea Peoples' challenge, despite their small numbers, lay in their new weapons, for these destructive migrants were the leading edge of the Age of Iron. Egypt's lack of iron ore probably contributed fatally to its military decline.

Egypt maintained continuity of tradition into the Late Dynastic Period (about 1079–525 B.C.E.). However, its independence came to an end with its successive incorporations into Nubian, Assyrian, and Persian empires.

Just as the pharaoh dominated the state, so the rulers controlled the predominantly agrarian economy, although departments of government or the priesthood of a temple often exploited the land and the king's serfs. Upper Egypt provided the bulk of farm produce that Lower Egypt exported to Mediterranean neighbors. In prosperous years, the pharaohs claimed up to half of the farm crops to support their building programs, especially funerary monuments. But in years of famine, dynasties fell and the state splintered into separate units.

Foreign trade was also a royal monopoly. The government obtained cedar from Lebanon, olive oil from Palestine, and myrrh from Punt, probably on the Somali coast. Since Egypt never developed a coinage, the pharaohs bartered for these imports with papyrus rolls (for writing), linen, weapons, and furniture. The pharaohs also exported gold from the eastern desert and copper from the Sinai peninsula. In addition, Egypt served as the carrier of tropical African goods—ebony, ivory, and animal skins—to the eastern Mediterranean.

Egyptian society was hierarchical, and at the top stood the pharaoh—the king and god incarnate. Because divine blood coursed through the ruler's veins, he could marry only within his own family. Tradition decreed that the Chief Queen, who was identified with the goddess Hathor, would produce the royal heir. If she failed to produce offspring, the successor pharaoh was selected from sons of the ruler's other wives or royal cousins. On rare occasions, when there was no suitable heir, the Chief Queen became the pharaoh, as did Hatshepsut [hat-SHEP-soot] in the New Kingdom.

Because there was no provision for a female king in Egyptian culture, the appearance of a female ruler is thought by scholars to signal a political crisis. Only four times in Egypt's three-thousand-year history was the king female; in contrast, there were more than two hundred male kings. Of the four female rulers, three appeared at the end of dynasties: Nitiqret in the Sixth Dynasty, Nefrusobk in the Twelfth, and Tausret in the Nineteenth. Hatshepsut's assumption of power was unique in that it occurred in the midst of a flourishing dynasty, though during the infancy of Thutmose III [thoot-MOH-suh], the heir apparent. Acting at first as regent to the young heir, she soon claimed the kingship in her own right and reigned for about ten years. After her death, Thutmose III obliterated her name and image from her monuments, though the reason for their removal is unclear. He may have been expressing hatred of her, or he may have wanted to erase the memory of a woman who had seized power contrary to *maat*, the natural order of things.

Ranked below the ruling family were the royal officials, nobles, large landowners, and priests, all generally hereditary offices. The pharaoh's word was law, but these groups were delegated powers for executing his will. On a lower level, artists and artisans worked for the pharaonic court and the nobility. Peasants and a small number of slaves formed the bulk of Egypt's population. Personal liberty took second place to the general welfare, and peasants were pressed into forced labor during natural disasters, such as floods, and at harvest time.

A Quest for Eternal Cultural Values

Until the invasion of the Hyksos, Egypt, in its splendid isolation, forged a civilization whose serene values and timeless forms deeply mirrored the religious beliefs of the rulers and the stability of the state. But as contact with other cultures and civilizations grew, Egyptian culture changed to reflect new influences. Writers borrowed words from other languages, for example, and sculptors displayed the human figure in more natural settings and poses. Still, Egyptian culture retained its distinctive qualities, and innovations continued to express traditional ideals.

Religion   Egypt was a **theocracy,** or a state ruled by a god. Believing that the deities had planned their country's future from the beginning, the Egyptians thought of their society as sacred. From the time that Menes first united Egypt, religious dogma taught that the king, as

god on earth, embodied the state. Egyptian rulers also identified themselves with the deities. For example, Menes claimed to be the "two ladies," the goddesses who stood for Upper and Lower Egypt. Other rulers identified themselves with Ra, the sun god, and with Ra's son, Horus, the sky god, who was always depicted as having the head of a falcon. Because of the king's divinity, the resources of the state were concentrated on giving the ruler proper homage, as in the Old Kingdom's massive tombs, designed on a superhuman scale to ensure his safe passage to the next life.

Egyptian subjects worshiped the pharaoh, but the pharaoh could venerate any deity he pleased. Hence, the shifting fortunes of Egypt's many cults depended on the ruler's preference. For example, Ptah (who, like the Hebrew God in Genesis, created through speech) became the god of Memphis, which was the capital of the Old Kingdom. The kings of the Fifth Dynasty, on the other hand, called themselves sons of Ra, the sun god, and they honored this celestial deity by building him temples more impressive than their own royal tombs. Later, the Twelfth Dynasty replaced Ptah with Amen (a word meaning "hidden one"), and a series of rulers adopted his name, as in Amenemhat [AH-men-EM-het]. Royal favor to a god generally increased the wealth and influence of the god's cult and priests. Consequently, by the time of the New Kingdom, society had become top-heavy with priests and their privileged religious properties.

Egypt came close to having a national deity during the New Kingdom when Akhenaten [ahk-NAHT-uhn] (r. about 1369–1353 B.C.E.) reshaped the royal religion at his capital, Amarna. Elevating Aten, the god of the sun's disk, to supremacy above the other gods, Akhenaten systematically disavowed the older divinities— a heretical view in tolerant, polytheistic Egypt. This innovation aroused the opposition of conservative nobles who supported the powerful priests of the Theban god, Amen. Akhenaten ultimately failed, and later pharaohs tried to erase his name and memory from history. The Amarna revolution, however, like the religious choices of the pharaohs generally, had little effect on the ordinary Egyptian, who continued to believe that the pharaoh could intervene with the other gods for the benefit of all.

The foremost distinguishing mark of Egyptian religion was its promise of immortality—a belief that generated a more optimistic attitude toward human existence than that found in Mesopotamia. At first, in the Old Kingdom, only the kings were accorded this reward. Eventually, nobles and royal officials were buried in the vicinity of the rulers' tombs, thereby ensuring their immortality as assistants to the risen god in the afterlife. By the First Intermediate Period, the nobles had claimed their own right to immortality by erecting tombs on which the royal funerary texts were

Figure 1.13 Egyptian Writing. *From the Old Kingdom onward, the hieroglyphs (in the top line) constituted the style of formal writing that appeared on tomb walls and in monuments. Religious and governmental scribes soon devised two distinct types of cursive script, a careful manuscript hand (in the middle line) and a more rapid hand (in the bottom line) for administrative documents and letters.*

Hieroglyphics				
Literary hieratic				
Swift hieratic				
Translation	*Amen* god of Memphis	*rôemt* mankind	*per-'o* Pharaoh	*hru* day

copied. Later, immortality was apparently opened to all Egyptians, although only the wealthy minority could afford the cost of a proper burial.

Writing and Literature Late predynastic Egypt learned the idea of writing, but not foreign words, from Mesopotamia. The Egyptians initially drew pictographs, called hieroglyphs, for such words as *hoe, arrowhead,* and *plow.* This early hieroglyphic script could also depict abstract words for which no adequate picture was available, but because such picture writing was time-consuming and clumsy to execute, the scribes soon made the pictographs function as signs, or clusters of consonants, for other words (Figure 1.13).

Egyptian literature produced no single great work that rivals *Gilgamesh,* but the Egyptian experience was rich in its variety of literary **genres,** or types of literature. For example, pyramid texts, the writings inscribed in burial chambers, formed the chief literary genre in the Old Kingdom. As this era gave way to the First Intermediate Period, new prose genres, such as prophecies and pessimistic writings, arose that addressed the prevalent political disintegration and social upheaval. Such was the tenor of the times that writers expressed views contradicting Egypt's otherwise optimistic attitudes to death and life. *The Dispute of a Man with His Soul* describes a desperate mortal finally choosing the emptiness of death rather than life in a materialistic and violent world.

The prophecies, **hymns** (songs of praise to the gods), and prose narratives of the Middle Kingdom constitute the classical period of Egyptian letters. The most famous work of the Middle Kingdom, as well as of all Egyptian literature, is the *Story of Sinuhe,* a prose tale that celebrates the ruler Senusert I and his subject, the hero named in the title. Fleeing Egypt, Sinuhe earns fame and fortune in Lebanon yet yearns for his beloved homeland. Sinuhe's exploits smack of the folk tale, for in one episode he subdues a taunting giant of a man, much as David defeats Goliath in the Old Testament story. Eventually, a gracious Senusert

writes Sinuhe, forgiving his wandering subject's unnamed crime and inviting him to return home. The travel yarn concludes with a homecoming scene in which a joyful Sinuhe is reintegrated into Egyptian court society.

The richest period in Egyptian letters occurred during the New Kingdom. In addition to songs praising the pharaoh, poets now composed lyrics telling of the pain of parted lovers, and new genres included model letters, wisdom literature, and fairy tales. Akhenaten's revolution led to unique forms of literary expression, as in the *Hymn to Aten,* which praised this universal god. Although the hymn has similarities to Psalm 104 of the Old Testament, Akhenaten's text, unlike the Jewish scriptures, was not a declaration of **monotheism,** the belief that there is only one god. Instead, the *Hymn to Aten* recognized a special link between Akhenaten and his family and the god of the solar disk while still acknowledging the worship of other deities.

Science and Medicine Natural philosophy, as a separate field of study, did not emerge in ancient Egypt. No term for either philosophy or science existed in the Egyptian language. Nevertheless, the Egyptians engaged in speculative thought, fueled by practical needs. For example, they invented a decimal number system, although using their cumbersome set of hieroglyphics. They devised problem-solving methods and related rules for measuring figures and calculating the volumes of solids. They kept accurate records of the annual floods of the Nile and built pyramids and other structures, which required knowledge of measurement and design.

Egyptians studied the movement of the stars, but Egyptian astronomy was not well advanced, being concerned primarily with casting horoscopes and the keeping of the civil calendar. Egypt's lasting contribution in this field was the calendar itself, which priests maintained for the celebration of religious rituals and festivals during the year. They divided the year into

SLICE OF LIFE
Life's Instruction Book for Egyptians

ANONYMOUS
From a Papyrus Text

Egypt's wisdom literature—aphorisms about the best way to live—culminated in The Instruction of Amenemope, *written in the late New Kingdom. In this work, the author stresses the ethical life rather than the amassing of personal wealth.*

Beginning of the teaching for life,
The instructions for well-being.

. . . .

If you make your life with these [words] in your
    heart,
You will find it a success;
You will find my words a storehouse for life,
Your being will prosper upon earth.

. . . .

Do not move the markers on the borders of fields,
Nor shift the position of the measuring-cord.
Do not be greedy for a cubit of land,
Nor encroach on the boundaries of a widow.

. . . .

Do not set your heart on wealth,
There is no ignoring Fate and Destiny;

. . . .

Do not strain to seek increase,
What you have, let it suffice you.

. . . .

Do not cheat a man (through) pen on scroll,
The god abhors it;

Do not bear witness with false words,
So as to brush aside a man by your tongue.

. . . .

Do not laugh at a blind man,
Nor tease a dwarf,
Nor cause hardship for the lame.

. . . .

Do not sit down in the beer-house
In order to join one greater than you,
Be he a youth great through his office,
Or be he an elder through birth.
Befriend a man of your own measure.

. . . .

Do not revile one older than you,
He has seen Re [the Sun God] before you;
Let (him) not report you to the Aten [the god of the
    sun's disk] at his rising,
Saying: "A youth has reviled an old man."

Interpreting This Slice of Life **What** are some of the "words to live by," which are offered in this piece of wisdom literature? **How** should old people be treated by the young? **What** is the author's teaching on wealth and materialism? **Compare** the advice in this work with the Ten Commandments (see Table 6.1). Do you think these rules are useful in today's world? **Discuss.**

---

twelve months of thirty days each, with five extra days at the end of the year. This calendar began each annual cycle on September 21, the autumnal equinox. Later, the Romans adopted the Egyptian calendar, with its twelve-month, 365-day cycle, and they in turn transmitted it to the modern world.

Practical matters made medicine another area of Egyptian scientific achievement. An ancient medical treatise, dating from about 1600 B.C.E. (but thought to be a copy of an earlier text from perhaps 3000 B.C.E.), is the world's oldest surviving medical textbook. This surgical treatise offers a comprehensive survey of the human body, detailing the diagnosis, treatment, and outcome of various maladies that can afflict the human organs. A second medical treatise, dating from about 1550 B.C.E., lists hundreds of magical incantations and folk remedies for numerous illnesses, such as crocodile wounds and ingrown toenails, along with advice on ridding the house of vermin, insects, and scorpions.

Architecture The classic Egyptian building was the pyramid, whose shape seemed to embody a constant and eternal order. During the Old Kingdom, the pyramid became the only building deemed suitable for a ruler-god's resting place preparatory to the afterlife. A modified version of the pyramid appeared first in about 2680 B.C.E. in the step pyramid of King Djoser [ZHO-ser] at Sakkareh, opposite Memphis (Figure 1.14). Later Egyptian rulers preferred the true pyramid form, and this design did not develop further.

The true pyramid appeared in the Old Kingdom when the Fourth Dynasty ruler Khufu [KOO-foo] erected the Great Pyramid at Giza, across the Nile from Cairo (see Figure 1.12). The anonymous architect executed this largest stone building in the world— 6.25 million tons—with mathematical precision. Many of the tomb's two million stones were quarried on the site, although most were obtained farther upstream

Figure 1.14 IMHOTEP. Step Pyramid of King Djoser. Ca. 2680 B.C.E. Sakkareh, Egypt.
Though isolated from its neighbors until about 1730 B.C.E., Egypt was influenced by surrounding cultures, as the design for the step pyramid at Sakkareh shows. Resting on a rectangular base and rising in six progressively smaller stages, this pyramid was modeled on Mesopotamia's ziggurat. But unlike the ziggurats, which were made of dried-clay bricks, it was built of cut stone, the first building to be so constructed in the world. The step pyramid has six levels on a 411-by-358-foot base and stands 204 feet high.

and ferried to Giza during the flooding of the Nile. The infinitesimally small deviation between the two sets of opposing base sides of the pyramid show the scientific spirit already at work in this early stage of Egypt's history. Later, two of Khufu's successors, Khafre [KAF-ray] and Menkure [men-KOO-ray], added their pyramids to make the complex at Giza the symbol of the Old Kingdom and one of the wonders of the ancient world.

The pyramids eventually gave way to funerary temples when the New Kingdom pharaohs began to construct splendid monuments for themselves that reflected Egypt's new imperial status. The temple of Queen Hatshepsut is perhaps the most beautiful example of this architectural development (Figure 1.15). Designed by the royal architect Senmut, the temple of Hatshepsut was carved into the face of the mountain at Deir el Bahri, across the Nile from Luxor. Senmut, adopting the post-and-lintel style of construction, gave the queen's temple two levels of pillared colonnades, each accessible by long sloping ramps. The most arresting feature of Hatshepsut's temple is its round columns, which are used alongside rectangular pillars in the **porticoes,** or covered entrances. These columns— with their plain tops and grooved surfaces—suggest the graceful columns of later Greek architecture, although some scholars dismiss this similarity as coincidental. Be that as it may, this Egyptian monument, like

the later Greek temples, shows a harmonious sense of proportion throughout its impressive colonnades.

Rulers in both Egypt and Mesopotamia created zoos and botanical gardens, the first in the world, though the earliest evidence of these developments comes from Egypt. Built for pleasure and prestige and to satisfy scientific curiosity, the menageries and gardens originated before 2000 B.C.E.

Sculpture, Painting, and Minor Arts The Egyptians did not understand art as it is defined today. Indeed, they had no word for art. Rather than being art for art's sake, Egyptian painting and sculpture served as a means to a religious end, specifically to house the *ka,* or spirit of a person or deity. Art was more than mere representation; images embodied all of the subjects' qualities.

In the royal graveyard at Giza, artisans of the Old Kingdom carved from the living rock a mythical creature that stirred the imagination of most peoples in the ancient world—a sphinx, half-lion and half-man (Figure 1.16). Although this creature often inspired feelings of dread, in actuality there was little mystery to the sphinx, since its original purpose was to guard the royal tombs, perhaps to frighten away grave robbers. Indeed, this first sphinx's face was that of Khafre, the Fourth Dynasty king whose pyramid stood nearby. Today, this crumbling relic stands as a reminder of the claims to immortality of the Old Kingdom rulers.

Figure 1.15   SENMUT. Hatshepsut's Temple. Ca. 1490 B.C.E. Deir el Bahri, across from Luxor, Egypt. *Hatshepsut's temple was planned for the same purpose as the pyramids—to serve as a shrine for the royal remains. In actuality an ascending series of three colonnaded courtyards, this temple provided a spectacular approach to a hidden sanctuary carved in the steep cliffs.*

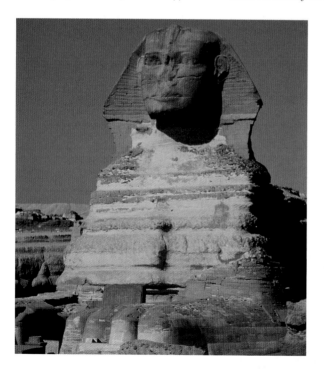

Figure 1.16   The Great Sphinx. Ca. 2560 B.C.E. Sandstone, 65′ high × 240′ long. Giza, Egypt. *Sphinxes, creatures part lion and part human, were often depicted in Egyptian art. The most famous sphinx is the one at Giza, carved from the rock on the site. The sphinx's colossal size prevented the anonymous sculptor from rendering it with any subtle facial expressions. More significant as a monument than as a great work of art, the Great Sphinx had a practical purpose—to guard the nearby pyramid tombs.*

The sheer size and mythical character of the Great Sphinx set it apart from Old Kingdom sculptures in the round, which favored human-scale figures and realistic images. The life-size statue of King Menkure and his Chief Queen, found beneath the ruler's pyramid at Giza, shows this art's brilliant realism (Figure 1.17). The sculpture embodies the characteristics of what became the standard, or classical, Egyptian style: their left legs forward, the king's clenched fists, their headdresses (sacred regalia for him and wig for her), their rigid poses, their serene countenances, and the figures' angularity. Designed to be attached to a wall, the sculpture was intended to be viewed from the front, so the couple has a two-dimensional quality.

In contrast to practices in the Old Kingdom, the wives of rulers in the New Kingdom acquired claims to divinity in their own right. A statue of Hatshepsut represents her in the clothing and with the sacred pose of pharaoh (Figure 1.18). Having first been Chief Queen to Thutmose II in the New Kingdom, after his death she seized leadership, probably with the cooperation of the powerful Theban priesthood of Amen. Although more than a thousand years separated this sculpture from that of Menkure (see Figure 1.17), in its expression of dignity and authority the statue of Hatshepsut bears a strong resemblance to the earlier work, thus demonstrating the continuity of the Egyptian style.

A major challenge to Egypt's traditional, austere forms occurred in Akhenaten's revolutionary reign. A low-relief sculpture of the royal family exemplifies the naturalism and fluid lines that this artistic rebellion favored (Figure 1.19). Akhenaten nuzzles one of his daughters in an intimate pose while his wife dandles another daughter on her knees and allows a third to stand on her left arm. The domesticity of this scene is quite unlike the sacred gestures of traditional Egyptian sculpture, but the religious subject of this relief remains true to that tradition, as the rays streaming from the disk of Aten onto the royal family indicate.

The most extraordinary artistic achievement of the Amarna period is the carved portrait head of Queen Nefertiti (Figure 1.20), a life-size sculpture discovered in 1912 by a team of German archeologists in the desert sands near the long-lost city founded by Akhenaten for the god Aten. This statue-head with its unfinished left eye, deliberate or accidental, is one of the most arresting images of world art. Painted in flesh tones and natural colors and imbued with the naturalism of the Amarna style, the queen has a vitality that is unsurpassed. A modern critic has called her the eternal female, ceaselessly watching.

Nefertiti's unusual headdress signifies her status as a potent force in this culture. Rising straight up from her forehead, this crown is decorated with the *uraeus*, the image of a cobra ready to strike. By custom, this powerful and protective symbol was part of the kingly **regalia** (tokens of royal authority) and could be worn only by rulers and their Great (principal) Queens. Modern scholars have proved that Nefertiti was the only Great, or Chief, Queen in Egypt's long history to share power with her husband. (Queen Hatshepsut actually ruled alone as pharaoh.) The prevalence of images of Nefertiti in so much of the art that remains from Amarna confirms this queen's importance on the political level and thus underscores her central role in the Amarna revolution.

Figure 1.17 *King Menkure and His Chief Queen.* Ca. 2525 B.C.E. Ht. 54½". Museum expedition. Courtesy Museum of Fine Arts, Boston. *This life-size slate sculpture of Menkure, a Fourth Dynasty ruler, and his Chief Queen was removed from its resting place beneath the king's pyramid at Giza (see Figure 1.12). In this sculpture, the figures are represented as being of comparable size, unlike the usual depiction of husbands as much larger than their wives, indicating their greater importance. The sizes here probably reflect the royal status of the Chief Queen. The queen's subordination to the king is subtly shown in her position on his left side, thought to be inferior to the right, and her arm around his waist, an indication that her role was to encourage and support.*

Just as Egypt's sculpture in the round developed a rigid **canon,** or set of rules, so did two-dimensional representations acquire a fixed formula, whether in relief sculptures or in wall paintings. The Egyptians never discovered the principles of perspective. On a flat surface, the human figures were depicted in profile, with both feet pointing sideways, as in a painting from a New Kingdom funerary papyrus (Figure 1.21). However, the artistic canon required that the eye and the shoulders be shown frontally, and both arms had to be visible, along with all the fingers. The artist determined the human proportions exactly, by the use of a grid. Throughout most Egyptian art history, the human figure was conceived as being eighteen squares high standing and fourteen squares high seated, with each unit equivalent to the width of one "fist"; anatomical parts were made accordingly proportional. The canon of proportions was established by the time of the Old Kingdom, and its continued use, with slight variations, helped Egyptian art retain its unmistakable style. Wall paintings, in contrast to relief sculptures, permitted a greater sense of space to be created, but the rules regarding the human figure still had to be observed (Figure 1.22). Given those stringent conventions, the Egyptian artists who worked in two dimensions were amazingly successful in creating the image of a carefree society bubbling with life.

Figure 1.18 *Hatshepsut.* Ca. 1460 B.C.E. Marble, ht. 6′5″. Courtesy Metropolitan Museum of Art. Rogers Fund and contribution from Edward S. Harkness, 1929. (29.3.2). *This sculpture is one of more than two hundred statues of Hatshepsut intended to adorn her massive and elegant funeral temple at Deir el Bahri in the western hills of Thebes. The authoritative pose and regalia convey her pharaonic status, and she is only subtly represented as a woman.*

Figure 1.19 *Family Scene: Pharaoh Akhenaten, Queen Nefertiti, and Their Three Daughters.* Ca. 1350 B.C.E. Limestone, 13″ high × 15⁵⁄₁₂″ wide. Altes Museum, Berlin. *The religious ideas associated with Akhenaten's reforms are expressed in the lines streaming from the sun's disk above the royal couple. Each ray of the sun ends in a tiny hand that offers a blessing to the royal family.*

Figure 1.20 *Nefertiti.* Ca. 1350 B.C.E. Limestone, ht. 20".
Altes Museum, Berlin. *This portrait head of Nefertiti is characterized by sleekness and charm, a look achieved through the sculptor's fusing of the fluid Amarna style with the formality of Egypt's traditional art. To create the image of sleekness, the sculptor has pushed Nefertiti's face forward like the prow of a ship cutting through the wind. The figure's charm emerges from the tension between the queen's dreamy, deeply hooded eyes (one eye is unfinished) and her lively, arched eyebrows. The artist has succeeded in representing Nefertiti as both a woman and a goddess.*

Figure 1.21 Opening of the Mouth Scene, Funerary Papyrus of Hunefer. Ca. 1305–1195 B.C.E. British Museum. *Egyptian painters and sculptors always depicted human subjects from the side, with the feet in profile, as in this painting on a papyrus manuscript deposited in a New Kingdom tomb. This painting's treatment of flesh tones of the human figures also typifies the Egyptian style. Egyptian men, represented here by the officiating priests, were consistently shown with red-brown, tanned skins at least partially reflective of their outdoor lives. Egyptian women, such as the mourners directly before the mummy, were usually painted with lighter complexions of yellow or pink or white. The Opening of the Mouth was a burial ritual, preparing the deceased to speak in the afterlife.*

28

Figure 1.22 Banqueting Scene. Ca. 1567–1320 B.C.E. Fresco, 23″ high × 27¼″ wide. British Museum. *In a small space, the Egyptian painter has created a delightful banqueting scene, a favorite subject in tomb decoration in the New Kingdom. No one eats at this ritual meal, for the purpose is to set the stage for the tomb owner's rebirth. The female figures, especially the young seminaked girls dancing (below) and serving (above), represent the female generative principle. The naked-girl motif in tomb paintings, which appeared at this time, was probably meant to ensure the tomb owner's fertility while living and the continuity of the family while the deceased was in the tomb awaiting rebirth. The lotus flowers on the heads of the female guests and musicians reflect the rebirth theme, since the lotus was used to symbolize the promise of immortality for the dead. The frontal pose of two of the lower figures is an artistic innovation. Faces were almost always shown in profile in Egyptian art (see Figures 1.19 and 1.21).*

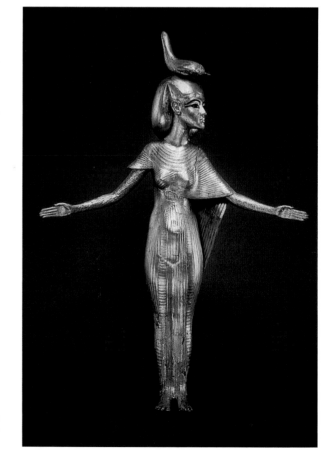

Figure 1.23 *Selket.* Ca. 1325 B.C.E. Wood, overlaid with gesso and gilded, ht. 53⅝″. Cairo Museum, Egypt. *This statue of the goddess Selket was discovered in King Tutankhamen's tomb in 1923, one of the great archeological finds of the twentieth century. Discovered by Egyptologist Howard Carter, the tomb held thousands of royal artifacts and art objects, including the pharaoh's gold funerary mask, a solid gold coffin, a gold throne, chairs, couches, chariots, jewelry, figurines, drinking cups, clothing, weapons, and games. The fascinating story of the discovery is told in Carter's book,* The Tomb of Tutankhamen.

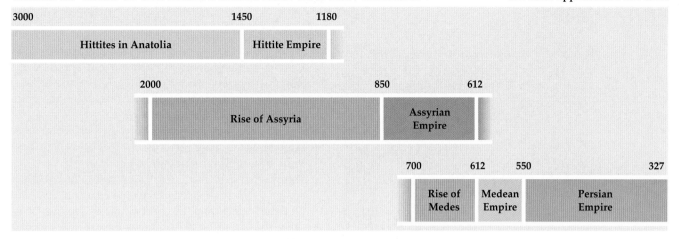

Royal tombs have yielded incomparable examples of Egyptian sculpture, as in the burial chamber of the New Kingdom pharaoh Tutankhamen [too-tahn-KAHM-en]. Of the thirty-four excavated royal tombs, only that of King Tut—as he is popularly known—escaped relatively free from violation by thieves in ancient times. A freestanding, life-size sculpture of the funerary goddess Selket was one of four goddess figures placed outside the gilded shrine that contained the king's internal organs (Figure 1.23). Her arms are outstretched in a protective fashion around her royal charge's shrine. A unique feature is the turn of Selket's head, a violation of the cardinal rule of three-dimensional Egyptian art that figures face frontward (see Figures 1.17 and 1.18). Selket's pose suggests that she was looking for intruders. The sculpture's style, with its naturalism and fluid lines, reflects the art of Amarna, the revolutionary style that flourished briefly in the fourteenth century B.C.E. before being abandoned and replaced by Egypt's traditional formal style.

HEIRS TO THE MESOPOTAMIAN AND EGYPTIAN EMPIRES

With the decline of Mesopotamian and Egyptian empires, successor kingdoms arose in the eastern Mediterranean, notably those of the Hittites, the Assyrians, the Medes, and the Persians. If the length of their rule and the richness of their achievements failed to measure up to those of Mesopotamian and Egyptian civilizations, they nevertheless brought degrees of law and order to numerous peoples over vast territories and spread various forms of civilized life (Timeline 1.4).

The Hittites

Starting in about 3000 B.C.E., the Hittites migrated into Anatolia from southern Russia. Slowly, by degrees and

through peaceful infiltrations, they established the Old Kingdom (about 1700–about 1500 B.C.E.). In 1595 B.C.E., they overturned the Babylonian state, which made them the most powerful and influential people in the area. During the New Kingdom or Empire (about 1450–about 1180 B.C.E.), they extended their control into eastern Anatolia and northern Mesopotamia and as far south as the borders of Egypt. They enjoyed many victories on the battlefield, due to their skills as charioteers and their forged iron weapons. Through diplomatic alliances and successful marriage contracts, they kept their enemies at bay for several centuries. A line of strong Hittite rulers consolidated their power, carried out social and political reforms, expanded their trade routes, and incorporated many of the area's deities and religious beliefs into the state religion. At the beginning of the twelfth century B.C.E., the Phrygians and other marauding tribes drove the Hittites from Anatolia into Syria. There, over the next few centuries, they mixed with the indigenous populations and reappeared scattered among the small city-states, now increasingly subject to the Phoenicians, the Egyptians, and the powerful Assyrians.

Except for their language, which survived beyond the Assyrian Empire, the Hittites left little legacy of their culture and civilization. Some examples have been excavated of small animal figurines, vases, and ornaments confirming the high skills of their metalworkers and potters. However, the most lasting works are the large scenes of animals, gods, and goddesses carved into rock walls near a number of Hittite urban centers. Also still visible and impressive are some temple structures, gateways, city walls, and extensive fortifications at Bogazkoy—at one time the capital of the Old Kingdom—in central Turkey.

The Assyrians

The earliest Assyrian tribes lived in the Upper Tigris region, in present-day Iraq. For several centuries, from

Figure 1.24 Human-Headed Winged Bull. Eighth century B.C.E. Gypseous alabaster, ht. 13'10". Louvre. *In Assyrian iconography, human-headed winged bulls—or lions—that guarded the entrances to royal residences and temples combined the characteristics of certain living beings. The head of a man represented intellectual power and the lord of creation; eagle wings were signs of speed and flight; the bull symbolized strength and fecundity, or, if the creature was a lion, then strength and the king of beasts. The carvings' five legs—an unnatural touch—gave each animal the appearance of either walking or standing still, depending on the perspective from which it was viewed. While their purposes are not fully understood, these guardian statues, with their imposing stance and symbolic meanings, made all who approached know that they were in the presence of a powerful ruler and forces. Other Near Eastern peoples adopted these hybrid creatures in their art, and Christians later claimed these images, converting them into Christian symbols of the four Evangelists (see Figure 9.19).*

about the twentieth to the thirteenth century B.C.E., they flourished under a series of kings who united their subjects and extended their territories. Over the next three hundred years, the Assyrians conquered Babylon and advanced westward to the Mediterranean Sea. In the ninth century B.C.E., they moved rapidly against their neighbors, defeating them on the battlefield, sending total populations into exile, and ruling with an iron fist and a policy of terror. At the height of their power, they controlled all the land between the Nile River in Egypt and the Tigris River in Mesopotamia. A vigorous and warlike people from the beginning, they sent their well-trained and highly disciplined armies to sweep through the enemy ranks. Supplied with the latest iron weapons and supported by swiftly moving chariot legions, they fought to total

victory, showing no mercy in executing prisoners and destroying their cities. Yet, just when it appeared the Assyrian Empire would continue for centuries, they were quickly defeated by the Medes and the Neo-Babylonians in 612 B.C.E., at Nineveh.

The Assyrians' military campaigns and cruel occupation policies manifested themselves in their civilization and art. Their cities were built as fortresses. The temples to their gods were huge and adorned. Their rulers' palaces were constructed on a magnificent and gigantic scale with open courtyards, terraces, and decorations. These royal residences expressed the empire's triumphs and sent a clear message to the Assyrian people and to subjected enemies. Among the ruins of the Assyrian palaces and sculpture, the portal carvings, or "guardians of the gates," and the wall reliefs remain as testaments to the glories and values of a fierce and proud civilization. The stone animals, placed as pairs at the entrances of palaces and temples, were there to impress visitors and to ward off evil forces. The human-headed winged bulls (Figure 1.24), found at several royal palaces, convey the power, aura, and mystery of the Assyrian kings. The stone reliefs covering the Assyrian palace walls also delivered symbolic messages, such as the glorification of war and the hunt (Figure 1.25).

The Medes

In 612 B.C.E., the Medes, an Indo-European people from the southwest Iranian plateau, sacked Nineveh, the Assyrian capital, and Assyria's empire passed into the hands of the Medes. Through conquest of nearby peoples, the Medes established a kingdom known as Media, which they governed from their homeland in the central Zagros Mountains. Media eventually covered most of northern and western Mesopotamia and eastern Anatolia. Crowned as King of Kings, the Median monarch shared power with rulers of other tribes in a confederation, which was often at war with its neighbors, especially the wealthy and culturally rich Lydians of western Anatolia and their independent-minded subjects, the Greeks of Asia Minor. The power of the Medes, however, proved to be short-lived. In about 550 B.C.E., their empire fell to the Persians, another nomadic Indo-European tribe.

The Persians

The Persians, under a series of highly successful rulers—and with masterful skill—forged the strongest and largest empire that the eastern Mediterranean had yet seen. At its height, Persian rule extended from Egypt in the south to central Russia in the north, and

Figure 1.25 Fugitives Swimming with Water-Skins. Ninth century B.C.E. Limestone, ht. 39". British Museum. *Assyrian artists were masters of relief sculpture, as in this detail of a battle scene, created for the palace of King Ashurasirpal II at Nimrud. The program for this Assyrian palace glorifies warfare and was meant to discourage Ashurasirpal's enemies. In this relief, archers pursue swimming fugitives, two of whom keep afloat with inflated animal skins (lower foreground). Despite the lack of depth and unconcern for relative dimensions, the relief vividly evokes Assyria's warrior culture and the king's brutality.*

from Cyprus in the west to the Indus River in the east. Of its neighbors in the eastern Mediterranean basin, only mainland Greece eluded Persia's grasp. Yet, it was from the Greek peninsula that Alexander the Great, the Macedonian warrior-king, in 327 B.C.E. launched his campaign to defeat the last Persian king, and his victory allowed the Greeks to assimilate the Persian lands.

During a two-hundred-year span, however, the Persian Empire and its culture had a brilliant run. Unlike their predecessors, the Medes, who had expressed little or no unique style, the Persians created a distinctive style that culminated in the monumental court art and architecture of the empire. This art reflected a multicultural ethos, a combination of their past and their present cultures. Persia's artistic heritage, dating from prehistoric times, had included distinctive vase painting and elegant metalworking but no tradition of stone architecture. Now, under the empire, artists and craftspeople, many of whom were new subjects, built on that heritage and, at the same time, borrowed from their own building traditions, mainly from Ionian Greece and Lydia. These borrowings included masonry methods, the finished appearance of buildings, treatment of architectural and sculptural details and decorations, as on columns, and some building types. In the end, Persian architecture became the first highly decorated style (between India in the east and Syria in the west) to use large dressed stone rather than brick.

Persian art was courtly and ceremonial and focused on heightening the dignity and authority of the king and his court. At the capital, Persepolis, located in the Persian homeland of Parsa (modern Fars, in south Iran), Cyrus the Great (about 585–about 529 B.C.E.), the founder of the Persian Empire, chose a site for a palace that would rival the great royal complexes of earlier kingdoms in Mesopotamia. His successor, King Darius I

[duh-RYE-us] (r. 522–486 B.C.E.), eventually built the first monumental palace there, and later rulers made splendid additions. Persepolis today is a ruin, having been looted during Alexander the Great's conquest in 330 B.C.E. Among the ruins, a magnificent decorative relief survives, depicting aristocrats as they offer tribute to the king on New Year's Day. Despite its battered condition, this relief attests to the stateliness of the Persian imperial style (Figure 1.26).

Persian visual arts also stressed contemplative themes with little action, as in the relief sculpture Darius Giving Audience Before Two Fire Altars (Figure 1.27). In this panel, originally installed in the Apadana, or Audience Room, at Persepolis, King Darius is represented on a throne before two fire altars, as he receives a court official. Bending slightly from the waist, the official covers his mouth with the tips of his fingers—a gesture of devotion. These two sculptures illustrate the limited range of subjects, namely the king and his court duties, employed in the art program of the Persian kings at Persepolis.

The fire altars depicted in the relief panel mentioned above are symbols of Zoroastrianism, the religion of the Persian prophet Zoroaster [ZOHR-uh-was-ter] (about 600 B.C.E.), or Zarathustra [zah-ra-THUSH-trah], which became the official faith of the Persian court at the time of Darius I. Zoroastrianism is the most original and enduring of Persia's legacies. Rejecting polytheism, Zoroaster called for a dualistic religion in which the god of light, Ahura Mazda (Persian, "Wise Lord"), engaged in a universal struggle with the god of darkness, Ahriman. According to Zoroaster, not only did those who led lives of purity gain favored treatment in the afterlife but their actions also ensured the triumph of the forces of good in the here and now. These teachings later had a profound impact on Western philosophy and religions (see Encounter in Chapter 4).

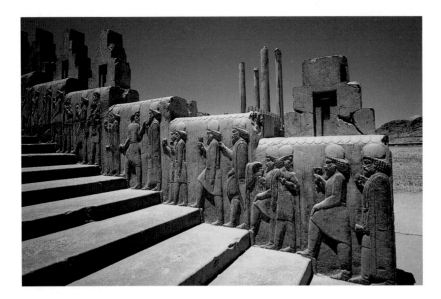

Figure 1.26 Nobles Marching Up the Stairs. Ca. 512–494 B.C.E. Persepolis, Iran. *This charming relief sculpture, carved on a wall facing a stairway at the Persian capital, Persepolis, depicts aristocrats mounting stairs to greet the king on New Year's Day, a sacred festival celebrated on the summer solstice and one of the major holidays in Mesopotamia. Each noble bears a flower offering as a tangible sign of his devotion to the monarch. The artist has humanized this courtly ritual by injecting an element of sly humor into the stately scene. One noble (the seventh from the left) sniffs his flower, and a second noble (the third from the left) turns to check on the progress of the procession behind him.*

Figure 1.27 Darius Giving Audience Before Two Fire Altars. Found in the Treasury, Persepolis. Ca. 512–494 B.C.E. Limestone, length 20′. Archeological Museum, Teheran. *This relief sculpture, carved on the walls of the Treasury at Persepolis, shows King Darius seated before two fire altars. In front of him is the master of ceremonies, with his hand raised to his lips in a gesture of devotion. Two bodyguards, holding spears, stand to the right. The Persian sculptural style is shown by the stylized hair and beards, precise folds in the clothing, and the formal poses of the figures.*

The Legacy of Early Near Eastern Civilizations

Mesopotamia and Egypt provide the earliest models of civilization in the West. In both, large numbers of people were organized into societies characterized by class stratification; a division of labor; complex political, economic, and religious forms; technological advances (in pottery and glass-making, the extraction and working of metals, textiles, woodworking, and building techniques); and cultural achievements. They weren't the only ancient civilizations—others developed in China, India, South America, and elsewhere—but they are the ones to which Westerners most directly trace their cultural roots.

Mesopotamia's gifts to Western civilization are impressive. In addition to writing, these societies established urbanism as a way of life in contrast to agrarian or village existence. In more practical matters, they created a mathematical system based on 60 that gave the world the 60-minute hour and the 360-degree circle. They also divided the seasons and devised a lunar calendar to mark off periods of days to aid them in their planting. Trade and commerce forced them to develop methods of counting, measuring, and weighing that became the standard procedures for other Near Eastern peoples for centuries. Mesopotamian myths, legends, and epics found their way into the folk tales and literature of other cultures.

Egypt made equally impressive contributions to the West. Egyptian bureaucrats, who wanted to predict the correct date for the rising of the Nile's waters, originated a solar calendar that is the basis of the Western calendar. The Egyptian model, which divided the year into twelve months of thirty days, with five days of holiday at the end of the year, was conveyed to Western culture by the Romans. In architecture, Egyptian builders devised the column with a decorated capital, which later Greek architects probably adopted. The Greek builders also borrowed the Egyptian tradition of sound engineering principles rooted in mathematics. Similarly, Greek sculptors owed a debt to Egyptian forms and poses. Indeed, the Egyptian idea of an aesthetic canon influenced both sculptors and artists in Greece.

In literature, the Egyptians explored a variety of genres—such as wisdom writing—and folk tales that influenced the Hebrews and the Greeks. In science, Egyptian physicians became renowned throughout the Near East for their medical learning and knowledge of drugs. Finally, with its priceless treasures, its mysterious pyramids, and its cult of the dead, Egypt inspired curiosity and excitement in foreigners from ancient times onward. One of the first Western tourists to visit Egypt was the Greek historian Herodotus, whose writings in the fifth century B.C.E. helped to create the Egyptian mystique. The world's fascination with the culture of ancient Egypt has not abated today.

KEY CULTURAL TERMS

culture
civilization
Paleolithic
Neolithic
homo faber
pictogram
ideogram
phonogram
cuneiform
polytheism
anthropomorphism
hieroglyphs
pantheism
stele
post-and-lintel
    construction
ziggurat
theocracy
genre
hymn
monotheism
portico
regalia
canon

SUGGESTIONS FOR FURTHER READING

KASTER, J., ed. and trans. *The Literature and Mythology of Ancient Egypt.* London: Allen Lane, 1970. An anthology that includes creation myths, rituals, stories, songs, proverbs, and prayers.

KRAMER, S. N. *History Begins at Sumer.* Philadelphia: University of Pennsylvania Press, 1981. A standard collection of original Sumerian sources by one of the most renowned modern Sumerian scholars.

PRITCHARD, J. B. *Ancient Near Eastern Texts Relating to the Old Testament.* Princeton: Princeton University Press, 1969. For the serious student, a collection of the most important nonbiblical texts, including myths, histories, prayers, and other types of writing.

SANDARS, N. K., ed. *The Epic of Gilgamesh.* New York: Penguin, 1972. The editor's informative introduction sets the tone for this famous ancient epic.

2 AEGEAN CIVILIZATIONS
The Minoans, the Mycenaeans, and the Greeks of the Archaic Age

Although Mesopotamia and Egypt offer successful models of civilization, the tradition of Greece is often the first in which Westerners feel they can recognize themselves. What ties most moderns to ancient Greece is the Greeks' vision of humanity, for they were the first to place human beings at the center of the universe. The Near Eastern cultures focused on deities and godlike rulers, paying little heed to the strivings of humanity. The Greeks, on the other hand, no longer saw mortals as the inconsequential objects of divine whim. Men and women assumed some importance in the scheme of things; they were seen as having some control over their destinies and some moral responsibility for their actions. By the fifth century B.C.E., the Greek philosopher Protagoras could proclaim, "Man is the measure of all things."

With their new way of thinking, the Greeks surged forward in all areas of creativity, ultimately reaching heights that some Western scholars think have never been equaled. Because of their grandeur and noble appeal, Greek poetry, sculpture, and architecture became the standard against which later works were frequently judged. From the Greeks the Western tradition has inherited many of its political forms and practices, its views on human behavior, its insistence on philosophical rigor, and its approach to scientific inquiry. In essence, through their human-centered consciousness and their cultural achievements, the Greeks laid the foundation of Western civilization.

Greek culture developed in the basin of the Aegean Sea (Map 2.1). On rocky coasts and rugged islands and peninsulas, the people coaxed a subsistence living from the thin, stony soil and turned to the sea for trade, conquest,

◀ **Detail** Acropolis, Athens.
View from the west.

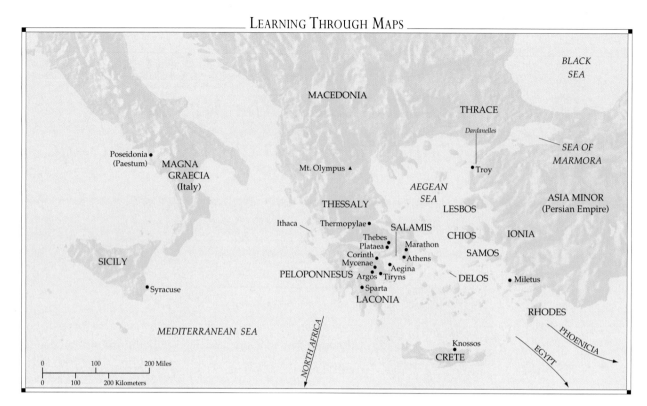

Map 2.1 THE AEGEAN WORLD, 479 B.C.E.
This map shows the location of the Minoan, Mycenaean, and Greek Archaic Age civilizations. **Consider** the role of the Aegean and Mediterranean Seas in shaping these three
civilizations. **What** were the centers of Minoan and Mycenaean civilizations? **Why** do
you think the location of Troy helped to make it a wealthy and strategic city? **Locate** the
major city-states of the Greek Archaic Age. **How** did geography influence the origins
and strategies of the Persian War?

and expansion. During the Bronze Age, the inhabitants
of the island of Crete and the Greek peninsula traded
with the Egyptians and the Hittites of Anatolia. The
early Greeks borrowed and adapted a writing system
from the Phoenicians. They were indebted to the
Egyptians for sculptural techniques and to other Near
Eastern civilizations for techniques in working with
metal and clay, for music and mathematics, and for
elements of their religious system.

The people we refer to as the Greeks were not the
first to thrive in the Aegean basin. Two other distinctive civilizations—the Minoan and the Mycenaean—
established centers of culture in the area and left their
mark on the Greeks of the Archaic Age (which dates
from about 800 B.C.E.) who followed (Timeline 2.1).

PRELUDE: MINOAN CIVILIZATION, 3000-1100 B.C.E.

While civilizations were flourishing in Egypt and
Mesopotamia, another culture was developing among
the Neolithic settlements on the island of Crete. By
about 2000 B.C.E., a prosperous and stable mercantile

civilization had emerged, and between 1700 and
1100 B.C.E., it reached its high point in wealth, power,
and sophistication. This society, labeled Minoan after
King Minos, a legendary Cretan ruler, was apparently
organized into a complex class system that included
nobles, merchants, artisans, bureaucrats, and laborers.
Noble life was based in palaces, and twentieth-century
archeological excavations of several palace sites indicate that communities were linked in a loose political
federation, with the major center at Knossos on the
north coast. Remarkably, no fortified walls protected
the Minoan palaces, suggesting that the cities remained at peace with one another and that the island
itself afforded adequate protection against invading
sea raiders. Crete's tranquil image is further supported
by the absence of weapons in excavated remains.

The palace at Knossos has revealed more about
Cretan life than has any other cultural artifact. The
ruins, though no longer paved or walled, still provide
a sense of the grandeur and expanse of this once-
magnificent site (Figure 2.1). It included an impressive
plumbing and drainage system and a complex layout
of rooms and passageways on several levels. Belowground, a storage area contained huge earthenware

Timeline 2.1 **MINOAN AND MYCENAEAN CIVILIZATIONS**   **All dates approximate and** B.C.E.

3000		2000		1700	1450	1100
Early Minoan			**Middle Minoan**	**High Minoan**	**Late Minoan**	

MINOAN CIVILIZATION, CRETE

		First destruction of palaces at Knossos and elsewhere	Rebuilding of palaces in grandiose style	Second destruction of palaces at Knossos and elsewhere

1900			1250	1100		800
	Mycenaean Dominance			**Dorian Invasions**	**Dark Ages**	

Mycenaeans arrive on Greek peninsula	**1500** Mycenaeans rule Greek peninsula	Trojan War, fall of Troy	Mycenaean civilization eclipsed	**800** Beginning of Archaic Age

1380
Mycenaeans rule
eastern Mediterranean

MYCENAEAN CIVILIZATION, PELOPONNESUS

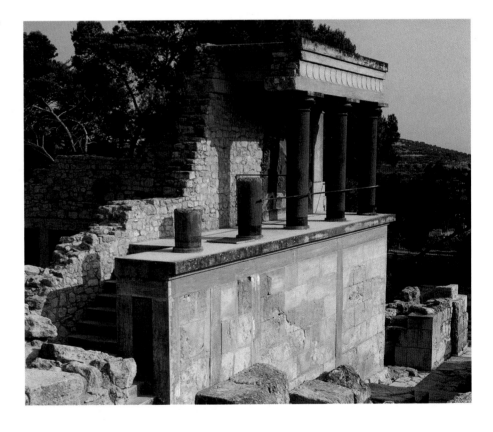

Figure 2.1 North Entrance, Palace of Minos, Knossos, Crete. Ca. 1750–1650 B.C.E. *The palace complex, with courtyards, staircases, and living areas, now partially restored, indicates that the royal family lived in comfort and security, surrounded by works of art. When British archeologist Sir Arthur Evans uncovered these ruins in 1902, he became convinced that he had discovered the palace of the legendary King Minos and labeled the civilization* Minoan—*a descriptive term now used interchangeably with* Cretan.

pots that held grains, oils, and wines, probably collected as taxes from the populace and serving as the basis of trade and wealth. Beautiful **friezes** (bands of designs and figures) decorated the walls of rooms and hallways. **Frescoes**—paint applied directly on wet plaster—of dolphins, octopuses, and other ocean creatures enlivened the palace walls.

The early Minoans developed a pictorial form of writing on clay tablets that was replaced in about 1800 B.C.E. by a still undeciphered script known as

Figure 2.2 Earth Goddess with Snakes. Ca. 1600–1580 B.C.E. Faience, ht. 13½". Archaeological Museum, Heraklion, Crete. *This cult figure was discovered in the Treasury of the Knossos Palace. Her triangular dress, with its apron and flounced skirt, is similar to those of Cretan youths in surviving frescoes.*

Figure 2.3 *Bull-Leaping. Ca. 1500 B.C.E. Archaeological Museum, Heraklion, Crete. This fresco (approximately 32 inches high) from the east wing of the palace at Knossos is one of the largest paintings recovered from Crete. The association of young men and women with bulls in this scene brings to mind the legend of the Minotaur, in which seven youths and seven maidens were periodically sacrificed to a monster, half-man and half-bull, who lived in an underground labyrinth, supposedly on Crete.*

Linear A. Linear B, which superseded Linear A, flourished from about 1400 to the decline of Minoan civilization in around 1300, though it remained in use in a few scattered places on the Greek mainland for about two hundred years. When Linear B was deciphered, it proved to be an early form of Greek. The Linear B writings revealed nothing of Minoan political, social, or philosophical systems but were used to record commercial transactions.

Minoan religion appears to have been matriarchal, centering on the worship of a mother goddess, or great goddess, creator of the universe and source of all life. Statues of a bare-breasted earth goddess with snakes in her hands show how the deity was portrayed by the Minoans, but the precise purpose of these statues is unknown (Figure 2.2). Minoans also honored numerous minor household goddesses and venerated trees and stone pillars, to which they probably attributed supernatural powers. Near the end of their era, the Minoans began to bury their dead in underground tombs and chambers, but neither the reason for the new burial practice nor its ritualistic meaning has been discovered.

What has been uncovered on the palace walls is a fresco depicting bull-leaping—a sport or ritual activity that perhaps was associated with a bull cult (Figure 2.3) and that apparently had deep religious significance. Regardless of its meaning, this daring act is probably more fiction than fact: The maidens (painted white) stand at either end of the bull while a male athlete (painted red) somersaults over the beast's back, a feat that is virtually impossible to accomplish.

Minoan trade dominated the eastern Mediterranean until about 1380 B.C.E., when the island was devastated by a natural catastrophe—perhaps a volcanic eruption on a nearby island, the second natural disaster to assault Crete in about 250 years. Weakened by Mycenaean incursions over the preceding centuries, Minoan civilization quickly fell to these raiders from the Greek mainland or to other invading seafarers. Late Minoan Crete (about 1400–1100 B.C.E.) was a blend of Cretan and Mycenaean elements, marked by decline in economic activity and artistic quality. Whatever the whole story, the Minoans disappeared suddenly and mysteriously, leaving few remnants of their peaceful civilization.

The Greeks of the later Archaic Age had no direct knowledge of Minoan civilization, but the Greek attitude toward the Minoans was shaped by mythology. Myths are usually considered fiction, but buried within them are often actual folk memories or deep psychological truths.

For example, Crete is traditionally the birthplace of the god Zeus. The Minoans worshiped a Zeus who was born in a cave, grew to manhood, and died. They venerated the site of his birth and honored him as a child. The later Greeks, however, believed Zeus to be the immortal father and ruler of the Olympian deities, and they were incensed by the Minoan belief that the god died. The grain of truth in this story may be that although the Greeks eventually dominated Crete in physical terms, elements of Minoan religion found their way into later Greek beliefs; thus, in a sense, the Olympian gods *were* born in Crete. Cretan influences on Greece may also be detected in language, social organization, and economic pursuits, although the Archaic Greeks did not regard the Minoan past as part of their heritage.

BEGINNINGS: MYCENAEAN CIVILIZATION, 1900–1100 B.C.E.

Unlike the Minoans, the Mycenaeans continued to live for the Greeks of the Archaic Age through the *Iliad* and the *Odyssey*. The events related in these two epic poems occur during the Mycenaean Age, and the stories furnished the Greeks with many of their heroes—Achilles, the doomed warrior, for example, and Odysseus, the tough and wily wandering sailor. Eventually, the Greeks traced their tradition to Mycenae, honoring its warriors as their ancestors and as models of ideal noble behavior and values.

Mycenaean civilization, named by archeologists for Mycenae, one of its most prominent fortress cities, developed on the rugged lower Greek peninsula known as the Peloponnesus. An aggressive warrior people, perhaps from the plains of southern Russia or from the Tigris-Euphrates valley, the Mycenaeans arrived on the peninsula in about 1900 B.C.E., and by about 1500 B.C.E., they ruled the entire Peloponnesus.

A feudal order similar to that found later in medieval Europe characterized the Mycenaean political system. Family ties and marriages, tentative alliances, and uneasy truces bound the local rulers in a confederation of petty kingdoms. The kings of these fortress states and their warriors controlled the surrounding countryside. A staunch loyalty developed between the kings and their noble allies, generating a rigid class structure that exploited those who were not warriors.

A royal tax system created a need for a large bureaucracy of collectors and civil employees. At the low end of the social scale stood the merchants, traders, artisans, small landowners, peasants, and slaves—the last, like the royal servants, probably captured in wars or raids.

The ruins of the Mycenaean fortress-palaces, with their massive double walls, narrow escape passages, and wide gateways, stand as mute testimony to the

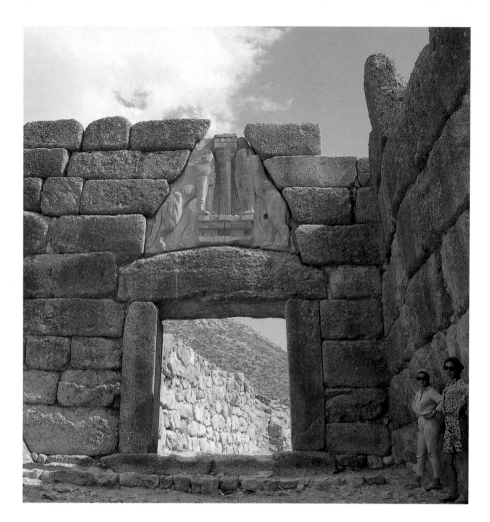

Figure 2.4 The Lion Gate at Mycenae. Ca. 1300 B.C.E. *The Lion Gate is a massive structure of four gigantic blocks—two posts and a beam forming the entrance and a triangular block on which are carved the two 9-foot-high lions and the central column. So impressive were the megalithic fortresses of the Mycenaeans to the later Greeks that they called them cyclopean, convinced that only a race of giants, the Cyclopes, could have built them.*

harshness of the militaristic life and the power of the local king. The best-known palace ruin, at Mycenae, contains the famous Lion Gate, constructed from four massive hewn stones, or **ashlars** (Figure 2.4). On one of these stones, two carved lions, separated by a column, face each other and stretch out their long, muscular bodies. Their heads, now missing, were made of metal, perhaps bronze or gold. Placed there to guard the fortress and to remind the populace of the ruler's power, the beasts must have intimidated all visitors who entered or left the citadel.

Within the fortresses and across the eastern Mediterranean, archeologists have found jars, containers, vessels, and terra-cotta figurines, revealing the high level of the Mycenaeans' artistic skill with clay and their wide-ranging trade and travel. The weapons and personal items crafted for the warriors show especially impressive artistic skills. A decorated sword blade depicting a lion hunt, inlaid in gold and silver, exemplifies the artisan's attention to delicate detail (Figure 2.5).

Mycenaean religion appears to have been a fusion of Minoan and local deities. Like the Minoans, the Mycenaeans venerated numerous household god-

desses and worshiped aspects of nature in caves and natural shrines. Local deities seem to have been of two kinds: Some were predecessors of the Olympian gods and goddesses worshiped by the later Greeks and had the same names; others were nature divinities and spirits. Six **shaft graves** have been excavated at Mycenae (Figure 2.6). These graves have yielded fabulous gold treasures. Similar finds have been discovered at Vapheio, near Sparta, including two famous Vapheio cups, from a sixteenth-century B.C.E. grave (Figure 2.7). The graves indicate that the Mycenaeans buried their dead with honor. Perhaps influenced by the Egyptians, they wrapped the bodies and surrounded them with precious objects and pottery. From such practices and attitudes evolved the worship of heroes, a central aspect of Greek culture.

Bronze was the preferred metal of Mycenaean artisans, as it was for the Minoans before them, but copper, tin, silver, and gold were also used. All these metals were available from mines and deposits in the Mediterranean basin, except tin, which came from the British Isles. Excavations at Knossos, Mycenae, and other sites indicate that the upper classes collected exquisite metal works and adorned their bodies with fine jewelry.

Figure 2.5 Lion Hunt. Ca. sixteenth century B.C.E. Bronze inlaid with gold and electrum. National Museum, Athens. *An anonymous artisan has decorated every part of this 9-inch dagger. Whether the weapon was ever used in battle is not clear, but its fine details and realistic figures must have made it a prized possession of a Mycenaean warrior. This dagger survived because it was buried alongside its owner in a funeral mound.*

Figure 2.6 Mycenae. Aerial view of the Acropolis. Ca. 1600–1200 B.C.E. *Set on top of a hill, this citadel occupied a commanding position over the surrounding countryside, and the fortified wall protected its inhabitants. Hilltop citadels such as this were typical for most cities in Mycenaean culture.*

Figure 2.7 Vapheio Cup. Ca. sixteenth century B.C.E. Gold, 3½" high. National Archaeological Museum, Athens. *This gold cup, one of two discovered in a tomb at Vapheio near Sparta, Greece, shows a man attempting to capture a bull. At the bottom of the image, the hunter tries to ensnare the bull by means of the net held in his outstretched arms. The curved line of the animal's arched back helps frame the scene, while the bull, with its size and muscular body, seems to be winning this ferocious struggle between man and beast. This cup is thought to be from the Mycenaean period, because its execution is less refined than the exquisite artistry of the other cup (not shown here), which is attributed to the Minoan style. However, both goldsmiths used the same technique: hammering out the scenes from the inside of the cup.*

The Mycenaean feudal system flourished for several centuries, and after 1380 B.C.E., when Crete fell, the Mycenaeans extended their raiding and trading activities throughout the eastern Mediterranean. In about 1250 B.C.E., they attacked the wealthy and strategic city of Troy, on the western coast of present-day Turkey, near the Dardanelles (see Map 2.1). Although similar expeditions had brought booty to the Mycenaeans on earlier occasions, this long, exhausting foray weakened them, leaving them open to conquest by more vigorous tribes. Ironically, this siege of the Trojan citadel probably inspired the *Iliad* and the *Odyssey*, Homer's enduring epics. Overwhelmed by the Dorians from the north, Mycenaean civilization faded, and by about 1100 B.C.E., the Age of the Mycenaeans had closed. A three-century hiatus in Greek history—called the Dark Ages—followed, when writing disappeared and cultural activities virtually ceased.

The Mycenaeans, as presented by Homer, gave the Greeks many of their ideals. Heir to three centuries of oral traditions about the Mycenaeans, Homer invented the Age of Heroes. He sang to the Greeks of a glittering past that both inspired and sobered them. In the *Iliad* and the *Odyssey,* the Greeks found a universe with a basic moral order and a people with a distinct ethos, or ethical code. The pursuit of excellence that Homer attributed to his Mycenaean heroes became an ideal of historical Greece. Many aristocrats even traced their ancestry back to Homer's warriors and, through them, to the gods and goddesses. So rich was Homer's world that art and literature drew on it for subjects and incentive throughout Greek history. Through him the Mycenaeans gave the Greeks their myths, their religion, their ethics, their perception of the universe, and their insight into human character.

Technology in Minoan Crete and Mycenae

The first Aegean civilizations—Minoan Crete and Mycenaean—built on the bronze technology of earlier Near Eastern models (see Chapter 1). Crete and Mycenae used bronze for weapons and everyday objects throughout their time, but both societies collapsed before the onset of the Iron Age, in about 1200 B.C.E.

In warfare technology, the Minoans and the Mycenaeans followed the lead of Near Eastern neighbors. Weaponry, such as daggers, swords, spears, and javelins, and body armor, such as shields, helmets, and leg and arm coverings, were all made of bronze. By 2000 B.C.E., the horse had been introduced into the Aegean basin, and, by about 1450 B.C.E., armed warriors were fighting in horse-drawn chariots. By 1300 B.C.E., the chariot had been redesigned so that the wheel spokes increased from four to six and the axle

shifted to rest under the rear platform where the warriors stood. These two innovations made the vehicle more stable and easier to maneuver. Combat was still limited to skirmishes and confined to small areas. Most wars involved soldiers only, while civilians lived in hilltop cities, protected behind massive stone walls with lookout towers. Battles were fought mainly in borderlands, usually for rich farming areas, or as part of seaport raids. Tactics, strategy, and weaponry changed very little over the years.

Advances in shipbuilding made Crete's and Mycenae's wealth possible. Minoan artisans improved sailing ship design by extending the height of the mast, enlarging the size of the sails, and redesigning the oar to increase rowing power. In their heyday, the Minoans plied the eastern Mediterranean, exchanging wine and olive oil for manufactured goods with their colonies and foreign ports. After the Minoans' abrupt decline, the Mycenaeans came to dominate the eastern Mediterranean with their well-constructed ships and heavily armored warriors, until they were overrun by invaders from the north.

INTERLUDE: THE DARK AGES, 1100–800 B.C.E.

With the fall of the Mycenaeans, a period known as the Dark Ages began, and life reverted to simpler patterns. People lived in isolated farming communities and produced only essential tools and domestic objects. Commercial and social interchange among communities, already made hazardous by the mountainous terrain, became even more dangerous, and communication with the eastern Mediterranean kingdoms nearly ceased.

Yet some fundamental changes were slowly occurring. Political power was gradually shifting from kings to the heads of powerful families, laying the foundation for a new form of government, and iron gradually replaced bronze in tools, weapons, and other crafted objects—thus ending the Bronze Age and beginning the Iron Age in Greece. Many Mycenaeans fled to the coast of Asia Minor, which later came to be called Ionia, thus paving the way for the formation of an extended Greek community around the Aegean and Mediterranean Seas.

THE ARCHAIC AGE, 800–479 B.C.E.

In about 800 B.C.E., the Greeks emerged from their long years of stagnation and moved into an era of political innovation and cultural experimentation. Although scattered and isolated, they shared a sense of identity

Figure 2.8 Acropolis, Athens. View from the west. *The Acropolis dominates Athens in the twenty-first century just as it did in ancient times when it was the center of Athenian ceremonial and religious life. Today it is the towering symbol of Athens's cultural heritage as well as the center of the local tourist industry. A landmark in the history of town planning, the Acropolis is the ancestor of all carefully laid-out urban environments from ancient Rome to Renaissance Florence to modern Brasilia.*

based on their common language, their heroic stories and folk tales, their myths and religious practices, and their commercial and trading interests. They claimed a common mythical parent, Hellen, who fathered three sons—the ancestors of the three major Greek tribes, the Ionians, the Aeolians, and the Dorians—and thus they called themselves Hellenes and their land Hellas. In the next three centuries, the Greeks would reconstruct their political and social systems, develop new styles of art and architecture, invent new literary genres, and make the first formal philosophical inquiries into the nature of human behavior and the universe. By the end of this period, they would have laid the foundations for a new world.

Political, Economic, and Social Structures

By the beginning of the Archaic Age (*archaic* is from the Greek and means "ancient" or "beginning"), the isolated farming community had evolved into the *polis* (plural, *poleis*), a small, well-defined city-state. Several hundred poleis lay scattered over the Greek mainland and abroad. Although each polis had its own separate history and unique traits, each shared certain features with all the others. An *acropolis*, or fortified hilltop, served as a citadel where the rulers usually resided (Figure 2.8). Temples and holy shrines stood on the acropolis or below in an *agora*. The agora, an open area where political leaders held forth, citizens assembled, and the populace congregated to conduct business and socialize, was the center of a polis. The pursuit of both public and private matters in an agora served to connect the citizens of a polis and to foster civic pride and loyalty. In effect, a polis, through its control of the religious, cultural, and psychological components of its relatively closed community, molded the citizenry into an organic body with a collective identity.

Simultaneously with the emergence of the polis, in about 800 B.C.E., the political system underwent a basic change. The kings had been deposed by the leaders of noble families who owned most of the land and possessed the weapons and horses. These wealthy warriors established **oligarchies,** or government by the few.

Although the oligarchies benefited the aristocrats, they were also characterized by exemplary leadership, civic idealism, and cultural and artistic patronage. However, most oligarchies eventually failed because of unforeseen and far-reaching military and economic changes.

New military tactics now made obsolete the aristocratic warriors in their horse-drawn chariots. Foot soldiers—armed with long spears, protected by shields and personal armor, and grouped in closed ranks called phalanxes—were proving more effective in battles. These foot soldiers, or hoplites, were recruited from among independent farmers, merchants, traders, and artisans, who were also profiting from an expanding economy. As their military value became evident, these commoners soon demanded a voice in political decisions.

At the same time, a growing population, beginning to strain the limited agricultural resources, led to an era of overseas expansion and colonization. The Hellenes sent citizens to join their earlier Ionian settlements and to establish new colonies along the coasts of Spain, North Africa, southern Russia (or the Black Sea), and Sicily and southern Italy, which became known as *Magna Graecia*, or Greater Greece.

Foreign ventures and expanded trade increased the wealth of the new middle class and reinforced their desires for more economic opportunities and political influence, but the entrenched aristocracy blocked their way to power. Frustrated by the inability of reform efforts to solve deep-seated problems, in the sixth century B.C.E. many poleis turned to rulers whom they entrusted with extraordinary powers to make sweeping economic and political changes. Many of these tyrants, as the Greeks called them, restructured their societies to allow more citizens to benefit from the growing economy, to move up the social scale, and to participate in the political process. However, some tyrants perpetuated their rule through heirs or political alliances and governed harshly for years, thus giving the word *tyrant* its modern meaning.

Regardless of the different results of the tyrants' reigns, by about 500 B.C.E. life was similar in many ways in all poleis. Citizens—freeborn males who could claim the right to enter into politics by virtue of family and wealth—voiced their opinions in a widening democratic process. They sat on juries, debated in the assemblies, and defended their polis in time of war. Civic responsibility, recognized as a central element in everyday life, was now passed on by the aristocrats to this new band of citizens.

Although horizons were expanding for the male citizens, other members of this predominantly middle-class society were severely restricted in political and economic matters. Women—except for priestesses such as Lysimache, who was priestess of Athena for sixty-four years in the later fifth and early fourth centuries, and a rare literary figure such as Sappho—were subservient to men. In Athens, for example, women possessed no legal or economic status, for they were by law under the control of the males in the household. Families often married off their daughters for economic gain, and, once married, the daughters were expected to be hardworking, loyal, and obedient.

Foreigners, with a few exceptions, were placed in special categories that restricted their personal rights and limited their economic opportunities. Some poleis, such as Sparta, simply barred most foreigners, whereas Athens was more tolerant. Slaves, on the other hand, had no rights and were treated as property, with little hope of future improvement.

The Greek Polis: Sparta and Athens

Of the hundreds of poleis that evolved during the Archaic Age, Sparta and Athens stand out for their vividly contrasting styles of life and their roles in subsequent Greek history. Sparta, the principal symbol of Dorian civilization, chose to guarantee its integrity and future through stringent and uncompromising policies. The earliest Spartans forcibly enslaved the *Helots*—the original inhabitants of the lower Peloponnesus. To prevent rebellions and to control the Helots, who outnumbered the Spartans ten to one, a vigilant Sparta was forced to keep its military always on the alert. Thus, Sparta created a rigid hierarchical society of well-trained, tough, and athletic men, women, and children. The Spartans also established a genuine oligarchy: a constitutional government operated by five officials elected annually by a small body of citizens. The ruling class, obsessed with keeping social order, passed laws forbidding immigration, limiting material possessions, and restricting creativity. Sparta was admired for its loyal, brave soldiers and its stable social order. But Sparta contributed little to the artistic enrichment of Greece.

In contrast, Athens, the symbol of Ionian civilization, reached greater artistic, intellectual, and literary heights than did any other polis. Athens, both the city and its surrounding countryside of Attica, was a more open society than Sparta. The Attican clans shared a sense of community with the Athenians and supported them in wartime.

The history of Athens echoes the general pattern of change in the poleis during the Archaic Age (Timeline 2.2). Aristocrats initially ruled Athens through councils and assemblies. As long as farming and trading sustained an expanding population, the nobles ruled without challenge. But at the beginning of the sixth century B.C.E., many peasant farmers were burdened with debts and were threatened with prison

Timeline 2.2   **THE ARCHAIC AGE IN GREECE**   **All dates** B.C.E.

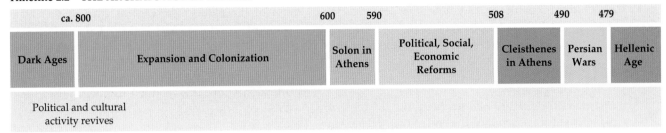

or slavery. Having no voice in the government, the farmers began to protest what they perceived as unfair laws.

In about 590 B.C.E., the Athenians granted an aristocrat named Solon special powers to reform the economy. He abolished debts and guaranteed a free peasantry, overhauled the judicial system, and recorded the laws. Solon also restructured the Athenian constitution by giving the lower ranks of free men—those without great name or noble family but with some property or wealth—the right to participate in government.

Solon's principal successor was Cleisthenes [KLICE-thu-neez], who established democracy in Athens beginning in 508 B.C.E. He broadened the governmental base by opening it to all free male citizens (called the *demos*) regardless of their property or bloodlines. Cleisthenes' democratic reforms, which lasted for almost two centuries, created an atmosphere in which civic pride and artistic energy were unleashed, inaugurating the Hellenic Age (sometimes called the Golden Age), which made Athens both the pride and the envy of the other Greek city-states.

For moderns, one of the most surprising contrasts between Sparta and Athens is the difference in the roles and status of women. In general, Spartan women, though expected to marry, spent their time outside and spoke freely to men; Athenian women were kept in seclusion and rarely talked with their husbands. What made Spartan women so independent was that, above all else, they were to be strong mothers of the vigorous males needed to maintain this warrior society. To that end, Spartan women, alone among Greek women, were given public education, including choral singing and dancing, and athletics, in which they stripped just as Greek men did. Spartan women were also unique in being able to own land and to manage their own property.

In contrast, the women of Athens pursued respectability as an ideal, which meant that they were supposed to marry and stay indoors, overseeing their households and performing domestic chores. It is not clear how strictly this ideal was imposed on them in daily life. Athenian drama contains many instances of female characters complaining about their powerless-

ness, as when a wife is abandoned (Euripides' *Medea*) or a woman is left during wartime (Aeschylus's *Agamemnon*). These examples probably reflected reality. Athenian women, lacking public education and excluded by law from government and the military, played a subordinate role to Athenian men.

Technology in Archaic Greece

Unlike the Minoan and Mycenaean cultures, the Archaic Greeks were an Iron Age civilization (though a few artisans continued to work sometimes with bronze in limited fields, such as artistic creation). As the Dark Ages gave way to the Archaic period, the Greeks built on the technology of the earlier cultures of Crete and Mycenae, using mainly iron and steel (a refined form of iron) to build weaponry and body armor. Metalworkers learned to reduce iron from its ore in charcoal-fed furnaces, intensifying the heat by means of a foot bellows. Harder and more readily available than copper and tin, iron soon drove out the general use of these softer metals. By 500 B.C.E., iron technology reigned across the Greek world.

Iron workers produced a range of tools besides weaponry, including farm implements (axes, hoes, and picks) and industrial devices (anvils, saws, and hammers). Iron's abundance made this metal cheaper than bronze, copper, or tin, thus making it possible for even the poorer classes to have access to this new technology.

Also important were the Greeks' improvements in sailing vessels. One such improvement was described by the Greek historian Herodotus, who wrote of a new light and quick ship powered by twenty-five oarsmen. This innovation in speed and efficiency spurred commercial development across their maritime reach. A second invention, the galley, a type of ship used just for fighting, helped make the Greeks masters of the Aegean waters. The first galleys, called *uniremes* (Latin, "oars"), had no decks and were powered by oars mounted in a single group, which made them extremely fast and elegant. From about 700 B.C.E. on, the uniremes were outfitted with a beak or a battering ram, to be used in sea battles. This ramming device forever changed the nature of sea warfare. Prior to this time, ships were designed only to carry warriors to fight a distant battle on land; now, they served as the site for the battles themselves.

The Persian Wars

Cleisthenes' domestic reforms were one of the two major events that heralded the end of the Archaic Age and the coming of Greece's Hellenic Age. The other event, the Persian Wars, was pivotal not only for Greece but also for Western civilization. If the autocratic and imperialistic Persians had won these wars, then the democratic institutions, the humanistic values, and the cultural landmarks that the Greeks were establishing would have been lost.

By the mid–sixth century B.C.E., the Persians ruled a huge empire in the Near East encompassing most of the ancient world and including the Greek poleis in Ionia. When Darius, king of the Persians in the late sixth century, demanded taxes from the Ionian Greeks, they revolted and looked to their homeland for support. A few poleis, including Athens, sent an expedition, which Darius defeated. To prevent future uprisings, Darius invaded the Greek peninsula and landed near Athens at Marathon in 490 B.C.E. The outnumbered Athenian army fought brilliantly, destroying many of the invader's ships and turning back the powerful Persian Empire.

However, the Persians soon found a new and determined ruler in Xerxes [ZIRK-seez], son of Darius, who overran much of northern Greece. Under Spartan leadership, the Greeks planned to trap the Persians at Thermopylae, a northern mountain pass, but they were annihilated by Xerxes' troops. Xerxes moved southward and sacked Athens, whose inhabitants escaped across the Saronic Gulf to the island of Salamis. The Athenians drew the Persian navy into the narrows of the gulf, where the swifter Greek ships outmaneuvered the cumbersome Persian craft. After witnessing the destruction of his fleet, Xerxes returned to Persia. The remainder of the Persian army was routed at Plataea in 479 B.C.E., thus ending this major threat to Greece. The Greeks' final victory over the mighty Persians created a euphoric mood in Athens and set the stage for the ensuing Hellenic Age.

THE EMERGENCE OF GREEK GENIUS: THE MASTERY OF FORM

During the Archaic Age, the Greeks developed a variety of literary, philosophical, and artistic forms that they used to probe the meaning of the universe and of human existence as well as to celebrate their joyous

sense of life. These cultural accomplishments, like those of the older Near Eastern civilizations, were associated with the religious beliefs and practices that played a central role in Greek life and history. In fact, the Greeks believed that creativity itself was a divine gift from the **muses,** the nine goddesses of artistic inspiration (Table 2.1). Guided by their muses, they created enduring works of art, literature, and theater, each with a universal appeal.

Religion

The Greeks made religion an ongoing part of their private and public affairs. Indeed, the polis and religion could not be separated, for in the eyes of the Greeks the fate of each community depended on the civic deity. Public rituals and festivals drew together the citizens, infused them with civic pride, and reminded them of their common heritage. During the Archaic Age, Greek religion—an amalgam of deities derived from the original settlers as well as invaders and foreigners—evolved into two major categories: the Olympian and the chthonian. The **Olympian deities** dwelled in the sky or on mountaintops and were associated with the Homeric heroes and the aristocracy. The **chthonian** [THOE-nee-uhn] (from the Greek *chthon,* meaning "the earth") **deities** lived underground and were associated with peasant life, the seasons and cycles of nature, and fertility.

The Olympian religion shared some traits with the polytheistic cults of the ancient Near East, including the notion that the deities intervene in daily affairs, the belief that they are like humans in many respects, and the idea of a pantheon of gods and goddesses. The

Table 2.1   THE NINE MUSES AND THEIR AREAS OF CREATIVITY

NAME	ART OR SCIENCE
Calliope	Epic poetry
Clio	History
Erato	Erotic poetry and mime
Euterpe	Lyric poetry and music
Melpomene	Tragedy
Polyhymnia	Sacred hymn
Terpsichore	Dance and song
Thalia	Comedy
Urania	Astronomy

Greeks endowed their deities with physical bodies and individual personalities, creating a fascinating blend of charm and cruelty, beauty and childishness, love of justice and caprice. These unruly and willful deities quarreled with one another and played favorites with their mortal worshipers as they pleased. Faced with such favoritism among the deities, the Greeks themselves developed a strong moral sense. They came to believe that as long as they recognized the divinities' power and did not challenge them—and thus become victims of **hubris,** or pride—they would survive and often prosper.

Homer's poems lay out the complex relations and kinships in the Olympic pantheon and explain the functions and roles of the twelve principal deities, but Homer by no means invented these supernatural beings; they had been around long before his time. Indeed, their confusing traits and characters are probably the result of a fusion of numerous gods and goddesses whose origins predate the Greeks. Notwithstanding the deities' erratic characteristics, however, the Greeks never forgot that the Olympian system reflected a moral order and a sense of justice.

Zeus, a sky god and first among the immortals, reigned as king on Mount Olympus, hurling thunderbolts and presiding over the divine councils. He sired both immortals and mortals, for his sexual appetite knew no bounds. Hera, probably the great goddess of earlier cultures, was the sister and wife of Zeus. She watched over the women who appealed to her for help and kept a close eye on her wandering husband. Zeus's two brothers controlled the rest of the universe, Poseidon ruling the seas, all waters, and earthquakes, and Hades guarding the underworld. Zeus's sister Hestia protected the hearth and its sacred flame. Zeus's twin offspring, Apollo and Artemis, symbolized the sun and the moon, respectively. Apollo, Zeus's favorite son, personified the voice of reason. Artemis watched over childbirth and guarded wild creatures. Zeus's lying son Ares delighted in fierce battles, and, as the war god, he possessed a quick temper and few morals. He and Aphrodite—Zeus's daughter and the goddess of love and beauty—were adulterous lovers. Ironically, Homer has Aphrodite married to Hephaestus, the ugly and lame son of Zeus who was a master smith and the patron of craftspeople.

Two other children of Zeus rounded out the Olympic roster. Athena, the goddess of wisdom and patron goddess of Athens, was associated with warfare, the arts, and handicrafts. She was worshiped as a virgin goddess. Hermes, the god of trade and good fortune, was also the patron of thieves, although he was best known as a messenger for his fellow deities (Table 2.2).

The chthonian gods and goddesses were probably derived from ancient earth and harvest deities. At first they were worshiped only by the lower orders, but as the demos grew in influence, chthonian rituals spread and were soon integrated into the civic calendar. Nevertheless, these cults were open only to initiates, who were sworn to silence; hence, they were called mystery cults, from the Greek word *mystos,* "keeping silent."

The chthonian practices originally invoked the powers of the earth to ensure a successful planting and a bountiful harvest. The two most important crops in Greece—grains and grapes, the sources of bread and wine, respectively—led to two major cults, those of Demeter and Dionysus. Demeter, a sister of Zeus, was a harvest goddess. She in turn had a daughter, Persephone, whom Hades abducted to his kingdom belowground. According to her cult legend, Demeter finally rescued Persephone, but not before Hades had tricked Persephone into eating a fruit that made her return to the underworld for part of each year. Thus, during the winter months, the earth is bare, but when Persephone and Demeter are together, the earth is fecund and the grains grow. At Eleusis, a small village in Attica, Demeter was the focus of a mystery cult. Prospective initiates from all over Greece traveled there, apparently to receive her promise of immortal life.

Whereas Demeter's followers honored her in a dignified manner, Dionysus's worshipers, through wild dancing and wine drinking, hoped to be reinvigorated by their god and born again. Dionysus came to represent the irrational, emotional, and uncontrolled aspects of human nature to the Greeks. In contrast, the

Table 2.2	THE OLYMPIAN DEITIES AND THE AREAS THEY RULED
GOD OR GODDESS	**DUTIES AND RESPONSIBILITIES**
Zeus	Chief deity and keeper of order on Olympus
Hera	Mother goddess, protector of women
Poseidon	Ruler of waters
Hades	Keeper of the underworld
Hestia	Protector of the hearth
Apollo	God of wisdom and moderation
Artemis	Virgin goddess who aided women
Ares	Amoral god of violence and warfare
Aphrodite	Goddess of passion, love, and beauty
Hephaestus	Patron of craftspeople
Athena	Goddess of wisdom and warfare
Hermes	God of merchants and thieves; messenger for the gods

rational, conscious, controlled aspects were associated with Apollo. The two aspects—Dionysian and Apollonian—were considered opposing but complementary. Eventually, a Dionysus cult arose in Athens, where his followers annually held ceremonies honoring his power as god of the vine (Figure 2.9). Over the years these rituals became civic festivals, which in turn spawned the competitive performances of tragic drama in Athens in the sixth century B.C.E.

Literature

During the Archaic Age, the Greeks recorded some of the greatest literature of our Western heritage, with stories as adventurous, amusing, and heartfelt as they are sophisticated, structured, and rich with many of the values we still hold dear today.

Epic Poetry   The originator of the major conventions of **epic poetry** is traditionally believed to be Homer (about 800 B.C.E.), a **bard,** or poet who sang his verses while accompanying himself on a stringed instrument. In the *Iliad* and the *Odyssey,* Homer sang of the events before, during, and after the Trojan War, stories that had circulated among the Greeks since the fall of Mycenae. Homer entertained an aristocratic audience eager to claim kinship with the Mycenaean past. For many years, his poems were transmitted orally by other bards, and they probably did not exist in written versions until the seventh century B.C.E. Homer's authorship and, indeed, even his very existence are established solely by tradition; nothing is actually known about him. Nevertheless, by the end of the Archaic Age, the appeal of Homer's poetry had embraced all social levels, and his authority approached that of a modern combination of television, Shakespeare, and the Bible.

The basic appeal of the Homeric epics lies in their well-crafted plots, filled with dramatic episodes and finely drawn characters. Set against the backdrop of the Trojan War, the *Iliad* describes the battle of Ilium, another name for Troy, and the *Odyssey* recounts events after the Greeks defeat the Trojans (Figure 2.10). The earlier of the epics, the *Iliad,* focuses on Achilles, the epitome of heroic Greek manhood. In contrast to the battlefield heroics of the *Iliad,* the *Odyssey* narrates the wanderings of the Greek warrior Odysseus after the fall of Troy. Moreover, the *Odyssey* celebrates marriage, for Odysseus, despite some amorous adventures, remains fixed on thoughts of his wife, Penelope, who waits for him in Ithaca.

In both poems, the deities merrily intrude into the lives of mortals, changing and postponing the fate of friend and enemy alike. So great was Homer's authority that his works made him the theologian of Greek religion. His stories of the gods and goddesses, although not completely replacing other versions of their lives, became the standard that circulated wherever Greek was spoken. Homer presented Zeus, the nominal protector of the moral order, as forever under siege by other gods seeking help for their favorite mortals. Although some later Greeks deplored Homer's inattention to moral issues, his roguish portraits of the deities remained indelibly imprinted in the minds of the general populace.

Homer's poetic expression also gave texture to the Greek language. Similes, figures of speech in which two unlike things are compared, help bring the dramatic, exotic events of the stories down to earth. For example, Homer creates a vivid image of Odysseus as a ferocious killer when he compares him to a lion "covered with blood, all his chest and his flanks on either side bloody." In a less violent simile, Homer has Achilles compare his fellow Greeks to "unwinged" baby birds and himself to their nurturing mother. Homer's images also provide a rich repertory of ready phrases and metaphors, known as **Homeric epithets,** such as "the wily Odysseus," "the swift-footed Achilles," and the "rosy-fingered dawn."

Besides shaping the language, Homer served as a guide to behavior for the Archaic Greeks. Because they became part of the Greek educational curriculum, his poems acquired an ethical function. A young man who took Achilles or Odysseus for a model would learn to maintain his well-being, to speak eloquently in company with other men, to give and receive hospitality, to shed tears in public over the death of his closest friend, to admire the beauty of women, to esteem the material wealth of other nobles, to appreciate songs of bravery, and, above all, to protect his reputation as a man and warrior. On the other hand, a young woman who imitated Penelope, the patient and faithful wife of Odysseus, would inhabit a more circumscribed world as she learned to weave at the loom, to manage a household, to cultivate her physical beauty, and to resist the advances of other men. Although much changed, life in the United States today still pays more than lip service to these values—men, esteeming material wealth, admiring women, and protecting their masculine position; women, cultivating beauty, remaining faithful, and keeping the home.

Lyric Poetry   Verses sung to the music of the **lyre** (a stringed instrument), or **lyric poetry,** became the dominant literary expression in the late Archaic Age, and **lyric** verses have dominated Western poetry ever since. Lyric poetry, which originated later than the

Figure 2.9 Exekias. *Dionysus Crossing the Sea.* Ca. 535 B.C.E. Clay, 12" diameter. Staatliche Antikensammlungen, Munich. *Painted in the basin of a circular drinking bowl, Dionysus, the god of wine, is depicted sailing alone in a fish-nosed boat. This work by Exekias, one of the most admired artists of the Archaic Age, illustrates the beautiful mastery of space—the making of a convincing pictorial image on a predetermined surface, such as a pot or a tomb—that characterized the best vase painting of the time. Dionysus reclines under a billowing sail, surrounded by gamboling dolphins. Sprouting from the boat is a vine carrying bunches of grapes—the symbol of the god of wine. Exekias's simple design is typical of Archaic painting.*

Figure 2.10 Signed by Exekias. *Achilles Killing the Amazon Queen Penthesilea.* Ca. 530 B.C.E. Clay, ht. of jar 16". British Museum, B 210. *Exekias painted this scene on an Athenian amphora, a vase with an oval body, cylindrical neck, and two handles, used for wine or oil. The scene is based on an episode from the Trojan War, which was Exekias's favorite source. Although not recorded by Homer in the* Iliad, *the event is part of the traditions of the siege of Troy. According to some of the stories, Penthesilea, whose warrior women were allies of the Trojans, outfought Achilles on several occasions before he killed her. At the moment he is about to kill Penthesilea, Achilles recognizes her beauty and falls in love. Exekias's skillful composition directs the viewer's eye to Achilles' spear, aimed at Penthesilea's throat. Both figures, simple and dignified, dressed in their armor, which Exekias details, are caught in a tragic scene of war and death, which Achilles' love cannot overcome. Exekias depicted Dionysus, holding an amphora, and his son, Oenopion, with a cup in his hand, on the reverse side. This work and Figure 2.9 are in the black-figure style, characterized by silhouetted figures on a reddish clay background. Greek artists later reversed this technique, creating the red-figure style of reddish figures on a black background (see Figures 3.1, 3.10, and 3.11).*

epic, expressed an author's personal, private thoughts, though the muse Euterpe was credited with the inspiration. The shift from epic to lyric poetry in the sixth century B.C.E. coincided with changes in the polis, where the rising democratic spirit encouraged a variety of voices to be heard.

Of the several types of lyric poetry, monody, or the solo lyric, became the most influential in Archaic Greece. Poets of monody achieved relative simplicity by using a single line of verse or by repeating a short stanza pattern. Unlike the Homeric epics, which survive relatively whole, the solo lyrics are extremely fragmented. For example, the bulk of what remains of Sappho's [SAF-oh] verses consists of random lines and references gleaned from later commentators and only one or two entire lyrics. And of the music, the whole has been lost. The ancients, however, regarded Sappho (about 600 B.C.E.) as the greatest of the writers of solo lyrics. The philosopher Plato hailed her as the tenth muse in a short lyric he dedicated to her. A truly original writer, Sappho apparently owed no debt to Homer or any other poet. Her work is addressed to a small

ENCOUNTER

Near Eastern Art and Greek Pottery

One of the great achievements of the Greek genius was in the minor art of vase painting, which culminated in the black-figure (see Figures 2.9 and 2.10; fl. about 700–530 B.C.E.) and red-figure (see Figures 3.1, 3.10, and 3.11; fl. from late sixth to late fourth century B.C.E.) styles. Before reaching this cultural climax, vase art evolved through many stages, sometimes influenced by the artworks of nearby peoples. During one of its most important phases, the **Orientalizing** *period (about 700–625 B.C.E.), the Greeks drew on the art of the Near East—thus, the name given this period in Greek history.*

Trade was the primary vehicle for cultural exchange between the Near East and Archaic Greece, and pottery, which held the liquid cargoes, such as oils, perfumes, unguents, and wine, was essential to this mercantile system. The merchants in the city-states of Euboea (the largest Greek island in the Aegean Sea) led the way in pottery making in the Greek world, as evidenced in the huge quantity of Euboean pottery discovered at sites in Anatolia (modern western Turkey). The wealthy city-states of Ionia, located on the south coast of Anatolia, as well as the mainland Greek city-states of Athens and Corinth, profited from this exchange of goods. These Greek and Near Eastern contacts happened mainly in the hinterland beyond the Ionian city-states and at Al Mina (modern Tripoli, in northern Lebanon), a thriving port on the Orontes River.

Greek artisans were inspired by the Near Eastern examples in metalwork vessels, jewelry, and perhaps, ultimately, textile designs. But the Greeks had little taste for Near Eastern pottery, including both the un-decorated types and the Phoenician style, which was indebted to Egyptian tradition.

Greek artists, in creating the Orientalizing style, borrowed artistic techniques, vessel forms, decorative motifs, and subjects. The adopted artistic techniques included new ways of representing human and animal figures. They learned to depict a body either by drawing it in outline or by painting it in silhouette with the head drawn in outline, and they learned a more naturalistic method of showing features on figures by painting muscles, ribs, and hair. Some Greek artisans preferred to incise, or cut, the features into their painted figures, and this process, when combined with the use of black paint to make a silhouette, led directly to the black-figure painting style. The Greek artists copied many types of Near Eastern vessels, including big round-bottomed pots balanced on stands, various forms of shallow dishes, and pots with animal-head spouts.

Near Eastern motifs, such as sphinxes, sirens, and griffins, now entered the Greek tradition. Hybrid creatures were a beloved feature of Near Eastern art (see Figure 1.24), but Greek tradition normally shunned them, preferring to depict human and animal forms in a natural manner. However, the Greek artists' genius and ability accommodated the exotic and monstrous into their own myths, legends, and folklore. For example, the sphinx—a hybrid of a lion and a man in Near Eastern art—became a riddle-asking winged female in the Oedipus legend. The siren—a bird-woman in Near Eastern myth—became the destructive winged women that lured sailors to their doom in the story of Odysseus. And the griffin—a winged monster with an eagle's head and a lion's body in Near Eastern lore—became part of a tale told by Herodotus about northern barbarians called Arimasps.

A final Near Eastern import into Greek art was a new subject, the animal frieze, which became a hall-mark of the Orientalizing style. In this frieze, the Greeks divided the vase surface into bands, separated by thin lines, and filled the bands with a linear parade of animals, including antlered beasts, geese, and wild goats (Encounter figure 2.1). The prominence of the wild goat caused these scenes to be called the Wild Goat Style of vase painting.

Learning from the Encounter **Explain** how trade led to a cultural exchange involving artistic styles. **Where** did the cultural exchange between Greece and the Near East take place? **What** artistic elements from Near Eastern art were adopted by Greek artists? **Discuss** the way that Greek art was changed by this encounter with Near Eastern traditions.

Encounter figure 2.1 Milesian Oinochoe (the Levy or
Marseilles Oinochoe). Ca. 640–630 B.C.E. Ht. approx.
15½". Louvre. Formerly in the Levy collection, purchased
1891. *This oinochoe, or wine vessel, was a popular form of pottery in ancient Greece. Its broad shape and its trefoil, or three-
lobed, mouth are typical of the form. This oinochoe depicts both
tame and wild animals in the two upper registers and mythic
creatures in the five lower zones. The choice of the goat as the
central figure reflects the creature's usefulness, as a source for
meat, drink, and, ultimately, cheese. Oriental influence also
abounds in the plant motifs, symbolic of the Tree of Life, with
rosettes, lotus blossoms, and intertwined vines. Decorated in a
workshop in Miletus, a city in Ionia, the vessel displays the
Orientalizing method the artist used—drawing the figures in
black silhouette, incising or cutting details into the image, and
adding white and purple colors to enhance the effect.*

circle of aristocratic women friends on her native island of Lesbos in the Aegean. She was deeply personal in her interests, writing chiefly about herself, her friends, and their feelings for one another. In her elegant but restrained verses, Sappho sang mostly about moods of romantic passion: of longing, unrequited love, absence, regret, dead feelings, jealousy, and fulfillment. Sappho's willing vulnerability and her love of truth made the solo lyric the perfect vehicle for confessional writing.

Philosophy, Science, and Medicine

The mental attitudes that partly accounted for the democratic challenge to established authority in the Archaic Age also brought forth thinkers who questioned the power and, ultimately, the existence of the gods. Just as the democrats constructed a human-centered state, so did the philosophers conceive of a world where natural causes and effects operated. These Greek thinkers invented what the Romans later called **natural philosophy,** a term that encompasses the fields we now call "philosophy" and "science." The close connection between philosophy and science persisted for twenty-two centuries, until the Newtonian revolution of the seventeenth century C.E. From that point on, science simply demonstrated what happened in nature without speculating about its purpose.

Natural Philosophy The origins of natural philosophy, like those of lyric poetry, are hidden in the incomplete historical record and distorted by the fragmented extant writings, but we can nevertheless say that formal Western philosophy began on the Ionian coast in the sixth century B.C.E. There, in the polis of Miletus, a set of thinkers known as the Milesian school speculated that beneath the ever-changing natural world was an unchanging matter (Table 2.3).

Thales [THAY-leez] (fl. 585 B.C.E.), the founder of the Milesian school, reasoned that the fundamental substance of the universe was water—an outlook that made him a materialist, because he thought that everything was made of matter. From the standpoint of modern science, Thales was wrong and so were the rest of his circle, who proposed other elements—air and "the infinite"—as the underlying essence. But more important than their conclusions regarding matter were their convictions that there is regularity in the universe and that human reason can ultimately understand the natural order. Their belief in rationality not only determined the direction of speculative thought but also initiated the steps that led to physics, chemistry, botany, and other sciences. Proposing that the

universe was governed by natural laws, these first philosophers questioned divine explanations for natural events, a development deplored by those who found the key to life in a divine spirit.

When the Persians conquered Asia Minor near the end of the sixth century B.C.E., the center of intellectual thought shifted to Athens and to southern Italy and Sicily, where a tradition had emerged that challenged the Milesian school. Pythagoras [puh-THAG-uh-ruhs] (about 580–about 507 B.C.E.), the leader of the Sicilian school, rejected the concept of an underlying substance. Instead, he proclaimed, "Everything is made of numbers," by which he meant that mathematical relationships explained the basic order in nature—an outlook that made him an idealist, because he thought that an immaterial principle was the root cause of things. His musical studies probably led Pythagoras to this conclusion. He may have observed that a plucked string vibrated, making a certain sound; if the string were cut in half and plucked again, then a new note an octave higher than the first, with twice as many vibrations per second, would be heard. Hence, mathematical ratios determined musical sounds. Pythagoras then concluded that "numbers" explained everything in the "cosmos," his term for the orderly system embracing the earth and the heavens. Later, ancient astronomers building on Pythagorean beliefs claimed that the planets, in moving through their orbits, made music—the "music of the spheres."

A third philosopher, Heraclitus [her-uh-KLITE-uhs] (about 545–about 485 B.C.E.), appeals more to the modern age than does any other thinker in Archaic Greece. Rejecting the materialism of Thales and the idealism of Pythagoras, Heraclitus pioneered a philosophic tradition that found truth in constant change, as in his well-known idea that a person cannot step twice into the

Table 2.3	PHILOSOPHERS OF THE ARCHAIC AGE	
PHILOSOPHER	*TIME*	*ACHIEVEMENT*
Thales	About 585 B.C.E.	First philosopher and founder of philosophic materialism
Pythagoras	About 580–about 507 B.C.E.	Founder of philosophic idealism
Heraclitus	About 545–about 485 B.C.E.	First dialectical reasoning; belief in continual flux

SLICE OF LIFE
The Worlds of Women and Men in Ancient Greece

By pairing these two very different perspectives, it is possible to see the chasm that lay between the worldviews of women and those of men in ancient Greece. Since there are no records of ordinary people from the Archaic Age, human reactions to Archaic life come almost exclusively from famous individuals, such as Sappho and Alcaeus. In the following poems, they express human emotions across time and class but their subjects are rather different. Sappho (about 600 B.C.E.) describes her intensely personal feelings, as in this ode to a lost love. In contrast, Alcaeus (about 620–about 580 B.C.E.) sings of his anguish when he was banished for political activities in the polis of Mytilene on the island of Lesbos—Sappho's hometown too.

SAPPHO
He Seems to Be a God

Sappho's lyrical poems reflect the circumscribed world of Greek women. In this ode, she describes the pangs of jealousy and grief she feels on seeing someone she loves respond to another.

He seems to be a god, that man
Facing you, who leans to be close,
Smiles, and, alert and glad, listens
To your mellow voice

And quickens in love at your laughter
That stings my breasts, jolts my heart
If I dare the shock of a glance.
I cannot speak,

My tongue sticks to my dry mouth,
Thin fire spreads beneath my skin,
My eyes cannot see and my aching ears
Roar in their labyrinths.

Chill sweat slides down my body,
I shake, I turn greener than grass.
I am neither living nor dead and cry
From the narrow between.
But endure, even this grief of love.

ALCAEUS
Longing for Home

Unlike Sappho, Alcaeus wrote about the world of men. His works were collected into ten books in antiquity, but only a few fragments survive today.

Plunged in the wild chaste-woods I live
a rustic life, unhappy me,
longing to hear Assembly called
and Council, Agesilaidas!

From lands my grandfather grew old
possessing, and my father too,
among these citizens who wrong
each other, I've been driven away.

An outland exile: here I dwell
like Onomacles, the Athenian
spear-wolf, out of the fray. To make
peace with . . . is no wise.
So to the precinct of the gods,
treading the dark earth . . .

. . . I live
keeping well out of trouble's reach.
Now Lesbos' long-robed girls are here for the beauty-
 contest. All around,
the women's wondrous annual cry,
the holy alleluia, rings.
When will the gods from all my trials
deliver. . . .

Interpreting These Slices of Life What emotions does Sappho express in her poem? **How** does she describe her body's reaction to jealousy? **What** does Alcaeus long for while he is away from his homeland? **Why** is Alcaeus away from home? **How** does the mood of these poems by Sappho and Alcaeus differ from the mood of Homer's poetry?

Figure 2.11   Elements of Greek Architecture

same flowing river. In addition, Heraclitus devised the earliest dialectical form of reasoning when he speculated that growth arises out of opposites, a fundamental tenet of dialectic thought. This original idea led him to argue that "strife is justice" and that struggle is necessary for progress. Heraclitus's dialectical reasoning anticipated certain nineteenth-century thinkers, and his notion of continual flux has attracted modern physicists.

Medicine   Medicine lagged behind natural philosophy in Archaic Greece. Greek healers, much in the manner of those in the Near East and Egypt, combined supernatural beliefs with practical knowledge in diagnosing and treating diseases. Since sickness was believed to be caused by the gods and goddesses, Asclepius, the god of healing, was invoked to help in a patient's recovery. The patient would pray to Asclepius or visit one of his shrines and join in a number of prescribed rituals, such as making sacrifices, taking baths, and sleeping outside the god's temple. At the temple, priest-healers would examine and diagnose the sick and injured and then administer herbal potions and medicines and apply ointments.

Architecture

The supreme architectural achievement of the Greeks, the temple, became the fountainhead of the building components, decorative details, and aesthetic principles that together have largely shaped Western architecture down to Post-Modernism in the early twenty-first century. In its origins during the Archaic Age, the temple was a sacred structure designed to house the cult statues of the civic deities. The early houses of worship were probably made of wood, which explains why no remains of these Greek temples have been discovered. However, as the Archaic Age gathered economic momentum and wealth accumulated, each polis rebuilt its wooden sanctuaries in stone.

A diagram of a typical temple illustrates how much the building has influenced Western architecture (Figure 2.11). Generic Greek architecture is called **post-beam-triangle construction** (also known as post-and-lintel construction). *Post* refers to the columns; *beam* indicates the horizontal members, or **architraves,** resting on the columns; and *triangle* denotes the triangular area, called a **pediment,** at either end of the upper building. Other common features include the **entablature,** which is the name for all of the building between the columns and the pediment; the **cornice,** the horizontal piece that crowns the entablature; and the **stylobate,** the upper step of the **stereobate,** the base on which the columns stand. A typical temple had columns on four sides, which in turn enclosed a walled room, called a **cella,** that housed the cult image. Each temple faced east, with the doors to the cella placed so that, when opened, they allowed the sunrise to illuminate the statue of the deity.

The earliest temple style in Greece was called **Doric,** both because it originated in the Dorian poleis

Figure 2.12 Greek Architecture of the Doric Order

and because the style's simplicity of design and scarcity of decorative detail reflected the severe Dorian taste (Figure 2.12). The Doric columns have plain tops, or **capitals,** and the columns rest directly on the stylobate without an intervening footing. On the entablature of each Doric temple is a sculptural band, called a *frieze,* which alternates three-grooved panels, called **triglyphs,** with blank panels, called **metopes,** that could be left plain or filled with **relief** sculptures. The triglyphs are reminders of the temple's origin as a wooden building when logs, faced with bronze, served as overhead beams.

An excellent example of the Doric style in the Archaic Age is the Temple of Hera in Poseidonia, now called Paestum, in southern Italy (Figure 2.13). The Temple of Hera is the oldest (about 550 B.C.E.) and best preserved of three cult sanctuaries on this site. Constructed from coarse local limestone, this large temple has a somewhat ungainly appearance, due in part to the massive architrave and the small spaces between the columns. The builders attempted to remedy this defect (without total success) by introducing refinements into the temple's design. The columns were made to appear strong and solid enough to support the entablature by enlarging the middles of the shafts, a technique known as **entasis.** The artisans also carved vertical grooves, called **fluting,** along the shafts to give the columns a graceful, delicate surface and enhance their visual three-dimensionality.

Eventually, after much experimentation, Greek architects overcame the awkwardness of the early Doric

Figure 2.13 Temple of Hera at Paestum. Ca. 560–550 B.C.E. Limestone. *This temple, with its heavy, squat columns, stands not only as a model of Archaic Greek architecture but also as a reminder of Greek wealth and expansion. Colonists from mainland Greece settled in southern Italy, the land they thought of as "Greater Greece," in the seventh and sixth centuries B.C.E., bringing with them the Olympian gods and goddesses and ideas of how to build temples in their honor.*

Figure 2.14   Temple of Aphaia, Aegina. 510 B.C.E. *The Temple of Aphaia in Aegina became the standard for the Doric temple style from its creation until it was superseded by the Athenian Parthenon in the 440s. Built of local limestone and covered in stucco and painted, the Temple of Aphaia gleamed like a jewel in its carefully planned site overlooking the Saronic Gulf. Constructed and decorated with strict attention to artistic refinements, such as the slender columns and the lifelike sculptures, this temple represents the climax of Archaic architecture.*

style by deciding that a temple's beauty was a function of mathematical proportions. The Temple of Aphaia—erected in 510 B.C.E. by the citizens of Aegina, Athens's neighbor and perennial enemy—seems to embody this principle (Figure 2.14). The architect of this temple achieved its pleasing dimensions by using the ratio 1:2, placing six columns on the ends and twelve columns on the sides. The Temple of Aphaia, with its harmonious proportions and graceful columns, became the widely imitated standard for the Doric style over the next half century.

Sculpture

Like the art of Mesopotamia and Egypt, Greek sculpture was rooted in religious practices and beliefs. The Greek sculptors fashioned images of the gods and goddesses to be used in temples either as objects of worship or as decorations for the pediments and friezes. Of greater importance for the development of Greek sculpture were the **kouros** (plural, *kourai*) and the **kore** (plural, *korai*), freestanding statues of youths and maidens, respectively. Before 600 B.C.E., these sculptures had evolved from images of gods, into statues of dead heroes, and finally into memorials that might not even relate directly to the dead person to whom they were dedicated.

What made the **Archaic** statues of youths and maidens so different from Egyptian and Mesopotamian art was the Greek delight in the splendor of the human body. In their representations of the human form, the Greeks rejected the sacred approach of the Egyptians and the Mesopotamians, which stressed

conventional poses and formal gestures. Instead, Greek sculptors created athletic, muscular males and lively, robust maidens. For the Greeks, the health and beauty of the subjects were as important as the statues' religious purpose.

The first Archaic statues of youths owed much to the Egyptian tradition, but gradually Greek sculpture broke free of its origins. An early example of the kouros type of sculpture is the New York Kouros (Figure 2.15), named for its present location in New York City's Metropolitan Museum of Art. Artistically, this marble statue of a youth with the left foot forward, the clenched fists, the arms held rigidly at the sides, the stylized hair, and the frontality—that is, the quality of being designed for viewing from the front—shows the Egyptian influence (see Figure 1.17). The Greek sculptor has moved beyond Egyptian techniques, however, by incorporating changes that make the figure more lifelike, such as by attempting to show the correct shape of the knees and suggesting an actual person's mouth. That the result is not a realistic or an idealized human figure is less important than that the sculptor has studied the human body with fresh eyes and endeavored to represent it accurately. With such groundbreaking works as the New York Kouros, the Greeks launched a dynamic tradition that later artists continually reshaped.

A generation after the New York Kouros, new sculptors expressed their changed notion of a beautiful living male body in such works as the Anavysos Kouros (Figure 2.16). This sculpture, which was probably a dedicatory offering to a god or a goddess, still shows a powerful Egyptian influence, but it takes a giant step forward to a greater sense of life. The taut

Figure 2.15 New York Kouros. Ca. 615–590 B.C.E. Marble, ht. 73½". Courtesy Metropolitan Museum of Art. Fletcher Fund, 1932. (32.11.1). *The New York Kouros is one of many similar statues dating from about the beginning of the sixth century* B.C.E. *During that century, the male and female statues evolved from stiff and stereotyped models to natural and anatomically correct forms.*

Figure 2.16 Anavysos Kouros. Ca. 540–520 B.C.E. Marble, ht. 76". National Museum, Athens. *The Anavysos Kouros possesses the distinguishing characteristics of all kourai: frontality, attention to bodily details, and a general formality. However, its subtle innovations—more precise musculature and more liveliness, as contrasted with Figure 2.15—foreshadow the Hellenic sculpture style.*

Figure 2.17   Auxerre Kore. Ca. 675–600 B.C.E. Limestone. Louvre. *The Auxerre Kore represents a fairly early stage in the development of this female form. The small size of the sculpture (about 29½″ high) suggests that it may have been part of a burial rite. Traces of red pigment on the bust indicate that this kore was once painted to make it appear more lifelike.*

Figure 2.18   Peplos Kore. Ca. 535–530 B.C.E. Marble, ht. 48″. Acropolis Museum, Athens. *The kore, a statue of a young draped female, was highly popular during the first phase of Greek art, the Archaic style, which set the standard for later Greek art. The Peplos Kore depicted here—with her beautiful face, elegant dress, and expectant countenance—represents the highest expression of this early style.*

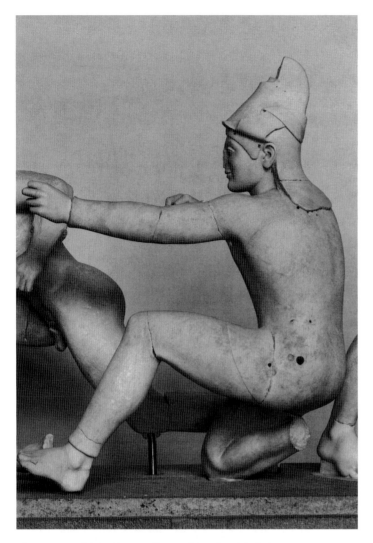

Figure 2.19 *Paris.* West pediment, Temple of Aphaia, Aegina. Ca. 500 B.C.E. Marble, ht. 41″. Staatliche Antiken-sammlungen, Munich. *The pedimental sculptures on the Temple of Aphaia illustrate the rapid changes that were occurring in artistic ideals and techniques in the period just preceding the Hellenic Age of Athens. The sculpture of Paris from the earlier west pediment is formal and stylized in comparison with its counterpart on the east pediment.*

Figure 2.20 *Herakles.* East pediment, Temple of Aphaia, Aegina. Ca. 490–485 B.C.E. Marble, ht. 31″. Staatliche Antikensammlungen, Munich. *The statue of Herakles from the east pediment of the Temple of Aphaia shows the advances made in sculpture in the ten to fifteen years after the figure of Paris was crafted for the west pediment. More realistic, detailed, and lifelike than Paris, Herakles is emotionally charged and tense, yet composed and restrained—a state admired and often depicted by Hellenic artists.*

body and massive torso convincingly reproduce the athletic qualities of an Olympic competitor, and the curious facial expression, known as the "archaic smile," gives an enigmatic quality to the marble figure.

The korai sculptures, like the statues of youths, evolved from a frozen, lifeless style toward a greater realism, although women were never depicted in the nude at this stage in Greek sculpture. The earliest draped korai sculptures mixed Mesopotamian and Egyptian traditions with Greek ideas, sometimes producing an interesting but awkward effect. Such an early work is the Auxerre Kore (Figure 2.17)—named for the museum in Auxerre, France—whose cylindri-

cal shape is copied from Mesopotamian models and whose stiff pose, wiglike hair, and thin waist are borrowed from Egypt. The Greek sculptor added the broad mouth and the Greek peplos (a loose-fitting outer robe) decorated with a meander pattern, but the Auxerre Kore, despite its charming details, is rigid and inert.

The Peplos Kore (Figure 2.18), dating from about a century later, expresses beautifully the exciting changes that were taking place in late Archaic sculpture. The statue wears a chiton, or tunic, over her upper torso, and a belted peplos. The sculptor has replaced the rigidity of the Egyptian pose with a more graceful one, as shown, for example, by the way the figure holds her right arm. Traces of a painted necklace may be seen, for the Peplos Kore, like all Greek sculpture, was painted to make the figure as true to life as possible. The often-awkward archaic smile is here rendered to perfection, giving this lovely maiden an aristocratic demeanor.

The Greek tradition of representing males nude and females clothed persisted throughout the Archaic Age and well into the succeeding Hellenic Age. The Greeks readily accepted male nudity, witnessing it in the army on campaigns, in the gymnasium during exercises, and in the games at Olympia and elsewhere, and this acceptance is reflected in their art. But they were much less comfortable with female nudity (except in Sparta, where women exercised in the nude), so women were usually depicted draped or robed.

The political turmoil brought on by the Persian Wars occurred simultaneously with the revolutionary changes in sculpture that were leading to a new style of art. The Temple of Aphaia at Aegina provides a laboratory setting for the transition from the Archaic to the Hellenic style (480–323 B.C.E.) because of the different ages of the building's statues: The sculptures for the west pediment (about 500 B.C.E.) were made some fifteen years earlier than those for the east pediment (about 490–485 B.C.E.). Their stylistic differences demonstrate the changes that were under way.

An earlier statue (from the west pediment) depicts the Trojan hero Paris as a nude, somewhat sensual bowman, poised, ready to release an arrow (Figure 2.19). Paris, his body and face revealing very little tension, might have been posing, rather than preparing for action. A later sculpture (from the east pediment) portrays the legendary hero Herakles as a clothed archer, in a stance copied from the *Paris* figure (Figure 2.20). But what a contrast! Herakles' more muscular body is tensed and ready for action. Although neither face registers emotion, Herakles' gaze and set jawline convey a more lifelike image of a warrior. The *Herakles* figure is a transitional work to the next style—the Hellenic.

The Legacy of Archaic Greek Civilization

The Archaic Age in Greece was a precious moment in the story of the arts and humanities. Inheriting survival techniques from Neolithic cultures, continuing the urban ways of Mesopotamia and Egypt, and, more important, drawing spiritual and psychological sustenance from the Minoans and the Mycenaeans, the Archaic Greeks developed a unique consciousness that expressed, through original artistic and literary forms, their views about the deities and themselves and how they interacted. A mark of the creative power of the Archaic Greeks is that at the same time they were inventing epic poetry, lyric poetry, the post-beam-triangle temple, the korai and kourai sculptures, and natural philosophy, they were involved in founding a new and better way to live in the polis.

The new way of life devised by the Archaic Greeks gave rise to what we call, in retrospect, the **humanities**— those original artistic and literary forms that made Greek civilization unique. But the cultural explosion of this brilliant age is inseparable from the Greeks' restless drive to experience life to the fullest and their deep regard for human powers. Having devised their cultural forms, the Archaic Greeks believed passionately that by simply employing these models, either through studying them or by creating new works, the individual became a better human being. In this way,

the Archaic Greeks' arts and humanities were imbued with an ethical content, thus suggesting for some— notably philosophers—an alternative way of life to that offered by religion.

Wherever we look in this age, we see creative energy, a trait that has characterized Western civilization through the ages. Even though the different cultural forms did not develop at the same pace during the Archaic Age—sculpture, for example, was not as expressive as lyric poetry—these early aesthetic efforts were fundamentally different from those of the earlier Near Eastern civilizations. The touchstone of the humanistic style developed by the Archaic Greeks was their belief in human powers, both intellectual and physical. Indeed, the most powerful literary voice of this age, Homer, was quoted over and over for his claim that mortals and divinities are part of the same family. Less confident people, hearing this assertion, might have reasoned that human beings are limited in their earthly hopes. But, for the Greeks of this period, Homer meant that humans are capable of godlike actions. The reverence that the Archaic Greeks expressed for all noteworthy deeds, whether in poetry, in warfare, or in the Olympic games, attested to their belief in the basic value of human achievement.

KEY CULTURAL TERMS

frieze	architrave
fresco	pediment
Linear A	entablature
Linear B	cornice
ashlar	stylobate
shaft graves	stereobate
oligarchy	cella
muse	Doric
Olympian deities	capital
chthonian deities	triglyph
hubris	metope
epic poetry	relief
bard	entasis
Homeric epithet	fluting
lyre	kouros
lyric poetry	kore
lyric	Archaic
Orientalizing	humanities
natural philosophy	
post-beam-triangle construction	

SUGGESTIONS FOR FURTHER READING

BARNSTONE, W., ed. and trans. *Greek Lyric Poetry*. New York: Bantam Books, 1962. Selections from literary fragments dating from the seventh century B.C.E. to the sixth century C.E.; includes helpful biographical notes.

HOMER. *Iliad*. Translated by R. Fagles. New York: Viking Penguin, 1998. The best recent modern translation of the story of the Trojan War.

———. *Odyssey*. Translated by R. Fagles. New York: Viking Penguin, 1996. The epic of Odysseus's adventures after the fall of Troy, again in Fagles's well-received translation.

Sappho, a Garland: The Poems and Fragments of Sappho. Translated by J. Powell. New York: Farrar, Straus & Giroux, 1993. This slim volume contains all of Sappho's existing verses, both whole and fragments, rendered into contemporary language.

WHEELWRIGHT, P., ed. *The Presocratics*. New York: Bobbs-Merrill, 1966. A collection of quotations from early philosophers that captures the flavor of sixth-century Greek thought.

Of all the many translations of Greek literature, the Loeb Classical Library (Harvard University Press) is probably the best.

3 CLASSICAL GREEK CIVILIZATION
The Hellenic Age

With the defeat of the Persians at Plataea in 479 B.C.E., the Greeks entered the **Hellenic** Age, a period that lasted until the death of Alexander the Great of Macedon in 323 B.C.E. During the more than 150 years of the Hellenic Age, the Greeks defeated the Persians for a second time and survived a century of destructive civil war, only to succumb ultimately to the Macedonians. But throughout those turbulent times, the Greeks never wavered in their supreme confidence in the superiority of their way of life.

The Greek world consisted of several hundred poleis (city-states), located on the mainland, on the Aegean Islands and the coast of Asia Minor, and in the lands bordering the Mediterranean and Black Seas (Map 3.1). Athens was the cultural center, but many poleis contributed both materially and intellectually to Hellenic civilization. The Hellenic Age was the first stage of Classical civilization, the highest achievement of the ancient Greeks. Chapter 4 describes the second stage of Classical civilization, the Hellenistic Age.

GENERAL CHARACTERISTICS OF HELLENIC CIVILIZATION

Despite diversity among the poleis, the Greeks of the Hellenic Age shared certain characteristics. Competitiveness and rivalry were certainly dominant features, as was an increasingly urban lifestyle (Figure 3.1). Most Greeks still lived in the countryside, but the city now dominated politics, society, and the economy.

◀ **Detail** *Poseidon (or Zeus).* Ca. 460–450 B.C.E. Bronze, ht. 6′10″. National Museum, Athens.

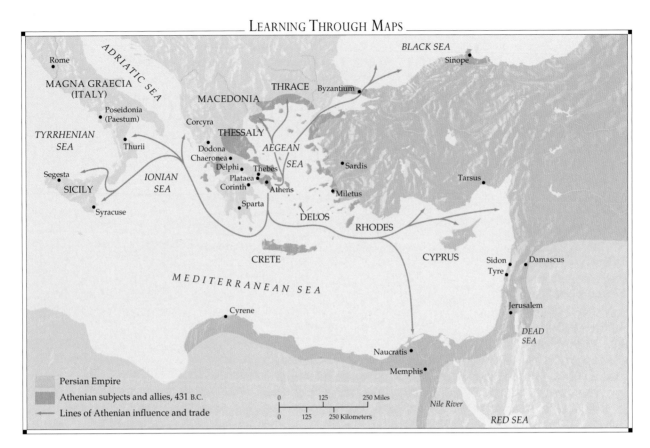

Map 3.1 THE ATHENIAN EMPIRE, 431 B.C.E.
This map shows the Athenian and Persian empires on the eve of the Peloponnesian War.
Compare the Athenian and Persian empires, with respect to size and sea and land con-
figuration. **Notice** the difference between Athenian and Spartan influence in the eastern
Mediterranean. **How** did the locations of Athens and Sparta influence their respective
naval and military policies? **In what way** did the distance between Sicily and Athens
affect the course of the Peloponnesian War? **Observe** that Macedonia's proximity to
Greece helped in its conquest of the late fourth century B.C.E.

Figure 3.1 *Torch Race.* Ca. 430–420 B.C.E. Clay, ht. 14³⁄₁₆″.
Arthur M. Sackler Museum, Harvard University Art Muse-
ums, Cambridge, Mass. (Bequest of David M. Robinson.)
*From the dawn of the Archaic period, about 800 B.C.E., sports, es-
pecially competitive sports, were integral to Greek life. In Hellenic
times, artists used sports contests as subjects, as in this painting
depicting a torch race, perhaps during the Panathenaea festival.
This vase painting is executed in the red-figure style, a reversal of
the black-figure style, which is illustrated in Figures 2.9 and 2.10.
The relatively uncluttered design, three figures with sparse details, perfectly fits into the small panel on the krater, a mixing
vessel.*

Popular attitudes toward the Olympian deities were also changing, and public worship began to be assimilated into civic festivals. The great art of the age reflected the fusion of civic and sacred in such works as the Parthenon, the temple of the goddess Athena, protector of Athens (Figure 3.2). With gods and goddesses playing increasingly ceremonial roles, religion became demystified and lost some of its personal value in people's lives. Religious dissatisfaction was also triggered by expanded civil rights: The more democratic poleis raised the collective hopes of their citizens but were unable to satisfy all their spiritual longings.

Another characteristic of Hellenic civilization was a high regard for the balanced life and for moderation in achieving it. In Athenian tragedy, a recurrent theme is the danger of great wealth and high position. According to the playwrights, riches and status bred pride and led to envy by other citizens or, worse, envy by the gods. A modest life was the safest way to avoid personal calamity.

The Greeks also sought a balance between two opposite aspects of human nature, symbolized by Apollo, god of moderation, and Dionysus, god of excess. As the god of light, Apollo embodied rational thought, ethical ideals, and aesthetic balance. Apollo's temple with its oracle at Delphi was one of the holiest shrines in Greece, second only to the island of Delos, his birthplace (Figure 3.3).

Dionysus, on the other hand, was the god of wine, drunken revelry, sexual excess, and madness. Women known as **maenads** followed and worshiped him, sometimes tearing apart beasts in their blind frenzy. By the Hellenic Age, these excesses were confined to rural areas, for the Dionysiac impulse was constantly being tamed by the Apollonian spirit and urban life. In Athens, the drunken worship of Dionysus was transformed into a civic festival, the **Dionysia,** from which tragedy, perhaps the highest expression of the Greek ethical genius, was born (Figure 3.4).

Figure 3.2 *Athena Parthenos.* Marble replica based on fifth-century B.C.E. statue by Phidias. Ht. 3'5⅜". National Museum, Athens. *Phidias's larger-than-life sculpture, which dominated the inner sanctum of the Parthenon, disappeared in ancient times, but numerous copies, such as this small figurine, have survived. Athena wears a peplos, gathered at her waist, and a helmet, ornamented with a sphinx flanked by two winged horses, and her left hand steadies a shield depicting Greek battle scenes. The statue was composed of gold and ivory sections joined together. A close examination of Athena's head demonstrates the shift from the Archaic to the Hellenic style of sculpture, since it does not have the Archaic smile and its features are idealized.*

Figure 3.3 *Apollo*. West pediment, Temple at Olympia. Ca. 460 B.C.E. Marble, ht. 10′2″. Olympia Museum. *Apollo's serene countenance in this splendidly crafted head reflects his image as the god of moderation. As the deity who counseled "Nothing in excess," Apollo was a potent force in combating the destructive urges that assailed the Greeks. This sculpture is executed in the Severe style, or the first stage of the Hellenic Classical style, which is evident by the turn of the head to the right. However, its wiglike hair indicates the lingering influence of the Archaic style.*

Figure 3.4 *Dionysus and His Followers*. Ca. 430 B.C.E. Staatliche Museen, Berlin. *Scrolling around a perfume vase, this painting depicts a bearded Dionysus seated on the right with his followers. Of his twelve devotees, eleven are maenads, young female revelers; the last is the bearded Silenus, the foster father and former schoolmaster of Dionysus. Silenus is depicted on the lower left in his usual drunken, disorderly state.*

Greek citizens of Hellenic times, then, were proud of their own polis, where they participated in civic functions and religious rites. However, despite the many commonalities among the Greek poleis—language, ancestry, history, and Homer—they never shared a politically united Greek world.

DOMESTIC AND FOREIGN AFFAIRS: WAR, PEACE, AND THE TRIUMPH OF MACEDONIA

On the eve of the Hellenic Age, the Greeks, having defeated the Persians, were united only in their continuing opposition to Persia and in their hostility to any polis that tried to control the others. Although they cooperated on short-term goals that served their common interests, goodwill among the poleis usually evaporated once specific ends were met.

Despite rivalries, the Greek economy expanded. A rising middle class took advantage of the economic opportunities created by the fluctuations of war and politics, causing manufacturing and commerce to flourish and advances in technology to be made. Although the economic base remained agricultural, people increasingly flocked to the poleis to make their fortunes, to participate in government, and to find stimulation.

Phases of the Hellenic Age

The Hellenic Age can be divided into four distinct phases: (1) the Delian League; (2) wars in Greece and with Persia and the ensuing Thirty Years' Peace; (3) the Peloponnesian War; and (4) Spartan and Theban hegemony and the triumph of Macedonia (Timeline 3.1). While these conflicts raged, life within the polis went on, and in some poleis, notably Athens, extraordinary

Timeline 3.1 PHASES OF HELLENIC HISTORY   All dates B.C.E.

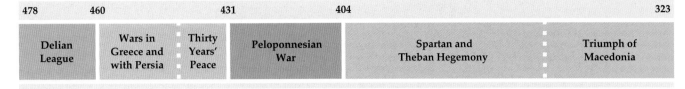

478	460		431	404		323
Delian League	Wars in Greece and with Persia	Thirty Years' Peace	Peloponnesian War	Spartan and Theban Hegemony		Triumph of Macedonia

political, cultural, and intellectual changes were occurring.

After defeating the Persians, the Greeks realized that a mutual defense organization was the key to preventing further Persian attack. In 478 B.C.E., a number of poleis formed the Delian League, a defensive alliance, with Athens at its head. But Athens soon began to transform the league into an instrument of imperialism. As the oppressive nature of Athenian policies emerged, Athens's independent neighbors became alarmed.

Athenian power, however, was restricted by strained relations with Sparta, by the continuing menace of Persia, and by the highly unstable Delian alliance. When a negotiated settlement finally resolved Persian claims, the Delian League fell apart, leaving Athens vulnerable to its enemies on the Greek mainland. First Thebes and then Sparta led attacks on Athens. The war dragged on, but in 445 B.C.E., when Sparta unexpectedly withdrew, Athens won a quick victory that forced its enemies to negotiate.

The ensuing Thirty Years' Peace (which lasted only fourteen years) brought the Hellenic Age of Athens to its zenith. Athenian democracy expanded so that even the poorest citizens were empowered with full rights (though women continued to be excluded). Artists and sculptors beautified the Acropolis, and the three great Athenian tragedians—Aeschylus, Sophocles, and Euripides—were active in the drama festivals. Drawing on the Delian treasury, Pericles [PER-uh-kleez], the popular leader and general, launched a glorious building program that was essentially a huge public works project (Figure 3.5). In a speech over Athens's war dead, Pericles offered an eloquent summation of Athenian democracy, praising its use of public debate in reaching decisions, its tolerance of diverse beliefs, its ability to love beauty without sacrificing military strength. His conclusion boasted that Athens was the model for Greece.

However, those poleis that were not enamored of Athenian aggression became convinced that war was the only way to protect themselves. Athens's foreign policy and its expansionism had given rise to an alliance system so delicately balanced that neither side could allow the other to gain the slightest advantage.

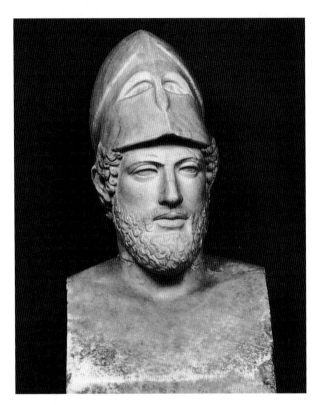

Figure 3.5 *Pericles*. Ca. 440 B.C.E. Marble, ht. 19¾". Vatican Museum. *Pericles possessed a vision of Athens as the political, economic, and cultural center of the Greek world. Even though this portrait bust is a Roman copy of the Greek original, it conveys Pericles' strong sense of leadership and determination.*

When Athens's neighbor Corinth went to war with Corcyra (present-day Corfu) in western Greece, Corcyra appealed to Athens for aid. Athens's initial victories frightened Corinth, whose leaders persuaded the Spartans to join together with them in the Peloponnesian League. The Peloponnesian War (431–404 B.C.E.) had begun.

Pericles knew the league was superior on land but thought the Athenians could hold out indefinitely within their own walls and win a war of attrition. However, a plague broke out in Athens in 430 B.C.E., killing many citizens, including Pericles. The first phase of the war ended in 421 B.C.E., when a demoralized and defeated Athens sued for peace.

Figure 3.6 *Alexander the Great. Ca. 200* B.C.E. *Marble, ht. 16⅛". Istanbul Museum. Alexander's youth and fine features, idealized perhaps in this portrait bust, add to the legends that have accumulated around one of the most famous conquerors in history. Later rulers measured themselves against Alexander, whose dream of a united world was cut short by his early death.*

soldier, Philip expanded Macedonia to the east as far as the Black Sea. He then moved southward, conquering the poleis of central Greece. The poleis hastily raised an army, but Philip's well-disciplined troops crushed them at Chaeronea in 338 B.C.E. After establishing a league between Macedonia and the poleis, he granted the Greeks autonomy in everything except military affairs. Philip then announced an all-out war against Persia but was assassinated before he could launch his first campaign.

Philip's nineteen-year-old son, Alexander, succeeded to the throne. Tutored in philosophy by the renowned thinker Aristotle, Alexander nevertheless had the heart of a warrior. When Thebes and other poleis attempted to take control at Philip's death, Alexander burned Thebes to the ground, sparing only the house of the poet Pindar. Placing a general in command of Greece, Alexander turned his sights to the east (Figure 3.6).

Alexander dreamed of a world united under his name and of a culture fused from Hellenic and Persian roots. His armies marched into Asia Minor, Egypt, and Mesopotamia, absorbing the great Persian Empire; then they swept east through Asia to the Indus River in India. As he conquered, Alexander destroyed and looted the great centers of Eastern civilization, but he also founded new cities and spread Greek culture.

Alexander's dream ended abruptly with his death in 323 B.C.E. at the age of thirty-two. Seizing the opportunity presented by his sudden death, the Greeks revolted against the Macedonian oppressors, but they were quickly overwhelmed. The Macedonians then occupied Athens and installed an aristocratic government. Thus ended democracy and Hellenic civilization—in Greece.

Technology

The Greeks of the Hellenic Age, like their predecessors, borrowed technologies from past and present societies in order to survive and to compete with rival states. The historical sources for these achievements are scarce, primarily literary records and a few artifacts, but the surviving evidence shows that the Hellenic Greeks made significant improvements to shipbuilding and warfare and these technologies endured for centuries.

Shipbuilding By 479 B.C.E., the Greeks had already improved on the designs and enlarged the size of the sailing vessels that they had adapted from Phoenicia, Syria, and Egypt. Like most seafaring peoples, the Greeks had replaced the unireme with *biremes,* ships powered by twenty oarsmen arranged in two banks.

The second half of the Peloponnesian War shifted from the Greek peninsula to distant Sicily and the west —a move that sealed Athens's fate. In 416 B.C.E., Segesta, a Sicilian polis, begged Athens for military assistance. The Athenians eventually sent help, but in trying to conduct a war so far from home, they were soundly defeated and never recovered their military and economic power.

In the early decades of the fourth century B.C.E., first Sparta and then Thebes emerged as the preeminent city-state, but these power struggles only further weakened the poleis and made them easy prey for an invader. At the northern edge of the civilized Greek world, that invader was gathering its forces. Macedonia was a primitive Greek state, governed by kings and populated with a people speaking a rough dialect of the Greek language. Their king, Philip, having been a hostage in Thebes when young, had become a *philhellene*—a lover of Greek civilization. A brilliant

Figure 3.7 *Athletes in the Palaestra.* Second quarter of the fifth century B.C.E. Marble, ht. 12½". National Museum, Athens. *This low-relief sculpture depicts athletes warming up in the open-air exercise area where spectators would congregate to urge on their favorites. The youth on the left is preparing for a foot race, and the one on the right tests his javelin. The pair in the center has just begun to wrestle. This relief was originally part of a sculptured base built into a wall that the Athenians constructed after the Persian Wars.*

However, the Greek biremes were longer and sat lower in the water, thus making them less top-heavy and easier to handle. One type of bireme, called a *penteconter,* a fifty-oar ship, was capable of going against strong currents, allowing it to sail the treacherous Hellespont, which is the narrow strait linking the Aegean Sea with the Sea of Marmara (the modern Dardanelles), and on into the Black Sea.

As the Hellenic Age began, the Greek bireme quickly gave way to the *trireme,* or triple-oared fighting ship. The Athenian trireme proved to be faster and more effective in sea battles due to its thin shell hull, larger keel, and cross ribbing. With a bronze ram mounted on the bow and a crew of up to two hundred men, including armed soldiers ready to board enemy ships, these Athenian triremes helped save the city-state in the famous Battle of Salamis (see Chapter 2).

Warfare   As the Hellenic Age dawned, similar dramatic changes were under way in the conduct of warfare. The old style of fighting had been skirmishes and occasional pitched battles or sieges, led by well-known warriors who often faced each other in personal combat—the style featured in Homer's *Iliad.* The new style of land warfare, as practiced in the recently concluded Persian Wars, was planned campaigns with well-supplied armies of trained and disciplined troops. These citizen-soldiers or, sometimes hired or enslaved men, fought in close formations or blocks, known as **phalanxes.** Earlier societies, including the Sumerians and Egyptians, had employed the phalanx, but the Greeks increased its size and reorganized its structure to make it one of their primary weapons.

The phalanx, when first used on the battlefield, could not maneuver very fast, but the Hellenic Age Greeks found ways to move large numbers of armored men in closed ranks in order to carry out mass frontal attacks or outflank opponents. The disciplined soldiers, wearing helmets and light protective armor and wielding small swords, daggers, pikes, and spears, often fought bloody and costly battles with heavy losses in lives and equipment. These foot soldiers, drawn from various social classes of the Greek poleis, were supported by proven military units, such as cavalry and light infantry, which, in their coordinated efforts, made warfare more complex and brutal.

THE PERFECTION OF THE TRADITION: THE GLORY OF HELLENIC GREECE

Throughout this era of shifting political fortunes, artistic and intellectual life flourished. Athens—bursting with creative energy—was the jewel of the Greek world. Atop its Acropolis, perfectly proportioned marble temples gleamed in the brilliant Aegean sun. Below, in the agora, philosophers debated the most profound questions of human nature. Hundreds of citizens congregated outdoors to serve in the assembly, where they passed laws or sat on juries that made legal rulings. Other citizens who were at leisure cheered on the athletes exercising in the open-air gymnasium (Figure 3.7). During drama festivals, the whole city

ENCOUNTER

The Representation of Blacks in Greek Art

Starting in the Archaic period, Greek artists began to depict black Africans in their art. For the rest of Greek history and subsequently in Roman history, artists continued this practice, thus making the representation of blacks a significant feature of Classical art. This change in Classical art is simply one of the ways that, over the centuries, the Western arts have been influenced by non-Western traditions, such as stylistic elements, artistic symbols, and motifs.

The Greeks, over the course of their history, encountered other peoples, but their contact with black Africans left the greatest visual legacy. Starting in the Archaic Age, Greek artists created a black type, which became a persistent theme in their tradition. Features that came to characterize the black type in art included black skin, tightly curled hair, broad nose, full lips, and projecting jaw. Once introduced, the black figure flourished for the rest of Greek history (see Figure 4.1) and became part of Roman art. Few life-size statues and heads of the black type have been found, but hundreds of small works, dating from all periods, reflect the enduring popularity of the type, including images on statuettes, vases, engraved gems, coins, lamps, weights, finger rings, earrings, necklaces, and masks.

The Greek word for a black person was *Ethiopian*, a term originally meaning "one with a sun-burned face." As Greeks encountered blacks at home and abroad, the word came to be applied to any dark-skinned person and had no special connection to the land below Egypt.

The black type probably originated in Naucratis, the city founded in Egypt's Nile delta by Greek settlers, in the seventh century B.C.E. There, artists, impressed by their contacts with black people, may have been the first to portray black figures in Greek art.

A critical date in the evolution of the black type was the arrival in Athens of black troops in the army of Persian king Xerxes in the Persian Wars (479 B.C.E.). The black type had previously emerged in mainland art, but the large number of blacks in Xerxes' defeated army deeply impressed the Greeks who saw them. Some may eventually have been enslaved and thus became a continuing presence in Greek life. Other blacks also made their way to Greece. Most came as prisoners of war, some as soldiers, diplomats, or members of trade delegations, and a few to study. Many black immigrants held menial positions, but others were soldiers, actors, and athletes.

The portrayal of blacks in Greek art arose from artistic and scientific interest, not from racial prejudice. The Greek world, just as the Roman, was free of color bias, unlike the modern world. The numerous images Greek artists created provide striking evidence of contacts between Greeks and black Africans throughout most of Greek history.

Encounter figure 3.1   Attic Head-Vase. 6th–5th centuries B.C.E. Berlin, Staatliche Museen, F4049. Courtesy Staatliche Museen, Berlin. *The head that forms this vase exhibits the typical features of the black type in Greek art, including black skin, curled, short hair, broad nose, and full lips. The vase was fashioned in Athens during the Archaic period.*

Learning from the Encounter   **What** circumstances enabled Greek artists to encounter black Africans in the Greek world? If we know that the first depiction of blacks may have occurred in the Greek city of Naucratis, in Egypt, **what** does the subsequent spread of the representation of blacks across Greek culture tell us about Greek art and society? **What** are some roles that blacks played in Greek society? **How** did Greek artists depict blacks in their art?

Figure 3.8 Theater at Epidaurus. Ca. 300 B.C.E. *The best-preserved theater in Greece is the one at Epidaurus. Although tragedy was created only in Athens, the popularity of the art form led to the construction of theaters all over Greece—a telling index of Athens's cultural imperialism. The acoustics in this ancient auditorium were remarkable. Performers' voices could be heard clearly throughout the theater even though it is in the open with fifty-four rows of seats accommodating 14,000 spectators.*

turned out to share a gripping tragedy or to laugh uproariously at the latest comedy.

The culture that flourished in Greece at this time is known as **Classic,** or **Classical,** a term with varied meanings. *Classic* means, first of all, "best" or "preeminent," and the judgment of the Western tradition is that Greek culture was in fact the highest moment in the entire history of the humanities. *Classic* also means having permanent and recognized significance; a classic work establishes a standard against which other efforts are measured. In this second sense, the aesthetic values and forms of Greek culture have been studied and imitated in all later stages of Western history. By extension, "the classics" are the works that have survived from Greece and Rome.

Classic also refers to the body of specific aesthetic principles expressed through the art and literature of Greece and Rome, a system known as **Classicism.** The first stage of Classicism, which originated in the Hellenic Age, emphasized simplicity over complexity; balance, or symmetry, over asymmetry; and restraint over excess. At the heart of Classicism was the search for perfection, for the ideal form—whether expressed in the proportions of a temple constructed in marble or in the canon of the human anatomy molded in bronze or in a philosophical conclusion reached through logic. Hellenic Classicism found expression in many areas: theater, music, history, natural philosophy, medicine, architecture, and sculpture.

Theater: Tragedy

One of the most prominent institutions of Greek civilization was the theater, in which the dramatic form known as **tragedy** reached a state of perfection. Greek theater originally arose in connection with the worship of Dionysus. The word *tragedy* in Greek means "goat song," and this word may refer to a prehistoric religious ceremony in which competing male **choruses**—groups of singers—sang and danced, while intoxicated, in homage to the god of wine; the victory prize may have been a sacrificial goat. Whatever its precise origins, during the Archaic Age theater in Athens had taken the form of a series of competitive performances presented annually during the Great Dionysia, celebrated in March.

Features of the Tragic Theater At first, the chorus served as both the collective actor and the commentator on the events of the drama. Then, in the late sixth century B.C.E., according to tradition, the poet Thespis—from whose name comes the word *thespian,* or "actor"—introduced an actor with whom the chorus could interact. The theater was born. Initially, the main function of the actor was simply to ask questions of the chorus. During the Hellenic Age, the number of actors was increased to three, and, occasionally, late in the fifth century B.C.E., a fourth was added. Any number of actors who did not speak might be on the stage, but

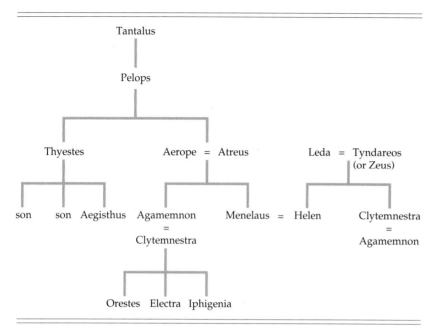

Figure 3.9 Genealogy of the House of Argos. *The tragic fate of the House of Argos (or the family of Atreus) was well under way before the opening scene of Aeschylus's tragedy* Agamemnon. *Thyestes seduced Aerope, the wife of his brother Atreus; in retaliation, Atreus killed Thyestes' two sons and served them to him in a stew. Thyestes then cursed the line of Atreus, and dire consequences followed. Most important, Agamemnon, the son of Atreus, sacrificed his own daughter to gain favorable weather for his planned invasion of Troy. Besides the* Oresteia, *three more tragedies survive that have plots based on the House of Argos—*Iphigenia in Taurus, Iphigenia in Aulis, *and* Electra, *all by Euripides—although they have no inner connection, as does Aeschylus's trilogy.*

only the three leading actors engaged in dialogue. In the fifth century B.C.E., the chorus achieved its classic function as mediator between actors and audience. As time went on, however, the role of the chorus declined and the importance of the actors increased. By the fourth century B.C.E., the actor had become the focus of the drama.

Because the focus of tragedy was originally the chorus, the need for a space to accommodate their dancing and singing determined the theater's shape. The chorus performed in a circular area called an **orchestra,** or "dancing place," in the center of which was a functioning altar, serving as a reminder that tragedy was a religious rite. The audience sat around two-thirds of the orchestra on wooden bleachers or stone seats under the open sky. The other third of the orchestra was backed by a wooden or stone building called the *skene* [SKEE-nee], which could be painted to suggest a scene and through which entrances and exits could be made (Figure 3.8).

Such simple set decorations may have provided a slight bit of realism, but Greek theater was not concerned with either realism or the expressiveness of individual actors. Ideas and language were crucial. The actors—all men, even in the female roles—wore elaborate masks designed to project their voices, platform shoes, and long robes, which helped give the dramas a timeless, otherworldly quality.

Plays were performed in tetralogies (sets of four) on successive days of the Great Dionysia. Each competing playwright offered three tragedies, not necessarily related in theme or subject, that were performed during

the day, and a satyr-play that was performed later. A **satyr-play** usually featured the indecent behavior and ribald speech of the satyrs—sexually insatiable half-men, half-goats—who followed Dionysus. That the Greeks liked to watch three deeply serious dramas followed by a play full of obscene high jinks demonstrates the breadth of their sensibility.

Tragic Drama   The essence of Greek tragedy is the deeply felt belief that mortals cannot escape pain and sorrow. The dramatists shared with Homer the insight that "we men are wretched things, and the gods . . . have woven sorrow into the very pattern of our lives." Although terrible things happened in the tragedies—murder, incest, suicide, rape, mutilation—the attitude of the play toward these events was deeply moral. Violence for its own sake was not the concern of the playwright, and violence was never depicted onstage.

The tragedies were primarily based on the legends of royal families—usually the dynasties of Thebes, Sparta, and Argos—dating from the Age of Heroes of which Homer sang in his epics (Figure 3.9). Since the audience already knew these stories, their interest focused on the playwright's treatment of a familiar tale, his ideas about its moral significance, and how his language shaped those ideas.

The plots dealt with fundamental human issues with no easy solutions, such as the decrees of the state versus the conscience of the individual or divine law versus human law. Humans were forced to make hard choices without being able to foresee the consequences of their decisions. Nonetheless, the dramatists af-

Figure 3.10 *Orestes Slaying Aegisthus.* Ca. late sixth century B.C.E. Kunsthistorisches Museum, Vienna. *This red-figure vase painting presents a different version of events in Argos from that given by Aeschylus in the* Libation Bearers, *the second play of the* Oresteia. *The vase painter portrays Clytemnestra bearing an ax (left), a detail Aeschylus omitted, and the sister between Orestes and his mother is not named Electra as she is in the* Oresteia. *However, painter and playwright agree that Orestes killed Aegisthus, his mother's lover.*

firmed that a basic moral order existed underneath the shifting tide of human affairs. The political leaders of Athens recognized and accepted tragedy's ethical significance and educative function and thus made the plays into civic spectacles. For example, the audience was composed of citizens seated according to voting precincts, and Athenian warriors' orphans, who were wards of the polis, were honored at the performances.

According to the Greek philosopher Aristotle, whose immensely influential theory of tragedy, the *Poetics*, was based on his study of the dramas of the Hellenic Age, the purpose of tragedy was to work a cathartic, or purging, effect on the audience, to "arouse pity and terror" so that these negative emotions could be drained from the soul. The tragic heroes were warnings, not models; the spectators were instructed to seek modest lives and not aim too high. Many tragedians pursued these themes and competed in the Dionysia, but the works of only three still survive—Aeschylus, Sophocles, and Euripides.

Aeschylus Aeschylus [ES-kuh-luhs] (about 525–about 456 B.C.E.), the earliest of the three dramatists,

won first prize in the Great Dionysia thirteen times. He composed about ninety plays, but only seven are extant. His masterpiece, the *Oresteia*, is the only trilogy that has survived, and even here the satyr-play is missing. The framing plot is the homecoming from Troy of the Greek king Agamemnon, who had sinned by sacrificing his daughter to gain military success; his murder by his vengeful and adulterous wife, Clytemnestra; and the dire consequences of this killing.

Aeschylus's treatment of these terrible events in the *Oresteia* embodies some of the principles of Classicism. In the first place, Aeschylus shows great simplicity by avoiding distracting subplots: The first play, *Agamemnon*, tells the story of the king's death and Clytemnestra's triumph; the second, the *Libation Bearers*, relates the vengeance murder of Clytemnestra by her son, Orestes; and the third, *Eumenides*, halts—with the help of the Olympians Athena and Apollo—the cycle of revenge by instituting an Athenian court to try such cases. The trilogy is symmetrical in that Agamemnon's murder in the first play serves as punishment for the sacrifice of his daughter, Clytemnestra's death in the second avenges her slaying of Agamemnon, and the courtroom drama of the third absolves Orestes of the crime of matricide.

Finally, Aeschylus shows great restraint inasmuch as all deaths occur offstage, and the chorus or messengers only describe them. However, for the Athenian audience, the *Oresteia* had moral significance as well as stylistic power. By transforming the Furies, the blind champions of vengeance killing, into the "Kindly Ones" *(Eumenides),* Aeschylus, in effect, affirmed the ethical superiority of the rational Olympians over the earthbound chthonian divinities (see Chapter 2). In the *Oresteia,* Aeschylus confronts and resolves the opposition between several seemingly irreconcilable polarities—Olympian and chthonian gods, divine and human justice, religious cult and civic ritual, and fate and free will (Figure 3.10).

Sophocles   Sophocles [SOF-uh-kleez] (about 496–406 B.C.E.), the most prolific of the great tragedians, wrote about 125 plays, but only 7 survive. He was popular among the Athenians, who awarded him first prize twenty-four times. Sophocles' *Antigone* (442 B.C.E.) expresses beautifully the principles of Classical tragedy. The simple plot treats the conflicts between King Creon and his niece Antigone. The principal, although not the sole, philosophical issue explored by the play is whether human or divine law should take precedence. Antigone's two brothers have killed each other in a dispute over the Theban crown. Creon decrees that Eteocles, who died defending the city, be buried with honor but that the body of the rebel Polyneices be left as carrion for wild beasts. Antigone, whose name in Greek means "born to oppose," defies his order and buries her brother in compliance with religious teachings. Arrested and imprisoned, Antigone hangs herself, and Creon's son and wife kill themselves. Too late, King Creon sees the light; he gives up his throne, saying, "There is no man can bear this guilt but I."

Several tensions are at issue here. Creon represents the typical tyrant, concerned only with "law and order." His son, Haemon, is the voice of democracy, opposing the tyrannical will of his father. Creon believes in the superiority of public power over domestic life, in the necessity of the state to seek power for its own sake, in the priority of war over the commands of love, and in the right of men to control women. When the king tries to persuade his son to renounce his love for the disobedient Antigone, they argue about all four of these issues. Whether the Athenian citizens sided with Creon or Haemon is unknown, but *Antigone* has become the classic example of a tragic dilemma where two rights confront each other. In his desire for balance, Sophocles gives equally powerful arguments to the play's opposing characters.

Sophocles returned to the history of the Theban dynasty in later plays about Antigone's ill-fated father, Oedipus. In *Oedipus the King,* he tells how the Theban ruler unwittingly kills his father and marries his mother and later blinds himself to atone for his guilt. Though fate has a pivotal role in Oedipus's story, the playwright also emphasizes the part the hero's weakness plays in his downfall. Aristotle's *Poetics* held up this work as a model of Greek tragedy. In *Oedipus at Colonus,* his last play, Sophocles portrays the former king at peace with himself and his destiny.

Euripides   By the time Euripides [yu-RIP-uh-deez] (about 480–406 B.C.E.) was writing for the stage, Athens was fighting for its existence in the Peloponnesian War. Euripides was in tune with the skeptical mood of the later years of this struggle, and by presenting unorthodox versions of myths and legends, he exposed the foolishness of some popular beliefs and, sometimes, the emptiness of contemporary values. When he staged *The Trojan Women* in 415 B.C.E., the Athenians could not have missed the parallel between the cruel enslavement of the women of Troy after the Greeks destroyed their city and the fate of the women of Melos, which Athens had just subjugated.

For his ninety or more tragedies (of which eighteen survive), the Athenians awarded the first prize to Euripides only five times, perhaps because his unorthodox plays angered the audience. But later ages, far removed from the stresses of Hellenic times, found his dramas more to their liking. Among the extant works, *The Bacchae* is his masterpiece, a gruesome tale about the introduction of the worship of Dionysus into Thebes. In this play, the bacchae, or bacchantes (another name for the followers of Dionysus), blinded by religious frenzy, kill the king of Thebes under the delusion that he is a wild animal. Euripides' dark tragedy may have been a warning to the citizens of Athens about the dangers of both excess and repression in religion and politics.

Euripides followed Classical principles in *The Bacchae,* using a single plot, offstage violence, and well-defined conflict, but he also extended the range of Classical drama with his unorthodox, even romantic, language and his skeptical treatment of familiar themes. Moreover, Euripides pointed the way toward a different sort of theater by having the severed head of the hero brought onstage at the end of the tragedy.

With Euripides, the creative phase of Classical theater came to an end. The playwrights who followed him seem to have read their works aloud rather than staging them with actors and choruses. The plays of all the Greek dramatists were presented frequently throughout Greece, however, as well as later in the Macedonian and Roman Empires.

Theater: Comedy

Comedies were performed in the Great Dionysia just as the tragedies were, and they were also entered in contests in another festival, known as the Lesser Dionysia, celebrated in late winter. The comedies refused to take anyone or anything seriously. They featured burlesque actions, buffoonery, slapstick, obscenity, and horseplay, and actors wore grotesque costumes with padded bellies or rumps to give a ridiculous effect. Comic playwrights invented their own plots and focused on contemporary matters: politics, philosophies, the new social classes, and well-known personalities. Even the deities were ridiculed and portrayed in embarrassing situations.

The freedom of the comic playwrights could exist only in a democracy. And yet the freedom was limited to a highly ritualized setting—the drama festivals—which allowed, even encouraged, the overturning of rules and the burlesquing of traditions. This controlled expression of the unspeakable provided a catharsis that strengthened communal bonds in the polis. At the same time, the authors demonstrated their faith in the basic good sense of the average citizen.

The comedies of Aristophanes [air-uh-STOF-uh-neez] (about 445–about 388 B.C.E.) are the primary source for what is known as **Old Comedy,** comic Greek plays with a strong element of political criticism. Aristophanes composed forty-four works in all, of which eleven are extant. Like Euripides, he wrote his plays for war-torn Athens, and he satirized famous contemporaries such as the thinker Socrates, depicting him as a hopeless dreamer. Aristophanes must have stepped on many toes, for the Athenians awarded him first prize only four times.

In *Lysistrata*, Aristophanes transcended the limitations of the comedic form and approached the timeless quality of the tragedies. A sexually explicit and hilarious comedy, *Lysistrata* points out the absurdity of the prolonged Peloponnesian War and, by implication, all war. In the play, Lysistrata, an Athenian matron, persuades the women of Athens and Sparta to withhold sex from their husbands until they sign a peace treaty. Filled with sexual innuendos, obscenities, and ridiculous allusions to tragic dramas, the play ends with stirring reminders to the Greeks of their common ancestry, their joint victory over the Persians earlier in the century, and their reverence for the same gods. First staged in 411 B.C.E., seven years before Sparta won the Peloponnesian War, this play commented on but failed to derail Athens's headlong rush to disaster (Figure 3.11).

After the Peloponnesian War and the restoration of a harsher democracy in 403 B.C.E., free speech was se-

Figure 3.11 Detail, Scene from a Comedy. Mid–fourth century B.C.E. Ht. of vase 15⅔". British Museum. *This scene, painted on a mixing bowl, portrays a situation from a Greek comedy. The actors on the right and left are outfitted in the grotesque costume of comedy with padded rumps and genitals. That these characters are onstage is indicated by the decorations at the bottom of the frame.*

verely repressed in Athens. Comedies still relied on burlesque and slapstick, but their political edge was blunted. For all practical purposes, the great creative age of Greek theater was now over.

Music

Like other peoples of the ancient Near East, the Greeks used music both in civic and religious events and in private entertainment. But the Greeks also gave music a new importance, making it one of the humanities along with art, literature, theater, and philosophy. Music became a form of expression subject to rules, styles, and rational analysis. One reason for this was that the Greeks believed music fulfilled an ethical function in the training of young citizens. They also believed that music had divine origins and was inspired by Euterpe, one of the nine muses (thus the word *music*).

Nevertheless, the vast library of Greek music has vanished. What knowledge there is of that lost heritage, which can be only partially reconstructed from surviving treatises on musical theory and references in other writings, shows a tradition that, despite some differences, became the foundation of Western music. Greek music apparently followed the diatonic system, which had been invented by Pythagoras, using a scale of eight notes, each of which was determined by its numerical ratio to the lowest tone. The Greek composers also devised a series of scales, called **modes,** which functioned roughly like major and minor keys in later Western music. The modes, however, were not interchangeable the way keys are, because the Greeks believed that each mode produced a different emotional and ethical effect on the listener. Thus, the Dorian mode, martial and grave in its emotional impact, was thought by the Greeks to make hearers brave and dignified; the tender and sorrowing Lydian mode, to make them sentimental and weak; and the passionate and wild Phrygian mode, to make them excited and headstrong. Believing that such emotional manipulation made free citizens difficult to govern, Plato banished virtually all music from his ideal republic. Modern research has been able to reproduce all the Greek modes, but otherwise this music remains a mystery.

Despite music's high ethical status in Greece, it had no independent role in Hellenic culture. Instead, music was integrated with verse, notably in epic and lyric poetry and in tragedy and comedy, with either the lyre (a stringed instrument) or the aulos (a wind instrument) providing accompaniment.

History

The study of history began in the fifth century B.C.E., when inquisitive and articulate Greeks started to analyze the meaning of their immediate past and to write down in prose the results of their research, or *historia*—the Greek word for inquiry. The Greeks before the Classical period had only a dim sense of their past; what they knew came from Homer, random artifacts, and the ruins of Mycenaean grandeur. Herodotus [he-ROD-uh-tuhs] (about 484 B.C.E.–about 430 B.C.E.) was the first to approach history as a separate study and the first to practice historical writing in anything like the modern sense. He was motivated by the belief that the present had its causes in the past and could be a guide for the future. His *Histories* recorded and analyzed the Persian Wars, which Herodotus interpreted as Europe versus Asia, or West versus East. In his desire to be fair to both sides, he traveled to Persia and recorded what he learned there.

The *Histories* have been criticized for implausible and inaccurate information, but Herodotus's clear prose style, his concern for research, his efforts to be impartial, his belief in historical cause and effect, and his desire to leave a record of the past as a legacy to future generations have justly earned him the title "Father of History."

Yet, for all his excellence, Herodotus pales in comparison with Thucydides [thew-SID-uh-deez] (died about 401 B.C.E.). His subject was the Peloponnesian War, of which he was an eyewitness at times. Thucydides was much more skeptical and inquiring than Herodotus, and although he was an avid democrat and an admirer of Pericles, he strove to be completely fair in his account of Periclean Athens. He saw the weaknesses of his beloved polis and realized the baleful effects of imperialism. In his *History of the Peloponnesian War,* he even wrote objectively of his own role as the losing admiral in a naval battle.

Thucydides also used ordinary events to illuminate human motives and fundamental causes and effects in history. Like the Greek dramatists, he showed that human weaknesses and flaws created the real-life tragedies he observed around him. His insight into human nature was penetrating as he chronicled how individuals shift loyalties and redefine their values to justify their actions.

This masterful writer rose above his narrative to give lessons to future generations, arguing that events that happened in the past would, at some time and in similar ways, recur. Yet he denied that history repeats itself simplistically, and he warned that his book must be read closely and thoughtfully if it was to be understood wisely.

Philosophy, Science, and Medicine

During the Hellenic Age, philosophy and science experienced a radical transformation. Both types of learning came to focus on the place of humans in society, rather than concentrating on the composition of the natural world. And both now approached their studies with the conviction that human behavior and the natural world could be understood, through the use of observation and reason.

When the Hellenic Age opened, natural philosophy remained divided into two major camps: the materialists and the idealists (see Chapter 2). The materialists, who perpetuated the inquiries of Thales and the Milesian school, believed that the world was made of some basic physical thing. The idealists, in contrast, whose thought stemmed from Pythagoras and the Sicilian school, were nonmaterialists, reasoning that the physical world was illusory and that behind it was a spiritual force or a metaphysical power.

By the mid–fifth century B.C.E., this simple pattern was being challenged by new philosophies, and by 400 B.C.E., a revolution in thought had occurred that overshadowed everything that had gone before. The

Table 3.1 PHILOSOPHY IN THE HELLENIC AGE	
PHILOSOPHY	EMPHASIS
Pre-Socratic	The physical world; nature; debate over materialism and idealism
Sophist	Humanistic values; practical skills, such as public speaking and logic
Socratic	Enduring moral and intellectual order of the universe; the psyche (mind/soul); "Virtue is Knowledge"
Platonist	Ideas (Forms) are the basis of everything; dualism, the split between the world of Ideas and the everyday world; rationalism; severe moderation in ethics
Aristotelian	Natural world is the only world; empiricism, using observation, classification, and comparison; "golden mean" in ethics

first assault came from Elea, in Sicily, where a new school of thinkers proposed to reconcile materialism and idealism. Then, in Athens, the Sophists questioned philosophical inquiry itself and the notion of absolute truth. The corrosive ideas of these figures provoked Socrates, the most revolutionary thinker of the entire ancient world, to respond to their claims. Socrates' life is regarded as a watershed in Greek thought. All Greek thinkers before him are now known as Pre-Socratics, and those who came after him—chiefly Plato and Aristotle in Hellenic Greece—followed his lead in studying the human experience (Table 3.1).

The Pre-Socratics   The major pre-Socratic thinkers were concerned with determining the nature of the physical world. For Parmenides [par-MEN-uh-deez] (about 515–? B.C.E.) and his followers in Elea, for example, the world was a single, unchanging, unmoving object whose order could be known through human reason. This attempt to reconcile materialism and idealism was modified by Parmenides' student Empedocles [em-PED-uh-kleez] (about 484–about 424 B.C.E.), who claimed that everything, animate or inanimate, originated in the four elements of earth, water, fire, and air. These elements were unchanging, but the opposing forces of Love and Strife could combine them in different ways, to the detriment or benefit of humans. This essentially metaphysical explanation of change later influenced Aristotle.

The Atomists, another school of pre-Socratic thinkers, believed that everything was composed of

atoms—eternal, invisible bodies of varying size that, by definition, could not be divided into smaller units—and the void, the empty space between the atoms. Atomic theory was developed most fully by Democritus [de-MOK-ruht-us] of Thrace (about 460–? B.C.E.). The movement and shape of the atoms were sufficient to explain not only physical objects but also feelings, tastes, sight, ideas—in short, every aspect of the physical world.

Anaxagoras [an-ak-SAG-uh-ruhs] (about 500–428 B.C.E.), although not an Atomist, also explained the world in terms of small particles. His unique contribution was the idea that the combinations and divisions of these particles were controlled by a nonphysical agency he called *nous* (reason or mind). Socrates praised him for the originality of this conception and then faulted him for seeing *nous* only as a mechanical force without religious significance.

The Sophists   The Sophists—from the Greek word *sophia*, or "wisdom"—scorned pre-Socratic speculation about atoms and elements as irrelevant and useless. These traveling teachers claimed to offer their students (for a fee) knowledge that guaranteed success in life. Their emphasis on the development of practical skills, such as effective public speaking, led their critics to accuse them of cynicism and a lack of interest in higher ethical values, but the Sophists were deeply serious and committed to humanistic values. Protagoras [pro-TAG-uh-ruhs] (481–411 B.C.E.), the most renowned of the Sophists, proclaimed in a dictum that "man is the measure of all things." This summed up the Sophists' argument that human beings, as the center of the universe, have the power to make judgments about themselves and their world. The Sophists helped free the human spirit to be critical and creative. If there was a danger in their teaching, it was a tendency toward unrestrained skepticism. By stressing that human beings had the power to shape the world, the Sophists opened themselves to charges of impiety and undermining traditional values, because the traditional Greek view was that the gods controlled everything.

The Socratic Revolution   Socrates [SAH-kruh-teez] (about 470–399 B.C.E.), the thinker who launched a new era in philosophy, did not hesitate to condemn the Sophists. He claimed to oppose everything they stood for, especially what he thought was the Sophist tendency to overvalue skepticism and thus undermine values without offering new ones in their place. But Socrates shared certain traits with the Sophists, such as his rejection of philosophizing about nature, his focus on human problems, and his desire to empower individuals to make their own moral choices. What basically separated Socrates from the Sophists was his

Figure 3.12 *Socrates*. Ca. 200 B.C.E.–100 C.E. Ht. 10½". British Museum. *This Roman marble copy of the original Greek statue supports the unflattering descriptions of Socrates by his contemporaries. By portraying the philosopher with a receding hairline and a dumpy body, the anonymous sculptor has made one of the world's most extraordinary human beings look very ordinary.*

passionate conviction that an enduring moral and intellectual order existed in the universe.

Socrates' method for arriving at true moral and intellectual values was deceptively simple yet maddeningly elusive. At the heart of his thinking was the *psyche* (mind, or soul); being immortal, the psyche was deemed more important than the mortal and doomed body. Those who want wisdom must protect, nourish, and expand their psyches by giving their minds the maximum amount of knowledge, but not just any knowledge. The knowledge the psyche acquired had to be won through stimulating conversations and debates as well as by contemplation of abstract virtues and moral values. Only then could the psyche approach its highest potential.

"Virtue is Knowledge," claimed Socrates; he meant that a person who knows the truth, acquired through personal struggle to self-enlightenment, will not commit evil deeds. And this moral dictum may be reversed: Those who do wrong do so out of ignorance. If people used their psyches to think more deeply and clearly, they would lead virtuous lives. His belief in the essential goodness of human nature and the necessity of well-defined knowledge became a central tenet of Western thought.

After having pointed out the proper path to wisdom, Socrates left the rest up to his students. Bombarding inquiring youths with questions on such topics as the meaning of justice, he used rigorous logic to refute all the squirming students' attempts at precise definition. Then—as shown by Plato's dialogues, the principal source for what we know about Socrates—the students, collapsing into confusion, admitted the serious gaps in their knowledge. Socrates' step-by-step questions, interspersed with gentle humor and ironic jabs, honed his students' logical skills and compelled them to begin a quest for knowledge in light of their self-confessed ignorance. The Socratic method was adopted by many teachers in Greece and Rome and remains an honored pedagogical device.

The Athenians of this era began to perceive Socrates as a threat to their way of life. This short, homely, and rather insignificant-looking man—as surviving statues reveal—aroused suspicion in the polis with his public arguments (Figure 3.12). When Athens fell to the Spartans in 404 B.C.E., opposition to Socrates began to swell. Many citizens now found subversion or even blasphemy in his words and in the behavior of his followers. Five years after the end of the Peloponnesian War, Socrates was accused of impiety and of corrupting the Athenian youth, and a jury declared him guilty and sentenced him to die. Plato, a former student, was so moved by Socrates' eloquent, though ineffective, defense and by the injustice of his death that the younger man dedicated the remainder of his life to righting the wrong and explaining the Socratic philosophy.

Plato also made Socrates' last days the subject of four works: the *Euthyphro* (a discussion of piety on the eve of his trial), the *Apology* (his defense before the court), the *Crito* (an explanation of his willingness to die for his beliefs), and the *Phaedo* (a deathbed scene with his argument in support of immortality).

Plato The spirit of Socrates hovers over the rest of Greek philosophy, especially in the accomplishments of his most famous student, Plato (about 427–347 B.C.E.). Plato's philosophy is the fountainhead of Western **idealism,** a thought system that emphasizes spiritual values and makes ideas, rather than matter, the basis of everything that exists. **Platonism** arose out of certain premises that were Socratic in origin—the concept of the psyche and the theory of remembrance. Like Socrates, Plato emphasized the immortal and immutable psyche over the mortal and changeful body. But Plato advanced a new polarity, favoring the invisible world of the Forms, or Ideas, in opposition to the physical world. The psyche's true home was the world of the Forms, which it inhabited before birth and after death—the time when the psyche was lost in wonder among the eternal Ideas. In contrast, the body lived exclusively in the material world, completely absorbed by the life of the senses. Once trapped inside the body, the psyche could glimpse the higher reality, or Forms, only through remembrance.

Nonetheless, Plato thought that through a set of mental exercises the psyche would be able to recall the Ideas to which it had once been exposed. The best training for the psyche was the study of mathematics, since mathematics required signs and symbols to represent other things. After the mastery of mathematics, the student proceeded, with the help of logic, to higher stages of abstract learning, such as defining the Forms of Justice, Beauty, and Love. By showing that wisdom came only after an intellectual progression that culminated in an understanding of the absolute Ideas, Plato silenced the Sophists, who claimed that knowledge was relative.

A major implication of Plato's idealism was that the psyche and the body were constantly at war. The psyche's attempts to remember the lost Ideas met resistance from the body's pursuit of power, fame, and physical comforts. This dualism especially plagued the philosopher, the lover of wisdom; but the true philosopher took comfort in recognizing that at death the psyche would return freely to the world of the Forms.

Plato identified the Form of the Good, the ultimate Idea, with God, yet the Platonic deity was neither the creator of the world nor the absolute and final power. Instead, Plato's deity was necessary for his idealism to

function; in his thought, God was the source from which descended the imperfect objects of the natural world. In a related theological notion, he, like Socrates, attributed the presence of evil to ignorance; but Plato added the psyche's misdirected judgment and insatiable bodily appetites as other causes of evil.

Socrates' death provoked Plato to envision a perfect state where justice flourished. The book that resulted from Plato's speculations—the *Republic*—sets forth his model state and, incidentally, launched the study of political philosophy in the West. Plato thought that a just state could be realized only when all social classes worked together for the good of the whole, each class performing its assigned tasks. Because of the importance of the psyche, social status was determined by the ability to reason, not by wealth or inheritance. A tiny elite of philosopher-kings and philosopher-queens, who were the best qualified to run the state, reigned. Possessing wisdom as a result of their education in the Platonic system, they lived simply, shunning the creature comforts that corrupted weaker rulers.

The two lower ranks were similarly equipped for their roles in society by their intellects and their training: A middle group provided police and military protection, and the third and largest segment operated the economy. In Plato's dream world, both the individual and the society aimed for virtue, and the laws and the institutions ensured that the ideal would be achieved.

Aristotle Socrates may have been revolutionary; Plato was certainly poetic; but Aristotle [AIR-uh-stot-uhl] (384–322 B.C.E.) had the most comprehensive mind of the ancient world. His curiosity and vast intellect led him into every major field of inquiry of his time except mathematics and music. Born in Macedonia, he was connected to some of the most glittering personalities of his day. He first studied philosophy under Plato in Athens and then tutored the future Alexander the Great back at Philip's court. After Philip's conquest of Greece, Aristotle settled in Athens and opened a school, the Lyceum, that quickly rivaled the Academy, the school Plato had established.

Although his philosophy owed much to Platonism, Aristotle emphasized the role of the human senses. To Aristotle, the natural world was the only world; no separate, invisible realm of Ideas existed. Nature could be studied and understood by observation, classification, and comparison of data from the physical world —that is, through the empirical method.

Aristotle rejected the world of the Forms because he believed that Form and Matter were inseparable, both rooted in nature. Each material object contained a predetermined Form that, with proper training or nourishment, would evolve into its final Form and ultimate

Figure 3.13 The Delphic Sanctuary. Aerial view. Late sixth century–late fourth century B.C.E. *The ruins of Apollo's temple—this is an active earthquake zone—are marked by a rectangular foundation and a few standing columns. A Sacred Way, or road, zigzagged up the mountain to the temple's entrance. During the fourth century B.C.E., a gymnasium, or school, for boys and a theater were established in the sanctuary, and a stadium was constructed for athletic contests.*

purpose. This growth process, in his view, was potentiality evolving into actuality, as when an embryo becomes a human or a seed matures into a plant. Thus, the philosopher could conclude that everything had a purpose, or end.

Aristotle's thought rested on the concept of God, which he equated with the First Cause. Aristotle's God was a philosopher's deity, purely rational, self-absorbed, and uncaring about the world or its inhabitants. Had this deity been anything else, Aristotle's God would not have been the supreme power, or First Cause.

Rejecting Platonic dualism and its exclusive regard for the psyche, Aristotle devised a down-to-earth ethical goal—a sound mind in a healthy body—that he called happiness. To achieve happiness, he advised, in his *Nicomachean Ethics*, striking a mean, or a balance, between extremes of behavior. For example, courage is the mean between the excess of foolhardiness and the deficiency of cowardice. Noting that actions like murder and adultery are vicious by their very nature, he condemned them as being unable to be moderated. Although Aristotle disavowed many of Plato's ideas, he agreed with his former mentor that the cultivation of the higher intellect was more important than that of the body.

Aristotle's ethics were related to his politics, for he taught that happiness finally depended on the type of government under which an individual lived. Unlike Plato, who based his politics on speculative thinking, Aristotle reached his political views after careful research. After collecting over 150 state constitutions, Aristotle, in his *Politics*, classified and compared them, concluding that the best form of government was a constitutional regime ruled by the middle class. His preference for the middle class stemmed from his belief that they, exciting neither envy from the poor nor contempt from the wealthy, would honor and work for the good of all.

Aristotle's influence on Western civilization is immeasurable. His writings formed the core of knowledge that Christian scholars later studied as they struggled to keep the light of civilization burning after the collapse of the Roman Empire. Likewise, Jewish and Moslem thinkers ranked his books just below their own religious scriptures. Today, Aristotelianism is embedded in the official theology of the Roman Catholic Church, and Aristotle's logic continues to be taught in college philosophy courses.

Medicine   Little is known of the life of Hippocrates [hip-OCK-re-teez] (about 460–377 B.C.E.), the major figure in Classical Greek medicine. Plato mentions him in two of his dialogues, and later Greek writers noted his contributions to medicine. In his own lifetime, he was

Figure 3.14 Second Temple of Hera at Poseidonia. Ca. 450 B.C.E. Limestone. *This temple of Hera is among the best-preserved structures from the ancient world. Since Hera may have been a chthonian goddess before becoming consort to Olympian Zeus, it is appropriate that this Doric temple, with its ground-hugging appearance, be her monument.*

highly regarded, and he apparently traveled extensively through Greece and Asia Minor, healing the sick and teaching aspiring physicians.

Hippocrates was born on the island of Cos in the Aegean Sea and probably taught at the medical school located there. In the second and third centuries C.E., many years after his death, scholars collected about seventy works attributed to him, known as the Hippocratic Collection, which ensured his future reputation. Today, Hippocrates is still known as the "Father of Medicine" and is identified with the Hippocratic Oath, which most medical students take at the commencement of their medical careers. This oath, which he certainly did not compose, spells out the duties and responsibilities of a physician and sets ethical standards and personal behavior practices.

Regardless of how little is known of Hippocrates, he is still recognized as one of the first individuals in medicine to reject supernatural explanations as causes of illness. Instead, he observed and studied the body and its parts from a scientific and clinical point of view. Most specifically, Hippocrates believed that diseases were caused by imbalances of the four "humors," which he identified as the four fluids—blood, phlegm, black bile, and yellow bile—within the physical body. He asserted that disease was not the invasion of evil spirits or controlling deities. If these humors were kept in balance—such as by administering drugs, prescribing diets, or removing excess blood or other humors—then the body would heal itself and the patient would recover.

In one of the works attributed to him, Hippocrates discusses the "sacred" disease, or what is now known as epilepsy. At the time, conventional wisdom explained epilepsy as a "divine affliction," a sign that the patient was favored by the gods. In contrast, Hippocrates argues that epilepsy has natural causes that can be identified and treated. He also comments on the brain, terming it the source of all emotions and senses and the "most powerful organ in the human body."

Architecture

Of all the Greek art forms, architecture most powerfully embodied the Classical ideals of the Hellenic Age. The stone temple, the supreme expression of the

Hellenic building genius, now received its definitive shape. Ironically, the Doric temple, which had originated in the Archaic Age, reached perfection in Ionian Athens. The versatile Athenians also perfected a new architectural order, the **Ionic,** which reflected more clearly their cultural tradition.

Sanctuaries Before there were temples, however, Greece had sanctuaries, places considered sacred to a god or a goddess. Of these sacred places, Apollo's shrine at Delphi was the oldest and the most famous (Figure 3.13). Delphi, thought to be the center of the earth, was hallowed ground to the entire Greek world, and the major poleis supported the god's priesthood there. Apollo's temple was the most splendid building on the site. Inside was Apollo's oracle—the only woman permitted at Delphi—to whom people journeyed from all over Greece with their questions.

With the rise of the poleis, the concept of a holy place set aside from the business of everyday life was adapted to the religious needs of each community. By the Hellenic Age, each polis had its own sacred area, usually built on a hill or protected by walls, which contained buildings and altars. Although each polis worshiped the entire pantheon of deities, one god or goddess was gradually singled out as a patron, and a temple was erected to house the statue of that particular divinity.

The Temple: The Perfection of the Form By Hellenic times, the Greek world was polarized between eastern (the mainland and the Aegean Islands) and western (Magna Graecia) styles of temple design, although in both styles the temples were rectilinear and of post-beam-triangle construction. Influenced by the Pythagorean quest for harmony through mathematical rules,

Figure 3.15 ICTINUS AND CALLICRATES. The Parthenon. Third quarter of the fifth century B.C.E. Pentelic marble. Athens. *A great humanistic icon, the Parthenon has had a long history since its days as a Greek temple. It served successively as a Christian church, a mosque, and an ammunitions depot, until it was accidentally blown up at the end of the seventeenth century C.E. Today, concerned nations are cooperating with the Greek government through UNESCO to preserve this noble ruin.*

the eastern builders had standardized six as the perfect number of columns for the ends of temples and thirteen, or twice the number of end columns plus one, as the perfect number of columns for the sides. These balanced proportions, along with simple designs and restrained decorative schemes, made the eastern temples majestically expressive of Classical ideals.

Architects in western Greece, somewhat removed from the centers of Classical culture, were more experimental. Their buildings deviated from the eastern ideals, as can be seen in the Second Temple of Hera at Poseidonia, built of limestone in about 450 B.C.E. (Figure 3.14). The best preserved of all Greek temples, this Doric structure does not have the harmonious proportions of the eastern version of this style. Although the Second Temple of Hera owed much to eastern influences, including the six columns at the ends and the porches, it had too many (fourteen)

Figure 3.16 CALLICRATES. Temple of Athena Nike. Late fifth century B.C.E. Marble. Athens. *Designed by Callicrates, one of the Parthenon's architects, this miniature temple was begun after 427 B.C.E. and probably completed before 420 B.C.E. Like the Parthenon, it was dedicated to the city's patron goddess, Athena, though here she was honored as Nike, goddess of victory. This temple's simple plan includes a square cella with four Ionic columns at the front and back and a sculptural frieze, devoted to scenes of mythic and contemporary battles, encircling the upper exterior walls.*

SLICE OF LIFE
Secrets of a Successful Marriage in Ancient Greece

XENOPHON
From *Oeconomicus*

With their boundless curiosity, it is not surprising that the Greeks were concerned with how to have a good marriage, as this piece by Xenophon (about 445–355 B.C.E.) demonstrates. A famous military commander, Xenophon was also a historian, essayist, and student of Socrates. Nonetheless, his discussion of marriage, taken from his essay on domestic economy, or home life, is considered a fairly accurate depiction of the marital ideal among well-to-do Greeks of the time. In this selection, he expounds his ideas through the characters of Socrates and Ischomachus, a rich landowner.

During Hellenic times, literacy increased among the Greeks, as compared with the achievements of earlier peoples of the Near East and Egypt. This growth in literacy was mainly the result of the rise of democracy, in which education became a major goal of the citizenry. Despite the increase, though, the survival of written records by ordinary Greeks is spotty. Hence, this Slice of Life is from the writings of a famous Greek author, not by an ordinary person.

I [Socrates] said, "I should very much like you to tell me, Ischomachus, whether you yourself trained your wife to become the sort of woman that she ought to be, or whether she already knew how to carry out her duties when you took her as your wife from her father and mother."

[Ischomachus replied,] "What could she have known when I took her as my wife, Socrates? She was not yet fifteen when she came to me, and had spent her previous years under careful supervision so that she might see and hear and speak as little as possible. . . .

"[A]s soon as she was sufficiently tamed and domesticated so as to be able to carry on a conversation, I questioned her more or less as follows: 'Tell me, wife, have you ever thought about why I married you and why your parents gave you to me? It must be quite obvious to you, I am sure, that there was no shortage of partners with whom we might sleep. I, on my part, and your parents, on your behalf, considered who was the best partner we could choose for managing an estate and for children. And I chose you, and your parents, apparently, chose me, out of those who were eligible. Now if some day the god grants us children, then we shall consider how to train them in the best way possi-

ble. For this will be a blessing to us both, to obtain the best allies and support in old age. But at present we two share this estate. I go on paying everything I have into the common fund; and you deposited into it everything you brought with you. There is no need to calculate precisely which of us has contributed more, but to be well aware of this: that the better partner is the one who makes the more valuable contribution. . . .

"'Because both the indoor and the outdoor tasks require work and concern, I think the god, from the very beginning, designed the nature of woman for the indoor work and concerns and the nature of man for the outdoor work. For he prepared man's body and mind to be more capable of enduring cold and heat and travelling and military campaigns, and so he assigned the outdoor work to him. Because the woman was physically less capable of endurance, I think the god has evidently assigned the indoor work to her. . . .

"'Because it is necessary for both of them to give and to take, he gave both of them equal powers of memory and concern. So you would not be able to distinguish whether the female or male sex has the larger share of these. And he gave them both equally the ability to practise self-control too, when it is needed. . . . [B]ecause they are not equally well endowed with all the same natural aptitudes, they are consequently more in need of each other, and the bond is more beneficial to the couple, since one is capable where the other is deficient.'"

Interpreting This Slice of Life Based on this selection, **what** was the role of women in marriage in Hellenic Greece? At **what** age was the wife in the selection married? **What** impact would the wife's youth have on the dynamics of the marriage? **Discuss** the role of material matters (money, property, and other forms of wealth) in Greek marriage, as depicted here. **What** attitude does the speaker, Ischomachus, have toward male and female intellectual abilities? **Why** does such advice on marriage appear in a work on domestic economy? **Compare and contrast** modern attitudes toward marriage with those represented in this selection.

columns on the sides, its columns were too thick, and the low-pitched roof made the building seem squat.

Between 447 and 438 B.C.E., the architects Ictinus [ik-TIE-nuhs] and Callicrates [kuh-LICK-ruh-teez] perfected the eastern-style Doric temple in the Parthenon, a temple on Athens's Acropolis dedicated to Athena (Figure 3.15). When completed, this temple established a new standard of Classicism, with eight columns on the ends and seventeen on the sides and with the numerical ratio of 9:4 used throughout, expressed, for

example, in the relation of a column's height to its diameter. Inside, the builders designed two chambers, an east room for a 40-foot-high statue of Athena and a smaller room housing the Delian League treasury. The rest of the Acropolis project, finally finished in 405 B.C.E., included the Propylaea, the gate leading to the sanctuary; the temple of Athena Nike, a gift to Athens's patron goddess thanking her for a military victory (Figure 3.16); and the Erechtheum, a temple dedicated to three deities.

Ictinus and Callicrates introduced many subtle variations, called refinements, into their designs so that no line is exactly straight, horizontal, or perpendicular. For example, the stepped base of the temple forms a gentle arc so that the ends are lower than the middle; the floor slopes slightly to the edges; and the columns tilt inward away from the ends. These and other refinements were no accidents but, instead, were intended to be corrections for real and imaginary optical illusions. The Parthenon's fame exerted such authority in later times that these refinements, along with harmonious proportions, became standardized as the essence of Greek architecture.

The second order of Greek architecture, the Ionic, originated in the late Archaic Age and, like the Doric, came to flower in Hellenic times. The Ionic style, freer than the Doric and more graceful, reflected its origins in the Ionian world; traditionally, the Ionians contrasted their opulence with the simplicity of the Dorians. In place of the alternating metopes and triglyphs of Doric buildings, the Ionic temple had a running frieze to which sculptured figures might be added. More decorated than the plain Doric, the Ionic columns had elegant bases, and their tops were crowned with capitals that suggested either a scroll's ends or a ram's horns. What solidified the Ionic temple's impression of elegance were its slender and delicate columns.

The Athenians chose the Ionic style for the exquisite, though eccentric, Erechtheum, the last of the great buildings erected on the Acropolis (Figure 3.17). The artistic freedom associated with the Ionic style may have led the architect, Mnesicles [NES-uh-kleez], to make the floor plan asymmetrical and to introduce so many design variations, but a more likely explanation was Mnesicles' need to integrate three existing shrines into a single building—those of the Olympians Athena and Poseidon and King Erechtheus, who introduced the horse to Athens. Mnesicles took the unusual step of stressing the site's unbalanced nature by adding two Ionic porches and the temple's crowning feature, the Porch of the Maidens. With his bold design, Mnesicles created a marvelous illusion of harmony that was in keeping with the age's Classical ideals.

Sculpture

Equally impressive is the Greek achievement in sculpture. Believing that the task of sculpture was to imitate nature, the Greeks created images of gods and goddesses as well as of men and women that have haunted the Western imagination ever since. They not only forged a canon of idealized human proportions that later sculptors followed but also developed a repertoire of postures, gestures, and subjects that have become embedded in Western art.

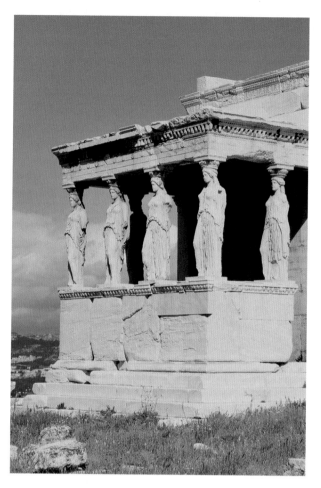

Figure 3.17 MNESICLES. The Erechtheum. View from the west. Ca. 410 B.C.E. Marble. Athens. *The Erechtheum was probably built to quiet conservatives who rejected Athena's new temple, the Parthenon, as a symbol of Athenian imperialism. Reflecting its ties with the past, the Erechtheum housed the ancient wooden cult statue of Athena, which pious Athenians believed had fallen from the sky. Its Ionic porches set the standard for the graceful Ionic order. The Porch of the Maidens (right), which was inaccessible from the outside, fronted the southern wall.*

During the Hellenic Age, Classical sculpture moved through three separate phases: the **Severe style,** which ushered in the period and lasted until 450 B.C.E.; the **High Classical style,** which coincided with the zenith of Athenian imperial greatness; and the **Fourth Century style,** which concluded with the death of Alexander the Great in 323 B.C.E.

Sculpture in the Severe style, inspired perhaps by its association with funeral customs, was characterized by a feeling of dignified nobility. The *Kritios Boy*—showing a figure fully at rest—is an elegant expression of this first phase of Classicism (Figure 3.18). Kritios [KRIT-ee-uhs], the supposed sculptor, fixed the mouth severely and altered the frontality, a feature of the Archaic style, by tilting the head subtly to the right and slightly twisting the upper torso. The flat-footed

Figure 3.18 *Kritios Boy.* Ca. 480 B.C.E. Ht. 33". Acropolis Museum, Athens. *This statue is carved from marble probably mined at Mt. Pentelicus in Attica. Two features—the treatment of the eyes, which were originally set with semiprecious stones, and the roll of hair—show that the Kritios sculptor was accustomed to working in bronze. The figure's beautifully rendered muscles and sense of inner life announce the arrival of the Hellenic style; the contrapposto, used sparingly here, foreshadows later developments in Greek sculpture.*

stance of the Archaic kouros has given way to a posture that places the body's weight on one leg and uses the other leg as a support. This stance is called **contrapposto** (counterpoise), and its invention, along with the mastery of the representation of musculature, helped to make the Classical revolution (Figure 3.19). Thereafter, sculptors were able to render the human figure in freer and more relaxed poses.

The central panel of the so-called Ludovisi Throne, another sculpture from the same period, conveys an air of quiet gravity (Figure 3.20). The subject is probably the birth of Aphrodite as she rises from the sea, indicated by pebbles under the feet of her attendants, the stooping figures on either side. This relief reflects a perfect blending of late Archaic grace (Aphrodite's stylized hair and the hint of Archaic smile) with the dignity of the Severe style (the delicate transparent draperies and the convincing realism produced by foreshortening the arms of the three figures).

In contrast to the Severe style, which accepted repose as normal, the High Classical style was fascinated with the aesthetic problem of showing motion in a static medium. The sculptors' solution, which became central to High Classicism, was to freeze the action, resisting the impulse to depict agitated movement, in much the same way that the tragic playwrights banished violence from the stage. In effect, the High Classical sculptors stopped time, allowing an ideal world to emerge in which serene gods and mortals showed grace under pressure. A striking representation of this aspect of High Classicism is the bronze statue of Poseidon or Zeus, found in the Aegean Sea off Cape Artemision. It captures to perfection High Classicism's ideal of virile grace (Figure 3.21). The god (whose maturity is signified by the beard and fully developed body), is shown poised, ready to hurl some object. In such sculptures as this, the Greeks found visual metaphors for their notion that deities and mortals are kin.

High Classical sculptors wanted to do more than portray figures in motion; some, especially Polykleitos [pol-e-KLITE-uhs] of Argos, continued to be obsessed with presenting the ideal human form at rest. In his search for perfection, Polykleitos executed a bronze male figure of such strength and beauty—the *Doryphoros*, or *Spearbearer*—that its proportions came to

86

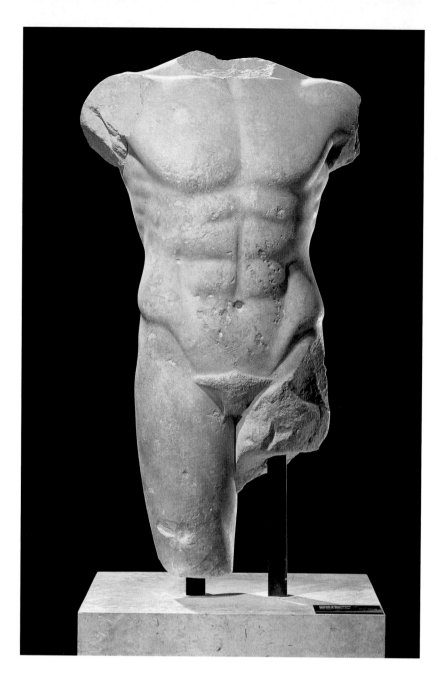

Figure 3.19 *Torso of Miletus.* Ca. 480–470 B.C.E. Marble, ht. 4'4". Louvre. *The torso is all that survives from a formerly life-size statue. Scars and plaster residue indicate that it was damaged and restored in antiquity. Although little is known of its origins and first use, the statue was eventually installed in a Roman theater in Miletus, Asia Minor. The torso shows the transition from the Archaic style, marked by frontality and nudity, to Classicism, characterized by well-defined musculature and the hint of contrapposto in the lightly flexed hips.*

Figure 3.20 *The Birth of Aphrodite (?).* Ca. 460 B.C.E. Ht. 2'9". Terme Museum, Rome. *The Ludovisi Throne, with its three relief panels, is a controversial work, because scholars disagree about its original function, the interpretation of its panels, and even its date. Discovered in Rome in the late nineteenth century, it probably was carved in Magna Graecia, perhaps for an altar, and brought to Rome in antiquity. The figure of Aphrodite was one of the first naked women depicted in large-scale Greek sculpture. The goddess is rendered in softly curving lines—a marked deviation from the Severe style and a forecast of the sensuous tendency of later Greek art.*

Figure 3.21 *Poseidon* (or *Zeus*). Ca. 460–450 B.C.E. Bronze, ht. 6'10". National Museum, Athens. *The Greek conception of the nobility of their gods is nowhere better revealed than in this magnificent bronze sculpture of Poseidon (or Zeus). Grace, strength, and intellect are united in this majestic image of a mature deity. Poseidon's eyes originally would have been semiprecious stones, and the statue would have been painted to create a more realistic effect.*

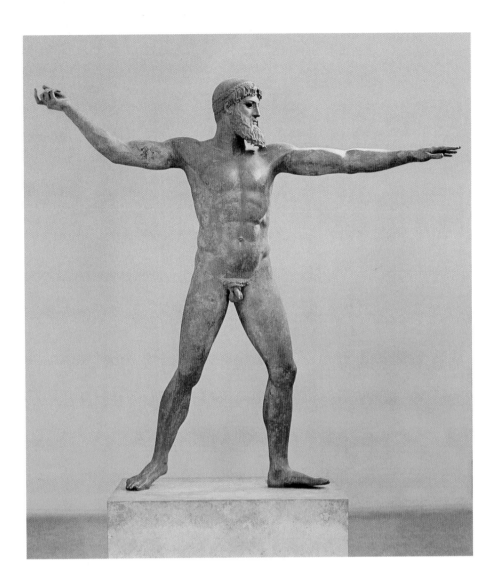

be regarded as a canon, or set of rules, to be imitated by other artists (Figure 3.22). In the *Doryphoros* canon, each of the limbs bears a numerical relation to the body's overall measurements; for example, the length of the foot is one-tenth of the figure's height. Other principles of High Classicism embodied in the *Doryphoros* include the slightly brutal facial features, which were typical of this style's masculine ideal; the relaxed contrapposto; and the controlled muscles.

Greek architecture reached its zenith in the Parthenon, and, similarly, Classical Greek sculpture attained its height in the reliefs and sculptures of this celebrated temple. Under the disciplined eye of the sculptor Phidias [FIHD-e-uhs], craftspeople carved patriotic and mythological subjects destined for various parts of the building. Taken as a whole, the sculptures revealed the Parthenon to be a tribute to Athenian imperialism as much as to the goddess Athena (Figure 3.23).

On the Parthenon's metopes—the rectangular spaces on the Doric frieze—sculptors portrayed scenes in the prevailing High Classical style. In panel after panel, the metope sculptors depicted perfect human forms showing restraint in the midst of struggle, such as Amazons against men, Greeks against Trojans, and gods against giants. The south metopes portrayed the battle between the legendary Lapiths and the half-men, half-horse Centaurs (Figure 3.24). For the Greeks, the struggle between the human Lapiths and the bestial Centaurs symbolized the contest between civilization and barbarism or, possibly, between the Greeks and the Persians.

Inside the columns, running around the perimeter of the upper cella walls in a continuous band, was a low-relief frieze. Borrowed from the Ionic order, this running frieze introduced greater liveliness into High Classicism. The 525-foot-long band is filled with

Figure 3.22 *Doryphoros.* Ca. 440 B.C.E. Marble copy of a bronze original by Polykleitos, ht. 6'6". Museo Nazionale Archeologico, Naples. *The* Doryphoros *expresses the classical ideal of balanced repose. The nude figure rests his weight upon the right leg. The left arm, extended to hold the now-missing spear, balances with the right leg. The left foot, barely touching the ground, balances with the relaxed right arm. Besides representing idealized repose, the* Doryphoros *was also recognized as the embodiment of human beauty with its ordered proportions, well-toned musculature, and rugged features.*

Figure 3.23 The Location of the Sculptures on the Parthenon. *This cutaway view shows the metopes on the Doric frieze, Ionic frieze, and pediments of the Parthenon, which were covered with sculptures celebrating the glory of Athens.*

Figure 3.24 *Centaur Versus Lapith.* Metope XXX, south face of the Parthenon. Ca. 448–442 B.C.E. Marble, ht. 56". British Museum. *This struggling pair was designed to fit comfortably into the metope frame, and thus the proportions of the figures in relation to each other and to the small space were worked out with precision. The intertwined limbs of the warrior and the Centaur visibly demonstrate the new freedom of High Classicism. The anguished countenance of the Lapith, however, is almost unique in High Classicism and is a portent of the more emotional faces of the Hellenistic style, the next major artistic development.*

depictions of hundreds of men and women, walking and riding horses, along with sacrificial animals for Athena and the rest of the Olympians. One of the most moving episodes on the frieze depicts two horsemen, one of whom turns to exhort the following procession by raising his left arm in a gesture of encouragement (Figure 3.25). The youths' tranquil faces, their sense of inner life, and the prevailing calm are the hallmarks of mature Classicism. The subject of this vivid scene is the procession of the Great Panathenaea festival, Athens's most important civic and religious ritual,

Figure 3.25 *Horsemen.* West frieze, Parthenon. Ca. 448–442 B.C.E. Marble, ht. 43". British Museum, London. *The Parthenon frieze offers an illusion of forward motion, starting with its western section, as the procession begins to form. In this illustration, from the west frieze, the procession is picking up steam, as the horsemen urge their horses along at a galloping pace. Although the scene shows great physical exertion, the bodies of the horsemen reveal little tension, nor do their faces show much emotion—typical qualities of the High Classical style. Their idealized bodies are also typical of the art of this period.*

The riding youths are probably meant to represent the sons of Athenian aristocrats, as members of this class would be the only ones in the city able to afford the steep expenses of the purchase and maintenance of a horse. Despite its democratic form of government, Athens remained a city where the aristocratic elite served in ceremonial and civic positions, as attested to by this illustration and other evidence.

Figure 3.26   PRAXITELES. *Hermes with the Infant Dionysus.* Ca. 350–340 B.C.E. Marble, ht. 85". Olympia Museum. *In this statue of Hermes, Praxiteles changed the look of Classical art with his rendering of the god's body. For example, Hermes' small head and long legs contributed to the Praxitelean canon for the male figure. The sculptor has also created a dramatic contrast between Hermes' well-muscled body and his soft face. As a direct result of Praxiteles' new vision, sculptors in the Hellenistic Age became interested in more frankly sensual portrayals of the human figure, both male and female.*

which was held every four years. This panoramic view of the thrilling procession concluded with a stunning group portrait of the twelve gods and goddesses, seated in casual majesty, awaiting their human worshipers. The entire Parthenon frieze was the most ambitious work of sculpture in the Greek tradition.

The transition to Fourth Century style coincided with the end of the creative phase of tragedy and the disintegration of the Greek world as it passed into the Macedonian political orbit. Sculpture remained innovative, since each generation seemed to produce a master who challenged the prevailing aesthetic rules, and free expression continued as a leading principle of Fourth Century style. But sculptors now expressed such new ideas as beauty for its own sake and a delight in sensuality. Earlier Classicism had stressed the notion that humans could become godlike, but the last phase concluded that gods and mortals alike reveled in human joys.

This new focus is apparent in Praxiteles' [prax-SIT-uhl-eez] *Hermes with the Infant Dionysus.* This sculpture, perhaps the only original work by a known sculptor that survives from Hellenic Greece, portrays two gods blissfully at play (Figure 3.26). Hermes, lounging in a casual yet dignified pose, probably dangled grapes before the attentive baby god. The contrapposto posture, beautifully defined in Hermes' stance, became widely imitated as the **Praxitelean curve.** Hermes' sensuous body, his intent gaze, and his delicate features are hallmarks of Fourth Century Classicism; by the next generation, Praxiteles' treatment of the male figure had superseded the more rugged *Doryphoros* canon.

KEY CULTURAL TERMS

Hellenic	Old Comedy
maenad	modes
Dionysia	idealism
phalanx	Platonism
Classic (Classical)	Ionic
Classicism	Severe style
tragedy	High Classical style
chorus	Fourth Century style
orchestra	contrapposto
skene	Praxitelean curve
satyr-play	humanism

The Legacy of Hellenic Civilization

Although Athens failed in its dream of political mastery of Greece, the Athenian miracle so impressed its contemporaries that Athenian culture dominated the Hellenic Age. Tragic poets, comic playwrights, and natural philosophers made the Athenian dialect the medium of expression for poetry and prose. The buildings on the Acropolis expressed visually the purity and restraint of the Athenian style. And Athenian democracy, which served as the exciting teacher of its citizens, was the envy of most of the other Greek poleis. After the fall of Greece to Macedonia, however, the idea of democracy fell into disrepute. Almost two thousand years passed before some in Europe were ready to give democracy a second chance.

But **humanism,** the other great creation of Athens, survived as a guide to refined living for the cultivated classes in the West. Athenian culture became the heart of the educational curriculum that was followed in Hellenistic civilization; that model was adopted by Rome and transmitted in the humanistic tradition to Europe. In time, the study and the practice of humanistic learning—literature, philosophy, theater, music, and the arts and architecture—became the crowning glory of Western civilization, affecting private individuals and entire societies.

Moreover, Classicism—the style of humanistic achievements in the Hellenic Age—had three great effects on the Western tradition. First, the principles of Greek Classicism—balance, simplicity, and restraint—set the standard by which the styles of other times are often measured. Second, the actual works of Classicism became basic building blocks of Western culture. In the realm of thought, the works of Plato and Aristotle quickly acquired a luster of authority and retained it until the seventeenth century C.E. Aristotle's literary criticism created a new writing genre, and his analysis of tragedy made this type of play the ultimate challenge to ambitious writers. The Greek tragedies themselves—of Aeschylus, Sophocles, and Euripides—are thought by many people in the West to be unsurpassed.

The comic plays of Aristophanes are less well known today, but their spirit still lives in period comedies and contemporary political satire. The histories of Herodotus and Thucydides retain their vitality as important sources for their respective eras, although modern research has cast doubt on some of their conclusions. Among Greece's accomplishments, architecture has had the most potent effect; the ruins on the Athenian Acropolis and elsewhere are eternal reminders of this Greek heritage. Finally, the idealized statues of men and women, such as the *Doryphoros*, have inspired Western artists with their vision of noble beings alert to the rich possibilities of human life.

The third and perhaps most important contribution of Classicism to the Western tradition was a skeptical spirit that was rooted in democracy. By asserting that the purpose of human life can best be realized in cities that are shaped by the citizens' needs, as Athenian humanism claimed, the humanists declared war on all tyrants, hierarchical societies, and divinely ordered states—in other words, the prevailing order of the ancient world. Because of this critical aspect of humanism, the Greek heritage has sometimes been called into question and, during repressive periods, been subjected to attack. However, the passion for questioning, for inquiry, which characterizes the skeptical spirit, is at the core of Western consciousness.

SUGGESTIONS FOR FURTHER READING

AESCHYLUS. *Oresteia*. Translated by R. Fagles. New York: Penguin, 1986. A good modern version of the only dramatic trilogy that survives from ancient Greece.

ARISTOPHANES. *Lysistrata*. Translated by J. Henderson. New York: Oxford University Press, 1987. This modern version captures the antiwar spirit and bawdy humor of the original comedy.

EURIPIDES. *The Bacchae and Other Plays*. Translated by P. Vellacott. New York: Penguin, 1972. An excellent collection of Euripides' dramas, in each of which strong-minded women play major roles.

HERODOTUS. *The Histories*. Translated by A. de Sélincourt. New York: Penguin, 1972. Prefaced with an informative introduction, this translation captures both the language and the narrative of the first history book in Western literature.

KAPLAN, J., ed. *The Pocket Aristotle*. New York: Washington Square Press, 1966. Edited selections from the *Physics*, the *Nicomachean Ethics*, *Politics*, and *Poetics* give a sense of Aristotle's method of inquiry.

ROUSE, W. H. D., trans. *Great Dialogues of Plato*. New York: New American Library, 1963. Includes the full text of the *Republic*, the *Apology*, *Phaedo*, and the *Symposium*.

SOPHOCLES. *The Theban Plays*. Translated by E. F. Watling. New York: Penguin, 1974. The three plays about the misfortunes of King Oedipus and his family; includes *Oedipus Rex* and *Antigone*. Unlike Aeschylus's Oresteian trilogy, Sophocles' Theban plays do not constitute a unified work; each was originally performed with other plays (now lost).

THUCYDIDES. *The Peloponnesian War*. Translated by R. Warner. New York: Penguin, 1970. A translation that captures the sweep and drama of the original.

4 CLASSICAL GREEK CIVILIZATION
The Hellenistic Age

The Hellenistic Age covers the relatively brief period from the death of Alexander the Great in 323 B.C.E. to the triumph of Rome over Macedonian Greece in 146 B.C.E. During this time, a new urban civilization developed in the eastern Mediterranean basin. In contrast to Hellenic Greece, this new civilization was dominated by large metropolitan centers linked by trade and commerce. More racially mixed and ethnically varied than Hellenic Greece, this civilization has come to be called **Hellenistic** because of the preeminent role Greece played in its development. Greece, for example, furnished the Hellenistic world with its diplomatic and commercial language, its bureaucrats, and most of its cultural forms. And yet Hellenistic culture was eclectic, for the subjects of the various states made their presence known (Figure 4.1). Several key motifs grew from oriental roots: the concept of a ruler who is also divine, the aesthetic ideal that identifies grandiosity with earthly majesty, and new religious cults that promised immortality.

Although the Hellenistic Age is sometimes overlooked, Alexander's dream of a world community united by a common leader has had an impact reaching into modern times. The multiracial and multicultural kingdoms of the Hellenistic period are the first examples of a type whose modern versions include the United States and the former Soviet Union. And, not least, Hellenistic achievements in philosophy, art, and architecture are considerable.

This creation of a worldly Mediterranean community destroyed the Hellenic political order in which poleis were guided by their citizens. The poleis were replaced mainly by large Hellenistic kingdoms, ruled by men who

◀ **Detail** *Aphrodite of Melos (Venus de Milo).* Ca. 160–150 B.C.E. Marble, ht. 6′10″. Louvre.

· more freedom for women

Figure 4.1 Black Youth. Third–second century B.C.E. Bronze. Metropolitan Museum of Art. *Beginning in the Archaic Age, Greek artists occasionally depicted black Africans in their works. During the Hellenistic Age, with the migration of peoples and the increased use of slaves, sculptors frequently chose black figures as subjects. This small bronze statue of a young African is an illustration of the racial diversity of the Hellenistic world. Despite the figure's exaggerated half-crouch, the statuette is probably not meant to represent an athlete, as he is not depicted fully nude. Note the sash around the waist, with the end draped down the upper thighs. The figure more likely was intended to represent a worker engaged in some task, as reflected in the object or objects (now lost) that he was holding in his hands.*

declared themselves deities. The Hellenistic economic order rested on specialized luxury crafts and professional occupations, international trade and banking, and an abundant and cheap supply of slaves. The large ports exported and imported basic agricultural commodities such as grain, olive oil, wine, and timber, exchanging them for expensive goods like pottery, silks, jewelry, and spices.

Class divisions in Hellenistic society were pronounced. For the rich, urban life was often luxurious and cosmopolitan, but most of society remained provincial. Those in the middle social ranks, primarily tradespeople and skilled artisans, struggled to keep ahead and hoped to prosper. However, for the poorest free classes—laborers, unskilled workers, and small landowners—life offered little. Slaves, whose numbers grew during the wars of this period, were expected to bear the brunt of all backbreaking labor.

Hellenistic women were affected by the period's growing cosmopolitanism. Women, along with men, moved to the newly conquered lands and created new lives for themselves in frontier towns. In Alexandria and other large cities, some restrictions of Hellenic Greece were maintained, but others were relaxed or discarded. For example, royal and non-Greek women were able to conduct their own legal and economic affairs, though nonroyal Greek women were still forced to use a male guardian in such cases. Dowries remained the custom among Greek families, but unmarried respectable women now had the option of working in the liberal arts, as poets and philosophers, and in the professions, as artists and physicians. Unmarried women who were unconcerned about their reputations served as courtesans and prostitutes, living outside the norms of respectable society. Hellenistic literature reflects changed mores, portraying women in carefree situations apart from the gaze of their husbands or fathers. In economic matters, some women became prosperous in their own right, and, just as men did, they made charitable bequests and erected impressive gravestones. Despite these changes, Hellenistic society was dominated by masculine thinking. The surest sign of women's subordinate role was that the Greek practice of infanticide, which was as old as Greek civilization, continued as a way for families to rid themselves of unwanted females.

THE STAGES OF HELLENISTIC HISTORY

The shadow of Rome hung over the Hellenistic world, although the rival states—mired in their quarrels and jockeying for power—were unaware that their fate depended on the rising western Mediterranean power.

Timeline 4.1   THE HELLENISTIC AGE

The events of this age fall into two stages: (1) the disintegration of Alexander's empire and the rise of the successor states; and (2) the arrival and triumph of Rome (Timeline 4.1).

The End of the Empire and the Rise of the States

The years from 323 to 307 B.C.E. saw the shattering of Alexander's dream of a united Greek and Persian civilization. Alexander left no designated successor. After his death, his chief generals (Antigonus, Seleucus, and Ptolemy) divided his empire into three dynastic kingdoms (known as the "successor states") that, along with a few minor states and leagues of Greek city-states, survived until Rome moved into the area. The era of the successor states (307–215 B.C.E.) was the zenith of Hellenistic culture. Politically the states were hardly ever at peace, but culturally they were united. Greeks and barbarians mingled freely, and an urban civilization began to emerge. A form of colloquial Greek, called *koine*, spread throughout the Hellenistic world and was spoken from Gaul to Syria.

The three successor states were based in Macedonia, in the former Persian Empire, and in Egypt (Map 4.1). The kingdom of Macedonia, that of Antigonus, controlled Greece until two leagues of poleis challenged Macedonian hegemony. The ensuing warfare with the Greek leagues ultimately weakened this state.

The Seleucid kingdom, that of Seleucus, was built on the ruins of the old Persian Empire. At its height, Seleucid power extended east to present-day Iraq. During the mid–third century B.C.E., however, the eastern region of the Seleucid kingdom broke away and formed the two smaller states of Parthia and Bactria, which would later prove to be prickly adversaries of Rome. In time, the Seleucid rulers, distracted by the invading Gauls, a wandering tribe of Celtic peoples from central and eastern Europe, lost control of their king-

dom and had to relinquish land in Asia Minor to a new kingdom known as Pergamum, named after an old Greek city.

The Ptolemaic kingdom, that of Ptolemy, included Egypt, the oldest civilization surviving in the ancient world. Although the Ptolemaic dynasty was marked by weak and corrupt rulers, Egypt enjoyed a resurgence as a unified and independent state. The capital, Alexandria, became the greatest urban center of the Hellenistic Age, enriched by the grains harvested in the Nile river valley and the goods and traffic that passed through its port.

The Arrival and Triumph of Rome

The second phase of Hellenistic civilization began in the late third century B.C.E. when Macedonia joined Carthage, a Phoenician state in North Africa, in its struggle against Rome. Thereafter, the unforgiving Romans used every opportunity to humiliate their Greek enemies. Between 215 and 148 B.C.E., Rome fought four wars with Macedonia, thus becoming entangled in Greek political and military squabbles. Finally, in 146 B.C.E., Rome brought the entire Greek peninsula under its control. The other Hellenistic kingdoms soon submitted. In 133 B.C.E., the ruler of Pergamum willed his state to Rome. The Seleucid kingdom was conquered by the Romans in 65 B.C.E. after three wars. Egypt maintained its freedom until 31 B.C.E., when Cleopatra and her forces were defeated by Octavian and the Roman navy.

URBAN LIFE IN THE HELLENISTIC AGE

Alexander's most enduring legacy to the Hellenistic world was his new image of the city. The city is as old as civilization, since urban life is by definition a

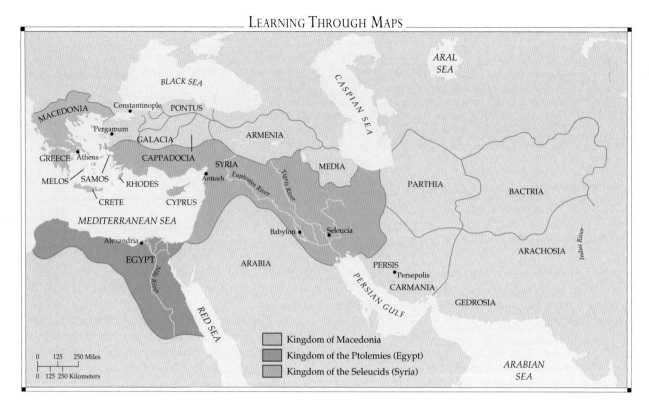

Map 4.1   THE SUCCESSOR STATES AND THE HELLENISTIC WORLD, AFTER 307 B.C.E.
This map shows the Hellenistic world and the successor states, which emerged after the breakup of Alexander the Great's empire. **Notice** the differing sizes of the successor states and the respective region controlled by each. **Consider** the impact of geography and regional cultural traditions on the three kingdoms. **Locate** the major cities of these kingdoms. **How** did Alexandria's location in Egypt help to make it the dominant city of the Hellenistic world?

component of civilized existence. For Alexander, cities were keystones holding together his diverse and vast empire—serving as centers of government, trade, and culture and radiating Greco-Oriental civilization into the hinterland. Alexander is reputed to have founded more than seventy cities during his conquests, many of which were named for him.

The burgeoning cities of the Hellenistic world accentuated the period's growing class divisions. As rural folk, both Greek and non-Greek, flocked to the cities seeking jobs and trying to better their economic condition, some succeeded, while others slipped into poverty and despair. Their failures divided the rich from the poor, thus intensifying class conflicts. How the rural migrants adjusted to urban ways also affected the values and beliefs of the times, in particular the various philosophies and religions (see "Philosophy and Religion"). And, in everyday life, a new survival strategy arose among upwardly mobile city folk as a way to avoid class conflict. That strategy was to shed their provincial ways and ethnic identity and to

adopt the ideal of the **cosmopolitan**—the Greek term for a citizen of a polis having a universal or worldwide view.

Greek migrants constituted a special challenge to Hellenistic culture. Greeks who left their home city-states to seek their fortunes in the successor states of Alexander's empire impacted every phase of life. Drawn to cities and ports across the eastern Mediterranean, Greek would-be traders, bankers, and seamen arrived, spreading their way of life and influencing the local culture—thus further blending the societies of the period. Many became government officials—bureaucrats, advisers, diplomats—or soldiers and sailors. Most, however, pursued business and professional careers or found work in the visual and performing arts. Their numbers and high-profile presence ensured that Greek culture and values would play a preeminent role in Hellenistic thought and art.

The expansion of trade within this diverse culture benefited Greek and non-Greek alike. The period's kings, seizing the opportunity to enrich themselves and their states, lengthened and improved existing overland trade routes and linked up with routes to India and into parts of Africa. After Egypt's king learned about the monsoon season in the Indian Ocean, regular sea trade with India began, thus ensuring the importance of Coptos, a city on the upper Nile, as the western terminal for this overseas trade.

Pergamum

During the Hellenistic period, Alexander's successors emulated him, establishing urban centers such as Antioch, on the Orontes River in southern Asia Minor, and Seleucia, the new capital of the Seleucid kingdom, near Babylon. The new city of Pergamum in western Asia Minor emerged as a brilliant center of art and thought, bringing together Greek and Persian civilizations. The Attalids, the ruling dynasty of Pergamum, decorated their city's acropolis with a splendid palace, a library second only to the one in Alexandria, and a marble temple to Athena. Scattered on the hillside beneath the acropolis were shrines, markets, and private dwellings of the more prosperous citizens. At the base of the hill, the tradespeople, artisans, and slaves lived crowded together (Figure 4.2).

Alexandria in Egypt

For all its claims to grandeur, however, Pergamum could not surpass the size, wealth, beauty, or culture of the premier Hellenistic city, Alexandria in Egypt, founded by Alexander (Figure 4.3). Under the Ptolemies, Alexandria grew to be a world city that attracted both the ambitious who sought opportunities and the apathetic who wanted to be left alone. Every desired attraction is said to have existed here, just as in the teeming cities of the twenty-first century. By the end of the first century B.C.E., Alexandria's population was about one million, and the city was divided into five sections, including one reserved for royalty and separate residential quarters for the Egyptians and the Jews, who were attracted by the city's opportunities and tolerant atmosphere. Whereas the polis of the Hellenic Age was self-contained, with a relatively homogeneous population, Alexandria's racially and ethnically diverse groups were held together by economic interests. With busy harbors, bustling markets, and international banks, the city became a hub of commercial and financial enterprises, similar to modern port cities.

Alexandria's economic vitality was matched by the splendor of its cultural achievements. The world's first university—a museum dedicated to the muses—was built here as a place for scholars to study and to exchange ideas. Nearby was the famed library, whose

Figure 4.2 Acropolis at Pergamum. Second century B.C.E. Reconstruction by H. Schlief. Staatliche Museen, Berlin. *Pergamum architecture was in the Hellenic style, but the city's mixed population and economy made it the commercial and political hub of a Hellenistic kingdom. Under Eumenes II, the capital and the country reached their height of power around 160 B.C.E.*

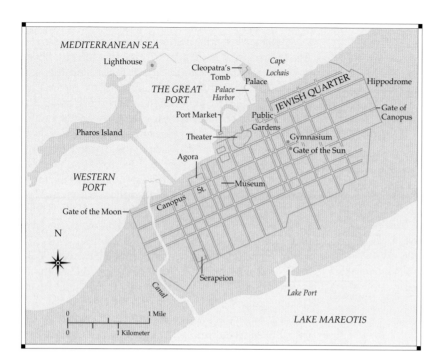

Figure 4.3   Plan of Ancient Alexandria. Third century B.C.E. *Designed by Deinocrates of Rhodes, Alexander's personal architect, Alexandria was laid out in a grid formed by intersecting avenues and streets. The entire city was enclosed by a wall, accessible by four massive gates at the ends of the major avenues. To the north lay two harbors that made the city the most vital port in the Mediterranean. The harbors were protected by an outer island, at the point of which stood the lighthouse of Pharos—now lost. Remarkable for its colossal size, the lighthouse was considered one of the wonders of the ancient world.*

staff, made up of poets and scholars, collected the classics of Greek civilization, including the works of Plato and Aristotle; the tragedies of Aeschylus, Sophocles, and Euripides; the comedies of Aristophanes; the works of Hellenistic scientists; and the treatises of Hellenistic philosophers. Some scholars in Alexandria wrote critical editions and commentaries on the works of earlier poets, among them Homer, Hesiod, and Pindar. One of the library's branches, the Serapeion, was open to all citizens. The Serapeion was a temple dedicated to Serapis, a god whose cult drew from the lore of other deities and who was favored by the Ptolemy rulers. At the time of the Roman conquest in the late first century B.C.E., the library contained nearly 700,000 volumes, the largest collection in the ancient world. By then, Alexandria had become a beacon for great minds, who were attracted by the city's rich intellectual life and cosmopolitan atmosphere.

THE ELABORATION OF THE GREEK TRADITION: THE SPREAD OF CLASSICISM TO THE HELLENISTIC WORLD

The Hellenistic world to some extent rejected the simplicity, balance, and restraint that had characterized Hellenism and embraced a more emotional, theatrical view of culture (Figure 4.4). The expansiveness of

Alexander's territorial conquests was echoed in the expansion of emotional and expressive content in the arts. As new energies, languages, and traditions were poured into old artistic and literary forms, the seriousness of Hellenism began to give way to a Hellenistic love of playfulness along with an interest in ordinary, everyday subjects.

Hellenistic culture also reflected the tastes and needs of the period's diverse states. Greek tragedy lost its vitality when separated from its roots in the independent polis, but comedy appealed to sophisticated urban audiences who were seeking diversion. Nondramatic literature became rather artificial as authors concentrated on perfecting their style or pursuing exotic scholarship. New philosophies and religions arose in response to the urban isolation and loneliness that many people experienced. And, finally, grandiose architecture addressed the propaganda needs of autocratic rulers, and realistic sculpture reflected the tastes of an increasingly urban, secular culture.

Nevertheless, the values of Hellenistic culture did not so much replace the standards of Hellenic Classicism as they enriched and elaborated the older ideals. Like Hellenism, the Hellenistic style depicted the realities of the physical world rather than finding truth in fantasy or abstraction. And Hellenistic artists and authors agreed with their Hellenic forebears that art must serve moral purposes, revealed through content and formal order.

SLICE OF LIFE
Street Scene in Hellenistic Egypt

THEOCRITUS,
From *Idylls*, third century B.C.E.

In Hellenistic Egypt, two society matrons, Gorgo and Praxinoa, each with her maid in tow (Eutychis and Eunoa, respectively), make their way through the crowded streets of Alexandria, on their way to the palace of Ptolemy II to hear a singer perform at the festival of Adonis.

[GORGO:] [C]ome, get your dress and cloak on,
　　and let's go to King Ptolemy's palace
　　and take a look at this Adonis.
　　The Queen, I hear, is doing things in style.
PRAXINOA: Oh, nothing but the best. Well, they can
　　keep it.
GORGO: But when you've seen it, just think,
　　you can tell those who haven't all about it.
　　Come on, it's time we were off.
PRAXINOA: Every day's a holiday for the idle.

• • •

[Out in the street.]
Ye Gods, what a crowd! The crush!
How on earth are we going to get through it?
They're like ants! Swarms of them, beyond
　　counting!
Well, you've done us many favours, Ptolemy,
since your father went to heaven.
We don't get those no-goods now, sliding up to us
in the street and playing their Egyptian tricks.
What they used to get up to, those rogues!
A bunch of villains, each as bad
as the next, and all utterly cursed!
Gorgo dear, what will become of us?
Here are the king's horses! Take care,
my good man, don't tread on me.
That brown one's reared right up!
Look how wild he is! He'll kill his groom!
Eunoa, you fool, get back!
Thank God I left that child at home.

GORGO: Don't worry, Praxinoa.
　　We've got behind them now.
　　They're back in their places.
PRAXINOA: I'm all right now.
　　Ever since I was a girl, two things
　　have always terrified me—horses,
　　and long, cold snakes. Let's hurry.
　　This great crowd will drown us.

• • •

GORGO: Look, Praxinoa! What a crowd at the door!
PRAXINOA: Fantastic! Gorgo, give me your hand. And
　　　　you, Eunoa, hold on to Eutychis.
　　Take care you don't lose each other.
　　We must all go in together. Stay close by us.
　　Oh no! Gorgo! My coat! It's been ripped
　　clean in two! My God, sir, as you hope
　　for heaven, mind my coat!
STRANGER: It wasn't my fault. But I'll be careful.
PRAXINOA: What a herd! They push like pigs.
STRANGER: Don't worry, madam, we'll be all right.
PRAXINOA: And may you, sir, be all right
　　forever and beyond, for looking after us.
　　What a charming man! Where's Eunoa?
　　She's getting squashed! Come on, girl, push!
　　That's it. "All safely in."

Interpreting This Slice of Life **What** is the "plot" in this story of life in the big city? **What** are some of the incidents that happen to the party of women as they move through the streets of Alexandria? **What** is the mood of the women in the story? Based on this vignette, **what** appears to be the position of women in Alexandrian society? **Describe** the relations between the women and their slaves. **Who** was the audience for this poem? **What** modern events are similar to this festival of Adonis? **Explain.**

Drama and Literature

In the Hellenistic Age, Greek comedy began to resemble modern productions. The grotesque padding worn by the actors gave way to realistic costumes; masks were redesigned to be representative of the portrayed characters; and the actors assumed a dominant status over the chorus. Comedies became a form of popular amusement, and Hellenistic playwrights developed a genre known as **New Comedy** to appeal to the pleasure-seeking audiences who were flocking to the theaters. Avoiding political criticism and casual obscenity, New Comedy presented gently satirical scenes from middle-class life.

The plays were generally comic romances on such themes as frustrated first love or marital misunder-

Figure 4.4 *Nike of Samothrace.* Front and side views. Ca. 190 B.C.E. Marble, ht. 8'.
Louvre. *The* Nike of Samothrace—*commonly called the "Winged Victory" because Nike was
the Greek goddess of victory—is a perfect symbol of the war-dominated Hellenistic Age. Carved
to appear to be striding into the wind, with wildly agitated draperies and soaring wings, this
sculpture embodies exuberant action, a defining feature of this turbulent age. Nike's costume also
illustrates this age's superb virtuosity; note the transparent band of "fabric" around the navel
and the draperies swathing the thighs and legs. Originally part of a sculptural group on the island of Samothrace, which included a war galley, a fountain, and a reflecting pool (now lost), the
Nike gives the impression of standing on the prow of a swiftly moving ship.*

standings, and although the endings were inevitably
happy and there was much formula writing—somewhat like today's situation comedies on television—
the plays reflected the comprehensive range of the
Hellenistic style. The characters, for example, were familiar types drawn from the rich diversity of Hellenistic society—the courtesan, the slave, the fawning
parasite. New Comedy remained steadfastly middle-

class, however, for the traditional social order always
prevailed in the end. For example, a favorite plot device of New Comedy hinged on discovering that a
seemingly lowborn character was actually from a respected—and often wealthy—family.

Both ancient and modern critics tend to regard
Menander [muh-NAN-duhr] (about 343–about 291
B.C.E.) as the leading author of New Comedy. He wrote

more than one hundred plays for the Dionysia festival in Athens, winning first prize for comedy eight times, and is credited with perfecting the **comedy of manners,** a humorous play that focuses on the way people interact in society.

The Woman from Samos is a robust example of his work. Dating from about 321 B.C.E., this comedy concerns the identity of an orphaned baby and features stock characters: a courtesan, a young lover, an old lover, a humorous neighbor, and two comic slaves. Menander first presents a household in which the father believes that he and his son are wooing the same woman, when, in actuality, the son is involved with the girl next door. Then, when a foundling appears, absurd misunderstandings arise and false accusations are made. The play ends happily with all characters reconciled, the son wed to his true love, and the father and mistress married in a joyous ceremony—a typical New Comedy resolution. Western comedy would be inconceivable without Menander. His style was assimilated into Roman comedy, which passed the spirit of his work into the dramas of the Italian Renaissance and from there into the comedies of Shakespeare and Molière.

In nondramatic literature, the Hellenistic Age produced a style known as **Alexandrianism.** The Ptolemaic rulers who built the library and the museum in Alexandria used state subsidies to lure scholars and poets to the city to study the works that found their way, by purchase or plunder, into the library's vast collections. The writers produced works of many types—poetry, history, biography, literary criticism, and essays on geography and mathematics—but their work is generally of historical interest only. Alexandrian literature is often obscure and ornate, derivative, and scholarly.

A writer who stands apart in the Alexandrian school is the poet Theocritus [the-OCK-ruht-us] (about 310–250 B.C.E.), who worked within the confines of the style but achieved genuine literary distinction. He created a new poetic form, the **pastoral,** which would influence later Classical and modern European literature. These poems describe the lives of shepherds and farmers in a somewhat artificial, idealized way. Theocritus drew his images from the memory of his earlier years in rural Sicily, and his charming, nostalgic verses appealed to many country folk who had also left the quiet rustic life for the excitement of the Hellenistic cities.

Theocritus also wrote what he called **idylls** (from the Greek word meaning "little picture"), which offered small portraits, or vignettes, of Hellenistic life. Some of these poems reveal much about everyday affairs, noting the common concerns and aspirations of all generations—love, family, religion, and wealth.

Philosophy and Religion

Hellenistic philosophy and religion, like the whole of Hellenistic culture, built on the achievements of Hellenic and Middle Eastern civilizations. Cities now became the crucible in which the meaning of life was studied. Alexandria emerged as the period's cultural center—taking over the role that Athens had played in the Hellenic Age. In Alexandria and other cities, some people found answers in new philosophies, while others discovered inner peace in mystery cults.

As life in Hellenistic cities became more multicultural, the sense of belonging that had characterized life in the Hellenic poleis was replaced by feelings of isolation, of loneliness, even of helplessness. As a consequence, two seemingly contradictory points of view grew up: individualism and internationalism. Those who held these attitudes were searching for continuity in a rapidly changing world; were seeking identity for the individual through common interests, values, and hopes; and were striving to understand events that seemed unpredictable and beyond human control.

Philosophies and religions offered answers that seemed as contradictory as the problems themselves. One philosophy urged a universal brotherhood of all human beings, united regardless of race, status, or birth; another, despairing of the world, excluded most people and appealed to a chosen few. Religions, similarly, provided varying answers. One faith preached salvation in a life after death, and another turned to magic to escape Fate—that blind force that controlled human life.

In the long run, such diversity of choice tended to foster tolerance, since no single set of beliefs prevailed or satisfied everyone (Figure 4.5). Having many alternatives spared society the anguish and bigotry that would have arisen had there been only two or three competing points of view. Because of the ease of communication and travel in the Hellenistic period, these new philosophies and religions quickly gained converts everywhere, regardless of class or geographic location.

The most enduring of this period's philosophies, Cynicism, Skepticism, Epicureanism, and Stoicism, attracted the better-educated and more influential groups in Hellenistic society. Of these four theories, Cynicism and Skepticism appealed to only a few, whereas Epicureanism and Stoicism had a much larger following (Table 4.1).

Cynicism Of the four schools, **Cynicism** had the least impact on Hellenistic civilization. The Cynics, believing that society diverted the individual from the more important goals of personal independence and

Figure 4.5 A Religious Ceremony. 159 C.E. Yale University Art Gallery, New Haven. *Although this relief is dated from the second century C.E., it is characteristic of Hellenistic religious practices that continued into Roman times. In the center is depicted Zeus Olympius–Baalshamin, a combination of Greek and Semitic deities. On the left is a priest burning an offering on an altar and dressed in Near Eastern garb; on the right is a priest wearing Greek clothing.*

Table 4.1 PHILOSOPHY IN THE HELLENISTIC AGE

PHILOSOPHY	EMPHASIS
Cynicism	True freedom arises from realizing that if one wants nothing, then one will never lack anything; *autarky* (self-sufficiency) is goal
Skepticism	Nothing can be known for certain; question all ideas; *autarky* is goal
Epicureanism	Only the atoms and void exist; pleasure is the highest good; death is final in its extinction of consciousness; the gods play no active role in human affairs
Stoicism	The world is governed by the divine *logos*, or reason, or nature; wisdom and freedom consist of living in harmony with the *logos*; all humans share in the divine *logos*; *autarky* is goal

freedom, denounced all religions and governments, shunned physical comfort, and advocated the avoidance of personal pleasure. In the Cynics' logic, true freedom came with the realization that if one wanted nothing, one could not lack anything. By isolating themselves from society, they gained a type of self-sufficiency the Greeks called *autarky* [AW-tar-kee].

The most prominent Cynic, Diogenes [die-AHJ-uh-neez] (about 412–about 323 B.C.E.), openly scorned the ordinary values and crass materialism of his society. His contrary personality so fascinated Alexander the Great that the ruler, upon being insulted by the Cynic, is reported to have said that if he were not Alexander, he would prefer to be Diogenes (Figure 4.6)! A few Cynics earned the respect of some thinkers, but the principles of Cynicism offended the educated, and its pessimism offered no hope to the masses.

Skepticism The proponents of **Skepticism** argued that nothing could be known for certain, an extreme conclusion they were led to by their belief that the senses were unreliable sources of knowledge. Thinking that everything was relative, the Skeptics maintained that all ideas must be questioned and that no single philosophy was true. When their critics pointed out that such unrelenting questioning was clearly not a practical answer to life's uncertainties, the Skeptics replied that certainty could be achieved only by admitting that truth was unknowable—a circular response. The Skeptics thought that if they recognized that intellectual inquiry was fruitless, then they could avoid frustration and achieve *autarky,* or self-sufficiency—the same goal as that of the Cynics and the Stoics.

The Skeptics, even though they attracted a smaller audience than the Cynics, had a greater impact on Western reasoning. Pyrrho [PEER-oh] of Elis (about 360–about 272 B.C.E.) founded Skepticism and pursued the native strain of Greek thinking to its logical conclusion, but he never recorded his ideas. Skepticism had some appeal for the early Romans, who brought the Greek philosopher and teacher Carneades [kar-NEE-uh-deez] (about 214–129 B.C.E.) to Rome in 155 B.C.E. Carneades shocked his pious Roman audience, who took his universal doubt as a denial of the stability and permanence of their state and its values. Although Skepticism faded after Carneades' death, the movement was revived during the Roman Empire and eventually passed into the mainstream of Western thought.

Epicureanism The strict and quiet way of life advocated by **Epicureanism** appealed to aristocrats who were more interested in learning than in politics. It began as the philosophy of the Greek thinker Epicurus [ep-uh-KYUR-uhs] (about 342–270 B.C.E.), who founded a school in Athens where pupils, including

Figure 4.6 *Diogenes and Alexander the Great.* First century C.E. Villa Albani, Rome. *This Roman relief shows that Diogenes and Alexander the Great, two figures of the Hellenistic Age, were living presences for the Romans. The philosopher Diogenes is carved sitting in his famous tub, a symbol of his contempt for creature comforts. The world-conqueror Alexander is on the right, pointing his finger at the Greek thinker. The dog portrayed on top of the tub is a reference to Cynicism (the word* cynic *is from the Greek word for "dog"). Diogenes asserted that humans should live simply—like dogs.*

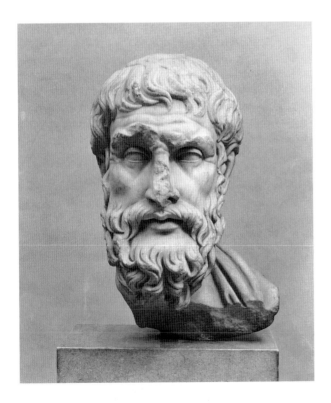

Figure 4.7 *Epicurus.* Ca. 290–280 B.C.E. Courtesy The Metropolitan Museum of Art. Rogers Fund, 1911. (11.90). *This marble bust of Epicurus, discovered in southern Italy and inscribed with his name, is a copy of the original bronze sculpture. Many busts and likenesses of Epicurus have been found, indicating the popularity of his philosophy in Hellenistic times and especially during the Roman era.*

slaves and women, gathered to discuss ideas (Figure 4.7). For Epicurus, the best way to keep one's wants simple, and thus to achieve happiness, was to abstain from sex and focus instead on friendship. Friendship was a mystic communion, based on shared need, in which men and men, men and women, rich and poor, old and young, of all nationalities and any class supported each other in trusting relationships. This vision guided Epicurus's school, where life became a daily exercise in friendship. It was an ideal that appealed to women since, in making them men's equals, it showed that there was more to their lives than bearing children and raising families.

Epicurus based his ethical philosophy on the Atomic theory of those Greek thinkers who saw the universe as completely determined by the behavior of atoms moving in empty space (see Chapter 3). Epicurus accepted this picture, but with one significant modification: He argued that because atoms on occasion swerved from their set paths and made unpredictable deviations, it was possible, even in a deterministic universe, for humans to make free choices. Like the Atomists, Epicurus also believed that the senses presented an accurate view of the physical world. Thus, by using the mind as a storehouse for sense impressions and by exercising free will in their choices, individuals could reach moral judgments and ultimately form an ethical code.

For Epicurus, the correct ethical code led to happiness, which was realized in a life of quiet—separated and withdrawn from the trying cares of the world. Furthermore, those who would be happy should keep their wants simple, not indulge excessive desires, and resist fame, power, and wealth, which only brought misery and disappointment.

Another characteristic of Epicurean happiness was freedom from fear—fear of the gods, of death, and of the hereafter. Although Epicurus believed that the gods existed, he also believed that they cared nothing about human beings, and therefore no one needed to be afraid of what the gods might or might not do. As for death, there was, again, nothing to agonize over because when it did occur, the atoms that made up the soul simply separated from the body's atoms and united with other particles to create new forms. With death came the end of the human capacity to feel pleasure or pain and thus the end of suffering. Consequently, death, rather than being feared, should be welcomed as a release from misfortune and trouble. Pleasure, in the Epicurean view, was the absence of pain. The happy Epicurean, standing above the cares of the world, had reached *ataraxia,* the desireless state that the Hellenistic Age deemed so precious.

Stoicism Both Epicureanism and **Stoicism** claimed that happiness was a final goal of the individual, and both were essentially materialistic, stressing the importance of sense impressions and the natural world. The Stoics, however, identified the supreme deity with nature, thus making the natural world divine and inseparable from the deity. The supreme being was also another name for reason, or *logos,* and hence nature was also rational. Since the Stoics' God was law and the author of law, this led to the notion that the workings of nature were expressed in divine laws.

The Stoics likewise discovered God in humanity. The Stoics' God, being identical with reason, gave a spark to each mortal's soul, conferring the twin gifts of

rationality and kinship with divinity. The Stoics thus believed that reason and the senses could be used jointly to uncover the underlying moral law as well as God's design in the world, proving God's wisdom and power over human life and nature.

There was in Stoicism a tendency to leave everything up to God. Stoics came to accept their roles in life, whether rich or poor, master or slave, healthy or afflicted, and such a resigned and deterministic outlook could (and did) lead to apathy or unconcern. However, the ideal Stoic, the Wise Man, never became apathetic. He overcame Stoicism's fatalistic tendency by stressing his own sense of and dedication to duty. Doing one's duty was part of following the deity's plan, and the Stoic willingly performed his tasks, no matter how onerous or laborious. The reward for living a life of duty was virtue. Having achieved virtue, the Stoics were freed from their emotions, which they thought only corrupted them. The Stoics had thus achieved *autarky,* the state of existence sought by many Hellenistic philosophers.

Stoicism was unique among the Hellenistic philosophies in holding out the promise of membership in a worldwide brotherhood. Perhaps inspired by Alexander the Great's dream, the Stoics advocated an ideal state, guided by God and law, that encompassed all of humanity of whatever race, sex, social status, or nationality in a common bond of reason. As humans carried out their duties in this larger community, they would rise above local and national limitations and create a better world.

Because of their practical optimism, the Stoics drew the largest number of followers among political leaders and intellectuals, who found the Cynics, the Skeptics, and the Epicureans too pessimistic. In the end, however, all four philosophies satisfied only a small portion of the vast Hellenistic population. They failed to appeal to persons who were confused by the intellectual theories or who derived no personal satisfaction from the teachings. Instead, the bulk of the people, spurred on by a growing sense of helplessness, began to believe that Fate ruled their lives.

Fate and the Mystery Cults The belief in Fate, a concept borrowed from Babylonia, gripped the lives of many people in the Hellenistic world. To them, Fate ruled the universe, controlled the heavens, and determined the course of life. Although no one could change the path of this nonmoral, predestined force, individuals could try to avoid the cruel consequences of Fate by various methods. The pseudoscience of astrology, also from Babylonia, offered one alternative. Magic was now revived, and many people used sacred objects to conjure up good spirits or to ward off evil ones. Nevertheless, it was the mystery cults—springing from the primitive chthonian religions of Greece (see Chapters 2 and 3) and elsewhere—that eventually emerged as the most popular and effective response to Fate.

During the Hellenistic Age, numerous chthonian cults spread from the Seleucid kingdom and Egypt to the Greek mainland, where they were combined with local beliefs and rituals to create religions that fused different beliefs and practices. By the second century B.C.E., converts were being attracted from all over the Hellenistic world to the well-established mystery cults of Orpheus and Dionysus in Greece and to the new religions from Egypt and the old Persian lands. The growth of these cults in turn sparked an increase in religious zeal after about 100 B.C.E., resulting in more ceremonies and public festivals and the revival of older faiths.

The Egyptian mystery cults grew, becoming quite popular across the Hellenistic world. Ptolemy I, the Macedonian founder of the Ptolemaic dynasty in 323 B.C.E., invented a new god, Serapis, in an effort to unite the Egyptians and the Greeks. Serapis became a favorite deity of the masses outside Egypt, and followers built shrines everywhere.

But the goddess Isis, already well known to the Egyptians, overshadowed the newly minted Serapis. For centuries, the Egyptians had worshiped Isis as the Great Lady who watched over the Two Lands of Egypt and the home. Isis possessed magical powers and ranked above all other deities. According to her cult legend, Isis rescued her husband-brother, Osiris, from his enemies and brought him back to life with her unwavering love. Osiris's resurrection symbolized to the faithful the new life awaiting them at death. Isis herself was identified with the annual flooding of the Nile, thus assuring the Egyptians of another year of survival. The pharaohs revered Isis as the Mother Goddess, and they claimed to be the incarnation of her son, Horus (Harpocrates). The Ptolemaic rulers, the successors to the pharaohs, also venerated her, and during the Hellenistic Age Isis became associated with many foreign goddesses, fusing with them to emerge as the most honored goddess of the ancient world (Figure 4.8).

From the Seleucid kingdom, the remnants of Babylonian and Persian cultures offered two radically different cults to the Hellenistic Age, the brutal religion of Cybele and the philosophical religion founded by Zoroaster (see Chapter 1). Cybele, the Great Mother goddess, appealed to many women and even a few men, despite the self-mutilation that male believers had to undergo to gain the promise of a new life. Under different names, the Great Mother goddess was worshiped throughout the Hellenistic world and in Rome. Later, Mithraism, an offshoot of Zoroastrianism, with its emphasis on duty and loyalty, caught the attention of Rome's soldiers, thereby ensuring the spread of this belief wherever Roman legions were stationed.

The secret rites of the mystery cults, which communicated the thrill of initiation and the satisfaction of belonging, answered deep psychological needs in their Hellenistic converts. This universal appeal cut across

Figure 4.8 Isis with Her Son Harpocrates (left) and God Anubis (right). First century C.E. Terra-cotta, ht. approx. 7". British Museum. *This small terra-cotta figurine—probably used as a votive—blends Greek sculptural style with Egyptian symbolism. The goddess is portrayed wearing an Egyptian headdress and is flanked by her son and the jackal-headed Anubis, the god of the dead. Greek features include the goddess's tightly curled hair, her slightly contrapposto pose, and the graceful drapery of her dress. The statue, fired on the Italian peninsula in the first century C.E., testifies to the goddess's popularity throughout ancient times and across the Mediterranean world.*

class and racial lines and attracted an ever-widening segment of the populace. With their promise of immortality, these rituals contributed to the atmosphere of the Roman world in which Christianity would later be born.

Science and Medicine

While Hellenistic scientists owed much to their Hellenic predecessors, they broke from the Classical school in many ways. They were more practical and less theoretical than the followers of Plato and Aristotle. They were interested in methodologies more than in speculation, and they tended to question, observe, and experiment rather than to offer explanations and quarrel over abstract issues. They focused on day-to-day matters, such as measuring distances, calculating navigation routes, designing war machines, and solving mathematical problems. And, finally, scientists and philosophers worked in isolation from one another, having little contact either as individuals or in groups. In working in these new ways, they were able during the Hellenistic Age to make scientific advances and discoveries unequaled in any other age—until Europe's Scientific Revolution in the 1600s (see Chapter 15).

The astronomer Aristarchus of Samos [air-uh-STAR-khus] (fl. about 270 B.C.E.) maintained that the sun was the center of the universe and that the earth rotated on its own axis. His conclusions, though considered correct today, were rejected by other ancient astronomers, who thought his views contradicted "common sense." Another astronomer, Eratosthenes [er-uh-TAS-thuh-neez] (about 276–about 194 B.C.E.) of Cyrene, who at one time headed the library in Alexandria, measured the circumference of the earth by creating a mathematical formula based on the differing angles cast by the sun's rays on the earth, when observed from two sites, separated by a known distance. He also devised a grid for measuring the earth, using lines running from north to south and east to west—a system implying that the earth was round.

Euclid [YU-klehd] (fl. about 300 B.C.E.), the most influential mathematician of his time, synthesized the works of earlier scholars to give the classic formulation of both plane and solid geometry. His clear writings laid out mathematical theories, axioms, propositions, and definitions. He was known as the "father of geometry," and Euclidean geometry became the basis of mathematical studies until the nineteenth century.

The best-known Hellenistic scientist, Archimedes [are-kuh-MEED-eez] (about 287–212 B.C.E.) was a mathematician, astronomer, and inventor. He made signal contributions in geometry, but he is best remembered for his studies in mechanics, hydrostatics, gravity, and the principle of buoyancy and for his many inventions. Among his inventions were the Archimedean screw for raising water; improved compound pulleys; and engines of war, including catapults and ramming towers. Many legends accrued to his life, including the famous story, undoubtedly apocryphal, in which he discovered the principle of buoyancy—the relation of fluid loss to weight displacement—while seated in his bath. Excited by the discovery, he leaped from his tub and ran naked down the street, shouting "eureka"—a Greek word meaning "I have found it."

Two physicians living in Alexandria, Herophilus [huh-RAF-uh-lus] (about 335–about 280 B.C.E.) and Erasistratus of Ceos [er-uh-SIS-truht-uhs] (fl. 250 B.C.E.), made breakthroughs in Hellenistic medicine. Like fellow scientists, they validated their work by empirical research. Both were anatomists, whose understanding of the human frame and its operations was based on the dissection of corpses. In studies of the brain, Herophilus was the first to distinguish between the motor and sensory nerves. He also prescribed drugs, a balanced diet, and gymnastics as cures for illnesses. None of his treatises has survived. The second physician, Erasistratus, founded a school of anatomy that flourished for centuries. He is often hailed as the "Father of Physiology," the study of the function of living organisms, based on his research into the circulatory and nervous systems.

Architecture

As in Hellenic times, architecture in the Hellenistic Age reflected the central role that religion played in the life of the people. Public buildings served religious, ceremonial, and governmental purposes, and the temple continued as the leading type of structure. The altar, which had originated in Archaic Greece as a simple structure where holy sacrifices or offerings were made, now became a major structural form, second in importance only to the temple, because of its use in state rituals.

Hellenistic architects modified the basic temple and altar forms inherited from Hellenic models to express the grandeur demanded by the age's rulers. These monarchs were mesmerized by Alexander the Great's claim to divinity, which had opened up a new vision of statecraft. As a result, Alexander's successors built temples and altars whose massive size and elaborate decoration manifested both their own earthly majesty and the divine authority of whatever deity with whom they claimed kinship.

The Corinthian Temple The **Corinthian** temple came to embody Hellenistic splendor. The Corinthian column had first appeared in the Hellenic period, when it was probably used as a decorative feature. Because it was taller, more slender, and more ornamented than either the Doric or the Ionic column, the Corinthian column was now used on the exterior of temples erected by Hellenistic builders for their kings. In time, Hellenistic taste decreed that the Corinthian column was appropriate for massive buildings. The Corinthian order later became the favorite of the Roman emperors, and it was revived in the Renaissance and diffused throughout the Western world, where it survives today as the most visible sign of Hellenistic influence.

The most outstanding Corinthian temples combined grandeur with grace, as in the Olympieum in Athens, now a ruin (Figure 4.9). Commissioned by the Seleucid king Antiochus IV [an-TIE-uh-kuhs], the Olympieum expressed his notion of a diverse, international culture united under Zeus, his divine counterpart and the lord of Mount Olympus. The temple, the first to use Corinthian columns, was constructed dur-

ing three different and distinct historical eras. The stylobate, or base, was laid in the late Archaic Age but then abandoned; the Corinthian columns were raised by Antiochus IV in about 175 B.C.E., after which work was suspended indefinitely; it was finally completed in 130 C.E. under the Roman emperor Hadrian, a great admirer of Greek culture. The temple is stylistically unified, however, because it was finished according to the surviving plans of its second-century B.C.E. architect. Despite its massive size and its lack of mathematical refinements, the Olympieum presented an extremely graceful appearance with its forest of delicate Corinthian columns, consisting of double rows of twenty columns each on the sides and triple rows of eight on the ends.

The Altar Before there were temples, there were altars, the oldest religious structure in the Greek world. The earliest altars were simple slabs, made wide enough to allow sacrificial animals to be slaughtered. During the Hellenistic Age, the altars were substantially

Figure 4.9 The Olympieum. Various dates: late sixth century B.C.E.; second quarter of second century B.C.E.; completed, second quarter of second century C.E. Athens. *The thirteen standing Corinthian columns were part of the original plan of the Olympieum's architect. After the temporary cessation of building in 164 B.C.E., some of this temple's unfinished columns were transported to Rome and reused in a building there. Their use in Rome helped to popularize the Corinthian style among political leaders and wealthy tastemakers.*

108

ENCOUNTER

The Invention of Parchment and the Birth of the Secular Library

The Hellenistic kingdom of Pergamum in northwestern Anatolia (modern Turkey) gave birth to an improved technology for writing surfaces—parchment—and a new civic institution—the secular library. Both achievements played a defining role in the heritage of the West.

Founded in the fifth century B.C.E. by Greek settlers, Pergamum emerged as an important state during the Hellenistic period. Under the Attalid dynasty, beginning in 263 B.C.E., Pergamum reached its zenith, holding sway over most of Anatolia. In 133 B.C.E., the last Attalid king, Attalos III [AT-uh-luhs], died without an heir, leaving his kingdom to Rome.

The peoples of Hellenistic Pergamum constituted a rich ethnic mixture. Besides the founding Greeks, the populace included many peoples from Anatolia, known collectively as Orientals. With differing languages, religions, and traditions, the Pergamenes were typical of the ethnic variety of the time. Faced with polyglot subjects, divided into many minorities and lacking a coherent majority, Pergamum's kings responded with creative cultural projects. Perhaps as a unifying point, they launched a building program to beautify their acropolis (see Figures 4.2 and 4.10). What was especially new about this project, and which appealed to Pergamum's multicultural ethos, was the building of a monumental library (now lost), which can be claimed as one of the first secular libraries in the world.

Libraries are as old as civilization. For example, the remains of a library have been uncovered in Mesopotamia, dating from about 2500 B.C.E. This and other early libraries housed writings preserved on either clay tablets (Mesopotamia) or rolled-up papyrus scrolls (Greece), and, in virtually all cases, the writing collections were meant to serve religious and/or civic purposes. The first librarians were priests.

That changed when Egypt's king, Ptolemy II Philadelphus (285–246 B.C.E.), founded his library at Alexandria. A repository of papyrus scrolls, it formed part of the research complex called the Alexandrian Museum. This library inspired envy in Pergamum's ruler, Eumenes II [YOU-muh-neez] (r. 263–241 B.C.E.), and a desire to establish his own library, thereby launching a race for manuscripts between the rival rulers. To defeat his Pergamene rival, Ptolemy II banned the export of papyrus from Egypt. In retaliation, Eumenes II encouraged anonymous craftspeople to develop parchment as a writing surface—an innovation that proved more durable and cheaper than papyrus. The word *parchment* evolved from its Latin name, *charta pergamena*, which pays homage to its invention in Pergamum.

Pergamum's library was a truly secular building, even though it housed a statue of Athena, the goddess of wisdom (Encounter figure 4.1). The library itself was neither attached to a temple nor part of a religious sanctuary. The link to Athena was for symbolic, not religious, reasons, and, hence, the library's basic purpose was as a repository for books. Pergamum's library, with its writings on parchment, set the standard for the secular libraries that followed.

The invention of parchment also revolutionized the acquisition of knowledge. **Parchment** is made from

enlarged. The biggest appears to have been the 650-foot-long altar, permitting the sacrifice of more than one hundred cattle at one time, funded by the tyrant of Syracuse in the third century B.C.E.

Although the Syracusan altar has disappeared, the dismantled altar of Zeus at Pergamum has recently been discovered and reassembled. It is easy to see why ancient travelers called it one of the wonders of the world (Figure 4.10). The actual altar, not visible in the photograph, stands lengthwise in a magnificent Ionic colonnaded courtyard. The courtyard itself is raised on a **podium**, or platform; below the courtyard, the sides of the structure are decorated with a sculptured frieze depicting the deities at war. The overall design—with the frieze below the columns—appears to be an inversion of the usual temple plan. Constructed by Eumenes II of the Attalid dynasty, this altar was but one part of a concerted effort to transform Pergamum into another Athens. Thus, the idea of a "new" Athens—a recurrent motif in the humanistic tradition—had already been formulated by the Hellenistic Age.

calf-, sheep-, or goatskins that have been treated to make a writing surface. Skins had been used for centuries for this purpose, but the Pergamenes improved the process, creating a supple surface capable of storing writing on both sides. With the double-sided page now possible, the door was open to a bound book—called a **codex** by the Romans. The codex made a basic change to the act of reading. Reading a codex required turning and closing the pages of a book, rather than unwinding and rewinding a papyrus roll.

Learning from the Encounter Describe the population mixture of Hellenistic Pergamum. **What** cultural impact did the diverse population of Pergamum have on the rulers? **How** did the Pergamene library differ from earlier libraries in the ancient world? **What** event led the Pergamene ruler to the use of parchment for manuscripts in his library? **What** is a codex? **Compare and contrast** reading from a papyrus scroll and reading from a codex. **Consider** the impact of technological changes on the act of reading, from reading a scroll to reading a book to reading a computer screen.

Encounter figure 4.1 *Athena.* From library at Pergamum. Second century B.C.E. Copy of a fifth-century B.C.E. original. Marble. Antikensammlung, Staatliche Museen, Berlin. *This statue of the goddess Athena is freely adapted from an original that stood in the Parthenon (see Figure 3.2). Although the original statue of Athena was intended for display within a religious sanctuary, this Pergamene copy is meant for a truly secular purpose: to be a symbol of learning within the library, where it stood. The Pergamene Athena is also executed fully in the round, thereby enhancing its status as a secular work of art. Such secular adaptations of earlier religious sculptures were a central feature of the art of the Hellenistic period.*

Sculpture

Like Hellenistic architects, Hellenistic sculptors adapted many of the basic forms and ideas of the Hellenic style to meet the tastes of their day. The Hellenistic sculptors perpetuated such Hellenic principles as contrapposto and proportion as well as the Hellenic emphasis on religious and moral themes. But Hellenistic art increasingly expressed a secular, urban viewpoint, and Hellenic restraint often gave way to realism, eroticism, and violence, expressed and en-

joyed for their own sake. Some of these Hellenistic qualities are apparent in the refreshingly naturalistic sculpture *Boy Struggling with a Goose* (Figure 4.11). At the same time, this work of art relates ironically to the age's values because it can be understood on two levels: Its subject is both an everyday scene and a mock-heroic battle; its playful nature masks a sense of violence; and its twisting forms and shifting planes seem overdone on such a small scale.

Between 230 and 220 B.C.E., King Attalos I of Pergamum dedicated in Athens a group of bronze sculptures

110

Figure 4.10 Altar of Zeus at Pergamum. (Reconstruction.) 170s B.C.E. Pergamum Museum, Berlin. *This masterpiece of Hellenistic architecture was erected in the 170s B.C.E. by Eumenes II, the king of Pergamum, to commemorate his victories over various barbarian states in Asia Minor. Eumenes believed himself to be the savior and disseminator of Greek culture, and this altar with its giant frieze was meant to suggest Hellenic monuments, such as the Athenian Parthenon.*

Figure 4.11 *Boy Struggling with a Goose.* Roman copy of a Greek original, dating from second half of second century B.C.E. Marble, ht. 33½″. Capitoline Museum, Rome. *When Hellenistic sculptors freed themselves from the ideals of Hellenic art, one of the results was the production of works on unhackneyed themes, as in* Boy Struggling with a Goose. *So popular was this genre scene that several versions of it are known from antiquity. Its popularity reflects the age's delight in childhood and its joys—perhaps an outgrowth of the rising status of women in Hellenistic times.*

Figure 4.12 *Dying Gaul.* Ca. 230–220 B.C.E. Roman marble copy of a bronze original, ht. 3′. Capitoline Museum, Rome. *The rulers of the Hellenistic kingdom of Pergamum preferred art that was showy and overwrought, a taste that perhaps stemmed from their insecurity at being a new dynasty. A Pergamene style of sculpture developed under these kings, in which gestures were theatrical and anatomical features were portrayed in exaggerated depth. The* Dying Gaul *is a superb example of this style.*

that celebrated his recent victory over the barbaric Gauls. By donating these bronzes to Athens, which was outside of Pergamum's political orbit, the Attalid ruler hoped to establish his cultural credentials as a defender of Greek culture and thus further his claims to rule over the entire Hellenistic world.

One of these pieces, *Dying Gaul* (which survives only in a Roman marble copy), shows a mortally wounded barbarian warrior (Figure 4.12). The torque, or twisted necklace, he wears identifies him as a Gaul. Lying close by are his sword and trumpet. The sculptor demonstrates his keen eye for realistic details in the open wound oozing blood from the warrior's rib cage and by the blank stare as he faces death. The Hellenistic style's appreciation of the melodramatic is evident in the tension between the warrior's sagging body and his efforts to prop himself up. But by treating a foreign enemy with such nobility, the anonymous sculptor perpetuated the deep moral sense that was central to Hellenic art.

A radically different subject is treated in the *Old Market Woman*, which, like a stock character from New Comedy, depicted a well-known social type (Figure 4.13). The old woman, who might have strolled out of the marketplace of any Hellenistic city, represented a

Figure 4.13 *Old Market Woman.* Third or second century B.C.E. Roman marble copy of a Hellenistic bronze, ht. 49″. Metropolitan Museum of Art. *Many Hellenistic sculptors depicted old women in pathetic situations, tired, drunk, or begging. Scholars are divided in opinion about whether these statues were meant to be admired for their truthfulness or whether they represented disdain for what Hellenistic aristocrats considered an ugly social phenomenon.*

genre subject, or a scene taken from everyday life. The original third-century B.C.E. bronze portrayed a stooped figure, straining under the combined weight of her groceries and her advancing years. In this Roman marble copy, the left arm is missing, but she carries a fowl and a brimming bucket. Her deeply lined and wrinkled face and her sagging breasts express the realism of Hellenistic style.

Among the masterpieces of Hellenistic art are the sculptures of the Pergamum altar frieze, which can be seen in Figure 4.10. The subject is a battle between the Olympian deities and the Giants, the monstrous race of pre-Greek gods and goddesses who were the offspring of Gaea (Earth) and Uranus (Sky, or the Heavens)—the first rulers of the universe. The Giants, having overthrown their parents, are then defeated by *their* own children, the Olympian deities. To the Greeks, the final triumph of the Olympian gods and goddesses symbolized the coming of a just and moral order both in the universe and in their own society.

Hence, when the Attalid rulers chose this subject for the altar frieze, they affirmed that they were continuing the values of Greek civilization. With the exception of the frieze on the Parthenon, the figures on this altar represent the most ambitious sculptural project in the ancient world.

Filled with high-powered energy, the Pergamum frieze displays figures that threaten to explode from the space in which they are barely contained. In one celebrated panel, Athena grasps the dying Giant Alkyoneus while her sacred snake bites him on the chest (Figure 4.14). Her agitated draperies appear to be billowing in a strong wind, so that the folds hang expressively rather than simply disclosing her body, as in the Hellenic style. The expression of pain on Alkyoneus's face—deeply furrowed brow and bulging eyeballs—and the straining muscles with prominent veins reflect the Pergamum school's taste for exaggeration.

The sculpture of the Hellenistic Age is also characterized by a frank appreciation of female beauty, a famous

Figure 4.14 *Athena Battling with Alkyoneus.* From the Great Frieze of the Pergamum altar, east section. 170s B.C.E. Marble, 7'6". Pergamum Museum, Berlin. *An unusual aspect of this relief is the diversity of the figures' bodily forms. For example, Alkyoneus's outspread wings identify him as a Giant and an offspring of Gaea, the goddess of the Earth, who is shown on the bottom right.*

example of which is the *Aphrodite of Melos*, perhaps better known as the Venus de Milo (Figure 4.15). This original sculpture, carved from Parian marble, shows many borrowings from the tradition of Praxiteles, as shown in his *Hermes with the Infant Dionysus* (see Figure 3.26). Both Aphrodite and Hermes exhibit exaggerated contrapposto; a sensuous, even erotic, modeling of the body; and a serene countenance with an unmistakable gaze. However, the Hellenistic sculptor, demonstrating a playful flair with the rolled-down draperies, calls attention to Aphrodite's exposed lower torso.

The *Aphrodite of Melos* was part of the growing influence of **Neoclassicism,** which swept the disintegrating Hellenistic world in the wake of Rome's rise to greatness. Neoclassicism, developing first in Athens in the late third century B.C.E. and later in Pergamum and other cities, was a kind of nostalgia for the glory days of the fifth and fourth centuries B.C.E. Another famous work in this style was the *Borghese Gladiator,* which combines the well-defined musculature perfected during the Hellenic period with a dramatic lunging pose so favored by Hellenistic taste (Figure 4.16). Probably commissioned by a Roman patron, this sculpture of a warrior standing on a plinth—a base for a statue—is thought to be either a copy of or inspired by a third- or second-century B.C.E. original. Its status as a copy is indicated by the tree trunk support—the place where the sculptor, Agasias of Ephesus (in modern Turkey), carved his name.

The *Horse and Jockey*, original bronzes that were retrieved in the twentieth century from a sunken ship in the Aegean Sea off Artemision, shows Hellenistic fluidity rather than the frozen style of Hellenic art (Figure 4.17). Whether the two figures are a true ensemble is a subject of scholarly debate. Arguing against their unity is the size disparity between the small jockey and the enormous horse, but the balance seems in favor of treating them as a group, especially when the jockey is seated on the horse. In this juxtaposition, the horse's forward motion seems to cause the jockey's cloak to blow behind him. The boy, contorting his face with the strain of the race, stretches out his left hand, as if to urge his mount on to victory. This sculptured pair shows other innovations in Hellenistic art. The boy athlete, who looks rather like a ragged street urchin, represents the new interest in children that arose in Hellenistic art, and the straining horse contrasts dramatically with the serene, well-proportioned horses on the Parthenon frieze.

Late Hellenistic Style: Rhodes

Although much of the Hellenistic world, including Greece, fell into Roman hands in 146 B.C.E., the Aegean

Figure 4.15 *Aphrodite of Melos (Venus de Milo).* Ca. 160–150 B.C.E. Marble, ht. 6′10″. Louvre. *This celebrated statue represents the classicizing tendency, derived from Greek tradition, in Hellenistic art. The head is executed in the pure Hellenic style, as seen in the serene countenance, the exquisitely detailed hair, and the finely chiseled features. However, the body, with its frank sensuality and its rumpled draperies, is clearly in the Hellenistic style.*

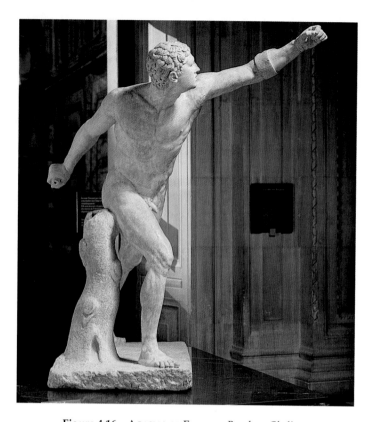

Figure 4.16 AGASIAS OF EPHESUS. *Borghese Gladiator.* Ca. 100 B.C.E. Marble, ht. 5′6½″. Louvre. *The subject here is not a gladiator, for the Greeks were ignorant of the circus games. Instead, based on the upturned gaze and the upraised left arm, the statue depicts a warrior on foot fighting for his life against an unseen opponent on horseback. The outmatched warrior is thus a figure of pathos, a beloved theme during the Hellenistic period. Yet Agasias has injected into this theme the rugged athleticism of the fourth century B.C.E. Lost in antiquity, the statue was acquired by a Borghese prince on its rediscovery in the seventeenth century C.E. Today, the* Borghese Gladiator, *newly restored in 1997, stands in a place of honor in the Louvre.*

island of Rhodes remained free for over sixty more years (see Map 4.1). During this period, independent Rhodes became a cultural center that rivaled the older cities of Pergamum, Alexandria, and Athens in concentration of scientists, artists, and humanists. The Rhodian style, which alternated between lighthearted and gay on the one hand and colossal and theatrical on the other, was influenced by the Pergamene school and was the final stage of Hellenistic art.

A graceful example of this statuary type is a Roman copy of one figure from a Rhodian sculptural group dating from the mid–second century B.C.E (Figure 4.18). The muse is probably either Melpomene, muse of tragedy, or Polyhymnia, muse of the choral hymn. She is portrayed as a young woman leaning against a support, lost in thought. Except for her left foot and left hand, she is swathed in draperies, a typically Hellenistic way of portraying women. The large number of statues of draped women surviving from the Hellenistic era reflects the rising social status of respectable women during this time.

The school of sculpture on Rhodes, even after the island's absorption into Rome, was still able to produce the sublime masterpiece of Rhodian and Hellenistic art, *The Laocoön Group* (Figure 4.19). The sculptors of this famous group, probably Hagesandros [haj-uh-SAN-drohs], Polydoros [pol-e-DOOR-uhs], and Athanadoros [ah-thay-nuh-DOOR-uhs], were all members of a local dynasty of sculptors. Their sculpture depicts the priest Laocoön and his sons. According to Vergil's *Aeneid*, the Roman epic, Laocoön, a priest of Neptune, warned the Trojans not to bring the wooden horse—which, unknown to him, concealed a party of Greek warriors—into their city. (Laocoön's admonition to beware Greeks bearing gifts has become

Figure 4.17 *Horse and Jockey of Artemision.* Mid–second century B.C.E. Bronze, ht. of jockey 33½″. National Museum, Athens. *The jockey and horse may have been intended by an athlete as a votive offering to a deity for victory in a competition. Such statues had been erected in Greece from the Archaic Age onward.*

Figure 4.18 *Muse (Melpomene or Polyhymnia [?]).* Roman copy, probably of a mid-second-century B.C.E. original by Philiskos of Rhodes. Ht. 4′11″ without plinth. Capitoline Museum, Rome. *The sculptor has portrayed the muse in a simple but dignified pose—leaning forward on a support, left foot upturned, chin resting on curved right hand—and swathed her in a thin mantle of fabric that falls into rhythmic folds. The contrast between the serenely meditative face and the dynamic drapery pattern is a typical effect of Hellenistic art (see Figure 4.14).*

Figure 4.19 HAGESANDROS, POLYDOROS, AND ATHANADOROS. *The Laocoön Group.* Ca. 50 C.E. Marble, ht. 8′. Vatican Museum. *Parallels are frequently made between the distorted features of the dying Laocoön and those of the mortally wounded Alkyoneus from the Pergamum altar (see Figure 4.14). This similarity points to some connection between the Rhodian and Pergamene schools of sculpture, though the exact relationship is a matter of controversy.*

proverbial.) As Laocoön finished his speech, sea serpents, sent by the gods, raced out of the sea and bit and crushed him and his two sons to death. The Trojans interpreted Laocoön's speech as an impious act against the gods, and they hauled the horse into Troy.

In the *Laocoön* sculptural group, the snakes, which grasp and bite the priest and his sons, serve to integrate the three figures into an image of unrelieved horror: Laocoön's face is contorted in anguish as the serpent bites him; on the left, one of his sons is already dead; and the other son seems to be disentangling himself from the serpentine coils. This celebrated work, with its technical virtuosity and its rhetorical violence, is a fitting climax to almost four hundred years of Hellenistic art. The *Laocoön* sculptural group vanished after the fall of Rome, only to be rediscovered in the early sixteenth century C.E., when it influenced the sculptor Michelangelo and the subsequent rise of Baroque art (see Chapters 12 and 14).

The Legacy of the Hellenistic World

In the Hellenistic Age, Athens and its culture achieved the status of an inspiring model to be honored and emulated. But the Hellenistic rulers had no interest in democracy; indeed, their larger political interests often conflicted with the needs of local subjects. Nor did these kings want to further humanism, which they regarded as either irrelevant to imperial goals or subversive of them. What appealed to the Hellenistic kings was a narrow, lifeless humanism, as exemplified by the dynasties of the Attalids in Pergamum and the Ptolemies in Egypt. The Hellenistic monarchs wanted to do no more than create new cultural centers that rivaled the fame of the old Athens. The great Hellenistic centers of Pergamum and Alexandria—with their libraries, poets, scientists, artists, schools of philosophy, marble buildings, and monuments—were perceived as politically useful to these ambitious rulers. In other words, they wanted to harness art to politics for propaganda purposes.

The Hellenistic world bequeathed the idea of a "new Athens" to Rome, which was, in part, inspired by its many cities, urban life, and civic culture. Rome in turn diffused the Greek heritage to the major cities of the entire Mediterranean area. After the fall of Rome, the medieval rulers adopted this tradition, making their governments responsive to the religious and, to a lesser extent, the cultural needs of their citizens. With the rise of the secular state in the eighteenth century C.E., governments began to dissociate themselves from the religious lives of their people. But state support of the arts and humanities increased and remains today a legacy of the Hellenistic Age to the modern world.

Hellenistic sculpture and architecture left their mark on later civilizations. Artists brought to their genre sculpture an invigorating realism that expressed emotions and individualism. They introduced the portrayal of female nudity, a practice that has persisted in Western art to the present day, with the exception of the Christian Middle Ages. Their emphasis on individualism influenced Roman sculptors, who, in carving many lifelike busts during the republic, preserved this tradition in Western art. The Corinthian temple, perfected in the Hellenistic era, set the standard in decoration and proportion for Roman temples and, along with the Doric and Ionic styles, was adopted and modified for many public structures.

A final legacy of the Hellenistic Age was its schools of philosophy—Stoicism, Epicureanism, Skepticism, and Cynicism. Although contradictory of each other, these schools of thought had a common appeal: the promise of a stable belief system and inner peace in the face of a hostile and chaotic environment. From Roman times to the present, these philosophies have attracted followers, but Stoicism has had the most enduring impact (on republican Rome, early Christianity, and the Enlightenment), with Epicureanism the next most influential (on the Scientific Revolution and the twentieth century). With their advice to disengage oneself from either the world or one's own passions, these four schools have provided solace in every age marked by overwhelming events and social disorder.

KEY CULTURAL TERMS

Hellenistic	Epicureanism
koine	*ataraxia*
cosmopolitan	Stoicism
New Comedy	*logos*
comedy of manners	Corinthian
Alexandrianism	parchment
pastoral	codex
idyll	podium
Cynicism	genre subject
autarky	Neoclassicism
Skepticism	

SUGGESTIONS FOR FURTHER READING

AUSTIN, M. M., ed. *The Hellenistic World from Alexander to the Roman Conquest: A Selection of Ancient Sources in Translation.* Cambridge: Cambridge University Press, 1981. Letters, decrees, and official pronouncements from the Hellenistic period; provides a real sense of the time.

SHAPIRO, H., and CURLEY, E., eds. *Hellenistic Philosophy: Selected Readings.* New York: Modern Library, 1965. Selections from writings on Epicureanism, Stoicism, Skepticism, and Neo-Platonism, with short introductions.

5 ROMAN CIVILIZATION
The Pre-Christian Centuries

Roman civilization is as ancient as Greek civilization, but it reached its peak later. From its legendary founding in 753 B.C.E., Rome grew steadily from a tiny city-state ruled by kings to a powerful republic, constantly adjusting to internal and external forces, and ultimately to a vast empire that controlled the known Western world. This chapter surveys Rome from its founding to its near collapse in 284 C.E. Chapter 7 follows the story of Rome through its rejuvenated and Christian period to the last days of the empire. Before that, Chapter 6 examines the Judeo-Christian tradition that wove itself inextricably into the Western heritage during the first centuries of imperial Rome.

THE COLOSSUS OF THE MEDITERRANEAN WORLD

In 248 C.E., the Romans celebrated the one-thousandth anniversary of the founding of their city. By that date, the Roman way of life had not only engulfed the peoples and cultures of the ancient Near East and the eastern Mediterranean but also brought the light of civilized existence to the tribes living in North Africa, in western Europe to the Rhine River, in central Europe to the Danube River, and in England (Map 5.1). So vast was Rome's dominion and so powerful its influence that until the eighteenth century, Rome was the exemplar of power and wealth, one that the nations of Europe could only dream of equaling. Roman civilization had a profound and lasting impact on life in the West.

◀ **Detail** Arch of Titus. Ca. 81 C.E. Marble, ht. 47′2″. Rome.

Map 5.1   THE ROMAN EMPIRE UNDER AUGUSTUS, 14 C.E.
This map shows the Roman Empire at the death of its founder, Augustus. **Notice** the wide-ranging lands incorporated into the Roman world. **Compare** this map with Map 1.1, Ancient Mesopotamia and Egypt, and Map 4.1, The Successor States and the Hellenistic World, and see which ancient civilizations were now included in the Roman Empire. **What** impact did these ancient civilizations have on Roman cultural life? **What** role did the Mediterranean Sea play in the Roman Empire? **How** did Rome's location make it a convenient site for the imperial government?

General Characteristics of Roman Civilization

Who were the Romans, and how did they create such a successful civilization? The Romans were, above all, a practical people, interested chiefly in what was useful. Possessed of a virile moral sense, they were inclined to view intellectual brilliance with suspicion. Furthermore, Roman authority figures cultivated the virtue known in Latin as *gravitas,* or gravity, meaning a deep-seated seriousness (Figure 5.1). By Greek standards, the Romans were a dull lot, too self-controlled and afraid of the imagination. But the Romans were ingenious at adapting borrowed cultural forms and had a gift for governing.

Early Rome was a minor city-state founded by herdsmen and farmers on seven low hills beside the Tiber River in central Italy. Over their long rise to world leadership, the Romans changed radically, but they never ceased to honor their agrarian roots. Ro-

man morality and Roman law both echoed a rural ethic by stressing the importance of nature and of living within one's means. Roman literary culture was also deeply imbued with a reverence for a rustic past. When Rome became prosperous, many writers bemoaned the corrupting power of luxury and appealed to the homespun values of Rome's founders.

Another important Roman value was the sanctity of the family. Divorce was unheard of until the late republican era, and even then family values continued to be eulogized by moralists and honored by leaders. Roles were strictly defined within the Roman family, which was guided by the father, the *paterfamilias,* who exercised legal power of life and death over his entire household, including his spouse, children, relatives, servants, and slaves (Figure 5.2). The paterfamilias wielded greater authority than his Greek counterpart, but, in contrast, the Roman matron was freer and had more practical influence than did the secluded wives

Figure 5.1 *Head of a Roman.* Ca. 80 B.C.E. Marble, life size. Palazzo Torlonia, Rome. *This Roman head is an excellent example of the highly individualized portraits that flowered in the Late Republic, beginning in about 100 B.C.E. Note the bald head, deeply lined and scarred face, sunken eyes, and clenched jaw— signs of an extremely realistic style. In cultural terms, the portrait personifies the period's reverence for great age, lack of vanity, and self-discipline—all traditional Roman virtues, greatly admired by the ruling elite. In artistic terms, the individuality of the face reflects the use of a funeral mask, a common custom of the period. With the coming of the empire, after 31 B.C.E., the realistic style became less pronounced, as the Romans explored earlier phases of Greek art.*

of Greece. In general, the Roman matron was conspicuously present in society, attending and presiding at gatherings along with her spouse and supervising the education of both her female and her male offspring (Figure 5.3).

Religion permeated family life, and each Roman household kept an undying fire burning on its hearth, symbolic of the goddess Vesta, to ensure the family's continuity. The family revered the deceased male ancestors, whose funeral masks adorned the walls and were regularly used in domestic rituals.

In sum, the Roman citizen was secure in the knowledge of both Rome's and his place in the world and in the cosmos. And the Roman matron, though lacking the voting rights citizenship gave to her spouse, played many roles that society and tradition demanded of her.

Figure 5.2 *Patrician with Busts of Ancestors (Barberini Togatus).* Early first century C.E. Marble, ht. 5'5". Palazzo dei Conservatori, Rome. *The stern and wrinkled faces of the anonymous patrician and his ancestors convey the quiet dignity and authority of the typical paterfamilias. Some scholars think that these portrait busts, with their unflattering realism, were modeled on death masks.*

Figure 5.3 *Eumachia.* Mid–first century C.E. Marble. Museo Nazionale, Naples. *This statue of Eumachia, which was found at Pompeii, shows that Roman matrons were involved in public life. The inscription on the statue's base praises her for having donated a building in the town's forum for the use of the fullers—workers involved in the making of woolen cloth. Her statue was paid for by the fullers' association in gratitude for her gift. Her idealized face reflects the Hellenic ideal preferred during the reign of Augustus in the first century* C.E.

Technology

Technology was the cultural sphere in which Rome's practical genius shone. Roman inventors, building on the heritage of prior Mediterranean peoples, created

the most advanced technological society in the ancient world. Warfare and construction, both essential for empire building, proved to be the technologies in which Rome cast the longest shadow.

Warfare   Pagan Rome's infantry was second to none in antiquity. Two major defeats, between 500 B.C.E. and 284 C.E., only served to energize the Romans, encouraging them to learn from their enemies: They were the virtual annihilation of an entire army at Cannae (in Italy) during the First Punic War, in 216 B.C.E.; and the loss at Carrhae in far-off Parthia (modern Iran), in 53 B.C.E. Rome's offensive weapons included swords, daggers, pikes, spears, maces, and bows. Defensive weaponry included shields, helmets, and body armor. Armor came in two styles, either scale (closely fitted pieces in metal, fishlike scales) or chain mail (small metal rings joined tightly together). Chain mail, being lighter, was more serviceable, thus allowing greater maneuverability. In this Age of Infantry, the cavalry played a secondary role, as the Roman military had not yet learned to armor its horses.

Roman ingenuity led to improved artillery in support of the infantry. The catapult (from Greek, *kata*, "to pierce," and *pelte*, "shield") became Rome's chief engine of destruction, striking terror into enemy hearts. At first, catapults comprised two types: one for hurling iron-tipped wooden javelins, to kill enemy troops; the other for throwing heavy stones to breach walls. In about 100 C.E., Dionysius of Alexandria devised a third type of catapult: a rapid-fire version capable of shooting short iron-tipped javelins—an ancestor of the machine gun. Catapults could be mounted on wheels, and pulled by oxen, if the terrain allowed. The Romans called their catapults *onagers*, "wild asses," because of their recoil, or "back kicking," effect.

From a humble start, Rome's navy grew to challenge and then defeat Greece and Carthage. At the end of the First Punic War against Carthage in 241 B.C.E., Rome ruled the Mediterranean. Its navy adopted the Greek trireme (see Chapter 3) and the Carthaginian quinquereme, an open galley with five banks of rowers, to convert both ship types into fighting machines. Each galley became a floating army, crammed with sailors and marines. Each galley was outfitted with a grappling hook, or *corvus*, for holding fast two battling ships, and a hinged gangplank, which served as a boarding ramp for the marines. Improved ship design and innovative fighting tactics eventually secured Rome's naval superiority. Specifically, by 133 B.C.E., the gangplank and the *corvus* were obsolete; the open galley was replaced by a fully decked galley with platforms for archers; and hand-to-hand combat gave way to artillery assault by archers. A final innovation was the liburnian, a fully decked bireme, powered by two sets of oarsmen, which helped Rome to victory at Actium, in 31 B.C.E. Thereafter, the liburnian was Rome's leading warship.

Construction Rome's construction technology made possible the spectacular structures that inspired the phrase "the grandeur of Rome." These building achievements are discussed elsewhere in this chapter (see "Architecture"). Besides these achievements, another memorable Roman structure is Hadrian's Wall, in southern Scotland. Built to keep barbarian invaders from Roman Britain, this largely stone barrier rose 18 feet in height and extended nearly 112 miles, from the North Sea to the Irish Sea. It was punctuated with forts, customs stops, signal posts, and, on either side, a 30-foot-wide moat for added protection. Soldiers were posted on its top, which functioned as a road. Using flares, the guards could send messages rapidly along the barrier's length. The wall's name memorializes Emperor Hadrian, who constructed it between 117 and 138 C.E.

The Romans developed other construction materials and techniques that set the standard for centuries. In brick technology, workers mass-produced bricks for imperial projects, as brickmaking became a state monopoly. In building construction, inventors developed a stronger truss—a triangular support, made of either timber or metal and used to stabilize a roof. In plumbing (from the Latin word *plumbum*, "lead"), the Romans introduced lead pipes to conduct freshwater, through a gravity system, from aqueducts to buildings and fountains, and to flush wastewater into rivers. In glass technology, glassblowing was invented, probably by Syrians, in the first century B.C.E. Other inventions followed, such as the first flat window glass and the method of blowing glass into molds to make flasks. And, in furniture technology, the Romans designed and built couches, chairs (with and without arms), folding chairs, stools, benches, tables (round and rectangular), and storage chests, all adapted mainly from the Greeks and built of wood, wickerwork, or bronze. These household items became the Western norm that home furnishings follow today.

The Etruscan and Greek Connections

Although the Romans took great pride in their native tradition, they were receptive to change and able to assimilate the contributions of superior cultures, as their experience with the Etruscans and the Greeks demonstrates. In the late seventh century B.C.E., Rome, still a small city-state, was subjugated by the Etruscans, a sophisticated urban people of obscure origins in northern Italy (Figure 5.4). The Etruscans excelled at commerce and conducted a brisk maritime trade with the advanced cultures of the eastern Mediterranean (Figure 5.5). Under Etruscan domination, Rome prospered and became a hub of commerce and transportation. Romans also began to put their spoken language into writing, using the Etruscan alphabet. Even what are called Roman numerals were invented by the Etruscans.

Whereas the Etruscans had conquered the Romans, it was the Romans who made the opening move in conquering the Greeks, beginning in 275 B.C.E. with the Greek colonies in southern Italy, or Magna Graecia. More conquests followed as Rome, between 146 and 31 B.C.E., assimilated the separate Hellenistic kingdoms into its overseas empire. Styling themselves after the defeated Hellenistic rulers, the Roman emperors eventually claimed to be immortal gods, turning the state into a divine monarchy. The emperors also adopted the civilizing mission of the Hellenistic kingdoms, thus giving Rome's domestic and foreign policies a new moral dimension.

The conquest of the Hellenistic kingdoms propelled Rome to the height of ancient civilization. However, in the end, Greek civilization conquered the conquerors, for when the Greek cultural forms (lyric and epic poetry, the arts, and architecture, among others) were imported into Rome, the Romans were forced out of their exclusively practical ways. The Romans coined the term *humanities* to refer to the artistic, literary, and philosophical activities the Greeks considered basic to civilized life. But the humanities themselves were Greek inventions, as was the belief that the study and practice of the humanities is stimulating to the soul (mind). Thus, the humanities, which originated among the artists and intellectuals of Archaic and Hellenic Greece, were preserved and transmitted by the Romans, an achievement that some historians regard as Rome's finest.

The Roman Empire was centuries in the making, and pre-Christian Roman history can be divided into three periods reflecting the prevailing type of government: monarchy (753–509 B.C.E.), republic (509–31 B.C.E.), and empire (31 B.C.E.–284 C.E.) (Timeline 5.1). In each period, earlier traits and values endured.

Rome in the Age of Kings, 753–509 B.C.E.

During the Age of Kings, some basic components of Roman political, social, and economic structures were established. The city-state, although ruled by kings, had a balanced system of government in which a council of landowners helped select the ruler and the entire people ratified its choice. This system ended in

Figure 5.4   *Tomb of the Leopards. Tarquinia. 480–470 B.C.E. Fresco. This wall fresco, from an Etruscan tomb, depicts a banquet scene. Reclining on couches, male and female diners talk together and share food and drink, as two male waiters serve the party (in the foreground). Because of such joyous scenes, the Etruscans are often described as an optimistic people in the face of death. Egyptian influence on Etruscan art is visible in the contrasting skin tones of the figures, with women paler than men (see Figure 1.21). Greek influence can be seen in the dining arrangement—a typical Greek banqueting scene.*

Timeline 5.1   THE ROMAN MILLENNIUM, 753 B.C.E.–248 C.E.

753 B.C.E.		509 B.C.E.		31 B.C.E.	284 C.E.
	Monarchy		**Republic**	**Empire**	
Founding of Rome	**ca. 600** Etruscan rulers	Founding of the republic		Founding of the empire	1,000th birthday of Rome

about 600 B.C.E. when the Etruscans imposed their rulers on Rome, but it became a model for government under the republic.

Also taking root at this time was another persistent feature of Roman political and economic life—class conflict. As Rome expanded, some urban dwellers, debarred from the aristocracy by poverty and birth, took advantage of commercial opportunities and began to engage in trade. The plebeians, as this class was called, accumulated wealth and began to challenge the social power of the landed aristocrats. When the aris-

tocrats abolished the monarchy and established the republic, they safeguarded their power by denying citizenship to the plebeians. This policy of exclusion laid the groundwork for centuries of class conflict.

The Roman Republic, 509–31 B.C.E.

In 509 B.C.E., the Roman aristocrats threw off their Etruscan overlords and founded a republic. Unlike the Greeks, whose political order consisted of short-lived

Figure 5.5 *Apollo of Veii.* Early fifth century B.C.E. Painted terra cotta, ht. 70". Museo Nazionale di Villa Guilia, Rome. *This magnificent striding statue of Apollo shows strong influences from the art of Archaic Greece, such as the proportion of the torso to the limbs and the enigmatic smile. But the superb mastery of movement achieved by the Etruscan artist is well in advance of the Greek style.*

leagues of city-states, the Romans established a republic whose provinces eventually reached the eastern Mediterranean and that lasted almost five hundred years. This republic, in contrast to Athens's direct democracy, was based on a system of representatives and a separation of powers. Rome's achievement is unsurpassed in Western history.

Rome's republic is divided into three principal periods: early, middle, and late. During these tumultuous periods, Rome became a world power (Timeline 5.2).

The Early Republic, 509–264 B.C.E. Two major crises, one domestic and one foreign, faced the Early Republic and threatened to overwhelm the fledgling state. The domestic issue stemmed from the division of society into two classes—the landed, aristocratic patricians and the unorganized, disenfranchised plebeians. As the patricians dismantled the monarchy and set up a republic, they continued to exclude the plebeians from political life. They placed executive power with two consuls, each with veto power over the other. They gave legal and fiscal power to magistracies—public offices—and legislative and judicial powers to an assembly. But real power resided with the Senate, the successor to the old council of landowners that had existed under the kings. The plebeians were given no part in these reforms, but, over the years, they steadily won concessions. By 287 B.C.E., they had gained all the rights of citizenship enjoyed by the ruling patricians.

The foreign crisis faced by Rome was the military conquest of the various peoples inhabiting the Italian peninsula. During these first foreign wars, the Romans originated the strategy that became the key to their military success. They permitted defeated peoples to remain self-governing, to keep their own religions, and, most especially, to satisfy obligations to Rome by providing troops for her armies instead of paying taxes. This strategy allowed the former foes some freedom and yet subtly tied them to Rome.

The Middle Republic, 264–133 B.C.E. Roman armies had conquered Italy, but up and down the peninsula restless tribes were not yet securely attached to Rome. The challenge was to convert them to the Roman way of life. By founding new towns and enticing settlers with offers of free land and full Roman citizenship, Rome eventually united the entire population. Roman law and the Latin language triumphed on the Italian peninsula.

509	264	133	31
Early Republic	Middle Republic	Late Republic	

Rome establishes republican form of government, subdues Italian peninsula	**264–241** First Punic War	**219–202** Second Punic War	**149–146** Third Punic War	**133–31** Rome acquires Hellenistic kingdoms; social, political unrest	**44** Julius Caesar assassinated **44–31** civil war

Beyond the peninsula, Rome faced the challenge of Carthage, a Phoenician state in North Africa that dominated the western Mediterranean and blocked Rome's expansion into that area. In the Punic Wars (from the Latin *poeni*, "Phoenician") (264–146 B.C.E.), a series of three separate but related conflicts, Rome overwhelmed and finally destroyed Carthage; later, in 29 B.C.E., the Romans refounded Carthage as the capital of the province of Africa. At the end of the Third Punic War, in 146 B.C.E., Rome added Sicily, Corsica, Sardinia, and North Africa to its realm.

The wars transformed both the Roman state and the Roman character. The republic's imperialistic ambitions were emboldened by its acquisition of new territories to the west. And during the Second Punic War, the Carthaginian general Hannibal had invaded Italy and ravaged the countryside for fourteen years. His scorched-earth policy devastated Italy's farm country, and small farms began to be replaced by huge ranches worked by slaves. Italy's social fabric was permanently changed.

Having made themselves masters in the west, the Romans moved quickly to conquer the Hellenistic kingdoms to the east. The Romans granted greater freedom to these older Hellenistic cultures, but they forcefully organized and civilized the western provinces. At the end of the Middle Republic, Romans could justly call the Mediterranean Mare Nostrum—"Our Sea."

The Late Republic, 133–31 B.C.E. Rome in the Late Republic was ruled by an oligarchy of patrician families who dominated the Senate and clung stubbornly to their rights and privileges. Although Roman power continued to spread throughout the Mediterranean basin, economic and social problems multiplied.

One problem was generated by the rise of the equestrian order (*equites* in Latin), a social class who had gained wealth during the Punic Wars but who lacked the political power of the patricians. By the mid–first century B.C.E., open warfare had broken out between the equites and the senators, contributing to the anarchy of the period.

At the same time, the nature of the masses was changing. Increasing numbers of independent farmers were pushed off the land by large estate owners, and many of them went to Rome, where they lived in perpetual poverty and sold their votes to the highest bidders. In an effort to pacify them, the government instituted free bread and public amusements, scornfully referred to by critics as "bread and circuses." The farmer-soldier ideal of early Rome now gave way to a new mentality, one more concerned with bloody sporting events such as gladiatorial contests than with political rights and duties.

The republic's last hope for substantive reform was Julius Caesar, a major figure in Roman politics from 60 to 44 B.C.E. Caesar had emerged as a great public hero by pacifying Gaul (France). The commander of a loyal and formidable army, he had defeated rival generals to become Rome's sole ruler in 48 B.C.E. He took his authority from the many titles and powers he held, including dictator for life, consul, and head of the armies. Future Roman emperors recognized him as their predecessor by calling themselves Caesar, or "ruler." With the possible exception of Alexander the Great, no other Western ruler has generated such praise or blame from philosophers, poets, and artists.

Caesar, though acting in the name of equestrian interests, held a lofty vision for Rome's future. He initiated building projects that gave work to the urban poor, allowed the Italians outside Rome more self-rule, and founded Rome's first public library. But Caesar's enemies in the Senate believed that the dictator wanted to be king—the dreaded fear dating back to Etruscan Rome. On the Ides of March (March 15) in 44 B.C.E., a band of senatorial assassins murdered Caesar, and Rome plunged into chaos.

A new leader emerged from the years of unrest that followed: Octavian, Caesar's great-nephew and adopted son. His accession to power in 31 B.C.E. marked the beginning of the Pax Romana (Roman peace), a two-hundred-year period of unprecedented tranquility and economic growth. But it also marked the gradual dismantling of the republic and the establishment of an autocratic empire.

Growing Autocracy: Imperial Rome, 31 B.C.E.–284 C.E.

When Octavian returned peace and order to Rome, he pledged to restore the republic. He maintained the government offices, the Senate, and the political

Figure 5.6 Timgad, Algeria. Ca. 100 C.E. *Timgad, strategically located at the intersection of six Roman roads in North Africa, was typical of the towns built from scratch by the Romans during the Pax Romana and populated by ex-soldiers and their families. The town was planned as a square with two main avenues crossing in the middle where the forum stood and all other streets intersecting at right angles. The so-called Arch of Trajan in the foreground marked one of the main thoroughfares, which was lined with columns. Temples, baths, fountains, markets, a theater, and private homes gave the city the reputation of being a pleasant place to live.*

machinery, but beneath the surface of the Roman state, power was being transferred to one man, the emperor. With no legal safeguards against the emperor's will, the citizens became subject to his personal whim, and political liberty was gradually strangled. Subsequent Roman emperors enhanced their power by stifling dissent and glorifying themselves, eventually adopting the Hellenistic practice of emperor worship.

The political structure forged by Octavian remained intact from 31 B.C.E. to 284 C.E. This span of almost three centuries may be broken into two parts: the two-hundred-year Pax Romana and nearly a century of civil wars.

Pax Romana, 31 B.C.E.–193 C.E. Octavian, who became known as Augustus Caesar, or "revered ruler," established his power by converting Egypt—Rome's wealthiest province—into his personal property and by making the military the loyal mainstay of his rule.

His armies pushed back Rome's frontiers, stopping at what he considered its natural borders, the Rhine and Danube Rivers. Augustus then extended the celebrated Pax Romana to the people whom he conquered. Governors were dispatched to rule and collect taxes, army camps were created to keep law and order, and colonies and municipalities were founded to provide more land for Romans. The amenities of urban life were also expanded: Temples, altars, schools, arenas, libraries, marketplaces, aqueducts, fountains, and baths were built, and paved roads linked each far outpost with Rome (Figure 5.6).

Under Augustus (r. 31 B.C.E.–14 C.E.), economic life also became centralized. Agriculture, industry, and trade flourished, and most social classes prospered. At the same time, Rome became a true melting pot. Except for the inhabitants of the Greek-speaking East, most people spoke Latin and followed Roman customs. Divisive social and ethnic issues had faded from memory as patrician power waned and equestrian power grew. Senators and emperors now came from the equestrian order as well as from the provinces of Greece and Spain.

Civil Wars, 193–284 C.E. Despite its economic success, however, the empire was profoundly hampered by a major problem: how to select a new emperor. Adoption and inheritance were both tried, often with disastrous results. The murder of the emperor Commodus in 193 C.E. ushered in decades of civil wars, military rule, violence, and chaos. Of the twenty-seven so-called Barrack emperors (rulers drawn from the ranks of the Roman legions) in the third century, only four died natural deaths.

The empire was beset by problems both inside and outside its boundaries. Searching for loot, implacable Germanic tribes began crossing the northern frontiers. Runaway inflation and a debased coinage wiped out fortunes and caused a return to barter exchange. The Roman army forcibly requisitioned food and supplies from civilians. In addition, a plague ravaged the empire, killing perhaps hundreds of thousands. In 284 C.E., Diocletian, a general from Illyricum (modern Croatia) seized power. In time, his reforms would snatch Rome from the brink of destruction, as described in Chapter 7.

THE STYLE OF PRE-CHRISTIAN ROME: FROM GREEK IMITATION TO ROMAN GRANDEUR

Hellenistic culture became the foundation of Roman civilization. Often, Rome simply expanded on Hellenistic ideas, but in areas for which the Romans had a special gift, as in lyric poetry and comedy, they created works that rivaled the Greek originals. And in architecture, the Romans made their greatest mark, because this art form naturally blends the utilitarian with the aesthetic.

As in any civilization, Roman cultural achievements were shaped by their political and social contexts. Especially notable in the long evolution of Roman culture is the shift in style that occurred as the republic gave way to the empire, a shift that can be seen in every area of cultural expression.

Under the republic, artistic achievements were inspired by the Greek model and appealed to the privileged few. Under the empire, a distinctive Roman style began to emerge in response to the tastes of the masses, and spectacle became important in Roman culture. In this atmosphere, philosophy survived mainly as an antidote to the restrictions of the imperial regime. Literature flourished among an educated elite, but flattery and propaganda crept into the works of

Table 5.1   THE CHIEF ROMAN GODS AND GODDESSES AND THEIR GREEK COUNTERPARTS

ROMAN	GREEK
Jupiter	Zeus
Juno	Hera
Neptune	Poseidon
Pluto	Hades
Vesta	Hestia
Apollo	Apollo
Diana	Artemis
Mars	Ares
Venus	Aphrodite
Vulcan	Hephaestus
Minerva	Athena
Mercury	Hermes

even the greatest writers. And architecture and sculpture became increasingly monumental and theatrical.

Roman Religion

The native Roman religion was deeply affected by the cults of neighboring and conquered peoples. **Syncretism,** the blending of religion, began in earliest times. After their initial contacts with the Greeks in southern Italy, the Romans started to intermingle their divinities with those of the Greek religious system, who seemed to be always either making mischief or making love (Table 5.1). Thereafter, the Greek deities enlivened Rome's religion and inspired her writers, musicians, and artists with thrilling stories. And even after the fall of Rome, the Greco-Roman gods and goddesses continued to live in the art, music, and literature of Europe.

From the Punic Wars onward, innovative cults sprang up in Rome. From Egypt came the worship of Isis (Figure 5.7), a religion that promised immortality, and from Asia Minor the cult of Cybele, a mother goddess. Army veterans returning from Persia brought back Mithra, the mortal son of the sun god, whose cult excluded women (Figure 5.8). Mithra's followers observed each seventh day as Sun Day and December 25 as the god's birthday; the faithful also underwent a baptism in the blood of a sacred bull.

Religious innovation was perpetuated in imperial Rome until Greek and oriental cults finally submerged

Figure 5.7 *Preparations for a Banquet.* Ca. 180–190 C.E. Detail. Mosaic, total size 7′4⅝″ × 6′10⅝″. Formerly in Carthage (Sidi-bou-Said), North Africa. Louvre. *This mosaic, depicting a slave-attendant at a banquet, probably decorated a room used by the Isis cult for ritualistic dinners, though no records have been found identifying the building in which it was discovered. The work's style, with its nearly life-size figure set against a plain white ground and the careful rendering of the human body, is typical of the mosaics of this period.*

the old Roman beliefs. Most of all, the emperor cult—the state policy of encouraging public worship of the ruler as a god—succeeded admirably, except among two groups of Roman subjects who refused to recognize the ruler's divinity—the Jews and the Christians, whose story of resistance and rebellion is told in Chapter 6.

Language, Literature, and Drama

Latin, the Roman language, was at first an unimaginative, functional language, suited only to legal documents, financial records, and military commands. But with the growth of law and oratory in the Early Republic, grammar was standardized, vocabulary was increased, and word meanings were clarified. As the Romans conquered, they made Latin the language of state, except in the Greek-speaking East. By the late empire, Latin had spread throughout the civilized world and was the common tongue for the vast majority of Roman citizens. Latin literature began to flourish in the Middle Republic (264–133 B.C.E.) with lyric and epic poetry, comedy, and tragedy, all in the Greek style, although writers were beginning to develop a distinctive Roman style. Roman literature changed with the changing times, evolving through several quite distinct periods.

Figure 5.8 *Mithra Slaying the Bull.* Third century C.E. Marble, ht. 2'10¼". Antiquario Comunale, Rome. *This relief depicts the defining moment of the Mithra cult, a standard representation found across the Roman Empire in statues and in paintings. Mithra, dressed in Phrygian cap, tunic, trousers, and flowing cloak, presses his right knee on the bull as he slays it. The various animals and humans surrounding this dramatic scene symbolize the themes of good and evil, light and dark, life and death, which are central to the religion.*

The First Literary Period, 250–31 B.C.E. The writing of the first literary period was noteworthy for its strongly Greek flavor and, in some writers, its grave moral tone. This period also saw the rise of a Roman theatrical tradition influenced both by roots in boisterous Etruscan religious celebrations and by contact with the Greek theater. Many educated Romans in this period could speak Greek, and many had seen performances of tragedies and comedies during their travels.

Plautus [PLAW-tuhs] (about 254–184 B.C.E.), a plebeian from Italy, launched Rome's great age of comic theater with his almost 130 plays. His genius lay in breathing fresh life into the stale plots and stock characters borrowed from Menander and other Hellenistic, New Comedy playwrights. In his hands, the mistaken identities, verbal misunderstandings, and bungled schemes seemed brand new. Rome's other significant comic playwright was Terence [TAIR-ents] (about 195–159 B.C.E.), a Carthaginian slave who was brought to Rome, educated, and set free. Although he wrote only six plays, he won the acclaim of Rome's educated elite, perhaps because of the pure Greek tone and themes of his works. Terence's highly polished style later inspired the magisterial Cicero.

As Roman comedy began to decline, superseded by the vast spectacles that the masses demanded, two major poets with distinctively different personalities and

talents appeared: Lucretius and Catullus. Both were heavily influenced by Greece. Lucretius [lew-KRE-shuhs] (about 94–about 55 B.C.E.) stands in the long line of instructive literary figures dating from Homer. A gifted poet, with his well-turned Latin phrases and imaginative and vivid language, Lucretius wrote *De Rerum Natura (On the Nature of Things)* to persuade the reader of the truth of Epicureanism, the philosophy based on scientific atomism that denied divine intervention in human affairs (see Chapter 4).

In contrast to Lucretius's lengthy poem, the verses of Catullus [kuh-TUHL-uhs] (about 84–about 54 B.C.E.) are characterized by brevity, one of the hallmarks of the Alexandrian school of the Hellenistic Age. Catullus's "small" epics, epigrams, and love poems also closely imitate the scholarly and romantic qualities of Alexandrianism. Catullus is best remembered for his love poems, which draw on the lives of his highborn, free-spirited circle in Rome, and which express his innermost feelings of desire, disappointment, and jealousy.

The efforts of Lucretius and Catullus pale, however, when placed beside those of their contemporary Cicero (106–43 B.C.E.). An equestrian from Italy, he dominated Roman letters in his own day so much that his era is often labeled the Age of Cicero. By translating Greek treatises into Latin, he created a philosophical vocabulary for the Latin language where none had existed before.

For centuries, Cicero's collected speeches served as models both of public oratory and of written argument. Similarly, his philosophical tracts set the agenda for generations of thinkers and reformers. Today's readers rank Cicero's collection of letters, most by him, some addressed to him (a few written by his son), as his masterpiece. These nearly nine hundred letters, frank in style and language, offer a unique self-portrait of a major public figure in ancient times (Figure 5.9).

The Second Literary Period: The Golden Age, 31 B.C.E.–14 C.E.   The second period of Roman literature coincided with the personal reign of Augustus and is considered the Golden Age of Roman letters. This period's three greatest writers, Vergil, Horace, and Ovid, captured the age's euphoric mood as peace and stability once more returned to Rome. Of the three writers, Vergil best represented the times through his vision of Rome and his stirring verses.

The works of Vergil [VUR-jill] (70–19 B.C.E.), an Italian plebeian, were inspired by Greek literary forms—idylls (or vignettes), didactic (instructive) poems, and epics—yet his use of native themes and his focus on the best traits in the Roman people give an authentic Roman voice to his work. Deeply moved by Augustus's reforms, he put his art in the service of the state. Vergil's pastoral poetry, the *Eclogues* and *Georgics*, celebrated rural life and urged readers to seek harmony with nature in order to find peace—advice that became a significant moral theme of the Western heritage. But Vergil is best known for the *Aeneid*, an epic poem in twelve books that he wrote in imitation of the Homeric epics. In this work, infused with Roman values and ideals, Vergil gave full voice to his love of country, his respect for Augustus, and his faith in Rome's destiny.

The *Aeneid* tells of Aeneas, the legendary Trojan hero who wandered the Mediterranean before founding Rome. In the first six books, Vergil models his tale on the *Odyssey*, writing of travel and love. The second half is modeled on the *Iliad*, stressing fighting and intrigue. The *Aeneid* became Rome's bible and its literary masterpiece. Children were often required to memorize passages from the poem to instill in them the values that had made Rome great. Aeneas served as the prototype of the faithful leader who would not be diverted from his destined path. The work's rich language led later poets to mine the *Aeneid* for expressions and images. As Homer inspired Vergil, so Vergil became the model for Western poets when imaginative literature was revived in late medieval Europe.

The second major poet of the Golden Age was Horace (65–8 B.C.E.), another Italian plebeian who welcomed Augustus as Rome's savior and offered

Figure 5.9 *Cicero.* First century B.C.E. Capitoline Museum, Rome. *The anonymous sculptor of this bust of Cicero has caught the character of the man as recalled in literary sources. Honored as one of Rome's finest intellectuals and a patriot devoted to rescuing the state from chaos, he is depicted deep in thought with stern and resolute features. This idealized portrait contributed to the mystique of Cicero as a hero of the Roman republic.*

patriotic sentiments in his verses. His poems, which were written to be read aloud, use Alexandrian forms such as odes and letters in verse. He helped to create a new poetic genre, the **satire,** which rebuked the manners of the age. Horace was at his best in addressing the heartbreaking brevity of life: "what has been, has been, and I have had my hour."

Ovid [AHV-uhd] (43 B.C.E.–about 17 C.E.), the third voice of the Golden Age, was a wealthy Italian equestrian who did not devote his verses to patriotic themes or pay lip service to conventional morality. Ovid's love poems speak of the purely sensual and fleeting quality of sex and ignore the enduring value of committed love. His *Art of Love* offers advice, in a manner bordering on the scientific, on how to seduce women, whether willing or not. Such advice contrasted with

SLICE OF LIFE
A College Student's Letter Home

MARCUS, SON OF CICERO

Marcus, the son of the famous writer-politician Cicero, having been accused of overspending his allowance, writes to Tiro, his father's secretary. Cicero, too busy to write himself, relies on his secretary to manage both personal and business affairs. In the following letter, written from Athens, 44 B.C.E., Marcus assures Tiro that he has mended his ways, knowing that this information will be shared with his skeptical father.

I had been looking for a letter when one finally came, forty-six days out. Its arrival brought me the keenest joy; for in addition to the pleasure I got from the kind words of my father your most delightful letter filled my cup of joy to overflowing. Accordingly, I was not sorry that there had been a break in our correspondence, but rather was I glad; for I profit greatly by your writing after my long silence. Therefore I rejoice exceedingly that you have accepted my excuses.

I don't doubt, my dearest Tiro, that you are deeply gratified over the rumors that are reaching your ears, and I will guarantee and strive that with the passing days this nascent good report may be increased twofold. You may, therefore, keep your promise of being a trumpeter of my good repute, for the errors of my youth have brought me such pain and sorrow that not only does my soul recoil at the acts themselves but my ear shrinks from the very mention of them. I know full well that you shared in the anxiety and worry of this experience.

Since I then brought you sorrow, I'll warrant that now I will bring you joy in double measure. Let me tell you that I am associated with Cratippus not as a disciple but as a son, for not only do I listen to his lectures with pleasure but also I am greatly privileged to enjoy him in person. I am with him all day and very often a part of the night since by much pleading I often succeed in getting him to dine with me. Now that he has got used to this habit, he often drops in on me at dinner time and, laying aside the severe demeanor of a college professor, he jokes with me like a human. See

to it, therefore, that you embrace the earliest opportunity of meeting the eminent gentleman, of finding out what he is like, and of becoming acquainted with his merry disposition.

What now shall I say of Professor Bruttius? I keep him with me all the time. He is a regular stoic in his habits of life but a jolly good fellow withal, for he is very much of a wit both in his lectures and in his discussions. I have hired lodgings for him next door, and, as best I may, out of my slender purse I relieve him in his slender circumstances.

Besides, I am studying public speaking in Greek with Cassius. I am planning to do the same with Bruttius in Latin. On Cratippus' recommendation I am on very intimate terms with certain learned gentlemen whom he brought with him from Mytilene. I also spend a good deal of time with Epicrates, the chief Athenian, Dean Leonidas, and other men of that sort. So much for what I am doing. . . . I am deeply grateful to you for looking out for my commissions; please send me as soon as possible a secretary, by all means one who knows Greek; he will save me much labor in copying out my notes. Of all things, be sure to take care of yourself that we may be able to pursue our studies together. I commend you to Anterus (the postman).

Interpreting This Slice of Life   What seems to have been Cicero's concerns about his son Marcus's behavior in Athens? **What** responses does Marcus offer to his father's concerns? Do you believe Marcus in his assertions in this letter? **Explain.** Sixteen hundred years later, Shakespeare (in the play *Hamlet*) has a father offer this advice to a son: "This above all, to thine own self be true." **Compare and contrast** this advice with that which Marcus seems to have received from his father. Based on this letter, **how** was education conducted in ancient Athens and Rome? **Compare and contrast** the life of a typical student today with that of Marcus.

Vergil's and Horace's attempts to raise the moral level of the Romans.

Ovid's masterpiece was the *Metamorphoses,* or *Transformations.* Somewhat irreverently, he breathed new life into more than two hundred Greek and Roman myths and legends that centered on the transformation of people into other forms. This work is the source of our knowledge of many Classical myths, and medieval and Renaissance poets turned to it continually for inspiration.

The Third Literary Period: The Silver Age, 14–200 C.E.
In the third literary period, the patriotic style of the previous era was replaced by the critical views of writers who often satirized Roman society and the state. Lacking the originality of the Golden Age, the writers of this era looked to their predecessors for models while they polished their phrases and reworked earlier themes. This shift in literary taste reflected a new educational ideal, which stressed skills in debate and oratory. As a result, moral considerations became secondary to aes-

thetic effects, with writers using rhetorical flourishes and exaggerated literary conceits.

One of Rome's outstanding Silver Age talents was Seneca [SEN-e-kuh] (4 B.C.E.–65 C.E.). Born into a wealthy equestrian family in Spain, Seneca became a powerful senator and one of the age's chief thinkers. He is best remembered as a dramatist, though his works failed to measure up to the Greek heritage. His ten extant plays relied on emotionalism, rhetorical excess, and stage violence—the perennial traits of Roman tragedy. After his day, the staging of tragedies ceased, not to be revived for more than fifteen hundred years.

The Silver Age produced Rome's last great Latin poet, Juvenal [JOO-vuh-nuhl] (about 60–about 140 C.E.), who trained his censorious gaze on the follies of the empire. Juvenal expressed his outraged observations in sixteen satires, the literary form originated by Horace and others. The voice that speaks in Juvenal's satires is embittered, perhaps a reflection of his obscure social origins. But the carefully crafted language— obscene, bilious, and evocative but always just right— made him the master of this genre in Rome, if not in world letters.

The leading historian of the Silver Age was Tacitus [TASS-i-tus] (55?–117 C.E.), famed also as an orator and politician. He honored the Greek tradition of historical writing, which dictated that history must be written according to literary rules, that the proper study of history is contemporary events, and that effects in history have human, not supernatural, causes.

Tacitus acquired his knowledge of statecraft as the governor of the province of Asia (present-day southwestern Turkey). Among his works are two that have earned him the front rank among Roman historians. The *Annals* focus on the rulers after the death of Augustus in 14 C.E. until the murder of Nero in 68. The *Histories* then pick up the story of Rome and carry it through 96, when the tyrannical Domitian was assassinated.

Tacitus was a master of the Latin language and had a flair for dramatic narrative. Like other Roman historians, he wrote history with a moral purpose, but his critical spirit set him apart from those who had nothing but glowing praise for Rome. Instead, Tacitus's perspective was that of a proud senator who could not conceal his distaste for Rome's loss of political freedom. In his works, he sought to uncover the origins of the misrule that had almost destroyed Rome in his day, and he ended by concluding that tyranny was an innate flaw in the imperial office.

Philosophy

The Romans adopted the ethical aspects of Greek thought, but they rejected philosophy itself as danger-

ous, fearing that its study would draw their young men away from the military to lives of dreamy speculation. As a result, Roman thought stressed rules of behavior with little regard for metaphysics.

In time, Roman versions of Epicureanism and Stoicism reached a wide audience, notably among influential aristocrats. Although Epicureanism had little impact, mainly because its focus on withdrawal from worldly cares contradicted the Roman sense of duty, Stoicism's effect was potent and lasting. Stoic values seemed to confirm the farmer-soldier ideal, suggesting that the early Romans were unintentional Stoics. In addition, Stoicism under the empire caused a few aristocrats to resist, if passively, the growing menace of autocracy; these hardy Stoics, some of whom, like Seneca, willingly sacrificed their lives for their ideas, believed that the natural law was superior to the earthbound justice of the rulers.

Stoicism Although Stoicism was introduced to Rome by Greek philosophers in the Late Republic, its greatest influence was achieved later, through the writings and teaching of Seneca, Epictetus, and the emperor Marcus Aurelius.

Seneca's fame as a philosopher rests on his *Letters on Morality*. These letters, which were usually written in response to pressing ethical problems, are filled with good advice, even though they break no new philosophical ground. Thus, for example, Seneca counseled a grieving acquaintance to maintain dignity and inner strength in the face of a loved one's death.

Seneca's *Letters* survived the fall of Rome in 476 C.E., but the works of most other thinkers temporarily disappeared. Consequently, Seneca became one of the great guides for Western thought when philosophy was revived in the Middle Ages. In the modern world, however, his reputation has suffered because of his closeness to Nero, an emperor of legendary cruelty. Despite Seneca's noble philosophy, doubt has been cast on his personal morality.

No such cloud hovers over Epictetus [ep-ik-TEET-uhs] (about 55–115 C.E.), who not only preached but also lived his Stoic creed. According to tradition, Epictetus, though a slave in Rome, won his freedom because of his teachings. He subsequently founded a school in Asia Minor and attracted enthusiastic converts. He did not write anything, but Arrian, a pupil, composed the *Discourses* and the *Handbook*, both in Greek, which together preserved the essence of his master's ideas.

Epictetus's philosophy reflected his own victory over personal misfortune. He advised patience in the face of trouble, indifference to material things, and acceptance of one's destiny. Although these ideas represented a rehash of basic Stoic beliefs, his moral wholeness gave them a special appeal.

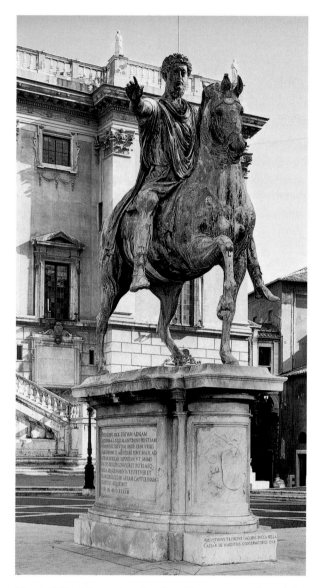

Figure 5.10 *Marcus Aurelius. Ca. 173 C.E. Bronze, ht. 16'8".* Piazza del Campidoglio, Rome. *The unknown artist has represented Marcus Aurelius as a warrior-emperor, but the militaristic image is offset somewhat by the Stoic ruler's face. Here we see revealed a human being lost in thought and far removed from pomp and power. This magnificent equestrian statue marked the climax of sculpture in the Roman Empire. In the eighteenth and nineteenth centuries, sculptors copied this statue's militaristic image to glorify European rulers.*

Stoicism's finest hour arrived in 161 C.E. when Marcus Aurelius became emperor (Figure 5.10). Converted to Stoicism in his youth, the emperor wrote an account (in Greek) of his daily musings—called *Meditations*—while he was engaged in almost continuous warfare against Germanic invaders. His journal came to light after his death and was soon recognized as a masterpiece of Stoicism.

Like all Stoics, the emperor admonished himself to play with dignity the role that providence had assigned. If a divine plan guides the universe, then he must accept it; if, however, the world is ruled by chance, then a well-regulated mind is the best defense. Such reasoning enabled Marcus Aurelius to avoid moral confusion. The emperor's death in 180 C.E. signaled the end of Stoicism. The next century witnessed the swamping of all philosophies in the military anarchy and oriental cults of the times.

Neo-Platonism Some Roman thinkers adopted Greek Stoicism; others were interested in blending the various Greek schools—Platonic, Aristotelian, and Stoic, among others—into a philosophic synthesis. The outstanding example of this latter trend was **Neo-Platonism,** a school of thought founded primarily by Plotinus [plo-TIE-nuhs] (205–270 C.E.) in the third century C.E. Neo-Platonism was the last major school of philosophy in the ancient world. The movement began as an attempt to correct the problem at the heart of Plato's system—the seemingly irreconcilable split between the absolute world of Ideas and the perishable material world. This Platonic dualism could and did lead to the notion that the everyday world has little purpose in the overall scheme of things. Plotinus now succeeded in bridging the two worlds with his theories, and his writings later influenced Christian thinkers in the Middle Ages and the Italian humanists of the Renaissance.

Plotinus resolved Platonic dualism not with logical analysis but with mystical insight, claiming that the union of the physical and spiritual worlds could be grasped only through an ecstatic vision. His retreat from philosophy into mysticism occurred during the turbulent era of the Barrack emperors, when many people fled from urban violence to the relative peace of their villas and estates in the countryside.

Science and Medicine

Unlike the Greeks, the Romans made few original contributions to science. Favoring the utilitarian over the philosophical, the Romans tended to reject Greek abstract thought and adapted only those Greek inventions that answered practical needs. A few Roman writers did acknowledge Greek science, and they incorporated some of the Greek findings into their historical and intellectual works. However, in medicine the Romans made some original contributions, advancing medical knowledge and helping shape medical studies and practices that were in place until the Scientific Revolution (see Chapter 15).

Rome's changing attitudes to disease, remedies, and the medical profession are preserved in a collection of writings and artifacts—the most extensive left by any

Western society prior to the Middle Ages. This collection includes medical records, experiments, and observations from physicians, personal accounts from doctors, speeches by politicians, and miscellaneous writings by literary figures. Other artifacts include assorted surgical instruments and examination tools, tomb inscriptions and public monuments, official decrees and laws, and archeological sites, such as military hospitals and camps and religious shrines for healing.

Roman medicine, like the rest of Roman culture, was indebted to the past. From the Etruscans and the Greeks, the Romans adopted an approach to medicine that combined religious elements with scientific analysis. The religious element, which survived until the end of Roman history, manifested itself in the many temples to Asclepius, healer of the sick, and to his daughter, Hygieia, the goddess of healing. Priests continued to treat diseases. There were sacrifices of animals to ensure good health, and **divining,** or interpreting, of animal entrails was done to predict the future.

The scientific aspect of Roman medicine went through three stages, over the course of the Roman millennium, from 753 B.C.E. to 284 C.E. (see Timeline 5.1). The first stage grew out of Rome's agricultural heritage. Remedies for sick farm animals, such as applying salves soaked in wool, were widely used on humans for generations. The paterfamilias, whose power over family and servants was almost complete, acted as a physician, using ancestral expertise and home remedies. As Etruscan and Greek medical knowledge became more widely known, Roman medicine entered its second stage. At first, out of suspicion for all things Greek, traditional-minded Romans tried to either suppress Greek doctors or condemn their practices. This initial reaction was understandable, since many of Rome's first Greek physicians were prisoners of war, usually members of the lower class or freed slaves, who were either poorly trained or outright charlatans. Some new arrivals found a following among the poor, and, as the doctors' reputations grew, their success attracted upper-class patients. By the start of the empire, in 31 B.C.E., Roman medicine had entered a third stage, as Greek and Roman medicine merged into a hybrid form—ranging from diagnostic procedures to pharmacology. In imperial Rome, the army, with its hospitals and surgeons, carried Roman medicine into all the corners of the empire. Based on their lasting influence, the two most important doctors from this period are Celsus and Galen.

The reputation of Celsus [SEL-suhs] (fl. first century C.E.) as a knowledgeable physician was enhanced by the encyclopedia he compiled, which included articles on philosophy, agriculture, and the military, as well as medicine. Only the section on medicine, *De medicina,* has survived into modern times. Much of what is known about early medical history and Roman medicine, such as surgical procedures, hygienic practices, and treatment of various diseases, is found in this work. Discovered in the early Renaissance (see Chapter 11), *De medicina* was, for several centuries, used by physicians to diagnose and treat illnesses and by European teachers as a textbook to train doctors.

Galen [GAY-len] of Pergamum (129–about 216 C.E.) was Rome's most famous medical authority. After studying medicine in Pergamum, Smyrna (modern Izmir, Turkey), and Alexandria, Galen settled in Rome. He soon became a fashionable physician, catering to Rome's elite. Several emperors, including Marcus Aurelius and Commodus, made Galen their court physician. Galen wrote more than five hundred medical treatises, covering such topics as anatomy, physiology, hygiene, exercise and diet, and pharmacology. In general, he followed scientific guidelines: collecting data, relying on experience and observation, and keeping to a set of general principles. His vast erudition and imperious writing style made him the West's chief authority on medicine, until about 1650 C.E. Later, his commanding status became a burden, when some of his findings on human anatomy, based on his dissection of dogs rather than humans, impeded the progress of medical knowledge.

Law

The most original contribution of the Roman mind was law. Rome's law created a notion of justice founded on such ideals as fairness for both citizens and subjects, as well as the presumption of innocence in criminal cases. These principles later became central to the Western legal tradition. But the most important facet of Roman law was born in Stoicism: the idea of **natural law,** or a higher justice than that made by human forces. This doctrine of natural law is the basis of the American Declaration of Independence.

Rome's law evolved over many centuries, starting in 450 B.C.E. with the first written code, the Twelve Tables. These tables, which represented a plebeian victory over the patricians, treated basic aspects of civil life such as personal and property rights, religious practices, and moral behavior. But this milestone did not rid Rome of class distinctions; it merely recognized conflicting rights and the necessity of a judge above both parties. Through the years, class divisions continued to affect the way the law was applied, since the dispensing of justice always favored the rich.

The branch of Roman law dealing with property rights was called civil law and developed through the office of the *praetor.* Each praetor, at the beginning of his term, issued an edict describing the legal procedures and precedents he would follow. The body of decisions handed down by the praetors eventually came to constitute Rome's civil law.

By the Late Republic, the development of law was enhanced by the advice of legal experts, called *jurisconsults* or *jurisprudentes*. They tended to broaden Roman justice with their Stoic views. The most creative phase of Roman law occurred in the second and third centuries C.E., when eminent jurisconsults helped to codify the law and extend its principles to cover all the citizens of the empire.

The Visual Arts

Architecture and sculpture dominated Rome's visual arts, but they were pressed into the service of practical needs. The Romans commissioned buildings and statues to serve the state, religion, or society, but they recognized that the practical did not have to forgo beauty, and many of Rome's engineering feats were beautiful in their functional elegance.

The early Romans learned lessons in architecture from the Etruscans, but after encountering the Greeks of Magna Graecia, they rebuilt Rome along Greek lines. By the second century B.C.E., wealthy Romans were collecting Greek statues in all styles—Archaic, Hellenic, and Hellenistic. Under Augustus, Hellenic style in sculpture and architecture became supreme, inching across the empire over the next two centuries. By the third century C.E., a new architectural style had arisen, blending Greek and Roman styles. This Greco-Roman style carried over into medieval civilization after the collapse of the Roman Empire in the West (see Chapter 7).

Architecture Over the years, the Romans used many types of materials in their public and private buildings. The architects of the Early Republic built with sun-dried bricks and used terra cotta, a fired clay, for roofs and decorations. As Rome's wealth grew and new materials were imported, the bricks retained an important though less visible role in buildings, chiefly in foundations and walls. By the Late Republic, two new products had been adapted from the Greeks, mortar and ashlars (massive hewn stones), which, in time, revolutionized the face of Rome.

Much of the impetus for the building revolution sprang from the Romans' improvement of mortar. They produced a moldable concrete by mixing lime, sand, small rocks, and rubble, but because the concrete was visually unappealing, the builders began to cover it with slabs of expensive and highly polished marble and granite imported from Greece or quarried in Italy.

The temple became one of Rome's chief architectural forms. The basic source for the Roman temple was the Greek model with its post-beam-triangle construction, although Etruscan influence was also significant. The Romans adapted the Greek column as either support or decoration, preferring the ornamented Corinthian order to the plainer Doric and Ionic.

The Romans' most significant innovations in architecture were made with the rounded arch, which already had a long history by the time they began to experiment with it. The Mesopotamians probably invented this arch, the Greeks knew about it, and the Etruscans used it in their drainage systems. The arch's basic round form is created with wedge-shaped stones called **voussoirs**. A **keystone** at the center of the semicircle locks the arch in place. The installed arch is amazingly strong, diverting the weight of the upper walls both outward and downward onto columns or other supports (Figure 5.11).

The Romans demonstrated their inventive genius by creating ceilings, or **vaults,** from arches—by transforming the simple rounded arch into barrel vaults, groined vaults, and domes. They created the **barrel vault**—named because it looks like a barrel divided lengthwise—by building a series of contiguous arches. They intersected two barrel vaults at right angles to produce a **groined,** or **cross, vault.** Finally, the dome, the crown jewel of Rome's architectural vocabulary, was constructed essentially by rotating an arch in a full circle (see Figure 5.11). They then placed the dome on a drum or enclosed cylinder. Architects later learned to seat domes on square bases (see Chapter 7). The Romans were also able to build arches more safely after they discovered the correct mathematical ratio (1:2) between the height of an arch and the width of its base.

The prototype of imperial temples is the well-preserved Maison Carrée in Nîmes, France, a major provincial city under Augustus. Built in about 16 B.C.E., the Maison Carrée incorporated Etruscan and Greek ideas (Figure 5.12). Raised on a platform in the Etruscan manner, this temple shows other Etruscan borrowings in the central stairway, the deep porch, and the engaged columns—that is, the columns built into the walls of the cella, the inner sanctum housing the cult statue. Greek influences are visible in the low gable—the triangular end of the building's roof—and the Corinthian columns. The Greek notion that beauty lies in mathematical harmony is also expressed in the predetermined ratio of the area of the cella to the area of the temple's porch. In the eighteenth century, Thomas Jefferson used the Maison Carrée as the model for the statehouse in Richmond, Virginia.

Besides perfecting their version of the rectilinear temple, the Romans also invented the round temple, as seen in the Pantheon, a sanctuary dedicated to all their deities. The Pantheon consists of three different

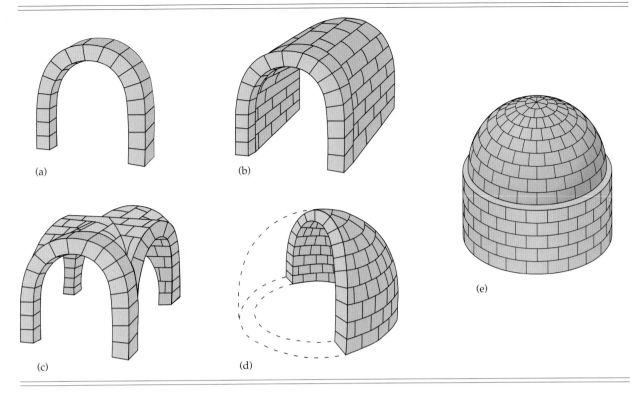

(a)

(b)

(c)

(d)

(e)

Figure 5.11 Structures Used in Roman Architecture. *Beginning with the basic arch (a), the Romans created the barrel vault (b) and the cross vault (c). These structural elements, along with the dome (d), which they formed by rotating a series of arches around a central axis, and the dome on a drum (e), gave the Romans the architectural elements they needed to construct their innovative temples and monuments.*

Figure 5.12 Maison Carrée. Ca. 16 B.C.E. Base 104′4″ × 48′10″. Nîmes, France. *This temple was probably modeled on temples in Rome, since buildings with Corinthian columns and similar overall designs were being constructed in the capital at this time. Reproducing architecture in the provincial cities was another way in which the Romans spread civilization throughout their conquered lands.*

Figure 5.13 Pantheon Exterior. 126 C.E. Rome. *In modern Rome, the Pantheon is crowded into a piazza where it faces a monument topped by an Egyptian obelisk. However, when built under the emperor Hadrian, the Pantheon was part of a complex of structures that complemented one another, and the temple's facade faced a set of columns in an open forecourt. Its original setting reflected the Roman sense that urban space should be organized harmoniously.*

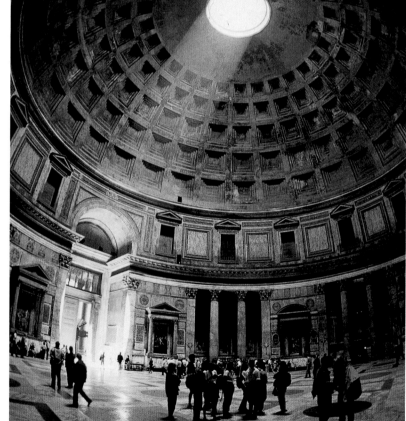

Figure 5.14 Pantheon Interior. 126 C.E. Rome. *The inner diameter of the dome is 144 feet. The height of the dome is 72 feet, or one-half of the total height (144 feet) of the building. The sunlight sweeps around the interior and plays on the dome's decorations as the earth turns, creating constantly changing patterns of light and design.*

units: the entrance porch, or portico, with its supporting columns; the huge drum, housing the sanctuary proper, which is attached to the porch; and the dome, set on top of the drum (Figure 5.13). This design showed the Romans' reliance on a native heritage, because the rounded shape was probably inspired by the circular religious shrines of the pre-Romans, as modern archeology has shown. The Pantheon also combined a religious with a secular image: The dome symbolized both the heaven of the deities and the vastness of the empire.

But the Pantheon did more than reflect the deep longings of the Roman people; its rich interior illustrated the Roman genius for decoration (Figure 5.14). A polychrome marble floor and a dome with recessed panels created a dazzling interior, and statues, decorative columns, triangular pediments, niches, and other architectural details alternated around the circular room. The most unusual effect of all was the round hole, thirty feet in diameter, called the **oculus,** or eye, which opened the dome to the sunlight and the elements. As the oldest standing domed structure in the world, the Pantheon is the direct ancestor of St. Peter's Basilica in Rome and St. Paul's cathedral in London.

Rome's architecture consisted of more than beautiful temples. The city of Rome was the center of government for the Mediterranean world, the nucleus of the state's religious system, and the hub of an international economy. And at the heart of the city was its **forum,** which functioned like the agora of Greek city-states. In the forum, citizens conducted business, ran the government, and socialized among the complex of public buildings, temples, sacred sites, and monuments (Figure 5.15). The high priest of Roman religion, the Pontifex Maximus, lived in the forum, and nearby stood the curia, or Senate house. Under the empire, the forum became a symbol of Roman power and civilization; the leading cities in each province had forums.

As part of his reforms, Augustus rebuilt and beautified much of the republican forum. Later emperors, such as Trajan [TRA-jen] (r. 98–117 C.E.), constructed their own forums, which not only served as new centers for trade and government but also perpetuated their names. Trajan's forum, which originally included

Figure 5.15   Roman Forum. Ca. 100 B.C.E.–ca. 400 C.E. *The forum was literally the center of the Roman world, for here the Romans erected the Golden Milestone, from which all roads led out across the empire. The temples and public buildings, crowded together in a relatively small area, were rebuilt over several centuries as rulers added to Rome's architectural legacy.*

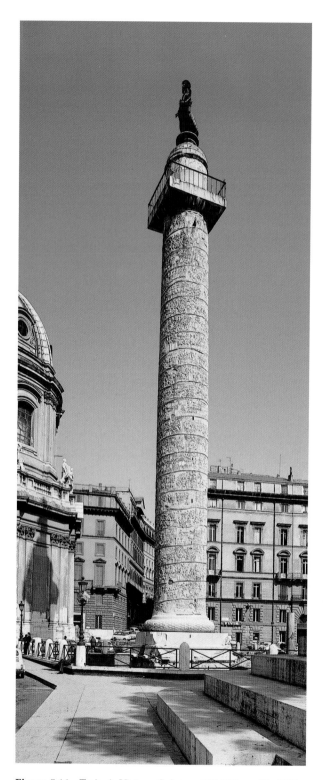

Figure 5.16 Trajan's Victory Column. 106–113 C.E. Ht. 125', including base. Rome. *Borrowing the idea of a victory column from Mesopotamia, the pragmatic Trajan used art to enhance his power in the eyes of the citizens. This work commemorated his conquest of Dacia—present-day Romania. The marble column, set on a foundation, enclosed a winding stairway that led to an observation platform and a statue of Trajan. Spiraling around the column's shaft was a stone relief sculpture that told the story of Trajan's victory in lively and painstaking detail.*

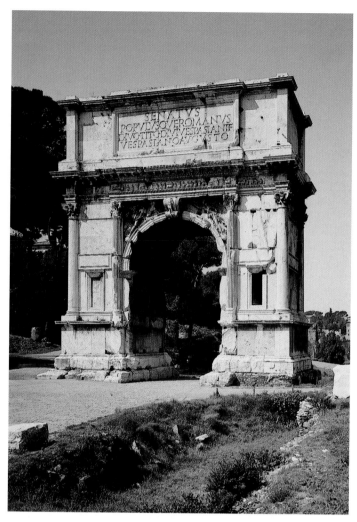

Figure 5.17 Arch of Titus. Ca. 81 C.E. Marble, ht. 47'2". Rome. *The Arch of Titus, like so many structures in Rome, was eventually incorporated into other buildings. Only in the early nineteenth century was the arch restored to its original splendor. Inspired by this arch, modern architects have designed similar structures throughout the Western world.*

a library, law courts, and plazas for strolling, has vanished except for one of the most significant monuments of the Roman Empire, a column commemorating Trajan's conquest of Dacia (modern Romania) (Figure 5.16).

Another symbol of empire, the triumphal arch, originated in the republic in the second century B.C.E. The Romans used both single and triple arches to celebrate military victories and erected them across the empire. The style of these memorials varied until the Arch of Titus, constructed in 81 C.E., became the accepted model. This arch, which commemorated the capture of Jerusalem by the then general Titus in 70 C.E., stood at the entrance to the Via Sacra, the thoroughfare of the Roman Forum (Figure 5.17). Inscribed

ENCOUNTER

Roman Conquests and Romance Languages

As the Romans expanded their empire, they encountered the Dacians and other peoples, making them part of the Roman world. Over time, political, commercial, and military needs led to the creation of hybrid languages that blended Latin with native tongues. Thus, in the sounds, words, and syntax of these new hybrid languages, the legacy of ancient peoples survives in the world today.

The Romans of the early empire, envisaging Cicero's call for "imperial glory," began to conquer neighboring peoples who threatened the Roman way of life. A superb example of this policy was Trajan's wars (101, 105–106 C.E.) against the Dacians, a people living in a territory roughly equivalent to modern-day Romania. With their strong, loyal tribal system and distinctive advanced material culture based on iron products and weapons, the Dacians refused to succumb to the Romans. Succeeding where other emperors had failed, Trajan conquered the Dacians and colonized the region, bringing in merchants, traders, and government officials.

The Romans, in varying degrees of success, followed their usual patterns of colonization in Dacia, transforming villages into provincial towns, constructing villas or country estates, and settling their veterans in the civic centers and rural areas. The colonizers set examples of the Roman way of life for the local populations, persuaded the tribal leaders to adopt Roman dress and other habits, encouraged them to finance and build amphitheaters, and made Latin the language of state.

Among the Dacians, a new language soon emerged, a language based on Latin but different from that of the invaders. The new tongue was a mingling of the local languages with the Latin spoken by the common Roman citizen—known as the vulgar, or ordinary, tongue—as opposed to the classical Latin used in official documents and writings. However, when the Western Roman Empire disintegrated, this new language lost its links to Rome and gradually evolved to become what is known as Romanian.

Romanian belongs to the Romance language family, which includes French, Spanish, Italian, Catalan, and Portuguese. These languages, though separate, share some vocabulary and grammar. As Europeans contacted and conquered many parts of the globe, the Romance languages spread so that today nearly 400 million people speak a Romance language. Romanian, which had it origins under Trajan, is still spoken by about 23 million inhabitants in Romania and by 2.5 million in Russia plus a half million others scattered across the Balkans and southeastern Europe.

Learning from the Encounter **Why** did the Romans initially have difficulty in conquering the Dacians? **Describe** the Roman pattern of colonizing their newly conquered territories. **What** were the basic characteristics of the new language? **How** has American English been transformed by the introduction of other languages? **Which** languages seem to have been the most influential on American English?

Encounter figure 5.1 Rome's War Against Dacia (modern Romania). *Trajan's victory over the Dacians was represented in Trajan's Column, which stands in the ruins of Trajan's forum in Rome. The continuous frieze narrates Trajan's two campaigns against the Dacians. The bottom scenes depict the Dacians attacking a Roman fort (left), the Dacians crossing the Danube (center), and the Romans ferrying troops over the Danube (right); the top scene shows the Romans attacking Dacian supply wagons.*

on the attic, or top story, of the arch is the dedication, and decorating the sides are composite columns, a Roman innovation that intertwined flowers in the capitals of Ionic columns. Inside the arch are reliefs of Titus's victorious march into Rome after subduing the Jews.

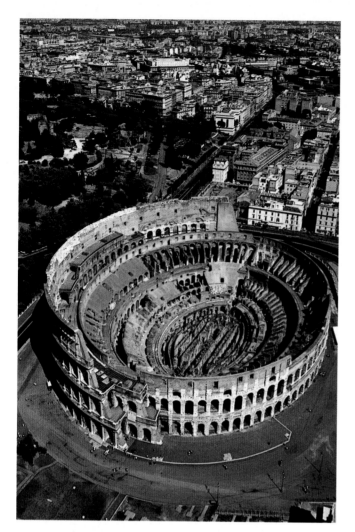

Figure 5.18 Colosseum. Ca. 72–80 C.E. Ht. 166'6". Rome. *Although the Flavians were a short-lived dynasty, starting with Vespasian in 69 C.E. and ending with Domitian in 96, they left Rome this structure, one of its most enduring landmarks. The Romans created the oval amphitheater (literally "theater on both sides") by joining two semicircular Greek theaters, another example of their ingenuity and practicality.*

▶

Figure 5.19 The Forum at Pompeii. Ca. 150–120 B.C.E. Pompeii, Italy. *This forum served as the civic center of this provincial town of 15,000 to 20,000 inhabitants. Four streets, from the north, south, east, and west, converged here, but no traffic was allowed in the central area.*

"sand"), was made of wood and usually covered with sand. A honeycomb of rooms, corridors, and cages ran underneath the wooden floor. The Colosseum's vast size and unusual features, such as its retractable overhead awning, made it one of the triumphs of Roman engineering, but the spectacular and brutal contests between men, and sometimes women, and wild beasts, in varied combinations, symbolized the sordid side of Rome.

Up and down the Italian peninsula and across the ancient world, the urban governments built forums, temples, and amphitheaters, laid roads, and engineered aqueducts in emulation of Rome. Sometimes old towns were made to conform to imperial standards. Pompeii, founded by the Greeks in southern Italy, was typical of the older provincial towns that the Romans remodeled to suit their needs. The Romans left Pompeii's earlier temples and public buildings standing, but a new forum gave the old city a modern look, with municipal offices, a business center, temples to the emperors and to Apollo, and a shrine honoring the civic deities (Figure 5.19). On the edge of town were such amenities as a palaestra—an exercise yard with swimming pool—and several markets. But disaster abruptly ended the urban renewal of Pompeii. In 79 C.E., nearby Mount Vesuvius, an active volcano, erupted and buried the city and most of its people—a horrible fate for the city, but one that produced a rich treasure for archeologists, who began excavations in the 1700s.

Like modern urban centers, Roman towns needed a continuous supply of water. In meeting the water demands of the cities, the Romans displayed their talent for organization and their preference for the practical by creating an elaborate network of aqueducts, sluices, and syphons that ran by gravity from a water source in nearby hills and culminated in a town's reservoirs and fountains.

The Romans started building underground aqueducts in about 300 B.C.E. and constructed the first elevated aqueduct in 144 B.C.E. Under Augustus, they completed an aqueduct across the Gard River near Nîmes in southern France (Figure 5.20). Known as the

In addition to forums, columns, and arches, the emperors commissioned amphitheaters as monuments to themselves and as gifts to the citizens. The amphitheaters were the sites of the gladiatorial contests and other blood sports that were the cornerstone of popular culture in the empire. The most famous of these structures was called the Colosseum, although it was actually named the Flavian amphitheater, in honor of the dynasty that built it (Figure 5.18). The name Colosseum, dating from a later time, referred to a large statue of the emperor Nero that stood nearby.

The exterior of the Colosseum was formed by stacking three tiers of rounded arches on top of one another; Greek columns were then inserted between the arches as decorations—Doric columns on the first level, Ionic on the second, and Corinthian on the third. A concrete and marble block foundation supported this immense amphitheater. The playing area, or arena (Latin for

▶

Figure 5.20 Pont du Gard. Ca. late first century C.E. Ht. 161'. Gard River, near Nîmes, France. *This aqueduct spanning the river was only one segment of the 31-mile system that supplied water to Nîmes. Between 8,000 and 12,000 gallons of water were delivered daily, or about 100 gallons per inhabitant.*

Figure 5.21 *Head of Brutus.* Ca. 350–50 B.C.E. Ht. 20". Palazzo dei Conservatori, Rome. *The finely detailed hair, beard, and facial lines are the work of a skilled sculptor, perhaps a Greek from southern Italy. The broad range of possible dates for this bronze head (ca. 350–50 B.C.E.) indicates that scholars still disagree over when it was cast.*

Pont du Gard, this aqueduct has a beautiful functional design. Six large arches form the base, and above them are eleven smaller ones supporting a third tier of thirty-five even smaller arches. Atop the third tier is the sluice through which the water flowed, by gravity, to Nîmes. This graceful structure is a reminder of how the Romans transformed an ordinary object into a work of art.

Sculpture   Unlike Roman architecture, Roman sculpture was deeply affected by the tastes of artists and patrons as well as by class interests. For example, certain trends in the republic ran along class lines: The patricians gravitated to the Greek styles and the plebeians favored the local art, called Italo-Roman. Under the empire, the same needs that gave rise to temples and amphitheaters were at work in changing the look of imperial sculpture.

Although Roman portrait sculpture never broke through to a distinct style during this period, it nevertheless passed through three definite phases. The first phase, lasting from the third to the first century B.C.E., was influenced by the death masks made for the family gallery as part of ancestor worship. This style can be seen in the *Head of Brutus* (Figure 5.21). Brutus, one of the great heroes who helped to turn out the last Etruscan king, is shown as a stern and resolute leader. In contrast, the artist who sculptured the *Republican Portrait of a Man* (Figure 5.22) captured the characteristic realism of sculpture in the Late Republic. The man's face, clearly troubled and aged, as indicated by the lines in his cheeks and around his eyes, was intended as a warning rather than as an inspiration to the viewer. This type of realistic sculpture, with its sense

Figure 5.22 *Republican Portrait of a Man.* Copy of an original from about 30 B.C.E. Marble, ht. 13". Museum of Art, Rhode Island School of Design, Providence, Rhode Island. *This bust reflects the upheavals of first-century B.C.E. Rome, as patricians reasserted their power over the crumbling state. Portraits of patrician leaders were characterized by wrinkled skin, clenched jaws, and determined expressions.*

Figure 5.23 *Augustus*, from Prima Porta. Ca. 14 C.E. Marble, ht. 6'7½". Vatican Collection. *This statue of Caesar Augustus (r. 31 B.C.E.–14 C.E.), the founder of the Roman Empire, was uncovered at Prima Porta, the villa of his wife, Livia. The statue closely resembled the ruler yet presented him as godlike. Augustus's imperial successors commissioned similar sculptures to convey a sense of their dignity and power.*

of unease, represents the second phase of Roman sculpture.

The third phase was shaped by the reign of Augustus. According to his biographer Suetonius, the emperor boasted that he found Rome a city of brick and left it a city of marble, and Augustus certainly did influence the direction of sculpture and architecture. Under his rule, imperial portraiture reverted to the idealism of Hellenic Greece, displacing the realistic art of the Late Republic. But Augustus's pure idealism did not prevail for long, for under his successors sculpture became more propagandistic—that is, more symbolic of imperial power. This move to symbolic idealism reflected the later emperors' need to find a highly visible way in which to overawe, and thus draw together, Rome's increasingly diversified masses.

Two major sculptural works associated with Augustus, the Prima Porta portrait and the Ara Pacis, or the Altar of Peace, helped to popularize the idealistic style. Augustus's statue, commissioned after his death, stood in a garden on his widow's estate, Prima Porta, just outside Rome (Figure 5.23). The pure Hellenic style is evident in Augustus's relaxed stance and ide-

alized face, both of which were modeled on the *Doryphoros* by Polykleitos (see Figure 3.22). However, the accompanying symbols reveal the propagandistic intent of the sculpture and were portents of the path that imperial portraits would take. For example, the cupid represents Venus, the mother of Aeneas, and thus Augustus is symbolically connected to the legendary origins of Rome.

The second idealistic sculpture, the marble Ara Pacis, was funded by the Senate as an offering of thanks to Augustus for his peacekeeping missions. The entire structure was set on a platform and enclosed by three walls. On the fourth side, an entrance with steps led to the altar (Figure 5.24). Relief sculptures decorated the interior and exterior walls, some in an idealized style and others in a realistic style (Figure 5.25). The resulting tension between realism and idealism marked this altar as an early work in the imperial style.

This type of sculpture reached its highest potential as a propaganda tool on triumphal arches and victory columns, such as the Arch of Titus and Trajan's Column. One of the reliefs from the Arch of Titus, the *March of the Legions*, portrays the army's victory march

Figure 5.24   Ara Pacis. 9 B.C.E. Marble, width 35'. Rome.
Like the Prima Porta statue, the Ara Pacis became a model for later emperors, who emulated its decorations, symbols, and size. The altar was rediscovered in the sixteenth century, excavated in the nineteenth and early twentieth centuries, and restored in 1938.

Figure 5.25 *Family of Augustus,* Ara Pacis relief. 9 B.C.E. Marble, ht. 63". Rome. *The figures in low relief, moving from right to left, are separated yet linked by their placement and clothing. The child to the right of center is given great prominence: He faces right while all the adults in the foreground are looking left and a man places his hand on the child's head. This singling out of the child may be an act of endearment or of recognition that he is to be the emperor.*

into Rome after the destruction of the Temple in Jerusalem in 70 C.E. (Figure 5.26).

The continuous frieze from Trajan's Victory Column is one of the sculptural marvels of the Roman world (Figure 5.27). This low-relief sculpture winds around the column like a long comic strip, telling the story of Trajan's campaign against Dacia. Scholars still study the carvings of campsites and fortifications on this relief, finding them a rich source for Roman military history.

The last great sculpture from this period is the equestrian statue of Marcus Aurelius (see Figure 5.10). This work reveals a falling away from Augustan idealism to a rugged, individualized style, although one

that was still highly propagandistic in its use of symbols. The symbols in this statue stress that Marcus Aurelius was a warrior-emperor, fighting enemies far from his capital in Rome.

Painting and Mosaics   Murals, or wall paintings, the most popular type of painting in Rome, have been found in private dwellings, public buildings, and temples. Surviving works hint at a highly decorative and brightly colored art. Originally the Romans applied tempera, or paint set in a binding solution, directly onto a dry wall. However, this quick and easy method produced a painting that soon faded and peeled. Later they adopted fresco painting as the most practical

Figure 5.26 *March of the Legions,* from the Arch of Titus. Ca. 81 C.E. Marble relief, approx. 6 × 12½′. Rome. *This rectangular marble relief occupies the south side of the Arch of Titus. It commemorates the Roman victory in the Jewish War of 66–70 C.E., when the Romans put down a rebellion by the Jews in Judea and subsequently dispersed them across the Roman world. In the relief, the Roman soldiers hold aloft the Jewish holy relics from the Temple as they seem to press forward and pass under the arch on the right.*

and lasting technique. Several coats of mortar, followed by coats of lime, were applied directly onto the wall. Paints were then mixed and worked into the freshly plastered wall. The colors dried into the wall, resulting in a nearly indestructible painting. The Romans were inspired by many subjects: Greek and Roman myths, architectural vistas, religious stories, ritual performances, genre scenes (everyday events), and landscapes.

Among the many landscapes painted by Roman artists are the splendid garden frescoes from the Villa of Livia at Prima Porta, a vast imperial estate outside of Rome (Figure 5.28). At Prima Porta stood the statue of the husband of Empress Livia, the emperor Augustus (see Figure 5.23). This fresco, depicting a distant garden, is framed by twin horizontal walls at its bottom and a jagged border at the top. Roman artists never mastered mathematical perspective; instead, they used the placement of objects, animals, and hu-

man figures to create a sense of space, as in this fresco. The patterned fence (foreground) and the stone wall (in the rear), with a walkway in between and a tree in the center, create the illusion of depth. The placement of the bushes, smaller trees, shrubs, fruits, and flowers behind the walls further augments the fresco's perspective. The vast array of identifiable plants and birds typifies two themes of Augustan art, as the art of the reign of Augustus is called. Those themes are prosperity and peace, thus suggestive of the propagandistic nature of the art of the period.

Figure 5.27 Detail of Trajan's Victory Column. 113 C.E. Marble, ht. of relief band approx. 36″. Rome. *Wrapped around the 100-foot-high column is the 645-foot relief carving with 2,500 figures depicting Trajan's two campaigns against the Dacians. Color was applied to heighten the realistic effect of the work, which, in its original setting, could be viewed from nearby buildings.*

149

Figure 5.28 *Garden Scene.* Villa of Livia, Prima Porta. Ca. 20 B.C.E. Fresco. Museo di Palazzo, Massimo, Rome. *This garden scene represents a particular style of Roman fresco painting that began in the first century B.C.E. and was still popular in the Age of Augustus. Labeled* **architectural,** *these paintings were often divided into three horizontal planes and framed by columns to give the sense of a wall opening or looking through a window onto a bucolic view of the world beyond the villa or house.*

The Romans learned to make **mosaics** from the Hellenistic Greeks in the third century B.C.E., but by the third century C.E., several local Roman mosaic styles had sprung up across the empire. Although subjects varied, certain ones seemed always to be in vogue, such as still lifes, landscapes, Greek and Roman myths, philosophers and orators, and scenes from the circus and amphitheaters. A mosaic from Tunisia (North Africa) shows the intricacy of design and variety of color that artisans achieved even in the Roman provinces (Figure 5.29).

Music

The absorption of the Greek tradition in music was so complete that later Roman music, in effect, simply perpetuated Greek forms and ideas. And yet the Romans used music only for practical purposes and rejected the Greek notion that music performed an ethical role in educating the soul or mind.

Not until imperial times did music come to play an important role in Roman life. Under the emperors, music became wildly popular, as all classes succumbed to its seductive charms. **Pantomimes**—dramatic productions with instrumental music and dances—became the spectacle favored by the Roman masses. In the long run, the pantomimes became a symbol of music's decadent trend under the empire. The largest of these productions featured three thousand instrumentalists and three thousand dancers, but the more common size was three hundred performers in each category. A more serious sort of music was kept alive by the wealthy classes, who maintained household orchestras and choruses for their private amusement. An even more cultivated audience encouraged poets such as Horace to set their verses to music, thus continuing the Greek tradition of lyric poetry.

Figure 5.29 Calendar Mosaic. Late second–early third century C.E. From the Maison des Mois at El Djem. Detail of 5 × 4′ mosaic. Sousse Museum, Sousse, Tunisia. *The El Djem Calendar comprises twelve small scenes, each representing a month, the name of which is inscribed in Latin. The Roman year began with March (top middle) and ended with February (top left corner). The months are symbolized by either religious or rural activities, such as in the September panel, which shows two figures standing in a vat crushing grapes.*

Although what Roman music actually sounded like remains a subject of conjecture, their musical instruments, borrowed from across the Mediterranean world, can be identified with some certainty. From Greece came the stringed instruments, the lyre and the kithara, along with such woodwinds as the single **aulos,** or oboe, and the double aulos—called by the Romans the tibia (Figure 5.30). From the Etruscans came the brasses. The Romans delighted in the harsh sounds made by these instruments, incorporating them into their military music just as the Etruscans did. The hydraulic organ, or water organ, was probably perfected in Hellenistic Alexandria, but in imperial Rome it became a crowd pleaser, adding deep, voluminous sounds to the pantomimes. The taste of the imperial Roman audience is evident in the water organ, which was impressive not for its musical qualities but as a feat of engineering expertise.

Figure 5.30 *The Street Musicians.* Ca. 100 B.C.E. 16⅞ × 16⅛". Museo Nazionale, Naples. *This mosaic may portray a scene from a comic play. Two masked figures dance and play the tambourine and the finger cymbals while a masked female figure plays the tibia, or double oboe. This mosaic was found in the so-called Villa of Cicero at Pompeii.*

The Legacy of Pre-Christian Rome

Western civilization is built on the ruins of Rome. Although no pre-Christian institutions survived to form a basis of European organization, other tangibles persisted in abundance so that the mark of Rome may still be seen and heard in countless ways. The very languages of western Europe bear the stamp of Rome, and Roman law forms the basis of the legal codes of many Western countries. Until the beginning of the twentieth century, the European educational ideal was based on the Roman curriculum, in which students studied the *trivium*—the three arts of grammar, logic, and rhetoric—and the *quadrivium*—the four sciences of arithmetic, geometry, music, and astronomy. Even today, this ideal persists at the heart of Western education.

Roman builders and engineers added to the Greek architectural tradition to create the Greco-Roman style, whose principal Roman components included domes, rounded arches, vaulting techniques, domed temples, temples on podiums, triumphal arches, amphitheaters, and victory columns. From the Renaissance, starting in 1400, until the twentieth century, the Greco-Roman style dominated Western architecture. Roman sculptors likewise helped to create the Greco-Roman style; their contributions included realistic portrait sculptures, propagandistic portraits of rulers, and equestrian statues. In literature and drama, Rome gave us the comic plays of Terence and Plautus, which influenced the rebirth of comedy in the Renaissance; the tragedies of Seneca, which inspired the tragedies of Shakespeare and other Renaissance dramatists; the contrasting satire genres invented by Horace and Juvenal, both of which spawned imitators through the ages; and the writings of Vergil, Horace, and Ovid, which became the classical standard for Europeans during the thousand years from the fall of Rome to the Renaissance, when Latin was in the ascendant and Greek had practically disappeared. In philosophy, Cicero taught the Christian West to write and think philosophically, since his works were known to the educated for centuries. And the ideas of Greek thinkers, though in summary or corrupt form, survived through Latin translations.

Rome's greatest legacy to the Western world was its shining image of a healthy civilization: a just and well-regulated society of multiethnic, multiracial citizens. The Idea of Rome, as we may call this achievement, was adapted from the Hellenistic rulers. However, the Hellenistic cities lacked the cohesiveness and longevity—and, most important, the vision—of the Roman creation. When the ancient world was swept away, the Idea of Rome remained a beacon in the darkness that descended over Europe.

KEY CULTURAL TERMS

syncretism	groined vault (cross vault)
satire	oculus
Neo-Platonism	forum
divining	mural
natural law	architectural painting
voussoir	mosaic
keystone	pantomime
vault	aulos
barrel vault	

SUGGESTIONS FOR FURTHER READING

APULEIUS. *The Golden Ass.* Translated by R. Graves. New York: Farrar, Straus & Giroux, 1951. A sound translation of one of the most lively and entertaining tales in ancient literature.

HORACE. *The Complete Works of Horace.* Introduction by C. Kraemer. New York: Modern Library, 1936. Masterly translations of the works that made Horace Rome's outstanding lyric poet.

JUVENAL. *The Sixteen Satires.* Translated by P. Green. New York: Penguin, 1970. Superb vernacular versions of Juvenal's bitter works.

VERGIL. *The Aeneid.* Translated by W. F. J. Knight. New York: Penguin, 1964. A sound English prose version of Vergil's poetic epic about Aeneas, the Trojan warrior whose conquests made possible the future supremacy of Rome.

6 JUDAISM AND THE RISE OF CHRISTIANITY

The great civilizations discussed so far—Mesopotamian, Egyptian, Greek, and Roman—were all wealthy, powerful, and culturally dynamic, and they contributed enormously to the Western heritage. Yet an even greater contribution, one that cannot be measured in buildings or governments, came from a politically insignificant people who lived in a tiny corner of the eastern Mediterranean during ancient times—the Jews. This people created a religion that helped to shape the character of the civilizations of the Western world. Through the Hebrew Bible—the Old Testament to Christians—Judaic beliefs were passed on to both Christianity and Islam and spread around the world. In addition, the fruitful interaction of the Judeo-Christian heritage with the Greco-Roman Classical ideals enriched and transformed the Western humanities.

JUDAISM

Judaism is one of the oldest living religions in the world. It originated in the third millennium B.C.E. among a tribal Middle Eastern people who placed themselves at the center of world history and created sacred texts for passing on their heritage. Unlike the history and religion of other ancient peoples, the history and religion of the Jews are so inextricably connected that they cannot be separated.

The People and Their Religion

In about 2000 B.C.E., many displaced tribes were wandering throughout the Middle East because of the political upheavals that accompanied the collapse

◀ **Detail** *Christ as the Good Shepherd*. Second–third century C.E. Fresco. Catacomb of Priscilla, Rome.

Timeline 6.1   JEWISH CIVILIZATION

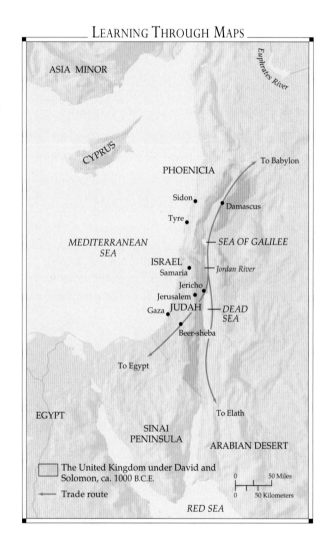

LEARNING THROUGH MAPS

Map 6.1   ANCIENT ISRAEL

This map shows the Hebrews' ancient kingdom, known as the United Monarchy, forged by the rulers David and his son Solomon. The map also shows the kingdoms of Israel and Judah, the two Hebrew states which emerged when the United Monarchy split on the death of Solomon, in 926 B.C.E. **Locate** the capitals of these two kingdoms. **How** was the cultural life and religious faith of the nation of Israel influenced by foreign neighbors? **What** impact did Israel's size and location have on its history and religious faith? **Notice** the scale of the map and compare it with the scale of Map 5.1, The Roman Empire Under Augustus.

One of these tribes, known as the Hebrews and led by the patriarch Abraham, occupied territory called Canaan, a region identified loosely with ancient Israel (Timeline 6.1). They settled in the hill country, where they tended their flocks and practiced their crafts (Map 6.1).

The Hebrews considered themselves unique, a belief based on the relationship between Abraham and a great supernatural being who spoke to him and whom he obeyed. This deity made a **covenant,** or solemn agreement (the outward sign of which was the circumcision of all male children), with Abraham to protect his family and bring prosperity to his offspring if they agreed to obey his divine commands. Although this Hebrew deity was associated with nature, he differed from other Mesopotamian deities in his commitment to justice and righteousness. He was an ethical god and sought to impose ethical principles on humans.

Egypt, Exodus, and Moses   The Hebrews prospered for decades in Canaan, but around 1500 B.C.E. a group migrated south into Egypt, which had recently been overrun by the Hyksos, a Semitic people with whom the Hebrews shared language and cultural traits. The Hebrews thrived over the next few centuries, until the

of the Akkadian kingdom and the coming of the Babylonians. Some of these nomads eventually settled along the eastern coast of the Mediterranean Sea that is part of the Fertile Crescent. These patriarchal tribes, under the guidance of the oldest and most respected male members, founded communities united by bloodlines, economic interests, and folk traditions.

Table 6.1   THE TEN COMMANDMENTS

1. You shall have no other gods before me.
2. You shall not make for yourself a graven image, or any likeness of any thing that is in heaven above, or that is on the earth beneath, or that is in the water under the earth. . . .
3. You shall not take the name of the Lord your God in vain. . . .
4. Observe the sabbath day, to keep it holy, as the Lord your God commanded you. . . .
5. Honor your father and your mother. . . .
6. You shall not kill.
7. Neither shall you commit adultery.
8. Neither shall you steal.
9. Neither shall you bear false witness against your neighbor.
10. Neither shall you covet your neighbor's wife . . . or anything that is your neighbor's.

Source: The Bible, Revised Standard Version, Deuteronomy 5:6–21.

Figure 6.1 Stone Menorah. Second century C.E. Ht. 18". Israel Museum, Jerusalem. *Although this particular menorah dates from the second century C.E., the seven-branched candelabrum had been in use as a religious symbol for centuries. According to Jewish beliefs, God gave Moses explicit instructions on how to craft the menorah, which was made for the tabernacle, or house of prayer. Later the menorah came to symbolize knowledge and understanding as well as the light of God protecting the Jews.*

Egyptians reconquered their land and enslaved both the Hyksos and the Hebrews. In about 1250 B.C.E., the extraordinary leader Moses rallied the Hebrews and led them on the Exodus from Egypt—one of the most significant events in Jewish history. Hebrew scriptures describe Moses as a savior sent by God.

As the Hebrews wandered in the desert on the Sinai peninsula, Moses molded his followers into a unified people under a set of ethical and societal laws, which they believed were received from God. The laws of Moses were unique among ancient peoples because they were grounded in the covenant between the Hebrews and God and because no distinction was made between religious and secular offenses. All crimes were seen as sins and all sins as crimes. Those who committed crimes could not simply make reparation to their victims; they also had to seek forgiveness from God. There were some crimes, such as murder, that were so offensive to God that they could not be forgiven by human beings alone. Furthermore, human life was seen as sacred, because it was given by God, who created and owned all things; individual humans were precious because they were made in God's image.

The core of Mosaic law was the Ten Commandments, which set forth the proper behavior of human beings (Table 6.1). The commandments became the basis of a renewed covenant, which was now extended beyond Abraham and his descendants to include the entire people. The Hebrew God tolerated no rivals; he was seen as the sole, omnipotent creator and ruler of the universe. If individuals followed his laws and wor-

shiped him alone, they would be rewarded, and if they strayed, they would be punished. Likewise, if the tribe followed the divine commands, they would prosper, and if they disobeyed, they would meet with adversity. As the mediator of the covenant between God and the Hebrew people, Moses played a crucial role in shaping Judaism into a comprehensive system of ethical monotheism.

As they wandered through the Sinai desert, the Hebrews carried with them a sacred decorated box called the Ark of the Covenant. Within were the stone tablets on which the Ten Commandments were carved. Details of how to craft the Ark and all the other sacred objects used in worship were dictated to Moses by God (Figure 6.1). In the desert, the deity also revealed a new name for himself—YHWH, a name so sacred that pious Jews never speak or write it. In the late Middle Ages, European scholars rendered YHWH as Jehovah, but today this term is generally considered a false reading of the sacred letters. In modern English, YHWH is usually rendered as Yahweh. In biblical times, Jewish priests called the deity Adonai, the Semitic term for Lord.

After forty years of wandering, followed by Moses' death, the Hebrews finally returned to Canaan, the Promised Land pledged by Yahweh to their forefathers. Over the next two centuries, the Hebrews won Canaan and became known as the Israelites.

The Kingdom of Israel   In about 1000 B.C.E., the Israelites established a monarchy, and from the late

Table 6.2 HISTORICAL STAGES OF THE TEMPLE OF JERUSALEM

NAME	CONSTRUCTION DETAILS	DATE DESTROYED
Solomon's Temple. Also called First Temple	Completed under King Solomon, 957 B.C.E.	587/586 B.C.E., by the Babylonians
Second Temple. Also called Herod's Temple after being rebuilt in 26 C.E.	Completed 515 B.C.E. Rebuilt at order of King Herod (d. 4 B.C.E.) between 20 B.C.E. and 26 C.E.	70 C.E., by the Romans. A section of the western wall (also called the Wailing Wall) survived; it was incorporated into the wall around the Muslim Dome of the Rock and al-Aqsa mosque in 691 C.E.

eleventh century to the end of the tenth century B.C.E., the nation flourished under a series of kings—Saul, David, and Solomon. The popular king David rallied the scattered Israelite tribes, centralized the government, and shifted the economy away from herding and toward commerce, trade, and farming.

Solomon, David's son, brought the Israelite kingdom to its pinnacle of power and prestige. He signed treaties with other states, expanded Israel's trade across the Middle East, and raised the standard of living for many of his subjects. He completed the building of Jerusalem begun by David, which, with its magnificent public structures and great Temple, rivaled the glory of other Middle Eastern cities. The Temple of Solomon, also known as the First Temple, housed Israel's holy relics, including the Ark of the Covenant, and became the focal point of the nation's religion, which required pilgrimages and rituals, based on the religious calendar (Table 6.2; Figure 6.2). The Hebrew religion required ritual offerings (sacrifices of animals on large altars and wine, incense, and grain mixed with oil on small altars) twice daily. These offerings were conducted by priests in the Temple in Jerusalem as a community ritual for the entire Hebrew nation; individuals could also arrange for sacrifices to be made on their own behalf. The early Hebrews sometimes were allowed to make sacrifices outside the Temple, but this practice was later forbidden.

King Solomon considered himself a patron of literature and the arts, and under his rule Hebrew culture

Figure 6.2 Horned Altar. Tenth century B.C.E. Carved limestone, ht. 26½". Oriental Institute, University of Chicago. *Middle Eastern peoples made sacrifices to their deities on altars, but the small horned altar, as pictured here, was unique to the Hebrews. Horned altars are described in the Bible, especially as a ritual object in the Temple in Jerusalem, built in the tenth century B.C.E. However, this horned altar was discovered at Megiddo, one of the cities of the Hebrew kingdom.*

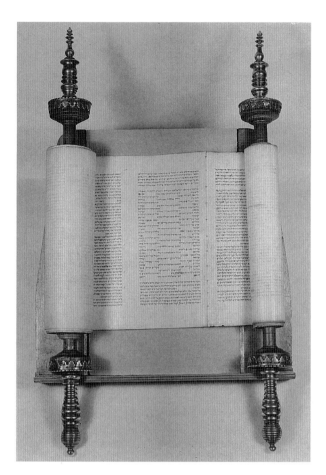

Figure 6.3 Scroll of the Pentateuch. *The ancient Hebrews recorded their scriptures on parchment scrolls. The scroll of the Pentateuch was wound on two staves. The scrolls were not decorated or illuminated with designs, animals, or humans because the Bible forbade any likeness of Yahweh and artistic expressions were not encouraged. However, some sacred books were illustrated and ornamented at various stages of Hebrew history. The carved staves on which the Pentateuch was wound were often embellished. Evidence exists that by the fifth century C.E., the scrolls might have been encased in a container of precious metal, and by the fifteenth century, they were enclosed in containers adorned with reliefs and Hebrew lettering.*

expanded, notably in law, writing, music, and dance. As the Hebrews' oral traditions gave way to written records, Hebrew authors wrote down their laws and their earliest histories, which are preserved in the first books of the Bible (Figure 6.3). These Hebrew works predate by five centuries the writings of the great Greek historians Herodotus and Thucydides, but, unlike the Greek writers, the Hebrew historians made God the central force in human history and thus transformed the unfolding of earthly events into a moral drama with cosmic significance.

Solomon's achievements came at a heavy price, however, for they undermined his people's religious foundations, intensified class divisions, and tended to divide the northern and southern tribes. When Solomon died in 926 B.C.E., the tensions between the regions intensified and the United Monarchy separated into two states: Israel in the north, with its capital at Samaria, and Judah in the south, with its capital at Jerusalem.

During the period of the two Hebrew kingdoms, a new type of religious leader, known as a prophet, appeared. The prophets warned of the fatal consequences of breaking Yahweh's commandments, and in predicting the downfall of surrounding non-Hebrew states, the prophets asserted that God was now using peoples other than the Hebrews to fulfill his divine plan in history. The prophets also demanded social justice for the helpless and the downtrodden. In the face of a widening gulf between rich and poor, the prophets predicted that if the well-off did not aid the less fortunate, Yahweh would bring down the evil rulers and, in the future, punish the selfish and reward the sufferers. But the words of the prophets, such as Hosea and Amos in Israel and Isaiah and Jeremiah in Judah, seemed to go unheeded.

The Babylonian Captivity and the Postexilic Period
Although Israel enjoyed its moments of prosperity and power, the larger empires, especially Egypt and Assyria, wanted to control the military and trade routes crossing this part of the Fertile Crescent. In 722 B.C.E., the tiny nation of Israel was destroyed by the Assyrians. Judah, to the south, endured for another two hundred years, but in 586 B.C.E., the Babylonians conquered Judah, destroying Solomon's Temple in Jerusalem and deporting most of the Hebrews to Babylonia. The approximately forty years of exile, known as the Babylonian Captivity, became one of the major turning points in Jewish history.

At the end of the sixth century, the Jews (as the Hebrews are called after the Babylonian Captivity) were freed by the triumphant Persians, who were sweeping across the ancient world under Cyrus (see Chapter 2). Returning to Judah, the Jews rebuilt their Temple, now known as the Second Temple, and their towns. Believing that God had rescued them, they established a theocratic state—a government ruled by those who are recognized as having special divine guidance and approval—and dedicated themselves to the correct formulation and observation of their religious beliefs. The Jews welcomed back many exiles, reestablished their commercial ties, and revived their handicraft industries. But many exiles remained outside the homeland and became known as Jews of the **Diaspora,** or the Dispersion.

After their return from Babylon, the Jews expanded their views of Yahweh. Probably under the indirect impact of the increasingly popular Persian religion,

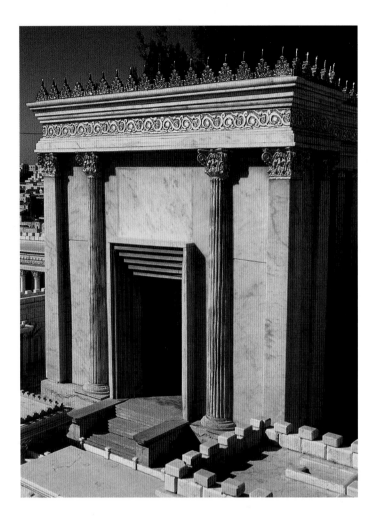

Figure 6.4   Model of the Reconstructed Second Temple (Herod's Temple) in Jerusalem. *This model of the Second Temple shows the strong influence of Hellenistic-style architecture, particularly in the colonnaded arcades, the decorative frieze, and the tall, slender Corinthian columns flanking the main entryway. The Second Temple was destroyed by Roman legions in 70 C.E., but one wall was left standing.*

Zoroastrianism—and its description of the twin forces of good and evil or Light and Dark—the Jews began to envision a cosmic dualism in their own beliefs. The Hebrews' earlier perception of themselves as a chosen people under a universal deity was reinforced as they concluded that Yahweh had used the Persians to free them. Furthermore, the Jews started to incorporate two new features into their religion: **eschatology,** or the concern with the end of the world, and an interest in **apocalypse,** prophecies about the coming of God and a day of judgment. This future world would be led by a **Messiah,** or Anointed One, who would bring peace and justice to all.

The Hellenistic and Roman Periods   Alexander the Great conquered Judah in 332 B.C.E., and after his

Figure 6.5   Masada, Israel. *This outcropping of rock in the forbidding terrain outside Jerusalem was a natural fortress. King Herod had built one of his palace-fortresses here in the years just before the birth of Christ. For three years the Zealots occupied its ruins, holding out against the Romans after the end of the First Jewish War in 70 C.E.*

Figure 6.6 *Moses Giving Water to the Twelve Tribes of Israel.*
Fresco. Synagogue. Third century C.E. Dura Europos, Syria.
Reconstructed in the National Museum, Damascus, Syria.
*This fresco is from a house-synagogue (a place of worship set up
within a private residence) that was discovered in the early twentieth century, after having been filled with rubble in 256 C.E., as
part of a defense plan for the city of Dura Europos. Only sections
of the walls survive. The room featured benches running around
the walls and a niche for the Torah scrolls in the western wall.
The paintings depict various events from the Hebrew Bible, most
having to do with national salvation, such as Samuel Anointing
David, the Ark Brought to Jerusalem, and the Exodus from Egypt.
Painted by anonymous artists, these works were executed in tempera, a medium made of pigments blended with egg yolks and water, applied to dry plaster.*
*This fresco was part of the Exodus group and was based on
biblical scripture (Numbers 2:2–12). It portrays Moses seated and
holding a staff, as he delivers life-giving water (via "tubes") to the
tribes, symbolized by twelve huts, each with a single figure. A
menorah stands in the center rear.*

death the area became part of the Seleucid kingdom, centered in Syria. Hellenistic culture and ideas prolif-erated and deeply affected Jewish life. Growing ten-sions between the Jews and the Hellenistic leaders erupted in 168 B.C.E. when the Seleucid king Antiochus IV tried to impose the worship of Greek gods on the Jews, placing a statue of Zeus in the Second Temple in Jerusalem. Antiochus's violation of the sacred place enraged the Maccabean clan, whose inspired leader-ship and bravery led to a successful revolt and the re-capture of the Temple. The Maccabean family ruled Judah as an independent commonwealth for approxi-mately one hundred years. Then, in 63 B.C.E., the Ro-mans conquered most of the Middle East. They subsequently incorporated Judah (in what was now called Palestine) into their empire as Judea and placed the Jewish lands under client kings.

Appointed to these kingships was the Herod dy-nasty, a family of Jews who had gained favor with the Romans. Herod the Great, who ruled from 37 to 4 B.C.E., rebuilt Jerusalem, including the Second Temple, and promoted Hellenistic culture (Figure 6.4). But con-ditions under the Romans became unbearable to the Jews, and in 66 C.E. a rebellion broke out. After four years of fighting, called the First Jewish War, the Ro-mans captured Jerusalem and destroyed the Second Temple (70 C.E.). A revolutionary group known as Zealots held out until 73 at Masada, a sheer-sided mesa on the shores of the Dead Sea (Figure 6.5). When their cause became hopeless, they committed suicide rather than surrender to the Romans.

One wall of the Second Temple in Jerusalem re-mained standing. Known as the Wailing Wall, it came to symbolize the plight of the Jewish people. As de-scribed in Chapter 5, Titus, the victorious Roman gen-eral and later emperor, returned to Rome with the holy Jewish relics (see Figure 5.26). To make sure the Jews would no longer be a problem, the Roman govern-ment in the late first century C.E. ordered the dispersal of the Jews throughout the empire. However, this sec-ond Diaspora did not end the Jews' cultural, intellec-tual, and religious existence. On the contrary, the Jewish way of life continued, though it changed. With the fall of the Temple in Jerusalem, Jews worshiped in synagogues, or congregations, which eventually were headed by rabbis, or teachers (Figure 6.6). Over the

SLICE OF LIFE
A Jewish Eyewitness to the Destruction of the Second Temple

FLAVIUS JOSEPHUS
A Jewish Soldier in the Roman Army

The Jewish historian Josephus (about 37–about 100 C.E.) was an eyewitness to one of the darkest days in Jewish history: the destruction of the Second Temple in Jerusalem on September 8, 70 C.E. Earlier, in 67 C.E., he had been made a captive of the Romans, but through his ingenuity, he had been given his freedom. He became an admiring, though sometimes reluctant, soldier in the Roman cause. Assigned to General Titus, he was among the troops that sacked and burned the temple on that fateful day. The following account is taken from Josephus's History of the Jewish War *(75–79 C.E.).*

At this moment one of the [Roman] soldiers, not waiting for orders and without any dread of such an act but driven on by some frenzy, snatched a brand from the blazing fire and, lifted up by a comrade, hurled the torch through the golden door which gave access to the buildings of the Temple Precinct from the north side. As the flames surged up, a great cry to match their feelings arose from the Jews, and they rushed to the defence, reckless of their lives and prodigal of their strength once they saw that the purpose of their previous watch was gone. . . .

As the fire gained strength, Titus found that he could not restrain the surge of his enthusiastic soldiers. . . .

Most were driven on by the hope of loot, for they thought that the inside of the building must be full of money if the outside, which they could see, was made of gold. One of those who had got in forestalled the attempts of Titus, who had rushed in to check them, and hurled a brand against the hinges of the door. Suddenly flames appeared from within, which forced back Titus and his officers, leaving those outside to kindle the blaze unhindered. In this way, though much against Titus's will, the Temple was burnt. . . .

Interpreting This Slice of Life   What was the source of conflict between the Romans and the Jews? **Do** you find Josephus's account credible, given that he was both a Jew and a Roman soldier? **Analyze** his account of the Temple's fall. **What** role does General Titus play in the assault? **How** are the Roman soldiers depicted? **How** does Josephus depict the Jewish rebels? **Are** there modern parallels to this type of eyewitness history?

---

centuries, the rabbis' teachings evolved into Rabbinic Judaism, based on the Torah and the Talmud (from Hebrew, "learning"), a collection of legal rulings and commentaries. Rabbinic Judaism established a mode of worship and moral code that Jews worldwide have followed down to modern times.

Societal and Family Relationships   From earliest times to the founding of the monarchy, Jewish families survived in an agrarian economy and society. Although the patriarchal structure set the pattern of life and ensured the dominance of the tribal chieftains, men and women shared duties and responsibilities because in a rural society a family's continuation and the preservation of its property required the efforts of all its members. Within the family, women exercised some freedom, mothers' and sisters' roles were taken seriously, and the family rights of wives and mothers were protected by law.

However, with the coming of the kingdom of Israel and during and after the Babylonian Captivity, the male leaders, in their efforts to protect the new political system, the integrity of their religion, and the He-

brew way of life, formally and informally limited the rights and powers of women. This trend accelerated in the Hellenistic period as urbanism and commercialism made inroads into the Jewish social order and family. Work was increasingly divided according to gender, with women being assigned domestic duties and subordinated and restricted within the economic, social, legal, and cultural system. The changing, and often conflicting, roles for women were reflected in the Hebrew Bible and other literature, which recorded instances of women serving as priestesses or influencing Hebrew officials, defined the qualities of a good wife, justified women's subservient status in a patriarchal order, and blamed them for human transgressions.

The Bible

The Jews enshrined their cultural developments in the Bible, their collection of sacred writings, or **scriptures.** Known as the Old Testament to Christians, the Hebrew Bible (from the Greek word for "book") contains history, law, poetry, songs, stories, prayers, and philosophical works. Evolving out of a rich and long oral tradition, the Bible probably began to take its earliest written form during the United Monarchy in the tenth century B.C.E. By then the Hebrews had an alphabet, which, like that of the Greeks, was probably derived from the Phoenicians. Having acquired a written language and a unified political state, the Hebrews shared a consciousness of their past and desired to preserve it. They assembled and recorded various historical accounts, songs, and stories, plus the sayings of the prophets. Sometime in the fifth century B.C.E., Jewish scholars and religious leaders canonized (officially accepted) parts of these writings as divinely inspired. They became the first five books of the Bible, known as the Torah or the Pentateuch. The Hebrew Bible's ultimate form was reached in 90 C.E. when a council of Jewish scholars added a last set of writings to the **canon.**

Another important development in the transmission of the Hebrew scriptures was their translation into other languages. In the third century B.C.E., after many Jews had been influenced by Hellenistic culture, a group of Alexandrian scholars collected all the authenticated Jewish writings and translated them into Greek. This Hebrew Greek Bible was called the Septuagint, from the Latin word for "seventy," so named because of the legend that it was translated by seventy scholars. Although traditionalist Jews initially rejected the Septuagint, it was gradually accepted as authoritative by Jewish intellectuals and early Christian scholars.

The final version of the Hebrew Bible is divided into three parts: the Law, the Prophets, and the Writings (Table 6.3). (Christians divide the Old Testament into four parts.) The Law, also called the Torah (from Hebrew, "instruction"), recounts the story of God's creation of the world and the early history of the Hebrews. More important, it details the establishment of the covenant and the foundation of the moral and ritualistic codes of personal and societal behavior that underlie Judaism.

The Prophets, canonized in the first century B.C.E., provide records about Israel and Judah and expand the Hebrews' ideas about God's nature and their relationship to him. They recount the conquest of Canaan, the events of the era of the Judges and the period of the United Monarchy, and the fate of Judah after the Babylonian Captivity.

The Writings reflect diverse viewpoints and contain many types of literature, including poetry, wise sayings, stories, and apocalyptic visions of the end of time. Some of these books, such as Job, Ecclesiastes, and Proverbs, reflect the influence of other cultures on Jewish beliefs. The Writings were not deemed canonical until 90 C.E., with the exception of Psalms, a collection of poems, which was given sacred status by 100 B.C.E.

There is also a body of Jewish literature outside the canon. The Apocrypha are books written between 200 B.C.E. and 100 C.E. that include wisdom literature, stories, and history, including the history of the Maccabees. Though not part of the Jewish canon, these books were included in the Septuagint, the Greek translation of the Hebrew Bible, and accepted by the Roman Catholic Church as part of the Christian Old Testament.

Copies of many Jewish works, both canonical and noncanonical, were found in a cave near the Dead Sea in 1947. These documents, dating from about 200 B.C.E. to 100 C.E. and known as the Dead Sea Scrolls, were almost a thousand years older than any other existing manuscripts of the Bible and confirmed that the books had been transmitted faithfully for centuries (Figure 6.7). The scrolls also provided scholars with material about nonmainstream Jewish religious practices in the period before and during the earliest Christian period.

The Hebrew Bible provided Judaism with many of its beliefs and values and much of its worldview. It contrasted a changing view of God with a consistently negative opinion of human nature. Examples abound of humans who, like Adam and Eve or David, failed to uphold their side of the covenant by disobeying Yahweh, worshiping other gods, exploiting the unfortunate, or breaking moral and social codes. The Bible implied that given the weakness of human nature and Yahweh's strict demands, most mortals were unlikely to attain happiness. Perhaps happiness would be reached when Yahweh's kingdom was established on earth, but no one knew when that would happen or in what form. The individual's life was made more perplexing because no mortal could comprehend the awesome power of Yahweh. Human beings could only try to follow Yahweh's commandments—knowing that they would sin—and hope for happiness through his forgiveness.

In biblical Judaism, the hope for happiness depended on another aspect of the covenant: Jews believed that they would be forgiven for their sins. Redemption by God had occurred over and over in history, and the Bible sustained human hope while revealing Yahweh's love and mercy. Yet such qualities often seemed inconsistent with the Lord's vengeful manner. Consequently, the hearts of worshipers were torn between hope and fear. Their hope was strengthened through the covenant's promise that Yahweh would protect humanity as long as they lived just lives.

Early Jewish Art and Architecture

Jewish culture was profoundly shaped by the Second Commandment, which forbids the making of images

Table 6.3   BOOKS OF THE HEBREW BIBLE AND THE CHRISTIAN BIBLE OLD TESTAMENT

HEBREW BIBLE		CHRISTIAN BIBLE OLD TESTAMENT	
The Law (Torah)		*The Pentateuch*	
Genesis	Numbers	Genesis	Numbers
Exodus	Deuteronomy	Exodus	Deuteronomy
Leviticus		Leviticus	
The Prophets		*The Historical Books*	
(Early Prophets)		Joshua	2 Chronicles
Joshua	2 Samuel	Judges	Ezra
Judges	1 Kings	Ruth	Nehemiah
1 Samuel	2 Kings	1 Samuel	Tobit*
(Later Prophets)		2 Samuel	Judith*
Isaiah	Micah	1 Kings	Esther
Jeremiah	Nahum	2 Kings	1 Maccabees*
Ezekiel	Habakkuk	1 Chronicles	2 Maccabees*
Hosea	Zephaniah		
Joel	Haggai	*The Poetical or Wisdom Books*	
Amos	Zechariah	Job	
Obadiah	Malachi	Psalms	
Jonah		Proverbs	
		Ecclesiastes	
The Writings		Song of Solomon (Songs)	
Psalms	Esther	Wisdom*	
Proverbs	Daniel	Sirach*	
Job	Ezra		
Song of Songs	Nehemiah	*The Prophetical Books*	
Ruth	1 Chronicles	Isaiah	Obadiah
Lamentations	2 Chronicles	Jeremiah	Jonah
Ecclesiastes		Lamentations	Micah
		Baruch*	Nahum
		Ezekiel	Habakkuk
		Daniel	Zephaniah
		Hosea	Haggai
		Joel	Zechariah
		Amos	Malachi

*Roman Catholics include these books in the canon and refer to them as deutero-canonical ("second canon"); Protestants sometimes place them in an appendix with other Apocrypha.

or likenesses of God. In art, this meant that Yahweh could not, by definition, be depicted in any recognizable form. Furthermore, creation and creativity are considered the exclusive domain of God and reserved for him alone. Thus, there is no official Jewish sculpture or painting.

The scattered surviving artifacts of the Hebrews from the period before the United Monarchy can seldom be distinguished from the works of their neighbors. Because of the early Hebrews' nomadic existence, what sacred objects they had were transportable and kept in tents. These early works were not for public display because of the very holiness of Yahweh and the Hebrews' sense of their deity's power. Only a few persons were even permitted to see or be in the vicinity of these sacred objects. Once the tribes

Figure 6.7 The Dead Sea Isaiah Scroll (detail). First century B.C.E.–first century C.E. *The Dead Sea Scrolls are believed to be the work of a Jewish sect known as the Essenes. Living in a monastic community called Qumran, this radical group rejected the leadership of the Jews in Jerusalem and practiced a militant, separatist form of Judaism. The scrolls represent their copies of the Hebrew Bible as well as previously unknown works. The Dead Sea Isaiah Scroll preserves all sixty-six chapters of the Bible's longest book.*

were united, however, Solomon enshrined the Ark of the Covenant and other ritualistic items in the splendid Temple that he built in Jerusalem. Solomon meant the Temple to be the central national shrine of the Hebrews and a symbol of his dynasty.

Solomon's Temple was destroyed by the Babylonians when they carried off the Jews in the early sixth century B.C.E. The description of the Temple in 1 Kings makes it sound similar to the "long-house" temples found in other civilizations of that time and probably indicated the influence of foreign neighbors. According to the Bible, Solomon's Temple was a rectangular building comprising three sections: a porch, a sanctuary, or main hall, and an inner sanctum that housed the Ark of the Covenant. Artists and craftspeople decorated the interior with carvings of floral designs and cherubs, highlighting these with gold. The building was made of ashlars, and two large freestanding columns were placed at the entranceway. The Temple may have been raised on a platform. A court surrounded the Temple, and a large altar stood inside the court.

When the Jews were released from the Babylonian Captivity by the Persians, they returned to their homeland and reconstructed the capital city of Jerusalem and its Temple. The Second Temple, completed in the late sixth century B.C.E., exhibited a simpler design and decoration scheme than did Solomon's Temple. Meanwhile, the Jews of the Diaspora gathered in Hellenistic cities to read the Torah and to pray in buildings that became synagogues, or houses of worship. No record survives of how these synagogues looked or how they might have been decorated until the third century C.E.

Greek influences became apparent in Jewish architecture during Hellenistic times. One Maccabean ruler, John Hyrcanus [hear-KAY-nuhs] (135–106 B.C.E.), constructed a fortress-palace at present-day Araq el Emir in Jordan that shows this influence clearly. The facade of the palace blended Greek columns and oriental carvings, typical of the Alexandrian architectural and decorative style. The edifice and its carvings were probably similar to the Second Temple in Jerusalem. One of the few decorations remaining from this palace is a lion fountain (Figure 6.8). Carved in high relief, the

Figure 6.8 Lion at the Palace of John Hyrcanus. Second century B.C.E. Araq el Emir, Jordan. *This lion, Greco-Oriental in style, was carved deeply into the stone's surface to create a high-relief work. The lion's tail, wrapped around his right rear leg, is balanced by the raised left front leg, creating a feeling of strength and agility.*

Figure 6.9   Tomb of Bene Hezir. Early first century B.C.E. Kidron Valley, Israel. *The Tomb of Bene Hezir (on the left) shows the influence of Greek architecture in its post-and-lintel construction and its Doric columns. Even though the area was subject to Roman impact at this time, Roman influence is not apparent in the architecture. The members of the priestly Hezir family, as recorded in 1 Chronicles 24, were buried in what has been determined to be the oldest tomb in Israel's Kidron Valley. Scholars disagree over whether the structure in the center with the pyramidal roof belonged to the Bene Hezir tomb.*

lion is well proportioned and conveys a sense of power with its raised front paw and open mouth.

The lingering influence of late Greek architecture on Jewish structures is also seen in a set of tombs dug out of the soft limestone rocks east of Jerusalem in the Kidron Valley. According to the inscription, these tombs contained the remains of priests from the Hezir family (Figure 6.9). The tomb on the left displays Doric columns, and the one in the center fuses Greek Ionic columns and an Egyptian pyramidal roof. Several other tombs in the vicinity reveal a similar melding of styles.

During the reign of King Herod the Great (r. 37–4 B.C.E.), architecture in Judea exhibited a further mix of Greek styles with Jewish motifs. King Herod's magnificent fortress-palace at Masada may have been a conscious blending of the two cultures in an effort to bridge the gap between the Roman and Jewish worlds (see Figure 6.5). The various buildings in Herod's complex contained many representative Greco-Roman features, including fluted Corinthian columns and marble facings (Figure 6.10). In Herod's palace, Classical pat-

terned mosaics were combined with traditional Jewish decorations of flowers, fruits, and intertwined vines and branches (Figure 6.11).

Herod also built palaces at Jericho and in Jerusalem, but they were destroyed, and their remains have not been uncovered. He also supervised the rebuilding of the Second Temple in Jerusalem (see Figure 6.4), whose large dimensions and impressive features were recorded in the writings of the Jewish historian Josephus in his works *The Jewish War* and *Jewish Antiquities*. Like the First Temple, this one contained many rooms, including the Holy of Holies with the menorah and the table where the priests placed the consecrated, unleavened bread eaten during Passover, the festival that commemorates the exodus from Egypt. Whatever may have been Herod's motives in constructing this new Temple, the results were short-lived. When the Romans finally crushed the Jewish revolt in 70 C.E., the Temple, except for the Wailing Wall, was destroyed, and its sacred objects were transported to Rome.

King Herod Antipas, son of Herod the Great, founded the city of Tiberias in about 20 C.E. on the Sea

Figure 6.10 Hall of Herod's North Palace. Late first century B.C.E. Masada, Israel. *These Corinthian columns were originally plastered over and painted. Carved directly out of the hill's rock, they formed a natural corridor around the banqueting hall. Herod built this and other splendid palaces to impress the Jews and win their political sympathy, but he failed to do either.*

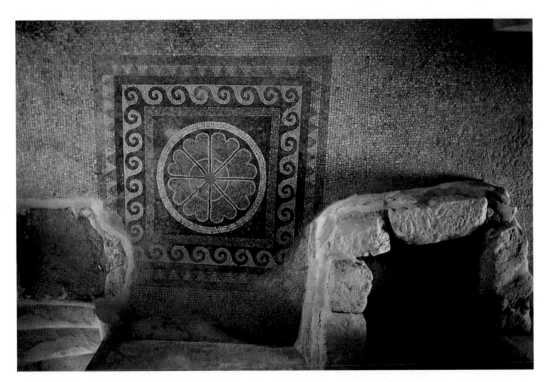

Figure 6.11 Mosaic from Herod's Palace. Late first century B.C.E. Masada, Israel. *The Greek practice of mosaic making was adopted by both the Romans and the Jews. The patterned designs around the borders of this mosaic from Herod's Palace are typically Greek, and the more organic image in the center is typically Jewish.*

ENCOUNTER

Baal, a Rival to the Israelites' God

When societies interact with one another, one of the most potentially dangerous consequences is the impact on religion. This is particularly true when religious beliefs and practices are deeply embedded in a people's history, as was the case when the Israelites encountered the people of Canaan. The Israelites were tempted by the religion of Baal, the Canaanite deity, and for many centuries Baal was Yahweh's most threatening rival for the hearts and minds of the people of Israel.

The origins and evolution of the Baal cult are similar to those of many other ancient polytheistic religions. According to texts on clay tablets discovered at Ugarit (modern Ras Shamra, Syria), which are dated from the second millennium B.C.E., Baal evolved into a fertility deity, the protector and guarantor of life for crops, animals, and humanity. As a fertility deity, Baal controlled the weather, planting, and harvests. His followers addressed him as Lord of Heaven (Baal means "master," "owner," or "lord"). Baal, according to one myth, ultimately became king of the gods, having challenged and defeated several deities, including Mot (death) and Yamm (the sea god). Many tribes across the Fertile Crescent, including the Canaanites, worshiped Baal, building temples and altars to him, paying homage in rituals and sacrifices, fabricating his image and symbols (human or animal), and incorporating the name Baal into individual names as a protection from evil.

The Israelites, led by Moses and his followers, wrested control of Canaan from the Canaanites and set up the kingdom of Israel with a moral and legal code based on Yahweh's teachings in *The Holy Scriptures.* Some Israelites, living among the conquered Canaanites, found Baal a satisfying alternative to Yahweh. They were drawn to the Baal cult's emotional practices, such as dancing and other frenzied rites, rather than to the staid rituals of Yahweh. Others were at-

tracted to the Baal cult's use of visible images, whereas Yahweh denounced this practice as idol worship. And a number of Israelite farmers and herdsmen found Baal's role as a fertility god, with a fairly lax moral code, more appealing than Yahweh's more distant status as Creator God and stern moral judge.

From the time of King Saul through the United Monarchy under Solomon, the Israelites tended to be loyal to Yahweh, though Baal's presence loomed in the background. With the fall of the United Monarchy in 926 B.C.E., Baal worship resurfaced in the northern kingdom of Israel and also in Judah, the southern kingdom. The Hebrew prophets, who were then emerging as a moral force, preached against the cult and its images, usually a bull or calf. Their message was that Yahweh, as Creator God, controlled all natural forces and brought the rains and the seasons but was not a nature god. Rather, Yahweh was the transcendent and universal deity, influencing historical events and affecting the lives of all peoples everywhere.

In Israel, the conflict between the two deities reached a climax during the time of King Ahab (r. about 874–about 853 B.C.E.). Ahab's wife, Jezebel of Phoenicia, built a temple to Baal in Samaria, the capital, and encouraged the Israelites to worship there. The prophet Elijah angrily denounced this movement, predicting that drought and famine would stalk the land until the Israelites gave up Baal and returned to Yahweh. The Hebrew Bible (1 Kings 18, 19) reports that Elijah and his supporters confronted Jezebel's priests and believers in a contest to end the drought, by having each side sacrifice a bull on separate altars. Each side prayed to its deity, asking that its altar fire be ignited spontaneously. Elijah's altar caught fire; Baal's altar did not. When the rains came, ending the drought, Yahweh was proved to be the one true deity, the ruler of the skies and all of nature. Thereafter, the

of Galilee. Named for Tiberius, the Roman emperor, the city attracted Roman and Greek settlers because of its baths and its site as a trade center. Jews, however, refused to move there, preferring to live in Hammat ("hot," in Hebrew), a village to the south whose origins date back to the Hellenistic Age. In the first century C.E., Tiberias expanded and absorbed several outlying settlements, including Hammat. Over the next two centuries, the growing Jewish population

turned Tiberias into a center of Jewish learning, and Jewish officials moved the Sanhedrin—the civil and religious supreme court—there. In the third century C.E., the local Jews built a synagogue, which was destroyed by an earthquake in 363 C.E. A more splendid edifice soon arose on its ruins. This second synagogue, in use to the fifth century C.E., was decorated with mosaics reflective of Greco-Roman influences. The mosaics in this synagogue included forbidden images worship of Baal in Israel tended to subside until the Assyrians overran the kingdom in 722 B.C.E.

In the southern kingdom of Judah, Yahweh remained locked in combat with Baal and other deities. During Judah's turbulent last years, the prophets constantly warned the rulers that their kingdom's end was near, condemned the followers of Baal, and implored the Hebrews to return to Yahweh. In 586 B.C.E., the Babylonians overpowered Judah and carried their Hebrew captives to Babylon, thus bringing Yahweh's rivalry with Baal to an abrupt end. When the Jews returned to their homeland at the beginning of the post-exilic period in 538 B.C.E., their faith had been transformed, as Yahweh's role expanded in public and private life, and they confronted new challenges to their religion.

Learning from the Encounter **How** were the origin and evolution of Baal similar to those of other ancient deities? **Why** were the Israelites attracted to Baal? **What** role did the prophets play in the rivalry between Baal and Yahweh? **How** does the story of Elijah's defeat of the Baal supporters symbolize larger issues in the

Hebrews' religion? **What** other religions have faced similar threats to their gods throughout history—and even today?

Encounter figure 6.1 Baal. Ca. 1700–1400 B.C.E. Louvre. Limestone, ht. 55". *This statue of Baal, discovered at Ugarit, shows the god, with his right arm raised, standing on a pedestal—a typical depiction of a weather god. The wavy lines below may represent mountains. He is dressed in a kilt fastened by a broad belt and cord from which hangs a sheathed dagger. He wears a sharp pointed helmet with a pair of bull horns on the front. In his upraised right hand, he holds a club or mace and in his left a spear with its top sprouting into a plant—a fertility symbol. In front, a miniature figure, who may be a Syrian king, pays homage. Although he was a Middle Eastern deity, Baal's delicate features and slim body hint at Egyptian influences. Striking what scholars call a "menacing god" pose, Baal's lordly appearance made him a rival to many other ancient gods, including Yahweh.*

such as human figures and non-Jewish themes, as well as depictions of sacred Hebrew symbols and objects (Figure 6.12).

CHRISTIANITY

Like Judaism, Christianity rose from obscurity and gained much of its power from the tremendous moral

force of its central beliefs and values. But Christianity went on to become the dominant religion of Western culture. From its origins among the Jews of Judea, Christianity slowly spread until, by the end of the fourth century C.E., it had become the official faith of Rome. When Rome lost control of the western provinces at the end of the fifth century C.E., Christianity's ideas and institutions survived as rays of hope in the surrounding darkness. In the following century,

Figure 6.12   Decorative Mosaic Floor Panel. Synagogue. Fourth century C.E. Hammat, near Tiberias, Israel. Israel Antiquities Authority, Jerusalem. *This decorative mosaic includes many objects associated with Jewish religious rites, tradition, and history. In the center stands the Ark, a cabinet partly covered by a draped curtain, which contained the Torah, the sacred scrolls on which were written the Pentateuch, the first five books of the Holy Scriptures. The Ark is the focal point of prayer in houses of worship, because it symbolizes the Holy of Holies of the Temple in Jerusalem. Other sacred objects in this mosaic include the menorah (seven-branched candelabrum), which was used in the Temple in Jerusalem; the shofar (ram's horn), which is blown at certain religious festivals, as a call to prayer; and an incense shovel, used in making offerings on altars (see Figure 6.2) in ancient Judaism. The two tall palm branches and the flowering citrons are agricultural symbols of the Festival of Tabernacles (in Hebrew, "Sukkot") or harvest festival—the last of seven such yearly festivals.*

Christians gradually gained the upper hand. Their triumph was powerfully symbolized in the Early Middle Ages when church authorities revised the old Roman calendar to make the birth of Christ the pivotal event in history. Thus, the period before Jesus' birth is known as B.C., or before Christ, and the era after his birth is termed A.D., or *anno Domini,* Latin words meaning "in the year of the Lord," the title of respect given to Jesus by Christians. Although Christianity and the church have declined from their zenith in the Middle Ages, the Christian calendar remains in effect throughout the West as well as in many other parts of the world—a symbol of the continuing power of this creed. In this textbook, reflecting today's multicultural world, the term B.C.E., "before common era," replaces B.C., and the term C.E., "common era," replaces A.D.

The Life of Jesus Christ and the New Testament

The surviving primary sources for the origin of Christianity are writings in Greek by early believers who were openly partisan. According to them, Christianity began within the Jewish faith among the followers of Jesus, a deeply pious and charismatic Jew who failed to purify his own faith but succeeded in founding a dynamic new religion.

Jesus was born to Mary and Joseph in Judea in about 4 B.C.E. (a date that reflects changes in the Christian calendar made since its inauguration). After narrating the events surrounding his birth, the accounts of Jesus' life are almost silent until he reaches the age of about thirty, when he commenced a teaching mission that placed him squarely in conflict with prevailing

Timeline 6.2   CHRISTIANITY TO 284 c.e.

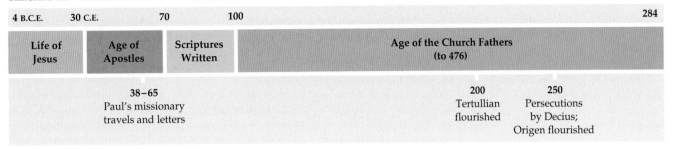

Jewish beliefs and authorities. The poor and outcast in Jewish society heard Jesus' message, and he soon had a small group of followers who believed that he was the Messiah, the Anointed One who would deliver the Jews, promised by God to the prophets. He was also termed the Christ, taken from the Greek for "the anointed one." Performing miracles and healing the sick, he preached that the apocalypse, or the end of the world, was near. In anticipation of what he called the coming of the kingdom of God, he urged his followers to practice a demanding and loving ethic.

Growing discord between the Jewish establishment and this messianic band caused Roman leaders to classify Jesus as a political rebel. In about 30 C.E., Jesus was crucified by the Romans (Timeline 6.2). Three days later, some of his followers reported that Jesus had risen from the dead and reappeared among them. His resurrection became the ultimate miracle associated with his teachings, the sign that immortal life awaited those who believed in him as the son of God and as the Messiah. After a few days on earth, Jesus ascended into heaven, though not before pledging to return when the world ended.

The outline of Jesus' life is set forth in the first three books, called **Gospels,** of the Christian scriptures. The early Christian community believed that the writers, known as Matthew, Mark, and Luke, were witnesses to Jesus' message; hence they were called **evangelists** after the Greek word *evangelion*—for those who preached the gospel, or the good news. The Gospels, although providing evidence for the historical Jesus, were not intended as histories in the Greco-Roman sense because they were addressed to Christian converts. Mark's Gospel was the earliest, dating from about 70; Matthew's account was written between 80 and 90; and an early version of Luke's narrative probably appeared at about the same time. These three works are known as the synoptic Gospels (from the Greek words *syn,* for "together," and *opsis,* for "view") because they take essentially the same point of view toward their subject. Between 90 and 100, a fourth, and somewhat different, Gospel appeared—that of John—

which treats Jesus as a wisdom teacher, a revealer of cosmic truths. The author of the Fourth Gospel has Jesus teach the possibility of being born again to eternal life.

Despite their similarities, the synoptic Gospels reflect a schism, or split, in the early Christian church. Peter, one of Jesus' original disciples, headed a Judaizing group that stressed the necessity of first becoming a Jew before becoming a Christian. Paul, a Jew who converted to Christianity after the death of Jesus, led a group that welcomed gentile, or non-Jewish, members. Mark's Gospel was written in part to support Paul's gentile faction and therefore takes a negative tone toward Jews. Matthew was written in part as a corrective to Mark and made Peter, according to Roman Catholic doctrine, the "rock" on which the church was founded—the biblical source for the belief that Peter was the first pope. Luke's Gospel was an effort by the early Roman church to deny, after the fact, that a schism had ever existed.

Luke also wrote the Acts of the Apostles, the earliest account of the fledgling Christian community. This work records the activities of Jesus' followers immediately after his resurrection and defines some of the church's first rituals and beliefs, including a rejection of Jewish dietary laws and the practice of circumcision. Acts also affirmed the opening of Christianity to gentiles, a policy that in the future would aid in the spread of Christianity. At the time Acts was written, however, Paul and other missionaries were preaching mainly to Greek-speaking Jews and Jewish converts scattered across the Roman Empire. Paul's Roman citizenship enabled him to move about freely.

The meaning of Jesus' life and teachings was further clarified by Paul, who had persecuted the Christians of Judea before joining the new faith. Between 50 and 62, Paul, who was familiar with Greek philosophy, addressed both local issues and broader theological concerns in epistles, or letters, the earliest writings among the Christian scriptures, although only seven of the fourteen so-called Pauline epistles are generally recognized as having been written by him. These epistles

LEARNING THROUGH MAPS

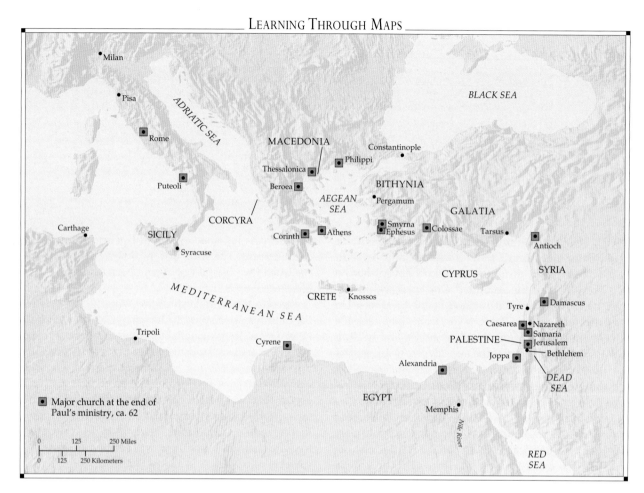

Map 6.2   THE EARLY CHRISTIAN WORLD
This map shows the spread of Christianity after the death of Jesus. **Identify** the major churches in existence by the end of Paul's ministry. **Which** of these churches did St. Paul found or visit? **Which** church was best positioned to become the mother church of Christianity? **Why? Consider** the impact of geography on the location of these churches. **Is** there a connection between the major cities on Map 5.1, The Roman Empire Under Augustus, and the location of the Christian churches in this map?

constitute Christianity's first **theology,** or the study of the nature of religious truth. Paul directed his letters to churches he either founded or visited across the Roman Empire: Ephesus and Colossae (Galatia), Philippi and Thessalonica (Macedonia), Corinth (Greece), and Rome (Map 6.2).

Paul's interpretation of the life of Jesus was based on the "Suffering Servant" section of the book of Isaiah in the Old Testament. The Suffering Servant was described as noble and guiltless but misunderstood and suffering on behalf of others. Paul set forth the doctrine of the Atonement, whereby a blameless Christ suffered on the cross to pay for the sins of humankind. Christ's life and death initiated a new moral order by

offering salvation to depraved human beings who otherwise were doomed to eternal death and punishment by Adam's first sin. But, according to Paul, human redemption was not automatically given, for a sinner must have faith in Jesus Christ and his sacrifice.

Paul's teachings also stressed that Christ's resurrection, which guaranteed everlasting life for others, was the heart of Christian beliefs, an argument that echoed the synoptic Gospels. Pauline Christianity made a radical break with Judaism by nullifying the old law's authority and claiming that the true heirs of Abraham were not the Jews but the followers of Christ. Paul also affirmed that obedience to Christ led to righteousness. Such righteousness demanded ascetic living, with particular stress on sexual chastity. From Paul's writing came the Roman Catholic Church's teaching that sexuality, except for reproductive purposes, was inherently sinful.

The final section of the Christian scriptures was the Book of Revelation, dating from about 95. This apocalyptic scripture projected the end of the world and the institution of a new moral order on the occasion of Jesus' return and final judgment. Revelation's picture of Rome as a corrupt Babylon destined for destruction reflected the early church's hatred of the existing political and social order. But the book, filled with enigmatic sayings and symbols, proved controversial, and not all ancient church communities accepted its authority.

By the mid–second century, the four Gospels, the Acts of the Apostles, the fourteen Pauline epistles, the seven non-Pauline epistles, and Revelation were accepted as the canon of Christian scriptures, or the New Testament (Table 6.4). Believing themselves to be the new Israel, the early Christians also retained the Hebrew scriptures, called the Old Testament. Although the spoken language of the Jews in Palestine was Aramaic, a Semitic tongue, the Christian canon was composed in Greek, like the Hebrew Septuagint. The use of Greek reflected the triumph of Paul and the gentile party as the church turned away from Jerusalem and toward the Greco-Roman world.

Table 6.4 BOOKS OF THE NEW TESTAMENT

Gospels

Matthew	Luke
Mark	John

Acts of the Apostles

Acts

Epistles

Romans	Titus
1 Corinthians	Philemon
2 Corinthians	Hebrews
Galatians	James
Ephesians	1 Peter
Philippians	2 Peter
Colossians	1 John
1 Thessalonians	2 John
2 Thessalonians	3 John
1 Timothy	Jude
2 Timothy	

Apocalypse

Revelation

Christians and Jews

Despite the distinctive features of early Christianity, many Jewish ideas and rituals contributed to the new religion. The Christian vision of Yahweh was rooted in Judaism: a single, creating, universal God who spoke through sacred texts (the canon) and who demanded moral behavior from all humans. Both Jewish and Christian ethical standards required social justice for individuals and for the community. Likewise, the Christian image of Jesus as Messiah was framed within the context of Jewish prophetic literature. Christian apocalyptic writing, such as Revelation, also shared a common literary form with Jewish models such as the book of Daniel.

Even when Christians rejected specific Jewish ideas, such as the sanctity of the Mosaic law, the early church continued discussions on human righteousness and sin in terms familiar to Jews. The Christians probably adapted their rite of baptism from a ceremony similar to that of the Jews of the Diaspora. Christians also kept the idea of the Sabbath but changed it from Saturday to Sunday, and they transformed the festival of Passover (a celebration of the Hebrews' escape from

Egypt) to Easter (a festival celebrating Jesus' resurrection). The church sanctuary as a focal point for prayer and learning evolved out of the Jewish synagogue, as did Christian priests from the Jewish elders. And the Christian **liturgy,** or the service of public worship, borrowed heavily from the Jewish service with its hymns, prayers, and Bible reading.

Judaism also influenced Christian thought by transmitting certain ideas from Zoroastrianism, including such dualistic concepts as Satan as the personification of evil, heaven and hell as the twin destinies of humankind, and a divine savior who would appear at the end of time. Jesus and the dominant Jewish sect, the Pharisees, though enemies, both integrated these Persian ideas into their religious outlooks.

Despite their common heritage, relations between Christians and Jews were stormy. After the Council at Jamnia in Judea in 90, when the Jews established the final version of their sacred canon, there was no place in Judaism for the Christian message. As revealed in Paul's letters, the Jews viewed the followers of Jesus Christ as apostates, people who had abandoned or renounced their true religion. Accordingly, the Jews tried to deny the Christians the protection that Jewish leaders had negotiated with Roman authorities regarding emperor worship and their own unique beliefs and rituals. In some cases, Jews resorted to reporting individual Christians to the Roman authorities. Until the end of the second century, Jews and Christians occasionally engaged in violent clashes. Possibly the strong anti-Jewish bias found in a few of the Christian books like the Gospel of Mark reflected these tensions.

Christianity and Greco-Roman Religions and Philosophies

Christianity also benefited from its contacts with Greco-Roman mystery cults and philosophies. Whether or not the rituals of the cults of Cybele, Isis, or Mithra directly influenced Christianity, they did share religious ideas—for example, salvation through the sacrifice of a savior, sacred meals, and hymns. Christianity, as a monotheistic religion, paralleled movements within the cults of the second and third centuries that were blending all deities into the worship of a single divinity. Among the Greco-Roman philosophies, both Stoicism and Neo-Platonism influenced Christianity as the church shifted from its Jewish roots and became hellenized; the Stoics taught the kinship of humanity, and the Neo-Platonists praised the spiritual realm at the expense of the physical world.

Christians in the Roman Empire

Eventually, the Romans viewed and treated Jews and Christians differently. The Romans initially regarded the Christians as a Jewish sect, but during the First Jewish War, the Christians evidently held themselves aloof. The Christian attitude seemed to be that the Jews had brought calamity upon themselves through their rejection of Christ. Similarly, Christians remained untouched during later persecutions of Jews by Romans in 115–117 and in 132–135.

As their faith expanded during the first century, individual Christians began to experience trouble from the Romans, though no state policy of seizing Christians was introduced. However, if suspected Christians came to the notice of secular officials, they were punished if they did not renounce their beliefs. The same pattern of localized, random persecution continued until the mid–third century, reminding the Christians of their vulnerability. The church, having by that time increased dramatically in membership and accumulated property in buildings and cemeteries, profited from the indifference of imperial and local authorities. As long as economic prosperity and political stability lasted, the Christians seemed safe.

However, as the chaos of the third century descended on Rome, the Christians were blamed for all the empire's troubles. The emperor Decius [DEE-she-uhs] (r. 249–251) mounted a wide-ranging political test that required all citizens (men, women, and children) to make a token sacrifice to the emperor. When the Christians refused to honor the emperor in this manner, hundreds of them died, including several of their local leaders, or bishops. Decius's sudden death ended this assault, but in 257 Valerian (r. 253–260) renewed the struggle, which resulted in the martyrdom of the bishop of Rome and the age's leading intellectual, Cyprian. Christians were beheaded, buried alive, or burned alive during this persecution. The killings eventually ceased, but for the rest of the century the survival of the Christian church was uncertain and depended on a muted existence.

Despite persecutions from the authorities, the Christian church drew much sustenance from Roman culture. The language of the church in the western provinces became Latin, and in the eastern provinces the religious leaders adopted Greek. The canon law that governed the church was based on the Roman civil law. Most important, the church modeled itself on the Roman state: The bishops had jurisdiction over territories called dioceses just as the secular governors controlled administrative dioceses.

In addition, the church was moving toward a monarchical form of government. Because the authority of the officeholders was believed to descend from Jesus' faithful supporters, those bishoprics established by apostles—such as the one in Rome that tradition claimed was founded by both Peter and Paul—emerged as the most powerful.

From an insignificant number of followers at the end of the first century, the church had attained a membership of perhaps five million, or about a tenth of the population of the empire, by the end of the third century. The smallest communities were scattered along the frontiers, and the largest congregations were in Rome and the older eastern cities. Social composition of the church evolved from primarily lower-class foreign women and slaves, particularly those recruited from among the Jewish communities of the Diaspora, to progressively higher classes. By the late second century, the middle classes, especially merchants and traders, were joining the church. Aristocratic women sought membership, but men of the highest classes tended to remain unconverted, although a few aristocratic converts prepared the way for future adherents.

Christianity's appeal to women was complex, though all seemed to respond to its promise of salvation and the Apostle Paul's egalitarian vision (Gala-

SLICE OF LIFE
A Christian Mother Faces Death from Roman Authorities

VIBIA PERPETUA
A Martyr in the Early Christian Church

Vibia Perpetua, an educated young woman from a wealthy Carthaginian family and a convert to Christianity, defied an edict against proselytizing issued by the non-Christian emperor in 202. She was jailed and died in the arena of Carthage in 203. This excerpt is part of her personal account of her last days before martyrdom.

A few days later we were moved to a prison [in Carthage]. I was frightened, because I had never been in such a dark place. A sad day! The large number of prisoners made the place stifling. The soldiers tried to extort money from us. I was also tormented by worry for my child. Finally, Tertius and Pomponius, the blessed deacons responsible for taking care of us, bribed the guards to allow us a few hours in a better part of the prison to regain our strength. All the prisoners were released from the dungeon and allowed to

do as they wished. I gave suck to my starving child. . . . I was permitted to keep my child with me in prison. His strength came back quickly, which alleviated my pain and anguish. The prison was suddenly like a palace; I felt more comfortable there than anywhere else.

Interpreting This Slice of Life Why was Vibia Perpetua being held captive by the Romans? **Describe** the conditions of her imprisonment. Since the Roman guards were eager for bribes, **what** does this reveal about their attitude toward Christians? **How** does Vibia Perpetua's faith sustain her in prison? **Compare and contrast** the religious conflict depicted here with religious conflicts in modern times. **Compare and contrast** conditions of prisons and prisoners then and now.

---

tians 3:28): "There is neither Jew nor Greek, there is neither bond nor free, there is neither male nor female: for ye are all one in Christ Jesus." Female converts also found the Christian community to be a refuge from the anonymity and cruelty of Roman society; the church formed a secret underworld of close relationships among people drawn together by an ascetic but loving way of life. That underworld promised to free women from the constraints of marriage and family life; it offered power by allowing them to influence others by their faith; it widened their horizons through intimate contacts with spiritual leaders; it gave them new identities through foreign travel and involvement in a cause that was life sustaining; and, for those who chose lives of chastity, it could serve as a means of birth control.

Early Christian Literature

By the late second century, the status of the church had attracted the attention of leading Roman intellectuals, such as the philosopher Celsus and the physician Galen. Celsus ridiculed the Christian notion of the resurrection of the body and the new religion's appeal to women and slaves. On the other hand, Galen found merit in Christianity because of its philosophical ap-

proach to life and its emphasis on strict self-discipline (see Chapter 5).

Christian literature was excluded from secular public discourse from its birth in Paul's letters until 284. But the work of Christian writers, which addressed the evolving needs of this underground religion, began to circulate among the faithful. Of the many Christian writers active during this time, Tertullian [tehr-TULL-yuhn] (about 160–about 230) and Origen [AHR-uh-juhn] (about 185–about 254) were important because they helped to define Christianity's relation to humanistic learning.

Tertullian's life and writings showed the uncompromising nature of Christianity. Trained in Stoic philosophy in Roman Carthage, he later converted to the new faith after he witnessed the serenity of Christians dying for their religion. The strength of his beliefs made him a spokesperson for North Africa, where a cult of martyrs made the area the "Bible belt" of the Roman world. Writing in Latin, he helped to shape the Western church's voice in that language. His diatribes against the pleasures of the theaters and arenas and his intense denunciation of women as sexual temptresses became legendary. In the severest terms he rejected the Greco-Roman humanistic heritage, preferring the culture of Christianity. Such fundamentalist thinking eventually drove this restless intellect into heretical, or

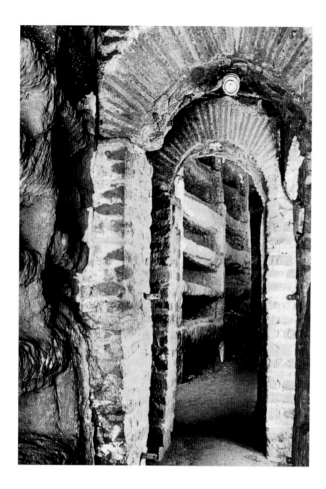

Figure 6.13 The Roman Catacombs: A Narrow Corridor with Niches for Burials. *Because of their belief in a bodily resurrection, proper burial loomed large in the minds of early Christians. Roman Christians joined with other citizens in burying their dead along subterranean passages underneath the city. In 400, when Christianity triumphed in Rome, the custom of catacomb burial ceased. Knowledge of the catacombs passed into oblivion until 1578, when they were rediscovered and became subjects of study and veneration.*

false, beliefs. His vehement detestation of the secular world and the institutional church proved to be an uncomfortable legacy for Christianity.

Origen of Alexandria shared Tertullian's puritanical zeal and his defiance of spiritual authority, but he did not repudiate humanistic learning. In his mature writings, composed in Greek, Origen brought Christian thought into harmony with Platonism and Stoicism. Origen's Jesus was not the redeemer of the Gospels but the *logos* of Stoicism (see Chapter 4). The *logos*, or reason, liberated the human soul so that it might move through different levels of reality to reach God. Origen's Platonism led him to reject the notion of the resurrection of the body as described in the Gospels and Paul's letters and to assert instead that the soul is eternal. Not surprisingly, Origen's ideas were condemned as heretical by later popes. Nevertheless, his philosophic writings, which were read secretly, helped free Christianity from its Jewish framework and appealed to intellectuals.

Christian women writers in this earliest period were very rare, because intellectual discourse was dominated by men. Women did play important roles in the new faith—such as Mary Magdalene, who waited at Jesus' empty tomb, and Lydia and Priscilla, whom Paul met on his travels—but their voices are al-

Figure 6.14 Christ as the Good Shepherd. Second–third century C.E. Fresco. Catacomb of Priscilla, Rome. *This fresco shows one of the popular religious symbols used by early Christians to disguise evidence of their faith from prying and perhaps hostile eyes. The "Good Shepherd" as an image of Jesus persisted in Christian art until the end of the fifth century.*

most always heard indirectly. In their theoretical writings, men often addressed women's issues, such as Tertullian's "The Apparel of Women." Nevertheless, the voice of one Christian woman from this period has come down to us: that of Vibia Perpetua (about 181–203 C.E.) of Carthage in North Africa, one of the first female saints. An anonymous account of the Christian martyrs' struggles includes a verbatim reproduction of Perpetua's writings in prison. Filled with heartbreaking detail, the account describes her prison ordeal as she awaited death while nursing her child. The sentence was imposed because she refused to obey an edict of the non-Christian emperor Septimius Severus (see Slice of Life).

Early Christian Art

Had Christians obeyed the Second Commandment, no Christian figurative art would have been produced. Indeed, the earliest Christian writers, including Tertullian and Origen, condemned the depiction of religious subjects as blasphemous. But pious Christians, attracted by the pull of humanism, commissioned frescoes for underground burial chambers and sculptures for their **sarcophagi,** or marble tombs. Christian painters and sculptors slowly fused their religious vision with the Greco-Roman tradition, a style that would dominate the art of the late empire. After the fall of Rome, religious values were central to Western art for almost a thousand years, until the Italian Renaissance.

In imperial Rome, citizens had the legal right to bury their dead in catacombs (underground rooms) beside the Appian Way, the city's chief thoroughfare (Figure 6.13). By the late second century, some of the tombs displayed Christian symbols and subjects, suggesting the increased confidence of the new religion in an otherwise hostile Roman environment. In the Catacomb of Priscilla, a second- or third-century fresco depicts a shepherd as a symbol of Jesus (Figure 6.14). This depiction, which is the most popular surviving image in the Christian art of this period, is based on the idea of Jesus as the kindly shepherd of his flock of followers, an image derived from many biblical sources, including the Twenty-third Psalm: "The Lord is my shepherd." Holding a sheep across his shoulders with his right hand, the shepherd stands in the center of a circle, flanked by two sheep. This circle in turn is surrounded by eight panels with alternating depictions of orants (praying figures) and scenes from the life of Jonah.

Even though the shepherd and sheep convey a Christian message, the image adapts a familiar Greco-Roman theme—known in both art and literature—that identified such diverse figures as the philosopher Pythagoras and the Orphic cult leader Orpheus with shepherds. The pose of the youth carrying an animal on his shoulders appeared in Archaic Greek sculpture as early as the sixth century B.C.E. (Figure 6.15). The

Figure 6.15 *Calf Bearer.* Ca. 570 B.C.E. Marble, ht. 65". Acropolis Museum, Athens. *This sixth-century B.C.E. Greek statue shows a young man carrying a calf probably intended for a ritual sacrifice. The statue is executed in the kouros style, popular in the Archaic Age, as indicated by the frontality, stiffness, and stylized beard. The shepherd image later became associated with Jesus in the early Christian period.*

Figure 6.16 *Christian Good Shepherd.* Second century C.E. Marble, ht. 39″. Vatican Museum. *This graceful statue blends Greek influences with a Christian subject. The casual pose of the shepherd with his easy contrapposto and dreamy gaze shows that the influence of Praxiteles, the fourth-century B.C.E. Greek sculptor, was still active after more than five centuries. The short cloak worn by the figure was a typical costume of shepherds in the art of the times.*

painter of the Good Shepherd ceiling fresco portrays the shepherd as a beardless youth without distinctive, godlike traits. A statue of a shepherd from the second century attests to the widespread use of this image (Figure 6.16). By such representations as these, the artists in effect declared the limits of their art in penetrating the mystery of Jesus as both God and man.

Catacomb paintings were rich in images, however disguised, of Christian resurrection, salvation, and life after death. The Jewish Bible was a source of subjects for Christian artists, as can be seen in Figure 6.17, *Three Hebrews in the Fiery Furnace.* The youths, Shadrach, Meschach, and Abednego, were rescued from certain death by divine intervention and thus symbolize redemption (Daniel 3). In the painting, they are depicted impressionistically, floating in abstract space. Their feet are hidden in swirls of red paint, representing the fiery torment of the furnace. Their arms are upraised as if praying and constitute an additional symbol: the invocation of God's blessing.

A relief panel sculpted on the marble sarcophagus, dating from about 270, in the church of Saint Maria Antiqua, Rome, reinforces the message that the Old and New Testaments are not in conflict but exist in religious harmony (Figure 6.18). Reading from left to right on the panel is the Old Testament story of Jonah: the Prayer in the Ship, Jonah and the Whale, and Jonah Under the Gourd Vine. The three days he spent in the belly of the whale are understood as prefiguring the time Christ spent in the tomb. The rest of the panel shows Christian symbols—a praying figure (with upraised arms), a philosopher (holding a scroll), the Good Shepherd, a baptism (a standing man places his hand on a smaller figure), and a fisherman (with a net). These images, found so often in Christian funerary art, attest to the saving power of their God.

Figure 6.17 *Three Hebrews in the Fiery Furnace.* Chamber of
the Velatio. Mid–third century C.E. 19½ × 34″. Cemetery of
Priscilla, Rome. *This catacomb painting of* Three Hebrews in
the Fiery Furnace *illustrates the practice of early Christian
artists drawing on Jewish stories to symbolize their beliefs. The
rescue of the Hebrew youths, who refused to bow down to the
golden image set up by the Babylonian king, becomes a symbol
of Christian refusal to engage in worship of Rome's emperor.
However, the Christian artist has changed the story, so that instead of being rescued by an angel, as recorded in Daniel 3:28, the
Hebrews are promised salvation by means of a bird bearing leaves
in its beak (above). This symbol probably derives from the Jewish
story of Noah and the Flood, in which a dove with an olive leaf
was a sign that the dry land had reappeared (Genesis 8:11).*

Figure 6.18 Early Christian Frieze Sarcophagus. Ca. 270 C.E. Marble. Saint Maria Antiqua, Rome. *Most sarcophagi were products of workshops; thus the artistic quality varied
greatly. However, this sarcophagus, carved by anonymous artists, exhibits a fairly sophisticated
artistic level in the treatment of human figures, such as the variety of poses and gestures, and
the attention to detail, such as the draperies and the varied objects used to identify each person.
The figures, despite their small size, possess limbs proportional to their bodies, except for the one
being baptized.*

The Legacy of Biblical Judaism and Early Christianity

The entire Jewish tradition has evolved from the early history of the Hebrews—their wandering without a homeland, their role as outsiders in other cultures, their brief period in control of the promised land of Canaan, and, above all, their deep and abiding sense of being the chosen people of the almighty God, Yahweh. Under the Romans, the Jews were punished for their religious views, a portent of the anti-Semitism and violent attacks that have dogged their existence down to the twenty-first century. Despite adversity, the Jews have survived and today have the longest continuous history of any group of people in Western civilization.

Unlike the Greco-Roman deities, who were seen as encouraging and supporting human achievement and excellence in many areas of life, the God of the Hebrews was primarily concerned with the ethical conduct of human beings and their obedience to his laws. Yahweh's jealousy extended to all forms of human expression insofar as they detracted from his worship. As a consequence, the arts and humanities, when allowed in Judaism, tended to be subordinated to religious concerns. Ultimately, Jewish culture found its voice in the ideals of the Bible, among the highest moral standards of any ancient people. The Jewish ethical vision, which even today drives Western reformers and revolutionaries, demanded social justice for every person, no matter how poor or powerless, within the human community.

Inheriting this conception of God and culture, the Christians reinterpreted it and gave it their distinctive stamp. After the fall of Rome, when Christianity emerged as the religion of the West, the Judeo-Christian tradition merged with the Greco-Roman heritage to form the basis of Western civilization. Following the teaching of Jesus, the early Christians perpetuated the Jewish emphasis on God's unity and omnipotence as well as the demands for stringently ethical behavior. Accordingly, Jesus' golden rule—to treat others as one would like to be treated—became the goal of devout Christians. The first Christians also laid great emphasis on taking care of the sick, the impoverished, and the homeless—a tradition that has given rise in Western civilization to a wide variety of private and public social relief programs.

The early Christians, rejecting the relatively closed nature of Judaism, turned their religion into a missionary faith; in the first generation of missionaries, Paul and other church leaders took Jesus' message to all people, addressing them as individuals regardless of their racial and ethnic backgrounds. Today, after two thousand years, nearly one-third of the world's population subscribes—at least nominally—to Christian beliefs.

Under the early Roman Empire, Christian thought also became a transnational, or international, belief system that expressed uncompromising hostility to Greco-Roman culture and to the Roman state. Those Christian writers who, like the author of the Book of Revelation, described Rome as "the great whore" and forecast that city's destruction simply expressed the collective yearnings of the faithful in the early church. Under the onslaught of the Roman persecutions, the Christians anticipated a new order ruled by God's values. Thus, early Christians adopted Greco-Roman ideas not for their own sake but for their usefulness to the Christian religion.

The hostility of the early church to humanism and secular thought was but the opening assault in a running battle between two ways of looking at the world. For the moment, in imperial Rome humanism was triumphant among the people who counted—the aristocrats, the intellectuals, and the ruling class. But by the end of the fourth century, the balance had swung over in favor of Christianity, and the non-Christian intellectuals were rapidly disappearing. This state of affairs prevailed until the Italian Renaissance; then, artists, writers, and intellectuals challenged the reigning Christian worldview by reviving humanistic learning and the Greco-Roman past. As the modern world has taken shape, Christianity has found itself assaulted from many sides and has never regained the preeminence that it held from the time of the fall of Rome to the coming of the Renaissance.

KEY CULTURAL TERMS

covenant	canon
Diaspora	Gospels
eschatology	evangelists
apocalypse	theology
Messiah	liturgy
scripture	sarcophagus

SUGGESTIONS FOR FURTHER READING

EUSEBIUS. *The History of the Church from Christ to Constantine.* Translated by G. A. Williamson. New York: Penguin, 1965. Though a partisan account written by a credulous observer, this work is the major source of early Christian history.

Holy Bible, New Testament, Old Testament. There are many translations of these sacred books, ranging from the King James version of the early seventeenth century to various twentieth-century translations based on recent scholarship. The Douay edition is the official Bible of the Roman Catholic Church.

JOSEPHUS. *The Jewish War.* Translated by G. A. Williamson. New York: Penguin, 1974. Josephus, a Jew who served Rome, wrote one of the few surviving accounts of this period.

7 THE CIVILIZATIONS OF LATE ROME, BYZANTIUM, AND THE EARLY MEDIEVAL WEST

◀ **Detail** *Diocletian's Tetrarchy.* Ca. 300. Porphyry, approx. 51". St. Mark's cathedral, Venice.

After 284, the Roman Empire underwent a radical transformation, sparked by political, social, and economic crises that increasingly seemed beyond human control. At the same time, Christianity was made the official state religion, the church became a prominent feature at all levels of life, and a new cultural ideal emerged that blended Christian beliefs with Classical humanism (Figure 7.1). When the empire fell in 476, Roman civilization as a unifying force around the Mediterranean basin came to an end, and within the power vacuum thus created, three new civilizations gradually emerged: Byzantium, the West, and Islam. All three civilizations borrowed features from Late Rome, and, most especially, Byzantium and the West adopted the cultural ideal of interweaving Christianity and Classical humanism.

Rome's fall meant the end of only the Western Roman Empire. The Eastern Roman Empire, known from this time onward as the Byzantine Empire, endured for nearly one thousand years longer, until 1453. (The Eastern Empire is called "Byzantine" because its capital, Constantinople, was founded on the site of the ancient Greek city of Byzantium.) Of Rome's successors, the Byzantine Empire, with its autocratic government, stable farm economy, Greek intellectual heritage, and what came to be called Orthodox Christianity, seemed to have the greatest prospects for dominance and longevity.

In contrast, the civilization of the West—the name given the surviving lands and peoples of the Western Roman Empire—was all but eclipsed in its first phase, the Early Medieval period. Its political and economic systems, inherited from Late Roman practices, were in disarray, and its people huddled

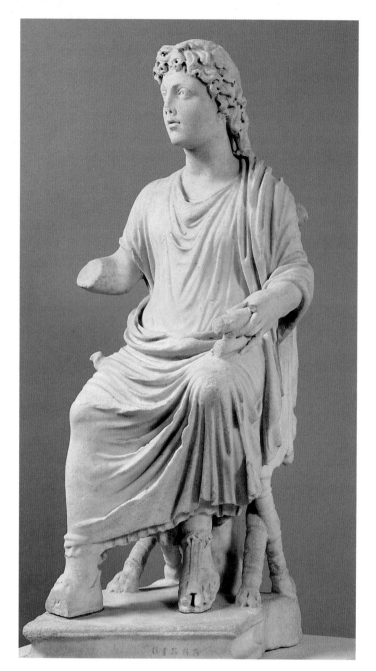

Figure 7.1 *Young Christ.* Third century. Marble, ht. 27½". Terme Museum, Rome. *Third-century church leaders, lacking a clear-cut tradition for portraying Jesus, simply borrowed from Classical art, making its tradition their own, as in this portrait of a young Christ. Like the gods on the Parthenon's frieze, Christ is portrayed as a beardless youth, dressed in a Greek garment and seated in repose, his left foot resting against a chair leg. The image of Christ as a beardless youth persisted in the church until the fall of Rome, when it was supplanted by the image of an older, bearded man.*

control army whose pressing needs intensified other threats to the state. For more than a century, the office of emperor depended on the army's approval, and increasing numbers of soldiers were recruited to defend the empire's borders. The army payroll drained the state treasury, which was already weakened by inflation and a declining economy. Urban population fell as thousands fled into the countryside to avoid military duty and heavy taxes. Many who stayed in urban areas still clamored for the amenities of Roman life, including bread and circuses, and that further drained precious state resources.

Christian converts presented another problem, for many valued their church membership more than Roman citizenship. They often refused to serve in the army on the grounds that killing was murder, an act forbidden by their faith. With the pool of potential troops reduced, the government recruited soldiers from the barbarians living within Rome's borders—a practice that weakened the loyalty of the military.

Faced with these problems, Diocletian began a series of reforms that virtually refounded the Roman state. Late Roman civilization may be divided into two phases: Diocletian's reforms and the triumph of Christianity, 284–395, and Christian Rome and the end of the Western Empire, 395–476 (Timeline 7.1).

Diocletian's Reforms and the Triumph of Christianity, 284–395

Diocletian (r. 284–305) stands as the creator of Late Rome just as Augustus does of the early empire. Unlike Augustus, however, Diocletian claimed to be divine, building on the sun-god cult and inflating the image of the emperor to enhance the power of the office. But whereas Diocletian may have ruled as a god, he had the soul of a bureaucrat when he turned to the problems facing Rome. He inaugurated reforms that reined in the rebellious army, contained barbarian incursions from beyond the borders, and restored modest economic prosperity for most of the fourth century.

Diocletian's efforts to restructure the government met with mixed success. His greatest reform was the division of the empire into two separate areas. In the

in wooden huts beside armed fortresses. In the midst of this chaos, however, a new world was being born, built on Classical ruins, spurred by Germanic energies, and animated by the new Christian ethos. This chapter surveys the civilizations of Late Rome, the Byzantine Empire, and the Early Medieval West (Map 7.1). Rome's third successor, Islam, will be covered in Chapter 8.

THE LAST DAYS OF THE ROMAN EMPIRE

When the Roman general Diocletian [die-uh-KLEE-shun] seized power as emperor in 284, the empire faced many problems, chief of which was an out-of-

LEARNING THROUGH MAPS

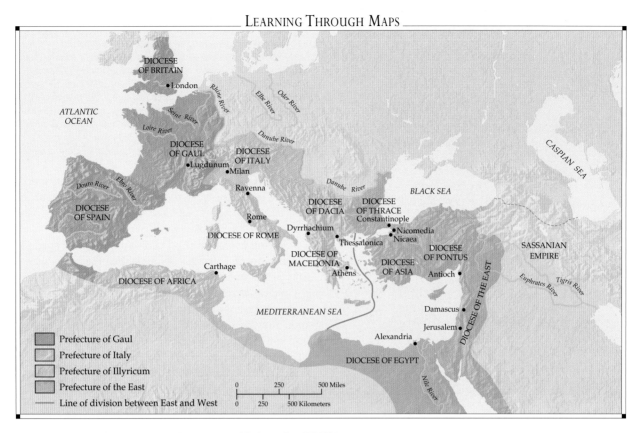

Map 7.1   THE ROMAN EMPIRE IN THE FOURTH CENTURY

This map shows the Roman Empire after the reforms of Diocletian and Constantine.
Notice the role of rivers and bodies of water in determining the empire's frontiers.
What was the impact of geography on establishing the pattern of governmental
dioceses? **Notice** also the dividing line between the Eastern and Western halves of the
empire. **Compare** the location of the Hellenistic kingdoms in Map 4.1, The Hellenistic
World, with the location of the same regions in this map.

Timeline 7.1   LATE ROME, 284–476

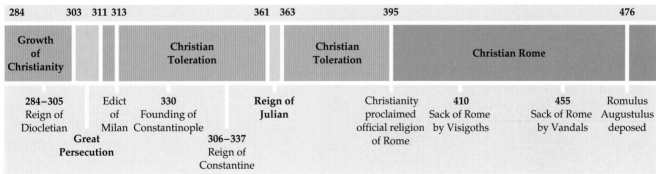

West, Rome remained the ceremonial capital, although
Ravenna became the imperial residence, and thus the
actual capital, for several decades. The Eastern Empire
was ultimately centered in Constantinople (now Istanbul, Turkey) by Diocletian's successor, Constantine (r.
306–337) (see Map 7.1). Diocletian's plan for administering the empire under a tetrarchy, or a rule by four,

proved unworkable, however. Each half of the empire
was to be governed by two tetrarchs, an Augustus
supported by a Caesar, but civil war among rival
tetrarchs only made an already confused situation
worse (Figure 7.2). A third reform—regrouping the
empire into four regional prefectures (each overseen
by an imperial prefect) and further subdividing these

Figure 7.2 *Diocletian's Tetrarchy.* Ca. 300. Porphyry, approx. 51". St. Mark's cathedral, Venice. *In this group portrait of the tetrarchs, the four rulers—two Augusti, or leaders, joined by their two Caesars, or successors—stand clasping shoulders to signify their unity and loyalty. By this time, the political leaders were no longer wearing imperial togas, as can be seen in the figures' cloaks, tunics, and hats; but the eagle-headed swords and decorated scabbards show that fine workmanship in armor was still practiced in Late Rome. Despite the solidarity suggested by the sculpture, the tetrarchy was not a successful reform of the imperial administration.*

into twelve dioceses (each controlled by an imperial vicar)—made the vast state more centralized. But the consequences were reduced efficiency and increased bureaucracy as officials multiplied at all levels.

Diocletian's social and economic reforms changed the nature of everyday Roman life. He froze wages and prices in a futile effort to control inflation. When the old tax system failed to produce adequate funds to support the enlarged army and the expanded state bureaucracy, he forced citizens to retain their occupations and sons to inherit their fathers' careers as well as their tax burdens—even if enslavement for debt resulted. Rural laborers coped with this new tax code by attaching themselves to landed estates, and thus the small independent farmer disappeared—the class that had made Early Rome great. Money virtually passed out of circulation, and the economy moved toward a barter system. Citizens now paid taxes in goods or labor or supplied recruits for the army.

One of Diocletian's reforms offers insight into the position of Roman women. Before Diocletian's reign, women, except for wealthy heiresses, were not counted in the state census, presumably because of male prejudice and because women were thought to contribute little to the overall economy. Diocletian now reversed that policy and included women and their wealth in census data. Still, women were not always counted as the equivalent of men; in rural Thrace, for example, two women counted as one man.

The Great Persecution and Christian Toleration At first, Diocletian's religious policy was to tolerate all faiths, but in 303 he began the Great Persecution, whose aim was to stamp out Christianity. Although Diocletian retired in 305, for eight years his successors

Figure 7.3 Colossal Statue of Constantine. Ca. 313. Marble. Palazzo dei Conservatori, Rome. *Like Diocletian, Constantine consciously nurtured the image of the emperor as a larger-than-life figure. To enhance this image, he commissioned a huge statue of himself, perhaps ten times life size, to stand in the gigantic basilica (which he had also built) in the Roman Forum. All that remains of the statue today are the head, which measures over 8 feet tall, a hand, and some pieces of the limbs. The monument signaled the climax of the emperor cult and the beginning of its decline. With the spread of Christianity, rulers were no longer viewed as gods.*

forbade Christian worship, destroyed churches and books, rebuilt pagan temples, arrested bishops, and imposed a religious test on all citizens (to offer a sacrifice to the pagan gods or face death). The number of Christians who died in this persecution is unclear, but the imperial policy ultimately failed, for the killings strengthened the church and the courage of Christian martyrs won many converts.

The Great Persecution suddenly ceased in 311, and in 313 toleration was restored to Christians by the Edict of Milan, also known as the Peace of the Church, at the order of the emperor Constantine, a convert to Christianity (Figure 7.3). Priests now joined army units, and bishops attended the imperial court. Across the empire, Constantine's policies expanded the restored faith, returned confiscated property to the church, built new churches, and gave tax exemptions to bishops.

Constantine, who after 324 ruled in both the East and the West, built his eastern capital, Constantinople, as a fully Christian city. Dedicated in 330, it was endowed with churches, a Senate building, and mansions for the senators. Standing on a peninsula between Europe and Asia and surrounded by thick walls and water, Constantinople was almost impregnable. It soon became one of Rome's most prosperous cities, thus attesting to the superior vitality and wealth of the East when compared with the Western Empire.

Christianity grew under Constantine's successors, and by 395 most Romans were nominally Christian. Conversions occurred for various motives. Many joined because the church adapted its message to Roman values, promising victory to Roman armies and a bountiful life for believers. Others, especially among the lower classes, found comfort in the Christian ideal of charity and its belief in the spiritual power of the poor.

Early Christian Developments   Christianity, unlike other Roman cults, developed a creed, or set of authorized doctrines, which church leaders imposed on believers. Those who differed were excommunicated as heretics. After the rulers became Christian, the state became entangled in the new religion's problems. Distressed by church squabbles, Constantine tried to end a major controversy over the relationship of Jesus to God. The followers of the Greek priest Arius [uh-RYE-uhs] (about 250–336) maintained that Jesus' nature was similar to God's divine nature, a belief that came to be known as Arianism. Those who supported deacon, later bishop, Athanasius [ath-uh-NAY-zhus] (about 293–373), a Greek prelate in Egypt, believed that the natures of Jesus and God were identical. For Christians, fundamental issues were at stake, such as whether Jesus was eternal and whether God had made the ultimate sacrifice for humanity. To resolve the dispute,

Constantine, in 325, called a church council at Nicaea in Asia Minor. Under his guidance, the council issued the Nicene Creed, which supported Athanasius.

Arianism, though condemned, divided the faith for decades and remained strong among church leaders. In addition, most of the Germanic tribes moving into the empire became Arian Christians through the efforts of Ulfilas [UHL-fuh-las] (about 311–about 382), a fellow German and an Arian bishop. Ulfilas's converts were treated as enemies of the true faith, for orthodox Christians recognized no difference between pagans and Christian heretics.

Despite these difficulties, Christianity remained vital. In the fourth century, an ascetic Christian movement began in Egypt and spread across the empire, taking two forms. Both forms taught that the world was evil and must be shunned, but they differed over the best way to earn salvation. Pachomius [puh-KOH-me-uhs] founded an isolated community where followers sought perfection through a life of self-denial and moral rigor. His contemporary Antony chose the solitary life of a hermit, seeking union with God through his individual efforts. Ultimately the dominant form of Christian asceticism became the community style—commonly known as monasticism.

Paganism ceased to be tolerated under Theodosius [the-uh-DOH-she-uhs], called the Great (r. 379–395). The ruler and the law courts ignored the rights of non-Christians, destroyed non-Christian images and temples, and made Christianity the state religion. Paganism disappeared in urban areas, but it survived in the countryside, kept alive by oral traditions, protected by ingrained conservatism, and hidden behind a Christian veneer.

Christian Rome and the End of the Western Empire, 395–476

Despite Diocletian's reforms, Rome ultimately faced insoluble problems: an increasingly non-Roman army, a growing state bureaucracy, and a shrinking tax base. When new waves of Germans began to sweep through the Western Empire in the fifth century, the government was overwhelmed. The Visigoths sacked Rome in 410, and a humbled Senate was forced to pay them a hefty ransom. About 450, the Saxons, Angles, and Jutes invaded Britain, ending its ties to Rome. The Vandals raged through France and Spain, creating a North African kingdom in 442 and sacking Rome in 455. Burgundians settled in central France after 430. Elsewhere, minor tribes exploited Roman weakness.

Western society changed radically. Town life virtually disappeared, leaving only noisy metropolises and the silent countryside. Landowners took over many state functions, and their isolated and relatively secure rural estates attracted desperate city people seeking refuge. Thus began the economic and social world of the Middle Ages.

The Roman Senate and the church responded to the disintegrating conditions quite differently. When Ravenna became the working capital of the Western Empire in the fourth century, the Senate was reduced to the status of a ceremonial body. Yet the senators still collected rents on their estates, doubling the fees when they could. In contrast, some church leaders used the crisis to stamp out troublesome heresies; but, more positively, others offered food and shelter to the homeless and comfort to the poor.

The end of the Western Empire came swiftly when Odoacer [oh-doh-AH-suhr] (about 433–493), the leader of a troop of Germans, defeated a Roman army in 476, deposed the young ruler, Romulus Augustulus (r. 475–476), and sent the symbols of office to the Eastern emperor in Constantinople, thereby signaling that centralized rule had ended in the West. Odoacer prepared to rule not as a Roman emperor but as a Germanic king in northern Italy. The Western Empire was in ruins, fractured into numerous independent Germanic kingdoms.

THE TRANSITION FROM CLASSICAL HUMANISM TO CHRISTIAN CIVILIZATION

Between 284 and 476, Roman civilization moved through two stages, both of which bristled with bitter pagan and Christian tensions. The first phase, which coincided with Diocletian's reforms, was paganism's last flowering; and the second phase, which began when the empire started to break apart after Constantine's reign, was a dynamic Christian age.

Literature, Theology, and History

During Rome's last two centuries, secular writers and Christian writers competed for the hearts and minds of educated Romans through poems, treatises, letters, and essays. The secular authors, who felt threatened by Christian activity and thought, preserved Classical forms and values in their writings. They turned to the humanistic tradition for inspiration and guidance because they believed that their morals and culture were undergirded by Rome's old religion and the farmer-soldier values. Nonetheless, these writers' romantic views of the past were distorted by nostalgia and veneration for a Rome that either was no more or had never been (Figure 7.4).

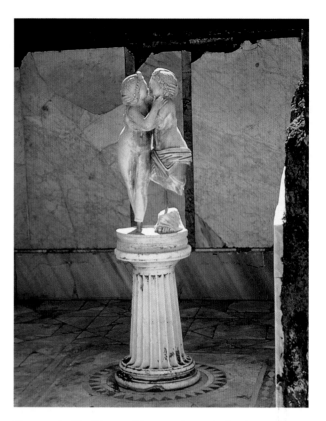

Figure 7.4 The House of Amor and Psyche (replacement copy of statuary). Fourth century. Ostia, Italy. *The non-Christian elite of Late Rome still revered their Classical past, as shown by this sculpture of Amor and Psyche, the famed lovers from Greek legend, found in the private residence of a wealthy Roman. The erotic pair stood in one of four elegantly decorated, intimate bedrooms, which were dimly lit by small windows and lined in white marble. The tale still caught the fancy of sophisticated Romans living in isolated splendor, perhaps reminding them of the glories of a former age.*

Secular literature declined in the late empire, and writers did not experiment with new styles or attempt to modify established forms. No one wrote plays, novels, or epics. As a group, the secular Roman authors reflected a growing sense of a lost age. With the exception of a few poets, they seemed unable to define or to analyze the profound changes occurring in their own lifetime.

In contrast, Christian writers looked to the future and a new world to come. They were convinced that Rome was not only dying but also not worth saving. After Constantine decreed toleration for Christians in 313, these authors moved into the mainstream and slowly began to overshadow their pagan rivals. The bitter differences of opinion between them and the pagans, which characterized the late fourth century, faded in the early fifth century. By then Christian literature had triumphed, though it remained deeply indebted to Greco-Roman thought and letters.

Figure 7.5 *Ambrose.* Ca. 470. Church of Sant'Ambrogio, Chapel of San Vittore in Ciel d'Oro, Milan. *This portrait of Ambrose conveys some of the spiritual intensity of the powerful fourth-century bishop of Milan. The work is one of few mosaics that survived the destruction brought by Germanic assaults in northern Italy. Although the artist shows some feeling for the shape and movement of the body, the mosaic strongly reflects the artistic ideals developing in the eastern provinces: frontality, flatness, enlarged eyes, and stylized pose.*

The Fathers of the Church By about 300, Christian writers began to find a large audience as their religion continued to win converts among the educated. Although they extolled the virtues and benefits of the new faith, they did not necessarily abandon Classical philosophy and literature; they believed that some of these writings conveyed God's veiled truth prior to the coming of Christ, and thus they combined Classical with biblical learning. No longer persecuted, these Christian writers lived either as interpreters of God's word or as bishops. Revered by later ages as the Fathers of the church, they set examples in their personal lives and public deeds. The three most renowned were Ambrose, Jerome, and Augustine. Because of their superior talents, resolute convictions, and commanding personalities, the Fathers not only were powerful figures within the church but also often intervened in secular matters, instructing the local authorities and even the emperors. Moreover, their writings laid the foundation of medieval Christian doctrine and philosophy.

The first of these men, Ambrose (about 340–397), devoted his life to affairs of the church (Figure 7.5). Born into a well-established Christian family (his sister was a nun), he was trained in the Greco-Roman Classics, from which he drew material for sermons, tracts, and letters. Ambrose vigorously opposed the Arian heresy, and as bishop of Milan he aided the urban poor and the victims of barbarian assaults. In scholarly sermons, he condemned the emperors for the social injustices of their reigns. His letters shed light on problems of church government, and his treatises analyzed controversies dividing the church. Ambrose's hymns, perhaps his most memorable contribution, introduced to the Western church another way for Christians to praise their God and enrich their ceremonies.

The second major church Father, Jerome (about 340–420), wrote extensively on religious issues, but his most enduring work was his translation of the Bible into Latin from Greek and Hebrew sources. The Vulgate (from *vulgus*, "common people"), as his version is called, was composed in the common speech of his day; the mark of his Bible's success is that, with some revisions, it remains the standard of the Roman Catholic Church today. Like Ambrose, Jerome received a Classical education. Later, after settling in Bethlehem, he founded a monastery, where he devoted most of his days to his translations of the scriptures. His reclusive habits and his harshly critical opinions of Roman society made him an unattractive figure to his enemies. Yet, as with the other Fathers, Jerome's ascetic life inspired both his own generation and later Christians to emulate his strict denial of personal pleasure.

Of all the Fathers, Augustine (354–430) exercised the greatest influence on Christianity. In his youth in North Africa, he studied Classical literature and thought, including Neo-Platonism (see Chapters 5 and 6). Augustine then journeyed, via Rome, to Milan, where he met Ambrose, whose persuasive sermons assisted in his conversion. Augustine, convinced of Christianity's intellectual integrity and spiritual vitality, retired to North Africa and dedicated himself to the spread of his new faith. However, his winning personality and administrative skills soon propelled him into church politics.

Augustine joined in the debates raging in the church. During his lifetime, his writing came to represent the voice of orthodox beliefs. He opposed the Donatists, who claimed that a priest's sin would make the sacraments useless. Augustine's position—that each sacrament worked in and of itself—became the church's official stance. But his greatest fury was against Pelagianism, which asserted that good works could earn salvation for a sinner. Augustine's argument—that salvation can be achieved only by God's grace—rested on his rejection of free will and his insistence on original sin. Once again, he spoke for orthodoxy.

During a long, active life, Augustine wrote many kinds of religious works, but looming over them all are his two major achievements: *The Confessions* and *The City of God. The Confessions,* written at the end of the fourth century, traces his search for intellectual and spiritual solace and details his dramatic conversion. In this spiritual autobiography, he castigates himself for living a sinful, sensual life. Although he was remorseful and laden with guilt for not having found God sooner, he came to believe that his efforts to understand the world by studying Greco-Roman philosophy, literature, and religion affirmed his desire to search for life's ultimate truths.

Augustine's conversion occurred in a garden in Milan, where a child's voice commanded him to read the scripture. Opening the Bible at random, he read from a letter of Paul, which directed him to arm himself with Jesus Christ as a way of combating the sins of the flesh. Upon reading this passage, Augustine wrote: "The light of confidence flooded into my heart and all the darkness of doubt was dispelled." Now certain of his faith, he dedicated himself to his new mission, adopted an ascetic style of life, and, ultimately, accepted church leadership as the bishop of Hippo, in North Africa. Augustine's convictions, so forcefully

expressed, helped to raise the standards of Christian literature in the final years of the Roman Empire.

Recent discoveries of two sets of unpublished writings by Augustine have led to a new look at his life and work. The first writings, numbering twenty-six sermons delivered at Hippo, where he was bishop, and at nearby towns, show him combating heresy and the vestiges of paganism—the chief challenges to orthodox Christian beliefs at the time. Augustine, in these sermons, dating from between 397 and 408, emerges as a patient, confident pastor, skillfully guiding unruly congregations made up of believers and curious pagans, with differing beliefs. The second writings, consisting of more than twenty letters, which date from between 418 and 428, depict Augustine in correspondence with church leaders. A rare insight from these letters is that Augustine was not yet a commanding figure in the church. Rather, he was more a person of humility, somewhat reconciled to being ignored, sometimes forgotten, by others, most of whom lived in the church's heartland, the eastern Mediterranean. From that vantage point, Augustine appeared to speak from a backwater, of both the Roman Empire and the Christian world.

Sometime between when he wrote the sermons and when he wrote the letters, Augustine wrote *The City of God,* a theological interpretation of human history. In this work, written soon after the Visigoths sacked Rome in 410, Augustine addresses the central question confronting the Romans of that generation: Why was their empire subjected to so many catastrophes? To those who blamed the Christians, he replied that the decline of Rome was part of God's plan to prepare the world for the coming of a divine kingdom on earth. If the city fell, it was best for the human race. Augustine expounded and reinforced this argument in the first ten books of *The City of God* as he attacked Greco-Roman philosophies and religions.

In the concluding twelve books of the work, he elaborated his view of world history, which relied on the Hebrew experience and Christian sources. At the heart of his argument lay what he called the two cities in history, the City of God and the City of Man. The inhabitants of the City of God were predestined to be saved, but the citizens of the City of Man were condemned to hell. Augustine predicted that the future would eventually expose the nature of the two cities: The City of Man would be destroyed, but the City of God—composed of Christians on their way to heaven—would last forever. In the City of God, the saved would enjoy an eternal happiness that paganism had promised but could not deliver.

Augustine completed *The City of God* shortly before his death and as the Vandals were approaching his city of Hippo. When Augustine's view of history seemed

SLICE OF LIFE
A Roman Delegate at a Barbarian Banquet

PRISCUS

In the fifth century, the Roman world was ravaged by Attila the Hun, the barbarian king who ruled a vast state in central and southeastern Europe (r. 434–453). Demanding tribute and holding prisoners for ransom, Attila and his fierce army invaded the Balkans and Greece in the east, and Italy and Gaul in the west. In 448, Theodosius II (r. 408–450), the Eastern Roman emperor, sent ambassadors to Attila's court to address certain issues, such as subsidies. The Greek historian Priscus (fl. 450–475), who was part of the Roman delegation, gives an eyewitness account of a banquet meeting.

When [three o'clock] arrived [Maximin, the head ambassador and I] went to the palace. . . . [A]ll the chairs were ranged along the walls of the room. . . . Attila sat in the middle on a couch; a second couch was set behind him, and from it steps led up to his bed, which was covered with linen sheets and wrought coverlets for ornament. . . . The places on the right of Attila were held chief in honour, those on the left, where we sat, were only second. . . . [A] cup-bearer . . . handed Attila a wooden cup of wine. He took it, and saluted the first in precedence, who . . . stood up, and might not sit down until the king, having tasted or drained the wine, returned the cup to the attendant. All the guests then honoured Attila in the same way. . . . [T]ables, large enough for three or four . . . were [then] placed next [to] the table of Attila. . . . A luxurious meal, served [by attendants] on silver plate, had been made ready for us . . . but Attila ate nothing but meat on a wooden trencher. In everything else, too, he showed himself temperate; his cup was of wood, while to the guests were given goblets of gold and silver. His dress, too, was quite simple, affecting only to be clean. The sword he carried at his side, the latchets of his . . . shoes, the bridle of his horse were not adorned, like those of the other[s] . . . with gold or gems or anything costly. . . . When evening fell torches were lit, and two barbarians coming forward in front of Attila sang songs they had composed, celebrating his victories and deeds of valour in war. When the night had advanced we retired . . . , not wishing to assist further at the potations [drinks].

Interpreting This Slice of Life Why was Priscus able to observe Attila the Hun in such an intimate setting? **Describe** the seating arrangement at the banquet. **Why** do Attila's personal dress and accessories differ from those of the other barbarians? **Is** there any evidence in this account of Attila's taste for personal luxury? Contemporaries of Priscus greatly feared Attila the Hun, giving him the nickname "the Scourge of God," because of the savagery of his military campaigns. That being the case, **how** do you account for Priscus's rather different picture of the barbarian king? **Do** you **detect** any cultural bias in Priscus's account? **Explain.**

---

to be validated by the fall of Rome, his fame began to mount. For many centuries, he was venerated by Christians as the supreme authority on nearly every major theological issue.

Church History In addition to theology, early Christian writing included a new literary genre—church history. Eusebius [you-SEE-be-uhs] (about 260–about 340), bishop of Caesarea in Palestine from 314 until his death, made no claims to impartiality in his *History of the Christian Church*. It makes the bishops the heroes, for Eusebius believed that they ensured the truth of Christianity. He also charted the church's spiritual, intellectual, and institutional life in its martyrs, thinkers, and leaders from its earliest days until 324. Although he is generally reliable in his discussions, modern scholars fault him for siding with the faction that was working to make the bishop of Rome the head of the church in the West.

Written in Greek, Eusebius's history was inspired by the secular Greco-Roman historians, and he followed them in quoting from written sources. He consulted both the Old and the New Testaments, Christian scholars, and the Greek classics, including Homer and Plato. Eusebius's historical account of the early church gained authority from his background. Having been jailed twice and having survived the Great Persecution, he appeared to prove God's power in the world. He also baptized Constantine and delivered the opening oration at the Council of Nicaea.

The Visual Arts

In Late Rome, secular and Christian art underwent major transformations. In terms of patronage, tastes shifted as the emperors' dictates were first challenged by the early Christian communities and then forced to

Figure 7.6 Diocletian's Palace. Ca. 300. Split, Croatia. *The peristyle, or colonnaded courtyard, screened off the buildings on the left and right, enhanced the enclosed atmosphere, and focused attention on the vestibule. Behind the peristyle, on the left, stood Diocletian's tomb (now a church) and, on the right, the Temple to Jupiter (now the Baptistery of St. John).*

bow to the triumphant church. In aesthetic terms, Classical forms and values yielded to a **symbolic realism** in imperial secular art and, later, to abstract spiritual values in Christian works. In geographic terms, church art and architecture in the Eastern Empire moved further away from Greco-Roman ideals, even though the artists and builders continued to modify Classical forms and subjects to fit their faith's themes and needs. A striking example of this trend is the art and architecture of Ravenna, the working capital of the Western Empire. Ravenna naturally had strong political ties with the East, and Ravenna's artistic monuments borrowed heavily from Eastern styles and schools.

Architecture   In the late third century, Diocletian revitalized architecture, following an unproductive period during the previous fifty years of political turmoil. As a part of his efforts to restore centralized rule, Diocletian used art, specifically architecture, as a sign of his new power. Constantine followed Diocletian's lead until the Edict of Milan in 313, after which he promoted Christian architecture and art. He then launched a building campaign of churches and shrines across the empire. Except for the brief reign of Julian (360–363), who renounced Christianity and tried to restore paganism, the later emperors patronized Christian forms and styles, and pagan tastes and schools disappeared.

During the fifth century, the bishops began to vie with the emperors in erecting Christian centers of worship. The invisible forms of the underground church—rooms in private homes, isolated buildings, and converted pagan temples—were abandoned in favor of new standardized structures such as baptisteries and basilicas. Architects, craftspeople, and artists traveled throughout the empire, directing their energies into glorifying the new official religion.

As part of his imperial reforms, Diocletian built a palace on the Dalmatian coast (modern Croatia), where he spent the last twelve years of his life. Strategically located halfway between the Western and Eastern centers of power, his residence resembled a Roman camp in its symmetrical layout. The palace serves as a fitting monument for this soldier who restored law and order to a world racked by civil war and incompetent rulers.

Visitors entered the palace by the main gate on the north side and walked along a path lined with columns across the central intersection and into the **peristyle,** or colonnaded courtyard (Figure 7.6). Those who traveled this far would be reminded of the emperor's presence by such architectural features as the long entranceway, the domed vestibule, and the grandiose courtyard. Beyond the vestibule, on the south side bordering the sea, were the imperial apartments, the guards' barracks, rooms for private audiences, and banquet halls. This residence incorporated nearly all the major designs and techniques, including the arch and mortar mixtures, known to Roman builders. More important, its impressive splendor symbolized divine authority combined with secular political power.

Just as Diocletian's palace was one of the last pagan edifices, the Arch of Constantine was literally the last pagan triumphal arch (Figure 7.7). The arch was erected to celebrate the emperor's victory in 312, which led to the issuing of the Edict of Milan. This well-proportioned monument with its triple arches evolved from the Arch of Titus with its single opening (see Figure 5.17). The circular **medallions** set between the detached columns on the side arches help to balance these smaller arches with the central arch. The decorated **attic,** or crown of the arch, with its statues of Germanic peoples, blends well with the lower sections. The Senate and the Roman people, according to the inscription, gratefully dedicated this arch to Constantine for his deeds as their liberator from civil war and as their new emperor.

Much of the decoration was borrowed from other monuments; for example, some of the reliefs and carvings came from works honoring the victories of Trajan, Hadrian, and Marcus Aurelius; and where a likeness of the emperor is intended, the original has been remodeled to resemble Constantine. Despite Constantine's celebrated conversion to Christianity, however, the arch clearly reflects a strong pagan influence. The symbols and figures stress human action, and only one small frieze hints at divine intervention.

The shift from pagan to Christian architecture began after 313 under Constantine's inspiration and patronage. He ordered the building of churches as places

Figure 7.7 Arch of Constantine. 312–315. Ht. 68'10". Rome. *The frieze that winds around the monument narrates the emperor's preparations for war, his victory, and his triumphant entry into Rome. The scenes depicted on the Arch of Constantine, like those on Trajan's Column, memorialized the Roman ruler's presence at every stage of a military campaign.*

Figure 7.8 Floor Plan of Old St. Peter's Basilica. Ca. 330. Rome. *Old St. Peter's Basilica was the most important structure in Christian Europe until it was demolished in the early sixteenth century to make way for the present St. Peter's. Constantine dedicated Old St. Peter's on the spot believed to be the burial site of Peter, whom the church considered the successor to Jesus. Of the original basilica nothing remains, but sixteenth-century drawings show that it was cruciform (cross shaped), had a wide central nave with two aisles on either side, and was fronted by an atrium, where worshipers washed their hands and faces before entering the sanctuary.*

of worship for congregations and as memorials at holy spots in Rome, Palestine, and other parts of the empire. Financed and supported by the state, this ambitious enterprise resulted not only in the spread of Christianity but also in the founding of new artistic values and architectural forms. The basic design of the churches that Constantine had constructed was derived from the **basilica,** a large enclosed rectangular structure that dated back to the second century B.C.E. and by the early empire was often built to house marketplaces or public assembly halls.

Although basilicas varied in detail, the basic form used for churches was simple: an oblong hall with an **apse,** or curved wall, at the eastern end. Two rows of parallel columns usually divided the hall into a central area, or **nave,** and two side **aisles.** The roof was taller over the nave section, and **clerestory windows** were set high in the outside nave walls to let in light. The apse, where ceremonies were performed or where the holy relics were placed, was often screened off from the worshipers, who stood in the nave. In some structures, there was an **atrium,** or open courtyard, in front of the main hall.

No fourth-century Roman basilica churches remain, but drawings, such as that of the floor plan of the basilica of Old St. Peter's, suggest their appearance (Figure 7.8). St. Peter's Basilica, built to mark the grave of the apostle who, by tradition, founded the church in

Figure 7.9   Constantine's Basilica in Trier. 310. Trier, Germany. *This basilica served first as an audience hall for Roman officials and then as a medieval castle; today it serves as a Lutheran church. Although it is an impressive 220 feet long, 91 feet wide, and 100 feet high, its plan is simple: a narrow hall without aisles and an apse at the eastern end. Around the exterior of the apse, two stories of round arched windows give a graceful appearance by creating the impression of an arcade. That such a monumental basilica was erected so far from the Roman capital showed the impact of imperial art in the distant provinces.*

Figure 7.10   Sta. Maria Maggiore. Interior, nave. 432–440. Rome. *As Germanic invaders were ending centralized rule in the West, Pope Sixtus III (r. 432–440) and his successors to 470 launched a Classical revival, drawing on the designs of late Classical Roman buildings of the second, third, and fourth centuries. The basilica of Sta. Maria Maggiore is the best surviving example of this revival, as evidenced in the nave's fusion of Classical features— Ionic columns, coffered ceiling, marble floor, clerestory windows topped with rounded pediments, and Classical entablature—into a majestic, symmetrical design.*

Rome, included a **transept,** or crossing section, that intersected the nave at the apse end of the building, making it **cruciform** (cross shaped). This first St. Peter's Basilica served as a shrine for thousands of pilgrims and, in its early years, as a burial ground for Christians.

Constantine ordered the construction of many similar buildings around the empire. In the provincial outpost of Trier, an important administrative and commercial center on the Moselle River (in modern Germany), he erected a complex of government buildings, including an imperial residence and a large basilica that was used as an assembly hall (Figure 7.9). Originally, an atrium fronted the basilica, and the hall connected to other buildings. Its heavily emphasized vertical supports, two tiers of rounded windows, and large apse established certain basic features that were incorporated into later churches, such as Sta. Maria Maggiore in Rome, built by a fifth-century pope (Figure 7.10). By this date not only had Christians taken over Classical learning as a tool for studying God's word, but they had also Christianized the pagan basilica. Sta. Maria Maggiore is typical of early churches in its Ionic columns and mosaics from the Greek tradition. By using existing models, Christians not only satisfied their own religious needs but also kept alive the Greco-Roman architectural tradition.

A second important design in Christian architecture was the round or polygonal structure topped by a dome. As these polygonal structures evolved, they came to serve primarily as **baptisteries**—that is, places set aside for baptism. The baptistery was usually separated from the basilica because Christians believed that the unbaptized were unworthy to enter the sanctuary and mingle with the church members. This design, which originated in the domed rooms of public baths and funerary architecture and whose most impressive realization was the Pantheon (see Figure 5.13), became standardized as an octagon with a domed roof (Figure 7.11).

Sculpture   During Diocletian's reign and before Christianity's conquest of the Roman arts, the late empire produced some unique and monumental works, such as the group portrait of Diocletian's tetrarchy, carved in red porphyry (see Figure 7.2) and the colossal statue of Constantine, a composite of marble and metal (see Figure 7.3). The generalized features of these figures show the trend to symbolic representation characteristic of the art of the late empire and the movement away from the idealized or realistic faces of Classical sculpture. These public works are clearly forms of propaganda art. But Roman artists also continued to execute statues for private citizens, whose changing tastes were typified in a statue of a bedraggled

Figure 7.11   Baptistery at Frèjus. Fifth century. Frèjus, France. *The Baptistery at Frèjus is one of the earliest surviving examples of the octagonal building. The eight-sided structure has a central dome resting on a solidly constructed drum pierced with windows. At one time it was believed that this style was imported from the East, but now evidence indicates it originated in the West, probably in France.*

Figure 7.12   *The Last Pagan.* Ca. 380–400. Marble, ht. 66". Museo Ostiense, Ostia, Italy. *Evidently this Roman, clad in the toga of an earlier era, has academic interests, since a set of bound books rests beside his right foot. The drapery is cut at severe angles, which increases the overall effect of this care-laden man. The statue is of Greek marble and stands just under 6 feet tall.*

scholar (Figure 7.12). Here the artist has fashioned a realistic work that delves into the psychology of his subject. The man's lined features, worried look, and weary slouch convey resignation and defeat. Symmachus (about 345–about 402), one of the last learned non-Christians, often visited Ostia, where this statue was found; the sculptor may have been depicting this Roman intellectual.

Christian sculpture was undergoing aesthetic changes similar to those taking place in secular art. By the end of the third century, Christian art was symbolic in content and **impressionistic** in style (see Chapter 6). Simple representations of Jesus and the apostles had become common in the underground church. In 313, when the Peace of the Church brought Christian art literally aboveground, artists began to receive the support of the Roman state.

Christian Rome's reshaping of the humanistic tradition can be seen in the carvings on sarcophagi. The Roman anxiety about life after death and the pursuit of intellectual matters easily evolved into Christian images and themes. The growing acceptance of burial rather than cremation and the resultant increased demand for sarcophagi afforded many artists new opportunities to express themselves. After about the second century, rich Roman families commissioned

artists to decorate the sides of these marble coffins and tombs with images of Classical heroes and heroines, gods and goddesses, military and political leaders, and scenes of famous events and battles. The Christians borrowed many of these subjects and transformed them into religious symbols pertaining to salvation and life after death. Thus, although the content of sarcophagus art became Christian after the Peace of the Church, the style remained Classical for some time.

Roman sarcophagi also depicted abstract concepts. For example, a carving of a seated philosopher, surrounded by attentive men and women, represents the life of the mind, its attention directed toward more important matters than earthly delights (Figure 7.13). The

Figure 7.13 The Plotinus Sarcophagus. Late third century. Marble, ht. 4'11". Lateran Museum, Rome. *This relief may depict Plotinus, a founder of Neo-Platonism, and his admirers. If so, then the scene is ironic, for Neo-Platonist philosophy rejected realistic art, claiming that art should be viewed with the inner eye. This Neo-Platonist belief influenced Christian mysticism, which in turn helped to create the symbolic art of the Middle Ages, an art that used traditional images to express religious faith.*

carvings, finely executed and well balanced, capture this philosophical idea through superbly realized human characters. On either side of the philosopher is a female follower. Neo-Platonism appealed to women because it welcomed them equally with men as students of philosophy. Women also responded favorably to its harsh moral code (sparse vegetarian diet, limited sleep, chastity) because it suited their intellectual striving and made them independent of men's sexual control.

Painting and Mosaics Unlike architecture and sculpture, painting exhibited no changes directly caused by the Peace of the Church. In the fourth century, Christian frescoes flourished in the Roman catacombs and continued the symbolic, impressionist style of the previous era (see Chapter 6). Non-Christian paintings are extremely scarce from the fifth century, except for a few works such as a collection of **miniatures**—small illustrations—for Vergil's *Aeneid*, probably painted for a wealthy patron. This extensive picture cycle (Figure 7.14), numbering over 225 scenes, recalls the style of earlier paintings, but it is also an early example of a new medium, the illustrated book. Books were now written on vellum, a parchment made from animal skins, and bound in pages rather than written on scrolls. In the Middle Ages, this type of decorated, or illuminated, book became a major art form. In the late empire, however, the form was in its infancy.

A more vital art form was the mosaic, which, as in other art forms, Christians ultimately turned to their own ends. Pagans continued to place mosaics on both floors and walls, but Christians more often put them

Figure 7.14 Illumination from Vergil's *Aeneid*. Fifth century. 6 × 6". Vatican Library, the Vatican. *This page from an illustrated manuscript of Vergil's* Aeneid *shows Dido, the Queen of Carthage (center), flanked by Aeneas (left) and a guest. The scene depicts the banquet, described at the end of Book I, that Dido gave in honor of the newly arrived Trojans. After the meal, Aeneas recounted his escape from Troy and seven subsequent years of wandering. Faithful to the* Aeneid's *description, the painting represents Aeneas speaking to Dido while she appears to be calling for the attendant, in the lower right corner, to wash the hands of the diners. That such works were being commissioned in fifth-century Christian Rome showed that not everyone was partaking of the new religion and its symbols. After the fall of Rome, however, decorated manuscripts became a favorite form of art for Christians.*

Figure 7.15 Loading the Wild Animals. Detail from mosaic. Early fourth century. Villa Romana del Casale near Piazza Armerina, Sicily. *This detail from the Corridor of the Great Hunt expresses the energy and activity found in nearly every mosaic on this site. Two workers struggle with the antelope on the gangplank, as sailors on deck prepare for the sailing. These mosaics were probably created by North African artists whose skills were well known during the Late Roman period. Many motifs and scenes, in particular those of the Great Hunt, were standard design elements employed in North Africa and across the Roman Empire. Given the repetition of some of the decorations and motifs, and the uniform quality of the mosaics, the entire project was likely done over a five- to ten-year period by the same design crew and skilled workers. Some stones were quarried locally, but the colored ones were imported from Africa.*

on the walls. Christian artists also replaced the stone chips with bits of glass that reflected light, thus adding a glittering, ethereal quality to the basilicas and other buildings.

In the Late Roman mosaics, the subject matter for pagan and Christian works stands in sharp contrast. Among the many pagan mosaics that survive are those at the Villa Romana del Casale, a Roman estate near the town of Piazza Armerina in central Sicily. The villa, built in the early fourth century on the ruins of a second-century structure, was the residence of either a rich Roman aristocrat or a high-ranking Roman official. The estate operated for over 150 years until the buildings fell into disuse when the Vandals and the Visigoths invaded Sicily. Over the next five centuries the area suffered successively under the Byzantines, the Arabs, and the Normans. In the twelfth century, the villa was destroyed by fire and then buried under an avalanche. Excavations, which started in the late nineteenth century and have continued into the twenty-first century, have, so far, uncovered the owner's large manor. Here he lived with his family, conducted his business, oversaw his estate, and welcomed his guests. Richly decorated then, this partially restored villa contains what is now considered the largest and most valuable collection of Late Roman mosaics in the world.

Over 35,000 square feet of mosaic flooring covers a complex of rooms, including baths, a gymnasium, guest quarters, peristyles or open courts, and long hallways. One of the hallways, the Corridor of the Great Hunt, over 200 feet long, depicts the hunting, capturing, and transporting of wild animals, which were typically found in the five provinces of the empire's diocese (administrative division) of Africa. These animals—antelopes, kids, lions, boars, and wild horses—were destined for Rome's Colosseum or arenas in other cities. Composed of two hunts, the narrative scene begins at either end of the corridor, with scenes of the hunters trapping or caging their prey. Then there are scenes at the ports where soldiers and slaves load the animals onto a ship, which is laden with crates, and, in the center of the hallway, the same ship is depicted as having arrived in Rome, where slaves unload the boxes and lead the animals away (Figure 7.15). The soldiers, slaves, and officials can be clearly identified by their dress and armor and their roles in the narrative. Their diverse facial features and multicolored skin tones indicate the diversity of the Roman Empire in the fourth century.

Figure 7.16 Putti *Harvesting Grapes.* Mosaic. Fourth century. Church of Sta. Costanza, Rome. *Besides alluding to communion, this scene illustrates the Christian scripture John 15:1, in which Jesus says, "I am the true vine, and my Father is the vinedresser." Putti are depicted trampling grapes and loading grapes into carts pulled by oxen; the rest of the scene is a labyrinth of vines, making up an arbor, amid which other putti are gathering grapes. This scene harkens back to representations of the cult of Dionysus; we know it is Christian only because it is in a Christian church.*

Among the many examples of life in the Late Roman Empire recorded in the pagan mosaics at the Villa Romana del Casale were various scenes of children, including young boys hunting animals and young girls gathering roses. These scenes, found in a floor decoration in the bedroom of the son of the owner, confirm that the pagans liked pictures of young children, or **putti,** in the role of adults at work or play or even in religious scenes. In the very first Christian art, some artists adopted this playful genre for scenes of grape harvesting, as in a mosaic from the Church of Sta. Costanza, Rome (Figure 7.16). In Christian art, however, the scene was a disguised representation of the Christian communion, in which wine made from grapes became the blood of Christ.

The *putti* genre proved not to be popular with Christians. More acceptable was art emphasizing the spiritual and otherworldly qualities of saintly figures, such as the mosaic of the church Father Ambrose (see Figure 7.5). Where the *putti*'s movements are fluid, Ambrose's pose is static, and where their bodies are celebrated, the shape of his body is completely concealed under his clothing, in accordance with the church teaching that the body is sinful and should be hidden from view.

Mosaics became one of the dominant art forms in the Eastern Empire and areas influenced by the Eastern rulers, beginning late in the fifth century. In Ravenna, the small cruciform tomb of Galla Placidia [GALL-uh pluh-SID-e-uh] (about 390–450), daughter

of Theodosius the Great, contains some splendid mosaics that prefigured the Byzantine style, which in succeeding centuries would dominate Christian art in the Eastern Empire. In the mosaics in the tomb of Galla Placidia, scrolls of vines and leaves wind around the ceiling; large flowers, or rosettes, decorate other sections; and animals and saints adorn parts of the curved walls. Over the entranceway stands the youthful shepherd watching over his flock (Figure 7.17). By the fifth century, the rich and the powerful, such as the relatives of Galla Placidia, were honoring the Good Shepherd in their sanctuaries as the giver of eternal life. The mosaics in the tomb of Galla Placidia clearly show the adaptation of Classical models to Christian purposes.

Music

The music of Late Rome was in decline, but Christian music was just beginning to take shape. The Christians took the principles of Greco-Roman music and integrated them with the Jewish tradition of singing the psalms and the liturgy to make music a dynamic part of their church rituals. In later times, this Christian practice gave birth to a rich body of sacred music that utilized both singers and instrumentalists.

In Late Rome, however, sacred music was limited to chanting and unaccompanied singing. The Antioch church, inspired by the congregational singing in Jewish synagogues, developed a new musical genre, the hymn, a song of praise to God. From Antioch the practice of hymn singing spread to Constantinople and Milan and eventually was integrated into the Christian liturgy everywhere. A few hymns survive from the period before Constantine, but only a fragment of musical notation has come to light. As with other ancient music, how it actually sounded can only be a matter of speculation.

Ambrose, bishop of Milan and a powerful influence at the imperial court, stands out among the earliest hymn writers as one of the founders of the Western sacred song. His hymns, which were written in Latin, coincided with a new era in the church; up until the fourth century, the liturgy of the early church was in Greek. Ambrose's Latin hymns were probably meant to be sung antiphonally—that is, with lines sung alternately between a leader and a chorus.

THE EASTERN ROMAN EMPIRE AND BYZANTINE CIVILIZATION, 476–1453

The end of centralized rule in Rome's western lands in 476 had little effect on the Eastern Roman Empire. During its one-thousand-year existence, the empire

Figure 7.17 *The Good Shepherd. Ca. 450. Mausoleum of Galla Placidia, Ravenna, Italy.
The young, beardless Christ, which was still the accepted image of the Christian savior in the
fifth century, supports himself with the cross and feeds the sheep, the symbol of the church, with
his right hand. Foliage and plants in the background tie in with similar decorations on the mausoleum's ceilings and walls. Upon entering the small tomb, worshipers would immediately be
confronted with this large figure of Christ.*

took its Roman heritage and became an autocratic, static entity in a world of great upheaval and movement of populations. The changing boundaries of the Byzantine world tell the story of an empire under continual siege. Byzantium's borders reached their farthest western limits in the sixth century and then contracted over the next eight hundred years. The empire lost territory to the Arabs in the east and to the Bulgars and other groups in the west. Finally, no longer able to defend even the city of Constantinople itself, the empire fell to the Ottoman Turks in 1453 (Map 7.2).

Although Byzantium was buffeted by rapid and sometimes catastrophic upheavals, great wealth and economic resources allowed the state to survive. The rulers tightly controlled their subjects' economic affairs, a policy that placed state interests above individual gains. A stimulating urban life developed, centered especially in Constantinople, the empire's capital and preeminent city (Figure 7.18). Beyond Constantinople, the countryside was dotted with walled towns and vast farming estates owned by aristocrats and tilled by *coloni*, or serfs. Agriculture remained Byzantium's basic source of wealth.

Even though the frontiers of the empire expanded and contracted over the centuries, its heartland in Greece and Asia Minor remained basically stable. Here, a relatively uniform culture evolved that differed markedly from Late Rome and the Medieval West. The Byzantine world gave up its pagan and Latin roots to become a Christian, Greek civilization. The Orthodox Church, led by the patriarch of Constantinople, emerged as a powerful force, but without the independence from secular rulers enjoyed by the Western church and the pope. Greek became the language of church, state, and scholarship, just as Latin served those functions in the West. But, like Late Rome and unlike the Medieval West, Byzantium remained characterized by ethnic and racial diversity; new peoples, such as the Serbs and the Bulgarians, helped to ensure this diversity as they were slowly assimilated into the Byzantine way of life.

History of the Byzantine Empire

Throughout its history, the Byzantine Empire's fortunes fluctuated depending on its relations with its hostile neighbors. From 476 to 641, the emperors made a valiant but ultimately futile effort to recover the lost western provinces and revive the empire (Timeline 7.2). The memorable emperor Justinian (r. 527–565)

200

ENCOUNTER

Ancient Globalization: Rome and the Silk Road

Globalization, while usually considered a contemporary phenomenon, did occur in the ancient world, mainly through trade, warfare, and travel. The greatest catalyst for globalization in antiquity was probably the Silk Road, the network of roads linking China with the Mediterranean and involving all the states in between these two distant points.

The Silk Road was not a single route, but a system of roads, crossing land and sea, that connected China to the West. On the overland route, merchants and their pack animals (horses, camels, and/or asses), organized into caravans for safety, stopped at the towns, cities, watering holes, and staging posts scattered across the 4,000-mile road. Since few traders traveled the full distance, middlemen, through a series of exchanges, transported the goods along the route. The routes fluctuated over time, not only due to escape raids by hostile nomads, rogue states, and bandits but also to avoid taxes to local rulers for goods in transit. Encounter map 7.1 shows the Silk Road, from its founding in the second century B.C.E. to one of its high points in the seventh century C.E.

China's Han dynasty (206 B.C.E.–8 C.E.) established this long-distance trade route for several reasons. Under the Han emperor Liu Ch'e (156–87 B.C.E.), embassies were sent to the western regions, hoping to forge trading and military ties with peoples then unknown. As the embassies pushed farther west, they found, already in place, flourishing contacts between Central Asia and the Mediterranean. For the first time, the Chinese learned about the wealthy states of Parthia (Persia), India, and Rome, or Lijian, Rome's Chinese name.

In China, the terminal points of the Silk Road were two cities of the Han dynasty: Luoyang, the capital of the Eastern Han (23–220 C.E.), and Chengdu, the capital of Sichuan province and, briefly, the capital of the Shu Han dynasty (221–263 C.E.). Equally important was Xi'an, or Chang'an, the capital of the Western Han (206 B.C.E.–8 C.E.).

China sent no ambassadors to Rome. Based on a disputed Chinese text, Rome may have sent an ambassador to China in 166 C.E. What is without dispute is that Rome became part of the Silk Road, because of Roman imperial goals, the Roman love of luxury, and Roman merchants' wish for new markets. As Rome absorbed the Hellenistic states, the old trade routes passed under Roman control, including the western entry points to the Silk Road: the Mediterranean ports of Alexandria in Egypt, Gaza, Tyre, and Antioch; and the Black Sea port of Trebizond. Through them, silk (yarn and cloth) entered the Roman world, becoming a prized luxury, comparable to gold and silver.

In Latin, silk is *ser*, derived possibly from the Chinese term for silk; the Romans called the Chinese *Seres*, that is, the people who make silk. The English word for silk production, *sericulture,* memorializes this early encounter between the West and China.

Sericulture was ancient in China, dating from Neolithic times, and the rulers made its production a state secret. By the dawn of the Silk Road, the Chinese were weaving varied silk textiles, such as gauze, brocade, and crepe. Rome first encountered silk in 53 B.C.E., when the shimmering silk tents of Parthian enemies dazzled the Roman soldiers. Later, in 46 B.C.E., Julius Caesar overawed the masses with silk banners during a military triumph in Rome. Caesar's example sparked a fad for silk in upper-class families. In 14 C.E., the Senate, fearing for public morals, forbade men to wear silk, claiming that it shamed them, and reserved its use exclusively to women. But the fad continued, despite the decree. Over time, the wealthy shifted from using small bits of dyed purple silk to enhance white tunics or togas to dressing fully in silk. Heliogabalus (r. 218–222) was the first ruler to dress completely in silk. In Late Rome, the Christian church began to enshroud the bodies of saints in pure silk, though Jerome, one of the church Fathers, denounced the wearing of silk by young women. Sericulture was introduced into the Byzantine world in the sixth century C.E.

Besides silk, the Silk Road brought other luxuries to Rome. Supplied by states along the route, these goods changed Rome's simple style of life. Most especially, aromatic and pungent spices, used variously for seasoning foods, as burnt offerings in temples and homes, as ingredients in medicines and perfumes, and in embalming, were imported from Arabia (myrrh and frankincense); from India (black pepper, cardamom, fennel, ginger, and turmeric); and from Southeast Asia (cinnamon, cloves, and cassia). From India also came two other luxury goods: pearls and cotton muslin textiles.

Rome offered many exports in exchange: wool (yarns and textiles), coral, amber, red cinnabar, lapis lazuli, colored glass, perfumes, copper and tin, linen, wines, and, perhaps to make up for the trade deficit, gold and silver.

The importation of silk and other expensive goods prompted Roman moralists, both pagan and Christian, who witnessed this type of consumerism and equated luxury with decadence to forecast the fall of their civilization.

Learning from the Encounter **What** was the Silk Road? **Why** was it termed the Silk Road? **Explain** how the Silk Road came into being. **What** role did the Chinese play in establishing the Silk Road? **What** brought the Romans into Silk Road commerce? **What** influence did silk have on the Roman people? **Was there** any difference between pagan and Christian attitudes toward the wearing of silk? **Describe** the spices imported into Rome and **explain** their various uses. **Note** the trade routes associated with the terminals in Alexandria in Egypt and Trebizond (see Encounter map 7.1). **What** goods would most likely pass through these port cities? **What** sorts of impressions would peoples at the eastern and western terminals of the Silk Road have of one another? **Why?**

Learning Through Maps

Encounter map 7.1 THE SILK ROAD, 200 B.C.E.–300 C.E.
Note the complexity of the road system that made up the Silk Road: one overland route and one via water, with various alternative paths along each way. **Note** also the Silk Road's end points, Luoyang and Guangzhou (Canton) in China and Antioch (in modern Turkey), Tyre (in modern Lebanon), and Red Sea ports in the eastern Mediterranean region. **Discuss** the value of silk cloth and spices to the Romans, given the difficulties (great distance, deserts, and mountains) of importing these goods from eastern sources. **What** impact would the Silk Road have on the Romans? the Chinese? the peoples situated between China and Rome? **Compare and contrast** China's presence in the Silk Road economy with China's presence in today's global economy.

LEARNING THROUGH MAPS

**Map 7.2   THE BYZANTINE AND CAROLINGIAN EMPIRES IN 814,
THE YEAR OF CHARLEMAGNE'S DEATH**

This map shows Charlemagne's empire during the Early Medieval period in the West,
along with the Byzantine Empire. **Consider** the impact of geography and regional cultural traditions on the two empires. **Compare** the size of the Byzantine and Carolingian
empires on this map with the size of the Roman Empire in Map 5.1. **Notice** the four
rivers in the Carolingian Empire. **What** influence would these rivers have? **What** is the
significance of the location of Charlemagne's capital in Aachen, rather than in Rome?

Figure 7.18   ISIDORE OF MILETUS AND ANTHEMIUS OF TRALLES.
Hagia Sophia, Exterior. 532–537. 270′ long × 240′ wide, ht. of
dome 180′. Istanbul. _The Byzantine emperors transformed their
capital into a glittering metropolis that easily outshone ravaged
Rome. The most magnificent building in the city was Hagia
Sophia ("Holy Wisdom"), originally built by Justinian as a
church. The building's 101-foot-diameter dome makes it the
largest domical structure in the world. Two half-domes at either
end double the interior length to more than 200 feet. The beauty
of Hagia Sophia made the domed church the ideal of Byzantine
architecture._

Timeline 7.2   **THE BYZANTINE EMPIRE**

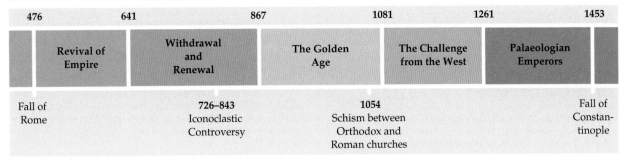

476	641	867	1081	1261	1453
	Revival of Empire	Withdrawal and Renewal	The Golden Age	The Challenge from the West	Palaeologian Emperors
Fall of Rome		726–843 Iconoclastic Controversy	1054 Schism between Orthodox and Roman churches		Fall of Constantinople

conquered several of the Germanic kingdoms that had arisen in the former Western Empire and extended the empire's borders to encompass Italy, southern Spain, and North Africa (Figure 7.19). Justinian's wars exhausted the state treasury, however, leaving his successors unable to maintain the empire.

Between 641 and 867, the second period of Byzantine history, a series of weak rulers lost all the western lands that Justinian had recovered. The emperors were also forced to yield much of Asia Minor to their Arab foes, and in 687 a Bulgarian kingdom was carved out of Byzantine territory in the Balkans. To repel these enemy assaults, Byzantium became more militarized. In the provinces, generals were given vast military and civil powers, and they began to replace the aristocrats as landowners. A style of feudalism—vast estates protected by private armies—slowly arose. Despite the changes in the social structure, important cultural developments occurred, including a major revision of the law code and the establishment of a second university in Constantinople.

With the reign of Basil I (r. 867–886), a new dynasty of capable Macedonian rulers led Byzantium into the Golden Age (867–1081). These rulers again expanded the borders of the empire and restored the state to economic health. Orthodox missionaries eventually tied the peoples of eastern Europe to the religion and civilization of Byzantium, and in the late tenth century they introduced Christianity to Russia. As a result, after the fall of Constantinople in 1453, the Russian state claimed to be the spiritual and cultural heir to Byzantine civilization.

In 1081 an exceptional feudal general, Alexius Comnenus [kahm-NEE-nuhs] (r. 1081–1118), seized the throne, and thus began a new period, characterized by increasing pressure from the West (1081–1261). Despite the energy of Comnenus and his successors, they were unable to solve the empire's social problems. Under the Comneni dynasty, Byzantium became fully militarized and feudalized. The free peasantry disappeared, having been transformed into a vast population of serfs forced to labor on the landlords' estates.

Figure 7.19 *Justinian and His Courtiers.* Mosaic. Sixth century. Church of San Vitale, Ravenna, Italy. *This mosaic represents a contemporary portrait of Justinian with his courtiers, including the patriarch of Constantinople, who is holding the bejeweled cross. The luxurious trappings of office—purple robes, jeweled crown, and golden scepter—were calculated to enhance the emperor's earthly dignity. The Byzantine Empire's union of church and state is symbolized by the juxtaposition of the soldiers on the emperor's right with the ecclesiastical officials on his left.*

The Comneni rulers tried vainly to win allies, but they were surrounded by enemies—Normans, Seljuk Turks, Hungarians, Serbs, Bulgars, and, after 1095, even the European Crusaders on their way to the Holy Land. In 1204 the soldiers of the Fourth Crusade conquered Constantinople and took over the remaining lands. The empire appeared to be finished except for some scattered holdings in Asia Minor. But in 1261 Michael Palaeologus [pay-lee-AHL-uh-guhs] (r. 1261–1282) regained Constantinople and breathed some new life into the feeble empire.

The Palaeologian dynasty ruled over the Byzantine world during the fifth and last phase of its history (1261–1453), but eventually it was forced to recognize that the empire was only a diminished Greek state. From 1302 onward, the Ottoman Turks built an empire

SLICE OF LIFE
A Father's Advice to His Sons

KEKAUMENOS
A Byzantine Aristocrat

Kekaumenos [kee-koh-MEE-nos], an aristocrat in the waning days of the Byzantine Empire, offered advice to his sons on how to deal with the emperor and hold on to their landed estates. His writings are known as the Strategikon *(about 1080), a collection of instructions, warnings, and illustrative stories. This work belongs to the literary genre called worldly wisdom, in which the head of a prominent family gives practical and scholarly advice to an upcoming generation.*

No one has ever dared to revolt against the emperor and the Roman Empire, breaking the peace, without destroying himself. That is why I counsel you, dear children whom God has given me, always to align yourself on the side of the emperor and in his service. For the emperor who sits in the city of Constantine always triumphs. . . .

If you have in your land fortified places or estates of which you are the owner and governor, do not let yourself be seduced by gold, by honorific titles, or by great promises of the emperors or cede your land to the emperor in exchange for riches and possessions. Not even if you will receive the quadruple part of its value; but preserve your own land, small as it might be or little in value. For it is better to be an independent friend than a servant without liberty. For in the eyes of the emperor and of all, you will remain a considerable personage, honored, esteemed, and noble, so long as you and your children and the children of your children remain in possession of your land and of your power. At the hour you lose your land and are despoiled of your power, you will still be loved by the emperor. But very soon you will be disdained by him and will count for nothing before him. You will understand then that you are no longer a friend but a servant. And from this moment, your inferior will also become formidable before you; if you displease him he will go to find the emperor and will accuse you of fomenting intrigues against him or of wishing to return to your former land. Perhaps you may not [later] even

be able to remember what you were accused of. It is better for you to be in your land. And honor the emperor and also love . . . all your fellows. . . .

There was a certain chief of the Arabs by name of Apelzarach who, coming before the Emperor Lord Romanus, was loaded with expensive gifts and honors and then released to return to his land by the emperor. And again he came to Constantinople, but the second time he was ignored. Slighted, he wanted to leave but was not allowed to do so by the emperor. He was then retained for two years in the Queen City, each year expecting exile and destruction. However, after two years the emperor released him to return to his own land. When he had arrived at and crossed the iron bridge beyond Antioch, he assembled all his servants and all those living in his house. Then, holding his head in both hands, he asked of them: "What is this?" "Your head, our master," they responded, laughing. "I give thanks to God," he replied, "that I passed Chrysopolis with my head on my body, and now I have reached the mountains of Arabia. For those who trip up their heels fall into their own traps."

Thus, now, it is necessary to tell you to speak truly and act honorably and be content with your lot. If you ever wish to go to render homage to the imperial power, in some way to make your devotions in the holy churches and to see the beauty and order of the palace and the city [Constantinople], do it once. But thereafter you will become a servant and not a friend.

Interpreting This Slice of Life Why might Kekaumenos be so concerned about his children's future at this time? **What** advice does he give his children in dealing with the emperor? **For what reasons** should his children hold on to their land? **Why** does Kekaumenos, who refers to an actual emperor, Romanus I (r. 920–944), include the illustrative story? **Explain** its lesson. **In what ways** are families today protective of their assets and reputation?

on the ruins of the Byzantine Empire. By 1330 this new state had absorbed Asia Minor, and by 1390 Serbia and Bulgaria were Turkish provinces. In 1453 the Turks took Constantinople, ravaging the city for three days, searching for booty and destroying priceless art treasures. Thus ended the last living vestige of ancient Rome.

Byzantine Culture: Christianity and Classicism

From Rome, Byzantium inherited a legacy of unresolved conflict between Christian and Classical ideals. In the wider Byzantine culture, this conflict was revealed in the division between secular forms of expression, which showed a playful or humorous side of

Byzantine life, and religious forms, which were always deeply serious. However, Byzantine culture, whether secular or religious, tended to stress Classical values of serenity, dignity, and restraint. This timeless and even majestic quality was cultivated, perhaps, in compensation for the beleaguered nature of the Byzantine state.

The Orthodox Religion   While the bishop of Rome (the pope) was the head of the Christian church in the West, the bishop (or patriarch) of Constantinople was the spiritual and doctrinal head of the Eastern (Orthodox) Church in Byzantium. Many differences existed between the two Christian churches. They disagreed over the issue of whether the pope or a patriarch should lead the church; they also differed in language (Latin in the West, Greek in the East), religious practices (Roman Catholic priests were celibate, Orthodox priests could marry), and fine points of religious doctrine. In 1054 the patriarch of Constantinople refused to yield to the Roman church's demand for submission, and a permanent schism, or split, ended all ties between the two faiths.

The patriarch of Constantinople had to deal with challenges from the pope, rival patriarchs in other Eastern cities, and the Byzantine emperors, who viewed the church as an extension of the government (the patriarchs never had the kind of power enjoyed by the popes). The Eastern Church was also plagued by internal dissension and a variety of heresies.

The most serious issue to confront the Orthodox Church was the Iconoclastic Controversy (726–843), which erupted when the emperor Leo III commanded the removal and destruction of all religious images. The iconoclasts, or image-breakers, claimed that the devotion paid to sacred pictures was blasphemous and idolatrous, a belief perhaps inspired by Judaism or Islam, which both strongly condemned the use of religious images. Siding with the iconoclastic emperors were the bishops, the army, and the civil service; opposed were the monks, many of whom lost their lives in the civil unrest that seized the empire. In the West, the papacy refused to join the iconoclastic frenzy. The controversy lasted for over one hundred years, and by the time the Byzantine rulers restored the veneration of icons, nearly all religious pictures had been destroyed by zealous reformers.

Monasticism, which furnished the chief foes of the iconoclastic emperors, was a basic expression of Orthodox piety. Like Western asceticism, Byzantine monasticism took two forms, hermitic (or isolated) and communal. The monastic communities were basically places where people retreated from the world to lead strictly disciplined lives. For centuries, the monasteries received immense gifts of land and wealth from rulers, merchants, and peasants alike, and eventually they achieved a powerful economic position in Byzantine society.

The most important monastic complex in Byzantium was at Mount Athos, founded in 963. This mountain retreat in northern Greece, which housed about eight thousand monks in the thirteenth century, achieved relative independence from the secular authorities. The style of Mount Athos—self-governing, self-contained, and committed to study and prayer—influenced monastic development in the Orthodox world.

Science and Technology   Byzantine science and technology, like other features of Byzantine culture, evolved from the Greco-Roman heritage. Byzantine monks and scholars saved, read, translated, and interpreted Greek and Roman philosophical treatises, medical tracts, histories, and literature. Byzantine emperors, bureaucrats, physicians, and generals read these works as they ruled the empire, managed the government, treated their patients, and waged war. The Greco-Roman influence faded over time, as the Byzantines made their own contributions in science, furthered architectural designs and building techniques, and developed new weapons.

Greek influence on Byzantine medicine was strong because Byzantine physicians relied on Greek medical works for training and in their practices. They were heavily indebted to the clinical findings and advice of Hippocrates (see Chapter 3) and Galen (see Chapter 5). One of the few Byzantine writers on medicine who made a lasting contribution was Paul of Aegina (about 625–690), himself a doctor. His seven-volume encyclopedia encompassed nearly all medical knowledge known at that time. In later years, his volume on surgery was utilized by doctors in the Arab world and the West. However, in most other scientific fields, the Byzantines made very few original contributions, and much of their understanding of the natural world followed Greek and Roman texts. As with the ancient world, the Byzantines used astrologers to foretell the future and to advise leaders facing critical decisions.

Byzantium's military might declined over its thousand-year-long history, going from initial triumphs and conquests to defeats and losses of territory in its twilight period. The early military policies, copying Greek and Roman practices, protected the empire until the eleventh century. Thereafter, with the rise of enemies using new military tactics, strategy, and weaponry, the Byzantine military proved unable to meet the challenge. The rulers also made a fatal mistake: They began to rely on foreign mercenaries. Nevertheless, before decline set in, the Byzantines made improvements in the technology of warfare, in both its navy and army, which helped to extend the life of the empire.

The Byzantine navy grew out of the Roman tradition. Inspired by Roman tactics and equipment, the Byzantines improved upon those models, with well-designed and heavily armed ships, trained and loyal crews, and a staff of qualified officers. From the sixth to the twelfth century, the navy's main vessel was the *dromon*, a warship manned by a crew of up to three hundred men and capable of carrying bowmen, catapults, and the metal tubes for Greek fire (see below). A smaller version of the *dromon*, speedy and maneuverable, was one of the navy's most lethal weapons. After 1100, the Byzantine navy was transformed, as Byzantine rulers contracted with the Italian maritime states, such as Venice and Genoa, for protection of the sea lanes and ports.

The Byzantine army likewise improved on its Roman heritage. The Byzantines continued to use the old Roman *onagers*, or "wild ass" single-armed catapults, and they invented more powerful machines capable of hurling huge stones and rubble against an enemy. They improved the crossbow, which many armies across the Middle East adapted and modified. Their most successful weapon was Greek fire, used by both army and navy. First employed in 673 against the Arabs at the siege of Constantinople, Greek fire came to be feared by Byzantium's enemies. Greek fire was heated and then pushed through a metal tube, by means of a pump, or was thrown from catapults in glass or breakable containers. Its exact ingredients have never been determined, but they were probably a mixture of crude oil, sulphur, nitre, lithium, and resin, which would burn on water and stick to a surface, making it a very effective weapon in naval battles. The Byzantines used Greek fire for centuries, up to the sack of Constantinople in 1453. But by that time cannons and gunpowder were rapidly replacing earlier weapons.

Law and History   From the viewpoint of Western culture, Byzantium's greatest accomplishment was the codification of the Roman law made under the emperor Justinian in the sixth century. The Justinian Code, which summarized a thousand years of Roman legal developments, not only laid the foundation of Byzantine law but also later furnished the starting point for the revival of Roman law in the West. This law code preserved such legal principles as requiring court proceedings to settle disputes, protecting the individual against unreasonable demands of society, and setting limits to the legitimate power of the sovereign. Through the Justinian Code, these Roman ideals permeated Byzantine society and served as a restraint on the autocratic emperors. When the West revived the study of Roman law in the Middle Ages, these princi-

ples were adopted by the infant European states. Today, in virtually all the Western states, these principles continue to be honored.

From the viewpoint of world culture, Byzantium was noteworthy for contributing one of the first known works of history by a woman: the *Alexiad*, by Anna Comnena [kawm-NEE-nuh] (1083–about 1153), daughter of Emperor Alexius I Comnenus. Joining Christian and Classical knowledge and following the rigorous method pioneered by the Greek historian Thucydides (see Chapter 3), the *Alexiad* is a scholarly study of the reign of Anna's father, Alexius. Despite the author's obvious bias toward her father and confused chronology, the work is the best source for this period in Byzantine history. Especially valuable for Western readers is its portrait of the soldiers, saints, and hangers-on of the First Crusade (1096) passing through Constantinople on the way to Jerusalem. To Anna Comnena's non-Western eyes, the European Crusaders were a crude, violent bunch, more greedy for loot than concerned about salvation.

Architecture and Mosaics   Besides law and history, architecture was the great achievement of the Byzantine world. Byzantine architecture was committed to glorifying the state and the emperors and to spreading the Christian message. Most of the Byzantine palaces and state buildings either were destroyed in the fifteenth century or have since fallen into ruins, but many churches still survive and attest to the lost grandeur of this civilization.

By the seventh century, the **Byzantine style** had been born, a style that drew from Greek, Roman, and oriental sources. The Greco-Roman tradition supplied the basic elements of Byzantine architecture: columns, arches, vaults, and domes. Oriental taste contributed a love of rich ornamentation and riotous color. Christianity fused these ingredients, provided wealthy patrons, and suggested subjects for the interior decorations. The **Greek cross,** which has arms of equal length, came to be the preferred floor plan for most later Byzantine churches.

Despite their borrowings, the Byzantines made one significant innovation that became fundamental in their architecture: They invented **pendentives**—supports in the shape of inverted concave triangles—which allowed a dome to be suspended over a square base (Figure 7.20). As a result of this invention, the domed building soon became synonymous with the Byzantine style, notably in churches.

The Byzantine obsession with the dome probably stemmed from its central role in the magnificent church Hagia Sophia, or Holy Wisdom, in Constantinople (see Figures 7.18 and 7.20). The dome had been

Figure 7.20 ISIDORE OF MILETUS AND ANTHEMIUS OF TRALLES. Hagia Sophia, Interior. 532–537. Istanbul. *Hagia Sophia was the mother church of the Orthodox faith. After the Ottoman conquest, the church became an Islamic mosque, and some of the trappings, such as the calligraphic writings, still survive from this stage of the building's life. Today, Hagia Sophia is a museum, and its striking mixture of Byzantine and Islamic elements makes it a vivid symbol of the meeting of West and East.*

employed in early Christian architecture (see Figure 7.11) and in important Roman temples such as the Pantheon (see Figure 5.13). Erected by Justinian, Hagia Sophia was intended to awe the worshiper with the twin majesties of God and the emperor. The central dome measures more than 101 feet in diameter and rests on four pendentives that channel the weight to four huge pillars. Half-domes cover the east and west ends of the aisles.

In the vast interior, the architects showed that they were divided about the Classical legacy. On the one hand, they used such Classical features as vaulted aisles, well-proportioned columns, and rounded arches. But they ignored the basic rules of Classical symmetry; for example, they failed to harmonize the floor columns with the columns in the second-story gallery. Their goal was not to produce a unified effect but rather to create an illusion of celestial light. Glittering walls covered with polychrome marbles and brilliant mosaics, which have since disappeared or been covered with whitewash, suggested shimmering cloth to early viewers and contributed to the breathtaking effect of this magnificent church.

Although many later Byzantine architects adopted Hagia Sophia as their model—a floor plan that unites the early Christian longitudinal basilica with a central square surmounted by a dome or domes set upon drums—they also built churches without a dome, particularly in Ravenna, on Italy's northeast Adriatic coast. Protected by marshes on the land side and with an escape route to the sea, Ravenna enjoyed the best of both Roman worlds. The Western emperors began to rule from there in 404 and to turn their new capital into an artistic jewel. In the late fifth century, Ravenna fell into the hands of Germanic invaders, who continued to add to the city's splendor. When the city became a Byzantine outpost under Justinian, new churches were built, including San Vitale, which was domed (Figure 7.21).

Mosaic making had experienced a lively flowering in Late Rome, and in Byzantium it became a major form of artistic expression. Unlike the Roman mosaics, which were of stone and laid in the floor, the Byzantine mosaics were usually of glass and set into the walls. Of the Byzantine mosaics, the most beautiful and the most perfectly preserved are those in the churches of Ravenna.

The church of San Vitale is home to a pair of impressive mosaics, one depicting Justinian and his courtiers (see Figure 7.19), the other depicting Justinian's empress, Theodora, and her retinue (Figure 7.22). In these mosaics, debts to Late Roman art may be seen in the full frontal presentation of each figure, their large and staring eyes, and their long gowns. But the two-dimensional rendering of the figures reveals the new Byzantine aesthetic; the rulers and their companions seem to float in space, their feet pointing downward and not touching any surface. In various ways, the mosaics compare Justinian and Theodora to Christ and the Virgin Mary. For example, Justinian is surrounded by twelve companions, and the lower edge of Theodora's robe shows the three Wise Men bearing gifts to the Christ child.

During the Iconoclastic Controversy, the emperors destroyed virtually all figurative religious art that was under their control. After the conclusion of the controversy, a formalized repertory of church decoration

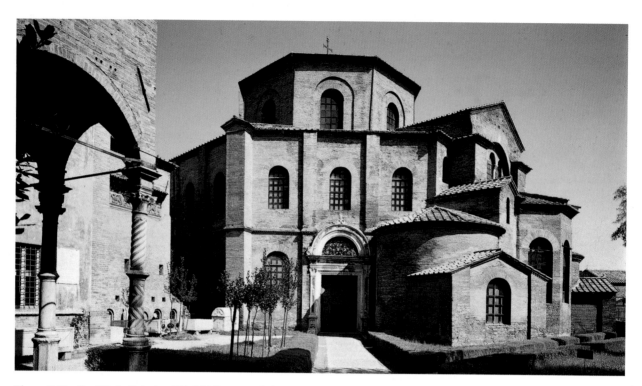

Figure 7.21   San Vitale, Exterior. 526–547. Ravenna, Italy. *Ravenna's church of San Vitale, with its octagonal plan and domed central core, is the prototype of the domed church that became standard in Byzantine civilization. From the outside, San Vitale's dome is not visible because it is covered by a timber and tile roof. This church inspired Charlemagne's Palace Chapel in Aachen (see Figure 7.27).*

evolved that characterized Byzantine art for the rest of its history. The aim of this religious art was strictly theological. For instance, Christ Pantocrator (Ruler of All) dominated each church's dome (Figure 7.23). In these portraits, Christ was presented as the emperor of the universe and the judge of the world. Accordingly, Byzantine art came to picture him with a stern and forceful countenance, in contrast to Western portrayals, which increasingly focused on his suffering.

THE EARLY MEDIEVAL WEST

Since the Italian Renaissance, scholars have described the fall of Rome as the end of the ancient world and the beginning of the thousand-year era known as the medieval period, or the Middle Ages. Although Renaissance intellectuals used the word *medieval* as a negative term, today's scholars believe the civilization of the Middle Ages to be as worthy of study as the an-

cient and modern worlds. This section is devoted to the first phase of this era, the Early Medieval period, dating from about 500 to about 1000.

The Early Middle Ages: A Romano-Germanic Christianized World

After the fall of Rome, life in the West was precarious for most people. There was a return to an essentially agrarian existence, accompanied by a decline in commerce and in the standard of living. Village life was simple and barter the primary medium of exchange. The little security that people had was provided by the Christian church, with its bishops and priests, its increasingly powerful pope in Rome, and its spreading network of monasteries and convents.

By about 500, Western life had stabilized to some degree. Three Germanic tribes occupied and ruled vast parts of the old Western Roman Empire: the Visigoths

Figure 7.22 *Theodora and Her Attendants.* Ca. 547. San Vitale, Ravenna. *This mosaic featuring the empress Theodora faces the panel of her husband, Justinian, with his courtiers (see Figure 7.19). Together, these mosaics communicate the pageantry and the luxury of this age. The man on Theodora's right draws back a curtain, inviting the imperial party into some unseen interior. His gesture may mean that this scene was part of a religious procession.*

Figure 7.23 *Christ Pantocrator.* Central dome, Church of Dafni. 1100. Dafni, near Athens. *In early Christian art, Christ had been portrayed as a beardless youth, often in the guise of the Good Shepherd (see Figure 7.17) or Orpheus. In Byzantine art, starting in the seventh century, Christ began to be depicted as a mature man with a full beard, as in this mosaic. Part of the change was a result of a fashion for full beards at this time, but, more important, the bearded figure reflected Orthodox theology's focus on Christ as the stern judge of the world.*

Timeline 7.3   **THE KINGDOM OF THE FRANKS**

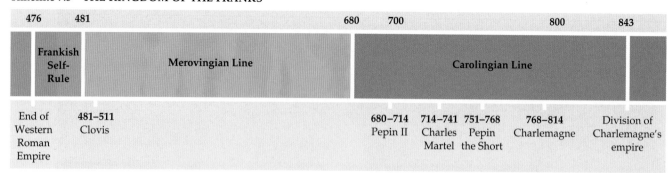

476	481		680	700		800	843
	Frankish Self-Rule	Merovingian Line			Carolingian Line		
End of Western Roman Empire	481–511 Clovis		680–714 Pepin II	714–741 Charles Martel 751–768 Pepin the Short		768–814 Charlemagne	Division of Charlemagne's empire

in Spain, the Ostrogoths in Italy and southern Germany, and the Franks in France and western Germany. The Angles and Saxons were dominant in England, the Vandals in North Africa, and the Burgundians in southern France; other Germanic tribes claimed land in central Europe, on the Scandinavian peninsula, and along the Baltic Sea. In Gaul (modern-day France), especially, life was being redefined in ways that would have a profound impact on Western civilization.

While a Germanic tribe known as the Lombards was gaining control of the Italian peninsula, the Franks were centralizing rule in Roman Gaul under Clovis (r. 481–511), the first important ruler of the Merovingian dynasty (Timeline 7.3). An early convert to Latin Christianity, through the persuasion of his wife, Clotilda (about 470–545), Clovis supported missionaries in newly conquered territories, strengthening political ties between Gaul and the pope.

During these years of political expansion in the Frankish kingdom, some security and order gradually developed, especially around the rulers' fortress-palaces. As the barbarian invasions subsided in the late sixth century, manorialism developed as a new economic system. Most of the Germanic invaders settled on the manors, or landed estates, of the Frankish warrior class. There they became serfs, indentured servants who were bound to the land. Their value as workers earned them the protection of the lord of the manor in time of war.

Frankish society was composed of three well-defined ranks: those who fought, those who prayed, and those who worked. Each social rank had a rigidly defined hierarchy of subgroups. The warrior class, headed by the king, consisted of the lords of the great manors and their families and, under them, their courtiers, the less wealthy knights, and the lords of small manors. The upper clergy, who shared the high social status of warriors, consisted of the archbishops, bishops, and abbots; the lower clergy comprised priests, monks, nuns, and clerical scribes and secretaries. The working ranks consisted of free farmers, artisans, and a few merchants; at the bottom was the vast population of peasants, serfs, and a few slaves.

In Frankish society, the status of women declined sharply from what it had been in the Roman world. On the manors, noblewomen enjoyed few personal or property rights, since, under Frankish law, land was passed through the male line. The noblewoman's primary function was the bearing of sons, and the peasant woman was simply another laborer. The only leadership role for women was in the nunneries, for women traditionally ruled themselves in these religious institutions.

After 700 the Merovingians gradually lost control of the Frankish kingdom to the Carolingian dynasty. Under Charles Martel ("Charles the Hammer") (r. 714–741), Carolingian troops halted the advance of the Muslims at the Battle of Tours in southern France in 732, thereby ensuring the future of Europe as a Christian land. In 751 Pepin the Short (r. 751–768), the son of Charles Martel, was declared king of the Franks, with the approval of the pope and the votes of the Frankish nobles. Three years later, a new pope crowned Pepin and anointed him as defender of the church. This ceremony, cementing an alliance between the popes and the Franks, set the course for church-state relationships in the West.

In exchange for papal recognition of his royal title, Pepin conquered the Lombards, who ruled most of Italy, and gave their lands in central Italy to the pope. These lands, which later became known as the Papal States, were conveyed in one of the most important documents of the Early Middle Ages, the Donation of Pepin. The alliance symbolized by the Donation of Pepin benefited both parties: The pope's authority and the church's economic foundation were enhanced, and the Frankish kings gained legitimacy and a claim to be the hereditary protectors of Rome. This alliance also redirected the church's interests away from the Eastern Empire and linked Rome's destiny with western Europe.

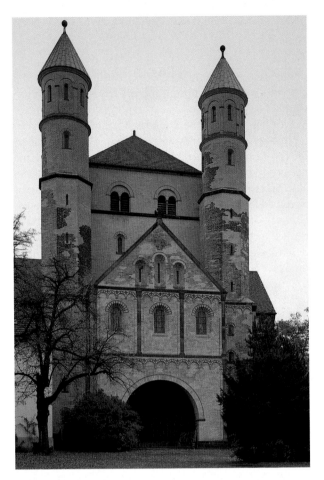

Figure 7.24 Church of St. Pantaleon. 966–980, restored 1890–1892. Cologne, Germany. *Otto the Great founded this church for a Benedictine monastery in Cologne where his brother was archbishop. As a builder of churches, Otto was following in Charlemagne's footsteps, identifying himself as God's chosen instrument intent on expanding both the Christian faith and his own empire. Of the original fortresslike church, only the westworks with three towers survive. Like many tenth-century churches, St. Pantaleon was flanked by two tall towers and an enclosed entrance. The rest of the church was restored in the late nineteenth century.*

Charlemagne created an efficient bureaucracy, instituted a fair judicial system, and brought learned people to his court as part of a revival of the arts and humanities. He granted large tracts of land to local warriors and then held them responsible for maintaining law and order in their domains. This administrative system fused the Roman approach to governing an empire with the Germanic warrior tradition, and it worked efficiently as long as Charlemagne lived.

The end of the Carolingian era began in 843 when Charlemagne's grandsons divided the empire into three parts, hastening the splintering of western Europe into smaller kingdoms. In the ninth and tenth centuries, a final wave of invaders entered western Europe—the Vikings from Scandinavia and the Magyars from the Hungarian plains. By the late tenth century, however, two new kingdoms—later to become modern France and Germany—were emerging from the political chaos.

France developed from the ambitions of Hugh Capet (r. 987–996), a noble landowner who was crowned king of the western Franks. From their power base in Paris, the Capetian kings consolidated their grip over the other feudal lords and their lands. The other emerging kingdom was that of Otto the Great (r. 936–973), who was elected king of the Germans and Saxons. A superb military leader and dedicated church reformer, Otto extended his kingdom into Italy. There he released the papacy from the control of corrupt Roman families and forced the pope, in return, to recognize him as emperor. Otto was clearly following the dream of Charlemagne—to restore the lost Roman world (Figure 7.24).

Religion and the Arts and Humanities in the Early Middle Ages

During the Early Middle Ages, literature, art, and architecture degenerated from the already low standards of Late Rome. There was a brief, bright moment in the early ninth century under Charlemagne and his successor when literature, learning, and the arts flourished, but by the middle of the ninth century this renaissance had faded in the wake of political disintegration and foreign invasions. Later, Otto the Great encouraged the cultivation of letters within his empire. Notwithstanding their sporadic nature, these intellectual and artistic developments helped to blend the Germanic and Greco-Roman worlds into an emerging Christian Europe.

Christianity: Leadership and Organization Regardless of internal dissension and external foes in the period between 500 and 1000, Christianity strengthened

Charlemagne ("Charles the Great") (r. 768–814), the son of Pepin the Short, established the first real empire in medieval Europe and challenged the Byzantine rulers' claims to the western Roman lands. Because Charlemagne was the most powerful ruler in the Early Middle Ages, historians have named a dynasty and an age for him—Carolingian, from *Carolus*, Latin for Charles. Charlemagne fought the Lombards in Italy, the Saxons in Germany, and the Muslims in Spain, colonizing most of these areas and converting the populace to Christianity. To reward Charlemagne's military and religious triumphs, Pope Leo III crowned him "Charles Augustus, Emperor of the Romans" on Christmas Day, 800. With this act, Leo may have hoped to assert the authority of the church over the state, but Charlemagne continued to believe in the supremacy of the state. The coronation enhanced Charlemagne's reputation, but it also widened the rift between Byzantium and the West (see Map 7.2).

Figure 7.25 Plan of St. Gall Monastery. Ca. 820. *One of the most prominent ninth-century monasteries was the Benedictine House at St. Gall in Switzerland. Although the monastery no longer exists, its original plan, perhaps by Linhard, has been preserved. The plan reveals the self-sufficient system of the monastery, with its school, hospital, dormitories, poorhouse, and various buildings and plots of land.*

ticular their sexual behavior, worked against the church's efforts to set high moral standards. Tradition claims he standardized the use of music in the service of worship, so that the Gregorian chants became synonymous with the medieval church. He encouraged the founding of new monasteries among the Germanic peoples. Abroad, he sent missionaries to England, thus ensuring the triumph of Christianity among the Anglo-Saxons. Despite their successes and reforms, however, Gregory and the later popes could not break the grip of secular power over church affairs.

The church found a new source of strength in monasticism. Western monks followed the guidelines that were laid down by St. Benedict (480–543) and observed in the Benedictine order's first monastery at Monte Cassino, south of Rome. Benedictines, after a period of rigorous intellectual training and self-denial, vowed to lead lives of chastity, obedience, and poverty. They divided their days into alternating periods of work, prayer, and study. The monks were known as the regular clergy, because they followed a *regula*, or rule. After the seventh century, women became part of the monastic system, using the Benedictine rules and sharing with monks the same facilities, then known as double monasteries. By the tenth century, separate facilities for women—nunneries—were being established by noblemen and noblewomen. Supervised by an abbess, some of these convents became important centers for women's concerns, and nearly all served as refuges for the devoted or for those forced by their families to take the veil as brides of Christ.

The monasteries and nunneries that spread across Europe served many purposes. They were havens for the populace during invasions. They were centers for copying ancient literary and philosophical texts, which were then studied in their libraries. The monks often established schools for the local young men, and the nuns schools for young women. These self-sufficient monasteries and nunneries were models of agricultural productivity and economic resourcefulness (Figure 7.25).

Literature, History, and Learning Writers during this period were more interested in conserving the past than in composing original works. Consequently, literature—all of it written in Latin—was eclectic, blending Christian ideas with Classical thought and often mixing genres, such as history, biography, science, philosophy, and theology.

The most highly educated scholar of the Early Middle Ages was Boethius [bo-E-the-uhs] (about 480–524), a Roman aristocrat and a courtier of Theodoric (r. 454?–526), the Ostrogoth king in Italy. A rarity in his age, an intellectual who knew Greek, Boethius translated many of Aristotle's vast writings into Latin. In

itself and its hold on society. The early popes faced heresy, disorganization, and a vast world of unbaptized men and women. The energetic and dedicated Pope Gregory the Great (pope 590–604) was the most successful of the early medieval pontiffs. He reformed the clergy, whose poor training and lax habits, in par-

SLICE OF LIFE
Marriage Diplomacy Nets a Diplomatic Insult

LIUDPRAND OF CREMONA

Bishop Liudprand (about 920–about 972) of Cremona, emissary of the German ruler Otto I (the Great), traveled (968) to Constantinople to arrange a marriage between Otto's son and a Byzantine princess. Here, he describes his strained meeting with the emperor to King Otto.

On the fourth of June we arrived at Constantinople, and after a miserable reception, meant as an insult to yourselves, we were given the most miserable and disgusting quarters. . . .

On the sixth of June, which was the Saturday before Pentecost, I was brought before the emperor's brother Leo, marshal of the court and chancellor; and there we tired ourselves with a fierce argument over your imperial title. He called you not emperor, which is Basileus in his tongue, but insultingly Rex, which is king in yours. I told him that the thing meant was the same though the word was different, and he then said that I had come not to make peace but to stir up strife. Finally he got up in a rage, and really wishing to insult us received your letter not in his own hand but through an interpreter. . . .

On the seventh of June, the sacred day of Pentecost, I was brought before Nicephorus himself in the palace called Stephana, that is, the Crown Palace. He is a monstrosity of a man. . . . He began his speech as follows:—

It was our duty and our desire to give you a courteous and magnificent reception. That, however, has been rendered impossible by the impiety of your master, who in the guise of an hostile invader has laid claim to Rome; . . . has tried to subdue to himself by massacre and conflagration cities belonging to our empire. . . .

To him I made this reply: "My master did not invade the city of Rome by force nor as a tyrant; he freed her from a tyrant's yoke, or rather from the yoke of many tyrants. . . . Your power, methinks, was fast asleep then; and the power of your predecessors, who in name alone are called emperors of the Romans, while the reality is far different. . . .

Interpreting This Slice of Life **What** is the purpose of the mission of Bishop Liudprand to the Byzantine court? **Why** was a churchman entrusted with this mission? **Discuss** church-state relations in both Byzantine and Early Medieval culture, based on the evidence of this Slice of Life. **Why** was Liudprand insulted by being addressed as the ambassador of a king? **What** were the issues at stake in this argument between Liudprand and the emperor's brother Leo? **Speculate** on the reaction of Otto to this report from his ambassador Liudprand.

the later Middle Ages, all that Latin scholars knew of Aristotle was through Boethius's translations.

Boethius fell from favor in Theodoric's court and was eventually executed. While in prison, he wrote the *Consolation of Philosophy*, a work widely read throughout the Middle Ages and beyond. In it he described his mental struggle with despair at life's cruel turn of events. He personified Philosophy as a learned woman with whom he argued many issues in search of the meaning of happiness. In the face of imminent death, Boethius finally concluded that true contentment was reserved for those who combined intellectual inquiry with Christian beliefs.

Although several scholars wrote historical chronicles, only Gregory of Tours and Bede can be classified as historians. Both consulted written documents and other sources and in general strove for (but did not always achieve) objectivity and historical accuracy. Gregory of Tours (about 538–593) left the single surviving record of the sixth-century Merovingian kingdom in his *History of the Franks*. Gregory's account

lacks historical cohesion and shows stylistic confusion, but he manages to capture the flavor of his times in his lively and humane character sketches of the Frankish rulers. In Anglo-Saxon England, Bede [BEED] (673–735), an English monk and scholar, composed *A History of the English Church and People*, which described the missionary activities that led to the founding of the English church. Written in a pure Latin style, his *History* is a major source for the chronology of this troubled age.

When Charlemagne came to power, cultural life enjoyed its greatest flowering in the Early Middle Ages. The Carolingian Renaissance, which represented Europe's first genuine rebirth of Classical studies within the context of Christian beliefs, had its roots in educational reform. Recognizing that ignorance posed a threat to his regime, Charlemagne founded a palace school at his residence at Aachen, in present-day western Germany. He invited the most learned men of the day to train his own staff and to teach the sons of the nobility. Leading scholars from England, Ireland, and

Italy settled in Aachen, where they pursued their scholarship. Foremost among them was Alcuin [AL-kwin] of York (735–804), who led the palace school, giving instruction in Latin, composing his own textbooks, and overseeing the copying of manuscripts.

Another important scholar and adviser at Aachen was Einhard [INE-hart] (about 770–840), who came from Gaul. His lasting contribution was his brief and simple biography of Charlemagne, the *Vita Caroli* (the *Life of Charles,* usually translated as *The Life of Charlemagne*). Modeled on the lives of the Caesars by the Roman historian Suetonius, this work is a major literary achievement of the Early Middle Ages and still gives today's readers a vivid portrait of Charlemagne and his times.

One of the important achievements of the palace school was a significant innovation in handwriting. Trained scribes developed a flowing style consisting primarily of rounded lowercase letters that became the standard form for all later handwriting styles in the West. With the development of this legible and uniform Latin script, known as Carolingian minuscule, educated men and women gained access to written material and monks, in transcribing books, were liable to make fewer errors (Figure 7.26).

During the turbulent ninth and tenth centuries, the light of civilization seemed to grow dimmer, except in monasteries in Ireland and Germany, where many monks and nuns kept the humanities alive. Especially noteworthy among the monastic scholars who balanced Christian faith with the Classics was Hrosvitha [rawts-VEE-tar] (about 935–about 1000), a canoness (a nunlike vocation that did not require vows for life) at the Gandersheim convent in Saxony. The first German playwright, Hrosvitha wrote six plays, in Latin, modeled on those of Terence, the Roman dramatist (see Chapter 5), but infused with erudite religious ideas. Rejecting the themes of Roman comedy as spiritually unhealthy, these Christian dramas focused on fall and conversion themes, as in *Abraham,* which tells of a prostitute rescued by a saintly monk. Literary exercises, these plays were probably never performed, except perhaps as recitations with mimed action. Hrosvitha's writings, forgotten until the Renaissance, were rediscovered about 1500 by German humanists who recognized them as major monuments of medieval drama.

Outside the walls of monasteries, storytellers captured the imagination of audiences at royal and aristocratic courts. Written in the first half of the eighth century, *Beowulf* recounts the adventures of a Danish fictionalized warrior hero. Spurred by his loyalty and daring, Beowulf not only kills monsters but also brings peace to his inherited kingdom. The poem, considered to be the finest achievement of Old English literature

Figure 7.26 Carolingian Minuscule. Ninth century. Bibliothèque Nationale, Paris. *Because Christianity relied heavily on written works, legible texts were important; but the prevailing style of writing, which used separately formed lowercase letters, was almost impossible to read. To overcome this difficulty, scribes during Charlemagne's reign perfected a new style of writing—the Carolingian minuscule—characterized by clearly formed letters linked into words, spaces between words, and capital letters at the beginning of sentences, as shown here. All subsequent Western handwriting styles follow from this tradition.*

and the most famous surviving epic poem in a European vernacular language, blends a surface of Christian values with a deep pagan fear of the forces of darkness.

Music Music became integral to the church liturgy during the Early Middle Ages and kept alive the Greek heritage of music as an art form. From this religious foundation ultimately arose all of the sacred and secular music of the modern West. The name of Pope Gregory the Great is preserved in the Early Medieval musical form the **Gregorian chant,** which became the official liturgical music of the early church—used in the Mass (the celebration of the Eucharist) and other services of the yearly cycle of public worship. The chants consisted of a single melodic line sung by male voices in unison—called **monophony**—without instrumental accompaniment. They had an impersonal, nonemotional quality and served religious rather than aesthetic or emotional purposes. Notwithstanding this aim, the chants cast a spell over their listeners, evoking in them feelings of otherworldliness, peace, and purity.

In the ninth century, one of the most important advances in music history occurred, the rise of polyphony—two lines of melody sounded at the same

Figure 7.27 Charlemagne's Palace Chapel. Ca. 792–805. Diameter over 50'. Aachen, Germany. *Odo of Metz designed the Royal Chapel for Charlemagne, and Pope Leo III probably dedicated it in 805. Although the chapel is inspired by Byzantine architecture, the decorative scheme and the roof design make it principally a Roman building. From the tenth to the sixteenth century, the Germans crowned their kings in this chapel.*

time. Polyphony, unlike the monophonic Gregorian chants, gave music a vertical as well as a horizontal quality. But further musical developments would have to await more settled social and political conditions.

Architecture   The overall decline of living conditions in western Europe took its toll in architecture and art as patronage evaporated, skills fell into disuse, and artistic talents were necessarily directed to more pragmatic ends. The few artisans and builders who were still in business traveled across western Europe constructing churches and chapels in protected places.

Charlemagne gave full support to the construction of impressive churches and palaces, especially his own royal residence. Today, most of the original apartments and offices of his palace are restored rather than original, but the Palace Chapel remains largely as it was first built (Figure 7.27). Inspired by the design of San Vitale in Ravenna, this magnificent room reflects the architect's reinterpretation of the graceful Byzantine style to incorporate the massive solidity of Roman

monuments and the vigor of Germanic taste. The octagonal chapel stands two stories high, and heavy square pillars support the second level, where galleries are framed by graceful arches and columns from Italy. The bronze gratings and mosaic floor were also brought to Aachen from Italy. An **ambulatory,** or passageway for walking, extends around the circumference of the central space behind the pillars. Spiral steps lead to the upper floor, where the tribune, or emperor's throne, was located. From here, Charlemagne observed and participated in church services and ceremonies and was in turn observed by his subjects, enthroned as Christ's representative on earth.

Painting: Illuminated Manuscripts   Although nearly all the murals, frescoes, and mosaics from this period have vanished, the surviving **illuminated manuscripts** offer an excellent view of the Early Medieval painting ideal. The art of manuscript illumination was influenced by the Germanic practice of decorating small objects and the Classical tradition of fine metalwork that had been maintained in Italy. During the Early Middle Ages, gifted artists and dedicated monks joined these disparate artistic elements to produce richly illustrated books and bejeweled book covers. Most of these decorated books were used in the liturgy of the Mass, such as the psalters, the collections of the psalms, and the gospel books, which were the texts of the first four books of the New Testament. For three centuries, in monasteries and abbeys from Ireland to Germany, scribes copied the Bible and their fellow artists adorned the pages with geometric and foliage designs, mythical animals, Christian symbols, and portraits of biblical characters and saints.

Manuscript illumination became both more symbolic and more realistic in the Carolingian Renaissance, partly because Italian artists were now influencing Frankish tastes. For example, the Gospel Book of St. Medard of Soissons follows Italian practice in being filled with Christian symbols and religious icons as well as making visual references to Classical architecture. Perhaps the most impressive of the Carolingian illuminated manuscripts was the St. Paul Bible, one of the presents Charles the Bald (r. 840–877), the grandson of Charlemagne, gave to win the pope's approval for his coronation as emperor in 875. Produced in an unidentified scriptorium in the city of Reims by a team of scribes and illuminators, the St. Paul Bible originally contained twenty-four (today, twenty-three) decorated full-page miniature paintings to introduce some of the books in the Old and New Testaments (Figure 7.28). It also included a dedicatory miniature of Charles the Bald (king of France 840–877; Holy Roman emperor 875–877) and his wife; a miniature based on the life of St. Jerome, translator of the

Figure 7.28 *Adam and Eve.* Genesis, from the St. Paul Bible. Ca. 870. San Paolo Fuori le Mura, Rome. *This miniature painting of Adam and Eve was intended to introduce the Book of Genesis. Divided into three bands, the painting presents, from left to right, the story of the first man and woman, beginning with the creation of Adam and ending with the exile of both from Eden. The decoration is brilliantly colored and extremely inventive, as in the final episode, where Adam is shown digging while Eve stands by suckling her firstborn, Cain. The treatment of the human figures, with carefully modeled limbs and appropriate expressions, shows a full mastery of the human form. The only sour note in the painting is the way the artist has rendered Eve's breasts as pendulous—perhaps a reflection of the artist's lack of access to live models or a conventional depiction of Eve copied by the artist.*

Vulgate Bible; and a treasure trove of decorated title pages and initial letters. The luxurious style of the St. Paul Bible was typical of the works commissioned by Charles the Bald, who is recognized today as the most important patron of the Carolingian Renaissance.

At the end of the Early Middle Ages, the style of manuscript illumination became even more elaborate and richer in tone, as in the Gospel Book of Otto III (r. 983–1002), a product of the German Reichnau school. This manuscript represents the enthroned figure of St. Luke in a state of religious ecstasy. The saint supports a host of Jewish prophets and heavenly messengers; books from the Old Testament are stacked in his lap. Hovering above St. Luke's head is his symbol, the ox (Figure 7.29).

Technology

The story of Early Medieval technology is largely an account of the preservation of prior achievements. However, Christianity, now the established faith of Europe, required many specialists in those areas under its control, thus ensuring the preservation of many older arts and crafts. In building churches, stonemasons, wood carvers, metalworkers (for bells), painters, and stained-glass artisans were needed. In monasteries—which were, in reality, self-reliant farms—farmers, blacksmiths, vintners, and millers were among the specialists needed. Charlemagne's decree that each monastery maintain a school, usually with a library attached, created a demand for workers with book publishing skills, such as calligraphers and manuscript illuminators. As in Late Rome, warfare and farming remained two areas in which some noted technological innovations were made.

Warfare In Europe, several changes in military technology now came into use, inspired by contacts with invading peoples. From various Germanic tribes, in the sixth century, there were the war saddle (helpful during violent action) and the curb bit (used in the horse's mouth, for control). From the Avars, invaders from central Asia, in the sixth and seventh centuries, came the stirrup; and, from the Arabs, in the seventh century, the superior Arabian warhorse. These new features were soon available across the land, thus making knightly culture possible (see Chapter 9).

Figure 7.29 *St. Luke*, from the Gospel Book of Otto III. Ca. 1000. About $13 \times 9\frac{3}{8}$". Bayerische Staatsbibliotek, Munich. *The biblical symbols and images, in colors of green, gold, and blue, dominate this illumination from the Gospel Book of Otto III. In the clouds above St. Luke, the anonymous painter has depicted not only Jewish prophets and heavenly messengers but also God (in the center), wearing a crown and holding what appears to be a scroll. The rays emanating from the clouds represent lightning. Below St. Luke are two lambs, symbolic of Christ as the Lamb of God and of the sacrament of baptism. The lambs drink from the springs that gush forth from the rocks, which probably represent the church. The flanking columns and arch, festooned with flowers and garlands, may refer to German folklore and its rural traditions and images.*

In a development related to warfare, Offa (r. 757–796), king of the Mercians, an Anglo-Saxon people living south of the Humber River (modern-day southern England), built a 120-mile-long stone dike as a bulwark against the fiery Welsh. Offa is considered the most able Anglo-Saxon ruler up to this time. Because of his wise policies, King Offa was highly respected by Emperor Charlemagne, and the dike (now in ruins) serves as a reminder of Offa's vision—his reign was a golden age for the people of Mercia.

Farming   Only modest advances were now made in farming technology, and the important changes tended to be north of the Alps. In about 900, for various reasons, settlers began to open new lands to cultivation by cutting down forests and, in the Netherlands, reclaiming land from marshes and the sea. A few improved implements appeared, such as a superior axe (for cutting trees), a more effective scythe (for harvesting grain and cutting grasses), and the earliest wheeled plow (in the tenth century).

The Legacy of Late Rome, Byzantium, and the Early Medieval West

Late Roman civilization created a synthesis of Christian and Greco-Roman values, which became its legacy to the Early Medieval West. Christian intellectuals valued Greco-Roman thought for the support it lent to the spiritual values that were now considered primary. Late Roman art and architecture also blended the two traditions.

Late Rome   The Late Roman synthesis of Christian and Greco-Roman values was supremely embodied in the Christian church. From the fall of Rome until the 1800s, the church's culture was nearly synonymous with the wider culture; to be Western was to be Christian. Church leaders were now the patrons of culture. They commanded artists to create only religious works, using a symbolic, impressionist style; they commissioned architects to build churches in the form of Roman basilicas adapted to religious needs and baptisteries based on round, or polygonal, designs; they asked composers to write music for the church liturgy; they authorized scholars to harmonize faith with Greco-Roman thought; and they ordered sacred books to be decorated—manuscript illumination—by gifted artist-clergy. Most notably, church leaders known as the Fathers left an impressive array of writings, including Jerome's Vulgate Bible, Augustine's vast theological works, and Ambrose's hymns, which soon became authoritative. And Eusebius, a church leader, created the literary form of church history, a popular genre in the Middle Ages.

From Late Rome came the structure of everyday life in the medieval world: the sharp division of society into aristocratic landowners and dependent agricultural workers, the church functioning as a state within the state, a barter economy, military power wielded by owners of large estates, farming and military technology, and the ideal of a multiethnic but Christian society. In effect, the late Classical world was the womb from which would emerge the next incarnation of Western institutions as well as Western humanities.

Byzantium   When Constantinople fell, Byzantine civilization left a profound legacy to the West, some of which is alive today. In eastern Europe, the Orthodox Church continues to influence the Slavic population. Western law owes a great debt to the Code of Justinian, which became the standard legal text studied in medieval universities. Elements of Byzantine art appeared in Renaissance art in Italy, and the Italian cities of Venice, Genoa, and Pisa became major cultural centers in the fifteenth century because of the wealth they had accumulated from Byzantine trade.

Byzantium also served conserving functions for the West. The Byzantine Empire acted as a buffer against the Arabs in the seventh century and against the Seljuk Turks in the twelfth century. Byzantine scholars preserved ancient Greek texts, many of which were carried to Italy, England, and elsewhere in the mid–fifteenth century. When these works were reintroduced into the West, they intensified the cultural revival already under way.

Early Medieval West   The Early Medieval West preserved the legacy of the ancient world, notably the Christian church, the papacy, the Latin language, the educational ideal of the arts and the sciences, building and artistic methods, farming implements and military weaponry, Greek thought, and Greco-Roman literary and artistic forms. The legacy was usually reshaped in some way, such as the reform of monasticism along Benedictine lines and the spread of female monasticism. Most important, this first medieval period added Germanic elements to the Classical and Christian legacy to forge a new civilization centered in Europe rather than in the Mediterranean basin. This new version of Western culture was born in the reign of Charlemagne, and its memory lingered in the monasteries and other isolated outposts. When the barbarian invasions ended, a more enduring Western culture was born.

KEY CULTURAL TERMS

symbolic realism	baptistery
peristyle	impressionistic
medallion	miniatures
attic	*putti*
basilica	Byzantine style
apse	Greek cross
nave	pendentive
aisles	Gregorian chant
clerestory windows	monophony
atrium	ambulatory
transept	illuminated manuscript
cruciform	

SUGGESTIONS FOR FURTHER READING

AUGUSTINE, SAINT. *The City of God.* Edited by D. Knowles. New York: Penguin, 1972. A monumental work that illustrates Augustine's blending of Classical and Christian thought.

———. *Confessions.* Translated by R. S. Pine-Coffin. New York: Penguin, 1966. One of the enduring books of Western literature; reveals the anguish and the achievements of this influential thinker.

BEDE. *A History of the English Church and People.* Translated by L. Sherley-Price. New York: Penguin, 1955. Written in 731, this account of the church in Saxon England is an important source for understanding early Christian society and attitudes in England.

BOETHIUS. *The Consolation of Philosophy.* Translated by V. E. Watts. New York: Penguin, 1969. An account, combining verse and prose and written in the early sixth century, that shows how Christian faith and pagan philosophy enabled the author to accept both his fall from power and death.

COMNENA, ANNA. *The Alexiad of Anna Comnena.* Translated and with a brief introduction by E. R. A. Sewter. New York: Penguin, 1979. A fresh, modern translation of this Byzantine classic work of history, with notes, a map, appendixes, and genealogical tables; some of the author's digressions are consigned to footnotes.

EINHARD and NOTKER THE STAMMERER. *Two Lives of Charlemagne.* Translated by L. Thorpe. New York: Penguin, 1969. A useful introduction and many footnotes enlighten the student about these two brief but important contemporary biographies by, respectively, the head of Charlemagne's palace school and a monk.

GREGORY, BISHOP OF TOURS. *History of the Franks.* Translated by L. Thorpe. New York: Penguin, 1974. An engrossing account of this chaotic time by an eyewitness.

HROSVITHA. *The Plays of Hrotsvit [Hrosvitha] of Gandersheim.* Translated and with an introduction by K. Wilson. New York: Garland, 1989. A lively and authoritative translation of these Early Medieval plays, with scholarly notes.

STANIFORTH, M., trans. *Early Christian Writings: The Apostolic Fathers.* New York: Penguin, 1968. Useful introduction to the issues and personalities of the early Christian church.

8 THE WORLD OF ISLAM
630–1517

The Byzantine Empire and the Early Medieval West were two of the three new civilizations that emerged in the power vacuum left by the fall of Rome in 476. Islamic civilization was the third. The word *islam* is Arabic for "submission" (to God); a *Muslim* is "one who has submitted," or accepted the beliefs and practices of Islam. At its largest, the Islamic Empire extended over an enormous area that included southern Spain, Sicily, North Africa, Syria, Palestine, Mesopotamia, Persia, and the Arabian peninsula (Map 8.1). Building on Arabic roots and the teachings of the prophet Muhammad while absorbing aspects of Greco-Roman and Persian cultures, Islamic civilization flourished from the mid–eighth to the thirteenth century. It was the source of numerous scholarly advances as well as a wealth of artistic achievements.

The date 630 marks the year when Muhammad's call for a new religion was accepted by the Arab leaders of Mecca and surrounding areas. The date 1517 marks the triumph of the Ottoman Turks, who had converted to Islam, and the beginning of a new era in Islamic history. Modern Islam is no longer identified with a particular country or region or with any one ethnic or racial group. The world's fastest-growing religion, with over one billion adherents around the globe, it is second in size only to Christianity (Figure 8.1).

The pre-Islamic Arabs inhabited the Arabian peninsula, a dry land wedged between the Red Sea and the Persian Gulf. In the north, nomadic Bedouin tribes herded sheep and goats across the higher plateaus and deserts. In the south, Arabs lived in farming communities and cities. Merchants prospered from trade on the southern caravan route, which began in India, crossed

◀ **Detail** Arches of the Great Mosque. Stone and brick columns, ht. 9′9″. Exterior: 590 × 425′. Eighth–tenth centuries. Córdoba, Spain.

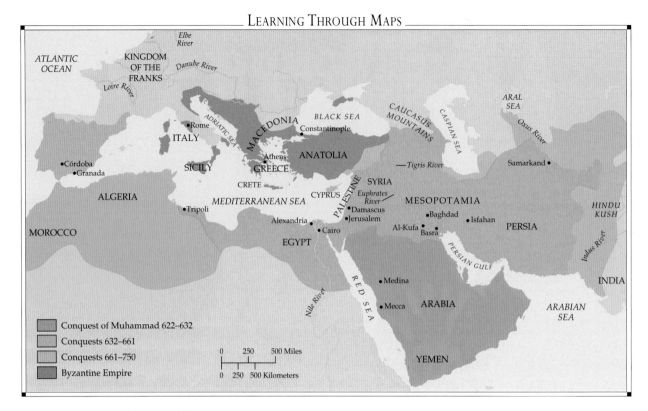

Map 8.1   THE WORLD OF ISLAM, 622–750
This map shows the successive expansion of the Islamic world, between 622 and 750.
Notice the three phases of expansion. **Consider** how the expansion of Islam threatened
the Byzantine Empire and the Kingdom of the Franks. **Identify** the three successive capitals of the Islamic Empire. **What** problems would the Muslims face in conquering so
much land so quickly and ruling such diverse peoples? **Compare** the size of the Islamic
holdings in 750 with those of the Roman Empire under Augustus in Map 5.1.

southern Arabia, and then followed the west coast
plateau along the Red Sea into the Roman Empire.

By the early seventh century, the Arabic language
had spread throughout the peninsula, binding the inhabitants with a common tongue and oral literary tradition. Jews and Christians, lured by the prospects of
wealth and trade, migrated into southern Arabia.
From them the Arabs acquired additional knowledge
of weaponry, textiles, food and wine, and writing. In
Mecca, the leading commercial city on the southern
trade route, Jews, Christians, and Arabs not only ex-
changed products and wares but also shared ideas and
values.

MUHAMMAD, THE PROPHET

Muhammad, the founder of Islam and one of the most
commanding figures in history, was born in the city of
Mecca in 570. His father was from a minor but respected clan within the city's most powerful tribe, the
Quraish or Quraysh. Apparently, Muhammad was orphaned when quite young and was reared by grand-
parents and other kinspeople. He is said to have been
a shepherd until he went to work for a caravan company owned by a wealthy widow, Khadija [kah-DE-
jah], his first wife. Their only surviving child, Fatima
[FAT-uh-mah], was to become a revered religious figure (Figure 8.2).

In 610, at the age of forty, Muhammad experienced
a spiritual transformation that convinced him that Allah had called him to be his prophet to the Arab people. Other revelations soon followed. Inspired by these
encounters, Muhammad slowly gathered a small band
of converts. As his fame grew, he became known simply as "the Prophet"—always written with an initial
capital letter as a sign of deep respect.

At first, the city leaders of Mecca paid scant attention to Muhammad. However, he became a controversial figure when, in the name of Allah, he declared that
there was only one God, attacked the polytheistic beliefs of his fellow Arabs, and condemned as idolatrous

Figure 8.1   The Pilgrimage to Mecca and the Circling of the *Kaaba*. J. Allan Cash photograph. *All Muslims are required to make a pilgrimage to Mecca at least once in their lives. There they circle the* Kaaba, *a sacred shrine, seven times in a counterclockwise direction, trying to touch or kiss its walls. On the ninth day of their pilgrimage, worshipers assemble on the plain of Arafat outside Mecca to make their stand before God. This ten-day journey and its ceremonies often mark the climax of a devout Muslim's life.*

Figure 8.2 *Fatima.* Chester Beatty Library, Dublin. *Fatima, veiled and dressed in white, kneels beside two of Muhammad's wives. Although Fatima is not mentioned in the* Qur'an, *her reputation grew over the years among the Shi'ite Muslims. She became the ideal woman, possessing extraordinary powers similar to those of the Virgin Mary for Roman Catholics. Devout Shi'ite women appeal to her for guidance and protection, and worship at her shrines.*

the *Kaaba* (cube), a local pagan shrine that housed a sacred black rock. Since the *Kaaba* was not only a holy place but also a source of revenue generated by the thousands of pilgrims who visited it each year, the Quraish tribal leaders feared that they were in danger of losing one of their most profitable attractions. They also considered Muhammad to be socially inferior and uneducated. Soon Quraish hostility turned to persecution. Fearing for his life, Muhammad and a few followers fled, in 622, to Yathrib, a neighboring city. This historic flight, or Hegira *(hijra)*, transformed Muhammad's message of reform into a call for a new religion.

And the date, 622 in the Christian Western calendar, marks the year 1 for Muslims.

According to tradition, Muhammad was welcomed into Yathrib and quickly made a name for himself by settling several disputes that had divided its citizens. He emerged as a judge and lawgiver as well as a military leader. In Yathrib, Muhammad was able to found his ideal community, where religion and the state were one. Yathrib became known as Medina, or "the City," a name that denoted its position as Islam's model city.

Before the Hegira, Muhammad had formulated the basic doctrines of Islam. In Medina, he put them into practice to solve social and legal problems and to offer guidelines for everyday life and social interactions. Muhammad, it is believed, also drew up a charter defining relations among the Medinese people, his own followers, and the Jews, who were influential in the city. Most important, this charter established several fundamental principles. Faith, not blood or tribe, unified the believers; Muhammad, as the voice of Allah, was a ruler and not a consensus builder; and Islam was the only source of spiritual and secular authority. In essence, a theocracy was in the making in Medina, as political and religious objectives blurred into one, and a unified, faith-based state government was envisioned. Eventually, tensions between the Jews and the followers of Muhammad reached the point where Muhammad exiled the Jews. At the same time, he expunged any rituals that might have had Jewish associations. Specifically, he changed the direction for praying from Jerusalem to Mecca, he called for pilgrimages to the *Kaaba*, and he moved the day of collective prayer from Saturday to Friday.

While Muhammad held sway in his newly adopted home, conflicts between Medina and Mecca grew as Medinese raiders attacked the caravans traveling over the trade routes from Mecca. Desert warfare soon erupted. From 624 to 628, the two cities fought three major battles. The last one resulted in a victory for Muhammad's forces. Now in full control of Medina and having repelled the Meccan army, Muhammad was ready to return to Mecca.

Muhammad and about one thousand of his followers set out as pilgrims to the *Kaaba* shrine. The Quraish leaders faced a dilemma. If they attacked or tried to prevent the pilgrims from worshiping, they would be violating their role as protectors of the shrine. But if they did nothing, they risked turning their city over to Muhammad and his supporters. As a way out of this impasse, a Quraish delegation negotiated a treaty that allowed Muhammad to visit Mecca the next year as a pilgrim in exchange for his returning to Medina. This peaceful solution convinced many Arab tribes that Muhammad's new faith and tactics were legitimate, and they soon converted to Islam.

In 629, Muhammad made his pilgrimage, winning new converts during a three-day visit. The next year, when the Quraish attacked one of Muhammad's allied tribes, he raised an army of ten thousand to march on Mecca. Faced with these odds, the Quraish opened the city, their leaders accepted the new faith, and the Prophet entered triumphantly. He destroyed the pagan idols at the *Kaaba*, and he forgave his enemies if they became Muslims. Nearby tribes sent delegations to Mecca, from which contacts Muhammad constructed a network of personal and political alliances across the Arabian peninsula based on recognition of Mecca's power and agreement not to attack Muslims and their allies. On the eve of his death in 632, he had achieved what no Arab leader before him had done. He had brought peace to Arabia and united its inhabitants; and, at the same time, he had given the Arabs a new faith based on revelation, an ethical code of conduct, and a monotheistic deity. Muhammad's personality, dedication, and resolve had ignited a unification movement that now was energized and directed by a vigorous and resourceful religion.

IMPERIAL ISLAM

Islam evolved through a series of dynasties in the first nine hundred years of its history. They can be divided into five major periods, which sometimes overlapped (Timeline 8.1).

The Post-Muhammad Years

After Muhammad's death, leadership was transferred to a series of caliphs. (*Caliph* means "representative" or "successor.") Those who personally knew the Prophet are identified as *rashidun*, or "rightly guided," to distinguish them from the more secular caliphs in later dynasties.

Abu Bakr [A-bu BAK-er] (573–643), the first of the four *rashidun* caliphs, had been Muhammad's close adviser, friend, and father-in-law. Rather than being elected, which was the custom among Arab tribes, he was picked by a small group of Muslims. Another faction supported Ali, Muhammad's cousin and son-in-law, who, in their view, was the true heir, since he was a blood relative. From this group would emerge the Shi'a party, or Shi'ites, who later challenged the Sunni, or mainstream, Muslims over succession, power, and legal matters. Today, most Shi'ites are found in Iran and southern Iraq.

During his brief rule, Abu Bakr suppressed a revolt of Arab tribes and launched numerous raiding parties beyond the Arab peninsula—a step that inaugurated

Timeline 8.1   THE WORLD OF ISLAM, 630–1517

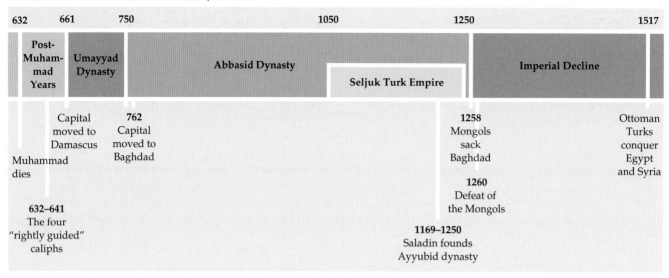

Islam's imperial period. His successor, Umar [u-mar] (about 586–644), continued the invasions. Although the Arabs took their share of loot, they neither destroyed towns or villages nor tried to convert their new subjects to Islam. Instead, they controlled the conquered peoples through existing governance and administrative systems—a wise policy that helped stabilize the Arab empire that was emerging. Umar's assassination in 644 opened a period of factionalism that ended with a leader from the Umayyad clan being chosen as caliph.

The Umayyad Dynasty

Muawiyah [mu-A-we-ya] (about 602–680) founded the Umayyad dynasty in 661, which lasted for about a century. Muawiyah moved the capital of his new empire from Medina to Damascus—a cosmopolitan trade center located more centrally in the Middle East— signifying an important shift in Arab politics and worldviews. During this dynasty, territorial expansion continued. Islam found converts more by example than by coercion, and those who did not convert were usually left to their own faiths. Nonetheless, they had to pay a special tax and were required to recognize the sovereignty of Islamic law and accept Arab political and military control.

The Abbasid Dynasty

During the 740s, a series of uprisings undermined the weakened Umayyad regime. In 750 an Arab Muslim army, led by a member of the Abbasid clan, defeated the last Umayyad ruler. The Abbasids, who claimed to be descendants of Abbas, the uncle of Muhammad, moved the capital from Damascus to Baghdad in modern Iraq—an old trading city that now became Islam's cultural center and the home of the caliphs. During the Abbasid period, Islamic peoples from other traditions began to play prominent roles in government, society, and culture. The Persians, a people with a centuries-old civilization, now exerted a strong influence in the arts and learning and set the tone and atmosphere at the Abbasid court. Persians also staffed the state bureaucracy and ran the government. Persian prime ministers, who ruled in the name of the caliph, made day-to-day decisions. Turks, Kurds, and other hired mercenaries replaced Arabs in the imperial armies.

The Seljuk Turk Empire

Internal weaknesses and breakaway kingdoms made the Abbasid Empire easy prey for the Seljuk Turks, a nomadic tribe who arrived from Central Asia after converting to Islam in the 990s. By about 1050, they ruled Baghdad in the name of the Abbasid caliphs and soon were in command of much of the Muslim world (Figure 8.3). Watching these events from Constantinople, the alarmed Byzantine rulers realized that the Seljuk Turks might destroy what remained of their empire. Consequently, they called upon the Christians in western Europe to rescue them, thus launching the first of nine crusades, which lasted from 1095 to 1272. Although the Crusades disrupted life in parts of the Muslim world, they proved to be more a nuisance than a danger.

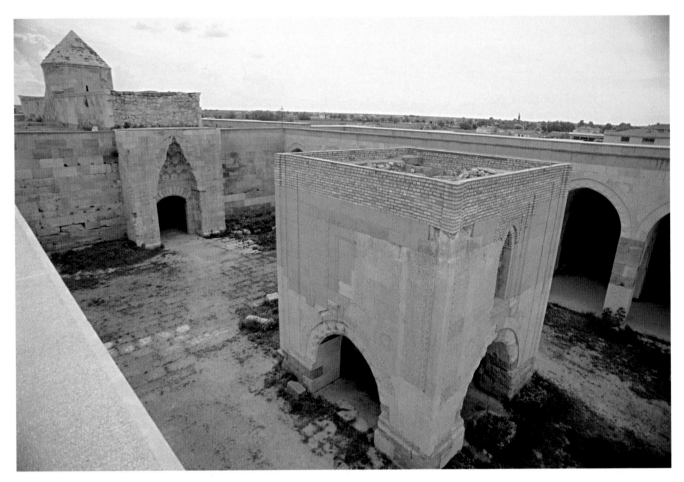

Figure 8.3 Courtyard and mosque. Sultan Han Caravanserai. Aksaray, Turkey. 1229, heavily restored. *This* caravanserai, *or way station for merchants, pilgrims, and other travelers, was built by the Seljuk sultan 'Ala' ad-Din Kayqubad.* Han *is Turkish for "caravanserai." Located along well-traveled caravan routes, at distances about a day's travel apart (about forty kilometers), caravanserais were usually heavily fortified and offered amenities, such as food and lodging for travelers, fodder and stables for the animals, and protection to all. The courtyard of the Sultan Han caravanserai is surrounded by an arcade that opens to a series of rooms on one side and covered places on the other. A small mosque stands in the center of the courtyard.*

The most famous of the Seljuk sultans was Saladin [SAL-ed-n] (about 1137–1193), who established the Ayyubid dynasty, which ruled in what are now modern Syria, northern Iraq, Palestine, and Egypt from 1169 to 1250. He made Cairo a new center for Islam and launched a golden age of learning in the city. Saladin then defeated the Crusaders in Palestine and restored Jerusalem to the Muslims.

Imperial Decline

Soon, however, Islam faced a powerful enemy from the east. The Mongols, a tribe of nomadic warriors out of the Mongolian Plateau in Asia, invaded and ravaged the Muslim lands, starting in the 1220s. In 1258 they sacked Baghdad and dethroned the last Abbasid caliph. The Turkish Mamelukes, who took control of Egypt and Syria after Saladin's death, defeated the Mongols in 1260. Islam had survived, but instead of a unified state there were smaller kingdoms and principalities. Islam's thriving commercial economy gave way to an agrarian system. In 1517 the largest of these kingdoms, located in Egypt and Syria, fell to the Ottoman Turks.

ISLAM AS RELIGION

Islam's fundamental characteristics—monotheism and revelation—are founded on its two central beliefs: There is but one God and Muhammad is his Prophet.

Figure 8.4 Kufic Calligraphy from the *Qur'an*. Ninth–tenth centuries. Ink and gold leaf on vellum, 8½ × 21". Nelson-Atkins Museum of Art, Kansas City, Missouri. Purchase: Nelson Trust. *Kufic calligraphy, which originated in the city of al-Kufa in Iraq, was used in mosque decoration and the writing of early copies of the* Qur'an. *Because Islam opposed the representation of figures in most art, calligraphy was one of the major forms available to Muslim artists.*

Muslims worship the same God as Jews and Christians, but Muslims alone recognize Muhammad as the final prophet of a tradition that dates from Abraham and Moses in Judaism, and that recognizes Jesus Christ, not as the son of God, but as the giver of the Christian prophecy. However, for devout Muslims, it is Muhammad's voice, above all others, that is the culminating revelation and perfects God's earlier message to Jews and Christians.

Muhammad's prophecies make up the text of the *Qur'an*, a word that literally means "recitation" (Figure 8.4). These prophecies were given final form in the generation after the Prophet's death. Nevertheless, for pious Muslims, the *Qur'an* is the uncreated or eternal word of God revealed through the angel Gabriel, or Gibril, to the Prophet. In the historical context, however, the *Qur'an* was created by a committee of Muslims between 640 and 650. They gathered the fragments of texts and sayings of Muhammad and compiled them into an official version of the word of God as had been revealed to the Prophet. They then destroyed all other sources or collections of sayings that might constitute rival texts. The *Qur'an* was now the only text, and it could not be questioned. Over time, Muslims came to believe that the *Qur'an* should be read only in Arabic. (Most Muslims today cannot read classical Arabic, the language of the *Qur'an*, so translations may be used for instructional purposes. For devotion, only the Arabic is allowed.)

The text of the *Qur'an* is arranged in 114 chapters, each called a *sura*, with the chapters printed accord-

ing to length, from the longest to the shortest. Each chapter is divided into *ayas*, or verses. The style resembles a type of rhymed prose. Muhammad's utterances reveal him to be a master of literary expression and rhetoric. Many converts came to Islam because they were swayed as much by the *Qur'an*'s evocative language as by its message. Its elevated tone and poetic qualities appeal to the faithful's soul, or inner being.

Within a century of Muhammad's death, another source of the Prophet's sayings, proclamations, instructions, and activities, along with those of his companions, appeared with the issuance of the *Hadith*, or the Tradition. Muslims use the *Hadith* as a supplement to the *Qur'an* and regard it as a source to explain their laws, rituals, and dogma. Today, the *Hadith*, the *Qur'an*, commentaries on the *Qur'an*, and the Arabic language make up the core curriculum taught in Islamic religious schools.

In early Islam, two types of schools soon emerged. The elementary school, maintained by a mosque (house of worship), offered boys basic religious education, along with training in how to read and interpret the *Qur'an*. Advanced learning took place in a **madrasah,** or university, the first of which was established in the ninth century in Fez, in modern Morocco. By the twelfth century, these universities had spread to most of the major cities of Islam. At first, their curriculum included only law, literature, philosophy, and theology, but, over time, mathematics, astronomy, and medicine were added (Figure 8.5). Some *madrasahs* be-

Figure 8.5   Scene from a *Madrasah*. Bibliotheque Nationale, Paris. (Ms. Arabe 5847 fol 5v.) *This manuscript page, with Arabic writing at the top and bottom, shows a Muslim scholar, the second person to the right holding an open book, explaining a particular text to his students. Behind the students and teacher are stacks of books set on open shelves, suggesting a library setting for the classroom. All students are male and have beards—as required by Islamic law. Adorning the room's upper level are typical decorative motifs of Islamic art, such as intricate foliage patterns and designs.*

Figure 8.6   Kutubiyya *Minbar*. Ca. 1137–1145. Bone and colored woods, ht. 12′10″, width, 2′10¼″, depth 11′4¼″. Kutubiyya Mosque, Marrakesh, Morocco. Islamic. Three-quarter view from the right. Photography by Bruce White. Photograph © 1998, The Metropolitan Museum of Art. *Richly decorated minbars, or portable pulpits, were used by local prayer leaders to address worshipers during Friday services. A minbar is basically a wooden staircase on wheels, with a seat at the top of the stairs for the prayer leader. This intricately detailed example was assembled from perhaps a million pieces of bone and fine African woods.*

came famous for particular areas of study, and local rulers often supported these schools in order to attract scholars and improve the university's reputation.

The *Qur'an* and the *Hadith*, as noted above, offer truth and guidance to the faithful. However, the core of Muslim religious life rests on the Five Pillars, or Supports, of the Faith—which include one verbal affirmation and four required devotional practices. The affirmation of faith states: "There is but one God, Allah, and Muhammad is his Prophet." The four acts of devotion are to pray five times a day facing Mecca (Figure 8.6), to fast from dawn to sunset during the month of Ramadan, to give alms to the poor, and to make a pilgrimage to Mecca at least once in one's life (see Figure 8.1).

Not one of the Five Pillars but central to the faith is the idea of *jihad.* Jihad basically means "to strive," or "to struggle," or "to make the utmost effort." Muslims

"struggle" against sinning, or doing evil, and strive to follow the demands of the *Qur'an* and the Five Pillars of the Faith. Thus, *jihad* is a moral or spiritual striving or fight within the individual to do the right thing. However, *jihad* has other meanings, such as Holy War, a definition often found in the Western media. Many modern Muslims reject the linkage between *jihad* and Holy War, but certain groups within Islam consider *jihad* to be a Sixth Pillar of the Faith. The belief that *jihad* means Holy War can lead, and has led, to military action on the part of individuals, of groups, or of states to protect the community, to defend the faith, or to promote Islam.

Figure 8.7 A Doctor Performing an Operation. Edinburgh University Library. *Muslim physicians normally did not operate on patients, preferring to use medicines and noninvasive procedures. Sometimes operations were necessary, as in this illustration of a woman having a cesarean section. The surgeon is helped by several attendants; on the right, one is holding the patient's head, while the one on the left is handing instruments to the doctor.*

In the eighth century, Muslim orthodoxy, also known as Sunni Islam, was challenged by the rise of Sufism, a mystical movement. Sufism emerged as both a reaction to the worldliness of the Umayyad dynasty rulers and a desire, on the part of some especially dedicated Muslims, to return to what they perceived to be the simpler faith that Muhammad had taught and practiced. They rejected the legalism and formalism that had crept into Islam, and they challenged the power and influence of the *ulama*, or those men who interpreted the *Qur'an* and guarded the tradition of the faith. A majority rejected the Sunni position that all revelations from Allah were now complete, for they felt that religious truths were to be found in many places, even in other faiths. The word *Sufi* comes from the Arabic word *su*, which means "wool," in reference to the coarse woolen garment worn by the Sufis as a symbol of their ascetic life and in memory of the simple garb worn by Muhammad. In some ways, Sufism resembled monasticism, which became so important in shaping Christianity's early growth and development (see Chapter 9).

Like most societies where codes of law are rooted in religious practice and tradition, the Muslim world established the holy law of Islam—the *Sharia*—on their faith. For Muslims, this body of sacred laws was derived, in its earliest forms, from the *Qur'an;* the *sunnah,* or habits and personal religious practices of Muhammad; and the *Hadith.* Although Muslim jurists, intellectuals, and scholars have added to the Islamic law over the centuries, the basic purpose remains the same—to tell the faithful what to believe and how to live their daily lives.

MEDIEVAL ISLAMIC CULTURE

From the ninth to the twelfth century, Islamic scholars, intellectuals and inventors made significant advances in medicine; in the humanities, including mathematics, philosophy, and history; and in technology. Muslim scholars tended to be highly versatile, often making contributions in more than one field of study. At the time of the Arabic expansion, they became the saviors and successors of the Greek learning tradition by translating Greek philosophy, mathematics, and science into Arabic, which they then passed on to other cultures (see Chapters 7 and 9). In addition, they used the Classical heritage as a foundation for numerous advances (see Encounter).

Medicine

Muslim doctors, whose skills were far superior to those of their Western contemporaries, obtained their knowledge from Greek texts that were translated into Arabic about the middle of the ninth century. In addition, Islamic medicine had a practical approach to the curing of disease, namely, through the use of observation and experimentation. Islamic medicine also made advances in ophthalmology, added new drugs to the pharmacopoeia, stressed the role of diet in the treatment of various maladies, and made the first clinical distinction between measles and smallpox. Surgeries, such as amputations, trepanning, or opening the skull, and cesarean sections were occasionally performed (Figure 8.7).

Muhammad al-Razi [al-RAY-zee] (about 865 to between 923 and 935) set the standard for medicine, both as a practicing doctor and as a scholar. A prolific writer, he compiled a twenty-volume medical encyclopedia in which he noted his own findings and took issue with the ancient Greeks and their medical tradition. Al-Razi also treated childhood diseases and wrote a treatise on them, earning the title "Father of Pediatrics." Most of his writings were translated into Latin and became part of the curriculum in Western medical schools until the nineteenth century.

Philosophy and History

The two most creative Muslim thinkers were Ibn Sina [IB-en SEE-nah] (980–1037), known in the West as

Avicenna [av-ah-SEN-ah], and Ibn Rushd [IB-en RUSHT] (1126–1198), known in the West as Averroës [uh-VER-uh-weez]. Both were well educated in the liberal arts, and although both were trained in medicine and became highly respected physicians, they wrote extensively not only in the area of medicine but also in metaphysics, theology, and religion.

Philosophy Avicenna and Averroës served at the courts of Islamic rulers where their careers rose and fell and where they engaged in heated controversies with other Muslim scholars. Their works influenced Western thought for centuries and are still revered among Muslim scholars today.

Avicenna, a Persian, spent most of his life in what is present-day Iran. By the age of twenty-one, he had mastered logic, metaphysics, and Islamic law and religion as well as medicine. Appointed court physician, he advised and served numerous Persian rulers. Over the years he wrote nearly two hundred works on medicine and other sciences, languages, philosophy, and religion. His *Canon of Medicine*, one of the most important books in the history of medicine, surveyed the achievements of Greek and Roman physicians, Arabic doctors, and his own findings. As Avicenna's reputation grew, Arabic and Western medical schools used his encyclopedia of Classical and Arabic medicine as their authoritative source for centuries. His philosophical works addressed Aristotelian philosophy and Neo-Platonism and attempted to reconcile both to Islam, including the *Qur'an* and other holy writings. Through these works Avicenna strived to understand the essence of God in the physical and metaphysical worlds. His writings on the nature of God later influenced Western Medieval thought, especially scholasticism (see Chapter 9).

Averroës, Islam's foremost thinker and one of the world's greatest minds, had even more of an impact on the West than did Avicenna. Born and reared in Córdoba, Spain, in a distinguished family, Averroës held important government positions, including chief judge of the judiciary system and personal physician to the caliph. Among his vast works, which he wrote while performing judicial duties, were comprehensive commentaries on Aristotle's writings, effectively reconciling the Greek thinker's ideas with Islamic thought. Western scholars used his Arabic versions of Aristotle, translated into Latin, to help reconcile Aristotelian and Christian thought. Ibn Rushd's writings remained basic texts in Western schools and universities until modern times.

History The study of history first played a role in Islamic thought because of the supreme significance of Muhammad's life to Islam. Biographies of the Prophet

and histories of his time appeared soon after his death. Later generations developed a taste for diverse historical genres, including accounts of territorial conquests, family genealogies, and town histories. However, Islamic history—and, indeed, the study of history—took a giant step forward in the works of Ibn Khaldun [IB-en kal-DOON] (1332–1406).

Ibn Khaldun's fame rests on a multivolume history of the world, especially the *Muqaddima* or *Prolegomena*, which serves as the introduction to his lengthy study. Ibn Khaldun examined ancient societies with an eye to identifying their characteristics and the stages of their evolution. He was one of the first thinkers anywhere to deal with supply and demand, the role and value of currency, and stages of economic development as a society evolves from an agricultural to an urban economy. In Ibn Khaldun's view, which echoes that of the Greek writer Thucydides, the best historical studies downplay the role of religion or divine forces and focus on the role of human activity. Historians, by probing beneath the surface explanations of human behavior, would discover that humans are governed not by religion or idealism but rather by status concerns and the desire to identify with certain groups. He also offered a theory explaining the rise and fall of civilizations: As a civilization decays, its social bonds weaken, and it falls victim to a more vigorous people from outside its frontiers. The outsiders overthrow the weakened civilization, become powerful, and then cycle into a state of decay, to be invaded by more powerful intruders—an outlook that reflected his knowledge of the dramatic impact of Seljuk Turk, Mongol, and other nomadic forces on Muslim life.

Technology

Islamic technology, like Islamic science and philosophy, continued and expanded the Greco-Roman heritage. As Islamic civilization spread from its Middle Eastern home, its technology borrowed new features from the Far East, Iran, and India. While making no dramatic breakthroughs, Muslim artisans were skilled at perfecting the achievements of others. And, over time, Muslim technology served as a bridge to Western technology. Medieval Muslim civilization made noteworthy technological advances in three areas: papermaking, hydraulics, and mechanical engineering.

Papermaking The art of papermaking originated in China, perhaps in the second century C.E. The first paper was made from old rags and organic fibers, softened by soaking in water; when the resulting mixture dried, it became sheets of paper. This innovation led to the building of paper mills on rivers. Because of its value to communication, China kept this art as a royal monopoly until the eighth century. In 793, Baghdad, on the Tigris River, became the site of the first paper mill in the Islamic world, an event that contributed to the Golden Age of Islam and made Baghdad the center of learning. In 1151, papermaking reached Muslim Spain, or al-Andalus, which had been converted to Islam as part of the Arab Conquest. There, in Jativa, situated on the Canyoles River, in the province of Valencia, the Moors (the Arab and Berber conquerors of Spain) built a large paper mill, to serve western Islam. From Jativa, historians speculate, European cities learned the art of papermaking, and paper mills began to be established in France, Germany, and Italy in the next century.

Hydraulics   From the Greek word meaning "water organ" or "water hollow tube," hydraulics is the branch of engineering concerned with water flow and the use of liquids to power machines. It was at the forefront of Muslim technology. Islam's newly conquered lands usually had irrigation systems in place, along with mills (for grinding grain into flour, crushing sugarcane, and sawing wood) and devices for raising water from a lower to a higher level, such as the hand-powered *shaduf* and the animal- or water-powered *noria*. These devices were utilized in cities and rural areas to raise the standard of living. For example, Baghdad's prosperity, during Islam's Golden Age, was ensured by a system of dams, canals, and mills that tapped the waters of the Tigris River. And, similarly, Córdoba, in Spain, enjoyed the benefits of an irrigation system, based on a 1,400-foot-wide dam over the Guadalquivir River, along with three mill houses and four flour mills. Another ancient technology, the water clock—powered by water moving through interlocking hollow tubes, which activated cams, shafts, pulleys, wheels, and wheels within wheels—became a hallmark of Muslim technology, such as those built in Toledo, Spain (1050), Damascus (1160), Baghdad (1235), and Fez, Morocco (fourteenth century). In one area of hydraulics the Muslims were actually pioneers: using dams for water supply. The best evidence here is the complex (now in ruins) in Valencia, Spain, where eight dams diverted water from the Turia River into canals for crops and to use as drinking water. Here, artisans also invented a desilting device for removing muck from water as it passed through channels—a basic invention to keep water moving without obstruction.

Mechanical Engineering   Muslim artisans worked in two distinctly different areas of mechanical engineering: one was to develop utilitarian devices employed in daily life and the other was to develop *automata*, or self-regulating machines, designed to entertain courtly audiences. The two leading utilitarian machines were used in mining and navigation. A pump, driven by a paddle wheel, pushed water through a web of gears, to remove water from mines—the first pump with actual suction pipes. The astrolabe, an ancient Greek device, was updated for telling time and determining the position of the sun or the stars, relative to both the horizon and the meridian. Mariners used it for timekeeping and navigation, and religious leaders for setting the hours of daily prayers. Automata, also improved from ancient models, included fountains, with mechanisms for discharging water at specific intervals; and the complex inner workings of water clocks, such as devices for opening doors on the hour and moving varied figures, signs, and motifs along a track. Many features of both types of machine technology were transmitted to Europe and incorporated into the mechanical clock (see Chapter 14).

Literature

In pre-Islamic Arabia, Arabic was basically a spoken language, developed by desert Bedouins and spread into urban areas by traders, who adapted it to their needs. Within this tribal culture, poets played a critical role, because they were thought to be wizards inspired by a *jinn*, or spirit. They eventually created a body of works that were transmitted orally by *rawis*, professional reciters of poetry. The preferred poetic form was the **qasida** (ode), composed in varied meters with a single rhyme. These poems, celebrating tribal life, personal glory, and love and wine, helped create a community identity and became the preferred model for poetic expression. Between 800 and 1300, Arabic became standardized as a written language. Called literary Arabic, or classical Arabic, it took the basic form of the language of the *Qur'an*, though modified to suit changing needs.

Critical to understanding Islam's literary culture is the concept of **adab**, an Arabic word initially meaning "rules of conduct," "manners," or "good habits." *Adab* first appeared in the eighth century as a literary genre, with the translation into Arabic of a Persian work on statesmanship. For several hundred years following, many works about *adab* were written, applying the term to all social classes. Among the elite, *adab* came to mean "refinement," which included having certain skills, such as the ability to swim and to ride horses, and, especially, having deep knowledge of Islamic poetry, prose, and history and of the Arabic language. In modern Arabic, *adab* simply refers to the whole of literature.

Poetry   Pre-Islamic poetry did not disappear with the advent of Islam. This poetry, consisting of several long and short odes, was now written down and survived to become the model for Islamic poets. The most famous surviving works are *al-Mu'allaqat* ("The Hanged Poems," or "The Seven Odes"), which, according to tradition, were suspended on the walls of the Kaaba while it was still a pagan shrine. The Prophet, though rejecting the pagan themes, recognized the poetry's power and called for poets to adapt the ode for religious ends.

Another genre that survived from pre-Islamic times was the elegy, or lament, especially for the dead. Usually composed by a woman, most often the dead hero's sister, the elegy became a favorite of Islamic poets. The best of these pieces were those by the female poet al-Khansa [al-kan-SAH] (d. after 630), who lived into the early Islamic period. Filled with the fatalistic outlook of the pre-Islamic world, these laments for her father and two brothers vividly capture her grief at the inescapable reality of death.

A new literary genre, the **ghazal,** or *ghazel,* a short lyric usually dealing with love, emerged in early Islamic Arabia. Composed in single rhyme, the *ghazal* often drew on the poet's personal life. Of these early poets, Jamil (d. 701) set the standard for later writers. His usual theme was impossible love: star-crossed lovers devoted to each other unto death. Persian, Turkish, and Urdu poets, adapting the *ghazal* into their languages, made it a popular genre in the Islamic world.

Two centuries later in Islamic Spain, Ibn Hazm [IB-en KAZ-um] (994–1064) produced the highly influential *The Ring of the Dove,* which blends poetry with prose and focuses on the art of love. In this work, he argues that the "true" lover finds happiness in pursuit of rather than in union with the beloved—a central idea of Arabic poetry that may have influenced the Provençal poetry of Europe.

The Persian-speaking region of the Islamic world produced the gifted poet Rumi (1207–1273), active in Afghanistan, Persia, and Anatolia (modern Turkey). A Sufi mystic, Rumi greatly influenced Muslim ascetic thought and writing and, most important, Turkish religious life. As part of prayer ritual, Turkish followers created a whirling dance called Whirling Dervishes in the West. Rumi's literary legacy is twofold: the *Diwan-e Shams,* a collection of poems addressed to a Sufi holy man and the poet's master; and the *Masnavi-ye Ma'navi* ("Spiritual Couplets"), a complex work, part Sufi handbook, part anthology of proverbs and folk tales. The theme of the *Diwan-e Shams* is the poet's deep love for his master, a metaphor for the Sufi idea of an all-consuming love for God. The *Masnavi,* written in rhyming couplets, a Persian genre, presents the Sufi "way" through pointed stories and anecdotes.

Prose   Literary prose in Arabic originated at the Abbasid court in Baghdad, mainly as the creation of clerks and translators. A vast literature gradually emerged, but the genres were limited because of Islam's moral objection to drama and pure fiction—drama because it "represented" reality and was thus not real, and fiction because it made no claim to truth. Early writings from the Abbasid court were collections of proverbs; tales of tribal warfare known as *ayyam al-'Arab,* or "The Days of the Arabs"; and, especially, "night conversations," or *musamarah,* which evoked lively communal evenings around desert campfires. Organized loosely about a well-worn theme, filled with puns, literary allusions, and colorful vignettes of tribal life, and, above all, animated by love of the Arabic language, the "night conversations" reminded urban Arabs of their past and inspired the *maqamah* genre, a major prose achievement.

The *maqamah* ("assembly") genre was created by al-Hamadhani [al-HAM-uh-tha-NE] (969–1008). Blurring the line between fact and fiction, his *maqamahs* are entertaining works, focusing on rogues, dreamers, and lowlifes, written in rhymed prose to display his learning and literary art.

The foremost writer in the *maqamah* genre was al-Hariri [al-ka-RE-re] (1054–1122), a government official in Basra and a scholar of Arabic language and literature. Al-Hariri's poems are noted for verbal fireworks, humor, and exquisite usage of Arabic language and grammar. In the *Maqamat,* or *The Assemblies of al-Hariri,* he focuses on the adventures of the learned rogue and vagabond Abu Zayd, as reported by a narrator, al-Harith. Abu Zayd, who resembles the author in his poetic powers and lively intelligence, repeatedly uses his skills as a storyteller to charm presents from wealthy victims.

During this time, the collection of stories known as *The Thousand and One Nights,* first translated into Arabic from Persian, was circulating in the Muslim world. It is perhaps the most famous example of the "tale within a framing tale" literary genre in all of literature. The framing tale, probably from an Indian source, tells of the woman Shahrazad (Scheherazade), who devises a storytelling plan to keep the vengeful King Shahryar from his mad scheme of murdering a wife a day because an earlier wife had betrayed him. The tales come from many lands, including India, Iran, Iraq, Egypt, Turkey, and possibly Greece, and represent various genres—fairy tales, romances, legends, fables, parables, anecdotes, and realistic adventures. Originally, fewer than a thousand tales existed, but as the stories grew in popularity, new ones were added to make the number exact. This collection has supplied the West with many legendary figures, such as Aladdin, Ali

ENCOUNTER

An International Community of Scholars

Islamic scholars during the Abbasid dynasty (750–1258), which is known as the Golden Age of Islam, preserved the works of Greek mathematicians, adopted and transmitted the contributions of the Hindus, and made original discoveries in mathematics and the sciences. They and western European scholars, often working together, passed this accumulated knowledge to western Europe during the twelfth and thirteenth centuries through oral communication and the creation of many new illuminated manuscripts.

Under the Abbasid dynasty, learned men gathered at Islamic centers of study scattered throughout the western reaches of the Muslim Empire. In Spain the university at Córdoba, famed for its tolerance and diversity, attracted monks and scholars from western Europe who studied the Arabic writings, made copies, and brought them back to their monasteries and schools. There, they were translated into Latin and studied by others.

Islam's Golden Age was the work of an international community of scholars. Al-Khwarizmi [al-KWAHR-iz-me] (780–850) advanced the field of algebra; he also introduced Hindu numerals, which became known as Arabic numerals, and used them to make calculations. His near contemporary al-Battani [al-ba-TAN-e] (about 858–929) corrected errors in the Ptolemaic planetary system and constructed an elaborate astronomical table. His writings on equinoxes and

eclipses, in which he showed the possibility of solar eclipses, were translated by European scholars into Latin, making him the best-known Arab astronomer in medieval Europe. Both al-Khwarizmi and al-Battani were associated with the "House of Wisdom" in Baghdad, the capital of the Abbasid dynasty. Another scholar, who spent his life in Cairo, Ibn al-Haytham [IB-en al-hi-THAM] (965–1039), studied the Ptolemaic system of planetary motions, expanded on the mathematical work of Euclid, and developed new ideas about optics and light rays. His works, available in Latin in the thirteenth century, later influenced the German astronomer Johannes Kepler and the French mathematician and philosopher René Descartes.

Western scientists and mathematicians during the Renaissance of the fifteenth and sixteenth centuries studied the Islamic works in translation and built upon their discoveries. By 1700 the West had assimilated the knowledge generated by Islamic civilization and applied it to their study of nature, especially the exploration, navigation, and mapping of the earth. Then Europeans, for the first time since the fall of Rome, took the lead in mathematics and science.

Learning from the Encounter **Name** three cities in the Islamic world associated with Islam's Golden Age, and the achievements made in each of them. **Which** dynasty ruled in Baghdad during Islam's Golden Age?

Baba, and Sinbad the Sailor. In the Arab world, however, Islamic scholars have not accepted *The Thousand and One Nights* as classical literature, criticizing it for colloquial language and grammar errors.

A significant prose form, popular from 1000 to 1400, was the "Mirror of Princes," a Persian genre, based on the idea of *adab*. A guide for enlightened rulers, this genre focused on real and legendary statesmen, presenting them as models of refinement and "good habits." This literature influenced a genre of the same name that flourished contemporaneously in the West.

Art and Architecture

Islamic art and architecture developed within a cultural setting dominated by the *Qur'anic* ideal that religion should govern all aspects of living. In an effort to

sanctify human life, this ideal made no distinction between the artistic and the practical, the private and the public, the secular and the divine. Thus, art and architecture, like the rest of Islamic culture, had no purpose beyond serving religious faith. Reality, of course, never fully realized this ideal, but it helped to define what Islamic artists and architects could and, of equal importance, could not do.

The *Qur'an* forbade the worship of idols. In time, this ban was extended to mean that artists were prohibited from representing all living things. Accordingly, large-scale paintings and sculptures were not produced, and lifelike figures, whether of humans or of animals, largely disappeared from art. Artists became abundantly inventive in the use of nonrepresentational forms. The **arabesque**—a complex figure made of intertwined floral, foliate (leaf shaped), or geometric forms—emerged as a highly visible sign of

What was special about the atmosphere in Córdoba, Spain? In **what** way was Islam's Golden Age produced by "an international community of scholars"? **What** Islamic achievements were transmitted into the Western tradition? **Compare and contrast** Islam's "international community of scholars" with the situation in the Western world today.

Encounter figure 8.1 In the 1570s, Arab astronomers, under the guidance of Taqi al-Din, the head astronomer of the Ottoman Empire, studied the heavens with various instruments at an observatory in Istanbul. To make their observations and calculations, they used astrolabes, hourglasses, globes, and a mechanical clock built by Taqi al-Din. Many of their instruments were similar to those later used by Western astronomers in the explorations of the universe.

Islamic culture (Figure 8.8). Geometric shapes, floral forms, and **calligraphy,** or writing, decorated walls, books, and mosaics (see Figure 8.4).

Islamic tenets allowed borrowing from other cultures, so long as what was borrowed was adapted to the teachings of the *Qur'an*. From Greco-Roman architecture came the column and the capital, the rib and the vault, and the arcade. From Byzantine architecture came the dome, the most prominent feature of the Islamic style, and the pendentive, the support feature that made the dome possible. From Persian art and architecture came miniature painting, the vaulted hall, the teaching mosque, the pointed arch, and floral and geometric ornamentation. And from Turkish art and architecture came a grand artistic synthesis, which raised Persian influence to a dominant role in Islamic art and architecture, in the zone stretching from Egypt eastward, after 1200.

Architecture The oldest extant Islamic monument is the Dome of the Rock in Jerusalem, a shrine for pilgrims dating from between 687 and about 691 (Figure 8.9). Located in a city already sacred to Jews and Christians, and built over a rock considered holy by Muslims and Jews, the shrine proclaimed by its presence that Islam was now a world religion. For Muslims, the shrine's rock marked the spot from which the founder of their faith, Muhammad, made his Night Journey to heaven. For Jews, it was identified with Abraham's planned sacrifice of his son Isaac. Because Muslims also claim Abraham as their ancestor, the site was thus given added meaning. Today, the Dome of the Rock remains one of Islam's holiest places, after Medina and Mecca.

The architecture of the Dome of the Rock draws mainly on Roman and Byzantine sources, but the aesthetic spirit reflects the new Islamic style. Its basic

Figure 8.8   The "Ardebil" Carpet. Formerly in the Mosque of Ardebil, Iran. 1539–1540. Woolen knotted carpet, 37'9½" × 17'6". Victoria and Albert Museum, London. *Arabesque leaves fill the yellow medallion at the center of this exquisite carpet. The medallion is surrounded by sixteen ogees (pointed ovals), which also contain arabesques. A section of this design is repeated in the corners of the interior rectangle. Praised as "the greatest example of carpet weaving in the world," this carpet of silk and wool was woven for a Persian mosque. At least thirty-two million knots were needed to complete it.*

liant interiors, the Dome of the Rock is a feast for the eyes throughout. Everywhere there are mosaics, tiles, and marble, much of which was added later. In obedience to the *Qur'anic* ban, there is no figurative art. Arabesques, foliated shapes, scrolls, and mosaics of purple and gold, inspired by Byzantine and Persian designs, animate the surfaces, and more than seven hundred feet of Arabic script—repeating passages from the *Qur'an*—are written on both interior and exterior surfaces. Sixteen stained-glass windows allow muted daylight to play across the interior surfaces. This shrine soon became fabled for its beauty, inspiring similar domed sanctuaries and saints' tombs across the Islamic world.

The Dome of the Rock, however, did not set the standard for Islam's dominant building type, the **mosque,** or in Arabic *masjid,* "place for bowing down." The Prophet himself established the basic mosque plan with the house of worship he constructed in Medina. This first mosque, now lost, reflected the simple values of early Islam. It consisted of a rectangular courtyard, covered by a roof that rested on palm trunks and enclosed by walls made of raw bricks. The wall facing Mecca, the direction for prayer, was designated the *qiblah* wall, and a pulpit was erected from which Muhammad led prayers, preached, decreed new laws, and settled disputes. The courtyard also functioned much as the Greek *agora* and the Roman forum, providing a public meeting space. In Muhammad's mosque, it became a gathering place for the Islamic community to discuss religion and any other vital concern. In huts opening onto the courtyard lived the Prophet and his wives. With its varied activities—judicial, political, social, and religious—this first mosque expressed the Islamic ideal of the unity of life.

Later mosque builders followed the example set by the Prophet. Plain in exterior ornament and rectangular in shape, mosques were distinguished from secular buildings by their interior features and spaces—basins and fountains for ritual hand washing, porticoes for instruction, a screened enclosure to shield the prayer

plan—an octagon covered by a dome—was rooted in Roman and Byzantine tradition, and the dome's support system—a tall **drum** or wall, resting on an **arcade,** or a series of arches supported by columns—was derived from Byzantine models. But, unlike the stone domes of Byzantine churches, this dome is made of wood covered with gold. The dome's splendor reflected the opulent aesthetic emerging in the Muslim world, as well as the ambitions of the Umayyad caliph who commissioned it.

The architectural aesthetic of the Dome of the Rock is echoed in its art program. Unlike Byzantine churches, whose plain exteriors contrasted with bril-

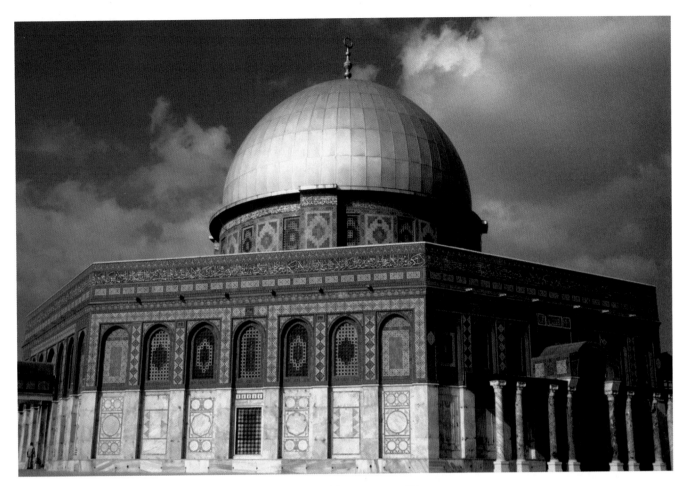

Figure 8.9 The Dome of the Rock. Ca. 687–ca. 691. Diameter of dome approx. 60′; each outer wall: 60′ wide × 36′ high. Jerusalem. *This Islamic shrine is filled with theological symbolism. The dome itself is a symbol of the heavens, and the dome's thrusting shape represents the correct path for the faithful to follow. The eight-sided figure on which the interior drum rests is an image of the earth, and the rock enclosed within this sacred space is the center of the world— a traditional Islamic belief. This belief arises, in part, because the Dome of the Rock stands on the Temple Mount—the location of Solomon's Temple and its successors. Thus, this building symbolizes Islam's claim to be the successor to and fulfillment of the Judaic and Christian faiths.*

leader, and an open area for the group prayers (Figure 8.10). Sometimes the mosque was crowned with a dome, as in the Byzantine churches, but the Islamic dome's high melon shape distinguished it from the more spherical Byzantine form. A thin pointed tower, or **minaret,** from whose top a Muslim official, the *muezzin,* called the faithful to prayer five times a day, also identified the mosque. Inside the mosque, from the earliest times, rich decorations reminded worshipers of the beauty of paradise. Brilliant mosaics and oriental carpets emblazoned the floors, facings and calligraphic friezes beautified the walls, metal or ceramic lamps cast a twilight glow onto the faithful at night, and richly decorated *minbars,* or pulpits (see

Figure 8.6), elevated the prayer leader above the worshipers. The mosque type inspired by Muhammad's example is called the **congregational mosque,** or **Friday mosque,** a horizontal structure that houses the Friday worshipers in a central courtyard with a domed fountain for ablutions. With the Arab conquests, mosques of this type were built across the Islamic world, from southern Spain and Morocco to China.

Early in the history of Islam, Abd al-Rahman (731–788), a member of the Umayyad dynasty who survived the Abbasid revolt, made his way to southern Spain, where he founded a new kingdom. In 786, he began to build the Great Mosque—an awe-inspiring example of the congregational mosque style. Constructed

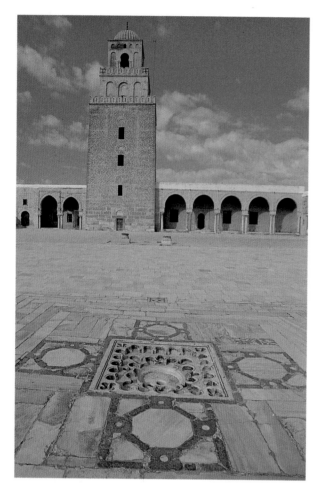

Figure 8.10 The Great Mosque of Kairouan, Tunisia. Ninth century. Stone, approx. 395 × 230′; ht. of minaret without finial 103′. *As in the other civilizations of this period, the dominant building type in Islam was the house of worship. This mosque, with its plain walls and square tower for calling the faithful to prayer, reflects the simple style of early Islam. Inside the walls, a large unadorned courtyard serves as a praying area.*

on the site of a Roman temple and a Christian church, the mosque was laid out in the traditional rectangular plan. During the next century, caliphs enlarged the Great Mosque four times to make it the largest sacred building in the Islamic world. The second expansion added an elaborately decorated *qiblah* and three domed chambers of Byzantine-inspired mosaics and gold ornamentation. But the most striking feature of the Great Mosque is the row after row of double-tiered horseshoe arches (Figure 8.11). The slender lower columns were salvaged from Roman buildings and Christian churches, and double-height arches were then placed on them. These rounded arches of red brick and yellow stone produce alternating patterns of light and color down the seemingly endless aisles.

The ninth-century Ibn Tulun mosque at Cairo is an imposing example of the congregational mosque (Figure 8.12). Four rows of arcades stand between the faithful and the east wall (the direction of Mecca), and portals of pointed arches open into the arcaded area. A minaret with a winding stair rises just beyond the mosque, which is built of brick faced with stucco. In later Islamic mosques, the pointed arches and decorated stucco work became basic features of this style. During the Christian Middle Ages, Western architects borrowed the pointed arch and adapted it to their own needs, using it to perfect the Gothic style of architecture.

In the twelfth century in the eastern Islamic lands ruled by the Seljuk Turks, a new type of mosque, inspired by Persian architecture but retaining the basic rectangular plan of the Friday mosque, emerged. The new mosque type was called a teaching mosque, because it provided distinctive areas for the *madrasah*, the religious school for advanced study. The teaching mosque proved to be a popular innovation, and between the twelfth and eighteenth centuries, architects built similar structures in Egypt, Central Asia, and India.

The most famous example of a teaching mosque is the Masjid-i Jami, or Great Mosque, in Isfahan (in modern Iran), the capital of the Seljuk dynasty in the eleventh and twelfth centuries (Figure 8.13). Four huge vaulted halls, or *iwans*, open into a central courtyard. Prayers are said in the *iwan* that opens toward Mecca, and the other three serve as areas for study, school, and rest. Viewed from the courtyard, the opening in each *iwan* constitutes a huge arch set into a rectangular facade, faced with blue tiles—a specialty of Persian artisans and the signature color of the Seljuk rulers.

Islamic builders also excelled in palace architecture, as exemplified by the Alhambra in Granada, the residence of the last Muslim rulers of Spain. Its exterior of plain red brick contrasts dramatically with its fantastic interior. The presence and sound of water everywhere—fountains, pools, and sluices—enhance the serenity and pleasure of the gardens and buildings. The Court of the Lions illustrates vividly the meaning of the term *arabesque*, with its calligraphic carvings, slender columns, geometric and floral shapes, and lacy

Figure 8.12 Ibn Tulun Mosque, Cairo. 876–879. Red brick covered with white stucco, exterior 531 × 532½′. *The finest surviving example of the congregational style, the Ibn Tulun mosque was imitated throughout the Islamic world. This view, from inside the courtyard, shows a domed fountain used for ritual washing. Outside the walls rises the spire of a four-story minaret, set on a square base with a cylindrical second story and an exterior staircase.*

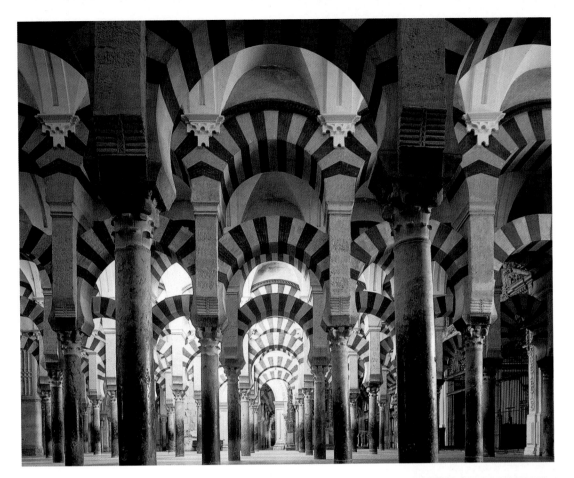

Figure 8.11. Arches of the Great Mosque. Stone and brick columns, ht. 9'9", exterior 590 × 425'. Eighth–tenth centuries. Córdoba, Spain. *The Great Mosque, nearly as large as St. Peter's Basilica in the Vatican, contains 850 pillars with nineteen aisles running north to south and twenty-nine going east to west. Although Spanish Christians, in 1236, converted it to a cathedral and constructed a high altar in the interior and, in the sixteenth century, added chapels around the quadrangle, the Great Mosque still stands as a monument to the Umayyad kingdom in southern Spain and a crowning achievement of Islamic architecture and decorative art.*

Figure 8.13. Masjid-i Jami (Great Mosque). Eleventh and twelfth centuries. Isfahan. *The view of the central courtyard and iwan (vaulted hall) of this teaching mosque is framed by the arched opening of the facing iwan. Various mosque facilities, including living quarters for teachers and students, are located in the areas around the iwans.*

240

SLICE OF LIFE
Fears of Assimilation in a Multicultural Society

PAUL ALBAR

In early-ninth-century Spain, the Umayyad rulers in Córdoba extended certain religious, legal, and civic rights to Christians, known as Mozarabs, and to Jews, who as dhimmi, or "people of the book," shared some religious beliefs with the Muslim community. However, in the 850s, peaceful relations between Muslims and Christians broke down after the government executed about fifty Christians for disrespecting Islam. In a contemporary account, the Christian layman Paul Albar laments how some young people in the Christian community were reacting to the government's crackdown. His account reveals the fear of assimilation to another culture and faith, and the subsequent loss of cultural and religious identity—a timeless issue in our multicultural society today.

The Christians love to read the poems and romances of the Arabs; they study the Arab theologians and philosophers, not to refute them but to form a correct and elegant Arabic. Where is the layman who now reads the Latin commentaries on the Holy Scriptures, or who studies the Gospels, prophets or apostles? Alas! all talented young Christians read and study with enthusiasm the Arab books; they gather immense libraries at great expense; they despise the Christian literature as unworthy of attention. They have forgotten their own language. For every one who can write a letter in Latin to a friend, there are a thousand who can express themselves in Arabic with elegance, and write better poems in this language than the Arabs themselves.

Interpreting This Slice of Life **Why** were the Spanish Muslims tolerant of Jews and Christians? **What** was the background to the conflict between the Muslims and Mozarabs? **Why** should we be careful in accepting Paul Albar's views on the Arabization of young Christians? **Why** were these young people attracted to Islamic culture? **Would** you be interested in joining another religion or culture? **Why or why not?**

decoration (Figure 8.14). The fountain surrounded by stone lions is a rare example of Islamic representational sculpture.

Painting Notwithstanding the *Qur'anic* prohibition, one branch of Islamic art—book painting, or the art of the book—usually depicted realistic scenes. A few surviving examples show that the art of the book was practiced in the early days of Islam. However, after 1100, in rapid succession, two brilliant schools of book painting emerged, each devoted to representational scenes. Little known in the West, the first school flowered in Syria and Iraq, and its artists were probably Arab, strongly influenced by Persian tradition. The second was the world-famous school of **Persian miniatures,** which flourished in Persia from the thirteenth to the seventeenth century.

Of the Arab painters whose works survive, Yahya ibn Mahmud al-Wasiti [YAK-yah IB-en mak-MOOD al-WAH-see-TEE] (fl. 1230s) is generally recognized as the best. Working in Baghdad, he illustrated al-Hariri's *Maqamat*, a twelfth-century work. Each picture depicts a colorful episode in the life of the con artist Abu Zayd, rendered with an eye to detail (Figure 8.15). The typical format on the page includes arranging the scene's focus into the frontal plane, keeping the background neutral in color, and creating a setting with the barest of details, such as a small hill or a single tree. Near Eastern tradition is apparent in the very large eyes, the dark outline of the figures, and the bunched drapery folds.

The Persian miniatures were produced under the patronage of the Mongol sultans, who had replaced the caliphs as rulers. Although the Mongols brought Chinese influences to the Persian miniatures, the Muslim artists rejected the openness of Chinese space and created their own ordered reality, as shown in a superb example from the fifteenth century (Figure 8.16). The painter records each object with painstaking naturalistic detail. The painting's high horizon and its rectangular format put the two figures in a precise setting. Like all Persian miniatures, this exquisite work is characterized by fine detail, naturalistic figures and landscape, and subtle colors.

These illustrated books were made from paper beginning around 800, when a Chinese prisoner of war revealed the secrets of papermaking to his Arab captors. Thereafter, a prodigious paper industry flourished, spreading from Samarkand to Baghdad, Damascus, Tripoli in Syria, Yemen, Maghrib, Egypt, and Spain. Christian Europeans eventually learned how to make paper from the Islamic industry in Spain.

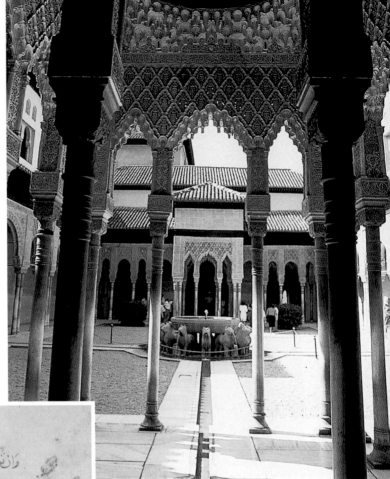

Figure 8.14 Court of the Lions. The Alhambra. Thirteenth and fourteenth centuries. Granada, Spain. *The Alhambra is the only Islamic palace surviving from the medieval period. A popular destination for European and American tourists, the ornate Alhambra has played a pivotal role in developing a taste for the arabesque among many Westerners.*

Figure 8.15 Yahya ibn Mahmud al-Wasiti. *Abu Zayd Preaching.* Book painting. 1237. *Abu Zayd, here disguised as a religious official, preaches to a group of pilgrims, including their camels. Islamic touches include the beards of male pilgrims and head coverings for both men and women. The artist creates a lively scene, much in the manner of street theater, in the way he shows the pilgrims' varied eye and facial movements, including an exchange of glances, stares into the distance, heads lifted upward, and a head looking down. No earlier pictorial source has been established for this lively and realistic art.*

Figure 8.16 Outdoor Entertainment Scene, from the *Khamsah (Five Poems)* of Amir Khosrow. 1463. Approx. 14⅓ × 9". Topkapi Sarayi Library, Istanbul. *The art of Persian miniatures achieved its classic expression during the fifteenth century, the age of the Mongol rulers in Persia. These small works are immediately recognizable by their rectangular designs, their representation of the human figure as about one-fifth the height of the painting, and their use of extremely refined detail. This painting illustrates a scene from the poetry of Amir Khosrow, an Indian poet, musician, and Sufi, whose works bridged elements of Muslim and Hindu culture.*

Music

Music has historically been a controversial topic in Muslim culture. Only a few musical genres have gained universal approval, such as the call to prayer *(adhan),* the chanting of the *Qur'an,* and the chanting of poems and prayers during certain religious events, including the Prophet's birthday, pilgrimages, and Ramadan. Clerics often question other musical forms, especially instrumental music, claiming such music undermines faith. And yet, music traditionally has thrived in the Muslim world.

Music was a constant presence in Muslim life, as heard in the five daily calls to prayer, echoing loudly from minarets in towns and cities across the Muslim world. A single male voice chants the call to worship, according to fixed rules, in which each phrase is followed by a longer pause. As the prayer unfolds, each phrase grows progressively longer and more ornamented in style. In each day's first prayer, the phrase "Prayer is better than sleep" is inserted into the sequence, before the last two statements.

The Islamic call to prayer, in English translation, is

"God is great" (repeated four times)

"I bear witness that there is no god except God" (twice)

"I bear witness that Muhammad is the Messenger of God" (twice)

"Hasten to the prayer" (twice)

"Hasten to real success" (twice)

"Allah is the Greatest" (twice)

"There is none worthy of worship but Allah"

Early Islamic music employs a microtonal system, in which the intervals, or distances between sounds (pitches) on a scale, are **microtones,** or intervals smaller than a semitone—the smallest interval in mainstream Western music before jazz.

Vocal music initially was dominant in Muslim culture, with instrumental music used only to support singing. Instrumental music later won its freedom under Spain's Umayyad rulers, who were great patrons of musicians and, most notably, of secular music (Figure 8.17). Meanwhile, religious music was given a new direction by the Sufi sect, who, in their pursuit of religious emotion, encouraged singing, chanting, and **recitative,** or vocal passages delivered in a speechlike manner. A major change arose in Turkey, where the Sufi order of Whirling Dervishes introduced music into their mosques.

Musicians across the Muslim world played many instruments, representing three groups of instruments and drawn from varied traditions. These included, from the string group, the *ud* (lute), the pandore (a bass lute), the psaltery (a trapezoidal-shaped zither), the harp, the *qithara* (guitar), and the *rabab* (rebec, a lute-shaped fiddle); from the wind group, the flute, the reed pipe, and the horn; and from the percussion group, tambourines (square and round), castanets, and various drums, such as *naqqara* (nakers, or small kettledrums) and *tabla* (a pair of wooden drums). Most of these instruments were adopted into Western music, especially as a result of cultural encounters during the Crusades.

The Legacy of Medieval Islam

The legacy of medieval Islam remains potent in the modern Muslim world. That medieval presence is apparent in distinctive architecture, which uses domes, vaulted halls, arcades, and pointed arches; in decorative patterns made with nonrepresentational designs, such as arabesques, calligraphy, and geometric, floral, and abstract forms; in a music tradition based on a microtonal system; in classical Arabic as a literary and scholarly language; in traditional clothing styles, along with beards for men and headscarves, and sometimes veils, for women; and in daily readings from the *Qur'an* on radio and television.

Medieval Islam also transmitted a legacy of suspicion toward the Christian West as a result of the Crusades; indeed, in parts of Islamic society today, the word *crusader* is a hate-charged term for a Westerner on Muslim soil. When the Greek heritage fell into disrepute in the Muslim world, medieval Islam changed the intellectual climate for scholars. As a result, the Muslim world, which after the fall of Rome had been the leader in scientific knowledge, began to lag behind the West, so that by 1800, Muslim science and universities had become irrelevant. Medieval Islam also transmitted a vision of a unified Islamic empire, stretching from Spain to China, inhabited by millions of Muslims, all worshiping Allah and obeying the *Qur'anic* laws—a vision that appeals to those dissatisfied with their place in today's Western-dominated world. Probably the major legacy of medieval Islam, and the feature of Islamic life that so differs from Western life, is the intermingling of religion and state. In the Muslim world, except for the secular state of Turkey, religion's dominant role is expressed in varied ways from law codes based on the *Qur'an*, mandating severe punishments for crimes such as adultery and theft, to separation of the sexes in public and private life.

Though perhaps not as strong as its impact on modern Islam, the influence of medieval Islam on the civilization of the modern West has been significant—ranging from architecture to literature to philosophy to mathematics to technology. Islam's direct legacy to Western civilization includes the pointed arch, which made the Gothic style possible; musical instruments from the string, the wind, and the percussion groups; poetic forms and themes that may have been imitated by the Provençal poets; love poetry, which inspired modern imitators; the poetry of the Sufi mystic Rumi, much admired by contemporary artists including the writer Doris Lessing and the composer Philip Glass; the tradition of reconciling religion with Aristotle's philosophy, which became the goal of Europe's scholastic thinkers; algebra and other original mathematical concepts, which became part of the Western educational curriculum; and a pump with actual suction pipes, a necessary feature used later in the steam engine.

Besides direct influence, medieval Islam has also had an indirect impact on the West by transmitting legacies from other cultures. Of these mediated legacies, the Classical heritage was probably the most important. Islamic scholars produced Arabic versions of most of the Greek and Roman scholarly writings, which Christian scholars then translated into Latin and used as the textbooks in medieval Europe's schools and universities. From the study of those textbooks, the West's modern scientific tradition was born. Other notable transmitted legacies include, from China, papermaking; from Greece, the astrolabe and various automata with intricate components; and, from India, the Hindu-Arabic numeral system along with other mathematical knowledge and probably the basic form of the *Arabian Nights*, though embellished with stories from various cultures.

244

KEY CULTURAL TERMS

madrasah	mosque
jihad	*qiblah*
qasida	minaret
adab	*minbar*
ghazal	congregational mosque
maqamah	(Friday mosque)
arabesque	*iwan*
calligraphy	Persian miniature
drum	microtone
arcade	recitative

SUGGESTIONS FOR FURTHER READING

Arabian Nights. Translated by J. Zipes. New York: Dutton Signet, 1991. Selections from the *Arabian Nights,* the alternative name for *The Thousand and One Nights,* by a noted authority on world folk tales.

Assemblies of al-Hariri. Translated and with an introduction by A. Shah. London: Octagon Press, 1981. An up-to-date translation of this classic of Arabic literature, telling of the adventures of the charming and learned rogue Abu Zayd. All fifty episodes, or "assemblies," are included.

The Essential Rumi. Translated by C. Barks and others. San Francisco: Harper San Francisco, 1997. Excellent American English free-verse renderings of the difficult poetry in the *Masnavi,* the masterpiece of the Sufi mystic Rumi. Includes selections of Rumi's love poems and teaching parables, along with Barks's insightful introductions.

IBN HAZM. *The Ring of the Dove: A Treatise on the Art and Practice of Arab Love.* Translated by A. J. Arberry. London: Luzac & Company, Ltd., 1953. A didactic work that blends a study of the characteristics and meaning of love, including examples, anecdotes, and poems, with a moral discourse on sinning and the virtues of abstinence.

IBN KHALDUN. *The Muqaddimah: An Introduction to History.* Translated by F. Rosenthal. Edited by N. J. Dawood. Princeton: Princeton University Press, 1969. Introduces the student to Ibn Khaldun's study of the origins and characteristics of civilization. An abridged edition of Rosenthal's three-volume translation.

The Koran [Qur'an]. Translated by N. J. Dawood. New York: Penguin, 2003. Easy to read, authoritative translation of Islam's holy book. Follows the *Qur'anic* tradition of arrangement of suras, or chapters.

The Seven Odes: The First Chapter in Arabic Literature. Translated by A. J. Arberry. London: George Allen & Unwin, 1957. An analysis, history, and modern translation of the earliest Arabic literary works—the seven odes, or *"hanged poems,"* which hung on the walls of the *Kaaba* before the time of Muhammad and the rise of Islam.

SUGGESTION FOR LISTENING

Islamic Call to Prayer. Perhaps the most familiar prayer in Islamic religion, the Call to Prayer is chanted five times daily, echoing around the world. Performed by a single male voice, according to traditional rules of expression.

◀ **Figure 8.17** Pyxis. Córdoba. 968. *The image on this* pyxis—*a vessel to hold cosmetics or perfumes—testifies to the high status held by instrumental musicians at the Umayyad court in Córdoba. At the center stands a musician, holding an* ud, *or lute, as he performs for the two young men flanking him. The listening youths, seated Muslim style, are royalty, as symbolized by the two lions below. The youth on the left holds a vessel and a flower, and the one on the right holds a fan. Executed in the all-over style of Islamic art, the surrounding space is enlivened with human, animal, and vegetal figures and abstract, meandering scrolls. An inscription identifies the* pyxis *as a gift to al-Mughira, the younger son of Abd al-Rahman III (r. 912–961), the first caliph of the West.*

9 THE HIGH MIDDLE AGES
The Christian Centuries

Although Charlemagne's ambitious hopes for Europe were thwarted by the invasions of the ninth and tenth centuries, society had grown more settled by the early eleventh century, and a brighter era began to unfold in the West. Between 1000 and 1300—the period called the High Middle Ages—a new foundation was laid that would support the future development of Western civilized life.

During this time, the Christian church became the dominant institution of the medieval world. At the same time, feudalism was established as the principal military, economic, and political system, and feudal monarchies in France, England, and central Europe were beginning to form what would become European states. Town life also revived in the West, and a new urban class was born. Situated midway between the feudal aristocrats and the peasants, this middle class included merchants, moneylenders, and skilled artisans—virtually all free persons associated with town life.

These momentous political, social, and economic changes were reflected in cultural interests. Theologians, writers, and architects worked to harmonize the two opposing trends of the time, the secular and the spiritual. They achieved a stunning but short-lived synthesis. Moving from rugged warrior values, supreme between 1000 and 1150, Western culture became more refined, more learned, and increasingly secular between 1150 and 1300. The earlier 150-year period is associated with monastic and feudal themes in literature and the Romanesque style in architecture. The later period saw a growing trend toward urban and courtly themes in literature and the rise of Gothic architecture, the most spectacular realization of which was the Gothic cathedral.

◀ **Detail** Western Facade. Notre Dame. Paris. 1220–1250.

FEUDALISM

Out of feudalism—a military and political system based on personal loyalty and kinship—arose a new social order, a code of conduct, and an artistic and literary tradition. In the beginning, feudalism restored law and order to western Europe, even though local lords often exploited those who fought or labored for them. But during the High Middle Ages, the feudal nobility slowly lost power to the feudal kings, who laid the foundations of the early modern national monarchies. By the early 1300s, feudalism no longer served its original function and was being superseded in many areas by different political, social, and economic forms.

The Feudal System and the Feudal Society

Feudalism evolved in the Early Middle Ages under the Franks and expanded under Charlemagne. As a military system, it offered some protection from invaders but at the cost of fragmenting society into rival states. As the feudal chiefs began to pass their lands on to their eldest sons, Europe became dominated by a military aristocracy (see Chapter 7).

Feudal wealth was reckoned in land; the feudal estate included lands, manor houses, and the serfs who worked the land. The feudal lords attracted warriors, called vassals, to their private armies by offering them estates, and thus feudalism depended on the manorial economy. The feudal estate, called a fief, provided the warrior with the means to outfit himself with the proper military equipment and attendants and to live in an aristocratic style.

Over the generations, feudalism became a complex web of agreements, obligations, and rituals. A written agreement spelled out the mutual duties and obligations of the lord and the vassal. Typically, the lord gave military protection to his vassal and settled quarrels among his supporters through his court. The vassal in turn furnished military or financial aid and sat as counsel in the lord's court. Conflicts between a lord and his vassal were sometimes settled by peers in the lord's court, but more often they escalated into civil wars.

The vassal–lord relationship was the heart of feudalism, but the form of the institution varied geographically. Feudalism's prototype was that of northern France, around Paris, but each area modified the French form to suit its local needs. Those who profited from feudalism retained the institution as long as possible, so that well into the twentieth century its vestiges were evident in central Europe and Russia and were eliminated only by revolution.

The hierarchical feudal social order was defined and elaborated in the unwritten rules of conduct known as the **chivalric code.** In the early eleventh century, chivalry (from the French word *cheval*, "horse") was largely a warrior code, although one rooted in Christian values. More an ideal than a reality, it nevertheless inspired the vassal to honor his lord and to respect his peers. He was also expected to protect the weak from danger and to practice his ideals—bravery, strength, and honesty—with all members of society. The French clergy refined the chivalric code by initiating the Peace of God, a call for an end to fighting at specified times, and other clerics encouraged the knights to treat women, clergy, and peasants more humanely.

By the twelfth century, both the Peace of God and the notion of protected classes—notably women—had been incorporated into the heart of a more refined and courtly version of the chivalric code. Especially influential in altering the status of women was the rise of courtly love, a movement that began in the aristocratic courts of southern France. The love of a lord for a lady (usually an unattainable lady, such as another man's wife) was seen as an ennobling emotion, encouraging the man to ever greater deeds. Aristocratic ladies were idealized and venerated with an almost holy respect, resembling that shown for the Virgin Mary (Figure 9.1). (However, a contemporaneous countertrend also identified women with Eve, who, by tempting Adam to eat the forbidden fruit, brought the burden of original sin to humanity.) Courtly love, one of the greatest contributions of medieval civilization, provided inspiration for much of the secular literature, art, and music of the High Middle Ages because it encouraged the intermingling of men and women in social settings, where dancing, music, and conversation were enjoyed in accordance with the rules of courtesy.

Whatever the image of woman in medieval society, however, on a practical level her position was determined by the social status of her husband or her father or by the support of a powerful family. A few women—such as Eleanor of Aquitaine, wife of King Henry II of England, in the twelfth century—sometimes influenced a spouse's decisions or wielded power on behalf of a son. But their rarity as rulers in their own right testifies to how little power women had in the Middle Ages, despite their exalted image.

Peasant Life

Feudalism and chivalry served the interests of the small noble classes. Life was quite different for the peasants, who constituted the vast majority of the population. Some were free, but many were bound in service. The

Figure 9.1 *Count Eckhart and Uta.* Naumburg cathedral. Ca. 1245. Limestone, life-size. Naumburg, Germany. *In this representation of a feudal lord and lady, the most striking features are the woman's chaste beauty, reflecting her role as the queen of chivalry and linking her to the Virgin Mary, and the man's great heraldic shield and sword, symbolizing his position as an aristocratic warrior and defender of honor. These two figures are among several that stand in Naumburg cathedral, representing noble men and women associated with the founding of the cathedral. The Naumburg statues are considered among the most beautiful sculptures from this period.*

two most common forms of servitude, slavery and serfdom, were legacies from Rome. Slaves were the personal property of the lord, whereas serfs were half-free but tied to the land. Serfs worked for the lord in exchange for living on his land. In eleventh-century Europe, slavery was dying out because the church's teachings had largely convinced the feudal lords of its inhumanity, but serfdom was firmly entrenched.

The routine of the serfs and the free peasants was dictated by custom and regulated by daily and seasonal events (Figure 9.2). With men and women occasionally working together in the fields, they eked out a bare subsistence from their tiny plots of land; they lived in wooden huts, raised their children, and found relief in the church's frequent Holy Days (the source of the modern term *holiday*) and feast days. As farming innovations were introduced (such as three-field crop rotation, which allowed the land to replenish itself), the plight of the serfs improved. Increasing the productivity of the soil brought economic benefits to the lord, who could then, if he wished, pay the peasants in coin and sell them tracts of land.

As serfs gained a few legal rights, they could become economically independent and gain their freedom from

Figure 9.2 Agricultural Laborers at Work. Aelfric writings, Canterbury. Eleventh century. *In the top panel, four men are depicted harvesting grain with various handheld tools, and, in the lower panel, five men carry bundles of grain. The scribe who painted these panels, as part of his copying duties, must have witnessed such scenes often in the harvest season. The laborers' costume—a loose-fitting tunic or gown, reaching below the knee, belted at the waist and with long sleeves and a round neck—was typically worn by both sexes in Europe, from the fall of Rome until fitted garments emerged, after 1340.*

Figure 9.3 Ambrogio Lorenzetti (active ca. 1319–1347). *Street Scene in Medieval Siena.* Detail from *Allegory of Good Government in the City.* 1338–1339. Fresco in the Sala della Pace, Palazzo Pubblico, Siena. *Although an idealized image, this painting is nevertheless an accurate representation of medieval Siena as a bustling country town built on a hill. Signs of prosperity abound. In the middle right and center, farmers, perhaps from the nearby countryside, lead pack animals loaded with sacks of wool and other goods. Nearby, three weavers are making textiles. On the lower right, a goatherd coaxes his flock, probably to the city market. In the middle left foreground, a shopkeeper arranges his wares. Through the large opening on the left may be glimpsed a classroom, where a seated teacher addresses his students. On the extreme right, two women, perhaps servants, carry objects, one, most noticeably, with a large bundle balanced on her head.*

the manorial system. These trends, however, were confined to western Europe, notably England and France. In some areas of central and eastern Europe, serfs continued to be exploited for centuries.

The Rise of Towns

A new trend began to counter the dominance of the feudal system: the rise of urban areas where free individuals pursued their own economic goals. Although rural manors provided work and security for 90 percent of the population at the beginning of the High Middle Ages, the population of Europe nearly doubled between 1000 and 1300, from thirty-five million to almost seventy million, and an increasing number of people sought economic opportunities in the new and revitalized urban areas (Figure 9.3). From that point on, the future of the West lay with town dwellers.

As towns grew larger and urban life became more competitive, the residents formed associations, called guilds, to protect their special interests. The artisan and craft guilds, for example, regulated working conditions, created apprenticeship programs, and set wages; the merchant and banking guilds approved new businesses and supervised trade contracts. These guilds often quarreled over issues inside the town walls, but they joined hands against the intrusions of the church and the local nobility.

Because urban economic life conflicted with the interests of the feudal system, urban dwellers, led by the guilds, founded self-governing towns, called communes, often with written charters that specified their rights in relation to the feudal lords. By about 1200, many towns in northern and western Europe had charters, and their political independence spurred economic growth.

Artisans and merchants needed buyers, secure trade routes, and markets for their products if they were to prosper. The earliest trade routes were the rivers and the old Roman roads. As demand increased in the West for luxury items from the East, new trade

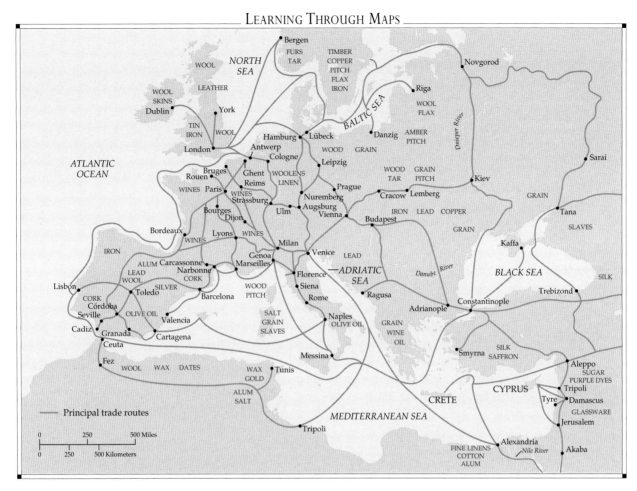

Map 9.1   PRINCIPAL TRADING ROUTES AND TOWNS OF EUROPE, 1300
This map shows the major towns and trading routes in Europe at the end of the
High Middle Ages. **Note** the important role played by sea trade. **Identify** some key
crossroads of trade. **How** did the location of the north Italian cities help to make them
leaders in trade? **Consider** the extensive nature of the long-distance trade between Europe and its neighbors. **Consider** also the impact of climate on the products made and
produced in various regions.

routes opened. Italian cities led this international commerce, trading the luxurious woolen cloth of Flanders
for the silks of China and the spices of the Middle East
(Map 9.1). Along the overland routes in Europe, local
lords guaranteed traders safe passage through their
territory for a fee. Some nobles and towns along the
way sponsored fairs to lure this rich international
trade.

As on the feudal manor, the position of women in
the medieval urban world was still subordinate to that
of men, even though urban women often worked
closely with their husbands in trade or crafts. Indeed,
in this hierarchical society gender roles became increasingly differentiated through custom and legisla-
tion. As a consequence, females could neither hold a
government office nor have any public voice in politics. The few women with economic power—such as

those directly involved in manufacturing and trade or
the occasional rich widow who kept her husband's
business afloat—were exceptions to this general exclu-
sionary rule.

The Feudal Monarchy

Politically, feudalism was leading to a new form of rule.
By about 1100, some powerful feudal lords had begun
to expand their holdings into larger kingdoms. As
these ambitious noblemen subdued weaker ones, they
often sealed their victories through marriages with the
conquered family. Over the ensuing generations, their
heirs extended and consolidated their lands, always
seeking to win the loyalty of their new subjects. The
greatest problem a feudal monarch faced was building

Timeline 9.1   THE FEUDAL MONARCHIES IN THE HIGH MIDDLE AGES

1000   1100   1200   1300

Capetian Line

FRENCH

- Chivalric code elaborated
- Peace of God
- Courtly love

1000   1100   1154   1200   1300

Anglo-Saxon Kingdom | **Normans Rule England** | **Angevin Line**

ENGLISH

- 1066 Battle of Hastings
- 1215 Magna Carta
- Formation of Parliament

1000   1039   1100   1125   1152   1200   1250   1273   1300

Saxon Line | **Salian Line** | **Hohenstaufen Line** | **Hapsburg Line**

HOLY ROMAN EMPIRE

- 1122 Concordat of Worms

1000   1100   1200   1300

1073–1085 Gregory VII | **1198–1216 Innocent III** | **1294–1303 Boniface VIII**

PAPAL

- 1059 College of Cardinals
- 1122 Concordat of Worms
- 1215 Fourth Lateran Council
- 1302 *Unam sanctam*

a centralized rule to keep the kingdom from disintegrating into a set of separate, warring states. During the High Middle Ages, four feudal monarchies dominated the West: France, England, the Holy Roman Empire, and the papacy, which was politically similar to the three secular monarchies (Timeline 9.1).

The French Monarchy   The origins of modern France stem from the reign of Hugh Capet (r. 987–996), the first of the Capetian rulers, who exercised power over a part of the old Frankish kingdom (see Chapter 7). By the early eleventh century, the Capetians, having de-

feated their rivals, had founded a feudal monarchy in central France, with Paris as its center.

During the twelfth and thirteenth centuries, a series of able monarchs managed to consolidate and expand the Capetian power base and control the great vassals by forming alliances with the lesser nobles, the middle class, the clergy, and the popes. The establishment of central authority in France was a slow process, but by the beginning of the reign of Philip IV in 1285, France was the most powerful feudal kingdom in Europe and the French tradition of royal absolutism was well established.

Figure 9.4 *These Men Wonder at the Star. Harold.* Panel from the Bayeux Tapestry. Third quarter of the eleventh century. Wool embroidery on linen, ht. 20". Bayeux, France. *Today housed in the cathedral of Bayeux, this famous embroidery provides an important historic record of the events leading up to the Battle of Hastings and presents a justification for the Norman conquest of England. Harold is cast as a villain who breaks his oath of allegiance to William and loses the English crown as a result of this treachery.*

Halley's comet, interpreted as an evil omen, appeared over England in February 1066. The comet is shown in the center of the upper border. On the left, men point to the comet, and on the right Harold also seems upset by the comet. Beneath Harold and his adviser are outlines of boats, implying a possible invasion by the Normans.

The English Monarchy The English monarchs also amassed power at the expense of the feudal landowners, but the English rulers never controlled their kingdom to the same degree as the Capetians. Moreover, because some English kings made grievous mistakes, England's feudal barons won pivotal battles against the monarchy. In addition, judicial reforms and advisory councils tended to limit, not to expand, the English kings' power.

Three major events determined English history during the High Middle Ages. The first was the Norman invasion of England. For five centuries, England had been ruled by an Anglo-Saxon monarchy, and when the king died in 1066 without a clear successor, Duke William, the ruler of the duchy of Normandy in northern France, invaded England to claim the throne. At the Battle of Hastings, in 1066, William conquered the Anglo-Saxon contender, Harold, and became king of England (Figure 9.4). For the rest of the High Middle Ages, England was ruled by Norman kings and their French (Angevin) successors, and conquerors and conquered were blended into one nation and one culture.

The second major event occurred in 1215 when the English feudal barons forced King John (r. 1199–1216) to sign the Magna Carta ("great charter"), a document that limited royal authority and gave the barons certain financial and governmental controls over the crown. In the long run, the Magna Carta was also a victory for all freemen because it gave them certain judicial rights, such as trial by jury. The third event was the creation of Parliament, which occurred during the reign of Henry III (r. 1216–1272). Faced with renewed

hostility from his English barons, Henry agreed to convene the ancient but little-used Great Council, comprising representatives from every county and town. This body became Parliament (from the French word *parler*, "to talk") and began to advise the king. Initially, Parliament was part of the royal government, but in time it represented the people against the crown, as England moved further toward a limited feudal monarchy.

The Holy Roman Empire Whereas France and England grew into unified feudal monarchies, the Holy Roman Empire, which began as the Saxon dynasty of Otto I in the late tenth century, failed to achieve a centralized state. From the early eleventh to the early twelfth century, the empire prospered and trade expanded, but a conflict with the papacy arose that would undermine the empire. It concerned the European-wide practice of lay investiture—the appointment of priests, bishops, and archbishops by local lords and nobles, often for money. Such appointments allowed the secular rulers some control over the wealth and influence of the church within their own territories. The central issue in the long and complicated conflict was whether the bishops and archbishops were the servants of the pope or of the secular rulers.

The issue of lay investiture was settled by the Concordat of Worms in 1122, which allowed the pope to confer spiritual authority on the clergy and the emperor to invest them with land and secular authority. But the rivalry between the Holy Roman rulers and the popes would not die. Under the Hohenstaufen dynasty, Frederick Barbarossa (r. 1152–1190) and Frederick II

Figure 9.5 Pope Urban II Consecrates the Great Abbey Church of Cluny (III). Book of Offices. Late twelfth century. Bibliothèque Nationale, Paris. *In this small manuscript painting, Pope Urban II (r. 1088–1099) consecrates the third version of the Great Abbey Church at Cluny. In the consecration service, the church is transformed into sacred ground and thus dedicated to the service of God. Framed by architectural features suggestive of the church's interior, the pope (the large standing figure on the left) offers a papal blessing before the high altar (under the domed center section). The artist has skillfully suggested a crowded church of worshipers, including Cluniac monks and nuns and various church officials. Pope Urban II, a member of the Cluniac order, preached the First Crusade in 1095.*

(r. 1212–1250) temporarily created an empire in central Europe, which included Italy. Their successors failed to maintain this empire, and the popes resumed their sway over Italian politics. The Holy Roman emperors ceased playing a major role in European affairs until after the coming of the Hapsburg line in 1273.

The Papal Monarchy   The papacy during the High Middle Ages closely resembled the feudal monarchies in Europe, except that it was guided by the ideal of Christendom—a universal state ruled by the popes under God's law. The church's most powerful claim to authority was that only through the clergy—those trained and ordained to administer the sacraments—could a Christian hope to gain everlasting life. The church defined society's moral standards at the same time that it participated in the politics of the period.

The key to the church's power was a reform movement that originated in the Benedictine monastery at Cluny, France, and swept through Europe in the 900s. Before this movement, the church had been riddled with scandal and corruption, and many clergy were poorly trained and lived less than exemplary lives. Because of lay investiture, bishops often acted as vassals of feudal lords rather than as agents of the church. The buying and selling of church offices, a practice known as simony, meant that positions often went to the highest bidder. Worst of all, many clergymen expressed blatant disregard for the sacraments.

The monks at Cluny, however, were free of feudal obligations and loyal only to the pope (Figure 9.5). Little by little, the Cluniacs impressed Europe with their spirituality, and as they established new monasteries and reformed others, the church began to revive, to eliminate corrupt practices, and to reimpose celibacy on the clergy. In 1059, the College of Cardinals was founded to elect the popes, thus freeing the papacy from German and Italian politics. By the late eleventh century, the political power of the reformed popes rivaled that of the feudal monarchs.

Of the great medieval popes, the two most powerful were Gregory VII and Innocent III. Gregory VII (pope 1073–1085), brought to the papacy by the Cluniac revival, purified the wayward clergy, demanding full obedience to canon law. Innocent III (pope 1198–1216) was probably the most powerful pontiff in the history of the church. He excommunicated kings; intervened in the secular affairs of England, France, and the Holy Roman Empire; and advocated crusades against the Muslims abroad and the heretics at home. Motivated by the ideal of Christendom, he aimed to unite Europe under the papal banner.

By his extravagant claims, Pope Boniface VIII (pope 1294–1303) unwittingly undid the three centuries' work of his predecessors to build papal power (see Figure 9.5). In 1302, he issued the papal bull (from the Latin word *bolla*, "seal") known as *Unam sanctam*, a proclamation of papal superiority over all secular rulers. The French crown swiftly sent an army to arrest the pope, and an unnerved Boniface VIII had to flee and died soon thereafter. This episode precipitated a decline in the prestige of the papacy from which it did not fully recover until the sixteenth century.

MEDIEVAL CHRISTIANITY AND THE CHURCH

In addition to its political significance, the institution of the church had incalculable influence in the High Middle Ages, bringing Christian values to bear on virtually all of medieval life. The church owed its influence not only to the maneuverings of the popes but also to the tireless work of the clergy and the powerful effect of Christian beliefs.

By this time in its history, the church had evolved an elaborate organization to carry out its work. The pope, as the spiritual leader of Christianity, stood at the head of a strict hierarchy. Supporting him was the papal curia—a staff of administrators, financial experts, secretaries, clerics, and legal advisers. A system of ecclesiastical courts handled the church's judicial functions and interpreted canon law, the church's law code based on the Bible. These courts were technically restricted to cases involving clerical personnel, but in actuality their jurisdiction was broader because of the huge number of people enmeshed in the workings of the church. The church's judicial branch rivaled the feudal courts in jurisdiction, and canon law sometimes challenged the authority of feudal law.

Tithes, taxes, and special collections provided funds for the church's daily operations and its charitable obligations. The system was relatively efficient, and as long as the church spent the funds wisely, the populace kept up its generous contributions.

Christian Beliefs and Practices

A great part of the immense authority of the church sprang from the belief shared by the overwhelming majority of the medieval population that the church held the keys to the kingdom of heaven and provided the only way to salvation. By attempting to adhere to the Christian moral code and by participating in the rituals and ceremonies prescribed by the church and established by tradition, Christians hoped for redemption and eternal life after death.

These rituals and ceremonies were basically inseparable from the doctrines of the religion. They had been derived from the teachings of Jesus and Paul, clarified by the church Fathers, particularly Augustine, and further defined by medieval theologians. Finally, the Fourth Lateran Council of 1215, under Pope Innocent III, officially proclaimed the sacraments as the outward signs of God's grace and the only way to heaven.

As established by the council, the sacraments numbered seven: baptism, confirmation, the Eucharist (Holy Communion), penance, marriage, last rites, and ordination for the priesthood. Baptism, the Eucharist, and penance were deemed of primary importance. In baptism, the parents were assured that the infant had been rescued from original sin. In the Eucharist, the central part of the Mass, the church taught that a miracle occurred whereby the priest turned the bread and wine into the body and blood of Jesus. That the outer appearance of the bread and wine remained the same while their inner nature changed was explained by medieval philosophers in the doctrine of transubstantiation. For the uneducated congregation, however, the Mass and the miracle were simply another sign of the church's spiritual power.

Penance evolved into a rather complicated practice. First, sinners confessed their sins individually to a priest; the priest conveyed God's forgiveness for the mortal penalties of sin so that hell could be avoided; the priest then directed that an earthly punishment—the penance—be carried out in an effort to erase the effects of the sin. Depending on the severity of the sin, penance could range from a few prayers to a pilgrimage or a crusade. This sacrament was made even more complex by its association with purgatory.

With the groundwork laid by Augustine in the fifth century and Pope Gregory the Great in the sixth century, the doctrine of purgatory was given more explicit form by the papacy and scholastic thinkers of the High Middle Ages. Neither hell nor heaven, purgatory was a third place, where those who had died in a state of

ENCOUNTER

Pagan Vikings Versus Christian Europeans

The ethnic composition of Europe changed dramatically during the Middle Ages (500–1500), with the assimilation of numerous barbarian peoples. These included various Germanic tribes, such as Angles and Saxons (in England), Franks (in France), Alemanni (in Germany), Visigoths (in Spain), and Lombards and Ostrogoths (in Italy); several Slavic groups, including Poles, Czechs, Slovaks, and Wends or Sorbs (in central and eastern Europe); and Magyars (in Hungary). The Vikings, a Germanic people, are the classic example of a barbarian people who not only were forever changed by assimilation but also effected indelible changes on European civilization.

The Vikings, the last Germanic people to be assimilated into European life, began the Early Middle Ages as pagans, linked by trade with Christian Europe but otherwise isolated, living in Norway, Denmark, and Sweden. Starting about 789, that changed, as peaceful coexistence gave way to sometimes violent encounters with European neighbors. For more than three hundred years, the Vikings launched hit-and-run raids, pillaging monasteries, churches, and other unfortified sites along the coasts and rivers of Britain, Ireland, northern France, and occasionally Italy; conquering Normandy, Sicily, and large parts of Russia and Britain; trading with Constantinople and Baghdad; discovering and colonizing Iceland and Greenland; and being the first Europeans to set foot in North America, on the coast of Newfoundland. Any hope for a far-flung Viking culture ended in the tenth and eleventh centuries, mainly because the Vikings converted to Christianity and thus lost their distinctive Scandinavian identity. By 1100, the Viking Age was over; they were now Christian Europeans.

The word *Viking* originally meant only those Scandinavians who went *vikingr,* or plundering, and it probably originated in Britain, where the first raids began about 789. Today, it is applied to all Early Medieval Scandinavians, whether they went "plundering" or not. However, the Viking Age was more than a time for looting. It was a period of migration of peoples, propelled by varied motives, including overpopulation, worsening climate and food supply, infighting among rival chieftains in which the losers were driven overseas, and the search for lucrative trading opportunities.

The Vikings unquestionably altered Western culture. They established the first towns in Ireland, Russia, and Scandinavia and made Iceland part of Europe by opening it to settlement. In France, they hastened the breakup of the Carolingian Empire and deeply influenced the history of France, England, and Italy by founding the duchy of Normandy. They set up the first

Encounter figure 9.1   Viking Raid. Tombstone. Lindisfarne (Holy Island). Ninth century. *This tombstone vividly depicts a Viking raid, through simple forms and expressive gestures. The ferocity of the attack is manifest in the massed warriors, each with one leg bent at the knee to suggest movement and one arm brandishing a battle-axe. Found in the monastery of Lindisfarne, on the northeastern coast of England, this image probably depicts the actual sacking of this monastery in 793. The attack on Lindisfarne, a major monastic center, caused some to believe that God was using the Vikings to punish Christians for some terrible sin.*

state in Russia; the word *Russia* is derived from *Rus,* the name given Scandinavians by the Slavic majority. They contributed about six hundred loan-words to modern English, including "cast," "knife," "window," and "egg," as well as certain plural pronouns, such as "they," "them," and "their." The Vikings' greatest impact was probably on Britain, where their small states, though short-lived, destroyed old governing units and thus prepared the way for the founding of the unified kingdoms of England and Scotland.

Learning from the Encounter   **What** is the popular stereotype of a Viking? **Assess** the truth of the Viking stereotype. **What** reasons led the Vikings to leave their homeland? **What** prompted the end of Viking culture? **How** were the Vikings changed by the process of assimilation? **List** five significant changes to European culture as a result of the Vikings' raids. **What** lessons may be learned from the assimilation of the Vikings into Western culture? **Is** there any modern non-Western people related to the West in the manner of the Vikings to the Medieval West? **Explain.**

grace could avoid damnation by being purged, or purified, from all stain of sin. All souls in purgatory were ultimately destined for heaven; penance was a means of reducing time in purgatory. Thus the living could do penance on earth in hope of spending less time in purgatory.

Confession and penance became widespread practices of the eleventh-century church. By 1300 both were integral to Christian rituals and beliefs. In political terms, penance, along with the Mass, was an effective means for controlling the moral behavior of church members.

Religious Orders and Lay Piety

Crucial to the workings of the church were the clergy, who were the most visible signs of the church's presence in everyday life. The "secular" clergy (from *saeculum*, Latin for "world") moved freely in society, and the "regular" clergy lived apart from the world in monasteries under a special rule (*regula* in Latin). The monasteries served as refuges from the world, as schools, and as places of study where manuscripts could be copied and traditional learning maintained. They also gave rise to the reform movements that periodically cleansed the church of corruption.

As noted earlier, the Cluniac monks originated the reform movement that helped to establish the moral and political authority of the medieval church. Other waves of reform followed, the most important of which was represented by the founding of the Cistercian order in the twelfth century. Bernard of Clairvaux [klair-VOH] (1090–1153), a saint, a mystic, and one of the most forceful personalities of the period, personally founded over 160 Cistercian abbeys. Unlike the moderate Cluniacs, the Cistercians observed a severe rule, living usually in isolated monasteries where the brothers worked with the local peasants. The Cistercians also simplified their worship services, eliminating elaborate ceremonies.

For women, the religious impulse found an outlet in convents and nunneries. Here, women could devote themselves to Christ and follow ascetic lives filled with prayer, contemplation, and service. Convents had existed since the time of Charlemagne, although seldom with the large endowments monasteries enjoyed or with as much influence in local affairs.

Convent life nevertheless did nurture several gifted women who influenced this age, most notably Hildegard of Bingen (1098–1179), founder and abbess of the Benedictine house of Rupertsberg near Bingen (modern Germany). Her writing and preaching attracted scores of supporters in Germany, France, and Switzerland, including most of her male superiors. She was

Figure 9.6 Hildegard's Awakening: A Self-Portrait from *Scivias. Ca.* 1150. *Hildegard's description of the moment when she received the word of God is effectively captured in this illumination: a "burning light coming from heaven poured into my mind." The Holy Spirit inflames her mind as she etches the word of God on a tablet; Volmar, the priest of the abbey and her loyal secretary, gazes at the event. The simplistic sketch of the towers and building is typical of twelfth-century illuminated manuscripts.*

highly influential with major figures of the time, as evidenced by her correspondence with Eleanor of Aquitaine (1122–1204), the Holy Roman emperor Frederick Barbarossa, and various popes. Hildegard wrote in the medical arts, theology, and the history of science, but it was mainly through visionary tracts that she had the most impact on her contemporaries. Her first book, entitled *Scivias* (translated variously as *May You Know* or *Know the Ways of the Lord*), included descriptions of her visions, the texts of liturgical songs, and a sung morality play, *Ordo Virtutatum (The Company of the Virtues)*, the first of its kind. She also illuminated manuscripts (Figure 9.6) and composed sacred poetry, which has survived in monophonic musical settings and has found new audiences today. Hildegard was a bold talent and left a superb legacy,

Figure 9.7 ATTRIBUTED TO GIOTTO. *St. Francis of Assisi's Trial by Fire Before the Sultan.* Before 1300. Fresco. Basilica of St. Francis, Assisi, Upper Church, nave. *This painting, from a cycle of twenty-eight frescoes detailing the life and miracles of St. Francis of Assisi, shows the saint (center, with a halo around his head) preaching before the enthroned Sultan al-Malik Kamil (r. 1218–1238), the last of the Ayyubid dynasty (right). The setting is Egypt, the center of the sultan's holdings, which included Syria and Palestine. Trying to convert the sultan to Christianity, St. Francis, backed by a second Franciscan friar, challenges the sultan's Islamic clergy to join in a walk through the blazing fire on the bottom left, as a test of their respective religious faiths. The sultan gestures toward the fire with his right hand, as four Muslim clergy prepare to leave on the far left. This fresco, completed perhaps seventy years after the saint's death, was painted during a time when Franciscan missionaries were active in Egypt and other Middle Eastern lands.*

especially given the belief of the time that it was dangerous to teach a woman to read and write, because it could lead to independent-mindedness and thus upset the social order.

Another type of religious order appeared in the thirteenth century with the rise of two major mendicant, or begging, orders, the Franciscans and the Dominicans. These new churchmen, called **friars,** were originally dedicated to working among the urban poor, but by 1250 most of them were also priests and they dominated higher education. For example, Thomas Aquinas, the age's leading scholar, was a Dominican friar. Although both orders made important

contributions, the Franciscans had a greater impact on medieval society, largely because of the gentle nature of the order's sainted founder, Francis (1182–1226). Many people still find Francis's piety, selflessness, and legendary humility the personification of a sublime Christian (Figure 9.7).

As monastic reform slowed in the late twelfth century, a wave of lay piety swelled up from the lower ranks of society, triggered by a mixture of religious protest and social and economic causes. Typical of these unorthodox movements were the beguines, independent communities of laywomen dedicated to good works, poverty, chastity, and religious devotion. Unlike nuns, who isolated themselves from the world, the beguines had regular contact with society—caring for the sick at home and in hospitals, teaching in both girls' and boys' schools, and working in the textile industry. The beguines first established themselves in northern France and then, along with male lay brethren called beghards, spread to Germany and the Netherlands, usually in proximity to Dominican monasteries. These lay communities became centers of freethinking, as some members turned their intellectual gifts to spiritual matters. For example, Mechthild of Magdeburg (about 1207–about 1282) wrote *The Flowing Light of the Godhead,* a mystical account of her religious odyssey. The beguine and beghard communities also provided the audience for medieval Germany's finest devotional writer and a great mystic of the Christian tradition, Meister Eckhart (about 1260–1328), who composed tracts and sermons to guide these laypeople's religious piety into orthodox ways.

Despite a reputation for freethinking, the beguines and the beghards won approval from religious authorities, but other lay groups were condemned as heretics, probably because they failed to amass enough property to found permanent residences and, hence, appeared to the church to be uncontrollable. The most powerful of these heretical sects was the Albigensian, which was centered at Albi in southern France. The Albigensians were also known as the Cathari, from the Greek word for "pure." Their unorthodox beliefs were derived partly from Zoroastrianism, the source of their concept of a universal struggle between a good God and an evil deity, and partly from Manichaeism, the source of their notion that the flesh is evil. The Albigensians stressed that Jesus was divine and not human, that the wealth of the church was a sign of its depravity, and that the goal of Christian living was to achieve the status of Cathari, or perfection.

These unorthodox beliefs spread rapidly across much of southern France, permeating the church and the secular society. In 1214, Pope Innocent III called for the destruction of the hated beliefs. His message appealed to the feudal nobles who were greedy for the heretics' lands. The Albigensians were repressed with incredible ferocity and cruelty. Many Cathari were slaughtered and their property was confiscated; others were tried by the Inquisition (the church tribunal set up to root out heresy [see Chapter 10]) and burned at the stake. Such actions reflected the less benign face of the medieval church and its immense power.

The Crusades

A defining feature of the High Middle Ages was the crusading movement. To free the Holy Land, or Palestine, from the Muslims, whom Christians then regarded as unbelievers, the Christian church preached nine Crusades between 1095 and 1272, all of which failed in their goal. Attracted by a complex set of motives—Christian zeal, the papal promise that all sins would be pardoned, and the anticipation of wealth from plunder—kings, bishops, and nobles, along with peasants, priests, workers, and prostitutes, sewed a cross on their garments (Crusader, "wearer of the cross") and walked and sailed the long, arduous, and dangerous journey to the Holy Land. Crusader victories proved to be temporary, as in the brief capture of Jerusalem from 1099 to 1187. Otherwise, the many sieges, sackings of cities, and pitched battles that marked the Crusades heightened hatred between the two sides, which resulted in mutual atrocities (Figures 9.8 and 9.9). Still, the crusading movement led to economic, social, intellectual, and cultural interchanges, which made Europe less provincial and enhanced medieval thought and learning.

THE AGE OF SYNTHESIS: EQUILIBRIUM BETWEEN THE SPIRITUAL AND THE SECULAR

Between 1000 and 1300, Christian values permeated European cultural life. The Christian faith was a unifying agent that reconciled the opposing realms of the spiritual and the secular, the immaterial and the material—as symbolized in many cities and towns by the soaring spires of the local **cathedral** (Figure 9.10). Medieval culture drew from the arts and humanities of the Classical world, the heritage of the various European peoples, and, to a lesser extent, the traditions of Byzantium and Islam. Because of these diverse influences, the culture of the High Middle Ages was by no means uniform. What many writers, thinkers, and artists shared was a set of common concerns and interests, most notably the quest for forms that could transcend the contradictions of the age.

Figure 9.8 and Figure 9.9   (top) Crusaders Attacking a Muslim Fortress. Twelfth century. Bibliothèque Nationale, Paris. Copyright The Bridgeman Art Library. (bottom) Muslims Burning Crusaders at the Stake. Twelfth century. Copyright Erich Lessing/Art Resource, N.Y. Twelfth century. *In the painting on the top, Crusaders, dressed in chain mail, catapult severed enemy heads into a Muslim fortress. Note the identifying cross on the banner at the top. In the painting on the bottom, Muslim warriors burn Christian captives at the stake. Mutual atrocities, such as depicted in these manuscript paintings, fueled horror stories of the Crusades and helped engender a legacy of mistrust that still complicates Western and Muslim relations today.*

A historical watershed occurred in the mid–twelfth century that was reflected in architecture, sculpture, music, learning, and literature. Before 1150, Western culture tended to express the rugged virtues of the feudal castle and the cloistered monastery; the militant warrior and the ascetic monk were the social ideals; and women were treated as chattel, or property. After

260

SLICE OF LIFE
When Love Knows No Boundaries

HELOISE
The Abbess of Le Paraclete, Founded by Abelard

The letters of Abelard, a monk, and his student Heloise (about 1101–1164), who later became a nun, are still read because they offer glimpses into the hearts of lovers whose devotion transcends any historical period or social context. In this letter, Heloise writes to Abelard after they have been forced to separate. His scholarly reputation has been tainted, and, for his transgression, Abelard has been castrated by men in the hire of Fulbert, Heloise's uncle and protector.

You know, beloved, as the whole world knows, how much I have lost in you, how at one wretched stroke of fortune that supreme act of flagrant treachery robbed me of my very self in robbing me of you; and how my sorrow for my loss is nothing compared with what I feel for the manner in which I lost you. Surely the greater the cause for grief the greater the need for the help of consolation, and this no one can bring but you; you are the sole cause of my sorrow, and you alone can grant me the grace of consolation. . . . God knows I never sought anything in you except yourself; I wanted simply you, nothing of yours. I looked for no marriage-bond, no marriage portion, and it was not my own pleasures and wishes I sought to gratify, as you well know, but yours. The name of wife may seem more sacred or more binding, but sweeter for me will always be the word mistress, or, if you will permit me, that of concubine or whore. I believed that the more I humbled myself on your account, the more gratitude I would win from you, and also the less damage I should do to the brightness of your reputation.

Interpreting This Slice of Life **What** are the relationships among Abelard, Heloise, and Fulbert? **What** is the treachery to which Heloise refers in her letter? **In what ways** does Heloise think Abelard can console her? **How** does Heloise describe her love and relationship to Abelard? **Why** do we still read their correspondence and love letters? **Does** this letter have a modern tone and message? **Why or why not?**

1150, the urban values of the new towns became paramount, along with a more courtly attitude toward women. The church indirectly encouraged this trend with the rise of the cult of the Virgin Mary; Mary's status became so great that she was revered almost as much as Christ.

Theology and Learning

From about 1000 onward, scholars revived the school system that had flourished briefly under Charlemagne in the Early Middle Ages. These monastic schools—along with many new cathedral schools—appealed to

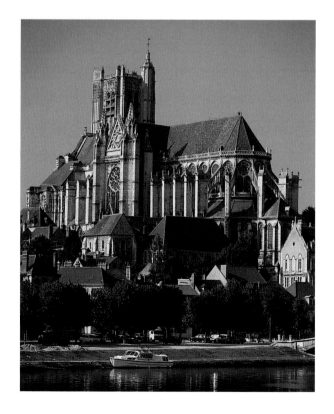

Figure 9.10 Auxerre Cathedral. Begun ca. 1225. Auxerre, France. *Looming over the town and dominating the countryside for miles around, the Gothic cathedral symbolized the preeminent role of the Christian church in medieval life. No other building could soar past its spires, either literally or figuratively. People worshiped inside it, built their houses right up to its walls, and conducted their business affairs within the shadows of its towers. Thus, the cathedral also symbolized the integration of the secular and the sacred in medieval life.*

an age that was hungry for learning and set Europe's intellectual tone until about 1200. During these two centuries, the only serious rival to the schools was a handful of independent scholars who drew crowds of students to their lectures in Paris and elsewhere. By 1200 new educational institutions had arisen—the universities—that soon surpassed the monastic and cathedral schools and forced the independent masters out of business. Since then, universities have dominated intellectual life in the West.

Cathedral Schools and the Development of Scholasticism   During the twelfth century, the new cathedral schools reached the height of their power, as Chartres and Paris led the way. Schooling, with rare exceptions, was the exclusive province of men who were preparing for careers in either the church or the dynastic states. For the next three hundred years, the curriculum stayed the same as that codified by Boethius in the sixth century: the trivium (grammar, logic, and rhetoric) and the quadrivium (arithmetic, astronomy, geometry, and music)—the seven liberal arts—which in turn were based on the works of the Classical authors and the early church Fathers. Teachers and pupils communicated in Latin, and students read the Christian works in the original Latin. In contrast, Classical writings were known only from misleading Latin summaries until they were replaced in the twelfth century with more accurate Latin versions made from Arabic translations (see Chapter 8).

The introduction of the new versions of the Classical texts, notably those of Aristotle, caused a revolution in education and elevated the Greek thinker to the status of an authority whose word could not be questioned. By 1300, Aristotle's writings virtually monopolized the curriculum at every educational level. The revival of Aristotle contributed to the development of **scholasticism.** In general, the aim of a scholastic thinker was to bring Aristotle's thought into harmony with the Christian faith. Scholasticism was also a system of reasoning that had been perfected in oral debates in the schools. In the scholastic method, a scholar divided each problem into three parts. First, a question was set forth for intellectual analysis; next, a discussion thoroughly summarized the arguments for and against the question, usually citing the Bible, the church Fathers, Aristotle, and other ancient authors; finally, a solution was offered, reinforced with support from religious and secular sources.

The scholastic method was not meant to discover new knowledge; rather, it used deductive logic to clarify existing issues and to explore the intellectual ramifications of a topic. This method, which tended to uphold rather than to question religious beliefs, was

discarded in favor of an inductive, mathematically based style of reasoning in the seventeenth century.

Peter Abelard   The primacy of the cathedral schools of Chartres and Paris in the twelfth century was challenged by a few independent masters who pitted their intellects against the authority of the faculty of these institutions. Of this daring breed of scholars, Peter Abelard [AB-uh-lard] (in French, Pierre Abélard) (1079–1142) was the most brilliant and controversial. More important, he was one of the first medieval thinkers to proclaim a clear distinction between reason and faith. Intellectually curious and reveling in provocative disputes, Abelard attended the lectures of William of Champeaux [shahm-POH] (about 1070–1121), the most revered teacher in the cathedral school of Paris. Dissatisfied with what he was hearing, Abelard began his own lecture series. He quickly became the sensation of Paris and his words found eager listeners. A master logician, Abelard demolished William's arguments and drove his rival into a monastery.

What divided Abelard and William of Champeaux was the problem of universals, the supreme intellectual issue between 1050 and 1150. This controversy revolved around the question of whether or not universals, or general concepts, such as "human being" and "church," truly exist. At stake in this dispute between the two schools of thought, known as **Realism and Nominalism,** were basic Christian ideas, such as whether Jesus' sacrifice had removed the stain of original sin from each individual. The Realists, following Plato, reasoned that universals do exist independently of physical objects and the human mind. Hence, "humanity," for example, is constantly present in every individual. In opposition, the Nominalists denied the existence of universals and claimed that only particular objects and events are real. Hence, "church" and "human being" exist only in particular instances.

In these debates, Abelard showed that William of Champeaux's extreme Realism denied human individuality and was thus inconsistent with church teachings. For his part, Abelard taught a moderate Realism that held that the universals existed, but only as mental words, and hence could be used as an intellectual convenience. Later in the century, when new translations of Aristotle became available, thinkers discovered that Abelard and the Greek genius agreed about universals, a discovery that further enhanced Abelard's fame. In the next century, Abelard's moderate Realism was adopted by Thomas Aquinas, the greatest mind of the High Middle Ages.

The Rise of the Universities   After 1100 a period of cultural ferment erupted that brought forth some of the finest achievements of medieval times, including the founding of the universities. By 1200 conditions were ripe for the rise of universities at Bologna, Paris, and Oxford, the first Western schools of higher education since the sixth century. Unlike the ancient universities in Athens and Alexandria, these medieval institutions were organized into self-governing corporations with charters. A century later, similar centers of learning were springing up elsewhere in Italy, France, and England, as well as in Spain, Portugal, and Germany. The University of Paris was the most celebrated institution of advanced learning during the High Middle Ages. Divided into faculties by specialization, it awarded degrees in civil law and canon law, medicine, theology, and the liberal arts. The liberal arts degree was basically devoted to mastering the new translations of Aristotle. Other universities taught a similar curriculum, but their faculties lacked the international renown of the Parisian professors.

Intellectual Controversy and Thomas Aquinas
More and more of Aristotle's works became available in the late twelfth and early thirteenth centuries. Between 1150 and 1200, a few hardy Christian scholars traveled to remote centers of learning, such as Muslim Sicily and Toledo, Spain, to meet Islamic and Jewish scholars and study Aristotle's writings. There they learned Arabic and translated the Greek and Arabic philosophical and scientific works into Latin, the form in which they entered the mainstream of European medieval thought.

At the University of Paris, the introduction of these improved and more complete versions divided the intellectual community. On one side was the theological faculty, who welcomed the Arabic writings but wanted to reconcile them to Christian thinking. Arrayed against them were the members of the arts faculty, who advocated that reason be fully divorced from faith or, in other words, that philosophy be separated from theology. The leaders of the arts faculty were called Latin Averroists because they claimed inspiration from the Arabic philosopher Ibn Rushd [IB-en RUSHT], known in the West as Averroës [uh-VER-uh-weez] (see Chapter 8).

Faced with the skeptical Latin Averroists, the Parisian theologians devised two ways to relate the new learning to orthodox beliefs. The more traditional view was set forth by Bonaventure [bahn-uh-VEN-chur] (1221–1274), who was later made a saint. Denying that knowledge was possible apart from God's grace, Bonaventure, following Augustine's mode of reasoning, argued that truth had to begin in the supernatural world and thus could not arise in the senses, as Aristotle had argued. A new and brilliant theological view, and the one that carried the day, was set forth

by Thomas Aquinas [uh-KWI-nus] (1226–1274), a Dominican friar who taught at Paris from 1252 to 1259 and again from 1269 to 1272. Within a generation of his death, he was made a saint, and six hundred years later, in 1874, the papacy declared his thought the official basis of Roman Catholic beliefs. Avoiding the pure rationalism of the Latin Averroists and the timidity of Bonaventure, Thomas Aquinas steered a middle path, or *via media*, which gave Aristotle a central role in his theology while honoring traditional Christian beliefs. Known as Thomism, this theological system in its complex design and sheer elegance remains one of the outstanding achievements of the High Middle Ages.

Of Thomas Aquinas's two monumental *Summas*—comprehensive summaries of Christian thought—the *Summa Theologica* is his masterpiece. In this work, he showed that God had given human beings two divine paths to truth: reason and faith. Following Aristotle, he made the senses the only source for human knowledge—a bold step that sharpened the difference between reason and faith. At the same time, Thomism escaped the strict rationalism of the Latin Averroists by denying that philosophy, or reason, could answer all theological questions. Aquinas claimed that reason based on sensory knowledge could prove certain truths, such as the notions that God exists and that the soul exists, but that reason had limits and that faith was necessary for those truths that were beyond sensory proof, such as the beliefs in the soul's immortality and the holy Trinity.

Thomas Aquinas's contributions to medieval thought extended beyond theology into political and economic matters. He saw the secular state as a natural and necessary support to human life. For Aquinas, politics had an ethical root, and this allowed him to write about everyday life in his *Summas*. For example, he reasoned that church law should be used to regulate economic behavior, putting controls on usury (the practice of charging exorbitant interest) and setting a just price for consumer goods.

Science and Medicine

Medieval science, like much of medieval learning, inherited Classical works and interpreted them within the framework of Christian theology. As noted above, by 1200, many Latin translations of Arabic versions of Greek scientific and philosophical works, as well as original writings by Muslim scientists and thinkers, were available in the West. Their arrival coincided with the birth of the universities. The spread of these writings encouraged scientific-minded scholars to explore the natural world. Although their findings were influenced by and subject to church doctrine and tradition, occasionally conflicts and differences occurred.

Science   Thomas Aquinas, while reconciling Aristotle's writings with Christian thought, was led to interpret the Greek thinker's scientific works, Muslim commentaries on these works, and original Muslim studies of the natural world. For Aquinas, the study of nature was not an end in itself but a means to understand God and his creation. Thus, any question about the natural world, such as motion, light, cosmology, or matter, would include Aristotle's and other thinkers' explanations, but the reason to explore these topics was to discover God's purposes, such as creating the universe (cosmology) or animals (matter). Usually the pursuits of medieval science were in direct relationship to their theological importance, such as studying light in order to account for a particular characteristic of God ("God is Light"). Medieval science played a major role in making Thomism the foundation of the age of synthesis, but eventually some medieval thinkers, whose works can be seen as forerunners to modern science, began to employ reason in ways that would ultimately undermine the integration of science, philosophy, and theology (see Chapter 10).

While medieval science never strayed far from Thomism, Aquinas and other thinkers held differing views on a number of subjects. Yet they all shared a confidence in human reason and its ability to comprehend the world—two traits of modern science. Even though the role of reason was carefully circumscribed within the context of Christian thought and often had to give way to revelation, a genuine and lasting rationalist tradition persisted throughout this period—one that originated in ancient Greece and passed through medieval Islam, then would be transmitted into Renaissance thought, and finally would help bring about the Scientific Revolution, which would inaugurate modern times.

Medicine   Medieval medicine also inherited beliefs and practices from the past while making significant advances. This blend of old—conjuring up spirits and casting spells—and new—improved medical schools—may seem primitive and "unscientific" by today's standards, but the preservation of ancient medical texts and the teaching of these works in the newly founded universities and hospitals paved the way for modern medicine.

Included in the vast number of Greek and Roman texts now made available to the learned were the writings of Hippocrates and Galen (see Chapters 3 and 5). Their works, along with *The Canon of Medicine,* by Avicenna, the Muslim scholar (see Chapter 8), became the basis of the curricula in the new medical schools. The

first prestigious medical schools were in Salerno, Italy, dating from the ninth century, and Montpellier, France, founded in about 1200; they were eclipsed in the Late Middle Ages by the new medical schools established by the universities in Paris and Bologna, Italy.

In these schools, aspiring doctors read medical works, attended lectures by scholars and practicing physicians, dissected human bodies (after the mid–thirteenth century), and learned to identify and treat certain disorders and diseases. Students were taught that the body is composed of four humors—black bile, phlegm, blood, and yellow bile—a belief of the ancient Greeks. Patients who suffered from certain maladies would be treated to correct the imbalance of Humors, such as by means of herbs, diet, or bleeding. Of the many teachers in these schools, perhaps the most influential was William of Saliceto [sah-le-CHAY-toe] (1210–1277), an Italian who taught at the University of Bologna and, later, was city physician (appointed medical officer) in Verona, Italy. In his book, *Cyrurgia,* or *Surgery,* the most advanced study on this subject in his day, he discussed surgical anatomy and advocated a union between medicine and surgery—a view that ran contrary to the prevailing medical wisdom that relegated surgery to the status of a craft.

That William of Saliceto became the city physician in Verona reflects the role played by new cities in attracting trained physicians. Most physicians attended wealthy urban clients who could afford the best of medical care. The physicians formed city guilds to set standards and regulate the profession; many became rich. The new cities also built the first hospitals in the West, often founded by religious orders or merchant or trade guilds. These hospitals were one of the few places women could be involved in medicine as nurses, since they were barred from medical school. Poorer city dwellers relied on untrained doctors or barbers who performed simple operations, while only a few of the impoverished were fortunate enough to be admitted to the hospitals as charity cases. Apothecaries sold drugs that were usually herbal or derived from animals or from minerals believed to possess healing powers; they also offered their own medical advice.

Outside urban centers, the peasants on manors and the village dwellers—who constituted most of the populace—were left to rely on local folklore, with its chants, incantations and rituals, prayers to local or popular saints, herbal potions, and untrained doctors or faith healers for medical care. If a nearby monastery had a hospital with spare rooms, it could accept the sick, but treatment in rural areas seldom equaled that found in the cities and larger towns. Thus, most people did not benefit from medical advances made during this period.

Literature

Beyond the rarefied atmosphere of scholastic thought, writing was finding its own way. The literature of the High Middle Ages falls naturally into two chronological parts, with the dividing line at about 1150. The first half, which coincides with Romanesque art, perpetuates the feudal and monastic values of the Early Middle Ages. The second half, which parallels the Gothic style, introduces urban and courtly themes while moving away from the world of the monasteries.

Monastic and Feudal Writing   Between 1000 and 1150, most authors were monks, writing in Latin and imitating Late Roman literary models such as hymns, sermons, lives of the saints, and historical chronicles. Perhaps most distinctive was the Latin lyric poetry composed during this time, which has been called the best literary work of the Latin-speaking Middle Ages. These poems were rich in metric subtleties, extremely learned in content, and filled with Classical and Christian allusions. Some of the poets have been identified as **goliards,** or roaming scholars, but most were probably clerics. Addressing an audience of church intellectuals, these poets often wrote on religious and moral topics. They also wrote lighthearted love poems, however, which appear to have had a wider audience and whose themes certainly appealed to more secular interests. Even though the love poems sang of carnal pleasure, these verses were not personal, nor were the poets' erotic yearnings directed toward real women.

While the monks sang of love in Latin, lay poets at the feudal courts of northern France were developing a new literary genre, the *chanson de geste,* or song of brave deeds. Written in the **vernacular,** or popular, spoken language, the *chansons de geste* chiefly honored the heroic adventures of warriors who had lived in France under Charlemagne and his heirs. These medieval epics often memorialized a minor battle or, more rarely, even a defeat. The epics were based on Christian values, but supernatural and magical elements were commonly a part of their plots. Of the many *chansons de geste,* the masterpiece is the *Song of Roland,* which became the standard for the genre (Figure 9.11).

Much of the *Song of Roland* was passed down orally for three hundred years, and it did not reach its final written form until about 1100. The narrative claims to be based on a historical event, telling of the destruction of a troop of Frankish warriors led by Count

Figure 9.11   Charlemagne Panels. Ca. 1220–1225. Stained-glass window, Chartres cathedral. Chartres, France. *The Song of Roland was so well known and well loved that scenes from the poem were depicted in the stained-glass windows of Chartres cathedral, constructed in the thirteenth century. Even though the Charlemagne panels were inspired by a secular poem, they were situated in the ambulatory behind the main altar, one of the cathedral's most sacred areas. In one scene, Charlemagne is shown arriving too late to save Roland's life. Other panels depict him donating a church and traveling to Constantinople.*

Roland, one of Charlemagne's vassals, and of Charlemagne's revenge for this massacre. Superimposed on this supposedly Carolingian tale are the later values of the High Middle Ages, such as chivalry, militant Christianity, and primitive nationalism. For example, Roland and his men obey the chivalric code, showing devotion to their ruler, to God, and to their personal honor—an ideal unknown in Charlemagne's day. Likewise, the religious zeal of Charlemagne's army against the Spanish Muslims probably derived from the First Crusade in 1095; indeed, modern scholars have shown that Charlemagne's actual enemies in Spain were Christians. Finally, this poem portrayed the Franks as ready to die for "sweet France," a sentiment that would have been incomprehensible to Charlemagne but that was encouraged by the twelfth-century French kings who used the popular *Song of Roland* to further their political ambitions.

Vernacular and Courtly Writing   Between 1150 and 1300, Latin continued to be the dominant language in the universities, but elsewhere lay writers, composing in the vernacular, were beginning to win new audiences and to develop new genres of **Vernacular Literature.**

For example, inspired by Latin lyric verse, and perhaps the love poetry of Islamic Spain (see Chapter 8), vernacular lyric poetry began to appear in the eleventh century in the Provençal tongue of southern France. This vernacular poetry reached its zenith in the next two centuries. Its supreme expression was the **canzone,** or love poem, the ancestor of all later Western love poetry. At the educated feudal courts of southern France, professional **minstrels,** or entertainers, sang the songs before the assembled court; the poems' composers—called **troubadors**—were often local nobles. Addressed to court ladies whose identities were thinly disguised in the poem, these troubador songs made devotion to a highborn woman the passionate ideal of the chivalrous knight. In the mature Provençal lyrics, adulterous passion was the central theme, and women were idolized and made the masters over men. Where previously adoration had been reserved for God, the troubadour lyrics now celebrated the worship of women.

As the influence of Provençal poetry spread, the status of women in Western literature was revolutionized, a development paralleled in the church, where the cult of the Virgin Mary was beginning to flourish. However, most real-life medieval women were unaffected by these literary and religious changes; their happiness depended on submitting to the limited roles that the masculine society allowed them to fill. After 1400, though, these cultural changes encouraged upper-class women to play a more prominent role in society, as hostesses and as arbiters of social decorum.

After 1150 courtly **romances** quickly replaced the feudal *chansons de geste* in popularity. The romances were long narratives of the chivalric and sentimental adventures of knights and ladies. The name *romance* arose from the mistaken belief that the medieval authors were imitating a Roman literary form. Their subjects derived from stories of ancient Troy and Celtic legends from the British Isles, the most enduring of which proved to be the Celtic stories of King Arthur and his knights of the Round Table.

The first poet to make Arthur and his court his subject was Chrétien de Troyes [KRAY-tyan duh TRWAH], whose versions set the standard for later romances. Chrétien (about 1148–about 1190) wrote his romances for the feudal courts of northern France. His treatment of the adulterous love of the knight Lancelot and Arthur's queen, Guinevere, is characteristic of the way romances combined aristocratic, courtly, and religious themes. In this version, Lancelot rescues Queen Guinevere after experiencing many adventures and personal humiliations for her sake; this humbling of Lancelot is necessary to teach him to love Guinevere with unquestioning obedience.

A curiosity for modern readers is that Chrétien identifies Lancelot with Christ, so that many episodes echo scenes of Jesus' suffering and death. Although the work avoids sacrilege, the net effect is unsettling in its mixing of the sacred with the profane. Chrétien describes Lancelot and Guinevere's passion without judging their behavior. Such moral neutrality was unacceptable to other Christian writers, who believed adultery to be a deadly sin. In an English prose version of this tale—Thomas Malory's *Le Morte d'Arthur*, published in 1485—the lovers are blamed for the collapse of Arthur's court. Perhaps because today's world tends to agree with Malory's more judgmental view, his story of Lancelot is the one better known now.

Another literary genre that flourished simultaneously with the romance was the **lay** (French, *lai*), a short lyric or narrative poem meant to be sung to the accompaniment of an instrument such as a harp. The oldest lays are the twelve surviving by Marie de France (fl. about 1170), a poet from Brittany who lived most of her life in England. Based on Celtic legends, including those of Lancelot, Marie de France's lays were stories of courtly love, often adulterous (for instance, a young wife kept under close watch by a jealous old husband), usually faced with conflict, always with a moral lesson. Writing in Old French, an early form of the French language, de France addressed the French-speaking nobility of post–Norman Conquest England, an audience that may have included King Henry II and Queen Eleanor of Aquitaine. De France's lays, along with her fables and other works, were part of the outpouring of writing in the twelfth century that made Old French literature the most influential in Europe until the rise of Italian literature in the age of Dante Alighieri.

Dante   Vernacular writing appeared late in Italy; not until the thirteenth century did Italian poetry begin to emerge. But, despite its later start, Italy had brought forth by 1300 the greatest literary figure of the High Middle Ages, Dante Alighieri [DAHN-tay ahl-egg-YEH-ree] (1265–1321). A native of Florence, in the province of Tuscany, Dante was the first of a proud tradition that soon made the Tuscan dialect the standard literary speech of Italy.

Born into a minor aristocratic family, Dante was given an excellent education with a thorough grounding in both Greco-Roman and Christian classics. Attracted to the values of ancient Rome, he combined a career in public office with the life of an intellectual—a tradition of civic duty inherited from the ancient Roman republic. When Dante's political allies fell from office in

1301, he was exiled from Florence for the rest of his life. During these years, poor and wandering about Italy, he composed the *Commedia,* or *Comedy,* which stands as the culmination of the literature of the Middle Ages. The *Comedy's* sublime qualities were immediately recognized, and soon its admirers attached the epithet "divine" to Dante's masterpiece.

Divided into three book-length parts, the *Divine Comedy* narrates Dante's fictional travels through three realms of the Christian afterlife. Led first by the ghost of Vergil, the ancient Roman poet, Dante descends into hell, where he hears from the damned the nature of their various crimes against God and the moral law. Vergil next leads Dante into purgatory, where the lesser sinners expiate their guilt while awaiting the joys of heaven. At a fixed spot in purgatory, Vergil is forced to relinquish his role to Beatrice, a young Florentine woman and Dante's symbol of the eternal female. With Beatrice's guidance, Dante enters paradise and even has a vision of the almighty God.

The majestic complexity of Dante's monumental poem, however, can scarcely be conveyed by this simple synopsis. Written as an allegory, the *Divine Comedy* was meant to be understood on several levels. Read literally, the poem bears witness to the author's personal fears as a moral sinner yet affirms his hope for eternal salvation. Read allegorically, the poem represents a comprehensive synthesis of the opposing tendencies that characterized medieval culture, such as balancing the Classical with the Christian, Aristotle with Aquinas, the ancient with the new, the proud with the humble, the profane with the sacred, and the secular with the spiritual.

Of the great cultural symbols that abound in the *Divine Comedy,* the richest in meaning are the central figures of Vergil and Beatrice, who represent human reason and divine revelation, respectively. In the poem, Vergil is made inferior to Beatrice, thus revealing Dante's acceptance of a basic idea of Thomas Aquinas—reason can lead only to awareness of sin; revelation is necessary to reach God's ultimate truth. Besides this fundamental Christian belief, the two figures convey other meanings. Vergil stands for Classical civilization and the secular literary life; Beatrice (Italian for "blessing") symbolizes spiritualized love and Christianized culture. By turning Beatrice into an image of God's grace, Dante revealed that the High Middle Ages were open to new symbols of Christian truth. (By the time of the Catholic Counter-Reformation in the sixteenth century, however, Dante's image was considered blasphemous and was censured by religious critics.)

Dante's spiritual odyssey is set during the season of Easter. The poet's journey through hell coincides with Jesus' descent into hell on Good Friday, and Dante's ascent up the Mount of Purgatory happens at Easter dawn—the time of Jesus' resurrection; the visit to heaven occupies the rest of Easter week. Thus, Dante's allegory has the religious aim of forcing his readers to meditate on the fate of their own immortal souls.

Dante's vision of the afterlife underscored his belief that humans have free will. Predestination had no place in his system, as his picture of hell shows. With one exception, all of the damned earned their fate by their deeds on earth. Excepted were the people consigned to Limbo—the pious pagans who lived before Jesus and thus were denied his message of hope. Moreover, those in Limbo, such as Aristotle and Plato, were not subjected to any punishment other than being removed from God's presence.

The intricate structure of Dante's massive poem owes much to numerology, a pseudoscience of numbers that absorbed the medieval mind. The numbers three and nine, for example, occur prominently in the *Divine Comedy.* Three is a common symbol of the Christian Trinity (the union of the Father, the Son, and the Holy Ghost in one God), and the poem is written in a three-line verse form called *terza rima* (an interlocking rhyme scheme in three-line stanzas, as *aba, bcb, cdc, ded,* and so on, ending in a rhyming couplet), which was Dante's invention. The other number, nine, symbolizes the Trinity squared. More important, Dante identified the number nine with the dead Beatrice, whose soul lived on in the ninth heaven, the one nearest to God. He also divides hell, purgatory, and paradise into nine sections each.

Despite its allegorical and theological features, the *Divine Comedy* is a deeply personal poem. Dante rewards and punishes his Florentine friends and foes by the location that he assigns each in the afterlife. He also reveals his private feelings as he enters into discussions with various saints and sinners along the way. Beyond his desire for salvation, his most cherished idea is to bring about a harmony between the church and the secular state on earth.

Architecture and Art

Just as scholars and writers devoted their efforts to exploring religious concerns and Christian values, artists, artisans, and architects channeled their talents into glorifying the Christian house of worship. Because the dominating physical presence of the church made it a ubiquitous symbol in both the countryside and the towns, architecture ranked higher than the other arts in medieval life. Indeed, the arts lacked an independent status, for they were regarded as mere auxiliary sources of church decoration—wall paintings, statues, and **stained-glass** windows, most of which portrayed saints and biblical heroes (Figure

Figure 9.12 Scenes from the Life of Christ. Detail. Ca. 1150–1170. Stained-glass windows, each panel: 40⅙" wide × 41⅓" high. West facade. Chartres cathedral. *The stained-glass windows of Chartres cathedral are renowned as the most beautiful examples of this craft to survive from the Gothic period. Of Chartres's windows, those in the west facade have been much praised for the brilliant effects created by their jewel tones of red, blue, and gold, as well as white, with small areas of green and lemon yellow. Taken from the central window of the west facade, this detail shows eighteen of its twenty-four panels, treating the life of Christ. Visible in the detail are panels depicting the annunciation (bottom left row), the visit of the three wise men (left and right, third row from bottom), and the flight into Egypt (left and right, sixth row from bottom). In the design, square panels alternate with roundel forms to frame each scene; red is the ground color for the squares and blue for the roundels. The windows can be awe-inspiring, as in the reaction of the scholar Henry Adams, who described the cathedral's interior as a "delirium of coloured light."*

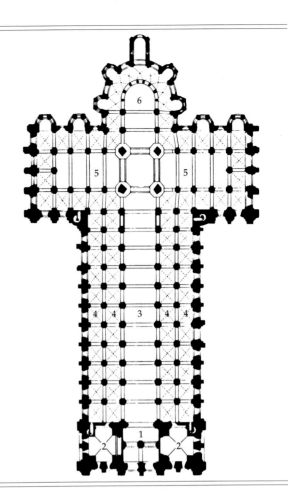

Figure 9.13 Floor Plan of a Typical Romanesque Church. *This floor plan identifies the characteristic features of a Romanesque church with its cruciform floor plan: (1) narthex, (2) towers, (3) nave, (4) side aisles, (5) transept, and (6) apse.*

9.12). In this respect, these art forms conformed to the church's teaching that the purpose of art was to represent Christian truth.

Even though the church dominated art and architecture, it did not prevent architects and artists from experimenting. In about 1000, an international style called the **Romanesque** emerged. The first in a succession of uniform styles to sweep over Europe, the Romanesque was carried along by the monastic revival until about 1200. But by 1150, the **Gothic style** was developing in Paris; it was to become the reigning style of the towns for the remainder of the Middle Ages, succumbing finally to Renaissance fashion in about 1500.

Romanesque Churches and Related Arts The Romanesque style, though based on the architectural language of ancient Rome, was not a pure Roman style but rather embraced elements inspired by Christianity, along with innovations made by builders between 1000 and 1200. From Roman architecture, Romanesque builders adapted the basilica plan, rounded arches, vaulted ceilings, and columns for both support and decoration (see Figure 7.8). Inspired by Christian beliefs, they pointed the basilicas toward Jerusalem in the east and curved each building's eastern end into an apse to house the altar. A transept, or crossing arm, was added at the church's eastern end to convert the floor plan into a cruciform shape to symbolize the cross (Figure 9.13). Other Christian beliefs dictated such practices as having three doorways in the western facade—to symbolize the Trinity—and building the baptistery apart from the church to keep the unbaptized out of sacred space. To Roman and Christian elements, Romanesque builders added innovative design features, such as the **narthex** (a porch or vestibule, usually enclosed, leading into the nave), vaulting techniques, and a wealth of ornamental detail, to create the most expressive and disciplined architectural style since the fall of Rome.

A representative Romanesque church is difficult to identify today for various reasons. Most original structures have been altered significantly over the years, and, of those that were not updated, many have been destroyed or fallen into ruins. The style itself, in its origin, allowed for great diversity and experiment, which reflected the taste of different regions, communities, and patrons; the types of stone available for building; and the knowledge and historical awareness of the master builders and their workshops. The style was also felt at all levels of society, underscoring the long reach of the church's arms into people's lives, ranging from simple parish churches and sumptuous urban cathedrals to both large and small monastic churches and vast pilgrimage churches.

Within this diversity, two stages of development can be identified: the First Romanesque, about 1000–1080, and the Second Romanesque, 1080–1200.

Figure 9.14 Santa Cruz de la Seros (Aragon), church of San Caprasio, Spain. View from the north. Last quarter of the eleventh century. *This church, though simple in the extreme, embodies the basic elements of the First Romanesque style. These elements include stone rubble walls, which have not been faced; a small number of windows; a flat, wooden roof; and both Lombard bands and Lombard arcades.*

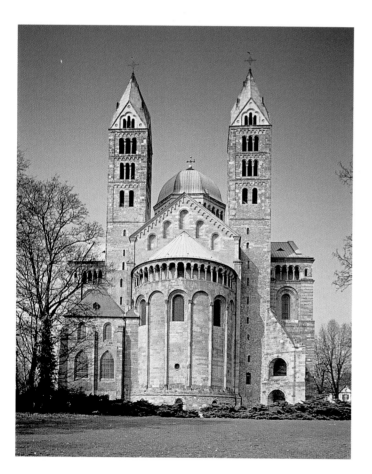

The **First Romanesque style** originated along the Mediterranean, in the zone ranging from Dalmatia (modern Croatia), across northern Italy and Provence (southern France), to Catalonia (northeastern Spain). Simple in design, the First Romanesque churches were built of stone rubble, a Roman technique, and covered with flat, wooden roofs. With high walls and few windows, they resembled fortresses, a trait that came to characterize both Romanesque styles. The defining exterior features of the First Romanesque churches were a web of vertical bands or buttresses along the sides and a sequence of small arcades below the eaves (Figure 9.14). Because these features may have been born in Lombardy (north central Italy), they are usually called **Lombard bands** and **Lombard arcades.** Later builders experimented with the Lombard bands and arcades, creating spectacular churches, such as the Speyer cathedral in Germany (Figure 9.15). At Speyer,

Figure 9.15 Speyer Cathedral. View from the east. Speyer, Germany. Begun about 1030, completed before 1150. *Speyer cathedral, whose massive size rivals that of the great mother church at Cluny, the home of the Cluniac order of monks, represents the climax of the First Romanesque, the first phase of Romanesque style.*

Lombard bands establish a rhythmic, vertical sequence on the walls of the apse. And variations on the Lombard arcade form include, on the lower part of the apse, the elongated, relatively windowless arcade attached to the wall; on the top part of the apse, the open, or "dwarf," arcaded gallery; and, on the wall above the apse, the arched niches arranged in stairstep fashion and the line of Lombard arches below the roofline.

The **Second Romanesque style** is associated with the Cluniac monastic order because the order's mother church at Cluny—Cluny III, founded 1088, the third church built on this site—in eastern France was constructed in this style (see Figure 9.5). Cluny III, though destroyed in the 1800s, was greatly admired in its day for its vast scale, including double transepts and crossing towers, towers at the ends of the transepts, a double-aisled nave covered with a barrel vault, and a rich decorative program of religious art, both inside and out. The spectacular success of the Cluniac movement in the eleventh and twelfth centuries led to the spread of the Second Romanesque style throughout Europe (Figure 9.16). In appearance, this style reflected both the needs of the monastic communities and the physical demands created by the unsettled conditions of the times. These churches were richly decorated and earth hugging, with massive walls and few windows, though more and larger windows than in the First Romanesque. They looked like the spiritual fortresses that they indeed were.

Many Second Romanesque churches were pilgrimage churches—destinations for pilgrims traveling vast distances to see and venerate holy relics, very often the supposed bones of saints. The foremost pilgrimage churches included ambulatories, or semicircular or polygonal aisles behind the apse, to accommodate the expected hordes of religious tourists.

A celebrated pilgrimage church in the Second Romanesque style is Sainte-Marie-Madeleine in Vézelay, France. Attached to a Cluniac convent, this church attracted penitents eager to view the bones of Mary Magdalene. Vézelay's builders followed a basilica design with a cruciform floor plan. Inside, the most striking feature is the nearly 200-foot-long nave, which could hold a large number of pilgrims as well as allow religious processions (Figure 9.17). Typical of Romanesque architecture, the nave is divided into sections called **bays.** Each bay is framed by a pair of rounded arches constructed from blocks of local pink and gray stones. These colors alternate in the overhead arches and create a dazzling effect for which this church is famous. The ceiling of each bay is a groin vault—a Roman building technique. The support system for the tall nave walls—an arcade, or series of arches resting on clusters of columns—was also taken

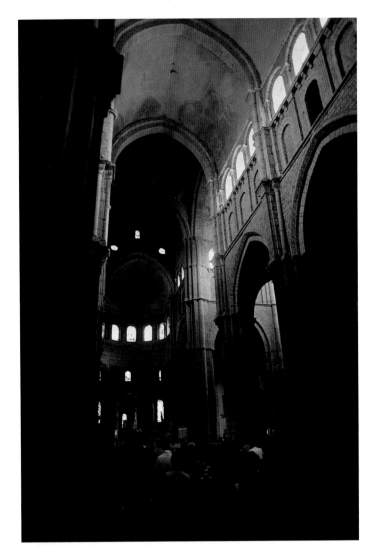

Figure 9.16 Basilica of Sacre-Coeur, formerly Abbey Church of the Virgin and St. John the Baptist, Paray-le-Monial, France, view of nave, looking east. Begun 1110s–1120s, completed mid–twelfth century. Nave height approx. 147'7½"; length approx. 72'2⅛". *The monastery at Paray-le-Monial became part of the Cluniac system in 999. Tradition links St. Hugh, abbot of Cluny (1049–1109), with the building of the Paray-le-Monial basilica. As head of the Cluniac order, Hugh commissioned Paray to be a scaled-down version of the great mother church, Cluny III. It replicates Cluny III's vaulting techniques, using barrel vaults in the nave and groin vaults in the aisles, combined with pointed arches—derived from Muslim architecture. (The pointed arches used at Cluny III and Paray-le-Monial were not related to the development of Gothic-style architecture.) As in Cluny III, the east end culminates in a semicircular arcade resting on slender columns. The nave, consisting of only three vaulted sections, is markedly shorter than Cluny III's nave, reflecting the lack of pageantry associated with the small monastic community at Paray-le-Monial.*

from Roman architecture. Vézelay's builders used sculpture to provide "sermons in stone" for illiterate visitors. Symbolic rather than idealistic, the Romanesque figures were designed to convey religious

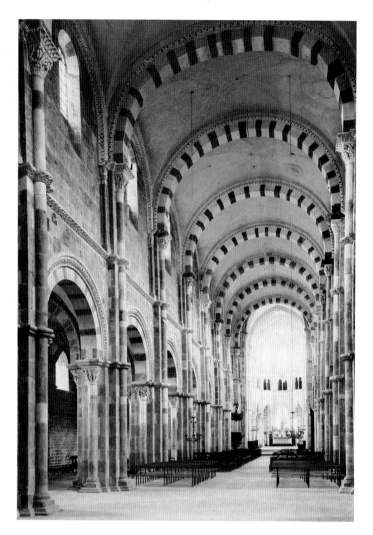

Figure 9.17   View of Nave, Looking East. Church of Sainte-Marie-Madeleine, Vézelay, France. Ca. 1089–1206. *Vézelay's nave was made unusually long so that religious pilgrims might make solemn processions along its length. A reliquary, or an area for displaying holy relics, was later set aside in the choir. Within the choir, the design of the ambulatory provided ample space for masses of pilgrims to view all the relics at one time.*

Figure 9.18   *Jacob Wrestling with the Angel.* Decorated column capital. Church of Sainte-Marie-Madeleine, Vézelay, France. Ca. 1089–1206. *The Vézelay capitals survive in near-immaculate condition. Late Medieval moralists considered their vivacity and gaiety inappropriate in God's house, and the offending sculptures were plastered over. When they were uncovered during a nineteenth-century restoration of the church's interior, the capitals were revealed in their charming originality.*

meanings. For example, instead of copying the ancient Greco-Roman columns, the artisans created their own style of decorated column. The capitals, or tops, of the interior columns are sculptured with religious scenes and motifs, such as one that shows Jacob, one of the Hebrew patriarchs (on the left), wrestling with the angel (Figure 9.18). The angel, clutching his robe in his left hand, raises his right hand to bless Jacob. The simple figures with their dramatic gestures and expressive faces accurately convey the message in Genesis (32:24–30) that Jacob has been chosen by God to lead the Hebrew people. The art is typically Romanesque: The feet point downward, the limbs are placed in angular positions, and the drapery folds are depicted in a stylized manner.

A more mature Romanesque style appears in the carvings on the **tympanum** over the south portal of the tower porch at Moissac, one of the two remaining elements of the twelfth-century abbey church that once stood here. The other surviving element is a **cloister,** a covered arcade surrounding a quadrangle, which originally connected the church to the monastic community. Although a subject of controversy, the tympanum carvings probably depict a vision of the Christian apocalypse, much of which is based on the Book of Revelation (Figure 9.19). Jesus is portrayed in glory, indicated by the cross-shaped symbol behind his head and the oval in which he sits enthroned, and wearing a crown. Immediately surrounding him are the four evangelist symbols, namely, man (Matthew), winged lion (Mark), winged bull (Luke), and eagle (John). These symbols date back at least to the eighth century B.C.E., when they appeared on Assyrian carvings and were later adopted by other Near Eastern societies (see

Figure 9.19 *Christ in Glory with Four Evangelist Symbols and the Twenty-four Elders.* Tympanum over south portal. Church of St. Pierre, Moissac, France. Ca. 1125. *The jam-packed imagery in this tympanum and surrounding space is typical of the allover patterns used in the Romanesque style. Nevertheless, there is artistic order here. Stylized floral forms are aligned rhythmically along the lintel and around the tympanum frame, and human and animal shapes encircle the seated Jesus, who is rendered four times larger than the Elders. The tympanum itself is divided into three zones by the horizontal lines of clouds below Jesus' feet and above the second row of Elders.*

Figure 1.24). Jesus and the four symbols are, in turn, encircled by ten of the twenty-four Elders listed in Revelation 4, while fourteen other Elders sit in a line below, gazing up at the Savior. The Elders hold cups and musical instruments as described in Revelation 5. This tympanum sculpture served as a warning about life's ultimate end to those who passed through the south portal.

Besides church building and church decoration, the Romanesque style was used in manuscript illumination. Originated in Late Rome and developed in the Early Middle Ages, this art remained a cloistered activity in this age of monasticism (see Chapter 7). Perhaps only cloistered painters had the leisure to pursue this painstaking skill. During the High Middle Ages, new local styles arose, inspired by regional tastes and by a knowledge of Byzantine painting brought from the East by Crusaders. The English monks probably developed the finest of these local styles.

The Bury Bible, painted at Bury St. Edmunds monastery, reflects an English taste that is calmer and less exuberant than Continental styles. Two panels from the Bury manuscript, set off by a border of highly colored foliage, show an episode in Moses' life (Figure 9.20). Borrowings from Byzantine art may be detected in the elongated figures, the large eyes, the flowing hair, and the hanging draperies. The naturalness of these scenes presented a vivid contrast with the spirited agitation of French Romanesque art.

Gothic Churches and Related Arts   The word *Gothic* was invented by later Renaissance scholars who preferred Greco-Roman styles. They despised medieval architecture, labeling it *Gothic*—meaning a barbaric creation of the Goths, or the Germanic peoples. Modern research, however, has shown that this Renaissance view is false. In fact, the Gothic grew out of the Romanesque and was not a German art. Nevertheless,

Figure 9.20 *Moses Expounding the Law of the Unclean Beasts.* The Bury Bible. 1130–1140. Approx. 20 × 14". Bury St. Edmunds, England. Master and Fellows of Corpus Christi College, Cambridge. *These panels depict Moses delivering the dietary laws to the ancient Hebrews. The responses of his audience reveal the sure hand of the artist, known only as Master Hugo. For example, in the upper panel one figure pulls at his nose, while a nearby companion looks skeptical. Moses' head is depicted with horns, which reflected a biblical mistranslation of the term for the radiance that surrounded him after receiving God's law.*

Figure 9.21 Principal Features of a Typical Gothic Church. *In this schematic drawing, the features are numbered from the nave outward: (1) nave arcade, (2) pointed arch, (3) vault, (4) clerestory, (5) flying buttress, (6) buttress, and (7) gargoyle.*

the term *Gothic* is still used today, although its negative connotation has long since been discarded.

Gothic architecture sprang from the religious revival of the twelfth century, when the clergy wanted to bring God's presence more tangibly to their urban congregations. As a result, clerics began to demand taller churches with more windows than were available in the relatively dark Romanesque churches. To the medieval mind, height and light were symbols of the divine. Another impetus behind the Gothic was the rise of the middle class, who wanted churches that reflected their growing economic power. Thus, spiritual

and economic forces were united in pushing architects to seek a new kind of architecture.

Two problems with the Romanesque stood in the way: The groin vaults were so heavy that the nearly windowless walls had to be extremely thick to support their great weight, and the rounded arches limited the building's height to less than 100 feet. During the early twelfth century, builders constantly sought solutions to these problems.

Eventually, between 1137 and 1144, the Gothic style was created by Suger [sue-ZHAY] (about 1081–1151), the abbot of the royal Abbey Church of St. Denis, near

Paris, and an adviser to the French kings. Suger's approach to architecture grew out of his religious faith, as in his words, "Through the beauty of material things we come to understand God." The brilliant innovation employed by Suger and the architects and artisans he hired was to change the vaulting problem from one of weight to one of stress. First, they replaced the groin vault with a **ribbed vault;** this step allowed lighter materials to be placed between the stone ribs, thus reducing the weight. Next, they abandoned the rounded arch in favor of the Muslim pointed arch. The combination of pointed arch and ribbed vault permitted an increase in the building's height as well as a rechanneling of the ceiling's stresses downward and outward to huge **piers** internally and, in later buildings, to **flying buttresses** externally, which formed a bridge between the upper nave walls and the nearby tall pillars (Figure 9.21). With the support skeleton transferred to the building's exterior, the builders could easily insert stained-glass windows into the non-weight-bearing walls.

The glory of the Gothic church—the **choir**—was all that remained to be built. The plan and inspiration for the choir (the part of the church where the service was sung) were the pilgrimage churches, such as Vézelay, that had enlarged their apses to accommodate religious tourists. In Suger's skillful hands, the east end of St. Denis was now elaborated into an oval-shaped area—the choir—ringed with several small chapels (Figure 9.22). At the heart of the choir was the apse, now arcaded; a spacious ambulatory area divided the apse from the chapels (Figure 9.23).

St. Denis gave only a foretaste of the triumphant art that was called Gothic. Between 1145 and 1500, the Gothic style presented an overwhelming image of God's majesty and the power of the church. A Gothic exterior carried the eye heavenward by impressive vertical spires. A Gothic interior surrounded the daytime worshiper with colored, celestial light; the soaring nave ceiling, sometimes rising to more than 150 feet, was calculated to stir the soul. In its total physicality the Gothic church stood as a towering symbol of the medieval obsession with the divine.

During the High Middle Ages, the Gothic style went through two stages, the Early and the High. The Early Gothic style lasted until 1194 and was best represented by Notre Dame cathedral in Paris. The High Gothic style flourished until 1300 and reached perfection in the cathedral at Amiens, France.

EARLY GOTHIC STYLE, 1145–1194 The cathedral of Notre Dame ("Our Lady," the Virgin Mary) in Paris made popular the Early Gothic style, making it a fashion for other cities and towns. Begun in 1163, the cathedral was the most monumental work erected in the

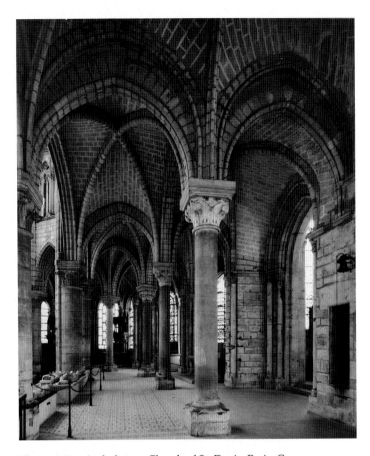

Figure 9.22 Ambulatory. Church of St. Denis, Paris. Ca. 1145. *This view of the choir of St. Denis shows a portion of the ambulatory that allowed pilgrims to view the chapels in the apse. The evenly spaced support columns and the pointed arches create this flowing, curved space. The ribbed arches in the ceiling are also central to the Gothic skeletal construction.*

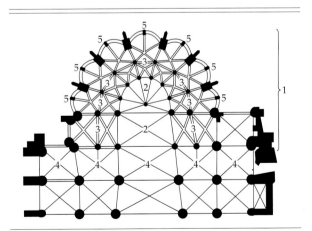

Figure 9.23 Floor Plan, Ambulatory. Church of St. Denis, Paris. Ca. 1145. *This floor plan, based on a similar design used in the pilgrimage churches, became the basis for the reordering of interior space in the Gothic choirs. The features include (1) choir, (2) apse, (3) ambulatory, (4) transept, and (5) chapel.*

Figure 9.24   Floor Plan of Notre Dame. Paris. 1163–ca. 1250. *This drawing shows the principal features of Notre Dame cathedral: (1) nave, (2) aisle, (3) transept, (4) apse, (5) choir, and (6) narthex, or vestibule.*

Figure 9.25   Western Facade. Notre Dame. Paris. 1220–1250. *In the gallery above the western portals are twenty-eight images of the kings of Judah, including David and Solomon. These sculptures, which are typical of Gothic churches, are more than decorations: They are reminders that Mary and Jesus were descended from royalty. In the medieval mind, this religious idea was meant to buttress the monarchical style of government.*

West to that time. Its floor plan was cruciform, but the length of the transept barely exceeded the width of the aisle walls (Figure 9.24). Part of Notre Dame's beauty stems from the rational principles applied by the builders, notably the ideal of harmony, best expressed in the integration of sculpture and decorative details with building units. For instance, the west facade is divided into three equal horizontal bands: the three doorways, the **rose window** and **blind arcades** (walled-in windows), and the two towers (Figure 9.25). Within each subdivision of this facade, figurative sculpture or architectural details play a harmonizing role, from the rows of saints flanking each of the portals to the **gargoyles,** or grotesque demons, peering down from the towers.

Inside Notre Dame, the spectacular nave reveals the awe-inspiring effects of Early Gothic art at its best (Figure 9.26). The strong vertical lines and the airy atmosphere represent the essence of this taste. With its ribbed vaults and pointed arches, the nave rises to a height of 115 feet from the pavement to the roof. Like the harmonious west facade, the nave is divided into three equal tiers: the nave and double aisles, the open spectator **gallery** above the aisles, and, at the top, the clerestory, as the window area is called.

Notre Dame reveals that the choir was coming to dominate the entire Early Gothic church. Notre Dame's choir is almost as long as the nave, so that the transept virtually divides the church into two halves. At first, the choir's walls had no special external sup-

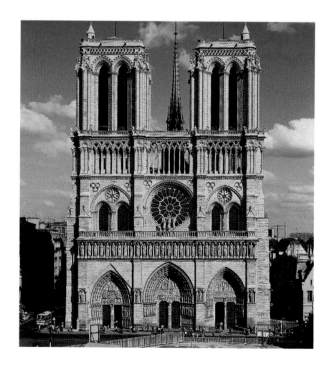

Figure 9.26 Nave. Notre Dame. Paris. View from the height of the western rose window. 1180–1250. Ht. floor to summit of roof, 115′. *The nave is clearly not aligned properly. The choir bends perceptibly to the north, which probably reflects the different building times for various parts of the cathedral. The transept and the choir were finished first, after which the nave and the double aisles were added. The western facade was completed last.*

ports, but as cracks began to appear in the choir's walls during the thirteenth century, flying buttresses were added to ensure greater stability—a feature that would later characterize High Gothic churches (Figure 9.27).

The Gothic sculptures that decorate Notre Dame differ from the exuberant Romanesque style. The Romanesque's animated images of Jesus have given way to the Gothic's more sober figures. In addition, the Gothic figures are modeled in three dimensions, and their draperies fall in natural folds (Figure 9.28). At the same time, the rise of the cult of the Virgin meant an increased number of images of Mary as well as of female saints. The name "Notre Dame" itself testifies to the appeal of the Virgin cult. Despite these visual differences, however, the Gothic remained true to the symbolic purposes of Romanesque art.

Before Notre Dame was finished, its architects began to move in new directions, refining the traditional features into a new style, called **Rayonnant,** or Radiant. In the Rayonnant style, the solid walls gave way

Figure 9.27 Notre Dame. Paris. View from the east. 1163–1182. *Notre Dame's choir, shown on the right, was originally built without chapels and flying buttresses—a sign of its Early Gothic origins. Paris's greatest church caught up with the High Gothic style in the fourteenth century, when these architectural features were added.*

Figure 9.28 *The Last Judgment.* Central portal, west facade. Notre Dame, Paris. Ca. 1210. *This tympanum represents Jesus enthroned and presiding over the Last Judgment. Surrounding him are the apostles, the prophets, the church Fathers, and the saints—arranged in descending order of their importance in relation to Jesus. Like all the sculptures of Notre Dame's first story, the entire scene was gilded with gold paint until the mid–fifteenth century.*

Figure 9.29 North Rose Window of Notre Dame. Paris. Ca. 1255. *This masterwork by Jehan de Chelles is the only original of Notre Dame's three rose windows. The nineteenth-century restoration genius Viollet-le-Duc recreated the other two. Measuring 43 feet in diameter, the window was installed after workers first removed sections of the existing wall. The bits of predominantly blue glass, encased in iron settings, were then placed inside the stone frame.*

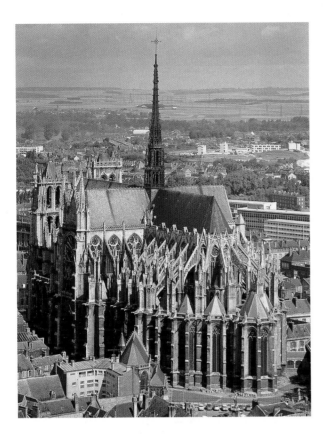

Figure 9.30 Amiens Cathedral. Amiens, France. Ca. 1220–1270. *This photograph shows the brilliantly articulated exterior skeleton of Amiens cathedral. The Gothic churches openly displayed the exterior support system that made their interior beauty possible. In the Renaissance, this aspect of Gothicism was decried for its clumsiness. Renaissance architects preferred Classical structures that hid their stresses and strains.*

to sheets of stained glass framed by elegant **traceries,** or rich ornamentation, of stone. This radiant effect was especially evident in the north transept facade, which was rebuilt in this new style. With the addition of this transept's imposing rose window, designed to suggest the rays of the sun, the cathedral's interior was bathed in constantly shifting colors, giving it a mystical atmosphere (Figure 9.29).

HIGH GOTHIC STYLE, **1194–1300** The High Gothic style is a tribute to the growing confidence of the builders of the thirteenth century. These builders took the Gothic ingredients and refined them, creating grander churches than had been erected earlier. In comparison with Early Gothic architecture, High Gothic churches were taller and had greater volume; artistic values now stressed wholeness rather than the division of space into harmonious units. Rejecting the restrained decorative ideal used in the Early Gothic style, the High Gothic architects covered the entire surface of their churches' western facades with sculptural and architectural designs.

The cathedral in Amiens is a perfect embodiment of the High Gothic style. Amiens was planned so that flying buttresses would surround its choir and march

along its nave walls (Figure 9.30). Instead of trying to disguise these supports, the architect made the exterior skeleton central to his overall plan. As a result, more spacious window openings could be made in the nave and the choir walls than had been the case in Notre Dame. Furthermore, the design of Amiens's nave was also changed so that the entire space was perceived as a homogeneous volume. The division of the nave walls into three equal horizontal bands was eliminated, and the system of arches and bays overhead became less emphatic (Figure 9.31). Amiens's overall floor plan was conservative, however, for it resembled that of Notre Dame; for example, its transept bisected a choir and a nave of equal length (Figure 9.32).

The western facade of Amiens shows how decoration changed in the High Gothic style (Figure 9.33). Amiens's western wall and towers are pierced with rich and intricate openings. The elegant tracery has the effect of dissolving the wall's apparent solidity. What surface remains intact is covered with an elaborate tapestry of architectural devices and sculptural figures (Figure 9.34).

The finest stained glass from the High Gothic era is from the cathedral in Chartres, a bishopric in Hugh Capet's old lands. Indeed, Chartres's windows are often recognized as the most exquisite of all Gothic stained glass. Chartres has 176 windows, and most are the thirteenth-century originals. Outstanding examples of this art are the Charlemagne panels depicting scenes from the *Song of Roland*, illustrated earlier in this chapter (see Figure 9.11). Each figure is precisely rendered, though many are cropped off at the edge of the pictorial space. The glass itself is brilliant, notably in the dominant blue tones.

High Gothic painting survives best in the manuscript illuminations of the late thirteenth century. By

Figure 9.31   Nave. Amiens cathedral. View from the west. Amiens, France. Ca. 1220–1236. Ht. floor to summit of vault, 139'. *Gothic architecture was built to appeal to the emotions. The overwhelming height and the celestial light were intended to create a spiritual environment. This spiritual feeling may be sensed even in a photograph. The dramatic contrast between the human elements—the chairs—and the voluminous space is a reminder of the frailty of mortals.*

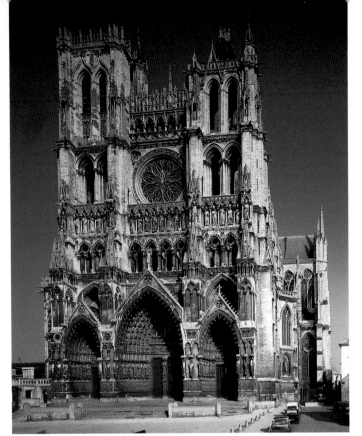

Figure 9.33 Western Facade. Amiens cathedral. Amiens, France. Ca. 1220–1236. *Comparison of Amiens's facade with that of Notre Dame in Paris (see Figure 9.25) shows how the High Gothic differs from the Early Gothic. The basic form remains the same, but Amiens's surface is richer in detail and more splendid overall. The pointed features, such as the arches over the portals and over the openings in the towers, are the most characteristic visual element in the High Gothic style.*

Figure 9.32 Floor Plan of Amiens Cathedral. Amiens, France. Ca. 1220–1236. *This drawing shows the principal features of Amiens cathedral: (1) nave, (2) aisle, (3) transept, (4) apse, (5) choir, and (6) narthex.*

Figure 9.34 *Golden Virgin.* Amiens Cathedral. Ca. 1260. Amiens, France. *The* Golden Virgin *of Amiens, so called because it was originally covered with a thin layer of gold, is one of the most admired works of Gothic art. The artist has depicted Mary as a loving earthly mother with fine features, a high forehead, and a shy smile. This sculpture shows the new tenderness that was creeping into art during the High Middle Ages as part of the rise of the cult of the Virgin.*

Figure 9.35 *Balaam and His Ass.* Psalter of St. Louis IX. 1252–1270. Bibliothèque Nationale, Paris. *The architectural details in this miniature painting show a correspondence with the Rayonnant architectural style: the two gabled roofs, the two rose windows with exterior traceries, the pointed arches, and the pinnacles. Just as Gothic architects emphasized the decorative aspects of their buildings, so did this anonymous miniature painter. The story of Balaam and his ass (Numbers 22:22–35 in the Old Testament) was a beast fable—a popular literary genre in the Middle Ages. In the biblical story, the ass could speak and see things of which his master, Balaam, was ignorant. In the painting, the ass turns his head and opens his mouth as if to speak.*

that time, these small paintings were being influenced by developments elsewhere in Gothic art. The Gothic illuminators abandoned the lively draperies of the Romanesque and instead showed gowns hanging in a natural manner. More important, they sometimes allowed the architectural frame to dominate the painting, as in the Psalter of St. Louis IX of France. Commissioned by the sainted French king (r. 1226–1270), this volume contains seventy-eight full-page paintings of scenes from the Old Testament. Of these paintings, *Balaam and His Ass* is a typical representation of the anonymous painter's style (Figure 9.35). The scene unfolds before a High Gothic church; two gables with rose windows are symmetrically balanced on the page. Although this painting owes much to changes in Gothic sculpture, the animated figures of the men, the angel, and the ass are reminiscent of the exuberant Romanesque style.

Music

As with the other arts, the purpose of music during the High Middle Ages was the glorification of God. At

first, the monophonic (single-line) Gregorian chants were still the main form of musical expression, but two innovations—the introduction of tropes and the development of polyphony—led the way to a different sound in the future.

Among the compositions of sacred music written during this period, the works of Hildegard of Bingen, the learned and gifted abbess of the Rupertsberg monastery on the Rhine River, have a lasting appeal. Hildegard composed within the tradition of Gregorian chant (see Chapter 7), though she, a devout mystic, claimed ecstatic visions as the inspiration for her musical ideas. The words for her texts were drawn from the Bible, her theological writings, and the church's liturgy.

Hildegard's works were unusual not only because they were written by a woman but also because they were performed by women singers before audiences of women—Hildegard's fellow nuns. Besides the previously mentioned sung morality play *Ordo Virtutatum (The Company of the Virtues)* (see page 257), she composed seventy-seven songs, chants, and hymns for the church's liturgy, including such works as *O Pastor Animarum (O Shepherd of Souls), Spiritui Sancto (Holy Spirit),* and *O Jerusalem.* She also wrote a kyrie (a chant sung during the Mass asking God for mercy) and an alleluia (a chant sung during the Mass offering praise), as well as two longer works composed specifically for women, one dedicated to virgins and the other to widows.

Hildegard's *O Pastor Animarum* is one of the seventy-seven songs in the collection known as the *Symphonia* (full name, *Symphonia armonie celestium revelationum,* or "Symphony of the Harmony of Celestial Revelations.") *Symphony* here means simply "collection" and should not be confused with the modern symphony, a musical form. *O Pastor Animarum* is an **antiphon,** a short prose text, chanted by an unaccompanied voice or voices during the liturgy. Addressed to God the Father, this antiphon reads, in Latin: "O Pastor animarum, / et o prima vox, / perquam omnes creati sumus, / nunc tibi, / tibi placeat, / ut degneris nos

Figure 9.36 Embellished Letter *B*. Psalter from Würzburg-Ebrach. Early thirteenth century. Universitäts Bibliothek, Munich. *In illuminated manuscripts, the initial letter of a sentence was often embellished with intricate details, drawn from the artist's imagination and experience. In this example from a thirteenth-century German psalter, the letter B is interwoven with a band of musicians playing instruments typical of the era: organ (with bellows), bells, ivory horn, flute, stringed instruments, and an instrument for bows. The artist who painted this miniature scene has captured the liveliness of a musical performance, depicting several players singing.*

281

outdoors. From the twelfth century onward, these works were staged in the area in front of the church as sacred dramas or mystery plays (*mystery* is derived from the Latin *ministerium,* "handicraft" or "occupation"). As their popularity increased, they began to be sung in the vernacular instead of Latin. Ultimately, the liturgical drama supplied one of the threads that led to the revival of the secular theater.

Gregorian chants were also being modified by the development of **polyphony,** in which two or more lines of melody are sung or played at the same time. In the early eleventh century, polyphony was extremely simple and was known as **organum.** It consisted of a main melody, called the *cantus firmus,* accompanied by an identical melody sung four or five tones higher or lower. By about 1150, the second line began to have its own independent melody rather than duplicating the first. During the thirteenth century, two-voiced organum gave way to multivoiced songs called **motets,** which employed more complex melodies. In the motets, the main singer used the liturgy as a text while up to five other voices sang either commentaries or vernacular translations of the text. The result was a complex blend of separate voices woven into a harmonious tapestry. By about 1250, the motet composers had laid the foundations of modern musical composition.

Notwithstanding these developments in sacred music, the church could not stop the rise of secular music any more than it could prevent the spread of courtly love. Indeed, the first secular music was associated with the same feudal courts where the *chansons de geste* and the troubador songs flourished in the twelfth century. At first, France was the center of this musical movement, but in the early thirteenth century, German poets took the lead. At the same time, music began to be practiced not just by aristocratic poets but also by middle-class minstrels, and new musical instruments—some, such as the **lute** (a multistringed instrument with neck and soundbox) and the bagpipe, banned by the church—started to find their way into secular music (Figure 9.36).

The High Middle Ages also gave rise to some innovations that made modern music possible. Guido of Arezzo [GWEE-doe/uh-RET-so] (about 995–about 1050), an Italian monk, modernized musical notation by his invention of the music staff, the set of five horizontal lines and four intermediate spaces on which notes may be drawn. Guido also began the practice of naming the musical tones by the syllables *ut* (or *do*), *re, mi, fa, sol,* and *la,* a step that greatly simplified the teaching of music. The music composed according to Guido's system can be reproduced by today's music historians; thus, Western music may be said to descend in an unbroken line from the music of this period.

liberare / de miseries et languoribus nostris" (in English, "O Shepherd of souls, / and o first voice, / through whom all creation was summoned, / now to you, / to you may it give pleasure and dignity, / to liberate us / from our miseries and languishing." Typically, Hildegard's antiphon is composed in **plainsong,** the Christian chant that dominated the period. The music shows her personal style: wide leaps of melody and ornamental features, especially **melismas** (groups of notes sung to the same syllable) and, to a lesser extent, **syllabic** singing (one note per syllable).

The **tropes,** or turns, were new texts and melodies inserted into the existing Gregorian chants. Added for both poetic and doctrinal reasons, these musical embellishments slowly changed the plainchants into more elaborate songs. Culminating in about 1150, this musical development coincided with the appearance of the richly articulated Gothic churches.

The tropes also gave a powerful impetus to Western drama. From the practice of troping grew a new musical genre, the **liturgical drama,** which at first was sung and performed in the church but gradually moved

Technology

As with the rest of Western culture, technology during the High Middle Ages recovered many valuable techniques from ancient Rome, and, by improving on this heritage as well as borrowing from Islam, the West was able to sustain Europe's burgeoning economy and society, as well as, in a few cases, to take steps forward. Probably the largest steps forward were made with the adoptions of papermaking and the astrolabe, both introduced from the Islamic world (see Chapter 8). However, the impact of these new technologies was relatively limited. Technology's strongest impact on the wider culture was made by further advances in warfare, the rise of watermills and windmills in the North, and new tools in farming.

Warfare   As this period began, the typical knight still fought much as in Late Rome, wielding a weapon or two (such as bow and arrows, sword, dagger, or spear), clad in armor (chain mail), and mounted on a horse. By 1300 improved technology had transformed the knight into a ferocious adversary. From Arab horse breeders in Spain, a large horse with great stamina was imported into Europe—thus making the feudal era possible. The knight was able to sit on, control, and protect this steed by means of a stirrup (see Chapter 7), padded saddle (see Chapter 7), spurs (introduced in the eleventh century), and horseshoes (inherited from Rome). Local artisans improved chain mail, covering a warrior in flexible fittings from neck to toe, with gauntlets (gloves) for the hands, the whole topped by a helmet. The knight's horse was similarly protected with chain mail. From northern Italy, starting in the tenth century, the metal crossbow soon became the weapon of choice, preferred because of its ability to pierce chain mail. For siege warfare, the catapult, a device for hurling missiles, was developed—a weapon of obscure origin, but similar to the Roman onager (see Chapter 5).

In the late 1200s, a new weapon was introduced to the West that later would revolutionize warfare: gunpowder, an explosive mix of saltpeter, carbon, and sulphur. In existence in China since about 900 C.E., the formula for gunpowder was known only there, where it was used for fireworks and signals and, only modestly, for explosives. But in 1242 the English scientist Roger Bacon set forth a recipe (though he seems to have never made an actual mixture). How gunpowder actually came to the West is unclear, but on arrival, its full meaning took decades to unfold (see Chapter 10). By 1300 gunpowder was being used in siege warfare, to undermine walls by setting off explosions and fires.

Water Power and Wind Power   In northern Europe in the High Middle Ages, a widespread adaptation of the waterwheel occurred, which allowed for the rise of grist mills, mills for grinding grains into flour. Water had been a source of power since ancient times (see Chapter 1), but now, mills, driven by waterwheels, were fully integrated into the medieval landscape. For example, in 1086, England was dotted with more than five thousand mills—as reported in the Domesday Book, a record of a survey ordered by William the Conqueror. England's example is typical of the era. Watermills—for land drainage and irrigation, as well as grinding grain—were vital to the period's subsistence economy, and sporadic improvements made them more efficient.

A second low-keyed revolution occurred as well: wind power, introduced in the twelfth century by returning Crusaders from the Muslim world. Mills, powered by wind, offered an attractive alternative to watermills for grinding grain, especially on larger estates. Thereafter, wind power, harnessed to perform various tasks, played a key role in the West until the advent of steam in the 1800s.

Farming   Also modestly revolutionary came the shift from the ox to the horse as the primary draft farm animal. Up until the twelfth century, farming required tilling the soil with iron-bladed plows, pulled by teams of oxen. But, with the invention of a rigid horse collar, all that changed. Made of leather and metal, this padded collar encircled the animal's neck, allowing it to breathe—and not choke—as it pulled a plow, wagon, or heavy load. This invention made the fast-paced horse more efficient than the slow-moving ox. Horses, of course, remained central to aristocratic culture, but, with the rigid collar, they also became a necessity in farm life. And, with horse-drawn plows, farmers could open new lands in northern Europe, since those soils were denser—and thus more difficult to till—than the sandy soils of the Mediterranean.

The Legacy of the Christian Centuries

The grandeur of this age of synthesis declined after 1300, when the secular and the spiritual began to go their separate ways. But the legacy of the Christian centuries survives, particularly in the writings of Dante, the theology of Thomas Aquinas, and the Gothic cathedrals. The *Divine Comedy* is Dante's most enduring gift to world literature; his poetic style and literary forms influenced Italian writers for centuries. Furthermore, Dante's love for Beatrice has deeply influenced Western literature by encouraging poets to seek inspiration from a living woman.

The Roman Catholic world is the most significant beneficiary of the philosophy of Thomas Aquinas. Since the late nineteenth century, Thomism has been regarded as the basis of orthodox beliefs. As for the Gothic style, it ceased to be practiced after about 1500, although it was revived in the nineteenth century as part of the Romantic movement, and even today universities often adopt Gothic elements in their architecture.

Besides these great gifts, the Christian centuries have left the modern world other significant cultural legacies. First and foremost was the birth of the courtly-love movement that glorified individual romantic affection—the idea that *this* man loves *this* woman. Vernacular literature finally found its voice during this time in the first European poetry. Of special note, the vernacular writers created one of the richest literary traditions in the West through the stories of King Arthur and the knights of the Round Table. The basic theoretical system for composing music was developed during this period under the auspices of the church. Outside the church, the ancestor of all Western love songs was invented by the Provençal poets. In Gothic sculpture, artists began to move away from symbolic representation to a more realistic art. In medicine, the hospital makes its first appearance in the West.

Notwithstanding these innovations, the Christian centuries transmitted many of the legacies that had been received from ancient and other sources. The liberal arts; the Christian religion; the rationalist tradition; schools, universities, and medical schools; water and wind technologies; cavalry warfare; Muslim science; and the entire Greco-Roman heritage are only the major ingredients of this invaluable legacy to later ages.

KEY CULTURAL TERMS

chivalric code	bay
friars	tympanum
cathedral	cloister
scholasticism	ribbed vault
Realism	pier
Nominalism	flying buttress
via media	choir
goliard	rose window
chanson de geste	blind arcade
vernacular language	gargoyle
Vernacular Literature	gallery
canzone	Rayonnant style
minstrel	tracery
troubador	antiphon
romance	plainsong
lay	melismas
terza rima	syllabic
stained glass	trope
Romanesque style	liturgical drama
Gothic style	polyphony
narthex	organum
First Romanesque style	motet
Lombard arcades	lute
Lombard bands	
Second Romanesque style	

SUGGESTIONS FOR FURTHER READING

CHRÉTIEN DE TROYES. *Arthurian Romances*. Translated by W. W. Comfort. New York: Everyman's Library, 1955. A good prose version of Chrétien's romances, including *Lancelot*.

DANTE. *The Divine Comedy. The Inferno. The Purgatorio. The Paradiso*. Translated by J. Ciardi. New York: New American Library, 1982. The best contemporary English translation.

HILDEGARD OF BINGEN. *Scivias*. Translated by C. Hart and J. Bishop. New York: Paulist Press, 1990. A modern, readable translation of Hildegard's writings.

The Lais of Marie de France. Translated and with an introduction by R. Hanning and J. Ferrante. Durham: Labyrinth Press, 1982. A modern, free-verse translation of these Old French poems; with notes and an extremely useful introductory essay.

The Song of Roland. Translated by F. Golden. New York: Norton, 1978. A readable and modern translation that still captures the language and drama of the original.

ST. THOMAS AQUINAS. *Summa Theologica*. 3 vols. Translated by Fathers of the English Dominican Province. New York: Benziger, 1947. A good English version of St. Thomas's monumental work, which underlies Roman Catholic theology.

TIERNEY, B. *The Crisis of Church and State, 1050–1300*. Englewood Cliffs, N.J.: Prentice-Hall, 1964. Primary documents linked by sound interpretations and explanations.

SUGGESTION FOR LISTENING

HILDEGARD OF BINGEN (mid–twelfth century). *O Pastor Animarum*. A plainsong setting of a prayer to God the Father, as part of the church's liturgy.

10

THE LATE MIDDLE AGES
1300–1500

Many who lived during what a modern historian has termed the "calamitous" fourteenth century believed that the biblical apocalypse had arrived, attended by plague, famine, and war. Amid this turbulence, the unique culture of the High Middle Ages, which blended the spiritual with the secular, began to unravel. In the Late Middle Ages, the church had to relinquish its dream of a united Christendom when faced with the reality of warring European states. New military tactics and weapons rendered chivalry obsolete, and the chivalric code began to seem a romantic fiction. In the universities, new intellectual currents drove a wedge between philosophy and theology, which had been so carefully integrated by Thomas Aquinas. And the balanced High Gothic style in art and architecture gave way to the florid Late Gothic style.

This chapter examines the third and final period of medieval civilization, between 1300 and 1500 (see Chapters 7 and 9). It also explores the rise of secularism in this contradictory age and the technological and artistic innovations that were guiding the Western world in a new direction (Figure 10.1). The specific developments in the 1400s that ushered in the Renaissance and the modern era will be the focus of the next chapter.

HARD TIMES COME TO EUROPE

Shortly after the opening of the fourteenth century, Europe entered a disastrous period of economic depression, accompanied by soaring prices and widespread famine. Against the backdrop of the Hundred Years' War between England and France (1337–1453), social unrest increased and renegade

◀ **Detail** LIMBOURG BROTHERS. Month of January, from the *Très Riches Heures du Duc de Berry*. 1413–1416. Approx. 8½ × 5½". Musée Condé, Chantilly, France.

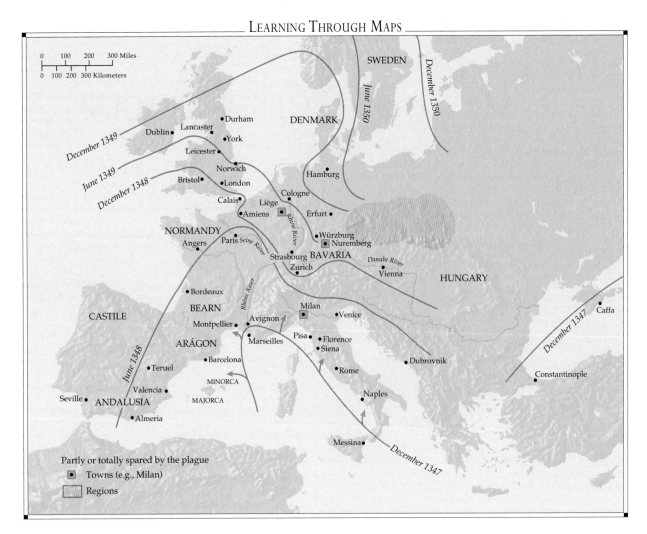

**Map 10.1 PROGRESS OF THE BLACK DEATH ACROSS EUROPE IN THE
FOURTEENTH CENTURY**
This map shows the spread of the plague across Europe in the mid–fourteenth century.
Notice how the dark lines mark the progress of the plague at a specific time. **Where** and
when does the Black Death appear in Europe? **Where** and **when** does it end? **What** regions and cities were partly or totally spared the plague? **Consider** the role of various
types of travelers in spreading the Black Death.

Figure 10.1 *Wine-Making.* Fifteenth century. Tapestry.
Cluny Museum, Paris. *Wine production became a specialty of
certain regions in the Late Middle Ages, as represented in this
fifteenth-century tapestry. In the center of the tapestry, two means
of wine-making are shown: above, a wine press, and, below, the
more traditional stomping of the grapes in a vat. In the left
foreground, the lord and lady of the manor, recognizable by their
rich gowns, supervise the making of the wine.*

Figure 10.2 *The Dance of Death.* Fifteenth century. *In the wake of the Black Death, art and literature became filled with themes affirming the biblical message that life is short and death certain. A vivid image of this theme was the* Danse Macabre, *or Dance of Death, which took many artistic and literary forms. In this example, a miniature painting taken from a fifteenth-century Spanish manuscript, the corpses are shown nude, stripped of their human dignity, and dancing with wild abandon.*

feudal armies ravaged much of western Europe. The church, in disgrace and disarray for much of this period, was unable to provide moral or political leadership. As old certainties evaporated, the optimistic mood of the High Middle Ages gave way to a sense of impending doom.

Ordeal by Plague, Famine, and War

Of all the calamities that now befell Europe, the worst was the plague, an animal-to-human illness, which first appeared in northern Italy in 1347 (Map 10.1). Imported from the East along newly opened trade routes, the plague bacillus was carried over sea and land by fleas. Fleas, infected from biting diseased rats, then transmitted the bacillus to other rats and humans. From Italy, the disease spread rapidly over most of Europe, halted by the frost line in the north. A few cities and areas—such as Milan and central Germany—were free of plague, but elsewhere it raged from 1348 until 1351, and further onslaughts occurred at random into the next century. So deadly was the disease that more than a third of Europe's seventy million people died in the first epidemic alone.

The mechanism of disease transmission was not fully understood, and the plague created panic. Using medieval accounts of the disease, modern researchers have detected three forms of plague: bubonic (infected lymph nodes), pneumonic (infected lungs), and septicemic (blood poisoning). All three forms were extremely painful, and death could result in a matter of hours or days. People in the Late Middle Ages referred to these disease types collectively as "the plague"; in

the sixteenth century, historians began to label the epidemic the "Black Death," which has become the common term.

The Black Death cast a long shadow over the Late Middle Ages. Many writers and artists reflected the melancholy times, occasionally brightening their dark works with an end-of-the-world gaiety. The age's leading image became the Dance of Death, often portrayed as a skeleton democratically joining hands with kings, queens, popes, merchants, peasants, and prostitutes as they danced their way to destruction. In the direct manner of medieval thinking, this symbol forcefully showed the folly of human ambition and the transitory nature of life (Figure 10.2).

The plague was compounded by growing famine conditions across the European continent. Starting in 1315, agricultural harvests failed with some regularity for more than a century. Besides raising the death rate, these famines weakened the populace and made them more susceptible to diseases.

War also disrupted the pattern of social and economic life. By 1450 the kings of Aragon in eastern Spain had defeated and replaced the French rulers of Naples, Sicily, and Sardinia. The increasingly powerful northern Italian cities waged war among themselves for commercial and political advantage. Farther east, from 1347 on, the Ottoman Turks had been on the move, occupying Greece and the Balkan peninsula, conquering Constantinople in 1453, and menacing Bohemia and Hungary as the century ended. During the same period in the West, England and France fought the seemingly endless Hundred Years' War, while the dukes of Burgundy attempted to carve out a "middle kingdom" between France and the German Empire.

One consequence of this almost constant warfare was a growing number of renegade soldiers who wandered the land. The countryside was filled with bands of roving knights—nobles, younger sons or bastards of aristocratic families, and outlaws—who blackmailed both landowners and peasants. Throughout Europe, these dangerous circumstances compelled town dwellers to retreat behind their city walls.

Depopulation and Rebellion

The chief consequence of the plagues, famines, and wars was depopulation, which affected the commercial centers of Europe. In general, the regions hardest hit economically were those that had benefited most in the earlier boom, particularly France. New centers rose to economic importance, including Bohemia, Poland, Hungary, Scandinavia, and Portugal. The northern Italian cities of Florence, Genoa, and Venice, the largest cities in Europe, rallied from the plague's devastating losses in the fifteenth century to make a remarkable economic recovery.

Population decline also caused dramatic social dislocations. Plague-free regions lost population as healthy people flocked to plague-stricken areas, where laborers were in great demand. The rural population decreased, and thousands of villages simply disappeared as peasants abandoned their farms and settled in the towns. A short-term effect of the population shift was the widening of the gap between rich and poor. As a once relatively homogeneous population began to split into antagonistic classes, the established social order broke down, and society experienced warfare between peasants and landowners, guildsmen and merchants, and town laborers and middle-class elites. These social uprisings often had an anticlerical element, with the rebels attacking church property and denouncing the collection of tithes.

Starting in Flanders in 1296, social unrest mounted across Europe. In 1358 the French Jacquerie, or rural renegades, made common cause with Parisian workers and killed many nobles. In England during the brief Peasants' Revolt in 1381, insurgents seized and occupied London. Among their demands was that the English king abolish the nobility (see Slice of Life). In the end, these uprisings failed to remedy the inequalities in the social order.

Although the immediate consequence of the demographic crisis was increased social unrest, the long-term effect was a higher standard of living for the survivors (see Figure 10.1). Peasants in western Europe found their labor more in demand and their bargaining positions with the landowners improved. Many broke free from servitude and became rent-paying farmers. Others, less fortunate, moved from the status of serf to that of sharecropper. As a result of all these changes, manorialism was dying out in most of western Europe by 1500. But in central and eastern Europe, where the plague had been less devastating and the landlords could hold firm, estate owners bound the serfs ever more tightly to their farm labors.

The Secular Monarchies

France and England maintained their leading positions in Europe, but they exhausted their economies with wasteful wars. The Hundred Years' War, as the group of conflicts between the mid–fourteenth and the mid–fifteenth centuries is called, arose over feudal and military rivalries dating from the High Middle Ages (Timeline 10.1). The war was fought entirely on French soil. The Valois dynasty had to contend not only with England but also with the dukes of Burgundy, who threatened to break their ties with the French crown and establish an independent kingdom on the northeast border of France. The Burgundian court at Dijon was the most brilliant in northern Europe, attracting the leading artists and humanists of the age. A heroic figure who emerged from this war was Joan of Arc (1412–1431), who rallied the French to victory, only to be burned at the stake by the English; in modern times, she became one of France's national heroines and a Roman Catholic saint.

Despite the ravages of the Hundred Years' War, the Valois kings ultimately increased their territory. Except for the port of Calais in northern France, England was forced to cede its overseas lands to the French crown. The dukes of Burgundy were brought under French control. And the northwestern region of Brittany, the last major territory that had escaped the French crown, was acquired through marriage. The contour of modern France was now complete (Figure 10.3).

While the Hundred Years' War raged on the Continent, life in England was disrupted by feudal rebellion, peasant unrest, and urban strife. Like France, England was emerging from the feudal system, but it was moving in a different direction. The English Parliament, which represented the interests of the nobles, the towns, and the rural counties, gained power at the expense of the king. Parliament also reflected popular feeling when it passed laws curbing papal power in England.

When Henry VII (r. 1485–1509) became king, however, it became apparent that a key reason for the dominance of Parliament had been the weakness of the kings. This founder of England's brilliant Tudor dynasty avoided the quarrels his predecessors had had with Parliament by abandoning foreign wars, living

Timeline 10.1   ROYAL DYNASTIES IN LATE MEDIEVAL FRANCE AND ENGLAND

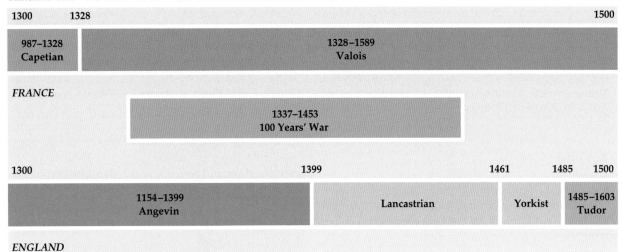

FRANCE

1300	1328		1500
987–1328 Capetian		1328–1589 Valois	

1337–1453
100 Years' War

ENGLAND

1300		1399		1461	1485	1500
1154–1399 Angevin			Lancastrian		Yorkist	1485–1603 Tudor

Figure 10.3   *An Archbishop Before a King of France. The Grand Coutumes of Normandy, the Coutumes of France.* **Fifteenth century. Law Library, Library of Congress, Washington, D.C.** *In addition to wars and marriage, the kings of France consolidated their power by establishing legal and judicial control over their newly acquired regions and territories. One of their tactics was to collect and codify the* coutumes, *or local customary laws. For centuries, provincial lawyers and regional courts had formulated and interpreted these local laws, and, by the fifteenth century, the* coutumes *had become the basis and the structure of the legal rulings and procedures in each province. Charles VII (r. 1422–1461), who, with the help of Joan of Arc, drove the English out of France during the Hundred Years' War, ordered in 1453 that the* coutumes *be codified and brought before him and his grand council for their examination and approval. Unlike other compilations,* The Grand Coutumes of Normandy *(ca. 1450–1470) were embellished with seven miniature paintings depicting various examples of the application and execution of the laws, which were common in Normandy and in England. In this example, the French king gives a document or charter to the archbishop of Normandy. Since such agreements between kings and church leaders were renewed many times in the fourteenth and fifteenth centuries, this miniature is likely symbolic, not representing an actual event. However, its message is clear—the crown holds the real power.*

off his own estates, and relying on his own advisers. Henry VII's policies deflated parliamentary power and made him as potent as his contemporaries in France.

The success of the French and the English kings in centralizing their states attracted many imitators. Their ruling style—with royal secretaries, efficient treasuries, national judiciaries, and representative assemblies—was adopted in part by other states. Spain was the most successful in achieving unity. Dynastic politics and civil war kept central Europe and Scandinavia from becoming strong and centralized. The Holy Roman Empire was the least successful of these political entities, and Germany remained divided into combative states. And, in the eastern Mediterranean, the Ottoman Turks, devotees of Islam, posed a threat to the whole of Christian Europe. Having consolidated rule over southeastern Europe and Anatolia (modern Turkey) by 1481, the Ottoman Empire now reached its height of power and wealth, and, at the same time, the Ottoman rulers began a century of expansive wars against European neighbors.

The Papal Monarchy

From its pinnacle of power and prestige in 1200 under Pope Innocent III, the church entered a period of decline in about 1300, and for the next century it was beset with schism and heresy. For most of the fourteenth century, the seat of the papacy was located in Avignon, a papal fief on the Rhône River, to escape from Rome's factional politics. Opponents of the relocation of the papacy, which had never happened before, claimed these popes were in the pocket of the French king. The chief success of the Avignonese popes was to centralize the papacy, an accomplishment comparable to what was happening in the secular kingdoms. These popes reorganized the church's financial system and changed payments from goods to money. At the same time, unfortunately, they rarely made moral reforms. Their reigns lapsed into worldliness and greed, which made the papacy more vulnerable to criticism.

The Avignonese papacy had barely ended in 1378 when a new calamity, the Great Schism, threw the church into even more confusion. Under Pope Gregory XI, the papacy had returned to Rome in 1377, and the cardinals had elected an Italian pope when Gregory died. The French cardinals did not approve of this pope, and they elected another pontiff to rule from Avignon. Western Christendom was thus divided into two obediences (as the area under papal control is called) with two popes, two colleges of cardinals, two curias, and two church tax systems. The rising power of the secular states became evident as rulers cast their support along political lines. France, Sicily, Scotland, Castile, Aragon, and Portugal rallied behind the Avignon pope; England, Flanders, Poland, Hungary, Germany, and the rest of Italy stayed loyal to the Roman pope. The papal office suffered the most; the pope's authority diminished as pious Christians became bewildered and disgusted.

The worst was yet to come. In 1409 both sets of cardinals summoned a church council in Pisa to heal the fissure. The Pisan Council elected a new pope and called on the other two to resign. They refused, and the church was faced with *three* rulers claiming papal authority. The Great Schism was finally resolved at the Council of Constance (1414–1418), which deposed the Avignon ruler, accepted the resignation of the Roman claimant, ignored the Pisan Council's choice, and elected a new pope, Martin V.

With the success of the Council of Constance, conciliar rule (rule by councils) as a way of curbing the power of the popes seemed to be gaining support in the church. But Martin V (pope 1417–1431) rejected this idea as soon as he was elected to the papal throne. Nevertheless, the conciliar movement remained alive until the mid–fifteenth century, when strong popes reasserted the monarchical power of their office. Although powerful, these popes failed to address pressing moral and spiritual concerns, for they were deeply involved in Italian politics and other worldly interests, ruling almost as secular princes in Papal States.

Technology

As farming life changed because of the growth of urban life, so did Europe's fledgling industrial life, and new technology, such as the suction pump, increased productivity in some industries. Older inventions, such as eyeglasses, mechanical clocks, and gunpowder, were improved in this age of rapid change. However, the most significant technological innovation of the Late Middle Ages was the development of printing with movable metal type in the mid–fifteenth century.

The Rise of Industries   Hand-loomed textile manufacturing remained the leading industry, but its production and distribution centers shifted. Cut off by war from their former wool supplies and their retail markets, the Flemish and French weavers were challenged by woolen manufacturers from the Rhineland, Poland, and the northern Italian cities of Florence, Genoa, and Venice. The greatest change in textile manufacturing, however, was ultimately precipitated by England's shift from the export of raw wool to the export of finished cloth, a change that disrupted the traditional rural way of life.

Wool merchants organized the new textile industry in England. Turning wool into finished cloth required many stages: shearing, carding, combing, spinning, weaving, fulling, felting, dyeing, and cutting. The merchants, who bought and owned the raw wool, created the "putting-out system," the assigning of tasks to families who worked at home—which came to be defined as the cottage industry. The workers tended to specialize in specific tasks. A new hand-operated machine, the spinning wheel—imported from India via the Middle East, perhaps during the Crusades—streamlined the spinning of wool into thread, or yarn. It replaced the ancient method, involving two hand-held sticks, called a distaff and a spindle. With the spinning wheel the worker stretched wool from a distaff onto a spindle, turning the wheel constantly so as to create a continuous thread. Women traditionally performed the spinning, hence the medieval terms *spinster* and *distaff side,* meaning "woman's work."

In England, merchant entrepreneurs invested in sites based on available grazing land for sheep and access to fast-flowing streams—the latter to power fulling mills, where wooden paddles washed and beat the cloth before it was stretched to dry outdoors. In some textile-producing areas, merchants, in order to ensure better cloth, recruited skilled workers from Flanders (modern Belgium) to perform the fulling and dyeing tasks. The importation of foreign workers could provoke social unrest, as in 1381, during the Peasants' Revolt, when the rioters massacred Flemish workers, accusing them of taking work from the local populace.

Other new industries also now emerged. Rag paper, a Chinese invention improved by the Arabs, was manufactured widely in Spain, Italy, France, and Germany; as part of papermaking, watermills turned wooden paddles, causing them to beat rags to soften them, in much the same way as was done in the fulling process for woolen textiles. Other new industries included silk fabrics, woven in impressive patterns in Florence, Venice, and Lucca, from the 1300s, and England and France, from the late 1400s. Salt was now distributed by Venice and Lisbon and used in the industries of tanning leather and preserving food. The iron industry arose to meet the demand for weapons, armor, and horseshoes.

The Printing Press   The German craftsman Johannes Gutenberg (1397?–1468) is often credited with the invention of the printing press, in about 1450, though it is nevertheless clear that his achievement rests on the shoulders of generations of craftspeople and tinkerers, working in various fields. Specifically, the model for his printing press came from similar devices used in the binding of books and the making of wine and paper. Gutenberg also had before him the model of printing from wood blocks (though without a printing press), invented in China in perhaps the sixth century C.E. and developed in the West after 1350, whereby pictures along with a brief text could be impressed onto a paper surface (see the section "The Print," later in the chapter).

Gutenberg's invention gave rise to the printing and publishing industries, with a host of related occupations, such as printers, engravers, compositors, typefounders (designers of typefaces), booksellers, editors, proofreaders, and librarians. Because it was cheaper to print a book than to have a text copied as a manu-

script, books became agents of democracy, with huge repercussions for education, literature, and society. Hints of the changes to come may be glimpsed in a survey of the perhaps forty thousand books, known as **incunabula** (from the Latin, "cradle"), which were printed before 1500: a mass of Christian texts, especially Bibles, prayer books, and lives of saints, in both Latin and vernacular languages; a flood of "how-to" manuals on topics such as etiquette; a horde of fictional works calculated to appeal to literate laypeople; a few books of music, showing lines and notes; and from Jewish-owned presses, an outpouring of works in Hebrew, including Bibles, prayer books, and almanacs.

THE CULTURAL FLOWERING OF THE LATE MIDDLE AGES

The calamitous political, social, and economic events of the Late Middle Ages were echoed in the cultural sphere by the breakdown of the medieval synthesis in religion, theology, literature, and art. New secular voices began to be heard, challenging traditional views, and the interests of the bourgeoisie started to have an impact on art and architecture. Although the church remained the principal financial supporter of the arts, rich town dwellers, notably bankers and merchants, were emerging as the new patrons of art (Figure 10.4). Conspicuous art patronage made them the equals of the most powerful figures in society, but they still had few political rights.

Religion

Monastic reform had been a major force within the church in the High Middle Ages, but such collective acts of piety were largely unknown in the Late Middle Ages. Dedicated and virtuous monks and nuns were increasingly rare, and their influence was waning. Innovative forms of religious expression came not from members of religious orders but from laypeople, inspired perhaps to protest and react against what they perceived as the increasing worldliness of the church and the declining commitment of many clergy.

Lay piety was thus one of the most significant developments in the religious landscape. By 1400, the Brethren and Sisters of the Common Life and the Friends of God were rising in the Rhineland, the Low Countries, and Flanders. This lay movement constituted the *devotio moderna,* or the "new devotion," with its ideal of a pious lay society. Disappointed with traditionally trained priests, members of these groups often rejected higher education and practiced the strict

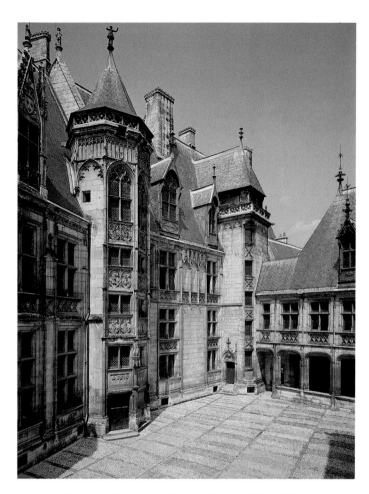

Figure 10.4 Jacques Coeur's House. 1443–1451. Bourges, France. *Coeur was an immensely successful entrepreneur who at one point bankrolled the French kings. His magnificent mansion at Bourges spawned many imitations among wealthy business-men across Europe. The building's spiky turrets, fanciful balconies, and highly decorated windows are all secular adaptations of the Late Gothic style more commonly seen in church architecture. Coeur conducted his Europe-wide financial and commercial dealings from this house, sending messages by carrier pigeons released through holes in the roof.*

Figure 10.5 *Flagellation Scene. Annales of Gilles Le Muisit.* Bibliothèque Royale Albert Ier, Brussels. *This miniature painting represents a familiar scene across Europe during the plague years. The penitents, depicted with bare backs and feet, marched through towns scourging themselves with whips. By this self-punishment, they hoped to atone for their own and society's sins and thus end the plague.*

discipline of the earlier monastic orders, but without withdrawing into a monastery. Among the most important expressions of this new devotion was *The Imitation of Christ*, by Thomas à Kempis (1380–1471). His manual, with its stern asceticism, reflected the harsh ideals of the Brethren of the Common Life, the group of which Kempis was a member.

Within the pietistic movement, extreme ascetic practices that verged on heresy increased in these turbulent years. The bizarre behavior of the flagellants, for example, was triggered by the plague. They regarded this disease as God's way to judge and punish an evil society. The flagellants staged public processions in which they engaged in ritual whippings in an attempt to divert divine wrath from the general population (Figure 10.5).

The flagellants managed to escape official censure, but those more openly critical of the church did not. The leaders who attempted to reform the church in England and Bohemia met stout resistance from the popes. The English reform movement sprang from the teachings of John Wycliffe (about 1320–1384), an Oxford teacher whose message attracted both nobility and common folk. Wishing to purify the church of worldliness, Wycliffe urged the abolition of ecclesiastical property, the subservience of the church to the state, and the denial of papal authority. The most lasting achievement of Wycliffe's movement was the introduction of the first complete English-language Bible, produced by scholars inspired by his teaching. After his followers (known as Lollards, because during religious frenzy, their tongues were said to "loll" out of their mouths) were condemned as heretical, the secular officials launched savage persecutions that resulted in the murder of those supporters who did not recant.

The Bohemian reformers in the Holy Roman Empire were indebted to Wycliffe, whom some had met at Oxford; but, more important, their strength was rooted in the popular piety and evangelical preachers of mid-fourteenth-century Prague. The heresy became identified with Jan Hus (about 1369–1415), a Czech theologian who accepted Wycliffe's political views but rejected some of his religious teachings. Hus was invited to the Council of Constance in 1415, where his ideas were condemned, and he was burned at the stake by state authorities. His death outraged his fellow Czechs, many of whom, including the powerful and wealthy, now adopted his views. Hussite beliefs became a vehicle for Czech nationalism, as Hus's ethnic comrades fought against German overlords and attacked church property. Because of the backing of powerful lay leaders, the Hussites survived into the next century. They gained more followers during the Protestant Reformation and exist today as the Moravian Brethren.

THE CULTURAL FLOWERING OF THE LATE MIDDLE AGES

Although the secular authorities, instigated by the church, could usually be counted on to put down the heresies, the church had a more powerful internal weapon at its disposal: the Inquisition (from the Latin *inquisitio,* "inquiry"). Born in the aftermath of the Albigensian heresy in the twelfth century (see Chapter 9), the Inquisition was a religious court for identifying and condemning heretics. The Inquisition reached its cruel height during the Late Middle Ages, particularly in Italy and Spain.

Because of its procedures, the Inquisition became the most notorious instrument ever created by the Christian church. Ignoring the basic ideals of Roman law, this church court allowed suspects to be condemned without ever facing their accusers. Confessions made under torture were also allowed to serve as evidence against other persons. Forbidden by the Bible to shed blood, the leaders of the Inquisition turned convicted heretics over to the state authorities, who then executed them by burning. By modern estimates, thousands of men and women perished in this way.

The Inquisition was also used to rid society of women—and to a lesser extent of men—who were suspected of being in league with the devil. The belief in witchcraft, an occult legacy of the ancient world, was next to universal during the Middle Ages. Many educated people sincerely believed that certain women were witches and that magical devices could protect the faithful from their spells. Consequently, hundreds of suspected individuals were killed by the Inquisition or by unruly mobs. Fear of witchcraft persisted as a dangerous part of popular lore into the eighteenth century.

Theology and Philosophy

Although the popes betrayed their spiritual mission in these years, the church was not without dedicated followers who cared deeply about theological issues. Many of these clerical thinkers were affiliated with the universities, principally in Paris and at Oxford. Their major disputes were over Thomism, the theological system of Thomas Aquinas, which in the Late Middle Ages was losing supporters and coming increasingly under attack. At the same time, the ongoing philosophical struggle between Realism and Nominalism finally ended with a Nominalist victory. In the long run, those who questioned Thomism and those who accepted Nominalism set philosophy and theology on separate paths and thus paved the way to the Renaissance and the Scientific Revolution.

The *Via Antiqua* Versus the *Via Moderna*   The opening round in the theological war against Thomism began soon after the death of Thomas Aquinas in 1274

and before the High Middle Ages were over. In 1277 church officials in Paris condemned the Latin Averroists at the local university for their rationalist ideas. As part of their attack on extreme rationalism, the church authorities rejected some of Aquinas's arguments. The censure of Thomism led to a heated controversy that raged for much of the Late Middle Ages among university scholars. In particular, Thomas's fellow Dominican friars waged an acrimonious battle with the Franciscan masters, their great rivals in theological studies.

During these theological debates, new labels were invented and assumed by the opposing sides. Aquinas's *via media* came to be termed by his opponents the *via antiqua,* or the old-fashioned way. Broadly speaking, the *via antiqua* followed Thomism in urging that faith and reason be combined as the correct approach to divine truth. In contrast, the *via moderna,* or the modern way, made a complete separation of biblical beliefs and rationalism. In time the *via moderna* prevailed, driving the *via antiqua* underground until it was rescued from oblivion in the modern period.

Duns Scotus and William of Ockham   The conflict between the *via antiqua* and the *via moderna* was best exemplified in the writings of John Duns Scotus and William of Ockham, respectively. The first of these commentators was sympathetic to the theology of Thomas Aquinas, but the second scholar was unmistakably hostile and tried to discredit Thomism.

Duns Scotus [duhnz SKOAT-us] (about 1265–1308), the most persuasive voice of the *via antiqua,* was a Scottish thinker who was trained as a Franciscan and lectured at the universities in Oxford, Paris, and Cologne. Even though he was a supporter of Thomism, Duns Scotus unwittingly undermined Aquinas's synthesis by stressing that faith was superior to reason, a shift in focus that arose from his belief in God's absolute and limitless power. Pointing out that God's existence could not be proven either through the senses or by reason, he asserted that only faith could explain the divine mystery. Furthermore, Duns Scotus concluded that because the theologian and the philosopher have different intellectual tasks, theology and science (that is, the study of nature) should be independent fields of inquiry.

What Duns Scotus unintentionally began, William of Ockham (about 1300–about 1349) purposely completed. Under the assaults of Ockham's keen intellect, the Thomist theological edifice collapsed. An Oxford-trained theologian, he recognized the importance of both reason and faith; but, like Scotus, he did not see how reason could prove God's existence. Both thinkers believed that only personal feelings and mystical experiences could reveal God and the divine moral order. Yet Ockham went further than Scotus by

SLICE OF LIFE
A Gossip Columnist of the Late Middle Ages

HENRY KNIGHTON
A View from the Provinces

The Chronicle *of Henry Knighton (?–1396) is an excellent source for the Late Middle Ages in England. An attentive observer of public affairs, Knighton recorded the gossip about the political and religious unrest of his age. He lived mainly in Leicestershire, far from London, but he had well-placed contacts and reliable sources. In the first excerpt, Knighton reports on the 1381 rebellion of Wat Tyler. In the second excerpt, he passes along a rumor about religious unrest, which may be related to the Lollards, who believed that women could be priests.*

1

The next day, which was Saturday [15 June 1381], they all came together again in Smithfield, where the king [Richard II] came early to meet them, and showed that although he was young in years he was possessed of a shrewd mind. He was approached by their leader, Wat Tyler, who had now changed his name to Jack Straw. He stood close to the king, speaking for the others, and carrying an unsheathed knife, of the kind people call a dagger, which he tossed from hand to hand as a child might play with it, and looked as though he might suddenly seize the opportunity to stab the king if he should refuse their requests, and those accompanying the king therefore greatly feared what might come to pass. The commons asked of the king that all game, whether in waters or in parks and woods should become common to all, so that everywhere in the realm, in rivers and fishponds, and woods and forests, they might take the wild beasts, and hunt the hare in the fields, and do many other such things without restraint.

And when the king wanted time to consider such a concession, Jack Straw drew closer to him, with menacing words, and though I know not how he dared, took the reins of the king's horse in his hand. Seeing that, [William] Walworth, a citizen of London, fearing that he was about to kill the king, drew his basilard and ran Jack Straw through the neck. Thereupon an-other esquire, called Ralph Standish, stabbed him in the side with his basilard. And he fell to the ground on his back, and after rising to his hands and knees, he died.

2

A woman in London celebrates mass. At that time there was a woman in the city of London who had an only daughter whom she taught to celebrate the mass; and she privily set up and furnished an altar in her own bedroom, and there she caused her daughter on many occasions to dress as a priest and in her fashion to celebrate mass, though when she came to the sacramental words she prostrated herself before the altar and did not complete the sacrament. But then she would rise for the rest of the mass and recite it to the end, her mother assisting her and showing her devotion.

That nonsense went on for some time, until it was revealed by a neighbour who had been admitted to the secret, when it came to the ears of the bishop of London. He summoned them to his presence and showed them the error of their ways, and compelled them to display the child's priestly tonsure in public, for her head was found to be quite bald. The bishop greatly deplored and bewailed such misconduct in the church in his time, uttering many lamentations, and put an end to it by enjoining penance upon them.

Interpreting This Slice of Life **What** particular demand did Wat Tyler make of Richard II, the English King? **Why** do you think Knighton singled out this demand in his account? **Why** might Wat Tyler have taken the pseudonym Jack Straw? **How** reliable is Knighton as a reporter? **Why** were the unnamed mother and daughter punished by the bishop of London? **What** bias may have motivated Knighton to report this London gossip to his patron? **Can** you draw a modern parallel to Henry Knighton and his *Chronicle*?

asserting that reason, the senses, and empirical evidence could enable human beings to discover and hence understand the natural world. To Ockham, faith and reason were both valid approaches to truth, but they should be kept apart so that each could achieve its respective end.

In the seemingly endless medieval debate between the Realists and the Nominalists, Ockham's reasoning swept Nominalism to its final victory. Like the Nominalists of the twelfth century, Ockham denied the existence of universals and claimed that only individual objects existed. He concluded that human beings can have clear and distinct knowledge only of specific things in the physical world; no useful knowledge can be gained through reason or the senses about the spiritual realm. Ockham's conclusion did not mean that human beings were cast adrift without access to the world of God. A corollary of his approach was that understanding of the spiritual realm rested solely on the truths of faith and theology.

In his reasoning, William of Ockham asserted a principle of economy that stripped away all that was irrelevant: Arguments should be drawn from a minimum of data and founded on closely constructed logic. "It is vain to do with more what can be done with fewer," he says in one of his works. Ockham's "razor" of logic eliminated superfluous information that could not be verified, thus enabling a student to cut to the core of a philosophical problem. The Ockhamites, following their mentor's logic and empiricism, challenged the Realists and dominated the intellectual life of the universities for the next two hundred years.

Science

Ockham's ideas broadened the path to modern science that had been opened by two thirteenth-century thinkers. In that earlier time, Robert Grosseteste [GROAS-test] (about 1175–1253), a Franciscan at Oxford University, had devised a scientific method for investigating natural phenomena; using step-by-step procedures, he employed mathematics and tested hypotheses until he reached satisfactory conclusions. Roger Bacon (about 1220–1292), another Franciscan and a follower of Grosseteste, advocated the use of the experimental method, which he demonstrated in his studies of optics, solar eclipses, and rainbows and in his treatises on mathematics, physics, and philosophy. From the modern standpoint, Bacon was perhaps the most original mind of this generally barren period in the history of science.

In the fourteenth century, other thinkers, with Grosseteste and Bacon as guides and Ockham's logic as a weapon, made further contributions to the advance of science. Outstanding among these men was one bold Parisian scholar who took advantage of the growing interest in the experimental method, Nicholas Oresme [O-REM] (about 1330–1382). Oresme answered all of Aristotle's objections to the idea that the earth moved. Using pure reason and applying theoretical arguments, he concluded that it was as plausible that the earth moved around the sun as that it was fixed. Having used reason to show that the earth may move, however, Oresme then chose to accept church doctrine, denying what he had demonstrated. Never-

Figure 10.6 DOMENICO DI BARTOLO. *Distribution of Alms.* 1440–1441. Fresco. Hospital of Santa Maria della Scala, Siena. *Hospitals, which originated in the High Middle Ages, continued to be founded across Europe. By the fourteenth century, in Siena, Italy, Santa Maria della Scala, which was located on the square of the cathedral, had grown into a highly reputable and richly endowed hospital. The friars and, later, the city of Siena managed it, nursing the sick, taking in orphans and abandoned children, and caring for the numerous pilgrims who traveled through the city on their way to Rome. Domenico di Bartolo's fresco, the* Distribution of Alms, *illustrates the life of this hospital, as it nurses its patients and performs its civic responsibilities. On the left, the rector (the hospital head) tips his hat to a well-dressed man, probably one of the wealthy donors; in the center, a man puts on clothes while other poor people wait in line, and, in the far right background, children receive bread. Above the figures, the facades of the cathedral and the bishop's residence may be seen. The painter's credible treatment of space and volume indicates his familiarity with the art innovations under way in Florence, where he probably studied.*

theless, Oresme's arguments, along with Ockham's separation of natural philosophy from theology and Bacon's formulation of the experimental method, foreshadowed the end of the medieval concept of the physical and celestial worlds (Figure 10.6).

Literature

The powerful forces that were reshaping the wider culture—the rising new monarchies, the growing

ENCOUNTER

A New Look at the Spread of Byzantine Scholarship in the West

Sudden and calamitous events are often seen by contemporaries as major turning points in history with both immediate and far-reaching consequences. Just such an event was the fall of Constantinople to the Ottoman Turks in 1453. While it remains true that this dramatic event spelled the end of the Eastern Roman or Byzantine Empire, modern research calls into question the old idea that the fall of Constantinople marked a transformational moment in the cultural life of the West. The reinterpretation of the meaning of the fall of Constantinople is a classic example of revisionist history.

Prior to the twentieth century, most historians believed that the fall of Constantinople forced the exodus of Byzantine scholars to the safety of Rome, Venice, and Florence, which, in turn, triggered a renewed interest in the Greek and Roman heritage—thus marking the start of the Renaissance in Italy. But today, evidence shows that, long before the Turks conquered Constantinople, Greek intellectuals and teachers went to Italy and spread their knowledge, and that religious thinkers and members of Italy's urban middle class welcomed them with open arms.

As early as the end of the fourteenth century, in about 1397, Manuel Chrysoloras [kris-uh-LOR-uhs] (about 1353–1415), a Byzantine aristocrat and scholar, came to Florence, at the invitation of the city-state government, to teach Greek (Encounter figure 10.1). After learning both Greek and Latin, his students studied the works of the Greek and Roman philosophers and

historians. Over the next few decades, more and more Byzantine scholars settled in Rome and Venice, where they taught Greek and rhetoric and translated Greek texts into Latin. They also brought along ancient Greek and Latin philosophical, literary, and scientific works and treatises by learned Byzantine writers, which had never been available in the West. In Venice, some of these scholars worked with the famous Aldine Press, which printed many Greek and Latin classics, only four decades after Gutenberg's invention.

Another encounter between Byzantine and Italian scholars occurred when church leaders from Rome and Constantinople held ecumenical councils in Ferrara and Florence (1438–1445). The Eastern Orthodox Church, based in Constantinople, which felt threatened by the Ottoman Turks and their Islamic faith, wanted to settle past disagreements with the papacy and reunite the two branches of Christianity. However, fundamental differences over ecclesiastical governance, dogmas, and liturgical practices doomed any hope for reconciliation (see Figure 11.21).

Although the church union failed, numerous intellectual exchanges took place between the conference delegates. Several Byzantine churchmen and scholars remained in Italy to teach and to translate more Greek and Latin manuscripts. The most influential of these men was John Bessarion (1403–1472), who was made an archbishop in the Eastern Church by the Byzantine emperor in 1437. Bessarion, who supported the union, first settled in Rome. There, he founded an academy,

---

national consciousness among diverse peoples, the emerging secularism, and the developing urban environment—were also transforming literature in the Late Middle Ages. The rise of literacy produced a growing educated class who learned to read and write the local languages rather than Latin, and a shift to vernacular literature began to occur. Two new groups—the monarchs and their courts, and the urban middle class—started to supplant the nobility and the church as patrons and audiences. And, most important of all, Gutenberg's printing press helped close the book on medieval civilization and signal the commencement of the modern world.

Northern Italian Literature: Petrarch and Boccaccio

New literary forms emerged in the areas where the chivalric and feudal modes were weakest—northern Italy and England. Petrarch and Boccaccio, both Flor-

entines, like Dante, grew up in a Christian world that was rapidly being secularized. These two writers captured the mood of this transition era as Florence and the other Italian city-states shed their medieval outlook. Both authors looked back to the Classical world for inspiration, and yet both found in the bustling world of the nearby towns the materials and characters for their stories. Of the two, Petrarch was the more dedicated Classicist and often used ancient themes in his writings.

Francesco Petrarch [PEE-trark] ("Petrarca" in Italian) (1304–1374), though Florentine by birth and in spirit, flourished in Avignon amid the splendor and learning of the papal court. As a diplomat for popes and Italian princes, he won fame and wealth, but his reputation arose from his career as a professional man of letters. Rejecting the age's trend toward the vernacular, he dedicated his life to Latin writing and to the re-

Encounter figure 10.1 ANONYMOUS. *Manuel Chrysoloras Teaching Greek in Florence. Drawing. Louvre. Although Chrysoloras's classroom teaching techniques are not known, today's scholars believe he would read aloud, in front of his students, a passage in Greek from some classical text and then analyze the work, drawing on sources from other Byzantine writers, a pedagogical device used in Constantinople. This portrait of Chrysoloras, perhaps done by one of his students, shows him teaching the Greek alphabet at the Florentine* studium, *or school, at which he taught.*

which translated Greek manuscripts and taught Greek philosophy. Recognizing his piety and learning, the pope, in 1439, made him a cardinal in the Western Church and sent him on several diplomatic missions. Later, he withdrew to Venice, where his reputation grew. When he died, he willed his personal library of Greek works to his beloved city of Venice. Bessarion—through patronage, his command of Greek, and his extensive collection of Greek manuscripts—played a central role in the Italo-Byzantine intellectual world well before the fall of Constantinople in 1453.

Learning from the Encounter What contributions did Byzantine scholars make to intellectual life in Italy prior to 1453? **How** did church councils lead to the exchange of ideas between the Byzantine and Italian scholars? **Why** should we look beyond immediate events and what often appears to be the obvious? **Can** you name a modern event that would benefit from a reexamination of our commonly held beliefs about its occurrence? **Discuss**.

covery of ancient manuscripts, although the work for which he is most renowned, a collection of love lyrics and sonnets called *Canzoniere*, or *Songbook*, is written in Italian. His devotion struck a responsive chord among his fellow Italians, who in 1341 proclaimed him poet laureate for his lyrics, sonnets, treatises, and epics. In many ways, Petrarch, despite a clerical training, shows the typical secular interests of his time. A conventional Christian, he only occasionally addressed religious issues in his works.

A religious theme is touched on in *Secretum*, or *My Secret*, in which Petrarch deals with the state of his soul. In this dialogue, "Augustinus," or St. Augustine, hounds "Franciscus," or Petrarch, about his innermost thoughts and desires, charging him with all the deadly sins. Freely admitting his moral lapses, Franciscus pleads that he is the same as any other man—driven by a love of learning, a weakness for fleshly attrac-

tions, and an appetite for personal comforts. Despite this confession, with its modern overtones, the dialogue shows that Petrarch could not liberate himself fully from medieval values.

Even more than his lifelong friend Petrarch, Giovanni Boccaccio [bo-KACH-e-o] (1313–1375) was a man of the world. The son of a banker, Boccaccio began his literary career by penning prose romances along with poetic pastorals and sonnets, many of which were dedicated to Fiammetta, a young woman who was both his consuming passion and his literary muse. His early efforts, however, were overshadowed by his Italian prose masterpiece, *The Decameron*. Written in about 1351, this work reflects the grim conditions of the Black Death, which had just swept through Florence. In *The Decameron* (from the Greek word for "ten days"), Boccaccio describes how ten young men and women, in their efforts to escape the plague, flee the city to a country villa, where they pass the time, each telling a story a day for ten days. Most of their one hundred tales were based on folk stories and popular legends. Although some tales deal lightly with social mores and a few contain moral messages, the majority simply entertain the listener. Boccaccio, speaking through a cross section of urban voices and relying on well-known stories, helped develop a form of literature that eventually led to the modern short story.

English Literature: Geoffrey Chaucer   Like its Italian counterpart, English literature rapidly matured into its own forms during the Late Middle Ages. The development of an English literary style was aided immensely by the evolution of a common language. Until this time, most educated English people read and spoke French, but a rising sense of national consciousness, triggered by the Hundred Years' War and by an emerging educated urban class, hastened the spread of English as the native tongue. England's kings came to see themselves as different from their French ancestors and purposely began to speak English instead of French; they also made English the official language of government.

By 1300 important works in English were beginning to appear, such as *The Vision of Piers Plowman*, a moral allegory, probably written by William Langland (about 1332–1400), that graphically exposes the plight of the poor and calls for a return to Christian virtues. This work provides insight into England's social and economic system and, through the author's anguish, reveals the social tension around the time of the Peasants' Revolt in 1381.

English literature was still establishing its own identity and a common language was slowly emerging when Geoffrey Chaucer (about 1340–1400) appeared on the scene. He wrote in an East Midland dialect of English that became the standard form for his generation as well as the foundation of modern English. The son of a wealthy London merchant, Chaucer spent his professional life as a courtier, a diplomat, and a public servant for the English crown. The profession of "writer" or "poet" was unknown in Chaucer's day. But his poetry brought him renown, and when he died he was the first commoner to be buried in Westminster Abbey, a favored burial spot for English royalty.

Chaucer began composing his most famous work, *The Canterbury Tales*, in 1385. He set the tales in the context of a pilgrimage to the tomb of Thomas à Becket, the twelfth-century martyr. Even though the journey has a religious purpose, Chaucer makes it plain that the travelers intend to have a good time along the way. To make the journey from London to Canterbury more interesting, the thirty-one pilgrims (including Chaucer himself) agree to tell tales—two each going and returning—and to award a prize for the best story told.

Chaucer completed only twenty-three tales and the general Prologue, in which he introduces the pilgrims. Each person on the pilgrimage not only represents an English social type but also is a unique and believable human being. In this poetic narrative about a group of ordinary people, the spiritual is mixed with the temporal and the serious with the comic.

Chaucer drew his pilgrims from nearly all walks of medieval society. The Knight, in this late stage of feudalism, personified much that was noble and honorable in the chivalric code; his bravery could not be questioned, but he was also a mercenary and cruel to his enemies. Certain representatives of the church are also somewhat skeptically treated. The Prioress, the head of a convent and from the upper class, is more concerned about her refined manners and polished language than the state of her soul. Similarly, the Monk lives a life of the flesh and enjoys good food, fine wines, and expensive clothing. The Friar seems the very opposite of his sworn ideals; he is eager to hear a confession for a fee, and he never goes among the poor or aids the sick. However, in the country Parson, Chaucer portrays a true servant of God who preaches to his parish, looks after the infirm and dying, and lives as simply as his church members. Among the secular travelers, the most vivid is the Wife of Bath. A widow five times over, this jolly woman is full of life and loves to talk. She has been on many pilgrimages and not only knows about foreign places but also has a keen insight into people (Figure 10.7).

As for the tales they tell, the pilgrims' choices often reflect their own moral values. The worthy Knight tells a chivalric love story, but the Miller, a coarse, rough man well versed in lying and cheating, relates how a young wife took on a lover and deceived her husband—an example of the popular medieval tale known as a *fabliau*. Thus the pilgrims' stories, based on folk and fairy tales, romances, classical stories, and beast fables, reveal as much about the narrators as they do about Late Medieval culture.

French Literature: Christine de Pizan   France was also touched by the winds of change blowing through Europe during the Late Middle Ages. Christine de Pizan [kris-teen duh pee-zuhn], the leading French writer of the day, began to explore in her works the status and role of women, giving voice in the process to one of the most prominent issues in the Post-Modern world (see Chapter 22). She also contributed to the triumph of vernacular over Latin language by writing in a graceful French with the learnedness of Latin.

Christine de Pizan (sometimes written as "de Pisan," or "of Pisa") (1364–about 1430) was by birth an

Figure 10.7 *The Wife of Bath.* Ellesmere Manuscript. Early fifteenth century. Bancroft Library, University of California at Berkeley. *In the Ellesmere Manuscript, an early edition of* The Canterbury Tales *issued soon after Chaucer's death, each story was accompanied by a sketch of the pilgrim who was narrating it. This portrait of the Wife of Bath shows her riding an ambler, a horse that walks with an easy gait, and wearing a wimple, the typical headdress of nuns as well as laywomen of the period.*

Italian whose literary gifts blossomed under the patronage of the French kings and dukes of Burgundy. She began a life of study and learning after the death of her husband, a royal official, in 1389, left her with a family to support. The first known Western woman to earn a living through her writings, de Pizan was a pioneer who blazed the trail for women authors.

De Pizan wrote on diverse topics, working within the well-established literary genres of her day, including love poems, lays, biography, letters, political tracts, and moral proverbs. Two themes dominate her writing: calls for peace and appeals for the recognition of women's contributions to culture and social life. Both themes reflect the era in which she lived—an age beset by civil strife because of the Hundred Years' War and a time in which women were scarcely allowed to express an opinion in public.

The work of de Pizan's that has excited the most interest among modern readers is *The Book of the City of Ladies* (1405), a book that forcefully tries to raise the status of women and to give them dignity. Offering one of the first histories of women and arguing that women have the right to be educated, based on her premise that women are moral and intellectual equals of men, this book seems almost feminist in a modern sense; however, a close reading shows that de Pizan is writing within a medieval framework. Nowhere in this book or in any other writings does she advocate that women abandon their traditional roles and strike out on a new path. It is proper, nevertheless, to claim that de Pizan is the first Western writer to raise the issue of women's rights in society and culture.

Art and Architecture

The Gothic style continued to dominate architecture throughout this period (see Chapter 9), but the balanced and unified High Gothic of the thirteenth century was now replaced with the ornate effects of the **Late Gothic style.** Virtuosity became the chief aesthetic goal, as the architects took basic forms and pushed them to the stylistic limits.

Late Gothic sculpture and painting also became more virtuosic. Statues and sculptured figures were given willowy, swaying bodies, rendered in exquisite detail, and illuminated manuscripts and painted wooden panels became ever more refined. At the same time, Giotto, an early-fourteenth-century Florentine painter, was revolutionizing art with a new approach to painting. The trend toward naturalism embodied in his works was the most significant new artistic development of this period and was destined to be the wave of the future.

Late Gothic Architecture France—the home of the Gothic style—remained a potent source of architectural innovation. French architects now abandoned the balanced ideal of the High Gothic and made extravagance their guiding principle, creating a Late Gothic style typified by ever greater heights and elaborate decoration. In the fifteenth century, this tendency culminated in the **Flamboyant style,** so named for its flamelike effects. French churches built in this style had sky-piercing spires, and their facades were embroidered with lacy or wavy decorations that obscured the buildings' structural components (Figure 10.8).

During the fourteenth century, the Late Gothic spread, becoming an international style. All across Europe, the focus shifted to fanciful designs: The churches were smaller, the roofs and towers taller, the naves wider, and the decorations more luxuriant. Regional tastes, however, made for local variations in the general style.

In England, the Late Gothic was called **Perpendicular** because of its dramatic emphasis on verticality. This

Figure 10.8 The Church of St. Maclou. 1435–ca. 1514. Rouen, France. *St. Maclou's exterior illustrates the ornate Late Gothic style. Its west facade, unlike a square High Gothic front, fans out to form a semicircular entrance. There are five portals (rather than the usual three), two of which are blind, and set above them are steeply pitched stone arches of intricate design.*

Figure 10.9 Choir of Gloucester Cathedral. Ca. 1330–1357. Gloucester, England. *The choir and apse of Gloucester cathedral were rebuilt in the Perpendicular Gothic style in about 1330, when King Edward III chose the church as the burial shrine for his murdered father, Edward II. The architects made the earlier Norman apse into a square and filled the east end with glass panels. Inside, the builders redesigned the support system, using thin vertical piers; these piers were attached to the walls and laced together on the ceiling, creating elaborate patterns that complemented the glass decorations.*

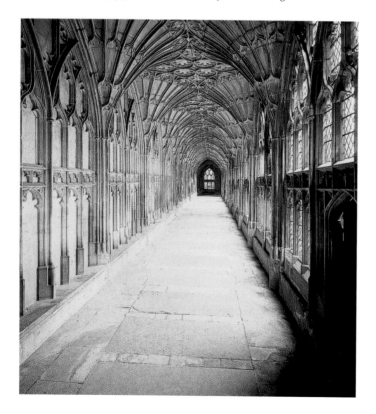

Figure 10.10 South Cloister of Gloucester Cathedral. Ca. 1370. Gloucester, England. *Fan vaulting, an intricate pattern in which ribs arch out from a single point in the ceiling, first appeared at Gloucester cathedral and inspired many imitations. Although the ribs may appear to be structurally necessary, they are really a richly decorative device carved from stone. In Gloucester's south cloister, the tracery fans out from the top of each column and then merges in the center of the ceiling, giving the impression of a delicate screen.*

Perpendicular style was characterized by an increased use of paneled decorations on the walls and overhead vaults, resulting in a variation of rib vaulting, called **fan vaulting,** in which stone ribs arch out from a single point in the ceiling to form a delicate pattern. This style also increased the number of window openings, which necessitated additional flying buttresses. The best example of the English Perpendicular is the cathedral in Gloucester. In the choir, the vertical lines, extending from the floor to the ceiling, where the tracery is interwoven, unite the building's interior into an upward-moving volume (Figure 10.9). Just as impressive as the interior is the nearby cloister with its fan tracery vaulting that weaves a pattern overhead while tying the walls and ceiling into a complex unit (Figure 10.10).

In Italy, the Gothic had put down only shallow roots because the Italians felt that the French builders had little to teach them about architecture. Italian Gothic has strong affinities with the Romanesque style—the large hall with its basilica floor plan and massive walls. In addition, most of the key Gothic features are missing from the Italian Gothic, such as the flying buttresses, the twin towers, and the vast numbers of stained-glass windows.

A key example of the Late Italian Gothic is the cathedral in Siena. Filled with civic pride, Siena's citizens urged their leaders to build a cathedral more splendid than those of their neighbors. Begun in the mid–thirteenth century, the cathedral was constructed over the next hundred and fifty years, and, as a result, the building complex shows a mixture of styles: The **campanile,** or bell tower, is executed in the Italian Romanesque, but the overall cathedral complex is Italian Gothic (Figure 10.11). The facade, for the first time in Italy, incorporated nearly life-size figures into the total design, thus heightening its resemblance to the French Gothic. However, many features distinguish the style of Siena from the French style. For example, the decorative statues on Siena's facade were placed above the gables, not set in niches. Furthermore, the Sienese builders put mosaics into the spaces in the gables and above the central rose window.

Florence, Siena's greatest military and trade rival, refused to be outdone by its nearby competitor. The Florentine city fathers asked Giotto [JAWT-toe] (about 1276–1337), the city's most renowned painter, to design a campanile for their own cathedral. Today, the first story of the bell tower—with its carvings, interlaced patterns of pink and white marble, and hexagonal inlays—still stands as conceived by Giotto (Figure 10.12). Giotto's plan, as left in a drawing, called for an open tower with a spire on top, as in a French Gothic tower. But later architects constructed a rectangular top instead and decorated it with marble—making it

distinctively Italian rather than reminiscent of the French.

Late Gothic Sculpture   During the Late Middle Ages, sculpture, like architecture, continued to undergo stylistic changes, among which two general trends may be identified. One trend centered in Italy, notably in Siena, where the Pisano [pee-SAHN-o] family began to experiment with sculptural forms that foreshadowed Renaissance art, with its return to Classical themes and values (see Chapter 11). Outstanding among the members of the gifted Pisano family was Giovanni Pisano (1245–1314), who designed the intricate Late Gothic facade of the Siena cathedral (see Figure 10.11). Giovanni's great artistic reputation is largely based on the massive marble pulpit that he carved for the cathedral at Pisa. Using Classical themes derived from Roman art (as Renaissance artists were to do), he designed the pulpit to rest on acanthus leaves at the top of eight Corinthian columns (Figure 10.13). The lions that support two of the columns were modeled on those on an ancient Roman sarcophagus. Just as Late Roman art blended Christian and Classical symbols, so Giovanni's treatment of the pulpit's base mixed images of the cardinal virtues, such as Justice and Temperance, with the figure of the Greek hero Herakles.

Pisano's octagonal pulpit includes eight panels in high relief that depict scenes from the lives of either John the Baptist or Christ. Of these panels, the scene depicting the Nativity ranks as his finest work. In this scene, he portrays a natural vitality through the careful balance and orderly spacing of the animals and people (Figure 10.14). The placement and the calm actions of the surrounding figures frame the Virgin and child so that the viewer's attention is focused on these two central figures. Giovanni's swaying figures with their smooth draperies were rooted in Late Gothic art, but their quiet serenity attested to his classicizing manner.

The other trend in sculpture during this time centered in Burgundy, where Philip the Bold (r. 1364–1404) supported scholars and artists at his ducal court in Dijon. Preeminent among these was Claus Sluter [SLUE-tuhr] (about 1350–1406), a sculptor of Netherlandish origin who helped to define this last phase of Gothic art. Sluter's masterly sculptures are still housed in a monastery near Dijon, and his most famous work, *The Well of Moses,* was commissioned for the cloister of this monastic retreat.

The Well of Moses, which was designed as a decorative cover for an actual well in a courtyard, is surrounded at its base with Old Testament prophets symbolizing the sacraments of communion and baptism. The most beautifully rendered of the surviving life-size statues is Moses, encased in a flowing robe

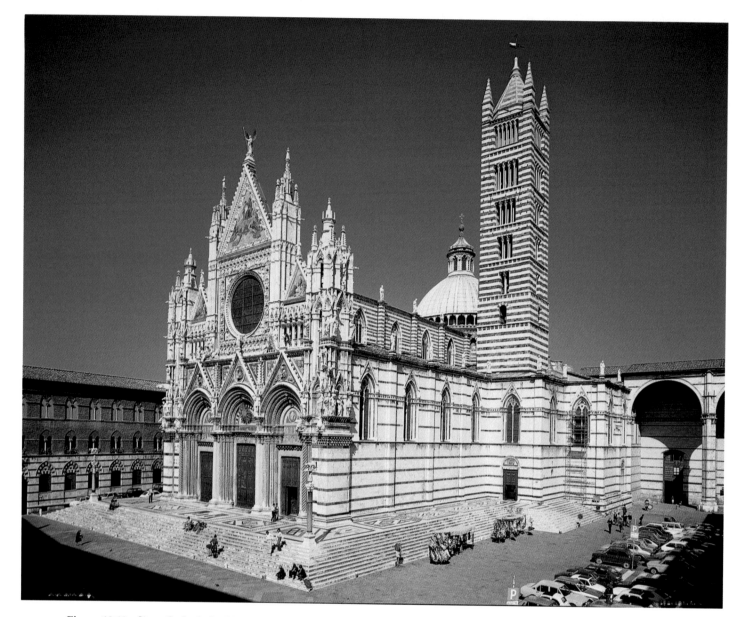

Figure 10.11 Siena Cathedral. 1250–1400. Siena, Italy. *Extant records and floor plans show that the Sienese changed their minds several times before deciding on the cathedral's final shape. At one time, in about 1322, a commission of architects advised that the existing cathedral be demolished because the foundations and walls were not strong enough to support new additions. Nonetheless, construction went forward, and the cathedral is still standing after more than six hundred years.*

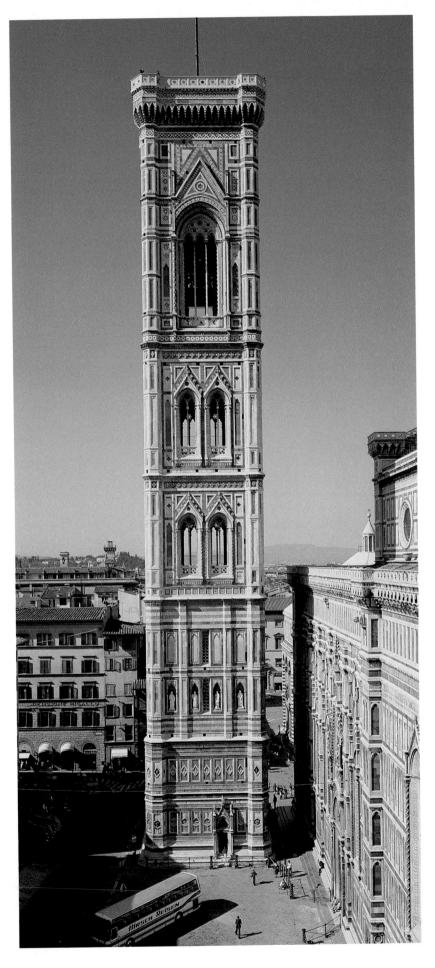

Figure 10.12 GIOTTO. Campanile of the Florentine Cathedral. Ca. 1334–1350. Ht. approx. 200'. Florence, Italy. *Giotto's Tower, as this campanile is known in Florence, is one of the city's most cherished landmarks. Today, its bells still toll the time. The two sets of windows in the central section and the taller openings at the top give the campanile a strong sense of balanced proportion. Thus, despite being built in the fourteenth century, the tower anticipates the Classical ideal that was revived in the Renaissance.*

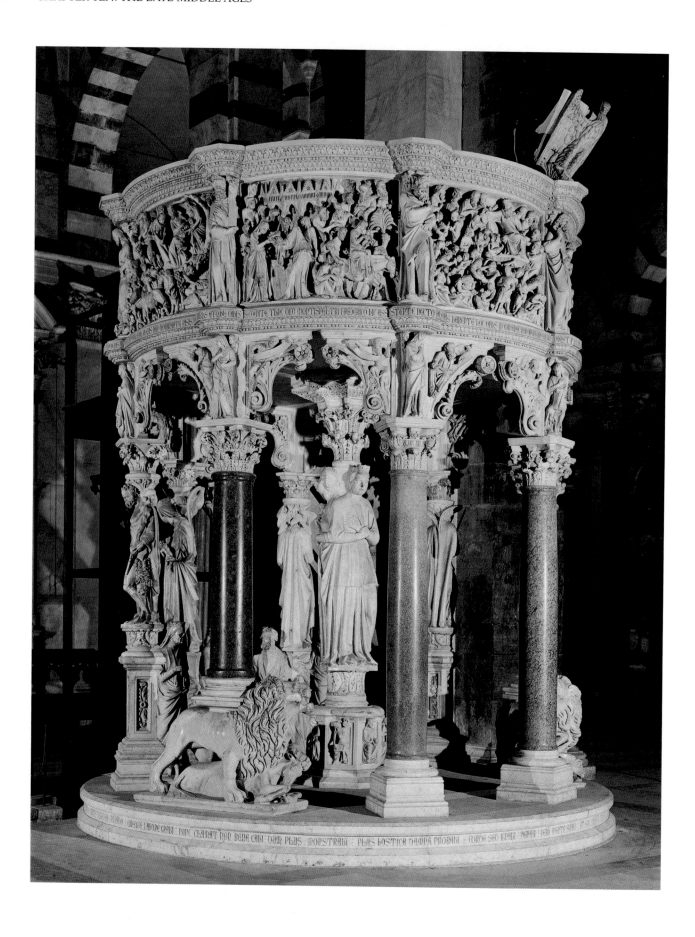

◀ **Figure 10.13** GIOVANNI PISANO. Pulpit in the Pisa Cathedral. Ca. 1302–1310. Pisa, Italy. *Pisano built and carved this massive (17-foot-high) pulpit at the height of his reputation. A superb artist but a quarrelsome man, Pisano recorded his frustrations in the lengthy inscription around the pulpit's base. In it he claimed that he had achieved much, had been condemned by many, and took full responsibility for this work of art. Pisano's advance from anonymity to a position of great artistic repute was typical of a new breed of artist appearing in fourteenth-century Italy.*

Figure 10.14 GIOVANNI PISANO. Nativity Scene. Pulpit in the Pisa cathedral. Ca. 1302–1310. 33½ × 44½". Pisa, Italy. *In this Late Gothic sculpture, Pisano cut deeply into the marble's surface to give a nearly three-dimensional effect. His many figures seem involved in their own tasks but are nevertheless linked with one another around the Madonna and child. For example, the two shepherds (the head of one has been lost) in the upper right corner appear to be listening to the angels approaching from the left, while at the far right, sheep rest and graze. Such balanced placements are evidence of Pisano's classicizing tendencies. Pisano's relief retains a prominent Gothic feature, however, by presenting the Virgin and child twice—in the central scene and in the lower left corner, where a seated Mary, balancing the baby Jesus on her right leg, stretches her left hand to test the temperature of the water in an elaborate basin.*

Figure 10.15 CLAUS SLUTER. *Moses*, from *The Well of Moses*. Ca. 1395–1406. Ht. of full figure approx. 6'. Chartreuse de Champmol, Dijon, France. *Sluter followed the allegorical tradition of medieval art in this portrait of the Hebrew prophet Moses. The book in Moses' right hand and the scroll over his left shoulder symbolize the Word of God. Sluter also depicted Moses with "horns" growing out of his forehead, as was characteristic in medieval representations.*

and standing erect with a finely chiseled head (Figure 10.15). Sluter's sense of the dramatic moment, of the prophet's personal emotions, and of the individual features makes the statue nearly an individual portrait. Sluter rendered Moses' beard and the unfurled scroll in precise detail and carved the figure with the head turned to the side, eyes looking into the future.

Late Gothic Painting and the Rise of New Trends
Of all the arts, painting underwent the most radical changes in the Late Middle Ages. Illuminated manuscripts maintained their popularity, but their themes became more secular under the patronage of titled aristocrats and wealthy merchants. At the same time,

painters of frescoes and wooden panels introduced new techniques for applying paint and mixing colors. Stylistically, painters preferred to work in the extravagant Late Gothic manner with its elegant refinement and its undulating lines. Nevertheless, as mentioned earlier, Giotto and other Italian painters discovered fresh ways of depicting human figures that started to revolutionize art.

ILLUMINATED MANUSCRIPTS The Burgundian court played a pivotal role in the production of one of the outstanding illuminated manuscripts of the medieval period, the *Très Riches Heures du Duc de Berry*. This famous collection of miniatures was painted by the three Limbourg brothers for the duke of Berry, brother of Philip the Bold of Burgundy. These illustrations stand above the others of their time for their exquisite detail, general liveliness, and intricately designed crowd scenes—some of the marks of the Late Gothic style.

The *Très Riches Heures*, or the *Very Rich Hours*, represents a type of small prayer book that was a favorite of nobles and businessmen. These personal books of worship, with their litanies and prayers, were often handsomely hand-illustrated to enhance their value. The duke of Berry's prayer book contained some 130 miniature paintings, including scenes from the life of Christ and the calendar cycle. In the calendar series, each tiny painting, finely detailed and colored in jewel-like tones, notes a seasonal activity appropriate for the month. Some represent the brilliant court life of the duke, and others depict the drudgery of peasant life, sharply differentiated from the court scenes by their action and color. The illustration for January shows the duke of Berry surrounded by his well-dressed courtiers and enjoying a sumptuous feast (Figure 10.16).

THE PRINT The print, a new artistic medium, developed in the Late Middle Ages in the Austrian-Bavarian regions, eastern France, and the Netherlands. Sparked by the growth of lay piety, the earliest prints were devotional woodcuts to be used as aids to personal meditation. The prints initially featured scenes from the lives of the Virgin and Christ. For the **woodcut print,** the artist drew an image on a woodblock, which was then cut by a woodcutter and printed by the artist; some were then hand-tinted by a colorist. By 1500 the new techniques of **engraving** (using a sharp tool to draw an image onto a metal plate overlaid with wax, dipping the plate in acid, and then printing it) and **drypoint** (marking an image onto a copper plate with a metal stylus and then printing it) were becoming increasingly popular.

Probably the outstanding set of prints dating from this period was that in the Medieval Housebook, a late-

Figure 10.16 LIMBOURG BROTHERS. Month of January, from the *Très Riches Heures du Duc de Berry*. 1413–1416. Approx. 8½ × 5½". Musée Condé, Chantilly, France. *This miniature painting provides insightful social history in its exquisite details. The duke, seated in the right center, is dressed in a blue patterned cloak and is greeting his guests for what was probably a New Year's celebration. Behind the duke stands a servant, over whose head are written the words "aproche, aproche," a welcome that is the equivalent of "come in, come in." Above this festive scene, the zodiac signs of Capricorn and Aquarius identify the month as January.*

fifteenth-century German manuscript. The so-called Medieval Housebook was a gathering of 192 prints, of which only 126 remain. Most of the prints are in black and white, though a few are partially colored. The printing techniques vary from drypoint and engraving to simple drawings on vellum. Stylistic differences indicate that at least three artists contributed to the work, thus suggesting that the Housebook may have been produced in a workshop. For convenience, however, the artist is called simply the Housebook Master.

Of the surviving 126 prints, the subjects range over Late Medieval life, from the workaday world to jousting scenes to court life. Some offer realistic views of medieval buildings, including barnyards, private dwellings, and palaces; most are highly detailed, showing hair and clothing styles. Others are lively and

Figure 10.17 HOUSEBOOK MASTER. *Leisure Time at the Bath*. Ca. 1475–1490. *Ink on vellum drawing, partially colored. Private collection. This print reveals the upper classes at play as well as the strict social order. On the left, young couples converse or flirt around a fountain in a courtyard; the pets (a falcon, two dogs, and a monkey) are indicators of the high status of their owners; a lady-in-waiting holds the skirt of her mistress. On the right, young aristocrats (a man and two women) enjoy bathing, while a third woman is entering the bathhouse. A servant serenades the bathers on a stringed instrument, as another waits in attendance. On the balcony, two servants enjoy a flirtatious moment. This Chaucerian-like scene, with its frank sensuality, indicates that within the increasingly secular world of the Late Middle Ages the pleasures of the flesh could be a fit subject for an artist.*

playful, depicting relations between the sexes and the classes (Figure 10.17).

NEW TRENDS IN ITALY: GIOTTO While the illuminated manuscript and the print were popular in northern Europe, a revolution in painting was under way in Italy. The paintings of Giotto are generally recognized as having established a new direction in Western art,

one that led into the Renaissance. In Giotto's own day, Dante praised him and the citizens of Florence honored him. Later, Vasari, the famous sixteenth-century painter and biographer, declared that Giotto had "rescued and restored" painting.

Giotto's revolution in painting was directed against the prevailing **Italo-Byzantine style,** which blended Late Gothic with Byzantine influences. He turned this

Figure 10.18 CIMABUE. *Madonna Enthroned*. Ca. 1280. Tempera on panel, 12'7½" × 7'4". Uffizi Gallery, Florence. *Although Cimabue was experiencing the same desire for freedom in art as the sculptor Giovanni Pisano, this painting of the Madonna shows that he was still strongly under the spell of the Italo-Byzantine tradition. Rather than showing the intense feeling of Giotto's portraits, Cimabue's Virgin and child remain medieval and mystical.*

painting style, with its two-dimensional, lifeless quality, into a three-dimensional art characterized by naturalism and the full expression of human emotions. Partly through the innovative use of light and shade and the placement of figures so as to create nonmathematical **perspective,** or depth, Giotto was able to paint realistic-looking figures, rather than the flat, or-

namental depictions found in most illuminated manuscripts or the Italian altar paintings.

A painting by one of Giotto's contemporaries, Cimabue [chee-muh-BU-ay] (about 1240–1302), the *Madonna Enthroned*, reveals the state of Italian painting at this time (Figure 10.18). The angels on the side are rendered stiffly, aligned vertically without any sense of

Figure 10.19 GIOTTO. *Madonna Enthroned.* Ca. 1310. Tempera on panel, 10'8" × 6'8". Uffizi Gallery, Florence. *Giotto's* Madonna Enthroned, *so revolutionary in its composition and spatial dimensions, has been called the most influential painting of the fourteenth century. Especially innovative in this altarpiece is the realistic treatment of the Virgin's eyes. They are shaped like ordinary eyes and peer out at the viewer rather than gazing into the distance, as in the Italo-Byzantine style.*

space between them, and placed flat on the wood panel without any precise relationship with the four prophets below them. Although Cimabue's angels were balanced in their placement and the depiction of the figures of the Madonna and Christ child offered some sense of rounded form, the overall effect of the work confirms its debt to the two-dimensional tradition of Italo-Byzantine art.

In contrast, Giotto's *Madonna Enthroned*, painted about thirty years after Cimabue's, shows how Giotto was transforming Florentine art (Figure 10.19). His Madonna seems to be actually sitting on her throne, and the four angels on either side of her chair are placed to give a sense of spatial depth, or perspective. The angels' distinctive gazes are highly expressive, suggesting feelings of wonder and respect. The Virgin resembles an individual woman and Christ a believable child, not a shrunken adult. Although Giotto uses Gothic touches—the pointed arch, the haloes, and the applied gold leaf—the natural rendering of the figures foreshadows great changes in art.

Giotto was a prolific artist whose paintings adorned churches in Florence and cities all over Italy. At the Arena Chapel in Padua, Giotto painted his masterpiece,

Figure 10.20 GIOTTO. *Pietà*, or *Lamentation*. Ca. 1305–1310. Fresco, 7'7" × 7'9". Arena Chapel, Padua, Italy. *Such works gained Giotto his reputation as the modern reviver of realistic art—a tradition that had been lost with the fall of ancient Rome. In this fresco, he created three-dimensional space in ways that even the Greeks and the Romans had not used. Giotto's illusion of depth was conveyed by surrounding the dead Christ with numerous figures and, in particular, by placing two mourners in the foreground with their backs to the viewer. Giotto's use of perspective was convincing to his generation even though it lacked mathematical precision.*

two sets of frescoes, one of the life of the Virgin and the other of the life of Christ. These thirty-eight scenes show Giotto at the height of his powers, rendering space with a sense of depth and organizing figures so as to create dramatic tension. An outstanding scene from the Padua frescoes is the *Pietà*, or *Lamentation* (Figure

10.20). This scene, which portrays the grief for the dead Christ, expresses total despair through the mourners' faces and gestures, from Mary, who cradles the body of Jesus, to John, who stands with arms outstretched, to the hovering angels. In the fresco's stark and rugged landscape, even nature seems to mourn, notably in the barren tree that symbolizes the wood of the cross on which Jesus was crucified. After Giotto died in 1337, no painter for the rest of the century was able to match his remarkable treatment of nature and human emotions.

FLEMISH PAINTING: JAN VAN EYCK AND HANS MEMLING
When Philip the Good (r. 1419–1467) became duke of Burgundy, he expanded his territories to include the wealthy counties of Holland, Zeeland, and Luxembourg, known as Flanders. Philip was the greatest secular patron of the arts of his day. Of the artists encouraged by his patronage, the brothers Jan and Hubert van Eyck are the most famous, and their religious works and portraits established the Flemish style of art. Little is known of Hubert, but Jan van Eyck [YAHN van IKE] (about 1370–1441) is considered the founder of the Flemish school.

As a general principle, Flemish art sought reality through an accumulation of precise and often symbolic details, in contrast to Italian art, which tended to be more concerned with psychological truth, as in Giotto's frescoes in the Arena Chapel. This national style, expressed primarily through painting with oils on wood panels, turned each artwork into a brilliant and precise reproduction of the original scene. The finest detail in a patterned carpet, the reflected light on

Figure 10.21   HUBERT AND JAN VAN EYCK. *Ghent Altarpiece.* Ca. 1432. Oil on panel, 11'3" × 14'5". St. Bavo cathedral, Ghent, Belgium. *This large altarpiece may seem to be a collection of separate paintings, but the work is united in themes and symbolism. What links the panels is their portrayal of Christ's redemption of humanity. From "The Sin of Adam and Eve" to the mystic "Adoration of the Lamb," all the paintings touch in some manner on Christ's sacrifice.*

a copper vase, and the wrinkled features of an elderly patron were laboriously and meticulously recorded. The Flemish style, with its close attention to detail, was widely appreciated and quickly spread to Italy and England.

Jan van Eyck, probably with his brother's help, painted an altarpiece for the cathedral at Ghent, Belgium (Figure 10.21). This large work—originally commissioned to beautify the high altar—still remains in its original place. The twenty panels are hinged together so that when opened twelve are visible. These twelve panels are divided into two levels—heavenly figures and symbols on the upper level and earthly figures on the lower level. On the ends of the upper level are nude portraits of Adam and Eve, next to angels singing and playing musical instruments. Mary on the left and John the Baptist on the right flank a portrayal of God the Father, resplendent in a jewel-encrusted robe and triple crown. Below, on the lower level, are human figures who are depicted as moving toward the center panel. On the left, knights and judges ride on horseback, while, on the right, pilgrims and hermits approach on foot.

The focus of the *Ghent Altarpiece*, when opened, is the lower center panel, the *Adoration of the Lamb*. In this work, the sacrificial death of Jesus is symbolized by the cross, the baptismal font in the foreground, and the blood issuing from the lamb into the communion chalice. The surrounding worshipers include holy virgins, martyrs, and prophets, plus the four evangelists and the Twelve Apostles, who stand and kneel in groups amid plants and trees (Figure 10.22).

Figure 10.22 HUBERT AND JAN VAN EYCK. *Adoration of the Lamb.* Detail of the *Ghent Altarpiece.* Ca. 1432. St. Bavo cathedral, Ghent, Belgium. *This lower center section of the opened altarpiece dramatically shows how the Flemish school could use religious symbolism to evoke a mystical effect. The refined details, which derived from the tradition of manuscript painting, make this scene both credible and otherworldly.*

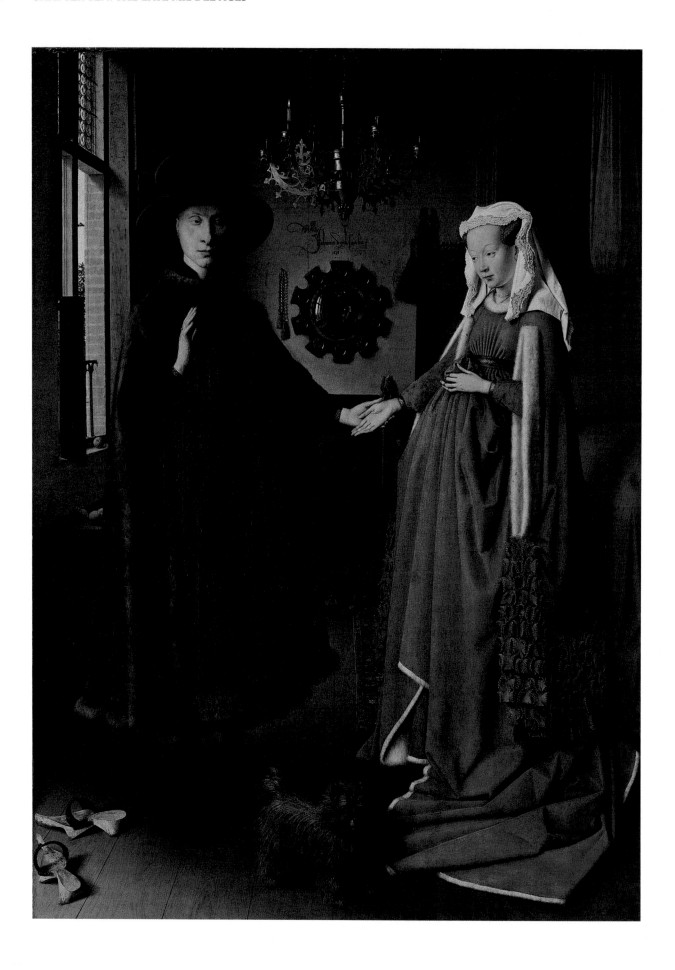

In contrast to this mystical work, Jan van Eyck painted a decidedly secular but still symbolic work in his *Arnolfini Wedding Portrait* (Figure 10.23). In this painting, nearly every object—the lighted candle, the shoes, the fruit, the dog—refers to a wedding custom or belief. Yet the details—for example, the mirror on the rear wall reflecting the couple's backs, the artist, and a fourth person—create a worldly setting. Van Eyck's painting is not an imaginary scene but a recording of an actual event, for Arnolfini was an Italian businessman who lived in Bruges. Thus, the commerce and wealth of Burgundy and the Italian cities are symbolically united by van Eyck in this wedding portrait.

A second outstanding artist working in Flanders during the Late Middle Ages was Hans Memling (about 1430–1494), the most popular painter of his day in Bruges. Long a northern commercial center, Bruges was now entering a period of decline, hastened by the displacement of the Burgundian ruling house by that of the Hapsburgs. Before settling in Bruges, the German-born Memling studied painting in Cologne and the Netherlands, where he fully absorbed the northern tradition. Memling's painting style, which borrowed heavily from that of Jan van Eyck and his generation, was characterized by serenity and graceful elegance, traits that stand in marked contrast to this turbulent era. After starting his workshop in Bruges, Memling grew wealthy from commissions, mainly for altarpieces and portraits, paid for by church leaders, local businesspeople, and resident foreign merchants. More than eighty of his works have survived.

Memling was particularly celebrated for the piety of his Madonna paintings, such as the *Madonna and Child with Angels* (Figure 10.24). Following the Flemish tradition, this painting is filled with religious symbolism, which reinforces the message that Christ died to atone for the sins of humankind. The baby Christ reaches for an apple held by an angel, the fruit symbolizing original sin. The second angel, dressed in a vestment associated with the High Mass, plays a harp,

possibly a reference to heavenly music. A carved vine of grapes, depicted on the arch, is an emblem of Holy Communion. On the left column stands David, an ancestor of Christ, and on the right column stands Isaiah, a prophet who foretold the birth of the Messiah.

The format and the details of Memling's enthroned Madonna harken back to Jan van Eyck, but without the intensity or sense of reality. Memling's style is static and somewhat artificial. The painting space is clearly arranged, but the landscape and architectural background function as a stage set; the figures are so composed that they constitute a veritable *tableau vivant*, a staged scene in which costumed actors remain silent as if in a picture. Each of the three figures is treated in similar fashion—thin bodies; oval faces; blank, emotionless stares. Adding to the air of artificiality is the absence of shadows, for the painting is bathed in unmodulated light.

Music

The forces of change transforming Europe in the 1300s also had an impact on the field of music (Figure 10.25). Sacred music began to be overshadowed by secular music, with the rise of new secular forms—such as the ballade and rondeau—based on the **chanson**, a song set to a French text and scored for one or more voices, often with instrumental accompaniment. Polyphony remained the dominant composing style, but composers now wrote secular polyphonic pieces that were not based on Gregorian chants. These changes were made possible by innovations that coalesced into what came to be called the *new art* (**ars nova** in Latin), particularly in Paris, the capital of polyphonic music. The innovations included a new system of music notation, along with new rhythmic patterns such as **isorhythm**—the use of a single rhythmic pattern from the beginning to the end of a work, despite changes in the melodic structure. The chief exponent of *ars nova* was the French composer and poet Guillaume de Machaut [gee-yom duh mah-show] (about 1300–1377).

Machaut, who trained as a priest and musician, first made his mark as a court official to the king of Bohemia. For his services, he was rewarded with an appointment to the cathedral in Reims (1337), where he worked for much of the rest of his life. His music circulated widely in his day, largely because he made gifts of his music manuscripts to wealthy patrons. Thus, he became one of the first composers whose works have survived. Reflecting the decline in church music, his output consists mainly of secular love themes. In England, his verses influenced the great poet Geoffrey Chaucer.

Figure 10.23 JAN VAN EYCK. *Arnolfini Wedding Portrait.* 1434. Oil on wood, 33 × 22½". Reproduced by courtesy of the Trustees, National Gallery, London. *This work is a perfect expression of the symbolic realism that dominated northern European painting in the Late Middle Ages. The wedding is celebrated in a room filled with religious symbols of the marriage rite. For example, the bride and groom stand shoeless, indicating that they are in holy space, and above them is a chandelier with a single lighted candle, a sign of God's presence.*

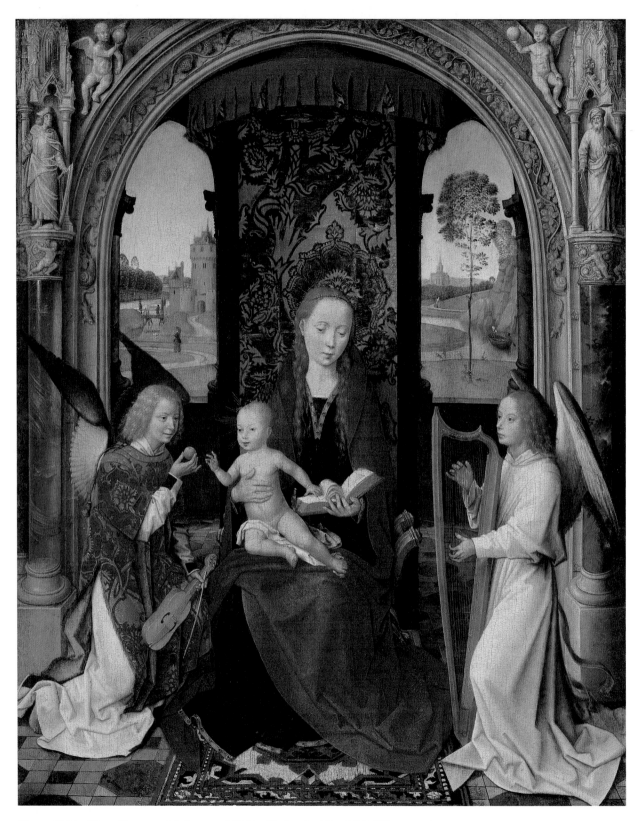

Figure 10.24   HANS MEMLING. *Madonna and Child with Angels.* After 1479. Oil on panel, 23⅛ × 18⅞". Andrew W. Mellon Collection. National Gallery of Art, Washington, D.C. (1937.1.41) Photograph © Board of Trustees. *Memling, though part of the Flemish tradition, appears to have been aware of developments in Renaissance Italy. He introduced some Italian elements into this painting, such as the* putti, *or small angels (used as decorations on the columns and arch), and the stringed musical instruments held by the angels.*

Although Machaut was famous for secular music, his reputation rests on his *Notre Dame* Mass, the first polyphonic version of the Mass Ordinary by a known composer. "Ordinary" refers to the five parts of the Mass that remain unchanged throughout the liturgical year, namely the kyrie ("Lord, have mercy"), gloria ("Glory"), credo ("the Nicene Creed"), sanctus and benedictus ("Holy" and "Blessed"), and Agnus Dei ("Lamb of God"). Written for four voices, some of which may have been performed by instrumentalists, Machaut's Mass made liberal use of isorhythm in most of its parts. Following his lead, composers for more than six hundred years made the Mass Ordinary the central point of choral music.

A short analysis of Machaut's Agnus Dei, from the *Notre Dame* Mass, shows the new polyphonic style. Its complex composition—four voices singing four parts simultaneously and using varied rhythms—means that the lead melody (sung by the tenor and based on an existing plainsong) is lost in a web of shifting sounds. The two lower voices, including the tenor, provide the ground for this piece. The two upper voices are the more inventive, ornamenting the text with melismas and syllabic singing, along with shifting rhythms, including **syncopation**—the accenting of a weak beat when a strong beat is expected. A prayer for mercy and peace, Agnus Dei is highly repetitive—a typical practice in the Christian liturgy. And it is divided into three parts, the symbol of the Trinity. Thus, Agnus Dei furthers Christian beliefs through words, musical sounds, and structure.

Agnus Dei reads, in Latin, "*Agnus Dei, qui tollis peccata mundi: misere nobis / Agnus Dei, qui tollis peccata mundi: Miserere nobis / Agnus Dei, qui tollis peccata mundi: dona nobis pacen,*" and, in English, "Lamb of God, who taketh away the sins of the world, have mercy on us / Lamb of God, who taketh away the sins of the world, have mercy on us / Lamb of God, who taketh away the sins of the world, grant us peace."

Figure 10.25. *Music and Her Attendants.* Fourteenth century. From Boethius, *De Arithmetica. This miniature painting, using both secular and religious imagery, artfully surveys the state of music in the Late Middle Ages. Court music, which flowered during this period, is represented by the seated lady playing a portable pipe organ, in the center, while around her other ladies perform with various instruments, including, starting from the top right and going clockwise: a lute; clappers; trumpets; nakers, or kettledrums; a shawm, an ancestor of the oboe; bagpipes; a tambourine; and a rebec, a precursor of the viol. Religious music, which had kept the legacy of ancient music alive after the fall of Rome, is represented by King David, visible in the circle at the top center, who is depicted playing a psaltery, a handheld type of harp, which is named after the Psalms—the book attributed to his authorship. As to the source of the instruments on view, Greco-Roman tradition supplied only the pipe organ, clappers, trumpets, and bagpipes, while all the others, including the psaltery, were imports from the Islamic world, either from Muslim Spain or from the Middle East during the Crusades.*

The Legacy of the Late Middle Ages

All historical eras are periods of transition, but the changes of the Late Middle Ages were especially momentous. The medieval world was dying, and the modern era was struggling to be born. Dating from this turbulent period were many of the cultural tensions that defined the history of Europe for the next four hundred years.

The most revolutionary happening in the Late Middle Ages was the release of a powerful secular spirit that began to make its presence felt everywhere. The upsurge of vernacular literature, the rise of literary themes questioning the low status of women, the increasing popularity of secular music, and the divergence of philosophy and theology are four examples of this new development. But the greatest impact of the rise of secularism on cultural life was that painting and sculpture began to be liberated from the service of architecture. The first stirrings of this change were expressed in the works of Giotto and other Italian and Flemish artists. By the next century, painting in Italy had freed itself from the tutelage of architecture and become the most important artistic genre in the West.

This period also saw the emergence of a new breed of secular ruler who was prepared to mount a sustained drive against the church's combined political and spiritual powers. The victories of the English and the French kings over the papacy—each ruler was able to secure control over his national church—were signs of the breakup of Christendom.

Another important legacy of these years is that the towns, led by their bourgeois citizens—the beginning of the middle class—began to exercise their influence over the countryside. From today's perspective, the growth of the middle class as a dominant force in society was perhaps the most critical development of this age. The first stirrings of industrialism, what has been called *protoindustrialism*, may be detected in the spread of pockets of manufacturing—paper, textiles, and books—over the face of Europe. This age also saw a strong upsurge in the West's continuing love affair with machines, with the inventions of the printing press and the spinning wheel. Finally, this period witnessed the unusual spectacle of the common people revolting against the aristocratic control of the culture and society. Their sporadic efforts failed, but the seeds of future revolution were planted.

KEY CULTURAL TERMS

incunabula   woodcut print
devotio moderna   engraving
via antiqua   drypoint
via moderna   Italo-Byzantine style
Late Gothic style   perspective
Flamboyant style   *chanson*
Perpendicular style   *ars nova*
fan vaulting   isorhythm
campanile   syncopation

SUGGESTIONS FOR FURTHER READING

BOCCACCIO, G. *The Decameron*. Translated by M. Musa and P. E. Bondanella. New York: Norton, 1977. An updated translation of the hundred stories—some learned, some coarse, but all humorous—that make up this work; first published about 1351.

CHAUCER, G. *The Canterbury Tales*. Edited by N. Coghill. New York: Penguin, 1978. Of many versions of these bawdy and lighthearted tales, Coghill's is one of the most readable and enjoyable; the original work dates from 1385.

CHRISTINE DE PIZAN. *The Book of the City of Ladies*. Translated by E. J. Richards. New York: Persea Books, 1982. An accessible, modern translation of this Late Medieval work, which argues that the political and cultural dignity of women depends on their being educated properly, just as men are; first published in 1405.

LANGLAND, W. *The Vision of Piers Plowman*. Translated by H. W. Wells. New York: Sheed and Ward, 1959. A good modern version of Langland's work criticizing the religious establishment of his day and calling for a new order; written between 1362 and 1394.

SUGGESTION FOR LISTENING

GUILLAUME DE MACHAUT. Machaut's innovations in rhythm helped inaugurate the *ars nova* style. His *Notre Dame* Mass, which employed isorhythms, is the first setting of the Mass Ordinary by a known composer.

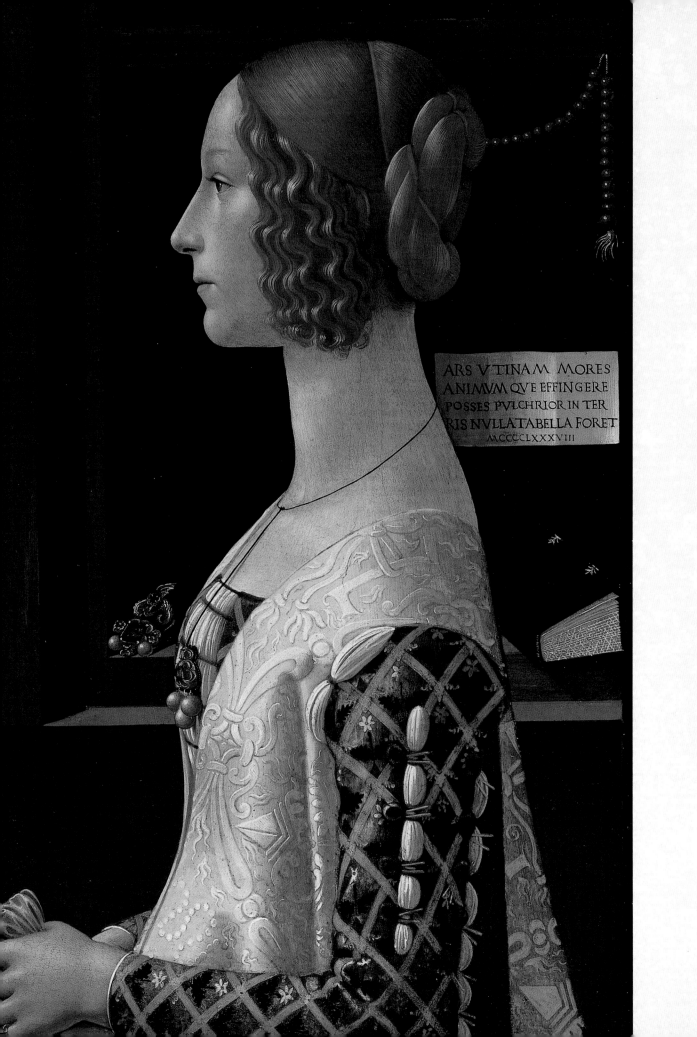

ARS VTINAM MORES
ANIMVM QVE EFFINGERE
POSSES PVLCHRIOR IN TER
RIS NVLLA TABELLA FORET
MCCCCLXXXVIII

11 THE EARLY RENAISSANCE
Return to Classical Roots
1400–1494

Believing they had broken radically with the past, Italian artists and intellectuals in the fifteenth century began to speak of a rebirth of civilization. Since the nineteenth century, the term *Renaissance* (meaning "rebirth") has described the cultural and artistic activities of the fifteenth and sixteenth centuries that began in Italy and spread northward. The Renaissance profoundly altered the course of Western culture, although scholars have differing interpretations of the significance of this first modern period.

THE RENAISSANCE: SCHOOLS OF INTERPRETATION

In the 1860s, Swiss historian Jacob Burckhardt, agreeing with the fifteenth-century Italians, asserted that the Renaissance was a rebirth of ideas after centuries of cultural stagnation. He maintained that a new way of understanding the world had emerged, as the Italians looked back to ancient Greece and Rome for inspiration and declared themselves part of a revitalized civilization that was distinctive and superior to the immediate past.

By the mid–twentieth century, Burckhardt's interpretation began to be viewed as too simplistic. According to some scholars, the Italians, after the fall of Rome, never lost sight of their Classical roots. These historians considered the revival of learning in the fifteenth century to be more of a shift in educational and cultural emphasis than a rediscovery of antiquity. They also noted that the Renaissance had at least two phases, the Early and the High, each with different contributions.

◄ **Detail** DOMENICO GHIRLANDAIO. *Giovanna degli Albizzi Tornabuoni.* Ca. 1489–1490. Tempera and (?) oil on panel, 29½ × 19¼". Madrid, Thyssen-Bornemisza Collection (cat. no. 46).

321

Figure 11.1 DOMENICO GHIRLANDAIO. *Old Man with a Child.* Ca. 1480. Panel 24½ × 18″. Louvre. *This double portrait summarizes many of the new secular values of the Early Renaissance, such as its human-centeredness and its preference for simple scenes. The work's subject, a man possibly with his grandchild, indicates the important role that the family played during the time. The age's commitment to direct observation of the physical world is evident in the treatment of the man's diseased nose (rosacea) and the landscape glimpsed through the open window.*

Since the 1960s, a third interpretation has dominated Renaissance studies. In this view, the Renaissance label should be used cautiously and only to describe what was happening in learning and the arts, not in politics and society. The authors of this book tend to agree with this third interpretation. In politics, economics, and society, Italy in the 1400s differed little from Italy in the 1300s; however, the Italians of the 1400s did start down a new *cultural* path (Figure 11.1).

This chapter examines the first phase of this new cultural style, the Early Renaissance (1400–1494); Chapter 12 is devoted to the brief High Renaissance (1494–1520) and to Early Mannerism (1520–1564), an anti-Classical phase of the Renaissance. Chapter 13 considers Northern Humanism, the Northern Renaissance, the early-sixteenth-century religious reformations, and Late Mannerism (1564–1603), when Renaissance style was slowly undermined by new trends (Timeline 11.1).

EARLY RENAISSANCE HISTORY AND INSTITUTIONS

For most of the fifteenth century, the city-states of northern Italy were prosperous and peaceful enough to sustain upper-class artists and writers. This supportive climate encouraged the innovations of Renaissance culture. By the end of the century, however, disputes among Italy's city-states and a shift in maritime trade from the Mediterranean to the Atlantic, coupled with the French invasion of Florence in 1494, had dimmed northern Italy's cultural preeminence.

Italian City-States During the Early Renaissance

The erratic fortunes of Italy's economy were a major factor in the region's politics in this period. The northern Italian city-states had emerged from the High Middle Ages in 1300 as Europe's leading commercial center and manufacturer of finished woolens (see Chapter 9), but by 1500 they had been eclipsed by various European nations to the north. In the 1300s, Italian population, productivity, and prosperity declined because of the Black Death and the birth of the English woolen industry. Although the Italians made a limited economic recovery in the 1400s, history was moving against them. Even their domination of international banking was challenged by German businessmen.

During the Early Renaissance, five Italian states competed for dominance: the Republic of Venice, the Duchy of Milan, the Republic of Florence, the Papal States, and the Kingdom of Naples (Map 11.1). Other small states, such as the artistic and intellectual centers of Ferrara and Modena, played minor but crucial roles. In the first half of the fifteenth century, the Italian states waged incessant wars among themselves, shifting sides when it was to their advantage.

The continuous warfare and the uncertain economy provided the conditions for the emergence of autocratic rulers called *signori,* who were from ruling families or elitist factions. Taking advantage of economic and class tensions, these autocrats pledged to solve local problems, and in so doing they proceeded to accumulate power in their own hands. What influence the guilds, the business leaders, and the middle class had wielded in the fourteenth century gave way to these despots, ending the great medieval legacy of republicanism in Venice, Milan, and Florence.

Under the *signori,* the conduct of warfare also changed. Technological developments improved weaponry, and battles were fought with mercenary troops led by *condottieri,* soldiers of fortune who sold their military expertise to the highest bidder. But the most significant change in Renaissance warfare was the

Timeline 11.1   STAGES OF THE ITALIAN RENAISSANCE

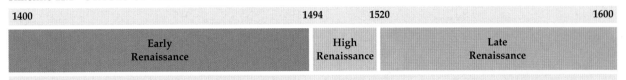

1400	1494	1520	1600
Early Renaissance	High Renaissance	Late Renaissance	

LEARNING THROUGH MAPS

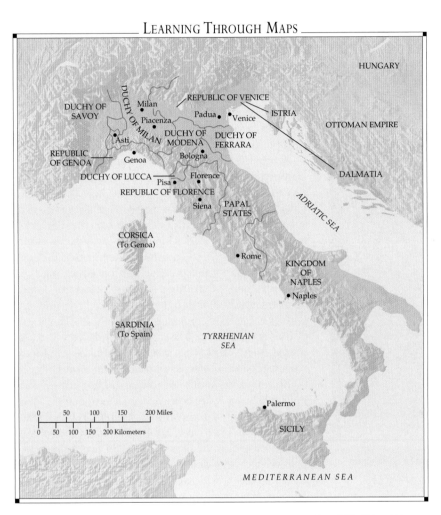

Map 11.1   THE STATES OF ITALY DURING THE RENAISSANCE, CA. 1494
This map shows the many states and principalities of Italy in the Early Renaissance. **Consider** the size of each state with its role in competing for dominance of the Italian peninsula. **Notice** the large number of states in the north as compared with the small number in the south. **Notice** also the four forms of government—duchy, republic, kingdom, and papal states. **Identify** the major ports of the Italian state system. **What** geographic advantage made the Papal States such a force in Italian politics?

emergence of diplomacy as a peaceful alternative to arms, a practice that gradually spread throughout the Continent. The Italian regimes began sending representatives to other states, and it soon became customary for these diplomats to negotiate peace settlements. In turbulent fifteenth-century Italy, these agreements seldom lasted long—with the notable exception of the

Peace of Lodi. This defensive pact, signed in 1454 by Milan, Florence, and Venice, established a delicate balance of power and ensured peace in Italy for forty years.

The Peace of Lodi came apart in 1494, when a French army led by Charles VIII (r. 1483–1498) entered Italy in the hope of promoting French monarchic

Figure 11.2 Pedro Berruguete (?). *Federico da Montefeltro and His Son Guidobaldo.* Ca. 1476–1477. Oil on panel, 4'5⅛" × 2'5⅞". Galleria Nazionale della Marche, Urbino. *Urbino, under the Montefeltro dynasty, was transformed from a sleepy hill town with no cultural history into a major center of Renaissance life. Federico, the founder of the dynasty and one of the greatest* condottieri *of his day, was created duke of Urbino and captain of the papal forces by Pope Sixtus IV in 1474. Federico then devoted his energies to making Urbino a model for Italian Renaissance courts. In this portrait, the seated Federico wears the armor of a papal officer while reading a book—symbols that established him as both a soldier and a scholar, later the ideal of Castiglione's Courtier. At the duke's right knee stands his son and heir, Guidobaldo, wearing an elaborate robe and holding a scepter, a symbol of power. Federico's dream ended with his son, the last of the Montefeltro line.*

At the Urbino court, artists combined Flemish and Italian styles, as in this double portrait. The internal lighting, emanating from some unseen source on the left, is adopted from the tradition pioneered by Jan van Eyck; the profile portrait of the duke follows the Italian practice, based on portrait heads rendered on medals. This double portrait was probably painted by Pedro Berruguete, Spain's first great Renaissance artist, who studied painting in Naples and worked briefly in Urbino before returning to his homeland.

ambitions. Outside Italy, three events further weakened the region's prospects for regaining its position as a major economic power: the fall of Constantinople in 1453, Portugal's opening of the sea route around Africa to India at the end of the century, and Columbus's Spanish-sponsored voyage to the New World.

These three events shifted the focus of international trade from the Mediterranean to the Atlantic. The fall of Constantinople to the Ottoman Turks in 1453 temporarily closed the eastern Mediterranean markets to the Italian city-states. At the same time, by virtue of the wide-ranging global explorations they sponsored, some European powers—most notably Portugal and Spain—were extending their political and economic interests beyond the geographic limits of continental Europe.

Before the Italian city-states were eclipsed by other European powers, however, upper-class families enjoyed unprecedented wealth, which they used to cultivate their tastes in literature and art and thus substantially determine the culture of the Early Renaissance (Figure 11.2). One reason for the importance these families gave to cultural matters is that they put high value on family prestige and on educating their sons for their predestined roles as heads of family businesses and their daughters as loyal wives and successful household managers (Figure 11.3). The courts of the local rulers, or *grandi,* became places where educated men—and, on occasion, women—could exchange ideas and discuss philosophical issues.

Although the status of women did not improve appreciably, more were educated than ever before. Many ended up behind the walls of a convent, however, if their parents could not afford the costly dowry expected of an upper-class bride. The few upper-class women with an independent role in society were those who had been widowed young. The women at the ducal courts who exercised any political influence did so because of their family alliances. One of the most powerful of these women was Lucrezia Borgia [loo-KRET-syah BOR-juh] (1480–1519), the illegitimate daughter of Pope Alexander VI. Married three times before the age of twenty-one, she held court in Ferrara and was the patron of many writers and artists. Most women who tried to exercise real power, however, found it unattainable.

Florence, the Center of the Renaissance

Amid the artistic and intellectual activity occurring throughout Italy, Florence, the capital of the Tuscan region, was the most prominent of the city-states. After 1300 Florence's political system went through three phases, evolving from republic to oligarchy to family

Timeline 11.2   THE EARLY RENAISSANCE IN FLORENCE, 1400–1494

1400							1494

			Early Renaissance				

1403–1424 Ghiberti's north doors, Florentine Baptistery	1425 Invention of linear perspective (Brunelleschi)	1424–1452 Ghiberti's east doors, Florentine Baptistery	1438–1445 Fra Angelico's *Annunciation*	1461 Completion of Pazzi Chapel by Brunelleschi	1473–1475 Verrocchio's *David*	1480s Botticelli's *Primavera* and *The Birth of Venus*	1483 Leonardo da Vinci's *The Virgin of the Rocks*
	1425–1428 Masaccio's frescoes for Santa Maria Novella	1430–1432 Donatello's *David*		1462 Founding of Platonic Academy, Florence			
		1435 Alberti's *On Painting*					

rule. During these turbulent political times, however, Florentine artists and writers made their city-state the center of the Early Renaissance (Timeline 11.2).

The republic, which began in the fourteenth century with hopes for political equality, fell into the hands of a wealthy oligarchy. This oligarchy, composed of rich bankers, merchants, and successful guildsmen and craftsmen, ruled until the early fifteenth century, when the Medici family gained control. The Medicis dominated Florentine politics and cultural life from 1434 to 1494, sometimes functioning as despots.

The Medicis rose from modest circumstances. Giovanni di Bicci de' Medici [jo-VAHN-nee dee BEET-chee day MED-uh-chee] (1360–1429) amassed the family's first large fortune through banking and close financial ties with the papacy. His son Cosimo

Figure 11.3 DOMENICO GHIRLANDAIO. *Giovanna degli Albizzi Tornabuoni*. Ca. 1489–1490. Tempera and (?) oil on panel, 29½ × 19¼". Madrid, Thyssen-Bornemisza Collection (cat. no. 46). *This likeness of Giovanna degli Albizzi Tornabuoni (1468–1486) embodies the Florentine ethos of family, city, and church. Her husband, Lorenzo Tornabuoni, a member of a prominent Florentine family, commissioned it as a memorial. Probably painted after his wife's death, it was much admired by Lorenzo, who, according to household records, kept it hanging in his bedroom, even after his remarriage. The subject's gold bodice is decorated with emblems—interlaced Ls and diamonds—which are symbolic of Lorenzo and his family. The brooch, the coral necklace, and the prayer book allude to Giovanna's high social status and piety. In the background, the Latin epigram "O Art, if thou were able to depict conduct and the soul, no lovelier painting would exist on earth" evokes the Renaissance ideal that equates physical beauty with moral perfection. The epitaph is based on a line from an ancient Roman poet.*

(1389–1464) added to the Medicis' wealth and outmaneuvered his political enemies, becoming the unacknowledged ruler of Florence. He spent his money on books, paintings, sculptures, and palaces, and, claiming to be the common man's friend, he was eventually awarded the title *Pater patriae,* Father of His Country—a Roman title revived during the Renaissance.

Cosimo's son, Piero, ruled for only a short time and was succeeded by his son Lorenzo (1449–1492), called the Magnificent because of his grand style of living. Lorenzo and his brother Giuliano controlled Florence until Giuliano was assassinated in 1478 by the Pazzi family, rivals of the Medicis. Lorenzo brutally executed the conspirators and then governed autocratically for the next fourteen years.

Within two years of Lorenzo's death, the great power and prestige of Florence began to weaken. Two events are symptomatic of this decline in Florentine authority. The first was the invasion by Charles VIII's French army in 1494. The invasion initiated a political and cultural decline that would eventually overtake Italy, whose small city-states could not withstand the incursions of the European monarchies. The French army drove the Medici family from Florence; they remained in exile until 1512.

The second event was the iconoclastic crusade against the city led by the Dominican monk Fra Savonarola [sav-uh-nuh-ROH-luh] (1452–1498). He opposed the Medicis' rule and wanted to restore a republican form of government. In his fire-and-brimstone sermons, he denounced Florence's leaders and the city's infatuation with the arts. He eventually ran afoul of the papacy and was excommunicated and publicly executed, but not before he had had an enormous effect on the citizens—including the painter Botticelli, who is said to have burned some of his paintings while under the sway of Savonarola's reforming zeal.

The Resurgent Papacy, 1450–1500

The Great Schism was ended by the Council of Constance in 1418, and a tattered Christendom reunited under a Roman pope (see Chapter 10). By 1447 the so-called Renaissance popes were in command and had turned their attention to consolidating the Papal States and pursuing power. Like the secular despots, these popes engaged in war and, when that failed, diplomacy. They brought artistic riches to the church but also lowered its moral tone by accepting bribes for church offices and filling positions with kinsmen. But above all, these popes patronized Renaissance culture.

Three of the most aggressive and successful of these church rulers were Nicholas V (pope 1447–1455), Pius

II (pope 1458–1464), and Sixtus IV (pope 1471–1484). Nicholas V, who had been librarian for Cosimo de' Medici, founded the Vatican Library, an institution virtually unrivaled today for its holdings of manuscripts and books. He also continued the rebuilding of Rome begun by his predecessors. Pius II, often considered the most representative of the Renaissance popes because of his interest in the Greek and Roman classics and in writing poetry himself, rose rapidly through the ecclesiastical ranks. This clever politician practiced both war and diplomacy with astounding success. As a student of the new learning and as a brilliant writer in Latin, Pius II attracted intellectuals and artists to Rome. His personal recollections, or *Commentaries,* reveal much about him and his turbulent times.

Sixtus IV came from the powerful and scheming della Rovere family, and he increased his personal power through nepotism, the practice of giving offices to relatives. He continued the papal tradition of making Rome the most beautiful city in the world. The construction of the Sistine Chapel, later adorned with paintings by Botticelli and Michelangelo, was his greatest achievement (see Chapter 12).

THE SPIRIT AND STYLE OF THE EARLY RENAISSANCE

Drawing inspiration from ancient Greek and Roman models, the thinkers and the artists of the Early Renaissance explored such perennial questions as, What is human nature? How are human beings related to God? and What is the best way to achieve human happiness? Although they did not reject Christian explanations outright, they were intrigued by the secular and humanistic values of the Greco-Roman tradition and the answers they might provide to these questions. They also rightfully claimed kinship with certain fourteenth-century predecessors such as the writer Petrarch and the artist Giotto (see Chapter 10).

Those artists, scholars, and writers who are identified with the Early Renaissance and who embodied its spirit were linked, through shared tastes and patronage, with the entrepreneurial nobility, the progressive middle class, and the secular clergy. Until about 1450, most artistic works were commissioned by wealthy patrons for family chapels in churches and for public buildings; later, patrons commissioned paintings and sculptures for their private dwellings.

Even though artists, scholars, and writers stamped this age with their fresh perspectives, some of the old cultural traits remained. Unsettling secular values emerged in the midst of long-accepted religious beliefs, creating contradictions and tensions within the society. In other ways, however, the past held firm, and certain values seemed immune to change. For example, Early Renaissance thought made little headway in science, and church patronage still strongly affected the evolution of the arts and architecture, despite the growing impact of the urban class on artistic tastes.

The artists, scholars, and writers who flourished in the Early Renaissance were almost exclusively men, in contrast with the Middle Ages, when women occasionally played cultural roles. Recent scholarship has pointed out that women living in the Italian Renaissance were subjected to new constraints, especially in well-to-do families. For example, the learned Laura Cereta [che-RAY-tah] (1469–1499), daughter of a prominent family in Brescia, silenced herself at eighteen years of age, after meeting a firestorm of harsh criticism for her outspokenness. Nevertheless, a volume of her published letters has survived, in one of which she defended herself against her critics, asserting the right of women to be educated the same as men.

Humanism, Scholarship, and Schooling

Toward the end of the 1300s, Italy's educated circles became fascinated by ancient Roman civilization. Inspired by Petrarch's interest in Latin literature and language, scholars began to collect and translate Roman manuscripts uncovered in monastic libraries and other out-of-the-way depositories. There was a shift in emphasis from the church Latin of the Middle Ages to the pure Latin style of Cicero, the first-century B.C.E. Roman writer whose eloquent essays established a high moral and literary standard (see Chapter 5).

In the 1400s, these scholars spoke of their literary interests and new learning as *studia humanitatis.* They defined this term, which may be translated as "humanistic studies," as a set of intellectual pursuits that included moral philosophy, history, grammar, rhetoric, and poetry. At first, the men who studied these disciplines read the appropriate works in Latin, but after the Greek originals began to appear about 1400 and the study of ancient languages spread, they learned from the Greek texts as well.

In response to the demand for humanistic learning, new schools sprang up in most Italian city-states. In these schools was born the Renaissance ideal of an education intended to free or to liberate the mind—a liberal education. To that end, study was based on the recently recovered Latin and Greek works rather than on the more narrowly defined curriculum of scholasticism and Aristotelianism that had been favored in the Middle Ages.

The first Renaissance scholars, who were primarily searching for original Latin manuscripts, were philologists—that is, experts in the study of languages and linguistics. In time, they came to call themselves humanists because of their training in the *studia humanitatis.* These early humanists created a branch of learning, now called textual criticism, that compares various versions of a text to determine which one is most correct or authentic. They recognized that knowledge of the evolution of language was necessary to make a critical judgment on the authenticity of a text. As a result of their studies, they revealed writing errors committed by medieval monks when they copied ancient manuscripts—revelations that, in the case of religious documents, raised grave problems for the church.

The most spectacular application of textual criticism was made by Lorenzo Valla (1406–1457), who exposed the Donation of Constantine as a forgery. Throughout the Middle Ages, this famous document had been cited by the popes as proof of their political authority over Christendom. By the terms of the document, the Roman emperor Constantine gave the popes his western lands and recognized their power to rule in them. But by comparing the Latin of the fourth century, when Constantine reigned, with the Latin of the eighth century, when the document first came to light, Valla concluded that the Donation must have been produced then and not in the fourth century.

Other humanists played an active role in the life of their states, modeling themselves on the heroes of the Roman republic. Outstanding among them is Leonardo Bruni (1374–1444), who typifies the practical, civic humanist. A one-time chancellor, or chief secretary, of Florence's governing body, or *signoria,* Bruni also worked for both the Medicis and the papacy and wrote the *History of the Florentine People*. This work reflected his humanistic values, combining as it did his political experience with his knowledge of ancient history. To Bruni, the study of history illuminated contemporary events. Bruni and the other civic humanists, through their writings and their governmental service, set an example for later generations of Florentines and helped infuse them with love of their city. Moreover, by expanding the concept of humanistic studies, they contributed new insights to the ongoing debate about the role of the individual in history and in the social order.

An important consequence of humanistic studies was the rise of educational reforms. Vittorino da Feltre [veet-toe-REE-no dah FEL-tray] (1378–1446) made the most significant contributions. Vittorino favored a curriculum that exercised the body and the mind—the ideal of the ancient Greek schools. His educational theories were put into practice at the school he founded in Mantua at the ruler's request. At this school, called the Happy House, Vittorino included

SLICE OF LIFE
Battle of the Sexes, Fifteenth-Century Style

LAURA CERETA
In Defense of the Education of Women

In this letter, dated January 13, 1488, eighteen-year-old Laura Cereta responds fiercely to a male critic whose praise she finds patronizing to her as a woman. She then sets him straight about the intellectual needs of women of that time.

My ears are wearied by your carping. You brashly and publicly not merely wonder but indeed lament that I am said to possess as fine a mind as nature ever bestowed upon the most learned man. You seem to think that so learned a woman has scarcely before been seen in the world. You are wrong on both counts. . . .

I would have been silent, believe me, if that savage old enmity of yours had attacked me alone. . . . But I cannot tolerate your having attacked my entire sex. For this reason my thirsty soul seeks revenge, my sleeping pen is aroused to literary struggle, raging anger stirs mental passions long chained by silence. With just cause I am moved to demonstrate how great a reputation for learning and virtue women have won by their inborn excellence, manifested in every age as knowledge. . . .

Only the question of the rarity of outstanding women remains to be addressed. The explanation is clear: women have been able by nature to be exceptional, but have chosen lesser goals. For some women are concerned with parting their hair correctly, adorning themselves with lovely dresses, or decorating their fingers with pearls and other gems. Others delight in mouthing carefully composed phrases, indulging in dancing, or managing spoiled puppies. Still others wish to gaze at lavish banquet tables, to rest in sleep, or, standing at mirrors, to smear their lovely faces. But those in whom a deeper integrity yearns for virtue, restrain from the start their youthful souls, reflect on higher things, harden the body with sobriety and tri-als, and curb their tongues, open their ears, compose their thoughts in wakeful hours, their minds in contemplation, to letters bonded to righteousness. For knowledge is not given as a gift, but [is gained] with diligence. The free mind, not shirking effort, always soars zealously toward the good, and the desire to know grows ever more wide and deep. It is because of no special holiness, therefore, that we [women] are rewarded by God the Giver with the gift of exceptional talent. Nature has generously lavished its gifts upon all people, opening to all the doors of choice through which reason sends envoys to the will, from which they learn and convey its desires. The will must choose to exercise the gift of reason. . . .

I have been praised too much; showing your contempt for women, you pretend that I alone am admirable because of the good fortune of my intellect. . . . Do you suppose, O most contemptible man on earth, that I think myself sprung [like Athena] from the head of Jove? I am a school girl, possessed of the sleeping embers of an ordinary mind. Indeed I am too hurt, and my mind, offended, too swayed by passions, sighs, tormenting itself, conscious of the obligation to defend my sex. For absolutely everything—that which is within us and that which is without—is made weak by association with my sex.

Interpreting This Slice of Life **Describe** the ways Cereta responds to her critic. **What** are some of the types of women she lists? **How** does she portray herself? According to Cereta, **what** are some of the talents God has given to women? **Compare and contrast** Cereta's arguments with those used by modern feminists.

humanistic studies along with the medieval curriculum. A major innovation was the stress on physical exercise, which arose from his emphasis on moral training. At first, only the sons and daughters of Mantuan nobility attended his school, but gradually the student body became more democratic as young people from all classes were enrolled. Vittorino's reforms were slowly introduced into the new urban schools in northern Europe, and their model—the well-rounded student of sound body, solid learning, and high morals—helped to lay the foundation for future European schools and education.

Thought and Philosophy

The Italian humanists were not satisfied with medieval answers to the perennial inquiries of philosophy because those answers did not go beyond Aristotelian philosophy and Christian dogma. Casting their nets wider, the Renaissance thinkers concluded that the ancients had given worthwhile responses to many of the same issues as Christians and that they should not be dismissed simply because they were non-Christian.

Renaissance scholars came to advocate more tolerance toward unorthodox beliefs and began to focus on the important role played by the individual in society. Individual fulfillment became a leading Renaissance idea and remains a central notion in Western thought today. During the Renaissance, the growing emphasis on the individual resulted in a more optimistic assessment of human nature—a development that in time led to a rejection of Christianity's stress on original sin.

Throughout the 1400s, a small group of scholars from the Byzantine world, living and working in Rome, Florence, and Venice, actively gave shape to the Italian Renaissance. As teachers of Greek, these overseas scholars introduced Italy's first generation of humanists to the many ancient manuscripts not seen in the West for nearly a thousand years. Then, in 1453, with the fall of Constantinople to the Ottoman Turks, a fresh wave of Byzantine scholars, teachers, and intellectuals arrived in Italy, bearing more precious manuscripts (see Encounter in Chapter 10). Thereafter, the humanists began to focus increasingly on Greek language, literature, and, eventually, philosophy. The philosophy of Plato found a home in Italy in 1462 when Cosimo de' Medici established the Platonic Academy at one of his villas near Florence. Here, scholars gathered to examine and to discuss the writings of Plato as well as those of the Neo-Platonists. In turn, these scholars would reinterpret Platonism in ways that would later influence early Christian theology. The academy was under the direction of the brilliant humanist Marsilio Ficino [mar-SILL-e-o fe-CHEE-no] (1433–1499), whom Cosimo commissioned to translate Plato's works into Latin.

In two major treatises, Ficino made himself the leading voice of Florentine Neo-Platonism by harmonizing Platonic ideas with Christian teachings. Believing that Platonism came from God, Ficino began with the principle that both thought systems rested on divine authority. Like Plato, Ficino believed that the soul was immortal and that complete enjoyment of God would be possible only in the afterlife, when the soul was in the divine realm. Ficino also revived the Platonic notion of free will—the power of humans to make of themselves what they wish. In Ficino's hands, free will became the source of human dignity because human beings were able to choose to love God.

Ficino had the most powerful impact on the Early Renaissance when he made Plato's teaching on love central to Neo-Platonism. Following Platonism, he taught that love is a divine gift that binds all human beings together. Love expresses itself in human experience by the desire for and the appreciation of beauty in its myriad forms. Platonic love, like erotic love, is aroused first by the physical appearance of the beloved. But Platonic love, dissatisfied by mere physical enjoyment, cannot rest until it moves upward to the highest spiritual level, where it finally meets its goal of union with the Divine. Under the promptings of Platonism, the human form became a metaphor of the soul's desire for God. Many Renaissance writers and artists came under the influence of Ficino's Neo-Platonism, embracing its principles and embodying them in their works. Sandro Botticelli, for example, created several allegorical paintings in which divine love and beauty were represented by an image from pre-Christian Rome—Venus, goddess of love (Figure 11.4).

Ficino's most prized student, Pico della Mirandola [PEE-koh DAYL-lah me-RAHN-do-lah] (1463–1494), surpassed his master's accomplishments by the breadth of his learning and the virtuosity of his mind. Pico—a wealthy and charming aristocrat—impressed everyone with his command of languages, his range of knowledge, and his spirited arguments. His goal was the synthesis of Platonism and Aristotelianism within a Christian framework that also encompassed Hebraic, Arabic, and Persian ideas. Church authorities and traditional scholars attacked Pico's efforts once they grasped the implication of his ambitious project—that all knowledge shared basic common truths and that Christians could benefit from studying non-Western, non-Christian writings.

Pico's second important contribution—the concept of individual worth—had been foreshadowed by Ficino. Pico's *Oration on the Dignity of Man* gives the highest expression to this idea, which is inherent in the humanist tradition. According to Pico, human beings, endowed with reason and speech, are created as a microcosm of the universe. Set at the midpoint in the scale of God's creatures, they are blessed with free will, which enables them either to raise themselves to God or to sink lower than the beasts. This liberty to determine private fate makes human beings the masters of their individual destinies and, at the same time, focuses attention on each human being as the measure of all things—a Classical belief now reborn.

Architecture, Sculpture, and Painting

It was in architecture, sculpture, and painting that the Renaissance made its most dramatic break with the medieval past. The **Early Renaissance style** was launched in Florence by artists who wanted to make a complete break with the Late Gothic style (Figure 11.5). Led by the architect Filippo Brunelleschi [bru-nayl-LAYS-kee] (1377–1446), this group studied the ruins of Classical buildings and ancient works of sculpture to unlock the secrets of their harmonious style. They believed that once the Classical ideals were rescued from obscurity, new works could be fashioned that captured the spirit of ancient art and architecture without slavishly copying it.

Figure 11.4 SANDRO BOTTICELLI. *The Birth of Venus.* 1480s. Tempera on canvas, 5'8" × 9'1". Uffizi Gallery, Florence. *With the paintings of Botticelli, the nude female form reappeared in Western art for the first time since the Greco-Roman period. Botticelli's* Venus *contains many Classical echoes, such as the goddess's lovely features and her modest pose. But the artist used these pre-Christian images to convey a Christian message and to embody the principles of Ficino's Neo-Platonist philosophy.*

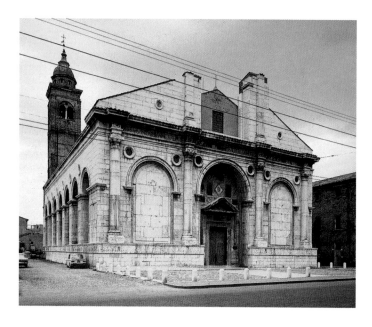

Figure 11.5 LEONE BATTISTA ALBERTI. Tempio Malatestiano (Malatesta Temple) (Church of San Francesco). Ca. 1450. Rimini, Italy. *Although unfinished, this church strikingly demonstrates the revolution in architecture represented by Early Renaissance ideals. Nothing could be further from the spires of Late Gothic cathedrals than this simple, symmetrical structure with its plain facade, post-and-lintel entrance, rounded arches, and Classical columns. Designed by the leading theoretician of the new style, the Malatesta Temple served as a model for artists and architects of the later Renaissance.*

Artistic Ideals and Innovations Guided by Brunelleschi's findings, architects, sculptors, and painters made the Classical principles of balance, simplicity, and restraint the central ideals of the Early Renaissance style. The heaviest debt to the past was owed by the architects, for they revived the Classical orders—the Doric, the Ionic, and the Corinthian. The new buildings, though constructed to accommodate modern needs, were symmetrical in plan and relied on simple decorative designs. The theoretician of Early Renaissance style and its other guiding light was Leone Battista Alberti [ahl-BAIR-tee] (1404–1472), who wrote at length on Brunelleschi's innovations and published a highly influential book on the new painting. Alberti believed that architecture should embody the humanistic qualities of dignity, balance, control, and harmony and that a building's ultimate beauty rested on the mathematical harmony of its separate parts.

Sculpture and painting, freed from their subordination to architecture, regained their ancient status as independent art forms and in time became the most cherished of the visual arts. Renaissance sculptors and painters aspired to greater realism than had been achieved in the Gothic style, seeking to depict human musculature and anatomy with a greater degree of credibility. Sculptors, led by this period's genius Donatello [dah-nah-TEL-lo] (about 1386–1466), revived Classical practices that had not been seen in the West for more than a thousand years: the freestanding figure; the technique of contrapposto, or a figure balanced with most of the weight resting on one leg (see Figure 3.22); the life-size nude statue; and the equestrian statue.

Whereas architecture and sculpture looked back to ancient Greek and Roman traditions, developments in painting grew from varied sources, including the Islamic world (see Encounter) and the Late Medieval world, though the most important influence was the art of the Florentine painter Giotto. In the early fourteenth century, Giotto had founded a new realistic and expressive style (see Chapter 10), on which Florentine painters began to build at the opening of the fifteenth century. Much of Giotto's genius lay in his ability to show perspective, or the appearance of spatial depth, in his frescoes, an illusion he achieved largely through the placement of the figures (see Figure 10.20). Approximately one hundred years after Giotto, painters learned to enhance the realism of their pictures by the use of linear perspective, the most significant artistic innovation of the age.

The invention of linear perspective was another of Brunelleschi's accomplishments. Using principles of architecture and optics, he conducted experiments in 1425 that provided the mathematical basis for achieving the illusion of depth on a two-dimensional surface (and, coincidentally, contributed to the enhancement of the status of the arts by grounding them in scholarly learning). Brunelleschi's solution to the problem of linear perspective was to organize the picture space around the center point, or **vanishing point.** After determining the painting's vanishing point, he devised a structural grid for placing objects in precise relation to each other within the picture space. He also computed the ratios by which objects diminish in size as they recede from view, so that pictorial reality seems to correspond visually with physical accuracy. He then subjected the design to a mirror test—checking its truthfulness in its reflected image.

When the camera appeared in the nineteenth century, it was discovered that the photographic lens "saw" nature according to Brunelleschi's mathematical rules. After the 1420s, Brunelleschi's studies led to the concept of Renaissance space, the notion that a composition should be viewed from one single position. For four hundred years, or until first challenged by Manet in the nineteenth century, linear perspective and Renaissance space played a leading role in Western painting (see Chapter 18).

A second type of perspective, atmospheric or aerial, was perfected by painters north of the Alps in the first half of the fifteenth century, although the Italian painter Masaccio was the first to revive atmospheric perspective in the 1420s, based on the Roman tradition. Through the use of colors, these artists created an illusion of depth by subtly diminishing the tones as the distance between the eye and the object increased; at the horizon line, the colors become grayish and the objects blurry in appearance. When atmospheric perspective was joined to linear perspective, as happened later in the century, a greater illusion of reality was achieved than was possible with either type used independently.

Again commenting on the innovations of Brunelleschi was Alberti, who published a treatise in 1435 that elaborated on the mathematical aspects of painting and set forth brilliantly the humanistic and secular values of the Early Renaissance. Alberti was an aristocratic humanist with both a deep knowledge of Classicism and a commitment to its ideals. In his treatise, he praised master painters in rousing terms, comparing their creativity to God's—a notion that would have been considered blasphemous by medieval thinkers. He asserted that paintings, in addition to pleasing the eye, should appeal to the mind with optical and mathematical accuracy. But paintings, he went on, should also present a noble subject, such as a Classical hero, and should be characterized by a small number of figures, by carefully observed and varied details, by graceful poses, by harmonious relationships among all elements, and by a judicious use of colors. These Classical ideals were quickly adopted by Florentine artists eager to establish a new aesthetic code.

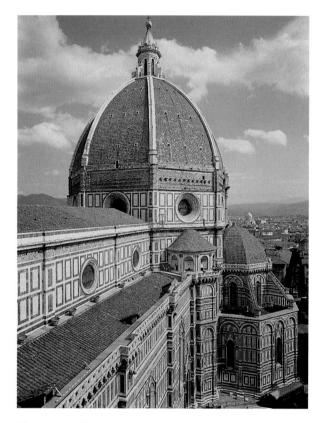

Figure 11.6   FILIPPO BRUNELLESCHI. Cathedral Dome, Florence. 1420–1436. Ht. of dome from floor 367'. *After the dome of the Florence cathedral was erected according to Brunelleschi's plan, another architect was employed to add small galleries in the area above the circular windows. But the Florentine authorities halted his work before the galleries were fully installed, leaving the structure in its present state.*

Figure 11.7   FILIPPO BRUNELLESCHI. Design for Construction of Dome of Florence Cathedral. *Brunelleschi designed the dome of the Florence cathedral with an inner and an outer shell, both of which are attached to the eight ribs of the octagonal-shaped structure. Sixteen smaller ribs, invisible from the outside, were placed between the shells to give added support. What held these elements together and gave them stability was the lantern, based on his design, that was anchored to the dome's top sometime after 1446.*

Architecture   In the High Middle Ages, most architects were stonemasons and were regarded as artisans, like shoemakers or potters. But by the fifteenth century, the status of architects had changed. Because of the newly discovered scientific aspects of their craft, the leading architects were now grouped with those practicing the learned professions of medicine and law. By 1450 Italian architects had freed architecture from Late Gothicism, as well as from the other arts. Unlike Gothic cathedrals adorned with sculptures and paintings, these new buildings drew on the Classical tradition for whatever simple decorative details were needed. This transformation became the most visible symbol of Early Renaissance architecture.

Although Brunelleschi established the new standards in architecture, most of his buildings have been either destroyed or altered considerably by later hands. However, the earliest work to bring him fame still survives in Florence largely as he had planned it— the dome of the city's cathedral (Figure 11.6). Although the rest of the cathedral—nave, transept, and

choir—was finished before 1400, no one had been able to devise a method for erecting the projected dome until Brunelleschi received the commission in 1420. Using the learning he had gained from his researches in Rome as well as his knowledge of Gothic building styles, he developed an ingenious plan for raising the dome, which was virtually completed in 1436.

Faced with a domical base of 140 feet, Brunelleschi realized that a hemispheric dome in the Roman manner, like the dome of the Pantheon, would not work (see Figure 5.14). Traditional building techniques could not span the Florentine cathedral's vast domical base, nor could the cathedral's walls be buttressed to support a massive dome. So he turned to Gothic methods, using diagonal ribs based on the pointed arch. This innovative dome had a double shell of two relatively thin walls held together by twenty-four stone ribs, of which only eight are visible. His crowning touch was to add a lantern that sits atop the dome and locks the ribs into place (Figure 11.7). The dome's rounded windows echo the openings in the upper nave walls, thereby ensuring that his addition would harmonize with the existing elements. But the octagonal-shaped dome was Brunelleschi's own creation and expresses a logical, even inevitable, structure. Today, the cathedral still dominates the skyline of Florence, a lasting symbol of Brunelleschi's creative genius.

Brunelleschi's most representative building is the Pazzi Chapel, as the chapter house, or meeting room, of the monks of Santa Croce is called. This small church embodies the harmonious proportions and Classical features that are the hallmark of the Early Renaissance style. In his architectural plan, Brunelleschi centered a dome over an oblong area whose width equals the dome's diameter and whose length is twice its width and then covered each of the chapel's elongated ends with a barrel vault. Double doors opened into the center wall on one long side, and two rounded arch windows flanked this doorway. A loggia, or porch, which Brunelleschi may not have designed, preceded the entrance (Figure 11.8). Inside the chapel, following the Classical rules of measure and proportion, Brunelleschi employed medallions, rosettes, **pilasters** (or applied columns), and square panels. In addition to these Classical details, the rounded arches and the barrel vaults further exemplify the new Renaissance style (Figure 11.9). His Classical theories were shared by Florence's humanist elite, who found religious significance in mathematical harmony. Both they and Brunelleschi believed that a well-ordered building such as the Pazzi Chapel mirrored God's plan of the universe.

The other towering figure in Early Renaissance architecture was Alberti. Despite the influence of his ideas, which dominated architecture until 1600, no completed building based on his design remains. A splendid unfinished effort is the Tempio Malatestiano in Rimini (see Figure 11.5), a structure that replaced the existing church of San Francesco. Rimini's despot, Sigismondo Malatesta (1417–1468), planned to have himself, his mistress, and his court buried in the refurbished structure, and he appointed Alberti to supervise the church's reconstruction.

Alberti's monument represents the first modern attempt to give a Classical exterior to a church. Abandoning the Gothic pointed arch, he designed this church's unfinished facade with its three rounded arches after a nearby triumphal arch. He framed the arches with Corinthian columns, one of his favorite decorative devices. Although the architect apparently planned to cover the church's interior with a dome comparable to Brunelleschi's on the Florentine cathedral, Malatesta's fortunes failed, and the projected temple had to be abandoned. Nevertheless, Alberti's unfinished church was admired by later builders and helped to point the way to the new Renaissance architecture.

Sculpture   Like architecture, sculpture blossomed in Florence in the early 1400s. Donatello, the leader of the sculptural revival, was imbued with Classical ideals but obsessed with realism. He used a variety of techniques—expressive gestures, direct observation, and mathematical precision—to reproduce what his eyes saw. Donatello accompanied Brunelleschi to Rome to study ancient art, and he adapted linear perspective as early as 1425 into a small **relief** called *The Feast of Herod* (Figure 11.10). The subject is the tragic end of John the Baptist, Florence's patron saint, as recounted in Mark 6:20–29. In Donatello's square bronze panel, the saint's severed head is being displayed on a dish to King Herod at the left, while the scorned Salome stands near the right end of the table. A puzzled guest leans toward the ruler, who recoils with upraised hands; two children at the left back away from the bloody head; and a diner leans back from the center of the table—all depicted under the rounded arches of the new Brunelleschian architecture. The sculpture's rich details and use of linear perspective point up the horror of the scene and thus achieve the heightened realism that was among the artistic goals of this era. The scene's vanishing point runs through the middle set of arches, so that the leaning motions of the two figures in the foreground not only express their inner turmoil but also cause them to fall away from the viewer's line of sight.

Donatello also revived the freestanding male nude, one of the supreme expressions of ancient art. Donatello's bronze *David*, probably executed for Cosimo de' Medici, portrays David standing with his left foot on the severed head of the Philistine warrior Goliath—a pose based on the biblical story (Figure 11.11). This sculpture had a profound influence on later sculptors, who admired Donatello's creation but produced rival interpretations of David (Figure 11.12). Donatello and his successors used the image of David to pay homage to male power—a major preoccupation of Renaissance artists and intellectuals.

Like other Renaissance masters, Donatello owed debts to Classical artists, but he also challenged them by adapting their principles to his own times. For example, the Roman statue of Marcus Aurelius (see Figure 5.10) inspired Donatello's bronze called the *Gattamelata*, the first successful equestrian sculpture in over twelve hundred years (Figure 11.13). As Donatello's *David* portrays the subtleties of adolescent male beauty, his *Gattamelata* pays homage to mature masculine power. This work honored the memory of Erasmo da Narni, a Venetian *condottiere* nicknamed Gattamelata, or "Honey Cat." The warrior's pose resembles the Roman imperial style, but in almost every other way, the sculptor violates the harmonious ideas of ancient art.

Figure 11.8 (Inset), FILIPPO BRUNELLESCHI AND OTHERS. Exterior, Pazzi Chapel, Santa Croce Church. 1433–1461. Florence. *The Pazzi Chapel's harmonious facade reflects the Classical principles of the Early Renaissance style: symmetry and simplicity. By breaking the rhythm of the facade with the rounded arch, the architect emphasizes its surface symmetry so that the left side is a mirror image of the right side. Simplicity is achieved in the architectural decorations, which are either Greco-Roman devices or mathematically inspired divisions.*

Figure 11.10 DONATELLO. *The Feast of Herod.* Ca. 1425. Gilt bronze, 23½″ square. Baptismal font, San Giovanni, Siena. *The first low-relief sculpture executed in the Early Renaissance style,* The Feast of Herod *is a stunning example of the power of this new approach to art. Its theatrical force arises from the successful use of linear perspective and the orderly placement of the figures throughout the three rooms.*

◀ **Figure 11.9** FILIPPO BRUNELLESCHI. Interior. Pazzi Chapel, Santa Croce Church. Ca. 1433–1461. 59′9″ long × 35′8″ wide. Florence. *Decorations on the white walls of the Pazzi Chapel's interior break up its plain surface and draw the viewer's eye to the architectural structure: pilasters, window and panel frames, medallions, capitals, and dome ribs. The only nonarchitecturally related decorations are the terra-cotta sculptures by Luca della Robbia of the four evangelists and the Pazzi family coat of arms, mounted inside the medallions.*

Figure 11.11 DONATELLO. *David.* Ca. 1430–1432. Bronze, ht. 62¼″. Bargello, Florence. *The David and Goliath story was often allegorized into a prophecy of Christ's triumph over Satan. But Donatello's sculpture undermines such an interpretation, for his* David *is less a heroic figure than a provocative image of refined sensuality, as suggested by the undeveloped but elegant body, the dandified pose, and the incongruous boots and hat. Donatello's* David *is a splendid modern portrayal of youthful male power, self-aware and poised on the brink of manhood.*

Figure 11.12 ANDREA DEL VERROCCHIO. *David.* 1473–1475. Bronze, ht. 4′2″. Bargello, Florence. *Verrocchio's* David *inaugurated the tradition in Renaissance Florence of identifying the Jewish giant-killer with the city's freedom-loving spirit. A masterpiece of bravado, Verrocchio's boyish hero stands challengingly over the severed head of Goliath. In its virility, this work surpasses the sculpture that inspired it, Donatello's* David *(see Figure 11.11). Florence's ruling council liked Verrocchio's statue so much that they placed it in the Palazzo Vecchio, the seat of government, where it remained until Michelangelo's* David *(see Figure 12.20) displaced it. Verrochio's* David *was restored in 2003, bringing back to the original the gold patina in the locks of hair, the borders of the clothes and boots, and the pupils of the eyes. With the restoration of the gold leaf gilding, restorers have concluded that the statue originally was intended for display indoors.*

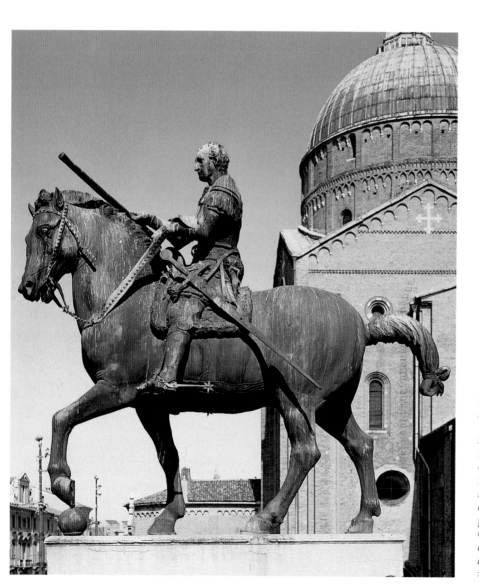

Figure 11.13 DONATELLO. *Equestrian Monument of Erasmo da Narni, Called "Gattamelata."* 1447–1453. Bronze, approx. 11 × 13′. Piazza del Santo, Padua. *This equestrian statue of the condottiere was funded by his family but authorized by a grateful Venetian senate in honor of his military exploits. Conceiving of the dead military leader as a "triumphant Caesar," Donatello dressed him in Classical costume and decorated his saddle and armor with many allusions to antique art, such as flying cupids and victory depicted as a goddess.*

Figure 11.14 DONATELLO. Detail of *"Gattamelata."* 1447–1453. Piazza del Santo, Padua. *Donatello deliberately designed the monument's stern, deeply lined, and serious face to conform to the Renaissance ideal of a strong military commander.*

Most significant, the rider's face owes its sharp realism—firm jawline, bushy eyebrows, widely set eyes, and close-cropped hair—to fifteenth-century sources, especially to the cult of the ugly, an aesthetic attitude that claimed to find moral strength in coarse features that did not conform to the Classical ideals (Figure 11.14). Since this work was commissioned after the hero's death and since Donatello had no way of knowing how the soldier looked, he sculptured the

face to conform to his notion of a strong-minded general. The massive horse, with flaring nostrils, open mouth, and lifted foreleg, seems to be an extension of the soldier's forceful personality.

The only serious rival to Donatello in the Early Renaissance was another Florentine, Lorenzo Ghiberti [gee-BAIR-tee] (about 1381–1455), who slowly adapted to the new style of art. In 1401 he defeated Brunelleschi in a competition to select a sculptor for the north doors of Florence's Baptistery. The north doors consist of twenty-eight panels, arranged in four columns of seven panels, each depicting a New Testament scene. These doors, completed between 1403 and 1424, show Ghiberti still under the influence of the International Gothic style that prevailed in about 1400. Illustrative of this tendency is the panel *The Annunciation* (Luke 1:26–38), which depicts the moment when Mary learns from an angelic messenger that she will become the mother of Christ (Figure 11.15). The Gothic quatrefoil, or four-leafed frame, was standard for these panels, and many of Ghiberti's techniques are typical of the Gothic style—the niche in which the Virgin stands, her swaying body, and the angel depicted in flight. Nevertheless, Ghiberti always exhibited a strong feeling for Classical forms and harmony, as in the angel's well-rounded body and Mary's serene face.

The artistic world of Florence was a rapidly changing one, however, and Ghiberti adapted his art to conform to the emerging Early Renaissance style of Donatello. Between 1425 and 1452, Ghiberti brought his mature art to its fullest expression in the east doors,

Figure 11.15 LORENZO GHIBERTI. *The Annunciation.* Panel from the north doors of the Baptistery. 1403–1424. Gilt bronze, 20½ × 17¾". Florence. *Ghiberti's rendition of the Annunciation was typical of his panels on the north doors. Mary and the angel are placed in the shallow foreground and are modeled almost completely in the round. The background details, including a sharply foreshortened representation of God on the left, are scarcely raised from the metal. The contrast between these design elements enhances the illusion of depth.*

338

the last of the Baptistery's three sculptured portals. These panels, larger than those on the north doors, depict ten scenes from the Old Testament. Most of the Gothic touches have been eliminated, including the framing quatrefoils, which are now replaced with square panels (Figure 11.16).

One of the sublime panels from the east doors is the one depicting the story of the brothers Cain and Abel (Figure 11.17), taken from the Book of Genesis. This panel shows, in many ways, Ghiberti's growing dedication to Classical ideals, seen, for example, in the graceful contrapposto of the standing figures and their proportional relationships. This work translates Albertian aesthetics into bronze by creating an illusion of depth. According to Ghiberti's *Commentaries*, the sculptor's purpose was not illusion for illusion's sake but, rather, an articulate visual presentation of the biblical story. Five incidents from the story of Cain and Abel are illustrated: (1) Cain and Abel as children with their parents, Adam and Eve, at the top left; (2) Cain and Abel making sacrifices before an altar, at the top right; (3) Cain plowing with oxen and Abel watching his sheep, in the left foreground and left middle, respectively; (4) Cain slaying Abel with a club, in the right middle; and (5) Cain being questioned by God, in the right foreground.

Painting The radical changes taking place in architecture and sculpture were minor compared with the changes in painting. Inspired by Classicism though lacking significant examples from ancient times, painters were relatively free to experiment and to define their own path. As in the other arts of the 1400s, Florentine painters led the way and established the standards for the new style—realism, linear perspective, and psychological truth (convincing portrayal of emotional states). This movement climaxed at the end

Figure 11.17 LORENZO GHIBERTI. *The Story of Cain and Abel.* Detail from the east doors of the Baptistery (the *Gates of Paradise*). 1424–1452. Gilt bronze, 31¼ × 31¼". Florence. *This exquisite panel from the Florence Baptistery's east doors is a testament to Ghiberti's absorption of Early Renaissance taste. He followed Brunelleschi's new rules for linear perspective by placing the vanishing point in the middle of the tree trunks in the center of the panel, and he adhered to Alberti's principle of varied details by adding the oxen, sheep, and altar.*

of the century with the early work of Leonardo da Vinci.

After 1450 Florence's dominance was challenged by Venetian painters, who were forging their own artistic tradition. Venice, having won its freedom from the Byzantine Empire only in the High Middle Ages, was still in the thrall of Byzantine culture (see Chapter 7). As a result, Venetian painters and their patrons showed a pronounced taste for the stylized effects and sensual surfaces typical of Byzantine art. However, a distinct school of Venetian painters emerged, which eventually was to have a major impact on the course of painting in the West.

North of the Alps, a third Early Renaissance development was taking place in Burgundy and the Low Countries. There, the painters pursued an art more religious than that of Italy and closer in spirit to the Late Gothic. The northern artists concentrated on minute details and landscapes rather than on the problems of depth and composition that concerned Italy's painters. This survey confines itself to the major figures in the Florentine school, which is divided into two generations, and to the founder of the Venetian school.

The guiding genius of the revolution in painting in the earlier Florentine school was the youthful Masaccio [mah-ZAHT-cho] (1401–1428), whose career was

◄ **Figure 11.16** LORENZO GHIBERTI. *Gates of Paradise.* East doors of the Baptistery. 1424–1452. Gilt bronze, ht. approx. 17'. Florence. *The ten scenes depicted on these doors are based on Old Testament stories, taken from the books of Genesis through Kings. Reading from top left to right, then back and forth, and ending at bottom right, the panels begin with an illustration of the opening chapters of Genesis followed by others representing events in the lives of Cain and Abel, Noah, Abraham, Isaac and Jacob, Joseph, Moses, Joshua, David, and Solomon. Taking heed of medieval artistic tradition, Ghiberti placed several dramatic episodes from the life of each biblical character in a single panel. Each panel was formed into a wax model, then cast in bronze, and gilded with gold. According to Giorgio Vasari, the Renaissance artist and writer, Michelangelo, on first seeing the doors, described them as "worthy of Paradise"—the name by which they are still known—the Gates of Paradise. In 1991 Ghiberti's original doors were moved inside to Florence's Duomo Museum and duplicate doors replaced them on the Baptistery.*

Figure 11.18 MASACCIO. *The Holy Trinity.* 1427 or 1428. Fresco, 21'10½" × 10'5". Santa Maria Novella, Florence. *Masaccio achieved a remarkable illusion of depth in this fresco by using linear and atmospheric perspective. Below the simulated chapel he painted a skeleton in a wall sarcophagus (not visible in this photograph) with a melancholy inscription reading, "I was once that which you are, and what I am you also will be." This* memento mori, *or reminder of death, was probably ordered by the donor, a member of the Lenzi family. His tomb is built into the floor and lies directly in front of the fresco.*

probably cut short by the plague. He adopted mathematical perspective in his works almost simultaneously with its invention by Brunelleschi. In the history of Western painting, Masaccio's *Holy Trinity* fresco is the first successful depiction in painting of the new concept of Renaissance space. His design for this fresco in the church of Santa Maria Novella, Florence,

shows that he was well aware of the new currents flowing in the art of his day. The painting offers an architectural setting in the style of Brunelleschi, and the solidity and vitality of the figures indicate that Masaccio had also absorbed the values of Donatello's new sculpture. Masaccio's fresco portrays the Holy Trinity—the three divine beings who make up the Christian idea of God—within a simulated chapel (Figure 11.18). Jesus' crucified body appears to be held up by God the Father, who stands on a platform behind the cross; between the heads of God and Jesus is a dove, symbolizing the Holy Spirit and completing the Trinitarian image. Mary and Saint John, both clothed in contemporary dress, flank the holy trio. Mary points dramatically to the Savior. Just outside the chapel's frame, the donors kneel in prayer—the typical way of presenting patrons in Renaissance art.

In the *Holy Trinity* fresco, Masaccio uses a variety of innovations. He is the first painter to show light falling from a single source, in this instance, from the left, bathing the body of Christ and coinciding with the actual lighting in Santa Maria Novella. This realistic feature adds to the three-dimensional effect of the well-modeled figures. The use of linear perspective further heightens the scene's realism. Finally, the perspective, converging to the midpoint between the kneeling donors, reinforces the hierarchy of beings within the fresco: from God the Father at the top to the human figures at the sides. In effect, mathematical tidiness is used to reveal the divine order—an ideal congenial to Florence's intellectual elite.

A second fresco by Masaccio, *The Tribute Money,* painted in the Brancacci Chapel of the church of Santa Maria del Carmine, Florence, is recognized as Masaccio's masterpiece (Figure 11.19). This fresco illustrates the Gospel account (Matthew 17:24–27) in which Jesus advises Peter, his chief disciple, to pay the Roman taxes. Because this painting depicts a biblical subject virtually unrepresented in Christian art, it was probably commissioned by a donor to justify a new and heavy Florentine tax. Whether the fresco had any effect on tax collection is debatable, but other artists were captivated by Masaccio's stunning technical effects: the use of perspective and **chiaroscuro,** or the modeling with light and shade.

The Tribute Money fresco follows the continuous narrative form of medieval art. Three separate episodes are depicted at the same time—in the center, Jesus is confronted by the tax collector; on the left, Peter, as foretold by Jesus, finds a coin in the mouth of a fish; and, on the right, Peter pays the coin to the Roman official. Despite this Gothic effect, the fresco's central section is able to stand alone because of its spatial integrity and unified composition. Jesus is partially en-

Figure 11.19   MASACCIO. *The Tribute Money.* Ca. 1425. Fresco, 8'2⅜" × 19'8¼". Santa Maria del Carmine, Florence. *This fresco represents the highest expression of the art of Masaccio, particularly in his realistic portrayal of the tax collector. This official, who appears twice, first confronting Christ in the center and then receiving money from Peter on the right, is depicted with coarse features—a typical man of the Florentine streets. Even his posture, though rendered with Classical contrapposto, suggests a swagger—a man at home in his body and content with his difficult occupation.*

circled by his apostles, and the tax gatherer, viewed from the back, stands to the right. In this central group, the heads are all at the same height, for Masaccio aligned them according to Brunelleschi's principles. Fully modeled in the round, each human form occupies a precise, mathematical space.

Painters such as the Dominican friar Fra Angelico (about 1400–1455) extended Masaccio's innovations. Fra Angelico's later works, painted for the renovated monastery of San Marco in Florence and partially funded by Cosimo de' Medici, show his mature blending of biblical motifs in Renaissance space. The *Annunciation* portrays a reflective Virgin receiving the angel Gabriel (Figure 11.20). Mary and Gabriel are framed in niches in the Gothic manner, but the other elements—the mastery of depth, the simplicity of gestures, the purity of colors, and the integrated scene— are rendered in the new, simple Renaissance style. The painting's vanishing point is placed to the right of center in the small barred window looking out from the Virgin's bedroom. The loggia [LOH-je-uh], or open porch, in which the scene takes place was based on a new architectural fashion popular among Florence's wealthy elite. Religious images abound in this painting; the enclosed garden symbolizes Mary's vir-

ginity, and the barred window attests to the purity of her life. Because of his gracious mastery of form and space, Fra Angelico's influence on later artists was pronounced.

One of those he influenced was Piero della Francesca [PYER-o DAYL-lah frahn-CHAY-skah] (about 1420–1492), a great painter of the second Florentine generation, who grew up in a Tuscan country town near Florence. His panel painting *The Flagellation* shows the powerful though mysterious aesthetic effects of his controversial style (Figure 11.21). The sunlight flooding the scene unites the figures, but the composition places them in two distinct areas. At the extreme left sits Pilate, the judge, on a dais. The painting's subject— the scourging of Christ before his crucifixion—is placed to the left rear. Reinforcing this odd displacement are the figures on the right, who are apparently lost in their own conversation. Aesthetically this strange juxtaposition arises because della Francesca has placed the horizon line around the hips of the figures beating Christ, causing the three men on the right to loom in such high perspective; thus the men in the foreground appear to be indifferent to Christ and unaware of his importance. The effect is distinctly unsettling in a religious scene. The modern world, which

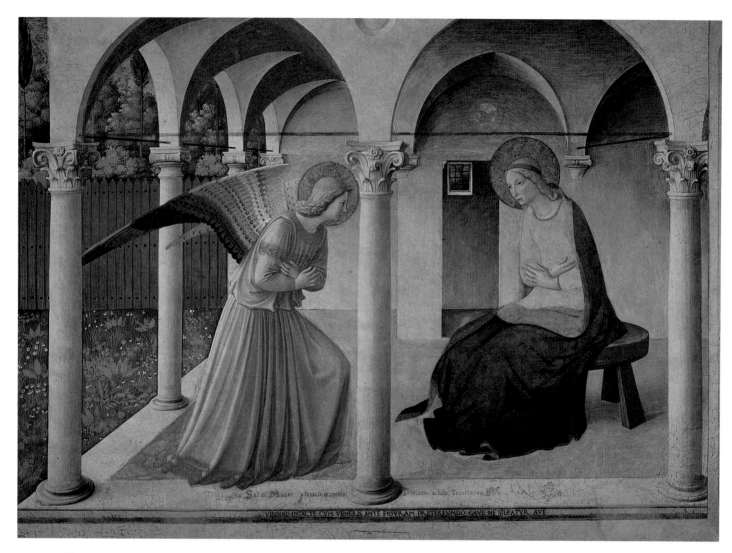

Figure 11.20   FRA ANGELICO. *Annunciation*. 1438–1445. Fresco, 7′6″ × 10′5″. Monastery of San Marco, Florence. *Fra Angelico's portrayal of the Virgin at the moment when she receives the news that she will bear the baby Jesus is a wonderful illustration of the painter's use of religious symbols. Mary's questioning expression and her arms crossed in a maternal gesture help to establish the painting's subject. Moreover, the physical setting of the scene, bare except for the rough bench on which she sits, suggests an ascetic existence—an appropriate detail for the painting's original setting, a monastery.*

loves conundrums, has developed a strong passion for the private vision of della Francesca as represented in his art.

Sandro Botticelli [baht-tuh-CHEL-lee] (1445–1510) is the best representative of a lyrical aspect of this second generation and one of the most admired painters in the Western tradition. One of the first Florentine artists to master both linear and atmospheric perspec-

tive, he was less interested in the technical aspects of painting than he was in depicting languid beauty and poetical truth.

Until the 1480s, Botticelli's art was shaped by the Neo-Platonic philosophy of the Florentine Academy, and thus he often allegorized pagan myths, giving them a Christian slant. Especially prominent in Neo-Platonic thought was the identification of Venus, the

Figure 11.21   Piero della Francesca. *The Flagellation.* 1460s. Oil on panel, 23 × 32″. Galleria Nazionale della Marche, Palazzo Ducale, Urbino. *A secondary religious message may be found in this work. In 1439 the Orthodox Church discussed union with Rome at the Council of Florence but later repudiated the merger when the Byzantine populace rioted in favor of Turkish rule. The hats on Pilate (seated at the left) and the third man from the right are copies of Greek headdresses that were worn at the council. In effect, these figures suggest that the Greek Church is a persecutor of true Christianity, for the papacy regarded the Greek Orthodox faith as schismatic.*

Roman goddess of love, with the Christian belief that "God is love." Botticelli, with the support of his patrons, notably the Medici family, made the Roman goddess the subject of two splendid paintings, the *Primavera* and *The Birth of Venus.* In this way, female nudes once again became a proper subject for art, though male nudes had appeared earlier, in Donatello's generation (see Figure 11.11).

Botticelli's *Primavera,* or *Allegory of Spring,* presents Venus as a Christianized deity, dressed in a revealingly transparent gown (Figure 11.22). At first glance, the goddess, standing just slightly to the right of center, appears lost amid the general agitation, but on closer view she is seen to be presiding over the revels. Venus tilts her head coyly and holds up her right hand, establishing by these commanding gestures that this

Figure 11.22   SANDRO BOTTICELLI. *Primavera*. Ca. 1482. Tempera on panel, 6′8″ × 10′4″. *Uffizi Gallery, Florence. Botticelli's lyricism is evident in his refined images of human beauty. His figures' elegant features and gestures, such as the sloping shoulders and the tilted heads, were copied by later artists. The women's blond, ropelike hair and transparent gowns are typical of Botticelli's style.*

orange grove is her garden and the other figures are her familiars, or associates, all of them symbolically linked with divine love.

Even though the *Primavera* is one of the most beloved works of Western art, in technical terms the painting shows that Botticelli was out of step with the Early Renaissance. He has placed the scene in the near foreground, stressing this area's extreme shallowness by the entangled backdrop of trees and shrubs. The figures are flattened, and the background appears more decorative than real.

An even more famous work by Botticelli, and one of the great landmarks of Western art, is *The Birth of Venus* (see Figure 11.4). Painted in an even more flattened style than the *Primavera*, this masterpiece was probably intended as a visual complement to it. In Neo-

Platonic terms, Venus is an image of beauty and love as it is born and grows in the human mind; the birth of Venus corresponds to the baptism of Jesus, because baptism is a symbol of rebirth.

In the 1480s, Florentine art was moving toward its culmination in the early works of Leonardo da Vinci (1452–1519). Leonardo is the quintessential representative of a new breed of artist: the Renaissance man, who takes the universe of learning as his province. Not only did he defy the authority of the church by secretly studying human cadavers, but he also rejected the Classical values that had guided the first generation of the Early Renaissance. He relied solely on empirical truth and what the human eye could discover. His notebooks, encoded so as to be legible only when read in a mirror, recorded and detailed his lifelong curiosity about both the human and the natural worlds. In his habits of mind, Leonardo joined intellectual curiosity with the skills of sculptor, architect, engineer, scientist, and painter.

Among his few surviving paintings from this period, the first version of *The Virgin of the Rocks* reveals both his scientific eye and his desire to create a haunting image uniquely his own (Figure 11.23). In this scene, set in a grotto or cave, Mary is portrayed with the infant Jesus, as a half-kneeling infant John the Baptist prays and an angel watches. The plants underfoot and the rocks in the background are a treasure of precise documentation. Nevertheless, the setting is Leonardo's own invention—without a scriptural or a traditional basis—and is a testimony to his creative genius.

Leonardo's plan of *The Virgin of the Rocks* shows the rich workings of his mind. Ignoring Brunelleschian perspective, he placed the figures his own way. He also developed a pyramid design for arranging the figures in relation to one another; Mary's head is the pyramid's apex, and her seat and the other three figures anchor its corners. Within this pyramid, Leonardo creates a dynamic tension by using gestures to suggest a circular motion: The angel points to John the Baptist, who in turn directs his praying hands toward Jesus. A second, vertical, line of stress is seen in the gesturing hands of Mary, the angel, and Christ. Later artists so admired this painting that its pyramidal composition became the standard in the High Renaissance.

No prior artist had used chiaroscuro to such advantage as Leonardo does in this work, causing the figures to stand out miraculously from the surrounding gloom. And unlike earlier artists, he colors the atmosphere, softening the edges of surfaces with a fine haze called **sfumato**. As a result, the painting looks more like a vision than a realistic scene. Leonardo's later works are part of the High Renaissance (see Chapter 12), but his early works represent the fullest expression of the scientific spirit of the second generation of Early Renaissance painting.

While the Florentine painters were establishing themselves as the driving force in the Early Renaissance, a rival school was beginning to emerge in Venice. The Venetian school, dedicated to exploring the effects of light and air and re-creating the sensuous effects of textured surfaces, was eventually to play a major role in the history of painting in Italy and the West. Founded by Giovanni Bellini, a member of a dynasty of painters, the Venetian school began its rise to greatness.

Giovanni Bellini (about 1430–1516), who trained in the workshop of his father, the Late Gothic painter Jacopo Bellini (about 1400–about 1470), made Venice a center of Renaissance art comparable to Florence and

Figure 11.23   LEONARDO DA VINCI. *The Virgin of the Rocks.* 1483. Oil on panel, approx. 6'3" × 3'7". Louvre. *Two slightly different versions of this work exist, this one dating from 1483 and a later one done in 1506 and on view in the National Gallery in London. The Louvre painting, with its carefully observed botanical specimens, is the culmination of the scientific side of the Early Renaissance. The painting's arbitrary features—the grotto setting and the unusual perspective—point ahead to the High Renaissance; the dramatic use of chiaroscuro foreshadows the "night pictures" of the Baroque period (see Figure 14.10).*

Rome. Ever experimenting, always striving to keep up with the latest trends, he frequently reinvented himself. Nevertheless, there were constants in his approach to painting. He combined the traditions of the Florentine school (the use of linear perspective and the direct observation of nature) and the Flemish school (the technique of oil painting, the use of landscape as background, and the practice of religious symbolism). Made aware of the importance of atmosphere by the Venetian setting, Bellini also experimented with a range of colors, variations in color intensity, and changes in light. In particular, Bellini perfected the

ENCOUNTER

The Influence of Islam on the European Renaissance

Can cultures learn from their enemies? Christian Europe and the Islamic world, despite mutually antagonistic religions, did engage in artistic borrowings in the period from 1300 to 1600. These borrowings, though modest for both cultures, were stronger and more enduring in Christian Europe, where Islamic influences helped give shape to the visual and decorative arts in the Renaissance, then in full flower.

Around 1400, at the beginning of the Early Italian Renaissance, Europe and Islam were locked in a centuries-old struggle, dating from the reign of Emperor Charlemagne in the early 800s. For Christian Europe, not only was Islam a false faith, but its leaders had unjustly conquered land, such as Spain and, especially, the Holy Land, or Palestine. For Islam, Christian Europe was the home of the infidel who refused to accept Muhammad as God's final revelation.

Intensifying the struggle between these cultures were their differing stages of economic growth. Islam, though past its Golden Age, was still flourishing, and its consumer goods appealed to Europe's elites. The West, whose industrial economy was in its infancy, was valued by the Islamic world only for its raw materials, such as furs and amber. Nevertheless, encounters occurred in the exchange of material goods—from the spoils of war, diplomatic gifts, and trade. These activities led to the acquisition of prized objects from both cultures, and this, in turn, inspired artistic borrowing between Islam and Europe.

Of these three types of encounters, conducting trade offered the best opportunity for cultural interchange, with Europe's taste for Islam's luxury goods turning the wheels of commerce. Venice led the way, followed by other Italian cities—Pisa, Lucca, and Siena—along with Sicily and southern Italy. These centers of commerce imported textiles, such as silks and embroidered cloth, carpets, metalwork, and other luxury goods from the Ottoman Empire (after 1453), Egypt, Syria, Iraq, and Persia.

These Islamic goods slowly changed the personal style of Europe's powerful and rich. For example, in 1003, Pope Sylvester II (pope 999–1003) was buried in a shroud made of Persian silk cloth. Islamic ceramic and metalwork goods became prestige objects, serving ritualistic purposes in churches and denoting the social aspirations of those who displayed them in their homes. The floors of royal and baronial courts, along with those of wealthy households, changed from being covered with rush matting to being dressed with woven carpets, especially in the Turkish and Persian styles. Carpets also were used as table covers and wall hangings.

As the Islamic luxury goods grew in popularity, Europe's decorative arts began to imitate them. In ceramics, southern Italian artisans copied Islamic models and motifs, such as geometric patterns, arabesques, and calligraphy that imitated Arabic writing. Venetian guildsmen imitated Ottoman models and designs in metalwork, varnished ware, and saddle decoration.

In the visual arts, painters began to incorporate elements, motifs, and design features from Islamic imported goods into both their secular and religious works—as symbols of opulence and high status. Italian painters started this trend, in the early 1300s, introducing images of carpets and some decorative motifs and patterns into their works. Artists across Europe followed their lead. For example, Hans Memling, in his painting *Madonna and Child with Angel,* depicts the Virgin and baby Christ, enthroned, with a Turkish carpet, identified as a "wheel carpet," placed before them (see Figure 10.24).

In contrast, Islam's borrowing from the West was more limited, confined to a few luxury goods, such as textiles, including velvets and cloths with gold and silver threads and pearls, from Florence, and undecorated glass, from Venice, to be finished with Islamic designs. However, one outstanding interchange between Islam and the West did occur during this time: the portrait of the Ottoman sultan who conquered

landscape format as a backdrop for foreground figures. A great teacher, Bellini founded a workshop where his methods were taught to young painters, including Giorgione and Titian (see Chapter 12).

An excellent example of Bellini's use of landscape may be seen in *St. Francis in Ecstasy* (Figure 11.24). This work, which depicts an ecstatic St. Francis displaying the stigmata (spontaneous appearance of open wounds, similar to those of the crucified Christ), shows Bellini's typical treatment of landscape. He divides the painting surface into zones, beginning with the area around the saint in the foreground, continuing through a second zone occupied by a donkey and a crane, to a third zone featuring Italian castles nestled into a hillside, and concluding with a fourth zone marked by a fortress and the sky. To heighten the realism, Bellini uses both a rich palette of colors and numerous objects to lead the viewer's eye into the vast distance. He adds to the realism by suffusing the scene with natural light. The landscape, with its vivid rendering of flora and fauna,

Constantinople, Mehmet II (r. 1444–1446 and 1451–1481), painted in about 1480 by the Venetian artist Gentile Bellini (Encounter figure 11.1). At that time, knowledge of the Renaissance art style was little known in Islam. Therefore, this portrait is a landmark, because it introduced Western perspective to the Ottoman court and its workshop of miniature painters.

Learning from the Encounter **Why** did Europe and Islam hold negative images of each other during the European Renaissance? **Compare and contrast** the economies of Europe and the Islamic world between 1300 and 1600. **Summarize** the influence of Islam on Europe during the Renaissance. **What** impact did the West have on Islam during the Renaissance? **Discuss** the interaction between the West and the Islamic world today.

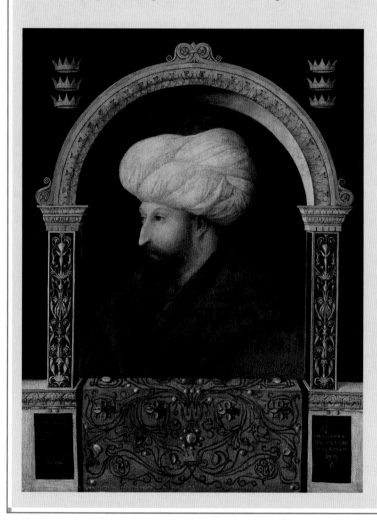

Encounter figure 11.1 Gentile Bellini. *Mehmet II. Ca. 1480. Oil on canvas, 27¾ × 20⅝". National Gallery, London. Bellini's commission for this portrait grew out of a diplomatic exchange between Venice and the Ottoman Empire. As a condition of making peace with Venice after a war, the sultan requested that a Venetian portrait painter be sent to his court. Bellini's portrait blends Western technique—the oil medium, the seated subject in profile, and the perspective—with Islamic touches—the rounded arch with an elaborate design, the sumptuous fabric draped over the balustrade, the turban and fur-lined robe, and the black background.*

expresses the Franciscan belief that humankind should live in harmony with the natural world (see Chapter 9).

Music

The changes affecting the cultural life of fifteenth-century Europe naturally also affected the music of the time. The impetus for a new musical direction, however, did not spring from Classical sources, because ancient musical texts had virtually perished. Instead, the new music owed its existence to meetings between English and Continental composers at the church councils that were called to settle the Great Schism (see Chapter 10) and the Continental composers' deep regard for the seductive sound of English music. The English composer John Dunstable [DUHN-stuh-bull] (about 1380–1453) was a central figure in the new musical era that began with the opening of the fifteenth century. Working in England and in France, he wrote

Figure 11.24 GIOVANNI BELLINI. *St. Francis in Ecstasy.* 1470s. Oil in tempera on panel, 49 × 57⅞". Frick Collection, New York. *In the foreground, Bellini renders his vision of the grotto at Alvernia, a mountain retreat near Assisi, where St. Francis went to pray and fast for forty days, in imitation of Christ's forty days in the wilderness. The artist reinforces the scene's religious significance through various symbols, such as the grapevine and the stigmata, alluding to the sacrifice of Christ, and the donkey (in the middle distance), emblematic of Jesus' entry into Jerusalem before the Crucifixion.*

Figure 11.25 Mass at the Court of Philip the Good in Burgundy. Bibliothèque Royal Albert Ier, Brussels. Fifteenth century. *This miniature painting shows a Mass being conducted at the court of Philip the Good of Burgundy (r. 1419–1467). Philip's patronage of the arts and music attracted leading painters and musicians to his court, which he conducted in cities across his holdings in modern-day Holland, Belgium, and France. John Dunstable, a composer of the Franco-Netherlandish school, was, on occasion, at the duke's court. In the painting, the priest prepares the sacraments at the altar, with his attendant behind him. On the right, the choir, dressed in white robes and gathered in front of the music stand, sings the Latin Mass. In the center background, dressed in black, stands a member of the Burgundian royal court, attended by two servants.*

mainly religious works—motets for multiple voices and settings for the Mass—that showed his increasingly harmonic approach to polyphony. The special quality of his music is its freedom from the use of mathematical proportion—the source of medieval music's dissonance.

Dunstable's music influenced composers in France, in Burgundy, and in Flanders, known collectively as the Franco-Netherlandish school. This school, which became the dominant force in fifteenth-century music, blended Dunstable's harmonics with northern European and Italian traditions. The principal works of this group were Latin **Masses** (Figure 11.25), or musical settings of the most sacred Christian rite; **motets,** or multivoiced songs set to Latin texts other than the Mass; and secular *chansons,* or songs, with French texts, including such types as the French ballade and the Italian madrigal, poems set to music for two and six voices, respectively. Together, these polyphonic compositions established the musical ideal of the Early Renaissance: multiple voices of equal importance singing **a cappella** (without instrumental accompaniment) and stressing the words so that they could be understood by listeners.

Between 1430 and 1500, the Continent's musical life was guided by composers from the Franco-Netherlandish school, the most important of whom was the Burgundian Josquin des Prez [zho-SKAN day PRAY] (about 1440–1521). Josquin was influential in his day and is now recognized as one of the greatest composers of all time. He was the first important composer to use music expressively so that the sounds matched the words of the text, thereby moving away from the abstract church style of the Middle Ages. One of his motets was described at the time as evoking Christ's suffering in a manner superior to painting. Josquin also began to organize music in the modern way, using major and minor scales with their related harmonies. All in all, he is probably the first Western composer whose music on first hearing appeals to modern ears.

Josquin's motet *Ave Maria . . . Virgo Serena (Hail, Mary . . . Serene Virgin,* 1502), a musical setting of a prayer to the Virgin Mary, shows the new expressive

Renaissance style as it breaks away from the abstract music of the Middle Ages. Based on a Gregorian chant, the opening section quickly gives way to an innovative melody. Divided into seven sections, the motet employs shifting voice combinations in each part. The opening section uses polyphonic **imitation,** a musical technique that functions like a relay race. The soprano begins with the phrase *Ave maria,* which, in turn, is restated by the alto, tenor, and bass. Next, there follows the second phrase, *gratia plena* ("full of grace"), sung to a different melody, which is also repeated among the voices. The musical effect in the first section is to create an overlapping tapestry of sound. The second section uses a duet of two upper voices, which is then imitated by the lower voices. Next, there is a four-voice ensemble, using expressive music that reflects the text, *nova laetitia* ("new joy"). Then, there follow four sections that shift voice groupings along with alterations in rhythms, ending with a brief pause. The motet ends with the group singing together in sustained chords: *"O mater Dei / memento mei. Amen,"* or "O Mother of God / remember me. Amen."

The Legacy of the Early Renaissance

Today, modern times are considered to begin with the Early Renaissance in Italy. This period saw the rebirth of the study and practice of the arts and the humanities and the rise of the idea of the "Renaissance man"—a term used today to define the supreme genius who makes all of human knowledge his province. Under the powerful stimulus of humanism, the liberal arts were restored to primacy over religion in the educational curriculum, a place they had not held for a thousand years, since the triumph of Christianity in the fourth century. With humanism also came a skeptical outlook that expressed itself in a new regard for the direct role of human causality in history and the rise of textual criticism. A new ingredient in Renaissance humanism was the drive to individual fulfillment, perhaps the defining trait of Western civilization from this point onward.

The greatest cultural changes took place in the arts and in architecture, largely under the spell of humanistic learning. Now freed from subordination to architecture, sculpture and painting became independent art forms. Fifteenth-century architects, inspired by the Greco-Roman tradition, adapted Classical forms and ideals to their own needs. For the next four hundred years, until the Gothic revival in the nineteenth century, Classicism was the ruling force in a succession of architectural styles. Sculpture also used its Classical roots to redefine its direction, reviving ancient forms and the practice of depicting male and female nudes. Of all the visual arts, painting was least influenced by the Classical tradition, except for its ideals of simplicity and realism. Perhaps as a consequence of its artistic freedom, painting became the dominant art form of this era and continues to hold first rank today.

KEY CULTURAL TERMS

Renaissance	chiaroscuro
studia humanitatis	*sfumato*
Early Renaissance style	Mass
vanishing point	motet
pilaster	a cappella
relief	imitation

SUGGESTIONS FOR FURTHER READING

CASSIRER, E., KRISTELLER, P. O., AND RANDALL, J., eds. *The Renaissance Philosophy of Man.* Chicago: University of Chicago Press, 1948. Selections from Pico, Valla, and other Renaissance scholars accompanied by a useful text.

PICO DELLA MIRANDOLA. *On the Dignity of Man.* Indianapolis: Bobbs-Merrill, 1956. A succinct statement on Renaissance thought by one of its leading scholars.

SUGGESTIONS FOR LISTENING

DUNSTABLE (or DUNSTAPLE), JOHN. Dunstable's sweet-sounding harmonies helped inaugurate Early Renaissance music. Predominantly a composer of sacred music, he is best represented by motets, including *Veni Sancte Spiritus—Veni Creator Spiritus* and *Sancta Maria, non est similis.* He also wrote a few secular songs, of which the two most familiar are *O Rosa bella* and *Puisque m'amour.*

JOSQUIN DES PREZ. Josquin's Masses, motets, and *chansons* all illustrate his skill at combining popular melodies with intricate counterpoint and his use of harmonies commonly heard today. The motet *Ave Maria,* the *chanson Faulte d'argent,* and the Mass *Malheur me bat* are good examples of his style.

12 THE HIGH RENAISSANCE AND EARLY MANNERISM 1494–1564

Between 1494 and 1564, one of the most brilliantly creative periods in Western history unfolded in Italy. During this span of seventy years, there flourished three artists—Leonardo da Vinci, Raphael, and Michelangelo—and a writer—Machiavelli—whose achievements became legendary. The works of these geniuses, and of other talented but less well-known artists and intellectuals, affected the basic Western concept of art and fundamentally influenced how we understand ourselves and the world (Figure 12.1).

The **High Renaissance,** lasting from 1494 to 1520, was the first phase of this creative period and was a time when the Classical principles of beauty, balance, order, serenity, harmony, and rational design reached a state of near perfection. The center of culture shifted from Florence, the heart of the Early Renaissance, to Rome, where the popes became the leading patrons of the new style in their desire to make Rome the world's most beautiful city. Florence even had to yield the services of Michelangelo, its favorite son, to the wealthy and powerful Roman pontiffs.

After 1520, however, the Renaissance veered away from the humanistic values of Classicism toward an antihumanistic vision of the world, labeled **Mannerism** because of the self-conscious, or "mannered," style adopted by its artists and intellectuals. Mannerist art and culture endured from 1520 until the end of the century, when the style was affected by religious controversy. This chapter covers the High Renaissance style and the Mannerist style through the end of its first phase in 1564, with the death of Michelangelo.

◄ **Detail** LEONARDO DA VINCI. *Mona Lisa*. 1503. Oil on panel, 30¼ × 21". Louvre.

THE RISE OF THE MODERN SOVEREIGN STATE

The most important political development in the first half of the sixteenth century was the emergence of powerful sovereign states in the newly unified and stabilized nations of France, England, and Spain. This process was already under way in the late fifteenth century (see Chapter 10), but it now began to influence foreign affairs. The ongoing rivalries of these aggressive national kingdoms led to the concept of balance of power—a principle that still dominates politics today.

From 1494 to 1569, Europe's international political life was controlled, either directly or indirectly, by France and Spain. France's central role resulted from the policies of its strong Valois kings, who had governed France since the early fourteenth century. Spain's fortunes soared during this period, first under the joint rule (1474–1504) of Ferdinand V and Isabella and then under Charles I (r. 1516–1556). In 1519 Charles I was also elected Holy Roman emperor as Charles V (he was of the royal house of Hapsburg), thus joining the interests of Spain and the Holy Roman Empire until his abdication in 1556. England kept aloof from Continental affairs during this time.

After 1591 the French and the Spanish rulers increasingly dispatched their armies and allies into the weaker states, where they fought and claimed new lands. As the sovereign monarchs gained power, the medieval dream of a united Christendom—pursued by Charlemagne, the popes, and the Holy Roman emperors—slowly faded away. These new states were strong because they were united around rulers who exercised increasing central control. Although most kings claimed to rule by divine right, their practical policies were more important in increasing their power. They surrounded themselves with ministers and consultative councils, both dependent on the crown. The ministers were often chosen from the bourgeois class, and they advised the rulers on such weighty matters as religion and war and also ran the developing bureaucracies. The bureaucracies in turn strengthened centralized rule by extending royal juris-

Figure 12.1 MICHELANGELO. *Dying Slave.* 1513–1516. Marble, approx. 7'5". Louvre. *Michelangelo's so-called* Dying Slave *embodies the conflicting artistic tendencies at work between 1494 and 1564. The statue's idealized traits—the perfectly proportioned figure, the restrained facial expression, and the body's gentle S-curve shape—are hallmarks of the High Renaissance style. But the figure's overall sleekness and exaggerated arm movements—probably based on one of the figures in the first-century C.E.* Laocoön Group *(see Figure 4.19), which had recently been rediscovered—were portents of Early Mannerism.*

diction into matters formerly administered by the feudal nobility, such as the justice system.

The crown further eroded the status of the feudal nobles by relying on mercenary armies rather than on the warrior class, a shift that began in the Late Middle Ages. To pay these armies, the kings had to consult with representative bodies, such as Parliament in England, and make them a part of their regular administration.

The Struggle for Italy, 1494–1529

Italy's relative tranquility, established by the Peace of Lodi in 1454, was shattered by the French invasion in 1494. For the next thirty-five years, Italy was a battleground where France, Spain, and the Holy Roman Empire fought among themselves, as well as with the papacy and most of the Italian states.

The struggle began when France, eager to reassert a hereditary claim to Naples, agreed to help Milan in a controversy involving Naples, Florence, and the pope. The French king, Charles VIII, took Florence in 1494 and then advanced to Rome and Naples. But the Italians did not relinquish ground easily. Joined by Venice and the pope and supported by the Holy Roman emperor and the Spanish monarch, they drove out the French. In 1499 the French returned to Italy to activate their claim to Milan, and the Spanish and the Germans joined with the Italians to defeat the French. Over the next several decades, however, France continued to invade Italy intermittently. In the course of their campaigns, the French rulers, who were enamored of the Italian Renaissance, brought its artistic and intellectual ideals to northern Europe (Figure 12.2).

In 1522 full-scale hostilities broke out between France and the Holy Roman Empire over Italy's future, a struggle that pitted the old Europe against the new. The Holy Roman Empire, ruled by Charles V, was a decentralized relic from the feudal age. France, under the bold and intellectual leadership of Francis I (r. 1515–1547) of the royal house of Valois, was the epitome of the new sovereign state.

The first Hapsburg-Valois war was the only one fought in Italy. In 1527 the troops of Charles V ran riot in Rome, raping, looting, and killing. This notorious sack of Rome had two major consequences. First, it cast doubt on Rome's ability to control Italy—long a goal of the popes—for it showed that the secular leaders no longer respected the temporal power of the papacy. Second, it ended papal patronage of the arts for almost a decade, thus weakening Rome's role as a cultural leader. It also had a chilling effect on artistic ideals and contributed to the rise of Mannerism.

In 1529 the Treaty of Cambrai ended this first phase of the Hapsburg-Valois rivalry. Years of invasions and

Figure 12.2 JEAN CLOUET. *Francis I.* Ca. 1525. Oil on panel, 37¾ × 29⅛". Louvre. *During his thirty-two-year reign, Francis I was a major force in sixteenth-century European affairs. He also embarked on an extensive artistic program, inspired by the Italian Renaissance, to make his court the most splendid in Europe. Under his personal direction, Italian artworks and artists, including Leonardo da Vinci, were imported into France. Ironically, this rather stylized portrait by Jean Clouet, Francis's chief court artist, owes more to the conventionalized portraits of the Gothic style than it does to the realistic works of the Italian Renaissance.*

wars had left most of Italy divided and exhausted. Some cities had suffered nearly irreparable harm. Florence, because it had so much to lose, fared the worst. In the 1530s, the Medici rulers resumed ducal power, but they were little more than puppets of the foreigners who controlled much of the peninsula. The only Italian state to keep its political independence was Venice, which became the last haven for artists and intellectuals in Italy for the rest of the sixteenth century.

Charles V and the Hapsburg Empire

By 1530 the struggle between the Valois and the Hapsburgs had shifted to central Europe. The French felt hemmed in by the Spanish in the south, the Germans

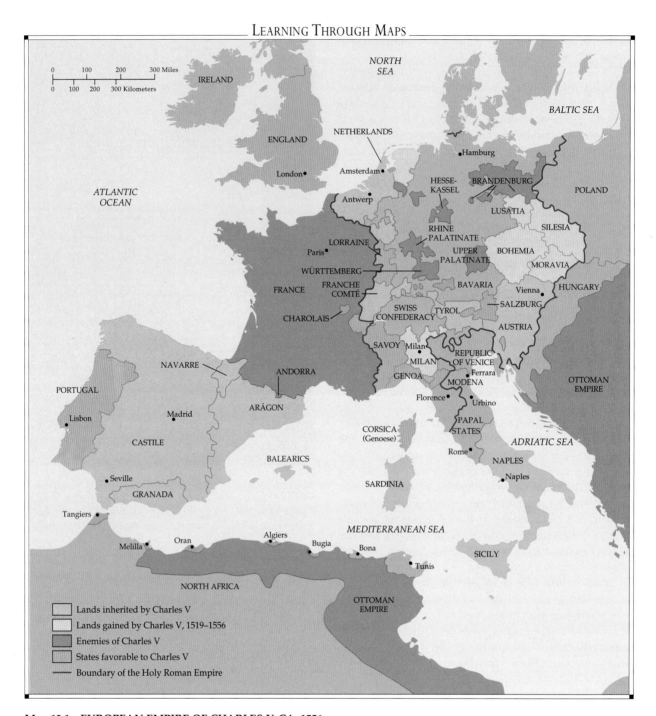

Map 12.1   EUROPEAN EMPIRE OF CHARLES V, CA. 1556
This map shows the extensive holdings of the Holy Roman emperor Charles V, also
known as King Charles I of Spain. **Notice** the lands inherited and the lands gained by
Charles V. **Identify** the boundaries of the Holy Roman Empire. **Who** were Charles V's
enemies within the Holy Roman Empire and elsewhere? **Consider** the challenges
Charles V faced in governing his widely scattered and culturally diverse empire. **What**
impact did geography have on France's attitude toward Charles V's empire?

to the east, and the Dutch to the north—peoples all
ruled by the Hapsburg emperor Charles V. In French
eyes, Charles had an insatiable appetite for power and
for control of the Continent. In turn, the Hapsburg

ruler considered the French king a land-hungry up-
start who stood in the way of a Europe united under a
Christian prince—in other words, the dream of Christendom. In 1559, after a number of exhausting wars

and a series of French victories, the belligerents signed the Treaty of Cateau-Cambrésis, which ushered in a brief period of peace (Map 12.1).

Charles V, the man at the center of most of these events, lived a life filled with paradoxes (Figure 12.3). Because of the size of his empire, he was in theory one of the most powerful rulers ever to live; but in actuality, again because of the vastness of his lands, he never quite succeeded in gaining complete control of his empire. In some ways, he was the last medieval king; in other ways, he foreshadowed a new age driven by sovereign kings, standing armies, diplomatic agreements, and strong religious differences.

Charles V's unique position at the center of Europe's political storm was the result of a series of timely deaths and births and politically astute arranged marriages. These circumstances had permitted the Hapsburg rulers to accumulate vast power, wealth, and land. Charles was born in 1500 to a German father and a Spanish mother, and he was the grandson of both the Holy Roman emperor Maximilian I and the Spanish king Ferdinand V. He held lands in present-day Spain, France, Italy, Germany, and Austria—along with the unimaginable riches of the recently acquired lands in the New World. By 1519 Charles V—simultaneously Charles I of Spain—ruled the largest empire the world has ever known.

For most of his life, Charles traveled from one of his possessions to another, fighting battles, arranging peace treaties, and attempting to unify his empire by personal control and compromise. His attention was often divided, and he found himself caught between two powerful foes—especially the French to the west and the Ottoman Turks in the east—who drained both his personal energies and his imperial resources.

Within the Holy Roman Empire, the princes of the German principalities often took advantage of his prolonged absences and his preoccupation with the French and the Turks. Their ability to gain political power at the emperor's expense increased after Martin Luther's revolt and the beginning of the Protestant Reformation (see Chapter 13). Charles also weakened his own position by his contradictory policies. At times he angered the disaffected German princes by meddling in their affairs and condemning Lutheran doctrines, and at other times he angered the popes by making concessions to the Protestants.

Exhausted and disillusioned by his inability to prevail in Europe, Charles abdicated in 1556 and retired to a monastery. His brother Ferdinand (r. 1558–1564) took control of the German-Austrian inheritance and was soon elected Holy Roman emperor. His son Philip (r. 1556–1598) assumed control of the Spanish Hapsburg holdings, including Spain, the New World territories, and the Netherlands. Thus ended Charles's vision of a

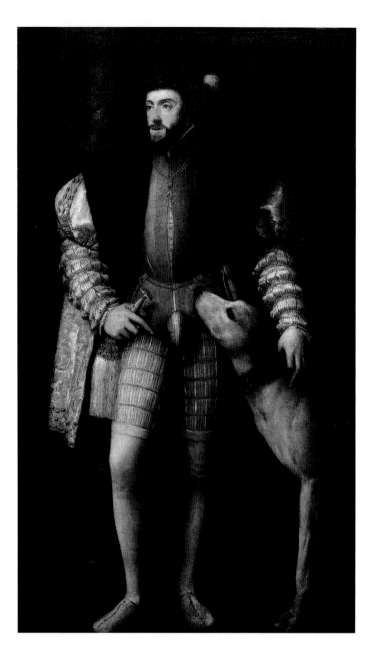

Figure 12.3 TITIAN. *Charles V with a Dog.* Ca. 1533. Oil on canvas, 6'3" × 3'8". Prado, Madrid. *Titian's full-length, standing portrait of Charles V was painted when the Hapsburg emperor was at the height of his power. By rendering the "ruler of the world" in contrapposto, his fingers casually holding the collar of his dog, Titian endows the emperor with a natural grace. The lighting that illuminates Charles from the dark background and the breathless hush that seems to envelop the man and dog are trademarks of Titian's style.*

united Europe and Christendom, which had turned into a nightmare of endless meetings, gory battles, and false hopes of peace and unity.

ECONOMIC EXPANSION AND SOCIAL DEVELOPMENTS

By the end of the fifteenth century, Europe had nearly recovered from the impact of the plague; the sixteenth century continued to be a time of growing population and increasing prosperity. The center of commerce shifted from the Mediterranean to the Atlantic coast, making cities like London and Antwerp financial and merchandising centers. Skilled craftspeople turned out quality products, and enterprising merchants distributed these finished goods across much of northwestern Europe. The daring sailing expeditions and discoveries of the late fifteenth and early sixteenth centuries provided new raw materials from America. Innovative manufacturing methods spurred economic growth and expanded worldwide markets.

Demographics, Prosperity, and the Beginning of a Global World

Although the data are scattered and often unreliable, evidence indicates that the population of Europe increased from about forty-five million in 1400 to sixty-nine million in 1500 and to about eighty-nine million by 1600. There was a major population shift from rural to urban areas, and the number of cities with populations over one hundred thousand grew from five to eight between 1500 and 1600. Rome, for example, grew from about fifty thousand in 1526—the year before the sack—to one hundred thousand by the end of the century.

Prosperity brought a higher standard of living to most of the urban middle class, but throughout much of the century prices rose faster than wages. Those who were not profiting from increased economic growth, such as poor peasants or impoverished nobility living on unproductive farms, suffered the most. In areas of Europe hardest hit by inflation or agricultural and commercial stagnation, economic crises often became intertwined with social and religious matters that intensified long-standing regional and local differences.

Yet the boom offered economic opportunities to some. Many merchants made fortunes and provided employment for others. These merchants and the bankers who offered loans were also accumulating capital, which they then invested in other types of commercial activity. The campaigns of Charles V were financed by wealthy bankers operating in a well-organized money market. The amassing of surplus capital and its reinvestment ushered in the opening phase of commercial capitalism that laid the foundation for Europe's future economic expansion.

During the first half of the sixteenth century, the abundance of raw materials and the vast market potential of the New World had just begun to affect Europe's economy. South American gold and silver played an important role in the upward price spiral. After 1650 New World agricultural products, such as tobacco, cotton, and cocoa, were used in new manufactured goods and profoundly altered consumer habits.

In the late 1500s, a major economic change had occurred that would make it possible to bring the natural resources of the New World to Europe. Some Europeans, taking advantage of the institution of slavery and the existing slave trade in western Africa, mercilessly exploited the local Africans by buying them and shipping them to European colonies in the New World. The Africans were forced to work in the gold and silver mines of Central and South America and on the cotton and sugarcane plantations in the West Indies, where they became a major factor in the production of these new forms of wealth.

Technology

The High Renaissance was a period of economic and social transformation, stimulated by advances in technology. The heroes of this age were the explorers and adventurers who dared to sail beyond the confines of Europe's shores, along with the inventors whose devices and discoveries opened the world for exploration. One of the most powerful agents of change was improved firearms, which rendered old forms of warfare obsolete and, gradually, affected the balance of power among the rising nation-states.

Sailing   Europe, starting in 1492, began to explore and then conquer much of the world. The pretext was religion and the spread of the Christian faith, but the motivation was gold, commodities, and riches. Based on a wealth of knowledge of the sea and the winds, the technology was now advanced for navigational instruments, ships, sails, and guns. Other societies, of course, had their religious faiths; they searched for wealth; they sailed the oceans; they possessed weapons and conquered other groups through warfare. But it was the Europeans, through chance, circumstances, and design, who started the Age of Exploration and dominated much of the globe until the late twentieth century.

By the late fifteenth century, European sailors were using the magnetic compass (to determine direction) and the astrolabe (to determine latitude), two inventions that allowed them to crisscross the oceans. They soon learned the path of prevailing ocean winds, especially in the Atlantic, which would take them first westward and then, catching other wind currents, eastward. This type of navigation would carry them toward the coast of Africa. As the mariners learned other wind patterns, they were able to sail farther and farther from Europe. In the early sixteenth century, the Portuguese navigator Fernao de Magalhaes [mah-GAHL-yeesh] (in English, Ferdinand Magellan) (about 1480–1521), aware of these wind patterns and acquainted with earlier explorations, circumnavigated the globe.

New types of sailing vessels also made these dangerous journeys possible. By the fifteenth century, *galleys* (long warships powered by oars and sails and loaded with armed boarding parties) were being replaced by square-rigged sailing ships outfitted with cannons. The Portuguese and the Spanish used the *caravel* (a three-masted vessel with a small roundish hull and a high stern and bow) for ocean travel and exploration, because the caravel could both carry cargo and be equipped with deck guns. The *galleon*, a much larger vessel, with greater maneuverability and firepower, replaced the caravel starting in the mid–sixteenth century. The galleon proved to be the mainstay for commerce and navies until the eighteenth century. The success of the caravel and the galleon resulted from having cannons mounted on the main deck, facing outward, so that each could fire through an opening cut into the ship's hull. Rows of these larger guns were installed on each side of the main deck, with galleons equipped usually with fourteen or more pairs. So successful were these heavily armed ships that, by 1700, the outcome of Europe's wars was often determined by battles on the open seas, as in England's triumph over the Spanish Armada in 1588.

Warfare The firepower of the sailing vessels had been made possible by the evolution of the cannon, which first appeared in Europe in the early 1300s. The first ones were siege cannons, packed with gunpowder and stones or pieces of metal and used to batter down the walls of castles and towns. Both iron and bronze guns were in service, but the bronze cannon soon proved to be the better weapon. Although a bronze cannon cost more due to materials and labor, it was easier to cast, its barrel did not rust, and it weighed less than an iron cannon.

As Europe's kings began to create the first modern sovereign states, they quickly recognized the need for a new type of army and better weaponry. Arsenals and foundries, turning out guns and shot, sprang up around Europe, and those nations with access to raw materials and innovative and skilled technicians and gunsmiths soon possessed the best-equipped armies. By 1700 military commanders were beginning to make a distinction between heavy siege guns and lighter field artillery. Light, more easily portable cannons with smaller caliber (the diameter of the gun's bore) not only were effective as a tactical weapon but also were well suited for the new warships—the galleons. The Spaniards held the lead during the sixteenth century, but the Dutch and English moved ahead in the early 1700s. Europe was now experiencing its first arms race: Amassing weapons had become an increasingly central need for each sovereign state, while new strategies and tactics were reshaping the nature of warfare.

Figure 12.4 LEONARDO DA VINCI. *Men Struggling to Move a Large Cannon.* Ca. 1488. Pen and ink, drawing. Windsor, Royal Library. *Leonardo's drawing of men trying to move a large cannon is more than just a scene of a sixteenth-century iron foundry. While much can be learned from its details—the use of winches and pulleys, the tools and equipment, and the differing models and sizes of cannons—the artist is also showing how machines are coming to control their human creators. Leonardo was fascinated by the machines of war, but he also understood how this large cannon (above) could wreak havoc, when he wrote, "With its breath it will kill men and ruin cities and castles."*

Among those who understood how weaponry could transform warfare was the artist-scientist Leonardo da Vinci (see the section "Painting"). He designed catapults, giant crossbows, and cannons. He calculated the trajectories of missiles fired by mortars and cannons and drew plans for armed vehicles on land, underwater craft, and flying machines. As a military engineer, he advised city planners on fortifications. Leonardo's curiosity and quest for knowledge led him not only to invent engines of war but also to speculate on how these destructive devices brutalized humans and destroyed nature (Figure 12.4).

Science and Medicine

While less pronounced in their immediate impact than the technological innovations, advances in science during this age would have long-lasting effects.

In the study of natural science, Leonardo again surpassed his contemporaries, in observation, in practices, and in understanding. Leonardo's genius was directed toward the study of nature in all of its forms, especially the human body. In the knowledge that he gained, he perhaps surpassed all those who had gone before him. He dissected human cadavers, took meticulous notes, described organs, bones, and muscles, and drew detailed anatomical studies. Although his writings and anatomical drawings were not made public during his lifetime, Leonardo's contributions to the understanding of the structure of the human body and the function of its skeleton, muscles, and organs reflected the Renaissance's desire to understand ourselves and the world.

During much of the sixteenth century, Italy's schools of medicine continued to be among the best in Europe. Italy also took another innovative step in medical care through the creative work of local administrators in the largest cities, officials who personified another characteristic of the Italian Renaissance, **civic humanism.** Civic humanism was an outgrowth of the Renaissance's cultivation of the culture of ancient Greece and Rome. Italy's civic administrators—dedicated men who were trained in the Greek and Latin classics—saw themselves as modern equivalents of civil servants in an ancient *polis,* or city. As such, they tried to establish responsible and efficient city governments. One of their projects, for example, which had a strong impact on medical care, was the setting up of citywide health boards, composed of physicians and medical personnel, to deal with public health issues, especially plague and other contagious diseases. Although lacking knowledge of the germ theory of disease, the health boards, nevertheless, could build on successful practices that had worked in the past. For example, they used controls and quarantines to isolate plague and prevent the spread of this and other contagious diseases among the populace. Such preventive methods were pioneered in the 1400s. Once established, the new city health boards soon made their presence felt in the areas under their jurisdiction, such as keeping records of each death and its cause, inspecting food markets, regulating city health conditions, and supervising burials, cemeteries, hospitals, and even beggars and prostitutes.

FROM HIGH RENAISSANCE TO EARLY MANNERISM

The characteristics of High Renaissance style were largely derived from the visual arts. Led by painters, sculptors, and architects who worshiped ancient Classical ideals, notably those of late-fifth-century B.C.E. Greece, the High Renaissance was filled with images of repose, harmony, and heroism. Under the spell of Classicism and the values of simplicity and restraint, artists sought to conquer unruly physical reality by subjecting it to the principle of a seemingly effortless order.

Although the visual arts dominated the High Renaissance, literary figures also contributed to this era. From Classicism, the High Renaissance authors appropriated two of their chief aesthetic aims, secularism and idealism. Like their ancient predecessors, historians showed that contemporary events arose from human causes rather than from divine action—unmistakable evidence of a mounting secular spirit. Actually, secularism more deeply affected the writing of history than it did the arts and architecture, where church patronage and religious subjects still held sway. A rising secular consciousness can also be seen in the popular handbooks on manners that offered advice on how to become a perfect gentleman or lady. Although they have no counterpart in ancient literature, these books nevertheless have the Classical quality of treating their subject in idealized terms.

What distinguished the High Renaissance preoccupation with the Classical past from the Early Renaissance's renewed interest in ancient matters was largely a shift in creative sensibility. The Early Renaissance artists, in the course of growing away from the Late Gothic style, had invented new ways of recapturing the harmonious spirit of ancient art and architecture. The geniuses of the next generation, benefiting from the experiments of the Early Renaissance, succeeded in creating masterpieces of disciplined form and idealized beauty. The High Renaissance masters' superb confidence allowed them to produce works that were in harmony with themselves and the physical world—a hallmark of Classical art.

In spite of its brilliance, the High Renaissance existed for only a fleeting moment in the history of Western culture—from the French invasion of Italy in 1494 until the death of Raphael in 1520 (preceded by the death of Leonardo in 1519) (Timeline 12.1). In this era, the Renaissance popes spared no expense in their patronage of the arts and letters. After the disasters of the fourteenth century, the papacy seemed to have restored the church to the vitality that it had enjoyed in the High Middle Ages. In reality, however, the popes of the early sixteenth century presided over a shaky ecclesiastical foundation. To the north, in Germany, a theological storm was brewing that would eventually split Christendom and destroy the papacy's claim to rule over the Christian world. This religious crisis, coupled with increasing tendencies to exaggeration in High Renaissance art and with the sack of Rome in 1527, contributed to the development of Mannerism and its spread through Italy and later across western Europe (Figure 12.5).

Timeline 12.1 ITALIAN CULTURAL STYLES BETWEEN 1494 AND 1564

1494		1520				1564
	High Renaissance		Early Mannerism			
French invasion of Italy	1508–1512 Michelangelo's Sistine Chapel ceiling frescoes	1519 Death of Leonardo da Vinci 1520 Death of Raphael	1532 Publication of Machiavelli's *The Prince*	1536–1541 Michelangelo's *Last Judgment* fresco	1550 Palladio's Villa Rotonda	1564 Death of Michel-angelo

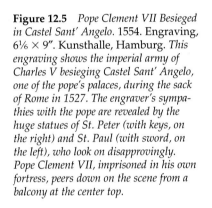

Figure 12.5 *Pope Clement VII Besieged in Castel Sant' Angelo. 1554. Engraving, 6⅙ × 9". Kunsthalle, Hamburg. This engraving shows the imperial army of Charles V besieging Castel Sant' Angelo, one of the pope's palaces, during the sack of Rome in 1527. The engraver's sympathies with the pope are revealed by the huge statues of St. Peter (with keys, on the right) and St. Paul (with sword, on the left), who look on disapprovingly. Pope Clement VII, imprisoned in his own fortress, peers down on the scene from a balcony at the center top.*

Mannerist painters, sculptors, and architects moved away from two of the guiding principles of the High Renaissance: the imitation of nature and the devotion to Classical ideals. In contrast to the High Renaissance masters, Mannerist painters deliberately chose odd perspectives that called attention to the artists' technical effects and their individual points of view. Mannerist sculptors, rejecting idealism, turned and twisted the human figure into unusual and bizarre poses to express their own notions of beauty. Likewise, Mannerist architects toyed with the emotions and expectations of their audience by designing buildings that were intended to surprise. Behind the Mannerist aesthetic lay a questioning or even a denial of the inherent worth of human beings and a negative image of human nature, along with a sense of the growing instability of the world.

Literature

The leading writers of the High Renaissance in Italy drew their themes and values from the Greco-Roman classics. Their artistic vision sprang from the Classical virtue of *humanitas*—a term coined by Cicero in antiquity (see Chapter 5) that can be translated as "humanity," meaning the wisdom, humor, tolerance, and passion of the person of good sense. With some reservations, they also believed in Classicism's basic tenet that human nature is inherently rational and good. One of the finest expressions of Classicism in Renaissance literature was the poetry of the Venetian Gaspara Stampa, whose lyric verses, though devoted to obsessive sexual love, asserted the moral worth of the lover.

But even as High Renaissance literature was enjoying its brief reign, the Mannerist works of the

ENCOUNTER

Portuguese Exploration Sets the Stage for a New World

Starting in the mid–fifteenth century, Portugal led the first wave of Europeans to export their peoples, traditions, and culture overseas. In response to their daring deeds, the poet Luis Vaz da Camoes, following the lead of the ancient poet Vergil, wrote an epic poem celebrating his adventurous countrymen and heralding the new Age of Exploration.

Portugal, located at the end of the Eurasian land mass, was the first European country to open trade routes from Europe to Africa, India, and the Far East. Portugal's arrival in these areas launched a new phase of international trade and commerce, stimulated racial, ethnic, and cultural interchanges, and altered the course of world history.

During the fifteenth century, the Portuguese explored islands in the Atlantic and traded along the west coast of Africa for gold and slaves. By the 1490s, they were at the southern tip of Africa—the Cape of Good Hope—and were searching for sea routes to Asia, which would bypass the Muslim trade system in the Middle East. In 1497, Vasco da Gama [VAS-co da GAH-ma] (about 1460–1524) sailed from Lisbon, rounded the Cape of Good Hope, came up the east coast of Africa, crossed the Indian ocean—with the aid of a Muslim mariner—and landed at Calicut (modern Kolkata, formerly Calcutta), India. Da Gama returned to Portugal two years later, his ships laden with pepper and spices. The Portuguese soon set up trading posts and forts along the coasts of Africa, throughout the East Indies, and in China. They monopolized the spice and pepper markets and tried to control the in-

ternational sea routes between Europe and the Far East. For most of the 1500s, this minor country, small in size and population, was the richest nation in Europe. However, Portugal's wealth and power lasted hardly a century, as the Portuguese soon overextended their empire and found themselves challenged by the Spanish, Dutch, French, and English, who were entering the European Age of Exploration.

Portugal's age of greatness, personified by Vasco da Gama's heroic and daring adventures, was recorded and praised by the country's first renowned poet, Luis Vaz de Camoes [LU-ees VAZH th KAE-moish] (about 1524–1580) (Encounter figure 12.1), in his epic poem *The Lusiads*. Descended from the lesser nobility, Camoes's father was a sea captain whose travels probably inspired the son. Camoes attended a Portuguese university, which was just coming under the influence of Renaissance thought, where he studied Latin, mythology, history, and Greek literature. He enjoyed life in Lisbon for a short time before being banished—for unclear personal or political reasons—from the capital in 1546. His adventurous life now began: soldiering in North Africa, traveling to India, serving his government in the Far East, and, finally, returning home in 1570. *The Lusiads*, which he composed over the years of his wandering, was published in 1572. In recognition of his epic poem, he received a small stipend from the state and lived in modest circumstances until he died from the plague, in 1580.

The Lusiads, named for *Lusus*, the mythical founder of Portugal, was modeled on Vergil's *Aeneid*. In ten

---

Florentine author Niccolò Machiavelli began to appear, and at the heart of his thought is an anti-Classical spirit. Despite his education in Classicism and his strict rationalism, Machiavelli concluded that the human race was irremediably flawed. The contrast between the idealizing spirit of the High Renaissance and the anti-traditionalist views of Mannerism can be clearly seen by placing the work of the diplomat and courtier Baldassare Castiglione beside that of Machiavelli. Each wrote a book that can fairly be described as a manual of behavior—but there the resemblance ends.

Gaspara Stampa   Gaspara Stampa (about 1524–1554) embraced the Classical tradition renewed by Petrarch in the 1300s; her work is thus typical of High Renaissance poetry. She adopted the Petrarchan sonnet as the preferred vehicle for her thoughts, and, like the earlier

poet, she used her poetic gifts to investigate the byways of love. Rather than glorifying the distant beloved, however, she asserted the moral worth of the suffering lover, thus transforming the essentially male Petrarchan ideal into a female point of view. Stampa poured out her heart in her verses, confessing vulnerability and lamenting abandonment. She portrayed the abandoned one as superior to the unresponsive loved one—the same lesson taught by Socrates in one of Plato's dialogues (see Chapter 3).

That Gaspara Stampa became a poet at all is testimony to the changing mores of Renaissance Venice, a city fabled for its love of luxury and pleasure. Her autobiographical poetry grew out of her situation in Venice's marginal world of writers, musicians, and artists, including aristocrats and high officials of church and state, who were notably indifferent to cantos, Camoes recounts Vasco da Gama's voyage to India. Along the route, da Gama and his men have many adventures. They encounter various enemies (usually Muslims), meet a friendly king to whom da Gama recounts the glorious history of Portugal, then sail across the Indian Ocean, establish trading outlets in India, and return home with their prizes and as triumphant heroes. As in the *Aeneid*, the author opens his tale *in medias res* (in the middle of events), with da Gama sailing up the east coast of Africa. Camoes then introduces the ancient Greek and Roman gods and goddesses, who play significant roles: Venus and Mars in aiding da Gama and Bacchus (the god of wine) in thwarting the explorer's journey.

Camoes was more than an accomplished storyteller: He was the voice of sixteenth-century Portugal and Europe. To him, Portugal had established itself as a great nation, acting as a harbinger for Europe's future, saving Europe from her enemies abroad, and helping spread the true Christian faith around the world. And, most important from a multicultural perspective, he linked Portugal's future, and, by extension, all of Europe's, to the hitherto little-known worlds overseas.

Learning from the Encounter **What** advantages enabled Portugal to become a nation of explorers? **What** were some consequences of the encounter between Portugal and the Far East? **Why** was Vasco da Gama seen as a hero? **Compare** *The Lusiads* with Vergil's *Aeneid*. **Discuss** the relationship between *The Lusiads* and the birth of a kind of multiculturalism in Europe.

Encounter figure 12.1 *Luis Vaz de Camoes.* Frontispiece from *The Lusiads.* 1655. *In this anonymous portrait, Luis Vaz de Camoes is dressed as a soldier and wears the laurel crown of the poet—an honorific symbol from Classical culture. The loss of his eye, he wrote, taught him about the expense of war and reminded him of the price he paid for adventure, heroism, fame, and his country's empire.*

Christian values. As a courtesan, or kept woman, she was a welcome member of this twilight world where sexuality was fused with art. Although she seems to have had several liaisons in her brief life, it was Count Collaltino di Collalto, a soldier, who won her heart. In time, Collaltino wearied of her, but Stampa transformed her hopeless love into some of the West's most touching poetry.

Castiglione The reputation of Castiglione [kahs-teel-YOH-nay] (1478–1529) rests on *The Book of Courtier* or, simply, *The Courtier*, one of the most influential and famous books of the High Renaissance. Intended for Italian court society, *The Courtier* was published in 1528 and translated into most Western languages by the end of the century. It quickly became the bible of courteous behavior for Europe's upper classes and remained so

over the next two hundred years. Even today, at the beginning of the twenty-first century, Castiglione's rules for civilized behavior are still not completely outmoded.

A Mantuan by birth, Castiglione (Figure 12.6) based his guide to manners on life at the north Italian court of Urbino, where, between 1504 and 1517, he was the beneficiary of the patronage of its resident duke, Guidobaldo da Montefeltro (see Figure 11.2). Impressed by the graceful conversations of his fellow courtiers and especially taken with the charms of Urbino's duchess, Elisabetta, Castiglione was moved to memorialize his experiences in writing. *The Courtier* is composed as a dialogue, a literary form originated by Plato and favored by Cicero. Castiglione's dialogue is set in Urbino over a period of four evenings and peopled with actual individuals for whom he invents

Figure 12.6   RAPHAEL. *Baldassare Castiglione.* 1514. Oil on canvas, 32¼ × 26½". *Castiglione, author of a famous book on manners, was memorialized in this handsome portrait by Raphael, one of the great portrait painters of the High Renaissance. Elegantly groomed and completely at ease, Castiglione appears here as the age's ideal courtier—an ideal that he helped to establish.*

courtier should be proficient in each of these areas. A sign that the Renaissance had raised the status of painting and sculpture was the group's expectation that a gentleman be knowledgeable about both of these art forms.

The Courtier also describes the perfect court lady. In the minds of the dialogue participants, the ideal lady is a civilizing influence on men, who would otherwise be crude. To that end, the perfect lady should be a consummate hostess, charming, witty, graceful, physically attractive, and utterly feminine. She ought to be well versed in the same areas as a man, except for athletics and the mastery of arms. With these social attributes, the cultivated lady can then bring out the best in a courtier. But she must not seem his inferior, for she contributes to society in her own way.

Castiglione's book turned away from medieval values and led his followers into the modern world. First, he argued that social relations between the sexes ought to be governed by Platonic love—a spiritual passion that surpassed physical conquest—and thus he rejected medieval courtly love and its adulterous focus. Second, he reasoned that women in society should be the educated equals of men, thereby sweeping away the barrier that had been erected when women were excluded from the medieval universities. In the short run, the impact of Castiglione's social rules was to keep women on a pedestal, as courtly love had done. But for the future, his advice allowed women to participate actively in every aspect of society and encouraged their education in much the same way as men's.

Machiavelli   In contrast to Castiglione's optimism, the Florentine Machiavelli [mak-ee-uh-VEL-ee] (1469–1527) had a negative view of human nature and made human weakness the central message of his writings. If *The Courtier* seems to be taking place in a highly refined never-never land where decorum and gentility are the primary interests, Machiavelli returns the reader to the solid ground of political reality. His Mannerist cynicism about his fellow human beings sprang from a wounded idealism, for life had taught him that his early optimism was wrong. His varied works, by means of their frank assessments of the human condition, were meant to restore sanity to a world that he thought had gone mad.

Except for Martin Luther (see Chapter 13), Machiavelli left a stronger imprint on Western culture than any other figure who lived between 1494 and 1564. His most enduring contribution was *The Prince,* which inaugurated a revolution in political thought. Rejecting the medieval tradition of framing political discussions in Christian terms, Machiavelli treated the state as a human invention that ought not necessarily conform to religious or moral rules. He began the modern

urbane and witty conversations that suit their known characters. Despite this realistic touch, his book's overall tone is definitely idealistic and hence expressive of High Renaissance style.

Castiglione's idealism shines forth most clearly in the sections in which the invited company try to define the perfect courtier, or gentleman. Under Duchess Elisabetta's eye, the guests cannot agree on which aspect of the ideal gentleman's training should take precedence: education in the arts and humanities or skill in horsemanship and swordplay. Some claim that a gentleman should be first a man of letters as well as proficient in music, drawing, and dance. In contrast, others believe that a courtier's profession is first to be ready for war, and hence athletics should play the central role. At any rate, both sides agree that the ideal search for a science of politics that has absorbed political thinkers and policymakers ever since.

Machiavelli's career in sixteenth-century Italy, like that of many writers in antiquity, was split between a life of action and a life of the mind. Between 1498 and 1512, he served the newly reborn Florentine republic as a senior official and diplomat, learning statecraft firsthand. During these turbulent years, he was particularly impressed by the daring and unscrupulous Cesare Borgia, Pope Alexander VI's son. In 1512, after the fall of the Florentine republic to the resurgent Medici party, Machiavelli was imprisoned, tortured, and finally exiled to his family estate outside the city. There, as he recounts in one of his famous letters, he divided his time between idle games with the local farmers at a nearby inn and nightly communion with the best minds of antiquity in his study. From this background emerged in 1513 the small work known as *The Prince,* which circulated in manuscript until after his death. In 1532 it was finally published.

Machiavelli had several motives in writing this masterpiece. Despairing over Italy's dismemberment by the French and the Spanish kings, he hoped the book would inspire an indigenous leader to unify the peninsula and drive out the foreigners. Enlightened by his personal experience in Florence's affairs, he wanted to capture in writing the truth of the politics to which he had been a witness. And, of equal importance, by dedicating *The Prince* to the restored Medici ruler, he hoped to regain employment in the Florentine state. Like other writers in this age, Machiavelli could not live by his wits but had to rely on secular or religious patronage.

Machiavelli's work failed to gain its immediate objectives: The Medici despot brushed it aside, and Italy remained fragmented until 1870. But as a work that exposed the ruthlessness needed to succeed in practical politics, *The Prince* was an instant, though controversial, success. The book was denounced by religious leaders for its amoral treatment of political power and read secretly by secular rulers for its sage advice. In the prevailing climate of opinion in the sixteenth century, which was still under the sway of Christian ideals, the name "Machiavelli" became synonymous with dishonesty and treachery, and the word *Machiavellianism* was coined to describe the amoral notion that "the end justifies any means."

From the modern perspective, this negative valuation of Machiavelli is both too simplistic and too harsh. Above all else he was a clear-eyed patriot who was anguished by the tragedy unfolding in Italy. *The Prince* describes the power politics that the new sovereign states of France and Spain were pursuing in Italian affairs. Machiavelli realized that the only way to rid Italy of foreigners was to adopt the methods of its successful

foes. Seeing his countrymen as cowardly and greedy, he had no illusions that a popular uprising would spring up and drive out Italy's oppressors. Only a strong-willed monarch, not bound by a finicky moral code, could bring Italy back from political chaos.

The controversial heart of Machiavelli's political treatise was the section that advised the ruler on the best way to govern. He counseled the prince to practice conscious duplicity, since that was the only way to maintain power and to ensure peace—the two basic goals of any state. By appearing virtuous and upright while acting as the situation demanded, the prince could achieve these fundamental ends. Machiavelli's startling advice reflected both his involvement in Italian affairs and his own view of human nature.

Painting

In the arts, the period between 1494 and 1564 was preeminently an age of painting, though several sculptors and architects created major works in their respective fields. The Classical values of idealism, balance, and restraint were translated by High Renaissance painters into harmonious colors, naturally posed figures with serene faces, realistic space and perspectives, and perfectly proportioned human bodies. After 1520, Mannerist tendencies became more and more evident, reflected in abnormal subjects, contorted figures with emotionally expressive faces, and garish colors.

Leonardo da Vinci   The inauguration of the High Renaissance in painting is usually dated from Leonardo's *The Last Supper,* which was completed between 1495 and 1498 (Figure 12.7). Painted for the Dominican friars of the church of Santa Maria delle Grazie in Milan, *The Last Supper* heralded the lucidity and harmony that were the essence of High Renaissance style. In executing the fresco, Leonardo unfortunately made use of a flawed technique, and the painting began to flake during his lifetime. Over the centuries, the work has been touched up frequently and restored seven times, with the most recent restoration completed in 1999. Nevertheless, enough of his noble intention is evident to ensure the reputation of *The Last Supper* as one of the best-known and most beloved paintings of Western art.

Leonardo's design for *The Last Supper* is highly idealized—a guiding principle of the High Renaissance. The fresco depicts the moment when Jesus says that one of the twelve disciples at the table will betray him. Ignoring the tradition that integrated this symbolic meal into an actual refectory, Leonardo separated the scene from its surroundings so that the figures would seem to hover over the heads of the clergy as they ate in their dining room. Idealism is also evident

Figure 12.7   LEONARDO DA VINCI. *The Last Supper.* (Restored.) 1495–1498. Oil-tempera on wall, 13'10" × 29'7½". Refectory, Santa Maria delle Grazie, Milan. *Classical restraint is one of the defining characteristics of this High Renaissance masterpiece. Instead of overwhelming the viewer with distracting details, Leonardo reduces the objects to a minimum, from the austere room in which the meal is being celebrated to the simple articles on the dining table. The viewer's gaze is thereby held on the unfolding human drama rather than on secondary aspects of the scene.*

in Leonardo's straightforward perspective. The artist makes Jesus the focal center by framing him in the middle window and locating the vanishing point behind his head. In addition, the arrangement of the banqueting party—Jesus is flanked by six followers on either side—gives the painting a balanced effect. This harmonious composition breaks with the medieval custom of putting the traitor Judas on the opposite side of the table from the others.

A final idealistic touch may be seen in the way that Leonardo hides the face of Judas, the third figure on Jesus' right, in shadow while illuminating the other figures in bright light. Judas, though no longer seated apart from the rest, can still be readily identified, sitting cloaked in shadows, reaching for the bread with his left hand, and clutching a bag of silver—symbolic of his treason—in the other hand. For generations, admirers have found Leonardo's fresco so natural and inevitable that it has become the standard version of this Christian subject.

Leonardo's setting and placement of the figures in *The Last Supper* are idealized, but his depiction of the individual figures is meant to convey the psychological truth about each of them. Jesus is portrayed with eyes cast down and arms outstretched in a gesture of resig-

nation, while on either side a tumultuous scene erupts. As the disciples react to Jesus' charge of treason, Leonardo reveals the inner truth about each one through bodily gestures and facial expressions: Beneath the visual tumult, however, the artistic rules of the High Renaissance are firmly in place. Since neither biblical sources nor sacred tradition offered an ordering principle, Leonardo used mathematics to guide his arrangement of the disciples. He divides them into four groups of three figures; each set in turn is composed of two older men and a younger one. In his conception, not only does each figure respond individually, but also each interacts with other group members.

Besides mastering a narrative subject like *The Last Supper*, Leonardo created a new type of portrait when he painted a half-length view of the seated *Mona Lisa* (Figure 12.8). As the fame of this work spread, other painters (and, later, photographers) adopted Leonardo's half-length model as a basic artistic format for portraits. This painting, perhaps the most famous portrait in Western art, was commissioned by a wealthy Florentine merchant. Avoiding the directness of *The Last Supper*, Leonardo hints at the sitter's demure nature through her shy smile and the charmingly awkward gesture of having the fingers of her right hand caress her left arm. In her face, celebrated in song and legend, he blends the likeness of a real person with an everlasting ideal to create a miraculous image. Further heightening the painting's eternal quality, the craggy background isolates the figure in space and time, in much the same way that the grotto functioned in Leonardo's *Virgin of the Rocks* (see Figure 11.23). Finally, he enhances the *Mona Lisa*'s mystery by enveloping the subject in the smoky atmosphere called *sfumato*—made possible by the oil medium—which softens her delicate features and the landscape in the background.

During the High Renaissance, Leonardo's great works contributed to the cult of genius—the high regard, even reverence, that the age accorded to a few select artists, poets, and intellectuals. *The Last Supper* earned him great fame while he was alive. The history of the *Mona Lisa* was more complicated, since it was unseen while he lived and found among his effects when he died in 1519. After his death, as the *Mona Lisa* became widely known, first as a possession of the king of France and later as a jewel in the Louvre collection, Leonardo was elevated to membership among the immortals of Western art.

Michelangelo While Leonardo was working in Milan during most of the 1490s, Michelangelo Buonarroti [my-kuh-LAN-juh-lo bwo-nahr-ROH-tee] (1475–1564) was beginning a career that would propel him to the forefront of first the Florentine and later the Roman Renaissance, making him the most formidable artist of the sixteenth century. Michelangelo's initial fame rested on his sculptural genius, which manifested itself at the age of thirteen when he was apprenticed to the Early Renaissance master Ghirlandaio and then, one year later, taken into the household of Lorenzo the Magnificent, the Medici ruler of Florence. In time, Michelangelo achieved greatness in painting and architecture as well as in sculpture, but he always remained a sculptor at heart.

Michelangelo's artistic credo was formed early, and he remained faithful to it over his long life. Sculpture, he believed, was the art form whereby human figures were liberated from the lifeless prison of their surrounding material. In this sense, he compared the sculptor's creativity with the activity of God—a notion that would have been judged blasphemous in prior Christian ages. Michelangelo himself, unlike the skeptical Leonardo, was a deeply pious man given to bouts of spiritual anxiety. His art constituted a form of divine worship.

Central to Michelangelo's artistic vision was his most celebrated image, the heroic nude male. Like the ancient Greek and Roman sculptors whose works he studied and admired, Michelangelo viewed the nude male form as a symbol of human dignity. In the High

Figure 12.8 LEONARDO DA VINCI. *Mona Lisa*. 1503. Oil on panel, 30¼ × 21". Louvre. *Leonardo's* Mona Lisa, *a likeness of the wife of the merchant Giocondo, illustrates the new status of Italy's urban middle class. This class was beginning to take its social cues from the fashionable world of the courts, the milieu described by Castiglione. Leonardo treats his middle-class subject as a model court lady, imbuing her presence with calm seriousness and quiet dignity.*

Renaissance, Michelangelo's nudes were based on Classical models, with robust bodies and serene faces. But in the 1530s, with the onset of Mannerism, the growing spiritual crisis in the church, and his own failing health, Michelangelo's depiction of the human figure changed. His later nudes had distorted body proportions and unusually expressive faces.

In 1508 Michelangelo was asked by Pope Julius II (pope 1503–1533) to decorate the Sistine Chapel ceiling. Michelangelo tried to avoid this commission, claiming that he was a sculptor and without expertise

Figure 12.9 MICHELANGELO. Sistine Chapel Ceiling. (Restored.) 1508–1512. Full ceiling 45 × 128'. The Vatican. *Michelangelo's knowledge of architecture prompted him to paint illusionistic niches for the Hebrew prophets and the pagan sibyls on either side of the nine central panels. Neo-Platonism inspired his use of triangles, circles, and squares, for these geometric shapes were believed to hold the key to the mystery of the universe. These various framing devices enabled him to give visual order to the more than three hundred figures in his monumental scheme.*

in frescoes, but the pope was unyielding in his insistence. The chapel had been built by Julius II's uncle, Pope Sixtus IV (pope 1471–1484), in the late 1400s, and most of the walls had already been covered with frescoes. Michelangelo's frescoes were intended to bring the chapel's decorative plan closer to completion.

The challenge of painting the Sistine Chapel ceiling was enormous, for it was almost 70 feet from the floor, its sides were curved downward, necessitating numerous perspective changes, and its area covered some 5,800 square feet. Michelangelo overcame all these difficulties, teaching himself fresco technique and working for four years on scaffolding, to create one of the glories of the High Renaissance and unquestionably the greatest cycle of paintings in Western art (Figure 12.9).

Michelangelo, probably with the support of a papal adviser, designed a complex layout (Figure 12.10) for the ceiling frescoes that combined biblical narrative, theology, Neo-Platonist philosophy, and Classical allusions. In the ceiling's center, running from the altar to the rear of the chapel, he painted nine panels that illustrate the early history of the world, encompassing the creation of the universe, the fall of Adam and Eve, and episodes in the life of Noah. Framing each of these biblical scenes were nude youths, whose presence shows Michelangelo's belief that the male form is an expression of divine power.

On either side of the center panels, he depicted Hebrew prophets and pagan sibyls, or oracles—all foretelling the coming of Christ (Figure 12.11). The pagan sibyls represent the Neo-Platonist idea that God's word was revealed in the prophecies of pre-Christian seers. At the corners of the ceiling, he placed four Old Testament scenes of violence and death that had been allegorized as foreshadowing the coming of Christ. Michelangelo unified this complex of human and divine figures with an illusionistic architectural frame,

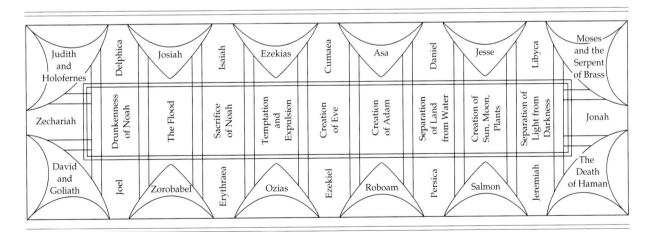

Judith and Holofernes	Delphica	Josiah	Isaiah	Ezekias	Cumaea	Asa	Daniel	Jesse	Libyca	Moses and the Serpent of Brass
Zechariah	Drunkenness of Noah	The Flood	Sacrifice of Noah	Temptation and Expulsion	Creation of Eve	Creation of Adam	Separation of Land from Water	Creation of Sun, Moon, Plants	Separation of Light from Darkness	Jonah
David and Goliath	Joel	Zorobabel	Erythraea	Ozias	Ezekiel	Roboam	Persica	Salmon	Jeremiah	The Death of Haman

Figure 12.10 Plan of Ceiling Frescoes, Sistine Chapel. 1508–1512. *The paintings on the Sistine Chapel ceiling may be grouped as follows: (1) the central section, which presents the history of the world from the creation (called "The Separation of Light from the Darkness") through the "Drunkenness of Noah"; (2) the gallery of portraits on both sides and at either end, which depict biblical prophets and pagan oracles; and (3) the four corner panels depicting Jewish heroes and heroines who overcame difficulties to help their people survive.*

Figure 12.11 MICHELANGELO. *The Libyan Sibyl.* (Restored.) Detail of the Sistine Chapel ceiling. 1508–1512. 12'11½" × 12'6". The Vatican. *Michelangelo, despite his manifold gifts as painter, sculptor, architect, and poet, always thought of himself as a sculptor, and this is quite evident in his portrait of the Libyan Sibyl, also known as Libica or Libyca (her Latin name). Her muscular back and shoulders are deviations from Classical sculptural ideals of feminine beauty and reflect, instead, Michelangelo's practice of using male models for female subjects. He was also fascinated by the anatomy of position, obvious in the Libyan Sibyl's rotated body, turned head, and outstretched arms. The Libyan Sibyl, according to the Sistine Chapel ceiling's Neo-Platonic plan, represented one of the Greek prophetesses often associated with Apollo. The church, by the end of the Middle Ages, had accepted twelve of these pagan seers. Like their counterparts—the prophets in the Old Testament—these adopted sibyls and their sayings foretold the coming of Jesus Christ. The book, which the Libyan Sibyl appears to be placing behind her, may symbolize these prophecies in writing.*

and he used a plain background to make the figures stand out.

The most famous image from this vast work is a panel from the central section, *The Creation of Adam* (Figure 12.12). In the treatment of this episode from the Book of Genesis, Michelangelo reduces the scene to a

Figure 12.12 MICHELANGELO. *The Creation of Adam.* Detail (restored) of the Sistine Chapel ceiling. 1511. 9'5" × 18'8". The Vatican. *One of the most celebrated details of this fresco is the outstretched fingers of God and Adam that approach but do not touch. By means of this vivid symbol, Michelangelo suggests that a divine spark is about to pass from God into the body of Adam, electrifying it into the fullness of life. The image demonstrates the restraint characteristic of the High Renaissance style. The Vatican's ongoing restoration of the Sistine Chapel frescoes has revealed the brilliant colors of the original, apparent in this detail.*

few details, in accordance with the High Renaissance love of simplicity. Adam, stretched out on a barely sketched bit of ground, seems to exist in some timeless space. Michelangelo depicts Adam as a pulsing, breathing human being. Such wondrous vitality in human flesh had not been seen in Western art since the vigorous nudes of ancient Greek art. In a bold move, Michelangelo ignored the Genesis story that told of God's molding Adam from dust. Instead, the artist paints Adam as half-awakened and reaching to God, who will implant a soul with his divine touch—an illustration of the Neo-Platonic idea of flesh yearning toward the spiritual.

By the 1530s, Michelangelo was painting in the Mannerist style, reflecting his disappointment with Florence's loss of freedom and his own spiritual torment. In this new style, he replaced his heroic vision with a fearful view of the world. A compelling example of this transformation is *The Last Judgment*, painted on the wall behind the Sistine Chapel's altar. This fresco conveys his own sense of sinfulness as well as humanity's future doom (Figure 12.13). Executed twenty-five years after the ceiling frescoes, *The Last Judgment*, with its images of justice and punishment, also reflects the crisis atmosphere of a Europe divided into militant Protestant and Catholic camps. In the center of the fresco, Michelangelo depicts Jesus as the divine and final judge, with right arm raised in a commanding gesture. At the bottom of the fresco, the open graves yield up the dead, and the saved and the damned (on Jesus' right and left, respectively) rise to meet their fate.

In this painting, Michelangelo abandons the architectural framework that had given order to the ceiling frescoes. Instead, the viewer is confronted with a chaotic surface on which a circle of bodies seems to swirl around the central image of Jesus. Michelangelo elongates the bodies and changes their proportions by reducing the size of the heads. There is no Classical serenity here; each figure's countenance shows the anguish provoked by this dreaded moment. Faced with judgment, some gesture wildly while others look beseechingly to their Savior. In this Mannerist masterpiece, simplicity has been replaced by exuberant abundance, and order has given way to rich diversity.

Raphael The youngest of the trio of great High Renaissance painters is Raphael [RAFF-ee-uhl] Santi (1483–1520). Lacking Leonardo's scientific spirit and Michelangelo's brooding genius, Raphael nevertheless had such artistry that his graceful works expressed the ideals of this style better than did those of any other painter. Trained in Urbino, Raphael spent four years (from 1504 to 1508) in Florence, where he absorbed the local painting tradition, learning from the public

works of both Leonardo and Michelangelo. Inspired by what he saw, Raphael developed his artistic ideal of well-ordered space in which human beauty and spatial harmony were given equal treatment.

Moving to Rome, Raphael had an abundance of patrons, especially the popes. At the heart of Raphael's success was his talent for blending the sacred and the secular, and in an age when a pope led troops into battle or went on hunting parties, this gift was appreciated and rewarded. Perhaps Raphael's most outstanding work in Rome was the cycle of paintings for the *stanze*, or rooms, of the Vatican apartment—one of the finest patronage plums of the High Renaissance. Commissioned by Julius II, the *stanze* frescoes show the same harmonization of Christianity and Classicism that Michelangelo brought to the Sistine Chapel ceiling.

Raphael's plan for the four walls of the Stanza della Segnatura in the papal chambers had as its subjects philosophy, poetry, theology, and law. Of these, the most famous is the fresco devoted to philosophy called *The School of Athens* (Figure 12.14). In this work, Raphael depicts a sober discussion among a group of ancient philosophers drawn from all periods. Following Leonardo's treatment of the disciples in *The Last Supper*, Raphael arranges the philosophers in groups, giving each scholar a characteristic gesture that reveals the essence of his thought. For example, Diogenes sprawls on the steps apart from the rest—a vivid symbol of the arch Cynic's contempt for his fellow man. In the right foreground, Euclid, the author of a standard text on geometry, illustrates the proof of one of his theorems. In his careful arrangement of this crowd scene, Raphael demonstrates that he is a master of ordered space.

The School of Athens has a majestic aura because of Raphael's adherence to Classical forms and ideas. The architectural setting, with its rounded arches, medallions, and coffered ceilings, is inspired by Classical architectural ruins and also perhaps by contemporary structures. Perfectly balanced, the scene is focused on Plato and Aristotle, who stand under the series of arches at the painting's center. Raphael reinforces their central position by placing the vanishing point just above and between their heads. The two thinkers' contrasting gestures symbolize the difference between their philosophies: Plato, on the left, points his finger skyward, suggesting the world of the Forms, or abstract thought, and Aristotle, on the right, motions toward the earth, indicating his more practical and empirical method. Raphael also uses these two thinkers as part of his ordering scheme to represent the division of philosophy into the arts and sciences. On Plato's side, the poetic thinkers are gathered under the statue of Apollo, the Greek god of music and lyric verse; Aristotle's half includes the scientists under the statue of Athena, the Greek goddess of wisdom.

Figure 12.13 MICHELANGELO. *The Last Judgment.* 1536–1541. 48 × 44'. Sistine Chapel, the Vatican. *This* Last Judgment *summarizes the anti-Classicism that was sweeping through the visual arts. Other painters studied this fresco for inspiration, borrowing its seemingly chaotic composition, its focus on large numbers of male nudes, and its use of bizarre perspective and odd postures as expressions of the Mannerist sensibility. This fresco was recently cleaned (completed in 1994), its colors returned to the vivid primary colors of Michelangelo's original design and the draperies removed (they had been added during the Catholic Reformation).*

Figure 12.14   RAPHAEL. *The School of Athens.* 1510–1511. Fresco, 18 × 26'. Stanza della Segnatura, the Vatican. *Much of Raphael's success stemmed from the ease with which he assimilated the prevailing ideas of his age. For instance, the posture of the statue of Apollo in the wall niche on the left is probably derived from Michelangelo's* Dying Slave *(see Figure 12.1). For all his artistic borrowings, however, Raphael could be very generous, as indicated by the conspicuous way he highlights Michelangelo's presence in this fresco: The brooding genius sits alone in the foreground, lost in his thoughts and oblivious to the hubbub swirling about him.*

Of even greater fame than Raphael's narrative paintings are his portraits of the Virgin Mary, or his Madonna series. They set the standard for this form of portraiture with their exquisite sweetness and harmonious composition. Raphael's Madonnas clearly show the influence of Leonardo, whose Virgin and Christ child paintings were well known by then (see Figure 11.23). Like many of the Madonna series, Raphael's *Madonna of the Chair* (Figure 12.15) is organized in a pyramidal structure, a design he likely adopted from Leonardo. The Virgin and Christ child are not enthroned, as in the traditional setting, but are sitting, lovingly cuddled together, in a chair, as is hinted by the carved spindle (on the left). To the right stands the child John the Baptist, who looks up adoringly at the Virgin and her son. The Virgin's simple piety comes through in the way Raphael captures her beauty and tenderness in a lovely image. Unlike many religious paintings, the *Madonna of the Chair* does not deliver a theological message, preach a sermon, or tell a story. Because of its familial and domestic setting, this image is considered one of the most natural of Raphael's Madonnas and remains one of his most popular paintings today.

The Venetian School: Giorgione and Titian   Venice maintained its autonomy during the High Renaissance both politically and culturally. Despite the artistic pull of the Roman and Florentine schools, the Venetian artists stayed true to their Byzantine-influenced tradition of sensual surfaces, rich colors, and theatrical lighting. The two greatest painters of the Venetian High Renaissance were Giorgione [jor-JO-na] (about 1477–1510), who was acknowledged to be Venice's premier artist at the end of his life, and Titian [TISH-uhn] (about

Figure 12.15 RAPHAEL. *Madonna of the Chair.* Ca. 1515. Oil on wood panel, diameter 2'5". Pitti Palace, Florence, Italy. *The Christ child caresses the Virgin's cheek—a conventional pose used by Renaissance artists for depicting the baby Jesus and Mary. Mary gazes at the viewer and seems to be contemplating her son's fate. Her head is covered in an oriental-inspired headdress (see Encounter in Chapter 11), and she wears a shawl over a red bodice. The Christ child sits on a blue pillow, the color mystically associated with the Virgin. The circular composition makes the three figures appear even more intimate, as it narrows the spaces between their bodies. Raphael probably painted the* Madonna of the Chair *for a church official.*

Figure 12.16 GIORGIONE. *The Tempest.* 1505. Oil on canvas, 31¼ × 28¾". Galleria dell' Accademia, Venice. *Giorgione's mysterious painting evokes the period—called an "anxious hush"—that sometimes attends the prelude to a violent thunderstorm. He creates this tense mood through atmospheric effects that suggest a gathering storm: billowing clouds; a flash of lightning and its watery reflection; and, in particular, the stark color contrasts between the harshly lighted buildings and the somber hues of earth, sky, and river. The mood is also heightened by the presence of two vulnerable figures, especially the nursing mother who gazes quizzically at the viewer, about to be engulfed by the storm. The painting has a typical Venetian feature in its carefully rendered textures—flesh, cloth, wood, stone, and foliage. Giorgione's painting blazed the path for later artists, chiefly in northern Europe, who took the landscape as a subject.*

1488–1576), who in his later years was revered as Europe's supreme painter.

Little is known of Giorgione's life until the last years of his brief career. A student of Bellini, he won early fame, indicated by the rich private and public commissions he was awarded. Although only a few of his works survive, Giorgione's influence on the course of European art was substantial. His two major innovations, the female nude and the landscape, contributed to the growing secularization of European painting. These developments helped to make Venetian art distinctive from that of Rome and Florence.

The Tempest (Figure 12.16) is probably his best-known work. Breaking free of Bellini's influence, Giorgione created a dramatic landscape, framed on the left by a soldier and on the right by a partly clothed mother nursing a child, that did not allude to mythology, the Bible, or allegorical stories. Whereas Bellini's *St. Francis in Ecstasy* (see Figure 11.24) made the saint the focus of the painting, in *The Tempest* the framing figures are overshadowed by the menacing storm. Thus, Giorgione's landscape, freed of storytelling elements, becomes the subject and should be appreciated on its own terms.

Titian's paintings were prized not only for their easy grace and natural lighting—characteristics of the Venetian Renaissance—but also for their masterful use of color to create dramatic effects (see Figure 12.3). Titian's adherence to the principles of High Renaissance style is evident in such narrative paintings as his *Martyrdom of St. Lawrence* (Figure 12.17). According to tradition, St. Lawrence, a Spaniard, died in Rome in 258. As a deacon who was in charge of the church's treasures, he gave them to the poor. When ordered by the pagan Romans to turn this wealth over to the authorities, he assembled the poor and announced that here were the treasures of the church. For this act he was condemned to die, but he became the patron saint of the poor and poverty-stricken.

Titian's careful arrangement of this complicated scene of torture and martyrdom reflects his commitment to the principle of simplicity. In the foreground, he depicted St. Lawrence being roasted on a grill; to the right, Titian painted a pagan temple, rendered in sharply receding perspective, thereby framing the early Christian saint's death scene. The juxtaposition of the dying St. Lawrence and the Classical temple reminds the viewer that the pagan Romans had failed to eradicate Christianity. Typical of his works, Titian's subtle modulations of color to create a sense of harmony made him a leading "colorist"—someone concerned more with color than with form—and an inspiration to future generations of painters.

The School of Parma: Parmigianino   Parma, in northern Italy, was another center of High Renaissance

Figure 12.17   TITIAN. *Martyrdom of St. Lawrence.* 1550s. Oil on canvas, 16′5½″ × 9′2″. Chiesa dei Gesuiti, Venice. *Even though Titian worked within the High Renaissance style, he was dissatisfied with the symmetry advocated by Classical rules and chose to deviate from their strict regularity in his works. In this painting, the temple's columns recede along a diagonal line, creating a sense of deep space in the foreground; within this space, he arranged objects in a triangular outline with the celestial light source at the apex. By using diagonal and triangular lines, as he often did in his religious works, Titian was able to achieve dramatic and emotional effects without forfeiting coherence or meaning. He heightened this effect even further by bathing the human figures in the light from the sky and the glow from the torches and the fire underneath St. Lawrence.*

art, but the city's best-known artist is a founder of Mannerism, Parmigianino [pahr-mee-jah-NEE-noh] (1503–1540). The *Madonna with the Long Neck* shows Parmigianino's delight in ambiguity, distortion, and dissonance and his love of eccentric composition (Figure 12.18). Mary is portrayed with sloping shoulders and long arms in the manner of Botticelli, and her sensuous figure is not quite hidden under diaphanous draperies—a disturbing mix of sacred and profane

Figure 12.18 PARMIGIANINO. *Madonna with the Long Neck.* 1534–1540. Oil on panel, 7'1" × 4'4". Uffizi Gallery, Florence. *This Madonna by Parmigianino is one of the landmark works in the rise of the Mannerist style. Ignoring Classical ideals, Parmigianino exaggerates the Virgin's body proportions, especially the slender hands and long neck, and elongates the body of the sleeping Jesus. This anti-Classical portrait was greatly at odds with the prevailing High Renaissance image of the Madonna established by Raphael.*

love. A similar confusion exists in the depiction of the infant Christ: The bald baby Jesus appears more dead than alive, so that the subject invokes the Pietà image of the dead Christ stretched on his mother's lap along with the image of the Virgin and Christ child. On the left, five figures stare in various directions. In the background, unfinished columns and an old man reading a scroll, perhaps an allusion to biblical prophecies of Jesus' birth, add to the feeling of multiple focuses and contradictory scales. Unlike the art of the High Renaissance, which offered readily understood subjects, this Mannerist painting, with its uneasy blend of religious piety and disguised sexuality, is enigmatic.

Sculpture

Michelangelo's art is as central to the High Renaissance style in sculpture as it is in painting. An early sculpture that helped to inaugurate this style was the *Pietà* executed when he was twenty-one (Figure 12.19). The touching subject of the **Pietà**—Mary holding the body of the dead Christ—struck a responsive chord in Michelangelo, for he created several sculptural variations on the Pietà theme during his lifetime.

The first *Pietà*, executed in 1498–1499, about the same time as Leonardo's *Last Supper*, shows Michelangelo already at the height of his creative powers. He has captured completely a bewildering sense of loss in his quiet rendering of Mary's suffering. Everything about the sculpture reinforces the somber subject: the superb modeling of Jesus' dead body, with its heavy head and dangling legs; Mary's outstretched gown, which serves as a shroud; and Mary's body, burdened by the weight of her son. Like some ancient funeral

Figure 12.19 MICHELANGELO. *Pietà.* 1498–1499. Marble, ht. 5'8½". St. Peter's, the Vatican. *This Pietà is the only one of Michelangelo's sculptures to be signed. Initially, it was exhibited without a signature, but, according to a legend, when Michelangelo overheard spectators attributing the statue to a rival sculptor, he carved his signature into the marble strap that crosses Mary's chest.*

SLICE OF LIFE
Artists and Their Critics: Michelangelo's Strategy

GIORGIO VASARI
From *Life of Michelangelo*

The writer Giorgio Vasari (1511–1574) actually studied painting with Michelangelo, but he is known today primarily for his accounts of the lives of Renaissance artists, sculptors, and architects. Medieval artists had been categorized with guild members, who were little more than skilled craftspeople and not high up in the social hierarchy. In this telling excerpt, Vasari shows Michelangelo as a full-blown Renaissance artist: proud, confident, and ready to take on critics, even the head of the Florentine republic.

Some of his [Michelangelo's] friends wrote to him from Florence urging him to return there as it seemed very probable that he would be able to obtain the block of marble that was standing in the Office of Works. Piero Soderini, who about that time was elected Gonfalonier for life [head of the Florentine republic], had often talked of handing it over to Leonardo da Vinci, but he was then arranging to give it to Andrea Contucci of Monte Sansovino, an accomplished sculptor who was very keen to have it. Now, although it seemed impossible to carve from the block a complete figure (and only Michelangelo was bold enough to try this without adding fresh pieces) Buonarroti had felt the desire to work on it many years before; and he tried to obtain it when he came back to Florence. The marble was eighteen feet high, but unfortunately an artist called Simone da Fiesole had started to carve a giant figure, and had bungled the work so badly that he had hacked a hole between the legs and left the block completely botched and misshapen. So the wardens of Santa Maria del Fiore (who were in charge of the undertaking) threw the block aside and it stayed abandoned for many years and seemed likely to remain so indefinitely. However, Michelangelo measured it again and calculated whether he could carve a satisfactory figure from the block by accommodating its attitude to the shape of the stone. Then he made up his mind to ask for it. Soderini and the wardens decided that they would let him have it, as being something of little value, and telling themselves that since the stone was of no use to their building, either

botched as it was or broken up, whatever Michelangelo made would be worthwhile. So Michelangelo made a wax model of the young David with a sling in his hand; this was intended as a symbol of liberty for the Palace, signifying that just as David had protected his people and governed them justly, so whoever ruled Florence should vigorously defend the city and govern it with justice. He began work on the statue in the Office of Works of Santa Maria del Fiore, erecting a partition of planks and trestles around the marble; and working on it continuously he brought it to perfect completion, without letting anyone see it. . . .

When he saw the David in place Piero Soderini was delighted; but while Michelangelo was retouching it he remarked that he thought the nose was too thick. Michelangelo, noticing that the Gonfalonier was standing beneath the Giant and that from where he was he could not see the figure properly, to satisfy him climbed on the scaffolding by the shoulders, seized hold of a chisel in his left hand, together with some of the marble dust lying on the planks, and as he tapped lightly with the chisel let the dust fall little by little, without altering anything. Then he looked down at the Gonfalonier, who had stopped to watch, and said:

"Now look at it."

"Ah, that's much better," replied Soderini. "Now you've really brought it to life."

And then Michelangelo climbed down, feeling sorry for those critics who talk nonsense in the hope of appearing well informed.

Interpreting This Slice of Life **Why** was Michelangelo eager to work on this particular block of marble? **What** does this story reveal about the character of Michelangelo? **Summarize** the exchange between Michelangelo and Soderini. **What** trick did Michelangelo play on Soderini? **Speculate** as to the motive behind Michelangelo's behavior. **Do** artists today show some of the same traits as those of Michelangelo in this piece? **Explain.**

---

monument, which the *Pietà* brings to mind, this sculpture of Mary and Jesus overwhelms the viewer with its sorrowful but serene mood.

In 1501, two years after finishing the *Pietà*, Michelangelo was given the commission by the city of Florence for the sculpture that is generally recognized as

his supreme masterpiece, the *David* (Figure 12.20). Michelangelo was eager for this commission because it allowed him to test himself against other great sculptors who had tackled this subject, such as Donatello in the Early Renaissance (see Figure 11.11). Moreover, Michelangelo, a great Florentine patriot, identified

Figure 12.20 MICHELANGELO. *David.* 1501–1504. Marble, ht. 14'3". Accademia, Florence. *Michelangelo's colossal David—standing more than 14 feet tall—captures the balanced ideal of High Renaissance art. The "closed" right side with its tensed hanging arm echoes the right leg, which supports the figure's weight; in the same way, the "open" left side with its bent arm is the precise counterpart of the flexed left leg. Further tension arises from the contrast between David's steady stare and the readiness of the right fist, which holds the stone. Through these means, Michelangelo reinforces the image of a young man wavering between thought and action.*

Figure 12.21 MICHELANGELO. *Pietà.* Before 1555. Marble, ht. 7′8″. Santa Maria del Fiore, Florence. *The rage that seemed to infuse Michelangelo's Mannerist vision in* The Last Judgment *appears purged in this* Pietà—*the work he was finishing when he died at the age of eighty-eight. Mannerist distortions are still present, particularly in the twisted body of the dead Christ and the implied downward motion of the entire ensemble. But the gentle faces suggest that serenity has been restored to Michelangelo's art.*

David with the aggressive spirit of his native city. Michelangelo's *David* was instantly successful, and the republic of Florence adopted the statue as its civic symbol, placing the work in the open square before the Palazzo Vecchio, the town hall. Damage to the statue through weathering and local unrest caused the civic leaders eventually to house Michelangelo's most famous sculpture indoors, where it remains today.

Michelangelo's *David*, rather than imitating Donatello's partly clothed and somewhat effete version, portrays the young Jewish warrior as a nude, Classical hero. Taking a damaged and abandoned block of marble, Michelangelo carved the colossal *David* as a muscular adolescent with his weight gracefully balanced on the right leg, in Classical contrapposto. The *David* perfectly represents Michelangelo's conception of sculpture; imagining a human figure imprisoned inside marble, he simply used his chisel to set it free.

Michelangelo also made minor deviations from Classical principles in his rendition of David in the name of higher ideals, just as ancient artists had done. David's large hands, for example, are outside Classical proportions and suggest a youth who has yet to grow to his potential. And his furrowed brow violates the Classical ideal of serene faces but reflects his intense concentration.

Michelangelo's later sculpture is Mannerist in style, as are his later paintings. A second *Pietà*—with Christ,

Figure 12.22 BRAMANTE. Tempietto. After 1502. Marble, ht. 46'; diameter of colonnade 29'. San Pietro in Montorio, Rome. *Bramante's Tempietto is the earliest surviving High Renaissance building and an exquisite example of this style. Fashioned from pure Classical forms, the building is almost devoid of decoration except for architectural features, and the separate parts—dome, cylindrical drum, and base—are brought into a harmonious whole. The only significant missing feature (since High Renaissance buildings were always planned in relation to their enveloping space) is the never-finished courtyard.*

Mary, Mary Magdalene, and Joseph of Arimathea—shows the change in his depiction of the human form (Figure 12.21). In this somber group, Michelangelo's anti-Classical spirit is paramount. Jesus' body is elongated and unnaturally twisted in death; the other figures, with great difficulty, struggle to support his dead weight. But rather than detracting from the sculpture's impact, the awkward body adds to the scene's emotional interest—an aim of Mannerist art, which did not trust the viewer to respond to more orderly images. Joseph, the rich man who, according to the Gospel, donated his own tomb to Jesus, has Michelangelo's face—a face that is more a death mask than a human countenance.

Architecture

The architectural heir to Alberti in the early sixteenth century was Donato Bramante [brah-MAHN-tay] (1444–1514), who became the moving force behind the High Renaissance in architecture. Trained as a painter, Bramante rejected the reigning building style, called **scenographic**, in which buildings are composed of discrete, individual units. Instead, by concentrating on space and volume, Bramante created an architecture that was unified in all its components and that followed the rules of the Classical orders.

The clearest surviving expression of Bramante's architectural genius is the Tempietto, or little temple, in Rome (Figure 12.22). This small structure was designed both as a church, seating ten worshipers, and as a building marking the site of the martyrdom of St. Peter. Copied from the circular temples of ancient Rome, this small domed building became the prototype of the central plan church popularized in the High Renaissance and later.

Bramante's design for the Tempietto sprang from ancient Classical principles. Foremost was his belief that architecture should appeal to human reason and that a building should present a severe appearance and not seek to please through specially planned effects. Further, Bramante thought that a building should be unified like a piece of sculpture and that ornamentation should be restricted to a few architectural details.

In accordance with this artistic credo, the Tempietto functions like a work of sculpture; it is raised on a pedestal with steps leading up to its colonnaded porch. In the absence of sculptural decorations, the temple's ex-

Figure 12.23 MICHELANGELO. Dome of St. Peter's. View from the southwest. 1546–1564. (Completed by Giacomo della Porta, 1590.) Ht. of dome 452'. Rome. *Its harmonious design and its reliance on Classical forms made Michelangelo's dome an object of universal admiration when it was completed in 1590, after his death. From then to the present day, other architects have used his dome as a model, hoping to reproduce its Classical spirit.*

terior is accented with architectural details: the columns; the **balustrade**, or rail with supporting posts; and the dome with barely visible ribs. The proportions of its various features, such as the ratio of column widths to column heights, were based on ancient mathematical formulas. Unfortunately for Bramante's final conception, the plan to integrate the small temple into a circular courtyard of a nearby church was never completed. Despite the absence of this crowning touch, the Tempietto is one of the jewels of the High Renaissance.

Bramante had been commissioned by Pope Julius II to rebuild St. Peter's Basilica, the world's most famous church, but he died before his plans could be carried out. The supervision of the rebuilding of St. Peter's fell to other architects; eventually Michelangelo, at the age of seventy-one, was given this vital task. From 1546 until his death in 1564, Michelangelo, among his other artistic tasks, was occupied with St. Peter's, especially with the construction of the dome. Over the years, other building projects had come his way, but nothing could compare with the significance of this one. Although the dome was completed after his death and slightly modified, it remains Michelangelo's outstanding architectural monument and a splendid climax to his career.

Michelangelo's sculptural approach to architecture was similar to that of Bramante. In an attempt to integrate the dome of St. Peter's with the rest of the existing structure, Michelangelo used double Corinthian columns as a unifying agent. Because the facade of St. Peter's was altered in the 1600s, Michelangelo's dome is best observed from the southwest (Figure 12.23). Beginning at ground level, the Corinthian order provides the artistic cement that pulls the entire building together. Sometimes as columns, sometimes as pilasters, and sometimes as ribs, the double Corinthian units move up the walls, eventually up the dome's drum, and up the dome itself.

This plan for St. Peter's shows that Michelangelo the architect differed from Michelangelo the painter and sculptor. In painting and sculpture, he had by the 1530s become a Mannerist in his use of exaggeration and expressive effects. But in architecture, he stayed faithful to the High Renaissance and its ideal of harmonious design.

The preeminent architect of the Mannerist style was Andrea di Pietro (1508–1580), known as Palladio [pah-LAHD-yo], whose base of operations was Vicenza, in northern Italy. The name Palladio derives from Pallas, a name for Athena, the goddess of wisdom. Palladio's artistic creed was rooted in Classicism, but his forte

Figure 12.24   PALLADIO. Villa Rotonda (Villa Capra). Begun 1550. (Completed in about 1592 by Vincenzo Scamozzi [1548–1616].) Ht. of dome 70'; villa 80' square. Vicenza. *Despite its harmonious proportions and Classical features, the Villa Rotonda belongs to the Mannerist style. Unlike High Renaissance buildings, which were designed to be integrated with their settings, this boxlike country house stands in an antagonistic relationship to its surrounding garden space. Furthermore, the Mannerist principle of elongation is apparent in its four long stairways. But the Villa Rotonda's most striking Mannerist feature is the surprise inherent in a plan that includes four identical porches.*

was the richly inventive way in which he could arrange the Classical elements of a building to guarantee surprise. He played with the effects of light and shadow, adding feature on top of feature, to create buildings that possess infinite variety in the midst of a certain decorative solemnity.

Palladio's most influential domestic design was the Villa Capra, more commonly called the Villa Rotonda because of its central circular area and covering dome (Figure 12.24). Inspired by ancient Roman farmhouses, the Villa Rotonda is a sixteenth-century country house built of brick and faced with stucco and located on a rise overlooking Vicenza. A dome provides a central axis from which four symmetrical wings radiate. Each of the four wings in turn opens to the outdoors through an Ionic-style porch raised on a pedestal. The porticoes, or covered porches supported by columns, then lead to the ground level through deeply recessed stairways. Statues stand on the corners and peak of

each of the four pediments, and others flank the four stairways.

Palladio's Mannerist spirit can be seen at work in the design of this building. Although the coldly formal porches are Classical in appearance, no Greek or Roman temple would have had four such identical porches, one on each side of the building (Figure 12.25). Palladio's design incorporates the unexpected and the contradictory within an apparently Classical structure.

Besides designing buildings, Palladio wrote about architecture in his treatise *Quattro libri dell'architettura*, or *The Four Books of Architecture*. Through its English translation, this work gained wide currency and led to the vogue of Palladianism in the English-speaking world. English aristocrats in the eighteenth century commissioned country houses built on Palladian principles, as did plantation owners in America's antebellum South.

Figure 12.25 PALLADIO. Floor Plan of the Villa Rotonda. *Palladio designed the Villa Rotonda to further the social ambitions of its wealthy Venetian owner, so he made its most prominent interior feature a central circular area, or rotunda. Surmounted by a dome, this area was ideal for concerts, parties, and other entertainments. Palladio surrounded the rotunda with four identically shaped sets of rooms on two levels, where the family lived and guests were housed. Passageways led to the four porches, where villa residents could obtain relief from the summer's heat and enjoy diverting views of the surrounding countryside.*

Music

No radical break separates the music of the High Renaissance from that of the Early Renaissance. Josquin des Prez, the leading composer of the dominant Franco-Netherlandish school, had brought to a climax the Early Renaissance style of music while he was employed in Italy by the popes and the local aristocrats (see Chapter 11). Josquin's sixteenth-century pieces, which consist chiefly of religious Masses and motets along with secular *chansons*, or songs, simply heightened the ideal already present in his earlier works: a sweet sound produced by multiple voices, usually two to six, singing a cappella and expressing the feelings described in the text. Despite his interest in music's emotional power, Josquin continued to subordinate the song to the words—thus reflecting the needs of the church, the foremost patron of the age. This balancing act between the music and the words, resulting in a clearly sung text, was also evidence of the Classical restraint of his High Renaissance style. A striking feature of this style was the rich multichoral effect produced when the singing group was subdivided into different combinations of voices.

Experimentation with choral effects was carried into the next generation by Adrian Willaert [VIL-art] (about 1490–1562), a member of the Netherlandish school and a disciple of Josquin's. After the death of his mentor, Willaert was probably Europe's most influential composer. He made his mark on musical history from his post as chapel master of the cathedral of St. Mark's in Venice, and he is considered the founder

of the Venetian school of music. Taking advantage of St. Mark's two organs and the Venetian practice of blending instruments with voices, he wrote music for two choirs as well. By a variety of musical mechanisms, such as alternating and combining voices, contrasting soft and loud, and arranging echo effects, Willaert created beautiful and expressive sounds that were the ancestor of the splendid church concertos of the Baroque era. A benefit of Willaert's innovations was that the organ was released from its dependence on vocal music.

Missa Christus resurgens (Mass, the Risen Christ, about 1536), composed for four voices, shows Willaert's beautifully expressive style. Based on a short polyphonic work of the same name by the Franco-Flemish composer Jean Richafort (about 1480–about 1547), Willaert's Mass creates an appealing tapestry of sound, using melismas and imitation, but ensuring faultless understanding of the text—the essence of "modern" sacred polyphony, his legacy. The short Agnus Dei (Lamb of God) begins with all four voices forming an ever-shifting ground, from which the tenor voice emerges, soaring above the rest, giving an ethereal sound and acting as a musical metaphor for Christ's rebirth.

Except for the stylistic perfection achieved by Josquin and Willaert, the musical scene during this period witnessed only minor changes from that of the Early Renaissance. Instrumental music still played a secondary role to the human voice, though Josquin and Willaert composed a few pieces for specific instruments, either transposing melodies that originally had

Figure 12.26   GIOVANNI DI LUTERO, KNOWN AS DOSSO DOSSI. *Apollo and Daphne.* Ca. 1538. Oil on canvas, 6′2″ × 3′9″. Galleria Borghese, Rome. *Dosso Dossi (about 1490–1542), who lived in Ferrara and was influenced by Giorgione, Titian, and probably Raphael, painted many allegorical and mythological scenes. His sense of color and understanding of light added to the magic and fantasy of his works. Apollo, the patron of poetry and music and leader of the Muses, is placed in the foreground, while Daphne, whom he constantly chased, is in the middle ground, fleeing from her pursuer. An Italian city, perhaps Bologna (identified by its Twin Towers), fills in the background. Apollo, rather than playing the lyre, an ancient Greek string instrument, is holding a violin. This painting may be one of the first to feature the violin, since it had only appeared about 1510. By the 1570s, Andrea Amati, who is recognized as the designer of the first violin, was making the instrument at his workshop in Cremona, a city within eighty miles of Ferrara. Antonio Stradivari and Andrea Guarneri, two of the most famous violin makers in history, were pupils of Niccolo Amati, Andrea's grandson. Antonio Stradivari brought violin making to its highest level of perfection. He produced 540 violins along with many other string instruments. Today, a Stradivari violin is considered one of the most precious musical instruments in the world.*

been intended for singers or adapting music forms from dance tunes.

Still, one development was the appearance of the violin, which evolved from the Arabic *rebec* and the medieval fiddle and its Italian cousin (Figure 12.26). A bowed, stringed musical instrument, the violin is probably the most popular musical instrument in the world today. By the end of the sixteenth century, Italian violin makers had determined the instrument's basic size and shape, though the number of strings continued to vary for several decades.

The development that had the most promise for the future was the invention of families of instruments, ranging from the low bass to the high treble, which blended to make a pleasant sound. In most cases, these families, called **consorts**, consisted of either recorders or viols. The consorts represented the principle of the mixed instrumental ensemble, and from this beginning would emerge the orchestra. Recorders and viols could also be blended to make an agreeable sound; when human voices were added to the mixture, the conditions were ripe for opera.

The Legacy of the High Renaissance and Early Mannerism

From a contemporary perspective, the seventy-year period during which the High Renaissance and Early Mannerism flourished is the Golden Age of the West in certain artistic and humanistic areas. In the visual arts—painting, sculpture, and architecture—standards were set and indelible images created that have not been surpassed. In political theory, this age produced the Mannerist thinker Machiavelli, who is the founder of modern political thought.

Beyond those achievements, three other important steps were being taken on the road to the modern world. On a political level, the beginnings of the modern secular state may be seen in the changes taking place in France, Spain, and England. What was innovative, even revolutionary, for these countries in the early sixteenth century has become second nature to the states of the twenty-first century, both in the Western world and beyond. On a social level, a new code of behavior appeared in the Italian courts and was in time adopted throughout Europe. Not only did the rules of courtesy finally penetrate into the European aristocracy and alter their behavior, but also they eventually trickled down to the middle classes. By our day, the behavior of Castiglione's courtier and lady, though in diluted form, has become the model for all Western people with any shred of social ambition. On the international level, the first stirrings of multiculturalism were being felt, as Portugal, followed by Spain, England, France, and the Netherlands, began to initiate contacts with societies beyond Europe—thus initiating the process of globalization that defines our world today.

Another new idea was beginning to develop now as well. The Classical and the medieval worlds had praised what was corporate and public, in conformity with traditional, universal values. But in the 1500s a few artists and humanists, along with their patrons, began to revere what was individual and private. The supreme example of free expression and of the "cult of genius" in the High Renaissance was Leonardo da Vinci, whose encoded notebooks were meant for his personal use, not for general publication. Early Mannerism carried individual expression to extremes by finding merit in personal eccentricities and unrestrained behavior. That patrons supported the new works of these artists and humanists demonstrates the rise of the belief that free expression is both a social and a private good. Both the High Renaissance and Early Mannerism encouraged the daring idea of individualism and thereby introduced what has become a defining theme of Western culture.

KEY CULTURAL TERMS

High Renaissance	Pietà
Mannerism	scenographic
civic humanism	balustrade
Machiavellianism	consort

SUGGESTIONS FOR FURTHER READING

CASTIGLIONE, B. *The Book of the Courtier*. Translated by G. Bull. New York: Penguin, 1967. A flowing translation; includes a helpful introduction and descriptions of characters who participate in the conversations recorded by Castiglione; first published in 1528.

MACHIAVELLI, N. *The Prince*. Translated by G. Bull. New York: Penguin, 1971. The introduction covers Machiavelli's life and other writings to set the stage for this important political work; written in 1513.

SUGGESTION FOR LISTENING

WILLAERT, ADRIAN. Willaert is particularly noted for his motets, such as *Sub tuum praesidium*, which reflect the Renaissance humanist ideal of setting the words precisely to the music. His *Musica nova*, published in 1559 and including motets, madrigals, and instrumental music, illustrates the complex polyphony and sensuous sounds that made him a widely imitated composer in the second half of the sixteenth century.

1500

A D

Albertus Durerus Noricus
ipsum me proprijs sic effin=
gebam coloribus ætatis
anno XXVIII.

GLOSSARY

Italicized words within definitions are defined in their own glossary entries.

abstract art Art that presents a subjective view of the world—the artist's emotions or ideas—or art that presents *line, color,* or shape for its own sake.

Abstract Expressionism Also known as *Action Painting,* a nonrepresentational artistic style that flourished after World War II and was typified by randomness, spontaneity, and an attempt by the artist to interact emotionally with the work as it was created.

abstraction In Modern art, nonrepresentational or nonobjective forms in sculpture and painting that emphasize shapes, *lines,* and *colors* independent of the natural world.

a cappella [ah kuh-PEL-uh] From the Italian, "in chapel style"; music sung without instrumental accompaniment.

Action Painting Another name for *Abstract Expressionism.* Action Painting referred to an artist's use of agitated motions while applying paint to canvas, such as Jackson Pollock's "drip paintings" or Willem de Kooning's slashing strokes. Inspired by *Surrealism's* reliance on automatic responses as a way to release the creative unconscious.

adab [ah-DAHB] An Arabic term. Originally, it meant good manners or good conduct. In the eighth century, it appeared as a literary *genre;* later, it indicated the possession of athletic skills and literary knowledge and applied especially to the elite. Today, *adab* refers to the whole of literature.

aesthete One who pursues and is devoted to the beautiful in art, music, and literature.

aisles The side passages in a church on either side of the central *nave.*

Alexandrianism [al-ig-ZAN-dree-an-ism] A literary style developed in the *Hellenistic* period, typically formal, artificial, and imitative of earlier Greek writing.

ambulatory [AM-bue-la-tor-e] A passageway for walking found in many religious structures, such as outdoors in a *cloister* or indoors around the *apse* or the *choir* of a church.

Anglicanism The doctrines and practices of the Church of England, which was established in the early sixteenth century under Henry VIII.

Angry Young Men A late 1950s and early 1960s literary movement in Great Britain, composed of novelists and playwrights, whose works expressed frustration and anger over their country's loss of empire and declining status on the world's stage. Most of the Angry Young Men were part of an emerging meritocracy, having been born in the lower classes but educated in the universities, including Oxford and Cambridge.

anthropomorphism [an-thro-po-MOR-fizm] The attributing of humanlike characteristics and traits to nonhuman things or powers, such as a deity.

antiphon [AN-te-fon] In music, a short prose text, chanted by unaccompanied voices during the Christian *liturgy.*

apocalypse [uh-PAHK-uh-lips] In Jewish and early Christian thought, the expectation and hope of the coming of God and his final judgment; also closely identified with the last book of the New Testament, Revelation, in which many events are foretold, often in highly symbolic and imaginative terms.

apse In architecture, a large projection, usually rounded or semicircular, found in a *basilica,* usually in the east end; in Christian *basilicas,* the altar stood in this space.

aquatint An early type of color print, made with a metal plate, which attempted to replicate the effect of a watercolor; originated in the Netherlands in about 1650. The golden age of the aquatint was from about 1770 to 1850. The print's name derives from nitrous oxide (*aqua fortis*), a chemical used in the printmaking process.

arabesque [air-uh-BESK] Literally, "Arabian-like"; decorative lines, patterns, and designs, often floral, in Islamic works of art.

arcade A series of arches supported by *piers* or columns, usually serving as a passageway along a street or between buildings.

Archaic style The style in Greek sculpture, dating from the seventh century to 480 B.C.E., that was characterized by heavy Egyptian influence; dominated by the *kouros* and *kore* sculptural forms.

architectural paintings A type of wall painting, which created the optical illusion of either a wall opening or the effect of looking through a window; popular in imperial Rome.

architrave [AHR-kuh-trayv] The part of the *entablature* that rests on the *capital* or column in Classical *post-beam-triangle construction.*

aria [AH-ree-uh] In music, an elaborate *melody* sung as a solo or sometimes a duet, usually in an *opera* or an *oratorio,* with an orchestral accompaniment.

ars nova Latin, "new art"; a style of music in fourteenth-century Europe. It used more secular themes than the "old art" music of earlier times, which was closely identified with sacred music.

art film A film *genre* marked by unusual narrative structures, violent action, and uplifting themes; associated with directors indebted to *auteurist* theory.

art song (lied) In music, a *lyric* song with *melody* performed by a singer and instrumental accompaniment usually provided by piano; made popular by Schubert in the nineteenth century.

ashlar [ASH-luhr] A massive hewn or squared stone used in constructing a fortress, palace, or large building.

assemblage art An art form in which the artist mixes and/or assembles "found objects," such as scraps of paper, cloth, or junk, into a three-dimensional work and then adds paint or other decorations to it.

ataraxia [at-uh-RAK-see-uh] Greek, "calmness"; in *Hellenistic* philosophy, the state of desiring nothing.

atonality [ay-toe-NAL-uh-tee] In music, the absence of a *key* note or tonal center and the use of the *tones* of the chromatic *scale* impartially.

atrium [AY-tree-uhm] In Roman architecture, an open courtyard at the front of a house; in Christian *Romanesque* churches, an open court, usually colonnaded, in front of the main doors of the structure.

attic The topmost section or crown of an arch.

audience The group or person for whom a work of art, architecture, literature, drama, film, or music is intended.

aulos In music, a reed woodwind instrument similar to the oboe, usually played in pairs by one player as the double aulos; used in Greek music.

autarky [AW-tar-kee] Greek, "self-sufficient"; in *Hellenistic* thought, the state of being isolated and free from the demands of society.

auteur [oh-TURR] French, "author"; a film director who imposes a personal style. The *auteurist* director "writes" with the camera to express a personal vision.

avant-garde [a-vahn-GARD] French, "advance guard"; writers, artists, and intellectuals who push their works and ideas ahead of more traditional groups and movements.

baldacchino [ball-duh-KEE-no] An ornamental structure in the shape of a canopy, supported by four columns, built over a church altar, and usually decorated with statues and other ornaments.

balustrade   In architecture, a rail and the row of posts that support it, as along the edge of a staircase or around a dome.

baptistery   A small, often octagonal structure, separated from the main church, particularly in Europe, where baptisms are performed.

bard   A tribal poet-singer who composed and recited works, often of the *epic poetry* genre.

Baroque [buh-ROKE]   The prevailing seventeenth-century artistic and cultural style, characterized by an emphasis on grandeur, opulence, expansiveness, and complexity.

barrel vault   A ceiling or *vault* made of sets of arches placed side by side and joined together.

basilica [buh-SILL-ih-kuh]   A rectangular structure that included an *apse* at one or both ends; originally a Roman building used for public purposes, later taken over by the Christians for worship. The floor plan became the basis of nearly all early Christian churches.

bay   A four-cornered unit of architectural space, often used to identify a section of the *nave* in a *Romanesque* or *Gothic* church.

bel canto [bell KAHN-toe]   Italian, "beautiful singing"; a style of singing characteristic of seventeenth-century Italian *opera* stressing ease, purity, and evenness of *tone* along with precise vocal technique.

Beat Generation   A literary movement in the United States, from about 1950 to 1970, made up of poets, novelists, and playwrights, who stood apart from the mainstream literary establishment, as reflected in their use of street language, experimental forms of literary expression, and liberal use of alcohol and drugs. While expressing solidarity with society's downtrodden—the source of the term *Beat*—the Beats criticized capitalism, bourgeois society and values, and the nuclear arms race.

blank verse   Unrhymed iambic pentameter (lines with five feet, or units, each consisting of an unaccented and an accented syllable).

blaxploitation film   A crime film *genre* that features a swaggering black hero, catering to black audiences.

blind arcade   A decorative architectural design that gives the appearance of an open *arcade* or window but is filled in with some type of building material such as stone or brick.

blues   A type of music that emerged around 1900 from the rural African American culture, was originally based on work songs and religious spirituals, and expressed feelings of loneliness and hopelessness.

Byzantine style [BIZ-uhn-teen]   In painting, decoration, and architecture, a *style* blending Greco-Roman and oriental components into a highly stylized art form that glorified Christianity, notably in domed churches adorned with *mosaics* and polished marble; associated with the culture of the Eastern Roman Empire from about 500 until 1453.

cadenza [kuh-DEN-zah]   In music, a *virtuoso* passage, usually for a solo instrument or voice, meant to be improvised or to have an improvised feeling.

Cajun   A descendant of French pioneers, chiefly in Louisiana, who in 1755 chose to leave Acadia (modern Nova Scotia) rather than live under the British crown.

calligraphy   Penmanship or handwriting, usually done with flowing lines, used as a decoration or as an enhancement of a written work; found in Islamic and Christian writings.

Calvinism   The theological beliefs and rituals set forth in and derived from John Calvin's writings, placing emphasis on the power of God and the weakness of human beings.

campanile   From the Latin "campana," bell; a bell tower, especially one near but not attached to a church; an Italian invention.

canon   A set of principles or rules that are accepted as true and authoritative for the various arts or fields of study; in architecture, it refers to the standards of proportion; in painting, the prescribed ways of painting certain objects; in sculpture, the ideal proportions of the human body; in literature, the authentic list of an author's works; in religion, the approved and authoritative writings that are accepted as divinely inspired, such as the *scriptures* for Jews and Christians; and in religious and other contexts, certain prescribed rituals or official rules and laws. In music, a canon is a *composition* in which a *melody* sung by one voice is repeated exactly by successive voices as they enter.

canzone [kan-ZOH-nee]   Latin, "chant"; a type of love poem popular in southern France during the twelfth and thirteenth centuries.

capital   In architecture, the upper or crowning part of a column, on which the *entablature* rests.

cathedral   The church of a bishop that houses a cathedral, or throne symbolizing the seat of power in his administrative district, known as a diocese.

causality   The idea that one event "causes" another; the relation between a cause and its effect.

cella [SELL-uh]   The inner sanctum or walled room of a *Classical* temple where sacred statues were housed.

chanson [shahn-SAWN]   French, "song"; a fourteenth- to sixteenth-century French song for one or more voices, often with instrumental accompaniment. Similar to a *madrigal*.

chanson de geste [shahn-SAWN duh zhest]   A poem of brave deeds in the *epic* form developed in France during the eleventh century, usually to be sung.

character   A person in a story or play; someone who acts out or is affected by the *plot*.

chiaroscuro [key-ahr-uh-SKOOR-oh]   In painting, the use of dark and light contrast to create the effect of modeling of a figure or object.

Chinese Rococo   A variation of the European *Rococo*, characterized by oriental shapes, materials, techniques, and design elements.

Chinoiserie (shen-WAZ-uh-ree)   French, "Chinois," China. A *style* and taste in the West for Chinese culture, embracing the decorative arts and, to a lesser extent, Chinese writings; most influential from 1740 to 1770, but lingering until about 1850.

chivalric code   The rules of conduct, probably idealized, that governed the social roles and duties of aristocrats in the Middle Ages.

chivalric novel   A Late Medieval literary form that presented romantic stories of knights and their ladies; the dominant literary form in Spain from the Late Middle Ages into the *Renaissance*.

choir   In architecture, that part of a *Gothic* church in which the service was sung by singers or clergy, located in the east end beyond the *transept*; also, the group of trained singers who sat in the choir area.

chorus   In Greek drama, a group of performers who sang and danced in both *tragedies* and *comedies*, often commenting on the action; in later times, a group of singers who performed with or without instrumental accompaniment.

Christian humanism   An intellectual movement in sixteenth-century northern Europe that sought to use the ideals of the *Classical* world, the tools of ancient learning, and the morals of the Christian *scriptures* to rid the church of worldliness and scandal.

chthonian deities [THOE-nee-uhn]   In Greek religion, earth gods and goddesses who lived underground and were usually associated with peasants and their religious beliefs.

civic humanism   An Italian *Renaissance* ideal, characterized by dedicated and educated citizens who served as administrators and civil servants in their cities; inspired by the period's *Classical* revival.

civilization   The way humans live in a complex political, economic, and social structure, usually in an urban environment, with some development in technology, literature, and art.

cladding   In architecture, a covering or overlay of some material for a building's exterior walls.

Classic, or Classical   Having the forms, values, or standards embodied in the art and literature of Greek and Roman *civilization*; in music, an eighteenth-century style characterized by simplicity, proportion, and an emphasis on structure.

Classical Baroque style   A secular variation of the *Baroque* style that was identified with French kings and artists, was rooted in *Classical* ideals, and was used mainly to emphasize the power and grandeur of the monarchy.

Classicism   A set of aesthetic principles found in Greek and Roman art and literature emphasizing the search for perfection or ideal forms.

clavier [French, KLAH-vyay; German, KLAH-veer]   Any musical instrument having a keyboard, such as a piano, organ, or harpsichord; the term came into general usage with the popularity of Bach's set of studies entitled *The Well-Tempered Clavier.*

clerestory windows [KLEER-stor-ee]   A row of windows set along the upper part of a wall, especially in a church.

cloister   In architecture, a covered walkway, open on one side, which is attached to the four walls of buildings that face a quadrangle; originated in medieval church architecture. Also, a monastery or convent dedicated to religious seclusion.

codex [KO-deks] (plural, **codices**)   The earliest form of a bound book, made of parchment pages, dating from about the first century B.C.E. in pagan Rome.

collage [koh-LAHZH]   From the French *coller*, to "glue"; a type of art, introduced by Picasso, in which bits and pieces of materials such as paper or cloth are glued to a painted surface.

color   Use of the hues found in nature to enhance or distort the sense of reality in a visual image.

commedia dell'arte [kuh-MAY-de-uh del-AR-teh]   Italian, "comedy of art"; an Italian theatrical *genre* from the sixteenth century, using puppets and stock characters, with a strong streak of improvisation. Highly influential later on live theater in Italy and elsewhere.

comedy   A literary *genre* characterized by a story with a complicated and amusing *plot* that ends with a happy and peaceful resolution of all conflicts.

comedy of manners   A humorous play that focuses on the way people in a particular social group or class interact with one another, especially regarding fashions and manners.

composition   The arrangement of constituent elements in an artistic work; in music, composition also refers to the process of creating the work.

concerto [kuhn-CHER-toe]   In music, a *composition* for one or more soloists and *orchestra*, usually in a symphonic *form* with three contrasting movements.

conceptual art   A *Late Modern* art movement in which the concept or idea of the proposed art is more important than the means for its execution.

congregational or Friday mosque   A type of *mosque* used for Friday prayers, inspired by Muhammad's original example. Characterized by a central courtyard along with a domed fountain for ablutions; found across the Islamic world.

consort   A set of musical instruments in the same family, ranging from bass to soprano; also, a group of musicians who entertain by singing or playing instruments.

Constructivism   A movement in nonobjective art, originating in the Soviet Union and flourishing from 1917 to 1922 and concerned with planes and volumes as expressed in modern industrial materials such as glass and plastic.

content   The subject matter of an artistic work.

context   The setting in which an artistic work arose, its own time and place. Context includes the political, economic, social, and cultural conditions of the time; it can also include the personal circumstances of the artist's life.

contrapposto [kon-truh-POH-stoh]   In sculpture and painting, the placement of the human figure so the weight is more on one leg than the other and the shoulders and chest are turned in the opposite direction from the hips and legs.

convention   An agreed-upon practice, device, technique, or form.

Corinthian   The third Greek architectural order, in which temple columns are slender and *fluted*, sit on a base, and have *capitals* shaped like inverted bells and decorated with carvings representing the leaves of the acanthus bush; this style was popular in *Hellenistic* times and widely adopted by the Romans.

cornice   In architecture, the crowning, projecting part of the *entablature.*

cosmopolitan   From Greek, "cosmos," world, and "polis," city; a citizen of the world, that is, an urban dweller with a universal, or world, view.

Counter-Reformation   A late-sixteenth-century movement in the Catholic Church aimed at reestablishing its basic beliefs, reforming its organizational structure, and reasserting itself as the authoritative voice of Christianity.

countersubject   In music, in the *fugue*, a contrasting variant to the *subject*; played in tandem with the *subject*, either below or above it.

covenant   In Judaism and Christianity, a solemn and binding agreement or contract between God and his followers.

Creole   An ambiguous term, sometimes referring to descendants of French and Spanish settlers of the southern United States, especially Louisiana; used by Kate Chopin in her short stories and novels in this sense. In other contexts, *Creole* can refer either to blacks born in the Western Hemisphere (as distinguished from blacks born in Africa) or to residents of the American Gulf states of mixed black, Spanish, and Portuguese ancestry.

crescendo [krah-SHEN-doh]   In music, an increase in volume.

cruciform [KROO-suh-form]   Cross-shaped; used to describe the standard floor plan of a church.

Cubism   A *style* of painting introduced by Picasso and Braque in which objects are broken up into fragments and patterns of geometric structures and depicted on the flat canvas as if from several points of view.

culture   The sum of human endeavors, including the basic political, economic, and social institutions and the values, beliefs, and arts of those who share them.

cuneiform [kue-NEE-uh-form]   Wedge-shaped characters used in writing on tablets found in Mesopotamia and other ancient *civilizations*.

Cynicism   A *Hellenistic* philosophy that denounced society and its institutions as artificial and called on the individual to strive for *autarky*.

Dada [DAH-dah]   An early-twentieth-century artistic movement, named after a nonsense word that was rooted in a love of play, encouraged deliberately irrational acts, and exhibited contempt for all traditions.

Decadence   A late-nineteenth-century literary *style* concerned with morbid and artificial subjects and themes.

Deconstruction   In *Post-Modern* literary analysis, a set of practices for analyzing and critiquing a text in order to "deconstruct" its actual meaning and language.

deductive reasoning   The process of reasoning from the general to the particular—that is, beginning with an accepted premise or first statement and, by steps of logical reasoning or inference, reaching a conclusion that necessarily follows from the premise.

Deism [DEE-iz-uhm]   A religion based on the idea that the universe was created by God and then left to run according to *natural laws,* without divine interference; formulated and practiced in the eighteenth century.

de Stijl [duh STILE]   Dutch, "the style"; an artistic movement associated with a group of early-twentieth-century Dutch painters who used rectangular forms and primary colors in their works and who believed that art should have spiritual values and a social purpose.

devotio moderna [de-VO-tee-oh mo-DER-nuh]   The "new devotion" of Late Medieval Christianity that emphasized piety and discipline as practiced by lay religious communities located primarily in northern Europe.

Diaspora [dye-AS-puhr-uh]   From the Greek, "to scatter"; the dispersion of the Jews from their homeland in ancient Palestine, a process that began with the Babylonian Captivity in the sixth century B.C.E. and continued over the centuries.

Dionysia [DYE-uh-NYSH-ee-ah]   Any of the religious festivals held in ancient Athens honoring Dionysus, the god of wine; especially the Great Dionysia, celebrated in late winter and early spring in which *tragedy* is thought to have originated.

divining   Predicting the future by "reading," or interpreting, the entrails of an animal or the behavior of birds; practiced by ancient Roman priests and religious leaders.

Doric   The simplest and oldest of the Greek architectural orders, in which temple columns have undecorated *capitals* and rest directly on the *stylobate.*

drum   In architecture, a circular or polygonal wall used to support a dome.

drypoint   In art, the technique of incising an image, using a sharp, pointed instrument, onto a metal surface or block used for printing. Also, the print made from the technique.

dynamics   In music, changes in the volume of a sound.

Early Renaissance style   A *style* inspired by *Classical* rather than *Gothic* models that arose among Florentine architects, sculptors, and painters in the late fourteenth and early fifteenth centuries.

electronic music   Music produced using electronic means, usually with a *synthesizer* and/or a computer.

empiricism   The process of collecting data, making observations, carrying out experiments based on the collected data and observations, and reaching a conclusion.

engraving   In art, the technique of carving, cutting, or etching an image with a sharp, pointed instrument onto a metal surface overlaid with wax, dipping the surface in acid, and then printing it. Also, the print made from the technique.

Enlightenment   The eighteenth-century philosophical and cultural movement marked by the application of reason to human problems and affairs, a questioning of traditional beliefs and ideas, and an optimistic faith in unlimited progress for humanity, particularly through education.

entablature [en-TAB-luh-choor]   In architecture, the part of the temple above the columns and below the roof, which, in *Classical* temples, included the *architrave*, the *frieze*, and the *pediment.*

entasis [EN-ta-sis]   In architecture, convex curving or enlarging of the central part of a column to correct the optical illusion that the column is too thin.

environmental art   A *Post-Modern* art form that uses the environment, including stone, earth, and water, so as to create a natural-looking artwork. Environmental art is ephemeral, as it tends to revert to its primary elements over time—thus echoing the ever-changing world of nature.

epic   A poem, novel, or film that recounts at length the life of a hero or the history of a people.

epic poetry   Narrative poetry, usually told or written in an elevated style, that recounts the life of a hero.

epic theater   A type of theater, invented by Brecht, in which major social issues are dramatized with outlandish props and jarring dialogue and effects, all designed to alienate middle-class *audiences* and force them to think seriously about the problems raised in the plays.

Epicureanism [ep-i-kyoo-REE-uh-niz-uhm]   A *Hellenistic* philosophy, founded by Epicurus and later expounded by the Roman Lucretius, that made its highest goals the development of the mind and an existence free from the demands of everyday life.

episode   In music, a short transitional section played between the *subject* and the *countersubject;* used in *fugal* composition.

eschatology [es-kuh-TAHL-uh-jee]   The concern with final events or the end of the world, a belief popular in Jewish and early Christian communities and linked to the concept of the coming of a *Messiah.*

evangelicalism   Historically, a nineteenth-century Protestant movement, mainly in the United States, which grew out of the Methodist tradition and emphasized personal piety and the working of the Holy Spirit. Evangelicalism dominated mainline Protestant America until about 1870. Today, evangelicalism is a term used for describing Protestants who emphasize *fundamentalism*, biblical inerrancy, and conservative social values.

evangelists   From the Greek *evangelion*, a term generally used for those who preach the Christian religion; more specifically, the four evangelists, Matthew, Mark, Luke, and John, who wrote about Jesus Christ soon after his death in the first four books of the New Testament.

evolution   The theory, set forth in the nineteenth century by Charles Darwin, that plants and animals, including humans, evolved over millions of years from simpler forms through a process of natural selection.

existentialism [eg-zi-STEN-shuh-liz-uhm]   A twentieth-century philosophy focusing on the precarious nature of human existence, with its uncertainty, anxiety, and ultimate death, as well as on individual freedom and responsibility and the possibilities for human creativity and authenticity.

Expressionism   A late-nineteenth-century literary and artistic movement characterized by the expression of highly personal feelings rather than of objective reality.

fan vaulting   A decorative pattern of *vault* ribs that arch out or radiate from a central point on the ceiling; popular in English *Perpendicular* architecture.

Faustian [FAU-stee-uhn]   Resembling the character Faust in Goethe's most famous work, in being spiritually tormented, insatiable for knowledge and experience, or willing to pay any price, including personal and spiritual integrity, to gain a desired end.

Fauvism [FOH-viz-uhm]   From the French "fauve," wild beast; an early-twentieth-century art movement led by Matisse and favoring exotic colors and disjointed shapes.

fête galante [fet gah-LAHNN]   In *Rococo* painting, the *theme* or scene of aristocrats being entertained or simply enjoying their leisure and other worldly pleasures.

First Great Awakening   The period of religious revivalism among Protestants that placed emphasis on a direct and personal relationship with God and undermined the traditional role and power of the established churches; centered mainly in the British American colonies during the 1730s and 1740s.

First Romanesque   The first stage of *Romanesque* architecture, about 1000–1080. First Romanesque churches had high walls, few windows, and flat wooden roofs, and were built of stone rubble and adorned with *Lombard bands* and *Lombard arcades*. Begun along the Mediterranean, in the area ranging from Dalmatia, across Northern Italy and Provence, to Catalonia.

Flamboyant style [flam-BOY-uhnt]   A Late French *Gothic* architectural style of elaborate decorations and ornamentation that produce a flamelike effect.

Florid Baroque style   A variation of the *Baroque* style specifically identified with the Catholic Church's patronage of the arts and used to glorify its beliefs.

fluting   Decorative vertical grooves carved in a column.

flying buttress   An external masonry support, found primarily in *Gothic* churches, that carries the thrust of the ceiling, or *vault*, away from the upper walls of the building to an external vertical column.

forms   In music, particular structures of arrangements of elements, such as *symphonies*, songs, concerts, and *operas*. In painting and sculpture, **form** refers to the artistic structure rather than to the material of which an artwork is made.

forum   In Rome and many Roman towns, the public place, located in the center of the town, where people gathered to socialize, transact business, and administer the government.

forte [FOR-tay]   Italian, "loud." A musical term.

fortississimo [fawrh-tis-ISS-e-moh]   In music, extremely loud; abbreviated fff.

Fourth Century style   The sculptural *style* characteristic of the last phase of the *Hellenic* period, when new interpretations of beauty and movement were adopted.

fresco   A painting done on wet or dry plaster that becomes part of the plastered wall.

friars   Members of a thirteenth-century mendicant (begging) monastic order.

frieze [FREEZ]   A band of painted designs or sculptured figures placed on walls; also, the central portion of a temple's *entablature* just above the *architrave*.

fugue [fewg]   In music, a *composition* for several instruments in which a *theme* is introduced by one instrument and then repeated by each successively entering instrument so that a complicated interweaving of themes, variations, *imitations,* and echoes results; this compositional technique began in the fifteenth century and reached its zenith in the *Baroque* period in works by Bach.

fundamentalism   Historically, an American Protestant movement that broke free of the *evangelicals* from about 1870 to 1970, stressing biblical inerrancy, "speaking in tongues," and opposition to certain modern scientific trends, such as evolution and higher criticism. Today, fundamentalism is often aggregated with *evangelicalism* and other socially conservative religious movements.

gallery   In architecture, a long, narrow passageway or corridor, usually found in churches and located above the *aisles,* and often with openings that permit viewing from above into the *nave.*

gargoyle [GAHR-goil]   In architecture, a water spout in the form of a grotesque animal or human, carved from stone, placed on the edge of a roof.

genre [ZHON-ruh]   From the French, "a kind, a type, or a class"; a category of artistic, musical, or literary composition, characterized by a particular *style, form,* or *content.*

genre subject   In art, a scene or a person from everyday life, depicted realistically and without religious or symbolic significance.

geocentrism   The belief that the earth is the center of the universe and that the sun, planets, and stars revolve around it.

ghazal [GUZ-l]   A short *lyric,* usually dealing with love, composed in a single rhyme and based on the poet's personal life and loves.

glissando [gle-SAHN-doe] (plural, **glissandi**)   In music, the blending of one *tone* into the next in scalelike passages that may be ascending or descending in character.

goliards [GOAL-yuhrds]   Medieval roaming poets or scholars who traveled about reciting poems on topics ranging from moral lessons to the pains of love.

Gospels   The first four books of the New Testament (Matthew, Mark, Luke, and John), which record the life and sayings of Jesus Christ; the word itself, from Old English, means "good news" or "good tales".

Gothic style   A *style* of architecture, usually associated with churches, that originated in northern France and whose three phases—Early, High, and Late—lasted from the twelfth to the sixteenth century. Emerging from the *Romanesque* style, Gothic is identified by pointed arches, *ribbed vaults,* stained-glass windows, *flying buttresses,* and carvings on the exterior.

Greek cross   A cross in which all the arms are of equal length; the shape used as a floor plan in many Greek or Eastern Orthodox churches.

Gregorian chant   A style of *monophonic* church music sung in unison and without instrumental accompaniment and used in the *liturgy;* named for Pope Gregory I (590–604).

groined vault, or cross vault   A ceiling, or *vault,* created when two *barrel vaults,* set at right angles, intersect.

happening   A *Late Modern* theatrical development, combining skits with outrageous events and involving performances by painters, actors, musicians, and audience members, so as to give the impression of spontaneity.

hard-edge In *Late Modern* painting, a technique used in color paintings, by which the areas of *color* are precisely delineated from one another.

harmony The simultaneous combination of two or more *tones,* producing a chord; generally, the chordal characteristics of a work and the way chords interact.

heliocentrism The belief that the sun is the center of the universe and that the earth and the other planets revolve around it.

Hellenic [hell-LENN-ik] Relating to the time period in Greek civilization from 480 to 323 B.C.E., when the most influential Greek artists, playwrights, and philosophers, such as Praxiteles, Sophocles, and Plato, created their greatest works; associated with the *Classical* style.

Hellenistic [hell-uh-NIS-tik] Relating to the time period from about 323 to 31 B.C.E., when Greek and oriental or Middle Eastern cultures and institutions intermingled to create a heterogeneous and *cosmopolitan civilization.*

hieroglyphs [HI-uhr-uh-glifs] Pictorial characters used in Egyptian writing, which is known as hieroglyphics.

High Classical style The *style* in Greek sculpture associated with the ideal physical form and perfected during the zenith of the Athenian Empire, about 450–400 B.C.E.

higher criticism A rational approach to Bible study, developed in German Protestant circles in the nineteenth century, that treated the biblical *scriptures* as literature and subjected them to close scrutiny, testing their literary history, authorship, and meaning.

High Renaissance The period from about 1495 to 1520, often associated with the patronage of the popes in Rome, when the most influential artists and writers of the *Renaissance,* including Michelangelo, Raphael, Leonardo da Vinci, and Machiavelli, were producing their greatest works.

high tech In architecture, a *style* that uses obvious industrial design elements with exposed parts serving as decorations.

hip hop In *Post-Modern* popular culture, after 1970, an eclectic trend among African Americans and Hispanic Americans, drawing on break dancing, graffiti art, rap rhyming, and disc jockeys playing with turntables and "scratch" effects; highly influential on today's youth culture, popular music, film, and dance styles.

holiness A nineteenth-century American Protestant movement, which came out of the Methodist tradition, emphasizing holy living and the need to be "born again" as a true disciple of Jesus Christ; part of the *fundamentalist* movement after 1870.

Homeric epithet A recurring nickname, such as "Ox-eyed Hera," used in Homer's *Iliad* or *Odyssey.*

homo faber Latin, "human fabricator"; an anthropological term used to describe humans as creators of tools and machines.

hubris [HYOO-bris] In Greek thought, human pride or arrogance that leads an individual to challenge the gods, usually provoking divine retribution.

humanism An attitude that is concerned with humanity, its achievements, and its potential; the study of the *humanities;* in the *Renaissance,* identified with *studia humanitatis.*

humanities In the nineteenth century, the study of Greek and Roman languages and literature; later set off from the sciences and expanded to include the works of all Western peoples in the arts, literature, music, philosophy, and sometimes history and religion; in *Post-Modernism* extended to a global dimension.

hymn From the Greek and Latin, "ode of praise of gods or heroes"; a song of praise or thanksgiving to God or the gods, performed both with and without instrumental accompaniment.

idealism In Plato's philosophy, the theory that reality and ultimate truth are to be found not in the material world but in the spiritual realm.

idée fixe [ee-DAY FEEX] French, "fixed idea"; in music, a recurring musical *theme* that is associated with a person or a concept.

ideogram [ID-e-uh-gram] A picture drawn to represent an idea or a concept.

idyll A relatively short poem that focuses on events and *themes* of everyday life, such as family, love, and religion; popular in the *Hellenistic Age* and a standard form that has been periodically revived in Western literature throughout the centuries.

illuminated manuscript A richly decorated book, painted with brilliant colors and gold leaf, usually of sacred writings; popular in the West in the Middle Ages.

illusionism The use of painting techniques in *Florid Baroque* art to create the appearance that decorated areas are part of the surrounding architecture, usually employed in ceiling decorations.

imitation In music, a technique in which a musical idea, or motif, is presented by one voice or instrument and is then followed immediately by a restatement by another voice or instrument; the effect is that of a musical relay race.

impasto [ihm-PAHS-toe] In painting, the application of thick layers of pigment.

Impressionism In painting, a *style* introduced in the 1870s, marked by an attempt to catch spontaneous impressions, often involving the play of sunlight on ordinary events and scenes observed outdoors; in music, a style of *composition* designed to create a vague and dreamy mood through gliding melodies and shimmering *tone colors.*

impressionistic In art, relating to the representation of a scene using the simplest details to create an illusion of reality by evoking subjective impressions rather than aiming for a totally realistic effect; characterized by images that are insubstantial and barely sketched in.

incunabula (singular, **incunabulum**) The collection of books printed before 1500 C.E.

inductive reasoning The process of reasoning from particulars to the general or from single parts to the whole and/or final conclusion.

installation art A boundary-challenging type of art born in the 1960s that creates architectural tableaux, using objects drawn from and making references to artistic sources (such as music, painting, sculpture, and theater) and the workaday world (such as everyday tasks, media images, and foodstuffs) and that may include a human presence. Associated with the work of Ann Hamilton.

International style In twentieth-century architecture, a *style* and method of construction that capitalized on modern materials, such as ferro-concrete, glass, and steel, and that produced the popular "glass box" skyscrapers and variously shaped private houses.

Ionic The Greek architectural order, developed in Ionia, in which columns are slender, sit on a base, and have *capitals* decorated with scrolls.

isorhythm In music, a unifying method based on rhythmic patterns rather than *melodic* patterns.

Italo-Byzantine style [ih-TAL-o-BIZ-uhn-teen] The *style* of Italian *Gothic* painting that reflected the influence of *Byzantine* paintings, *mosaics,* and icons.

iwan [eye-van]   In Islamic architecture, a vaulted hall. In the 4-*iwan mosque,* one *iwan* was used for prayers and the other three for study or rest.

jazz   A type of music, instrumental and vocal, originating in the African American community and rooted in African, African American, and Western musical forms and traditions.

Jesuits [JEZH-oo-its]   Members of the Society of Jesus, the best-organized and most effective monastic order founded during the *Counter-Reformation* to combat Protestantism and spread Roman Catholicism around the world.

jihad [JEE-HAD]   Originally, this Arabic term meant "to strive" or "to struggle" and, as such, was identified with any pious Muslim combating sin and trying not to do evil. In modern times, radical Islamic states and groups have given the term new meaning as "Holy War" and have used it to justify military and other violent action against their enemies. A central belief in Islam.

key   In music, a tonal system consisting of seven *tones* in fixed relationship to a tonic, or keynote. Since the *Renaissance, key* has been the structural foundation of the bulk of Western music, down to the *Modernist* period.

keystone   The central stone at the top of an arch that locks the other stones in place.

koine [KOI-nay]   A colloquial Greek language spoken in the *Hellenistic* world that helped tie together that *civilization.*

kore [KOH-ray]   An *Archaic* Greek standing statue of a young draped female.

kouros [KOO-rus]   An *Archaic* Greek standing statue of a young naked male.

Late Gothic style   A *style* characterized in architecture by ornate decoration and tall cathedral windows and spires and in painting and sculpture by increased refinement of details and a trend toward naturalism; popular in the fourteenth and fifteenth centuries in central and western Europe.

Late Mannerism   The last stage of the *Mannerist* movement, characterized by exaggeration and distortion, especially in painting.

Late Modernism   The last stage of *Modernism,* characterized by an increasing sense of existential despair, an attraction to non-Western cultures, and extreme experimentalism.

lay   A short *lyric* or narrative poem meant to be sung to the accompaniment of an instrument such as a harp; based on Celtic legends but usually set in feudal times and focused on courtly love *themes,* especially adulterous passion. The oldest surviving lays are those of the twelfth-century poet Marie de France.

leitmotif [LITE-mo-teef]   In music, and especially in Wagner's *operas,* the use of recurring *themes* associated with particular characters, objects, or ideas.

liberalism   In political thought, a set of beliefs advocating certain personal, economic, and natural rights based on assumptions about the perfectibility and autonomy of human beings and the notion of progress, as first expressed in the writings of John Locke.

liberation theology   A reform movement, which began in the late 1960s among Roman Catholic priests and nuns in Latin America, blending Christian teachings on social and economic justice with Marxist theory. After this movement went global, the Vatican withdrew its support in the 1980s, though liberation theology remains an underground force in some parts of the world today.

libretto [lih-BRET-oh]   In Italian, "little book"; the text or words of an *opera,* an *oratorio,* or a musical work of a similar dramatic nature involving a written text.

line   The mark—straight or curved, thick or thin, light or dark—made by the artist in a work of art.

Linear A   In Minoan *civilization,* a type of script still undeciphered that lasted from about 1800 to 1400 B.C.E.

Linear B   In Minoan *civilization,* an early form of Greek writing that flourished on Crete from about 1400 until about 1300 B.C.E. and lasted in a few scattered places on the Greek mainland until about 1150 B.C.E.; used to record commercial transactions.

liturgical drama   Religious dramas, popular between the twelfth and sixteenth centuries, based on biblical stories with musical accompaniment that were staged in the area in front of the church, performed at first in Latin but later in the *vernacular languages;* the mystery plays (*mystery* is derived from the Latin for "action") are the most famous type of liturgical drama.

liturgy   A rite or ritual, such as prayers or ceremonies, practiced by a religious group in public worship.

local color   In literature, the use of detail peculiar to a particular region and environment to add interest and authenticity to a narrative, including description of the locale, customs, speech, and music. Local color was an especially popular development in American literature in the late nineteenth century.

logical positivism   A school of modern philosophy that seeks truth by defining terms and clarifying statements and asserts that metaphysical theories are meaningless.

logos [LOWG-os]   In *Stoicism,* the name for the supreme being or for reason—the controlling principle of the universe—believed to be present both in nature and in each human being.

Lombard arcades   In architecture, a sequence of decorative *arcades* beneath the eaves of a building. First used in churches in Lombardy (North Central Italy). A defining feature of the *First Romanesque.*

Lombard bands   In architecture, a web of vertical bands or buttresses along the sides of a building. First used in churches in Lombardy (North Central Italy). A defining feature of the *First Romanesque.*

luminism   In nineteenth-century American landscape painting, a group of artists, who were inspired by the vastness of the American west and influenced by *Transcendentalism,* approached their work by consciously removing themselves from their paintings.

lute   In music, a wooden instrument, plucked or bowed, consisting of a sound box with an elaborately carved sound hole and a neck across which the (often twelve) strings pass. Introduced during the High Middle Ages, the lute enjoyed a height of popularity in Europe from the seventeenth to eighteenth century.

Lutheranism   The doctrine, *liturgy,* and institutional structure of the church founded in the sixteenth century by Martin Luther, who stressed the authority of the Bible, the faith of the individual, and the worshiper's direct communication with God as the bases of his new religion.

lyre   In music, a handheld stringed instrument, with or without a sound box, used by ancient Egyptians, Assyrians, and Greeks. In Greek culture, the lyre was played to accompany song and recitation.

lyric   A short subjective poem that expresses intense personal emotion.

lyric poetry   In Greece, verses sung and accompanied by the *lyre;* today, intensely personal poetry.

Machiavellianism [mahk-ih-uh-VEL-ih-uhn-iz-uhm]   The view that politics should be separated from morals and dedicated to the achievement of desired ends through any means necessary ("the end justifies the means"); derived from the political writings of Machiavelli.

madrasah [mah-DRASS-ah]   An Arabic term meaning a religious school for advanced study; a forerunner of the Islamic university. Today, *madrasahs* are schools for Islamic youth, and their curriculum is based on the *Qur'an.*

madrigal [MAD-rih-guhl]   A *polyphonic* song performed without accompaniment and based on a secular text, often a love *lyric;* especially popular in the sixteenth century.

maenad [MEE-nad]   A woman who worshiped Dionysus, often in a state of frenzy.

magic realism   A literary and artistic *style* identified with Latin American *Post-Modernism* that mixes realistic and supernatural elements to create imaginary or fantastic scenes.

Mannerism   A cultural movement between 1520 and 1600 that grew out of a rebellion against the *Renaissance's* artistic norms of symmetry and balance; characterized in art by distortion and incongruity and in thought and literature by the belief that human nature is depraved.

maqamah [mah-kah-mah]   In Arabic, "assembly." A Muslim literary *genre,* intended for educated readers, that recounted stories of rogues and con men; filled with wordplay, humor, and keen usage of Arabic language and grammar. Created by al-Hamadhani in the tenth century.

Mass   In religion, the ritual celebrating the Eucharist, or Holy Communion, primarily in the Roman Catholic Church. The Mass has two parts, the Ordinary and the Proper; the former remains the same throughout the church year, whereas the latter changes for each date and service. The Mass Ordinary is composed of the Kyrie, Gloria, Credo, Sanctus, and Agnus Dei; the Mass Proper includes the Introit, Gradual, Alleluia or Tract, Sequence, Offertory, and Communion. In music, a musical setting of certain parts of the Mass, especially the Kyrie, Gloria, Credo, Sanctus, Benedictus, and Agnus Dei. The first complete Mass Ordinary was composed by Guillaume de Machaut [mah-SHOH] (about 1300–1377) in the fourteenth century.

mass culture   The tastes, values, and interests of the classes that dominate modern industrialized society, especially the consumer-oriented American middle class.

medallion   In Roman architecture, a circular decoration often found on triumphal arches enclosing a scene or portrait; in more general architectural use, a tablet or panel in a wall or window containing a figure or an ornament.

medium   The material from which an artwork is made.

melody   A succession of musical *tones* having a distinctive shape and rhythm.

melisma   In music, in *plainsong,* a style of singing in which a group of notes is sung to the same syllable; the opposite of *syllabic* singing.

Messiah   A Hebrew word meaning "the anointed one," or one chosen by God to be his representative on earth; in Judaism, a savior who will come bringing peace and justice; in Christianity, Jesus Christ (*Christ* is derived from a Greek word meaning "the anointed one").

metope [MET-uh-pee]   In architecture, a panel, often decorated, between two *triglyphs* on the *entablature* of a *Doric* Greek temple.

mezzotint   Also known as half-tone. An early type of color print, made with a metal plate, characterized by subtle gradations of shadings and clear definition of *line;* developed in about 1650 in the Netherlands.

microtone   In music, an interval, or distance between a sound (pitch) on a scale, that is smaller than a semi*tone*—the smallest interval in mainstream Western music prior to *jazz.* Muslim music uses a microtonal system.

minaret   In Islamic architecture, a tall, slender tower with a pointed top, from which the daily calls to prayer are delivered; located near a *mosque.*

minbar [min-bar]   In Muslim *mosque* architecture, a pulpit with steps, sometimes on wheels for portability; used by a cleric for leading prayers and giving sermons.

miniature   A small painting, usually of a religious nature, found in *illuminated manuscripts;* also, a small portrait.

minimalism   A trend in *Late Modern* and *Post-Modern* art, architecture, and music which found beauty in the bare essentials and thus stripped art, buildings, and music to their basic elements. The minimalist aesthetic was a strong influence in the architecture of Mies van der Rohe, many art styles, including *conceptual art, environmental art,* and *Op Art,* and the music of Philip Glass.

minstrel   A professional entertainer of the twelfth to the seventeenth century; especially a secular musician; also called "jongleur."

minuet and trio   In music, a *Classical* music form, based on two French court dances of the same name, dating from the seventeenth and eighteenth centuries; often paired in the third section of *symphonies* in the *Classical* period. Typically, the minuet was in ¾ time and with a moderate *tempo,* while the trio provided contrast but had no standard form.

Modernism   A late-nineteenth- and twentieth-century cultural, artistic, and literary movement that rejected much of the past and focused on the current, the secular, and the revolutionary in search of new forms of expression; the dominant style of the twentieth century until 1970. In Roman Catholic Church history, *Modernism* was a liberal movement among progressive churchpeople, 1850 to 1910, which applied new findings in history, philosophy, and psychology to traditional church teachings; condemned by the Vatican in 1907.

modes   A series of musical *scales* devised by the Greeks and believed by them to create certain emotional or ethical effects on the listener.

monophony [muh-NOF-uh-nee]   A *style* of music in which there is only a single line of melody; the *Gregorian chants* are the most famous examples of monophonic music.

monotheism   From the Greek *monos,* single, alone, and the Greek *theos,* god; the belief that there is only one God.

mood   In music, the emotional impact of a *composition* on the feelings of a listener.

mosaic   An art form or decoration, usually on a wall or a floor, created by inlaying small pieces of glass, shell, or stone in cement or plaster to create pictures or patterns.

mosque   A Muslim place of worship, often distinguished by a dome-shaped central building placed in an open space surrounded by a wall.

motet   A multivoiced song with words of a sacred or secular text, usually sung without accompanying instruments; developed in the thirteenth century.

mural   A wall painting, usually quite large, used to decorate a private or public structure.

muse   In Greek religion, any one of the nine sister goddesses who preside over the creative arts and sciences.

music drama   An *opera* in which the action and music are continuous, not broken up into separate *arias* and *recitatives,* and the music is determined by its dramatic appropriateness, producing a work in which music, words, and staging are fused; the term was coined by Wagner.

narrative voice In literature, the *narrator*, a key element in fiction. An omniscient narrator, usually in the third person, knows everything about the *plot* and *characters*, regardless of time and place—typical of nineteenth-century novels. In *Modernist* fiction, the narrative voice tends to be disjointed, unreliable, and often in the first person.

narrator The speaker whose voice we hear in a story or poem.

narthex The porch or vestibule of a church, usually enclosed, through which worshipers walk before entering the *nave*.

Naturalism In literature, a late-nineteenth-century movement inspired by the methods of science and the insights of sociology, concerned with an objective depiction of the ugly side of industrial society.

natural law In *Stoicism* and later in other philosophies, a body of laws or principles that are believed to be derived from nature and binding on human society and that constitute a higher form of justice than civil or judicial law.

natural philosophy Science based on philosophical speculation and experiments or data, founded in Ionian Greece in the sixth century B.C.E.; a term that embraced both science and philosophy until about 1800 C.E.

nave The central longitudinal area of a church, extending from the entrance to the *apse* and flanked by *aisles*.

Neoclassical style In the late eighteenth century, an artistic and literary movement that emerged as a reaction to the *Rococo* style and that sought inspiration from ancient *Classicism*. In the twentieth century, between 1919 and 1951, *Neoclassicism* in music was a style that rejected the emotionalism favored by *Romantic* composers as well as the dense orchestral sounds of the *Impressionists;* instead, it borrowed features from seventeenth- and eighteenth-century music and practiced the ideals of balance, clarity of texture, and nonprogrammatic works.

Neoclassicism In the late third century B.C.E., an artistic movement in the disintegrating *Hellenistic* world that sought inspiration in the Athenian Golden Age of the fifth and fourth centuries B.C.E.; and, since 1970, *Neoclassicism* has been a highly visible submovement in *Post-Modernism*, particularly prominent in painting and architecture, that restates the principles of *Classical* art—balance, harmony, idealism.

Neoexpressionism A submovement in *Post-Modernism*, associated primarily with painting, that offers social criticism and is concerned with the expression of the artist's feelings.

Neolithic Literally, "new stone"; used to define the New Stone Age, when human *cultures* evolved into agrarian systems and settled communities; dating from about 10,000 or 8000 B.C.E. to about 3000 B.C.E.

Neo-orthodoxy A twentieth-century Protestant movement, dedicated to recentering orthodox theology in Christian thought and emphasizing the central role played by God in history. Founded after World War I in opposition to the *Social Gospel*.

Neo-Platonism A philosophy based on Plato's ideas that was developed during the Roman period in an attempt to reconcile the dichotomy between Plato's concept of an eternal World of Ideas and the ever-changing physical world; in the fifteenth-century *Renaissance*, it served as a philosophical guide for Italian humanists who sought to reconcile Late Medieval Christian beliefs with *Classical* thinking.

Neorealism A submovement in *Post-Modernism* that is based on a photographic sense of detail and harks back to many of the qualities of nineteenth-century *Realism*.

Neoromanticism A *Post-Modern* movement in music, starting after 1970, which rejects *atonality* and draws inspiration from the music of the *Romantic* period.

New Comedy The style of comedy favored by *Hellenistic* playwrights, concentrating on gentle satirical *themes*—in particular, romantic *plots* with stock *characters* and predictable endings.

nihilism The denial of any objective ground of truth, and, in particular, of moral truths.

Nominalism [NAHM-uh-nuhl-iz-uhm] In medieval thought, the school that held that objects were separate unto themselves but could, for convenience, be treated in a collective sense because they shared certain characteristics; opposed to *Realism*.

Northern Renaissance The sixteenth-century cultural movement in northern Europe that was launched by the northward spread of Italian *Renaissance* art, culture, and ideals. The Northern Renaissance differed from the Italian Renaissance largely because of the persistence of the *Late Gothic style* and the unfolding of the *Reformation* after 1520.

Nouvelle Vague French, "New Wave"; a *Late Modern* movement in French film, featuring innovative narrative structures and various experimental cinematic techniques. French word for "New Wave" films in the post–World War II period which experimented with new ways to capture scenes and events.

octave In music, usually the eight-tone interval between a note and a second note of the same name, as in C to C.

oculus [AHK-yuh-lus] The circular opening at the top of a dome; derived from the Latin word for "eye."

Old Comedy The style of *comedy* established by Aristophanes in the fifth century B.C.E., distinguished by a strong element of political and social satire.

oligarchy From the Greek *oligos*, "few"; a state ruled by the few, especially by a small fraction of persons or families.

Olympian deities In Greek religion, sky gods and goddesses who lived on mountaintops and were worshiped mainly by the Greek aristocracy.

Op Art A *Late Modern* art movement, using *abstract*, mathematically based forms to create stimulating images for the eyes, such as optical patterns, lingering images, and whirling effects.

opera A drama or play set to music and consisting of vocal pieces with *orchestral* accompaniment; acting, scenery, and sometimes *choruses* and dancing are used to heighten the dramatic values of operas.

oratorio A choral work based on religious events or *scripture* employing singers, *choruses*, and *orchestra*, but without scenery or staging and performed usually in a church or a concert hall.

orchestra In Greek theaters, the circular area where the *chorus* performed in front of the audience; in music, a group of instrumentalists, including string players, who play together.

organum [OR-guh-nuhm] In the ninth through the thirteenth centuries, a simple and early form of *polyphonic* music consisting of a main *melody* sung along with a *Gregorian chant*; by the thirteenth century it had developed into a complex multivoiced song.

Orientalizing A phase of Greek art, particularly Greek vase painting, lasting from about 700 to 530 B.C.E., which drew inspiration from Near Eastern art, including artistic techniques, vessel forms, decorative motifs, and subjects.

Paleolithic Literally, "old stone"; used to define the Old Stone Age, when crude stones and tools were used; dating from about 2,000,000 B.C.E. to about 10,000 B.C.E.

pantheism The doctrine of or belief in multitudes of deities found in nature; a recurrent belief since prehistoric times. Prominent in nineteenth-century Romanticism.

pantomime In Roman times, enormous dramatic productions featuring instrumental music and dances, favored by the masses; later, a type of dramatic or dancing performance in which the story is told with expressive or even exaggerated bodily and facial movements.

paradigm shift The exchange of one worldview or perspective for another, as, for example, the shift from earth-centered astronomy to sun-centered astronomy between 1550 and 1700; a **paradigm** is an unconsciously agreed-on pattern of thought in a scientific discipline and, by extension, any shared set of beliefs and habits of thought; a term coined by Thomas Kuhn.

parchment A writing surface, prepared from calf-, sheep-, and goatskins, developed in ancient Pergamum. Parchment's supple surface allowed the storing of writing on both sides of a page and thus opened the door to the first books.

pastoral A type of *Hellenistic* poetry that idealized rural customs and farming, especially the simple life of shepherds, and deprecated urban living.

pavane [puh-VAHN] A sixteenth- and seventeenth-century English court dance of Italian origin; the dance is performed by couples to stately music. Ravel based *Pavane for a Dead Princess* (1899) on this *Baroque* dance form.

pediment In *Classical*-style architecture, the triangular-shaped area or gable at the end of the building formed by the sloping roof and the *cornice.*

pendentive [pen-DEN-tiv] In architecture, a triangular, concave-shaped section of *vaulting* between the rim of a dome and the pair of arches that support it; used in Byzantine and Islamic architecture.

performance art A democratic type of mixed-media art born in the 1960s that ignores artistic boundaries, mixing high art (such as music, painting, and theater) and popular art (such as rock and roll, film, and fads), to create a unique, nonreproducible, artistic experience. Associated with the work of Laurie Anderson.

peristyle [PAIR-uh-stile] A colonnade around an open courtyard or a building.

Perpendicular style The highly decorative *style* of *Late Gothic* architecture that developed in England at the same time as the *Late Gothic* on the European continent.

Persian miniature A style of *miniature* painting that flourished in Persia from the thirteenth to the seventeenth century; characterized by rectangular designs, the depiction of the human figure as about one-fifth the height of the painting, and refined detail.

perspective A technique or formula for creating the illusion or appearance of depth and distance on a two-dimensional surface. **Atmospheric perspective** is achieved in many ways: by diminishing color intensity, by omitting detail, and by blurring the lines of an object. **Linear perspective,** based on mathematical calculations, is achieved by having parallel lines or lines of projection appearing to converge at a single point, known as the *vanishing point,* on the horizon of the flat surface and by diminishing distant objects in size according to scale to make them appear to recede from the viewer.

philosophes [FEEL-uh-sawfs] A group of European thinkers and writers who popularized the ideas of the *Enlightenment* through essays, novels, plays, and other works, hoping to change the climate of opinion and bring about social and political reform.

phonogram A symbol used to represent a syllable, a word, or a sound.

Physiocrats [FIZ-ih-uh-kratz] A group of writers, primarily French, who dealt with economic issues during the *Enlightenment,* in particular calling for improved agricultural productivity and questioning the state's role in economic affairs.

piano Italian, "soft." In music, softly. Also, the usual term for *pianoforte.*

pianissimo Italian, "very softly," a musical term.

pianoforte [pee-an-o-FOR-tay] A piano; derived from the Italian for "soft/loud," terms used to describe the two types of sound emitted by a stringed instrument whose wires are struck with felt-covered hammers operated from a keyboard.

picaresque novel From the Spanish term for "rogue." A type of literature, originating in sixteenth-century Spain, that recounted the comic misadventures of a roguish hero who lived by his wits, often at the expense of the high and mighty; influenced novel writing across Europe, especially in England, France, and Germany, until about 1800; the anonymous *Lazarillo de Tormes* (1554) was the first picaresque novel.

pictogram A carefully drawn, often stylized, picture that represents a particular object.

pier In architecture, a vertical masonry structure that may support a *vault,* an arch, or a roof; in *Gothic* churches, piers were often clustered together to form massive supports.

Pietà [pee-ay-TAH] A painting or sculpture depicting the mourning Virgin and the dead Christ.

Pietism A religious reform movement among German Lutherans, which stressed personal piety, along with support for social programs for the poor; part of the general religious ferment of western Europe in the late 1600s and early 1700s and a catalyst for the *First Great Awakening* in British Colonial America in the 1700s.

pilaster [pih-LAS-tuhr] In architecture, a vertical, rectangular decorative device projecting from a wall that gives the appearance of a column with a base and a *capital;* sometimes called an applied column.

Pinteresque In the theater, a dramatic style, attributed to the British playwright Harold Pinter; characterized by enigmatic *plots* and, especially, long pauses in the dialogue.

Platonism The collective beliefs and arguments presented in Plato's writings stressing especially that actual things are copies of ideas.

plainsong Also called *plainchant.* In music, the *monophonic* chant sung in the *liturgy* of the Roman Catholic Church.

plot The action, or arrangement of incidents, in a story.

podium In architecture, a low wall serving as a foundation; a platform.

poetry Language that is concentrated and imaginative, marked by meter, rhythm, rhyme, and imagery.

Pointillism [PWANT-il-iz-uhm] Also known as Divisionism, a *style* of painting, perfected by Seurat, in which tiny dots of paint are applied to the canvas in such a way that when they are viewed from a distance they merge and blend to form recognizable objects with natural effects of color, light, and shade.

polyphony [puh-LIF-uh-nee] A style of musical *composition* in which two or more voices or melodic lines are woven together.

polytheism [PAHL-e-the-iz-uhm]   The doctrine of or belief in more than one deity.

Pop Art   An artistic *style* popular between 1960 and 1970 in which commonplace commercial objects drawn from *mass culture,* such as soup cans, fast foods, and comic strips, became the subjects of art.

portico   In architecture, a covered entrance to a building, usually with a separate roof supported by columns.

post-and-lintel construction   A basic architectural form in which upright posts, or columns, support a horizontal lintel, or beam.

post-beam-triangle construction   The generic name given to Greek architecture that includes the post, or column; the beam, or lintel; and the triangular-shaped area, or *pediment.*

Post-Impressionism   A late-nineteenth-century artistic movement that extended the boundaries of *Impressionism* in new directions to focus on structure, composition, fantasy, and subjective expression.

Post-Modernism   An artistic, cultural, and intellectual movement, originating in about 1970, that is more optimistic than *Modernism,* embraces an open-ended and democratic global *civilization,* freely adapts elements of high culture and *mass culture,* and manifests itself chiefly through revivals of earlier styles, giving rise to *Neoclassicism, Neoexpressionism,* and *Neorealism.*

Post-Structuralism   In analytical theory, a set of techniques, growing out of *structuralism,* which were used to show that meaning is shifting and unstable.

Praxitelean curve [prak-sit-i-LEE-an]   The graceful line of the sculptured body in the *contrapposto* stance, perfected by the *Fourth Century style* sculptor Praxiteles.

primitivism   In painting, the "primitives" are those painters of the Netherlandish and Italian schools who flourished before 1500, thus all Netherlandish painters between the van Eycks and Dürer and all Italian painters between Giotto and Raphael; more generally, the term reflects modern artists' fascination with non-Western art forms, as in Gauguin's Tahitian-inspired paintings. In literature, primitivism has complex meanings; on the one hand, it refers to the notion of a golden age, a world of lost innocence, which appeared in both ancient pagan and Christian writings; on the other hand, it is a modern term used to denote two species of cultural relativism, which either finds people isolated from civilization to be superior to those living in civilized and urban settings, as in the cult of the Noble Savage (Rousseau), or respects native peoples and their cultures within their own settings, yet accepts that natives can be as cruel as Europeans (the view expressed by Montaigne).

problem play   A type of drama that focuses on a specific social problem; the Swedish playwright Ibsen was a pioneer of this *genre,* as in *A Doll's House* (1879), concerning women's independence.

program music   Instrumental music that depicts a narrative, portrays a *setting,* or suggests a sequence of events; often based on other sources, such as a poem or a play.

prose   The ordinary language used in speaking and writing.

proverb   A pithy saying, thought to convey folk wisdom or a general truth.

Puritanism   The beliefs and practices of the Puritans, a small but influential religious group devoted to the teachings of John Calvin; they stressed strict rules of personal and public behavior and practiced their beliefs in England and the New World during the seventeenth century.

putti [POOH-tee]   Italian, plural of *putto;* in painting and sculpture, figures of babies, children, or sometimes angels.

qasida [kah-SEE-dah]   In Arabic, "ode." An ode composed in varied meters and with a single rhyme; that is, all lines end in the same rhyming sound. The leading poetic *genre* in Muslim literature.

qiblah [kee-blah]   In Islamic *mosque* architecture, a niche, often richly decorated, pointing the direction for prayer, that is, toward the Kaaba in Mecca.

ragtime   A type of instrumental music, popularized by African Americans in the late nineteenth and early twentieth centuries, with a strongly syncopated rhythm and a lively *melody.*

Rayonnant [ray-yo-NAHNN]   A decorative *style* in French architecture associated with the High *Gothic* period, in which walls were replaced by sheets of *stained glass* framed by elegant stone *traceries.* Also called *Radiant.*

Realism   In medieval philosophy, the school that asserted that objects contained common or universal qualities that were not always apparent to the human senses but that were more real or true than the objects' physical attributes; opposed to *Nominalism.* In art and literature, a mid- to late-nineteenth-century style that focused on the everyday lives of the middle and lower classes, portraying their world in a serious, accurate, and unsentimental way; opposed to *Romanticism.*

recitative [ress-uh-tuh-TEEV]   In music, a rhythmically free but often stylized declamation, midway between singing and ordinary speech, that serves as a transition between *arias* or as a narrative device in an *opera.*

Reformation   The sixteenth-century religious movement that looked back to the ideals of early Christianity, called for moral and structural changes in the church, and led ultimately to the founding of the various Protestant churches.

refrain   In music, a recurring musical passage or phrase; called *ritornello* in Italian.

regalia   Plural in form, often used with a singular verb. The emblems and symbols of royalty, as the crown and scepter.

relief   In sculpture, figures or forms that are carved so that they project from the flat surface of a stone or metal background. **High relief** projects sharply from the surface; **low relief,** or **bas relief,** is more shallow.

Renaissance [ren-uh-SAHNS]   From the French for "rebirth"; the artistic, cultural, and intellectual movement marked by a revival of *Classical* and *humanistic* values that began in Italy in the mid-fourteenth century and had spread across Europe by the mid-sixteenth century.

representational art   Art that presents a likeness of the world as it appears to the naked eye.

Restrained Baroque style   A variation of the *Baroque* style identified with Dutch and English architects and painters who wanted to reduce *Baroque* grandeur and exuberance to a more human scale.

revenge tragedy   A type of play popular in sixteenth-century England, probably rooted in Roman *tragedies* and concerned with the need for a family to seek revenge for the murder of a relative.

ribbed vault   A masonry roof with a framework of arches or ribs that reinforce and decorate the *vault* ceiling.

rocaille [roh-KYE]   In *Rococo* design, the stucco ornaments shaped like leaves, flowers, and ribbons that decorate walls and ceilings.

Rococo style [ruh-KOH-koh]   An artistic and cultural *style* that grew out of the *Baroque* style but that was more intimate and personal and emphasized the frivolous and superficial side of aristocratic life.

romance A story derived from legends associated with Troy or Celtic culture but often set in feudal times and centered on *themes* of licit and illicit love between noble lords and ladies.

Romanesque style [roh-muhn-ESK] A *style* of architecture, usually associated with churches built in the eleventh and twelfth centuries, that was inspired by Roman architectural features, such as the *basilica,* and was thus Roman-like. Romanesque buildings were massive, with round arches and *barrel* or *groined vault* ceilings, and had less exterior decoration than *Gothic* churches.

Romanticism An intellectual, artistic, and literary movement that began in the late eighteenth century as a reaction to *Neoclassicism* and stressed the emotional, mysterious, and imaginative side of human behavior and the unruly side of nature.

rondeau [RON-doh], pl. (rondeaux) A French verse form, consisting of 13 lines, or sometimes 10 lines, dating from the Late Middle Ages.

rose window A large circular window, made of *stained glass* and held together with lead and carved stones set in patterns, or *tracery,* and located over an entrance in a *Gothic cathedral.*

sacred music Religious music, such as Gregorian chants, *masses,* and hymns.

sarcophagus [sahr-KAHF-uh-guhs] (plural, **sarcophagi**) From the Greek meaning "flesh-eating stone"; a marble or stone coffin or tomb, usually decorated with carvings, used first by Romans and later by Christians for burial of the dead.

satire From the Latin, "medley"—a cooking term; a literary *genre* that originated in ancient Rome and was characterized by two basic forms: (a) tolerant and amused observation of the human scene, modeled on Horace's style, and (b) bitter and sarcastic denunciation of all behavior and thought outside a civilized norm, modeled on Juvenal's style. In modern times, a literary work that holds up human vices and follies to ridicule or scorn.

satyr-play [SAT-uhr] A comic play, often featuring sexual *themes,* performed at the Greek drama festivals along with the *tragedies.*

scale A set pattern of *tones* (or notes) arranged from low to high.

scenographic [see-nuh-GRAF-ik] In *Renaissance* architecture, a building style that envisioned buildings as composed of separate units; in the painting of stage scenery, the art of *perspective* representation.

scherzo [SKER-tso] From the Italian for "joke"; a quick and lively instrumental *composition* or movement found in *sonatas* and *symphonies.*

scholasticism In medieval times, the body or collection of knowledge that tried to harmonize Aristotle's writings with Christian doctrine; also, a way of thinking and establishing sets of arguments.

Scientific Revolution The seventeenth-century intellectual movement, based originally on discoveries in astronomy and physics, that challenged and overturned medieval views about the order of the universe and the theories used to explain motion.

scripture The sacred writings of any religion, as the Bible in Judaism and Christianity.

Second Romanesque The second and mature stage of *Romanesque* architecture, about 1080–1200. Second Romanesque churches were richly decorated and built on a vast scale, including such features as double *transepts,* double *aisles,* crossing towers, and towers at the ends of the *transepts;* associated with Cluniac monasticism.

secular music Nonreligious music, such as *symphonies,* songs, and dances.

serenade In music, a lighthearted piece, intended to be performed outdoors in the evening; popular in the eighteenth and nineteenth centuries.

serial music A type of musical composition based on a *twelve-tone scale* arranged any way the composer chooses; the absence of a tonal center in serial music leads to *atonality.*

setting In literature, the background against which the action takes place; in a representational artwork, the time and place depicted.

Severe style The first sculptural style of the *Classical* period in Greece, which retained stylistic elements from the *Archaic* style.

sfumato [sfoo-MAH-toh] In painting, the blending of one *tone* into another to blur the outline of a form and give the canvas a smokelike appearance; a technique perfected by Leonardo da Vinci.

shaft graves Deep pit burial sites; the dead were usually placed at the bottom of the shafts; a burial practice in Mycenaean Greece.

skene [SKEE-nee] A small building behind the *orchestra* in a Greek theater, used as a prop and as a storehouse for theatrical materials.

Skepticism A *Hellenistic* philosophy that questioned whether anything could be known for certain, argued that all beliefs were relative, and concluded that *autarky* could be achieved only by recognizing that inquiry was fruitless.

slave narrative A literary *genre,* either written by slaves or told by slaves to secretaries, which emerged prior to the American Civil War; the genre was launched by the *Narrative of the Life of Frederick Douglass, an American Slave* (1845); the harsh details of the inhumane and unjust slave system, as reported in these narratives, contributed to *Realist* literature.

social contract In political thought, an agreement or contract between the people and their rulers defining the rights and duties of each so that a civil society might be created.

Social Gospel A Protestant movement, mainly in the United States, whose heyday was from 1880 to 1945, which stressed social improvement rather than personal piety; the religious equivalent of *liberal* politics.

socialism An economic and political system in which goods and property are owned collectively or by the state; the socialist movement began as a reaction to the excesses of the factory system in the nineteenth century and ultimately called for either reforming or abolishing industrial capitalism.

Socialist Realism A Marxist artistic theory that calls for the use of literature, music, and the arts in the service of the ideals and goals of socialism and/or communism, with an emphasis in painting on the realistic portrayal of objects.

solipsism In philosophy, the sense that only one's self exists or can be known.

sonata [soh-NAH-tah] In music, an instrumental *composition,* usually in three or four movements.

sonata form A musical *form* or structure consisting of three (or sometimes four) sections that vary in *key, tempo,* and *mood.*

stained glass An art form characterized by many small pieces of tinted glass bound together by strips of lead, usually to produce a pictorial scene of a religious theme; developed by *Romanesque* artists and a central feature of *Gothic* churches.

stele [STEE-lee]   A carved or inscribed vertical stone pillar or slab, often used for commemorative purposes.

stereobate   In Greek architecture, the stepped base on which a temple stands.

Stoicism [STO-ih-sihz-uhm]   The most popular and influential *Hellenistic* philosophy, advocating a restrained way of life, a toleration for others, a resignation to disappointments, and a resolution to carry out one's responsibilities. Stoicism appealed to many Romans and had an impact on early Christian thought.

stream-of-consciousness   A writing technique used by some modern authors in which the narration consists of a *character's* continuous interior monologue of thoughts and feelings.

structuralism   In *Post-Modernism,* an approach to knowledge based on the belief that human behavior and institutions can be explained by reference to a few underlying structures that themselves are reflections of hidden patterns in the human mind.

studia humanitatis [STOO-dee-ah hu-man-ih-TAH-tis] **(humanistic studies)**   The Latin term given by *Renaissance* scholars to new intellectual pursuits that were based on recently discovered ancient texts, including moral philosophy, history, grammar, rhetoric, and poetry. This new learning stood in sharp contrast to medieval *scholasticism.*

Sturm und Drang [STOORM oont drahng]   German, "Storm and Stress"; a German literary movement of the 1770s that focused on themes of action, emotionalism, and the individual's revolt against the conventions of society.

style   The combination of distinctive elements of creative execution and expression, in terms of both *form* and *content.*

style galant [STEEL gah-LAHNN]   In *Rococo* music, a *style* of music developed by French composers and characterized by graceful and simple *melodies.*

stylobate [STY-luh-bate]   In Greek temples, the upper step of the base that forms a platform on which the columns stand.

Sublime [suh-BLIME]   In *Romanticism,* the term used to describe nature as a terrifying and awesome force full of violence and power.

subject   In music, the main *theme.*

Suprematism [suh-PREM-uh-tiz-uhm]   A variation of *abstract art,* originating in Russia in the early twentieth century, characterized by the use of geometric shapes as the basic elements of the composition.

Surrealism [suh-REE-uhl-iz-uhm]   An early-twentieth-century movement in art, literature, and theater, in which incongruous juxtapositions and fantastic images produce an irrational and dreamlike effect.

swing band   A 15- to 16-member orchestra, which plays ballads and dance tunes; dominated popular music in the United States and in large cities in western Europe, from the early 1930s until the early 1950s.

syllabic   In music, in *plainsong,* a style of musical setting in which one note is set to each syllable.

symbolic realism   In art, a *style* that is realistic and true to life but uses the portrayed object or person to represent or symbolize something else.

symphony   A long and complex *sonata,* usually written in three or four movements, for large *orchestras;* the first movement is traditionally fast, the second slow, and the third (and optional fourth) movement fast.

syncopation [sin-ko-PAY-shun]   In music, the technique of accenting the weak beat when a strong beat is expected.

syncretism [SIN-kruh-tiz-uhm]   The combining of different forms of religious beliefs or practices.

synthesizer [SIN-thuh-size-uhr]   An electronic apparatus with a keyboard capable of duplicating the sounds of many musical instruments, popular among *Post-Modernist* composers and musicians.

tabula rasa [TAB-yuh-luh RAH-zuh]   "Erased tablet," the Latin term John Locke used to describe the mind at birth, empty of inborn ideas and ready to receive sense impressions, which Locke believed were the sole source of knowledge.

technique   The systematic procedure whereby a particular creative task is performed.

tempo   In music, the relative speed at which a *composition* is to be played, indicated by a suggestive word or phrase or by a precise number such as a metronome marking. (A metronome is a finely calibrated device used to determine the exact tempo for a musical work.)

terza rima [TER-tsuh REE-muh]   A three-line stanza with an interlocking rhyme scheme (*aba bcb cdc ded,* and so on), used by Dante in his *Divine Comedy.*

texture   In a musical composition, the number and nature of voices or instruments employed and how the parts are combined.

theater of the absurd   A type of theater that has come to reflect the despair, anxieties, and absurdities of modern life and in which the characters seldom make sense, the plot is nearly nonexistent, bizarre and fantastic events occur onstage, and *tragedy* and *comedy* are mixed in unconventional ways; associated with *Late Modernism.*

theme   The dominant idea of a work; the message or emotion the artist intends to convey; used in music, literature, and art.

theme and variations   In music, a *technique* in which a musical idea is stated and then repeated in variant versions, with modifications or embellishments; used in independent works or as a single movement in a *symphony, sonata,* or chamber work.

theocracy   From the Greek *theos,* "god"; a state governed by a god regarded as the ruling power or by priests or officials claiming divine sanction.

theology   The application of philosophy to the study of religious truth, focusing especially on the nature of the deity and the origin and teachings of an organized religious community.

tone   A musical sound of definite pitch; also, the quality of a sound.

tone color   In music, the quality of a sound, determined by the overtones; used for providing contrasts.

tracery   Ornamental architectural work with lines that branch out to form designs, often found as stone carvings in *rose windows.*

tragedy   A serious and deeply moral drama, typically involving a noble protagonist brought down by excessive pride (hubris) and describing a conflict between seemingly irreconcilable values or forces; in Greece, tragedies were performed at the festivals associated with the worship of Dionysus.

Transcendentalism   A literary and philosophical movement that emphasized the spiritual over the material, the metaphysical over the physical, and intuition over empiricism. Its central tenet identified God or the divine spirit (Transcendence) with Nature; popular in early and mid-nineteenth-century New England.

transept In church architecture, the crossing arm that bisects the *nave* near the *apse* and gives the characteristic *cruciform* shape to the floor plan.

tremolo In music, the rapid repetiton of two pitches in a chord, so as to produce a tremulous effect.

triglyph [TRY-glif] In Greek architecture, a three-grooved rectangular panel on the *frieze* of a *Doric* temple; triglyphs alternated with *metopes*.

trill In music, the rapid alternation of two notes, a step apart; used as a musical embellishment.

triptych [TRIP-tik] In painting, a set of three hinged or folding panels depicting a religious story, mainly used as an altarpiece.

trope [TROHP] In *Gregorian chants,* a new phrase or *melody* inserted into an existing chant to make it more musically appealing; also called a turn; in literature, a figure of speech.

troubador [TROO-buh-door] A composer and/or singer, usually an aristocrat, who performed *secular* love songs at the feudal courts in southern France.

twelve-tone scale In music, a fixed *scale* or series in which there is an arbitrary arrangement of the twelve *tones* (counting every half-tone) of an octave; devised by Arnold Schoenberg.

tympanum [TIM-puh-num] In medieval architecture, the arch over a doorway set above the lintel, usually decorated with carvings depicting biblical themes; in *Classical*-style architecture, the recessed face of a *pediment*.

ukiyo-e [oo-key-yoh-AY] A type of colorful Japanese print, incised on woodblocks, that is characterized by simple design, plain backgrounds, and flat areas of color. Developed in seventeenth-century Japan; admired by late-nineteenth-century Parisian artists, who assimilated it to a Western style that is most notable in the prints of Mary Cassatt.

Utilitarianism [yoo-til-uh-TARE-e-uh-niz-uhm] The doctrine set forth in the social theory of Jeremy Bentham in the nineteenth century that the final goal of society and humans is "the greatest good for the greatest number."

vanishing point In linear *perspective*, the point on the horizon at which the receding parallel lines appear to converge and then vanish.

vault A ceiling or roof made from a series of arches placed next to one another.

vernacular language [vuhr-NAK-yuh-luhr] The language or dialect of a region, usually spoken by the general population as opposed to the wealthy or educated elite.

vernacular literature Literature written in the language of the populace, such as English, French, or Italian, as opposed to the language of the educated elite, usually Latin.

via antiqua [VEE-uh ahn-TEE-kwah] The "old way," the term used in Late Medieval thought by the opponents of St. Thomas Aquinas to describe his *via media*, which they considered outdated.

via media [VEE-uh MAY-dee-ah] The "middle way" that St. Thomas Aquinas sought in reconciling Aristotle's works to Christian beliefs.

via moderna [VEE-uh moh-DEHR-nah] The "new way," the term used in Late Medieval thought by those thinkers who opposed the school of Aquinas.

video art A type of art made with a video monitor or monitors; produced using either computerized programs or handheld cameras; can be ephemeral or permanent.

virtuoso [vehr-choo-O-so] An aristocratic person who experimented in science, usually as an amateur, in the seventeenth century, giving science respectability and a wider audience; later, in music, a person with great technical skill.

voussoir [voo-SWAR] A carved, wedge-shaped stone or block in an arch.

woodcut In art, the technique of cutting or carving an image onto a wooden block used for printing; originated in the Late Middle Ages. Also, the print made from the technique.

word painting In music, the illustration of an idea, a meaning, or a feeling associated with a word, as, for example, using a discordant *melody* when the word *pain* is sung. This technique is especially identified with the sixteenth-century *madrigal;* also called word illustration or madrigalism.

ziggurat [ZIG-oo-rat] A Mesopotamian stepped pyramid, usually built with external staircases and a shrine at the top; sometimes included a tower.

CREDITS

INDEX

Page numbers in *italics* indicate pronunciation guides; pages numbers in **boldface** indicate illustrations. For readers using the two-volume set of *The Western Humanities*, page numbers 1–383 (Chapters 1–12) refer to material in Volume I: *Beginnings through the Renaissance* and page numbers 384–736 (Chapters 11–22) refer to material in Volume II: *The Renaissance to the Present*.